Doctor To The World Champions

Order this book online at www.trafford.com/06-3020
or email orders@trafford.com

Most Trafford titles are also available at major online book retailers.

© Copyright 2007 Dr. Neil Phillips

All rights reserved. No part of this publication may be reproduced, stored in a retrieval system, or transmitted, in any form or by any means, electronic, mechanical, photocopying, recording, or otherwise, without the written prior permission of the author.

Note for Librarians: A cataloguing record for this book is available from Library and Archives Canada at www.collectionscanada.ca/amicus/index-e.html

Printed in Victoria, BC, Canada.

ISBN: 978-1-4251-1261-5

We at Trafford believe that it is the responsibility of us all, as both individuals and corporations, to make choices that are environmentally and socially sound. You, in turn, are supporting this responsible conduct each time you purchase a Trafford book, or make use of our publishing services. To find out how you are helping, please visit www.trafford.com/responsiblepublishing.html

Our mission is to efficiently provide the world's finest, most comprehensive book publishing service, enabling every author to experience success. To find out how to publish your book, your way, and have it available worldwide, visit us online at www.trafford.com/10510

Trafford
PUBLISHING

www.trafford.com

North America & international
toll-free: 1 888 232 4444 (USA & Canada)
phone: 250 383 6864 ♦ fax: 250 383 6804
email: info@trafford.com

The United Kingdom & Europe
phone: +44 (0)1865 487 395 ♦ local rate: 0845 230 9601
facsimile: +44 (0)1865 481 507 ♦ email: info.uk@trafford.com

10 9 8 7 6 5

For Margaret,
Shelagh, Ann and Michael

"Margaret, and the Three Degrees"

The Four, Who Always Gave Me
More Love Than I Ever Deserved.

Contents

1. Home, Is Where My Heart Is 1
2. Schooldays 37
3. Medical School 75
4. I'm A Proper Doctor 120
5. General Practice 150
6. I Become A Football Club Director 182
7. Triumph and Disaster 226
8. Who wants to be a Millionaire? 254
9. Promotion For Me 273
10. The Medical Teams 316
11. If You Can't Stand The Heat 356
12. It Takes Time To Be Accepted 372
13. Acclimatisation, 1970 Style 392
14. The Competition Proper 422
15. With Hindsight Everything Is Easy 443
16. The Lull Before The Storm 458
17. Jack Charlton–A Matter of Trust 479
18. Phenomenal Success & Utter Despair 510
19. My International Resignation 548
20. Epilogue 568

ACKNOWLEDGEMENTS

Aged seventeen, I received a severe head injury playing rugby for my Grammar School. Following the injury, I was ill for some six months, with double vision and severe headaches. The love, care and encouragement given to me daily by Mam and Dad, throughout my long recuperation, was exceptional. I shall always be grateful to them for caring for me so well. It exemplified their love for me.

My enthusiasm for professional football commenced following my qualification as a doctor, when I was appointed House Surgeon to Mr. Blacow Yates. Blacow was not only Sheffield's senior surgeon at the time, but also Chairman of Sheffield United Football Club. I really enjoyed our post match chats following his team's home games. Blacow not only taught me well about clinical surgery and professional football, but, more importantly, taught me about life.

My first introduction to a professional footballer was when I met Bob Dennison, the then Manager of Middlesbrough Football Club. Bob took me under his wing and we travelled the country together, on a weekly basis, watching innumerable football matches. Always the gentleman, Bob introduced me to so many fellow Managers, Coaches and Trainers, as he endeavoured to involve me in the professional game.

It was through Bob I met and became a close friend of Harold Shepherdson, the Middlesbrough Assistant Manager and England Trainer. Harold guided and advised me, on innumerable occasions, when I was a director at Middlesbrough Football Club. We travelled the world together with the England team and were great companions. We always worked well together.

By responding to an emergency medical call, I met and became a friend

ACKNOWLEDGEMENTS

of Walter Winterbottom, the England Manager. My views on Sports Medicine, at a time when the speciality did not exist in England, intrigued Walter. It was Walter's persistence, with the Middlesbrough directors, that persuaded them to co-opt me onto the Board at Middlesbrough Football Club. He also involved me on The Football Association medical courses at Lilleshall. Attending those courses gave me so much pleasure over many years. My thanks are extended to all the Managers, Coaches and Trainers who made me so welcome every time I visited there.

Without doubt, the man to whom I owe the greatest debt is Sir Alf Ramsey. He believed in me, when I was very young and inexperienced in Sports Medicine. He appointed me as one of his Team Physicians and involved me as a member of his England squads for a period of twelve years. It was an honour and privilege to work for him. Of all the people I have worked with and for in my life, Alf stood out as a solitary beacon. For twelve years of my life, when we worked together, he was my best friend. His love of football was immeasurable.

"We don't do this job for the money,"
he often told me.
"We do it for the love of the game and for the players."
His integrity was beyond question. He was an honest, understanding, compassionate man. I miss him greatly.

Without the co-operation of my partners in General Practice at Redcar, the twelve years, I was involved with England, would not have been possible. Consequently, I am most grateful to Ian Mackinlay, Reg Cutts, David Whitehouse and Cameron Davidson for their immeasurable help and understanding in allowing me to do my job with England. To each and every one of my Medical Team, who advised me, in my preparation of the England team for Mexico, I shall always be grateful. They gave their time, expert knowledge and support freely and with great enthusiasm.

I would also thank the managers, staff, and players with whom I worked daily at Middlesbrough Football Club. Raich Carter, Stan Anderson and Jack Charlton were great people to be associated with. My daily working, with Jimmy Headrige and George Wright, in the treatment room at

ACKNOWLEDGEMENTS

Middlesbrough, was always a pleasure. The treatment they provided was of the highest quality and, as a threesome, we worked exceptionally well together. I know, the Middlesbrough players appreciated the high quality of care we provided for them.

I shall always be grateful to three managers of the England teams I attended as an Honorary Team Physician while on tour. John Harris of Sheffield United, Bill Nicholson of Tottenham and Joe Mercer, when he came out of retirement. As Alf wished, these three managers accepted me as just another member of the squad and I learnt much from them.

Football, however, is, above all, about the players. I am particularly grateful to the innumerable players, too numerous to mention individually, both at Middlesbrough and England who accepted me as 'just another member of the squad'. My daily contact, throughout my many years with them, will always be cherished.

Throughout this whole experience my wife Margaret, and our three children, always encouraged me in my role. As my three children frequently remind me,

> "We never saw our Dad until we were 'teenagers – he was always away with England."

In writing this book however, I must pay particular thanks to those who have given me permission to write about details of our friendship and medical consultations. In this regard I am particularly grateful, to the late Les Cocker, Terry Cooper, George Cohen, Sir Geoff Hurst, Harry Charlton, Gordon Jones, Bill Gates, the late Willie Maddren, Alan Peacock, Kathy Peters, Frank Spraggon and Glenys Young. Medical confidentiality is often quite an embarrassment in football, as most injuries to players are accurately reported in the daily, local and national press. Where medical information has been divulged to the media, usually by Managers and players, I have merely confirmed what was already known in the public domain. Where I believed further medical details would be of interest, I have sought the views of the people concerned, who were, after all, patients of mine. Some of them preferred me not to publish our encounters and consultations. I fully appreciate their decisions and have respected their wishes.

ACKNOWLEDGEMENTS

My thanks are also given to the photographers, particularly Jim Larkin of Middlesbrough and Derek Fellows of Sheffield, for giving me so many photographs, three of which I have used in the book. I am also grateful to Mirror Newspapers for agreeing to my publishing three photographs taken by my good friend Monte Fresco.

Finally, I am not a writer. English was never a strong subject of mine at school in Wales. My wife Margaret has endeavoured over many years to correct many, if not all, of my writing errors. She has read and re read the text and advised me accordingly. Nevertheless, the tales I have told are mine and mine alone. I am entirely responsible for them. They do however contain a miniscule of fiction, in certain places, to enhance my tale. All have been verified by the notes I routinely made at the time. The quotations are as I recall them, though word for word they may be slightly imperfect. If anyone involved with me over my life is upset by what I have written, I apologise in advance. The story, I believed, was too good not to tell.

1

Home, Is Where My Heart Is...

Few, if any, of my readers will have visited Tredegar. Many will not know where the town, with its present day population of sixteen thousand, is even situated. Unless one has relatives or friends living in Tredegar, it is unlikely you will visit the town in the future.

Tredegar is situated at the northern end of the Sirhowy valley in South Wales. Unfortunately, the construction of the new modern roads ensures travellers, by road, bypass the town in every direction. To the north of the town, the 'Head of the Valleys' road, which meanders from Abergavenny in the east to Neath in the west, bypasses the town by several miles. Previously, a road, signposted to Tredegar from the 'Head of the Valleys' road, went straight through the centre of the town, circling around its famous clock, which is almost one hundred feet high and surprisingly, for any building in South Wales, bears the Royal Arms of England on its north facing side. Unfortunately, the newly constructed bypass, travelling south through the valley to Newport, skirts around the town on the eastern slope of the valley, ensuring the centre of the town is again left isolated. In the twenty-first century, a visit to the town has to be planned, as the traveller is very unlikely to pass through the centre of the town. The new road systems ensure Tredegar is bypassed in every direction. It is a shame, as the town's history has much to interest the reader.

At the beginning of the nineteenth century, there was no Tredegar. At the northern end of the Sirhowy valley there were just four small settlements, namely Trefil, Dukestown, Scrwfa and Sirhowy. Trefil, the most northerly settlement, lies some one thousand feet above sea level. Surrounded by moorland, Trefil overlooks the Duffryn and Usk valleys. It was here, in the north, where the land, owned by the then Duke of Beaufort, was found to contain rich seams of limestone, coal and iron ore. The discovery of such minerals in the soil, quickly led to the industrialisation of the area. Tredegar and South Wales, became one of the largest coal and steel producing areas in the British Isles. The discovery of limestone led to the development of limestone quarries at Trefil. In the year eighteen hundred, with iron ore so plentiful in the ground, the first Iron Works, with its many furnaces, was built at Sirhowy. Six years later, in Dukestown, the first coal mine was sunk. These four northern settlements became the catalyst for the development of one of the great industrial areas of South Wales. The mining of limestone, coal, and iron ore became the focus for the town's residents. As a result, the town of Tredegar was born and grew at an alarming pace. The town's prosperity would be built on the minerals found below the soil.

As the nineteenth century progressed, Tredegar became a boom town. At the commencement of the century, the town's population was a little over one thousand. By the latter part of the century, the population was over thirty-four thousand. Houses were built in terrace formation on both sides of the valley to accommodate the influx of new workers and their families. Virtually all the men, migrating to Tredegar, were employed in the mining of coal or the production of steel. By the mid nineteenth century, The Tredegar Iron Company employed over two thousand men, working at the numerous furnaces and steel producing mills in the town. Coal mines were sunk at Dukestown, Sirhowy, Pochin, Ty Tryst, and Bedwellty. Their big black wheels, on the surface of each pit, demarcated the extraction of coal below the surface. At the end of the nineteenth century, Tredegar had become a booming industrial town, producing tons of coal and large amounts of steel. Two railway lines were built. One to the north of the town connected Merthyr in the west to Abergavenny in the east. This railway line included the four hundred and fifty feet long viaduct known as 'The Nine Arches'. A second railway line was developed, at the southern end of the town. This line connected Tredegar with Newport, meandering, in a southerly direction, throughout the entire length of the Sirhowy valley.

During the nineteenth century, the industrialisation, which had occurred in Tredegar, rapidly spread westwards throughout the valleys of South Wales. As the people of the valleys realised the extent of the mineral wealth lying below the surface of their land, coal mines and steel works were developed throughout the region. The sea ports of South Wales, particularly Barry and Cardiff, became one of the biggest exporters of coal and steel in the world. This rapid industrialisation of South Wales was not achieved without the development of many community problems. Miners and steelworkers worked six days every week. Their only non working day was the Sabbath. Sunday was the day of rest for the miners and steelworkers of Tredegar. Whether working in the coal mines or in the steel works, their work was extremely hard, dangerous and thirst provoking. Fluid intake was essential. Inevitably drunkenness on Sundays became a major problem. With the six day working week, the workers were paid on a Saturday. With money in their pockets, their day of rest, became the day to refresh their thirst and consume large quantities of alcohol. Drunkeness, on the Sabbath became a community disease. Surprisingly, the favourite tipple of the workers was gin. Absenteeism from work on a Monday, due to the inevitable hangovers, became a major problem. On Sundays, large amounts of gin were consumed by many workers who gathered in groups relaxing on the hillsides of the valley. The problem became so acute that, in eighteen-thirty, the government of the day introduced a heavy tax on gin with the sole intention of curtailing the drinking of gin by the workers in South Wales. The tax increase on gin worked. The consumption of gin was greatly reduced. The workers stopped drinking gin. The government however had failed to increase the tax on beer. Inevitably the workers switched to drinking beer. Many argue, the drunkenness, prevalent amongst the workers of South Wales, was the reason for the formation of the Temperance Movements. This is difficult to understand, as the first temperance organisation was The Racobites. They were founded at Salford in Lancashire in 1835, over a hundred miles from South Wales. The formation of the Racobites was followed, five years later, by yet another temperance movement named the Band of Hope. The Band of Hope was closely associated with the Methodist Church. With the development of these two temperance movements those who joined the organisations were encouraged to 'Sign the Pledge'–never to allow alcohol to pass their lips. Many people joined one or more of the Temperance Movements and, more importantly for the communities in South Wales, signed the pledge. This inevitably led to the local communities, throughout South Wales, becoming polarised. The communities were strictly divided into those who drank alcohol and those who did not. Churches and chapels, became the religious and social centres for those who had signed the pledge. The public houses were where the remainder of the population spent their leisure time. In the small town of Tredegar there were over twenty churches and chapels and a similar number of public houses. Both the chapels and the pubs would be full to overflowing. The polarisation of beliefs gave an indication as to how the mining and steel communities, and even families, became completely divided into those who drank alcohol and those who did not. Despite the original intention of the government, the consumption of alcohol, by the workers, continued unabated throughout the second half of the nineteenth century The government however remained resolute in its desire to reduce the consumption of alcohol in South Wales, aided and abetted by the owners and managers of the coal mines and steel works, who wanted to reduce the absenteeism amongst the workers on every Monday. In eighteen-eighty-one, the government introduced the Sunday Closing Act. This act banned the opening of shops on a Sunday and prohibited the sale of alcohol at any establishment, other than at a private members club. Surprisingly, the government excluded the county of Monmouthshire from the act. Tredegar, because of its geographical position in the county, was thus excluded. Despite the act, life continued as previously in the town. Many residents, from other towns in South Wales overcame the government's restrictions by migrating temporarily, to Monmouthshire on a Sunday. Making the short journey to Monmouthshire from their homes in South Wales, they were able to enjoy their alcoholic drink on the Sabbath. It was not until forty years later, in nineteen-twenty-one, that the government included

Monmouthshire in the Sunday Closing Act. This subsequent government action was a further attempt to restrict the consumption of alcohol on Sundays. With the introduction of the 1921 act, the whole of South Wales and Monmouthshire became so- called "Dry". For the members of the Temperance Movement, life became one of teetotalism and strict observance of the Sabbath. The churches and chapels of South Wales and Monmouthshire were full on a Sunday and so were the private, members only, drinking clubs. The divisions in the community were absolute.

The rapid expansion of the coal and steel industries in South Wales continued throughout the whole of the nineteenth century and the first half of the twentieth. Coal mines prospered throughout the valleys and the majority of men living in South Wales worked in the pits in appalling conditions. The development of so many coal mines led to a shortage of wooden pit props, which the miners required in abundance to support the roofs as they extracted coal underground. Due to the shortage of suitable wood, a decision was taken to import timber from the Apennine mountains of northern Italy. The Italian timber was cut down in abundance from the Valchano hills, surrounding Bardi in northern Italy, and exported to South Wales through the port of Genoa. The demand for timber for South Wales became so great, the people of Northern Italy began to believe that South Wales was the promised-land, with its streets paved with gold. Many Italians believed South Wales was the country that could give them a much better life than the hard agricultural, poorly paid life, they experienced in Northern Italy. A migration of Italians ensued. The romantics would have you believe that some of the early Italians walked across Europe to find the promised-land. Whatever their method of migration it is generally agreed that Bracchi was the first Italian to migrate to South Wales. Bracchi was closely followed by Rabbaiotti, Berni and Rossi. Of course the Italians soon found that South Wales was not the promised-land they had come to believe. The streets of South Wales were not paved with gold. Nevertheless, in the early part of the twentieth century, many Italians saw a wonderful business opportunity in every town of South Wales. With half the South Wales communities signed up to the pledge, the Italians opened Temperance Cafes. The cafes would sell no alcohol, but would concentrate on providing a social environment for the teetotallers in the community. It would be in the Italian cafes where the teetotal, chapel members would socialise, drink their Italian coffee, or soft drinks with or without an Italian ice cream or the innumerable varieties of sweets available. Italian cafes sprang up in every town of South Wales. Tredegar was no exception. The two prominent Italian cafes in the town were Berni's and Rabbaiotti's. The Italians were quickly integrated into the South Wales communities. Their café businesses prospered.

While Tredegar, during the nineteenth century, was predominately noted for its industrial development, the century saw the introduction of two of its most famous sons; one at the beginning century and the other towards the end of the century. The first son of note was Thomas Ellis. Ellis was a very intelligent engineer who, because of the town's steel industry, worked on the first ever steam railway locomotive. Additionally, in eighteen hundred and five, he was the main contributor in the development of the tram road link between Tredegar and Newport. Many believe Ellis was the inspiration for the development of the Darlington to Stockton railway, in the northeast of England, and Stevenson's Rocket steam railway engine. Arguably however, Tredegar's most famous son was born in Charles Street towards the end of the nineteenth century. Aneurin Bevan, later became the town's Member of Parliament and Secretary of State for Health. Aneurin is widely regarded as the one person responsible for introducing, in nineteen forty eight, the National Health Service to Great Britain. Before his career in parliament, Aneurin grew up and was educated in the town. Like many of the young men of Tredegar, at a very early age, he went to work in one of the town's coal mines. His political career developed with various elected appointments in the town prior to his election to parliament. For me personally however the most famous person born in Tredegar during the nineteenth century was my dad. He was born at forty-four Charles Street, a few doors away from Aneurin's house. Dad and Aneurin would grow up together as youngsters in the town. My dad was born in eighteen ninety-seven and christened John. At that time, Tredegar, with its several pits, mining coal, and its iron ore works, producing steel, was a thriving industrial community. Most males, born in Tredegar at that time, left school at the age of twelve to work underground. A few stayed at school to follow a career in education. Aneurin left school to work underground in the coal mine. My dad stayed at school, embarking on a career in education. Most of the townsfolk were born in the town, lived their lives in the town and died in the town. For many, it seemed a sad and sorry existence, yet they all seemed happy. I believe it was because they knew of nothing better. The escape mechanism, from the life of a miner or steel worker, for the male adolescents of the town was education. The advice, given to the young schoolboys of the town, was always the same,

> "If you don't want to spend your life underground, working as a miner, work hard at school; go to college and become a teacher."

It was the escape route several of the town's youngsters followed, my dad included. At the commencement of the Great War in nineteen fourteen, my Dad was a student at Caerleon Teachers Training College. All such students were allowed to complete their studies prior to entering the services. My Dad entered the navy at the completion of his studies in nineteen sixteen. He was based at Milford Haven, serving as a wireless operator on H.M.S. Hecate.

Not surprisingly, both Mam and Dad were born into miners' families. Dad was the first child of Samuel and Mary Phillips. Sam was a miner, spending his working life cutting coal at the coal face, with a pick and shovel, in difficult and dangerous surroundings. Sam died at an early age, but not before he had sired eight children; five boys and three girls. Whilst seriously ill throughout the war, with recurring chest infections, he soldiered on working underground until the last month of his life. My Dad eventually returned to his home in Tredegar from his naval duties on Thursday December 5th nineteen eighteen, to find his father Sam dying from Pneumonia. My dad spent his first night at home at his father's bedside It was the last night they would spend together. Sam died the following morning at six o'clock. Sam's death certificate stated that he had died of Pneumonia. Certainly for many years, prior to his death, he suffered with a persistent cough and shortness of breath. As the years passed by, his shortness of breath and persistent cough became progressively worse. Many believed he died of Pneumoconiosis, his lungs full of coal dust, but his death certificate said otherwise. There is no doubt however that Sam's work underground, cutting coal at the coalface, daily breathing in uncontrolled amounts of coal dust, contributed to his death. Sam was not the only miner in South Wales to die in similar circumstances. The graveyards of South Wales are full of such miners. The underground conditions for the miners were intolerable but, for the great majority, it was the only work available.

Mam's parents were Joe and Emily Hodges. Mam was born in 1898. Her father, Joe, initially worked as a miner, cutting coal at the coalface. Joe left school at the age of twelve to commence work at Ty Trist colliery. In his early twenties he sustained a nasty accident underground. He was off work for over a year. When he eventually returned to work he was given a new job as a check- weigher. Joe worked, for the rest of his working life, above ground, checking and weighing the coal cut by others. Joe's chest benefited from his unfortunate accident. Joe lived well into his eighties. He died from a stroke.

With my father being the eldest of the eight children and with his father dying so young, the responsibility for bringing up his four brothers and three sisters, after the Great War, fell heavily upon him and his mother. Dad's youngest sister, Edna, was seven years old when her father died. Whilst carrying out his naval duties, in the First World War, as a naval rating, my dad qualified as a radio operator. He spent most of the war on H.M.S. Hecate. The ship was part of the Dover patrol. Their role was escorting merchant ships up and down the Bay of Biscay. My father's naval career was greatly influenced by one of the ship's officers, a Lieutenant Napier. It was Napier who convinced my father that he was intelligent enough to further progress his academic career as a schoolteacher. When my dad was discharged from the navy he had promised Napier he would eventually aim to become a headmaster. He would be spared from spending the rest of his life working underground.

Edith, my Mam, was also the eldest child in her family. Mam had one brother and two sisters. Edith was destined to become a teacher from a very early age; her father saw to that. Realising his eldest daughter was bright at school, Joe Hodges ensured her adolescence was spent studying for a better life. My mam was admitted to the teachers' training college at Barry; one year before my dad went to Caerleon.

On qualifying as teachers Edith and John were both appointed to teaching posts in a school at Hollybush, a village some five miles south of Tredegar. They would frequently walk the five miles to and from school each day. It was there that they met and fell in love. They married in nineteen twenty four at Commercial Street Primitive Methodist Chapel. Initially they lived in rented accommodation in Bourneville Terrace prior to moving into forty-two West Hill, a Tredegar property they bought for four hundred pounds with a loan they received from Edith's father. They didn't realise then, but they both would spend their lives working as teachers in the Sirhowy valley. They were both dedicated chapel people and, as such, had both signed the pledge. No alcohol would pass their lips. In fact, alcohol would not find a place in their home.

John and Edith's first child was born two years after their marriage on the twentieth of April. A son, he was christened John, after his father, and Dayton was his second name. It is unclear when John and Edith made the pact but a pact was certainly made between the young married couple. Both Edith and John had realised early on in their teaching careers that they were at a disadvantage, compared to other teachers in that they had no university degree, merely a teacher training qualification. Both wanted to go to university, but the finances of their families would not allow it. Shortly after their marriage, or may be it was before, they made a pact that any child of theirs would have to attend university. Anything less was unacceptable. Dayton was therefore programmed from a very early age along such an academic career. It would be six more years before Edith and John would have a second child.

The Italians from Northern Italy continued to infiltrate into the valleys of South Wales. Temperance cafes were evident throughout the principality.. Knowing that many of his friends from the Apennine mountains had emigrated to South Wales, a young medical student at Bologna university determined that he too would emigrate to South Wales. He would practice his medicine in the valleys. After qualifying as a doctor in Bologna, he initially took up an appointment at a hospital in Wolverhampton, but he, Ugo Zanazi, was very quickly appointed as an assistant to Dr. Richards, a general practitioner in Bargoed, situated in the Rhymney valley. Zanazi settled in well at Bargoed and was well liked by his patients. Dr. Richards was also very impressed with his medical knowledge and bedside manner. Through the good offices of Dr. Richards, Zanazi was introduced to Margaret Bevan, a very attractive lady from Griffithstown and the daughter of Moppy Bevan a close friend of Dr. Richards. Margaret Bevan and Zanazi fell in love. With certain reservations from Margaret's mother, Ugo Zanazi and Margaret Bevan married. They set up house in Bargoed, while Zanazi himself completed his assistantship with Dr. Richards. Zanazi was so contented with his life in the valleys, that he sought a permanent appointment, as a general practitioner, in South Wales.

Tredegar's medical services were provided by the Miners' Medical Aid Society, a precursor of the National Health Service, and one with which Aneurin Bevan was closely involved. The Miners' Medical Aid Society received its income from the working miners. An agreed amount of money was deducted every week from the miners' pay and transferred to their Medical Aid Society. The society was thus able to employ the general practitioners who provided free medical care for the miners and their families in the town. Other non mining residents of the town were able to receive medical care from the society's doctors, but paid for the services provided. The general practitioner services were provided in two surgeries owned by the society. Park Place Surgery was at the southern end of the town and Church Street Surgery catered for the residents in the north of the town. A general practitioner vacancy occurred at The Church Street Surgery in the spring of nineteen thirty one and Dr. Zanazi decided to apply. My dad was a friend of Moppy Bevan, the young Mrs. Zanazi's mother. I wish I could tell you how that friendship, between Moppy and my Dad, had developed, but I have no knowledge of its history. Moppy Bevan lived in Griffithstown, some twenty miles from Tredegar, and my Dad had no car to visit her on a regular basis. Their friendship however was plain to see. It had endured over many years. Moppy and Dad were very close. With her daughter's husband seeking a medical post in Tredegar, it seemed quite natural for Moppy to contact my Dad. Moppy enquired if my father would use his good offices, in the town, to canvas the members of the Medical Aid Committee to appoint Dr. Zanazi. My Dad duly obliged. He met with Dr. Zanazi and escorted him to the homes of various committee members, prior to his interview for the post. Dr. Zanazi was appointed a General Practitioner in the town, employed by the Miners' Medical Aid, and based at the Church Street surgery. He commenced his duties on the first of March nineteen thirty one. Doctor and the young Mrs. Zanazi moved into a large detached house close to Sirhowy Bridge, at the northern end of Church Street. My dad had met Doctor Zanazi on only three occasions.

It is an indication of the closeness of the friendship between Moppy Bevan and my Dad that, throughout the remainder of nineteen thirty one, Dad endeavoured to make the new doctor and his wife comfortable in their new home. My Dad seized every opportunity to ensure that the Italian doctor and Moppy Bevan's daughter were accepted into the community of Tredegar. With Doctor Zanazi busy at his work, my Dad became his gardener, painter and decorator, and handyman around the house. By the end of nineteen thirty one, Mam and Dad were very close friends of the Zanazis enjoying each others company in the innumerable visits they made to each others houses. Moppy Bevan was most grateful to my Mam and Dad. They had supported the young doctor's wife throughout her move to Tredegar and ensured, as best they could, that she had integrated well into the town. Needless to say, Dr. Zanazi became John and Edith's family doctor.

The midwife closed her notebook. A wave of tiredness swept over her. She examined her face in the mirror of the dressing table. Dimly lit, by the single candle, the mirror confirmed her feeling of total exhaustion. Despite her tiredness, she had an inner feeling of complete satisfaction. The feeling that comes from a job well done. She gathered up her midwifery bag. It was time to leave.

Edith, the mother, was in a very deep sleep. Dr. Zanazi had injected her with sedatives. At the bedside, the newly born baby lay quietly in a brown, wicker basket. Sister Thomas took one last look at the baby. She checked his breathing and his colour, now a healthy pink, before quietly leaving the bedroom. She descended the stairs. John, the father, slept soundly in a chair. He too had become exhausted with the efforts and stresses of the past three days. Sister Thomas tiptoed past him out into the cold midnight air. Her pushbike was leaning against the wall of the house. She placed her midwifery bag in the bike's wire basket, before mounting it and cycling away into the cold, wintry night.

Three days previously, on the twelfth of January nineteen thirty two, John had called at Sister Thomas's house. His message was simple. Edith, his wife, had commenced in labour. It seemed, at the time, a routine call. It was Edith's second pregnancy. Her first baby had been born six years previously. That pregnancy and childbirth had been quite straightforward. It had resulted in an eight-pound baby boy. This second pregnancy had also progressed normally throughout the antenatal period. Sister Thomas anticipated no problems with the delivery. Events would prove otherwise.

Edith's labour pains, during the first twenty-four hours, were weak. She slept for most of the time. Sister Thomas left Edith for long periods while she continued her routine work around the town. With the rupture of the membranes, on the second day, Sister Thomas anticipated the labour pains would become stronger ensuring the labour would be quickly established. In the event, the labour pains did not intensify. The delivery process was slow and little progress appeared to be made. On the evening of the fourteenth, some forty-eight hours after Sister Thomas had first been called, labour was still not properly established. The midwife was concerned at the lack of progress. She decided to call in the local general practitioner. Doctor Zanazi was a giant of a man. Italian by birth, he had trained in the northern Italian University of Bologna. Like many of his fellow Italians, he had travelled to South Wales in search of a better life. In the nineteen twenties, the valleys of South Wales had received many such Italians. With their opening of Temperance Cafes, they were readily accepted and integrated into the mining communities. An Italian doctor, working in the valleys, was however unique. Although Zanazi had only been working in Tredegar for nine months, he was already renowned for the high quality of care he provided for his patients. The townsfolk of Tredegar loved him.

Zanazi called to see Edith late at night on the fourteenth. He had experienced another busy day in the practice and was anxious to go home to his beloved Margaret. At first he was unable to give a satisfactory reason why Edith's labour had not progressed. He discussed the clinical details with Sister Thomas. They both came to the conclusion that, apart from the fact the labour pains had been weak and infrequent, everything was quite normal. Edith remained quite comfortable. The baby's heart rate was normal; there was no evidence that the unborn child was in any distress. Zanazi saw no reason to intervene, deciding to allow nature to take its course. Almost as an afterthought, he decided to carry out an internal vaginal examination in order to establish the position of the baby's head and the dilatation of the neck of the womb. The cervix was not dilated. His examination of the baby's head however revealed it was lying in a posterior position. The baby' face was facing forwards in the pelvis, instead of backwards. Zanazi confirmed that this was the case subsequently, by re-examining the mother's abdomen. He cursed himself for not diagnosing the baby's abnormal position on his previous abdominal examination. Zanazi now decided it was necessary to ensure that the labour be properly established. He instructed Sister Thomas to give Edith a small enema. The deed was quickly performed. From that moment, Zanazi and Sister Thomas realised the labour would be prolonged and difficult. Close observation of the mother and the unborn baby would be essential. As this labour now progressed, the baby's head would need to rotate, while it descended through the pelvis. Such a rotation of the baby's head during labour was always difficult and usually accompanied by complications. The next few hours would be critical. Zanazi instructed Sister Thomas to stay with the patient, as the mother's condition and the baby's heart rate would need to be closely monitored for any evidence of maternal or foetal distress.

Edith awakened at dawn on the fifteenth of January. It was the third day of her labour. The labour pains were now severe. The pains returned regularly, at five minute intervals. Edith and Sister Thomas realised that labour had now begun in earnest. Each painful contraction, of Edith's uterus, endeavoured to push the baby downwards in the pelvis rotating the baby's head as it did so. Zanazi called at Edith's home before his morning surgery. He confirmed that the labour was now firmly established. The baby's heart rate remained within normal limits. There was no evidence to suggest the baby was in any way distressed. Zanazi prescribed a sedative and gave Edith an injection of Pethidine to ease the pain. He advised Edith to rest as much as possible between the pains. Zanazi knew the labour would be prolonged and difficult. The rotation of a baby's head, from a posterior position, as it descended through the pelvis, was always difficult. Having sedated Edith and administered a pain relieving injection, Zanazi left for his morning surgery leaving Sister Thomas in charge.

By mid afternoon the labour pains were strong, extremely painful and almost continuous. Edith was now quite distressed. While the baby's heart rate remained quite normal, Edith was exhausted. Sister Thomas concluded that Edith was now in grave danger. John was despatched to the Church Street Surgery to request Zanazi's presence immediately. With no telephone in the house, John ran to the surgery. Zanazi's large Austin car arrived at four o'clock in the afternoon. The doctor's examination revealed the cervix to be now fully dilated. The baby's head had descended into the pelvis. The head had rotated to a degree, but now lay in the transverse position. The head lay across the pelvis, with the baby's face pointing to the left. Zanazi's worst fears were confirmed. The baby's head and the mother's pelvis were too tight a fit. With the baby's head lying in this transverse position across the mother's pelvis there was no room for it to progress further. Zanazi decided to give Edith another injection of Pethidine to ease her pain. Edith was so exhausted Zanazi knew her own life was now in danger. Despite the severe labour pains, little progress had been made with the rotation of the baby's head. The head was now fixed in this transverse position across the mother's pelvis. In medical terms 'a deep transverse arrest' had occurred. Zanazi had no option but to intervene. He would attempt to disengage the baby's head from the pelvis, rotate the head himself into the correct position and then deliver the baby by using forceps.

At such times, Zanazi wished for the facilities of a maternity hospital, but Tredegar had no such hospital. The nearest maternity hospital was some twenty miles away at Newport. Zanazi had no other option but to attempt the forceps delivery in the bed where Edith lay. Copious supplies of hot water would be required. John was deputed to ensure a continuous supply. The difficulty of a forceps delivery at home was further complicated by the fact that Zanazi would need to act both as the Anaesthetist and as the Obstetrician. Fortunately, Zanazi was an expert at Chloroform and Ether anaesthesia. It was a technique at which he was experienced. With Edith stretched across the bed, he anaesthetised her with what is commonly known as the rag and bottle. The technique consists of a facemask covered with gauze onto which is dropped the Chloroform and Ether mixture. In minutes, Edith was fully anaesthetised and asleep. Zanazi's role now changed from that of Anaesthetist to one of Obstetrician. His first task was to disengage the baby's head from the mother's pelvis by pushing the baby's head back up out of the pelvis and into the abdomen. Having disengaged the head, he then rotated it in his hand until it lay in the correct position with its face lying to the back of the pelvis. Considerable force was required to achieve this obstetric manoeuvre. The beads of sweat on Zanazi's brow gave indication to the hard work required. Sister Thomas handed Zanazi the two forceps blades. With the skill of an experienced practitioner the forceps were successfully applied to the baby's head. Considerable traction on the forceps was then required by the doctor to deliver the baby's head. Once free of the pelvis, the baby delivered easily. Sister Thomas wrapped the newborn baby in a towel, while Zanazi continued to supervise the delivery of the afterbirth. Sister Thomas sucked the mucous from the baby's mouth with a small pipette. Zanazi was relieved to hear the baby cry heartily from the corner of the bedroom. The mother's bleeding was slight. Only three sutures were required in the perineal tear.

DOCTOR TO THE WORLD CHAMPIONS

Zanazi was pleased with his efforts and delighted the birth had been accomplished with such a pleasing outcome. John and Edith now had two sons. Edith remained deeply anaesthetised. She was totally oblivious to what had happened. Zanazi examined the baby. He then gave the mother a strong sedative injection. Edith would sleep for a considerable time. Her joy would come later.

The cold January night air blew across Sister Thomas's face. In a state of extreme tiredness, she was grateful the cycle ride home was downhill. Once West Hill was negotiated, there were the hills of Glandovey and Union Street on which she could freewheel before reaching her terraced house in Harcourt Terrace. She was pleased she was not travelling in the reverse direction. As the cold night air rushed across her face, she reflected on the happenings of the past three days. She marvelled at the medical skill of Zanazi. Not only was he a compassionate and caring doctor, but his practical skills were outstanding. Sister Thomas wondered if the townsfolk appreciated their good fortune in having a doctor of the calibre of Zanazi. Edith and John Phillips were indeed fortunate that Zanazi had supervised and orchestrated the delivery of their second son. Sister Thomas knew, only too well, that if other doctors from the town had been in charge, the outcome might not have been such a happy one. Edith and John certainly owed a debt of gratitude to Doctor Zanazi. The Harcourt Terrace house was in total darkness. Sister Thomas knew the absence of light indicated her father was fast asleep. There were no messages on the hall table. In minutes Sister Thomas was in her own bed, fast asleep.

Edith did not wake until seven the following morning. As she awoke, she felt the comfort and security of John's hand in hers. John sat on the edge of the bed. The newborn baby was asleep. John and Edith smiled at each other. John was the first to speak.

"I know you wanted a little girl, but God has blessed us with another son. He's fine, but how are you?"

Edith could not disguise her disappointment. The tears streamed down her face.

"I did so want a girl."

"I know, but let us be grateful that our second son is fit and perfectly normal. You've had a terrible time and you need to rest. I'll go and make you a cup of tea."

John left Edith sobbing with her obvious disappointment. John knew it would take time for her to happily accept that she now had two sons, instead of the one son and daughter she so desperately wanted. John had told his wife often, during the pregnancy, not to make all the baby's clothes in pink. Edith however was convinced the baby would be a girl. She had pressed on regardless with her dressmaking. It would now be a matter of dressing their new son in pink. John resigned himself to the fact that, for a few weeks, their new son would be dressed in the frilly pink dresses of a girl.

Zanazi breezed into Edith's bedroom at eight o'clock. He carried out his routine postnatal examinations. The blood loss was minimal. The abdominal examination revealed a firm, well-contracted uterus. Edith's pulse, blood pressure and temperature were normal. Zanazi crossed the bedroom to examine the new baby. The baby cried, as its sleep was disturbed, and continued to cry as Zanazi examined its heart and lungs with his stethoscope. The remnants of the umbilical cord were dry and not bleeding.

"He's all complete Edith, and in good working order. It was a very difficult birth and I apologise for putting you to sleep. I can assure you it was all very necessary. I don't think this son of yours was very keen to be born. I needed to give him a little help. Between us we made it, and he now seems fine in every respect."

Such a modest assessment of the delivery was something Edith could not appreciate. Zanazi considered no further explanation of the obstetric difficulties was appropriate and he gave none.

"What are you going to call him?" enquired Zanazi.

"I was going to call him Emily, after my mother. I was certain he was a girl. We haven't considered any boy's names. John and I will need to talk about a boy's name."

A single tear rolled down her cheek, which Zanazi's keen sense of observation noted. He made no comment. He excused himself by saying he would be late for his morning surgery.

Downstairs, Zanazi joined John and Sister Thomas for a cup of tea in the kitchen.

"They both seem fine to me" Zanazi informed Sister Thomas.

"Quite remarkable when one considers the difficulties of yesterday. I never enjoy dealing with a transverse arrest. The outcome is so precarious. We must be thankful it all turned out so well."

With a few gulps of his tea Zanazi departed, leaving Sister Thomas to provide the nursing care for Edith and the baby.

"A quite remarkable man" commented Sister Thomas.

"I have to say Mr. Phillips that without Zanazi's expertise, there would be no live, healthy baby today. You might even have lost your wife in the process. Zanazi makes everything look so simple. He truly is a great doctor."

"Dr. Ugo Zanazi"

Having received her nursing care from Sister Thomas, Edith gave the baby its first breast-feed. Mother and baby then slept for most of the morning. The neighbours and close family called, but John, under instructions from Sister Thomas, kept them all at bay. Even Edith's parents were politely turned away. It was essential Edith rest. There would be plenty of time for visitors. It was early afternoon when John brought his wife lunch; a bowl of homemade soup and a tomato sandwich. Edith propped herself up in bed with John's help. She enjoyed her lunch.

"Silly really isn't it?"
she said at last.
"Here we are, two qualified teachers and we haven't given a thought to our baby boy's name."
"There are plenty of names to choose from."
said John.
"There's Gareth, or Bryn. Mervyn, Alan, Jenkin, Thomas, Dewi or, even at a push, Aneurin. We could call him Joseph, after your father, or Samuel after mine. There are plenty of names to choose from."
"Sister Thomas has told me how lucky I was yesterday. 'Very fortunate' is what she said. She doubted that I would have been alive today, if it had not been for Doctor Zanazi. Sister Thomas feels he saved my life and that of the baby. I can't remember anything about it. It's all very strange. All I can remember is Zanazi asking me to breathe in and out while he placed a mask over my face. The next thing I remember, John, is waking up holding your hand. It's all so very strange."
"Maybe we should name the baby after Doctor Zanazi. It would be a nice way to remember the doctor forever."
said John.
"But then, I've always fancied 'Neil' as a boy's name."
"Zanazi Phillips." murmured Edith and then she was asleep.
John took the tray, with its empty soup dish and plate. He satisfied himself the baby was well and went downstairs to wash the dishes.

Zanazi arrived, as usual, at his Church Street Surgery an hour before his surgery was due to commence. He used that hour to write up his notes relating to the previous day's home visits. Edith Phillips' notes required some thought and were expressed in detail. It was not every day that a transverse arrest occurred in a second pregnancy. It was not every day that Zanazi worked as an Anaesthetist and an Obstetrician. As he wrote the detailed notes of the case, he reflected on how well he had been taught the skills of Obstetrics in The University of Bologna. He had much to be grateful for. The lecturers and teachers of the Bologna Medical School had taught him well. There was so much that could have gone wrong with Edith's delivery. As he wrote,

"Mother and baby appeared well at the completion of the forceps delivery."

he felt an inner sense of deep satisfaction at the outcome and genuinely felt a sense of pride in his achievement. As a final flourish to his notes, he added

"Both mother and baby appeared well",

without realising, in his enthusiasm, he had repeated himself.

Sister Thomas and Zanazi usually met together each day immediately before evening surgery. At that time, they would exchange information on patients and programmes of patient care would be jointly agreed. The report on the Phillips family was satisfactory. Mother and baby continued to do well. As a result, Sister Thomas was happy to continue with the care alone. There was no immediate need for Zanazi to carry out daily visits.

The new baby was six days old when Zanazi next visited. Dressed in a pink frilly dress, the baby slept peacefully in its wicker basket. Zanazi decided not to disturb the baby's sleep. He carried out his routine examination of Edith and satisfied himself that all was well.

"You can now get up more and more each day, but no venturing outside for another four days."

John had stood at the end of the bed during the examination. He was pleased that Edith was making a full recovery and expressed his thanks to

Doctor Zanazi.

> "I wonder if Edith and I could have a word? We both are extremely grateful to you for the care and kindness you have shown to us. Without your skill and expertise we both realise the baby and Edith would not be here today. We are so grateful. We wondered if you would give permission for the baby to be called after yourself."

John realised he had not phrased his request very well. Edith broke the silence that followed.

> "We would like to call the baby Ugo, after yourself, and Neil, as John and I like that name. We wish, with your permission, to call the baby 'Ugo Neil'."

Zanazi was stunned. He was overcome with pleasure.

> "Of course. Whatever you wish. I'm greatly honoured. It is an honour and a pleasure. Ugo Neil Phillips. What a nice name. Of course I shall call him Ugino; the little Ugo; but you must call him Ugo. In Italy, whenever a baby is called after someone, he is always 'the little one'."

Zanazi crossed the room to look at the baby. He repeated Ugino several times to himself, to indicate his pleasure.

> "It is a great honour."

he said again and left to carry on with his practice work.

Edith insisted on registering the birth of Ugino herself. The Registrar's office was in Bedwellty Park. Edith walked there on the twenty-seventh of February nineteen hundred and thirty two. The baby was six weeks old. It was the first time Edith had ventured into the town.. The little Ugino, still dressed in a pink frock, accompanied her in the pram. Edith registered the baby as Ugo Neil Phillips, but Edith would always call him Ugino. The name would be, to say the very least, unusual. Although he would grow up in the valleys of South Wales surrounded by boys whose names would be the true names of Wales namely Gareth, Bryn, Mervyn and Mostyn, her boy would be known as Ugino. Edith was pleased. She would remember Doctor Zanazi forever.

And so it was, I was named 'Ugo Neil', for I was that baby. Mam would always call me Ugino. She spoke my name as
"Who-Geen-Oh", with a hard g.
Throughout my early years, and well into my teens, Mam always called me,
"Who-Geen-Oh".
Although my parents were both schoolteachers, and therefore intelligent adults, it is doubtful if they ever gave a thought to the effect the name Ugino would have upon me in the valleys of South Wales. It is also surprising that they should agree to call their son after a man they had only known for nine months. They were very grateful to Zanazi. I can visualise Mam now, standing on the door step of our home in West Hill, Tredegar, shouting down the street :
"Who-Geen-Oh. It's time to come in."
When I played rugby,
"Pass the ball to Who-Geen-Oh,"
was not a phrase my fellow rugby players found easy to flow from their tongues. In crueller moments at school, when fellow pupils knew my real name was Ugo,
"You go-I come back",
would be a constant taunt. Mam and Dad were however immensely proud that Zanazi had agreed to the naming of their baby as Ugo. I would always be their Ugino. Ugino was to be my name. The pink dresses disappeared with time, but the name Ugino remained. Mam would always refer to me as Ugino and by so doing, she would always remember Zanazi. He had saved her life and mine. Before my birth, Mam and Dad were very friendly with Ugo and Margaret Zanazi. After my birth, the four of them were inseparable. I became an adopted member of the Zanazi family. Like it or not, I was saddled with the name
"Who-geen-oh".
I too would remember Zanazi forever. Sadly, Ugino would be a name I would grow to hate.
Every year of his life, from nineteen eighteen until he died, in nineteen sixty-three, my Dad kept a daily diary. Those diaries encapsulate

his own, and his family's life. His innumerable diaries are one of my most valuable possessions. My first recollection is going to school when I was five. My dad's diaries therefore give a great insight into the happenings within my family in those first five years of my life, when I recall nothing.

Following my birth, the friendship between my parents and Margaret and Ugo Zanazi flourished. There is no doubt that my presence was largely responsible for that friendship. Mam and dad were frequent visitors to the doctor's house. Mam regularly pushed me in my pram to visit Margaret Zanazi for afternoon tea. Dad continued to carry out renovations and improvements to the Zanazi house. They visited each other frequently, often having supper in each other's house. Over those early years of my life, their friendship became much more involved. When I was aged four however, Margaret Zanazi developed fulminating Tuberculosis. Although immediately admitted to a sanatorium in Breconshire, she died on the fourth July nineteen thirty six. Margaret was just in her thirties. I was four years old. I have no recollection of Margaret Zanazi, merely a photograph of me as a small baby sitting on her lap. An indication of the level of friendship that had developed between my Dad and Ugo Zanazi was, when Margaret died, my Dad was asked, by Zanazi, to make all the funeral arrangements for Margaret's burial in Panteg Cemetery. The burial took place on the eighth of July. Ugo Zanazi was devastated by the death of his young wife. His grief would be buried in his work as a General Practitioner in Tredegar. His mother, Mama Zanazi, came to Tredegar on a permanent basis to care for her son. Mama would act as his housekeeper.

Many years have rolled by since those events occurred. Outside today, it is a typical January day. It is cold, wet and misty. Fortunately, I am inside, enjoying the warmth of my home. Occasionally, the rain lashes against the windowpane. I am glad to be in the comfort of my own house. The passage of many years, has made me realise the pleasures of home in such conditions. However, it was not always the case. As a child, I would have been making incessant requests of my parents throughout the cold, rainy, and misty day. The request would always be the same.

"Can I go out to play."

Play was the most important part of my life. The rain and wind were no barrier to the enjoyment of my play. If a storm broke, while I played on the hills above Tredegar, and the rain lashed against my face, I could think of no greater pleasure. My parents invariably thought otherwise. On such days, my parents would confine me indoors. I hated being indoors. Today, as I write this story, it is different. The warmth of my own home surrounds me. Much older now, I am happy and content to be indoors. Gemma sits at my feet. Gemma is my Border collie bitch. Disabled, by deafness since birth, she is confined to a world of silence. Noise does not disturb her. I am unable to verbally communicate with her. In spite of her severe disability, she is extremely obedient. We communicate with hand signals, and she is an expert at understanding them. On walks in the fields, or on the hills, she always keeps one eye on me. The moment she sees my hand signals, she immediately responds. She is obedient, loyal and has a quiet disposition. We love each other. Her greatest pleasure is to be curled up at my feet. Today she is pleased it is a cold, miserable, January day. We are together in the warmth of our home. She sleeps peacefully at my feet.

The family have always had a dog. Chippy, a thoroughbred, black, cocker spaniel, was the first. He was the family pet when I was born. Good looking, with long, black ears encircling his sad, appealing face, Chippy was my brother's dog. Although I possess photographs of myself, as a very small child, with Chippy, I have no personal memories of him. Chippy died when I was five. Dogs have always been a part of our family life. In my life, I have enjoyed the companionship of Bryn, a majestic Golden Retriever, who rejoiced in the pedigreed name of Boltby Victor. Sniffer, so called after Allan Clarke, the Leeds United footballer and my son's favourite player, would follow Bryn. Sniffer was a Border Collie. My present dog, Gemma, followed him. Probably, because of her deafness, Gemma is the most good-natured of them all. She lives in a world of peace. There is no doubt, however, that my favourite dog was, and always will be, Bonzo. Bonzo will always be the best. As I write these words, Gemma looks into my face with her sad, brown eyes, as if to ask why a mongrel dog, with scraggy, curly, black hair, can take precedence over her. It is however true. Of all the dogs I've owned, Bonzo was the best. Bonzo was the dog of my childhood. In reality he was the first dog I ever had. It was as a boy that I developed my relationship with him. The most important element in any relationship is having time to spend together. Bonzo and I had all the time in the world. It was the vast amount of time we spent together that made our relationship so special.

When I was a child, all our days were spent in each other's company. We were inseparable. We had a great affection for each other. Bonzo was my best friend and I was his. Whatever I did as a child, Bonzo was always with me. Playing on the hills, or in the streets, he was always there. On cold, rainy days he would sit at my feet eagerly awaiting the signal that we could both go out to play. Bonzo was my constant friend and companion. If I left home without him, he would sit on the wall at the front of the house until my return. As I entered the street and whistled, he would leap from the wall, his tail wagging in delight as he raced toward me. It was a welcome we mutually enjoyed.

Weekends, as a child, were always divided into two distinct halves. Saturday was the day for playing: Sunday the day for chapel. As a boy, I loved Saturdays. In the summertime, the western slopes of the Sirhowy valley were my playground. The dirty, grey and black shale tips, overlooking the town, beckoned. My days were spent in those hills. In the small valleys, between the shale tips, were the mountain ponds. There I would fish. A tree branch was my rod. Mam's black cotton made my line. The float was an old matchstick. The hook, a bent pin. The bait was always an earthworm, dug from the back garden of our house. The fishing gear was primitive, but I spent many happy hours fishing at those filthy, stagnant, ponds. I recall with pride, the rare occasions I actually caught a fish and hurriedly returned home with the solitary stickleback in my jam jar. The jam jar would have pride of place in the kitchen until the inevitable happened. The fish died. Dead fish always floated upside down in the jar. I would always cry when my fish died. Bonzo did not like fishing. It was boring for him. There was no pleasure for a dog sitting hour after hour by the side of a pond. While I fished, Bonzo would wander off into the hills, leaving me to my fishing. Bonzo always returned and, when he was completely fed up, he would show his hatred of fishing, by leaping into the pond near my float. The splash he made in the pond always succeeded in frightening the fish away. It was his way of saying,

"Let's do something more enjoyable than fishing."
Bonzo preferred playing in the rush fields.

Towards Cefn Gola, the shale tips gave way to the lush green rush fields. In the heat of summer, I would collect the rushes from the fields and bind them together. From the rushes, I would make a rush whip. The whip had no purpose, but it gave me the satisfaction of making something with my own hands, even if the final product was useless. Bonzo and I would race each other through the rush fields. He out in front and me running behind. Occasionally he would lead me into a bog. With ease, he would extract his four legs from the bog. Inevitably my feet often sank. My shoes and stockings covered in mud. On such days, when we returned home, Mam would not be pleased.

"Ugino, don't let that dog in the house, until you have washed his feet."
she would forcibly say.

"Ugino! (Who-Geen-Oh). Take those shoes and socks off before coming into the house."
Bonzo and I never objected to her scolding. We had always had a very enjoyable time running together through the rush fields.

Lying between the Pear and Dead Dog ponds was the flat expanse of red shale we called the Red Ground. That red stony ground was our Cardiff Arms Park. It was there I learned to play cricket and rugby. All our important matches were played on the Red Ground. Uneven, and covered with loose red shale, from the town's iron ore works with not a blade of grass in sight, it was, for the children of West Hill, their stadium. I enjoyed playing there. The uneven bounce, the unpredictability of any ball on the surface added to the pleasure. It taught me a fundamental principle of all ball games. The principle of keeping one's eye on the ball at all times. In later years, I would be privileged to play on grounds with lush green turf and cricket squares reminiscent of billiard tables, but the pleasure that red, uneven, shale tip gave me lingers on. At cricket, Bonzo was one of our best fielders, particularly when the ball was hit into one of the ponds. He was a great retriever.

The hills of the valley were the places for flying kites. With a prevailing westerly wind, my homemade kite would soar out over the valley, flying higher than the hills themselves. My kite was always made out of a wooden cross of bamboo sticks, tied together with string. The four corners of the cross I would also link with string. The whole structure I covered in brown paper, and then sealed it all with flour and water paste. To give the kite stability in flight, a long piece of string was attached to its lower end, interspersed with bows of brown paper and a final duster tail. The flying of a homemade kite from the western hills of Tredegar was an exhilarating experience. Like fishing, kite flying was not one of Bonzo's favourite games. He was, however, always with me. He seemed to know how much pleasure those pastimes gave me. He somehow tolerated his own boredom when I was doing things he didn't enjoy. It was if he knew how much pleasure fishing and flying kites gave me. He was my true friend.

There was little, if any traffic, in the streets of Tredegar in my youth. The traffic mainly consisted of Billy Bevan's horse and cart. Billy brought the milk in large metal churns. Occasionally, a pedal cycle would venture into the street. On many occasions the street of West Hill became our playground. Cricket, rounders, hopscotch, skipping, bat and catty, and rugby were played there, long into the summer evenings. When playing cricket, a wooden box would be placed in the middle of the street, to represent the wickets and very competitive cricket matches would follow. Adults would stand out on the pavements or sit on their front window ledges watching the children play. They also made the occasional catch thus preventing the tennis ball going through their front window. The street frequently became our rugby pitch. Too poor to buy a proper rugby ball, our ball was a magazine, or some newspapers, tied together with string. We always played touch rugby. Proper tackling was not allowed. Conversions were made over the street's gas lamps. I gained many international caps of Wales in that street. When rugby was played, it was always Wales versus England. I can never recall an England victory. If England were leading in any game, we would all agree to change sides in the last minutes thus ensuring Wales' unbeaten run against the English continued. After all, Welsh pride was at stake! A fall, whilst playing touch rugby in the street, had severe consequences. The gravelled road was unkind to human skin. Deep cuts and abrasions were commonplace. Like all my friends, the scars on our knees bear testimony to the commitment we all gave to those games. We all believed we were playing for Wales. It was essential to keep the English at bay! Personal injury was a small price to pay. When Bonzo joined in, we called him an All Black!

My childhood days were happy days. I was grateful to Bonzo and my parents for making them so. As a boy, I loved Saturdays. It was a special day. Saturday was the day I treasured. It was always the day of complete enjoyment. It was my play day. Friends have told me that going to the pub, for the first time in their teens, with their dad was one of their greatest pleasures when growing up. The experience, they believed, was recognition by their father, of moving from childhood to manhood. It signalled, for them the arrival of a more equal relationship between their father and themselves. I did not experience any such pleasure. I feel no regrets or bitterness at missing out on a visit to the pub with my Dad. Father was teetotal. Throughout his life, he never once entered a public house. An hotel maybe, but never a public house. In the town, residents had a stark choice; the pub or chapel. If the choice was chapel, the pubs became a no go area. Chapel people were teetotal. In the days of my childhood, Tredegar, population eighteen thousand, had more chapels than pubs and all the chapels were well attended. We grew up in the town as chapel people. The chapel was the centre of our spiritual and social life. Chapels, in Tredegar, were at every street corner. Baptist, Congregational, Primitive Methodist, Wesleyan Methodist, Tabernacle; the variety of chapels seemed endless. The 'posh' people went to the Anglican Church in Church Street. Our chapel was Commercial Street Primitive Methodist, although father went, on his own, to Castle Street Congregational Chapel. Commercial Street Primitive Methodist Chapel is no more. It has been demolished. The Gwent Shopping Centre has replaced it. Throughout my youth it was the centre of my spiritual upbringing. Sunday was for chapel and only for chapel. Each Sunday, Mam would take my brother and me to chapel, not once or twice, but three times. On beautiful summer days, or in the midst of winter, with lashing rain or falling snow, the Sunday ritual never varied. I cannot recall a Sunday, when Mam would not ensure my brother and I were at morning service, Sunday school and evening service. We were never excused. The climb back up the western slope of the Sirhowy valley was made three times every Sunday. Mam would never accept a reason for missing chapel. To add to the solemnity of Sundays, games were never played outside or inside the house. The radio was silent. Sunday papers were not allowed. No comics could be read. The Lord, my brother and I were told, had declared Sunday as a day of rest. The ritual remained the same throughout my childhood. Bonzo never came to chapel.

Lunch on Sundays was never at home. After morning chapel, my brother and I went to forty-seven West Hill. Our Sunday lunch was always with Gramma and Grandpa Hodges, my mother's parents. On rare occasions five grandchildren would appear for lunch. Our three cousins, Barbara, Pam, and Alan, would join us. Usually it was just my brother and me with our grandparents. Each Sunday, before lunch, we congregated around the harmonium in the front room. Dayton, my brother, played the harmonium. Grandpa Hodges would select the hymns. We sang the hymns with great gusto, while Gramma prepared our lunch. The ritual never changed. It was as regular as Sunday itself.

If I missed out on the pubs, I didn't notice. Our 'pub' was the Italian Temperance Cafes. Coffee, Oxo, Sarsaparilla, and ice cream were on the menu at those cafes and how I loved them. There were two Italian cafes in Tredegar; Berni's was below the town clock, on the corner of Morgan Street, and Rabbaiotti's was at the junction of Castle Street with Commercial

Street. These two cafes were our meeting places. It was there Dad and I shared our drinks together. Berni's and Rabbaiotti's were the places where we discussed together the issues of the day. Chapel people met in the Italian Temperance Cafes. It was there Dad and I drank our Cappuccino Coffees. The hiss and bubble of the machine making our Cappuccino; the taste of real Italian ice creams, I easily recall today. I loved their coffee. I always licked their Italian ice cream with childhood delight. I did not miss the drink in the pub with my father. I was, of course, always a favoured visitor at the two Italian cafes. With the name of Ugino, I was half Italian anyway! Berni and Rabbaiotti always called me Ugino. I always received special treatment at their cafes. It was the only benefit from having the name Ugino. My Italian connection did not go unnoticed with the local Italians.

"Mam taking Ugino to Sunday School"

It was January nineteen forty. The snow lay thickly on the roads and hillside. It was my birthday. I was eight. The country had been at war with Germany for four months. In the valleys of South Wales, apart from the nightly blackouts, the effects of war had not been noticed. The air raids, with their wailing sirens and the drone of the German bombers overhead, as they made they way to the Midlands, were yet to come. My birthday would proceed as normal, war or no war. Doctor Zanazi always visited me on my birthday; he never missed. My eighth birthday would be no exception. Despite the war, my eighth birthday proceeded as normal. My friends came for tea. They had left hours ago. I was tired after a long, exhausting, but happy day. The family sat at home; Mam, Dad, my brother Dayton, Bonzo, and myself. We waited patiently for Zanazi's visit. He came after evening surgery. He enthused over me, as usual–his beloved Ugino. He towered over me, yet made me feel important and proud. After all, I was his little Ugo. Although only a small eight year old, he made me feel tall. He brought me a birthday card from Mamma Zanazi and some of her home made cake. A card from himself and a delightful picture of Venice that, in years to come, I would cherish and derive much pleasure from. Zanazi then spoke directly to me.

> "This year, I have a special present for you Ugino. I've spoken with your parents and they have agreed. Every Saturday, after morning surgery, I will collect you in my car and take you on my home visits around. the town. We shall have lunch together at my home, cooked by Mamma. When lunch is over, I shall bring you back home. We will spend Saturdays together, and I shall look forward to your company."

"How wonderful!" exclaimed my mother.

"Say thank you to the doctor."

"Thank you", I said, but I was far from pleased. I do hope my face did not convey my disappointment to Zanazi. My Saturdays would now be ruined. I could see the new routine flashing before my eyes. I would not be allowed out to play on Saturday mornings, before Doctor Zanazi arrived to collect me. The early hours of Saturday would be spent making me presentable for the doctor. My Friday evening in the bath, would be switched to Saturday morning. Mam would insist I was perfectly clean to accompany the doctor. I would need a new jacket to wear. My hair would need to be brushed and combed. There would be no time to spend on the hills; no time for games in the street; no time for fishing; no time for flying kites; no time for Bonzo; no time for touch rugby and no time for my friends. No time for anything. Saturday and Sunday would now both become dressing up days. The weekend would now become two days on which to wear my best clothes. Two days when I would always be expected to be on my best behaviour. The thought did not please me. My eighth birthday had turned into a miserable affair. I hoped and prayed my visits with Zanazi would not last.

The Saturday morning routine proved worse than expected. I was not allowed to play. My weekly bath, in front of the kitchen fire, became a regular Saturday morning ritual. My hair was repeatedly combed and brushed by Mam throughout the morning.

I didn't receive a new jacket, but was given one of my brother's. My shoes were cleaned and polished, until they shone like never before. When ready, I was then subjected to the inevitable final close inspection by Mam. I was then ordered to sit still and wait for Doctor Zanazi. I seemed to wait for hours. Oh, how I wished I could be out playing with Bonzo and my friends.

Doctor Zanazi had an Austin Twelve car. There were few cars in the town. Everyone seemed to know the doctor's car. When Zanazi arrived at a house, I was left alone in the car, sitting, waiting until his return. I often sat alone in the car for thirty minutes or more. Sitting and thinking how much nicer it would be playing games with my friends. The arrival of the doctor's car in any street always evoked curiosity amongst the neighbours. Indiscreet women, I frequently saw surreptitiously pulling the corner of their curtain back, to verify which house the doctor was visiting. When Zanazi entered the patient's house, the local children surrounded his car. A car was a novelty to them. To see a dressed up eight-year-old sitting in the front seat alone was something they could not understand. I frequently became the subject of taunts and abuse from those children. I was always glad when the visits were finished, for then we made our way to Zanazi's house. Mamma Zanazi's lunches were wonderful. I was always hungry. It was there that I learnt the delights of Italian food. A delight I have carried into my adult life. Mamma Zanazi's spoken English was excellent. I enjoyed listening to her reminiscing with her son about the beauty of northern Italy.

Mamma was a beautiful and gracious lady. I cannot recall her being dressed in anything other than a long, flowing, black, lace dress. Tightly fitting in the bodice and at the waist, it flowed into layer upon layer of black lace that made up the skirt. Her body was tall, elegant and erect. Her face, gently wrinkled with age, always carried a welcoming smile. Her head was covered with thick, silver hair. She glided through the house, but the rustle of her skirt always gave the clue to her whereabouts. I came to enjoy lunch at Zanazi's. Mamma treated me like her grandson. After all I was her Ugino. She loved me, as if I was her own.

It was Spring, and for four months I had spent every Saturday in Zanazi's company. I longed to spend my Saturdays playing cricket with my friends. I had given up sixteen Saturdays, when I could have been playing, to go on visits with Zanazi. The Saturday ritual at home remained the same. The morning bath was followed by dressing up. I then sat still, waiting for the doctor to arrive. The journey around town saw me sitting in the front seat of the doctor's car, prior to lunch with Mamma. The only part I enjoyed was Mamma's Italian food and Mamma. I always returned home with Doctor Zanazi in mid afternoon. Invariably it was too late to go out to play. As always, Zanazi brought me into the house and reported to my parents.

"What a good boy Ugino has been."

Today however was different. My father wanted to talk with Zanazi. Dad seemed very serious. Dad and Zanazi departed together to the front room. The door was quickly closed. I was in the process of going upstairs to change my clothes, when I decided to sit on the stairs listening to what my father and Zanazi were discussing. I feared there maybe another scheme they were plotting for me. I heard my Dad raise his voice.

"You have to become English. You have to become a naturalised citizen. Give up being Italian. Become British and you will be safe."

Zanazi's response was subdued.

"I am an Italian, John. I do not agree with what Italy is doing. I have come to hate Mussolini, but I am an Italian. I shall always remain an Italian. You must realise, I am what I am. I cannot change."

The front room door opened. Dad pleaded with Zanazi.

"Please become British. The consequences otherwise could be disastrous."

"I'm sorry John. I appreciate your concern. I am, and always will be an Italian. I cannot become British."

I quietly climbed the stairs. I don't believe either my father or Zanazi saw me or were aware that I had overheard their conversation. As I changed my clothes, I thought 'what a stupid father.' Doctor Zanazi is Italian. How could he become British? Did my Dad now want me to have English food from Mamma on a Saturday? I had developed a liking for Mamma's Italian food. I wanted her meals to continue.

It was the evening of June 10th nineteen hundred and forty. I was eight years and five months. For those five months I had missed playing on Saturdays. Some twenty Saturdays had been spent with Ugo and Mamma Zanazi. My geography of Italy had improved. My taste for Italian food was well established. Dad left the house in a hurry. Italy had declared war on the United Kingdom. The British government had planned that, in the event of Italy entering the war, all the adult male Italians in the country would be arrested. Initially they would be placed in local jails, prior to internment in prisoner of war camps. It seemed to many astonishing that the British government considered all the adult male Italians to be fifth columnists and a danger to the country's security. Ugo Zanazi, Berni and Rabbaiotti were our friends. How could they be a danger to our country? The Tredegar police, had been aware of the government plans for several days. The government's instructions had been received at the police station. The instructions were explicit.

> "In the event of Italy declaring war on the United Kingdom, all adult male Italians were to be arrested and placed in custody to await further instructions."

The police constables were sent out in pairs to arrest the Italians living in Tredegar. Berni and Rabbaiotti were arrested at their homes. When the police arrived at Zanazi's house in Church Street, Zanazi was not at home. Mamma answered the door. When the police asked her questions however her sole response was.

"Me no speaky the language."

Zanazi was arrested by the police walking on the mountain between Tredegar and Rhymney. Many believed he was trying to escape. He would spend the night, with the other local adult male Italians, in Georgetown jail. It was an unbelievable situation. The town's beloved doctor and the owners of the two Temperance Cafes had been arrested. The town would lose Zanazi forever. My wish had been granted. Saturday would revert to become my day for playing. Saturdays would now be spent on the western hills of Tredegar. I could play games again. I would fish, run through the rush fields, fly kites, play cricket and touch rugby. However, I would always wish Ugo Zanazi had remained our doctor and Mamma had remained my friend.

The following morning, at breakfast, Dad tried to explain to me why the Italians had been arrested. I could not understand how Berni, Rabbaiotti and, most of all, Zanazi were a danger to us. Zanazi had been such a kind considerate man. I couldn't believe he was a danger to anyone. How could he be arrested and taken to prison, when he had done so many good deeds in the town. It didn't make any sense. Our family would have a new doctor. There would be no more birthday presents from Zanazi. No more Saturdays spent touring the streets of the town in his car. No more lunches with Mamma enjoying her Italian food. My weekly bath would revert to a Friday evening. There would be no need for me to dress in my best clothes on a Saturday. I would be free to play again on Saturdays, but I never realised how I would miss Mamma and Doctor Zanazi. Dad decided to walk me to Georgetown jail to say my goodbyes to Zanazi. It was a long walk as the jail was situated on the eastern slope of the valley. When Dad and I arrived at the jail, I was refused admission.

"Too young"
the policeman said. My Dad was allowed in. I sat and cried on the steps outside the jail. The police later revisited Zanazi's home to question Mamma. Then, in her eighties, her answer to the police was always the same.

"Me no speaky the language!"
Dad visited her every day, before she left Tredegar forever. She went to live initially with Italian friends in Cardiff, prior to moving to some other friends in London. Sadly she died without seeing her son again. I had no opportunity to say goodbye to Mamma. Saturdays became the day for me to play again. Games would be the order of my day, but the memory of Ugo and Mamma Zanazi would remain forever.

2

Schooldays..................

Mam and Dad first became parents in nineteen twenty six, with the birth of my elder brother. He was born on the twentieth of April, one day before Queen Elizabeth the second. From a very early age, both our parents had been indoctrinated with the town's belief that,

> "If you don't want to spend the rest of your life working underground as a miner; work hard at school; go to college and become a teacher."

Our parents had however progressed this philosophy. As teenagers they both had followed the town's philosophy. On leaving school, both Mam and Dad had attended teacher-training college and qualified as teachers. In the working world of education however, they had discovered that university trained teachers had distinct advantages over those trained at a teachers training college. Mam and Dad both agreed that any of their children would have to go to university. Teachers Training Colleges would just not be good enough for their children. University would provide their offspring with the best education possible. Whatever their children wanted to become in life, as parents, they insisted, it would have to involve a university education. Dayton was destined for university, as far as our parents were concerned, from the day he was born. His education was always Mam and Dad's main concern.

Dayton grew up in West Hill, the highest street on the western slope of the valley. Above West Hill there were just open mountains. Earl Street was the street below West Hill. The local elementary school was in Earl

Street; the schoolyard was visible from our front bedroom window. All the children of West Hill went to Earl Street School. From our house it was less than a five-minute walk away. At the time of Dayton's birth, Dad taught at Georgetown School, on the eastern slope of the valley. His school was a two-mile walk away from home. If Dayton was to succeed on the academic, university path his parents had planned for him, he would, his parents believed, have a distinct advantage if he was at the same school where his father taught. Mam and Dad decided that Dayton would attend Georgetown School. All Dayton's friends attended Earl Street. Dad and Dayton would walk the two miles every day to Georgetown School. Mam and Dad were thus able to personally monitor Dayton's progress through elementary school. Dayton was a great success at elementary school. He passed the eleven plus examination heading the examination list. He took up a grammar school place at Lewis' School Pengam, some twelve miles away in the Rhymney valley. Mam and Dad continued to closely supervise Dayton's progress through grammar school. Academically he did exceptionally well. Always in the A forms, Dayton invariably was at, or near, the top of his class. He was an outstanding academic pupil. His parents ensured that each evening, on returning from school, he worked hard at his studies. Sport and games, not to mention girls, were considered by his parents, an irrelevant distraction. Dayton did not enjoy the joys of rugby football at school; Mam and Dad convinced him playing sport was an irrelevance. Dayton's main aim in life was obtaining a place at university. At seventeen years of age, Dayton was admitted to Cambridge University. He would study Mechanical Engineering. Mam and Dad were delirious.

I was born six years after Dayton. At the time of my birth, Dayton was already attending Georgetown School. At the age of five, when I commenced primary school, Dayton was eleven. He was already at grammar school, travelling the twelve miles by bus every day. In our childhood, Dayton and I grew up seeing very little of each other. For two boys, the six-year age difference between us was too big. I was a little pest to my elder brother. Whether it was a conscious decision by my parents, or whether the education authority would not allow it, I know not. Whatever the reason, at the age of five, I went to Earl Street School. I was saved the embarrassment of being a pupil in the school where my father taught. I was delighted. All my friends went to Earl Street School. I was therefore spared the daily two-mile walk to Georgetown with my Dad. At no time did I receive an explanation from my parents, as to why they chose different schools for their two sons. I never enquired. I just accepted my parents' decision. I had a happy time at Earl Street School. I really enjoyed my five years there. Those five years coincided, almost totally, with Dayton's years at grammar school. In those years, I was always conscious of how hard my parents expected Dayton to work and study. Dayton was never allowed to play out in the streets, with the other children, as I did. All Dayton's evenings were spent revising, or doing homework under the supervision of one or other of our parents. Strangely, on those evenings, I was always allowed out to play. Maybe my absence from home out playing, was to allow my brother a more quiet time in which to study. I never questioned my parent's decision. They seemed so intent on ensuring my brother was an academic success. In any event, I enjoyed playing in the street too much.

I sat the eleven plus examination a year early. I entered the same grammar school as my brother, when I was ten years and nine months old. My brother was a prefect in the second year six. We would be together at the grammar school for just one year. At school we always remained apart.

From my very first day, I hated life at Lewis' School Pengam. As each subject master took the names of the pupils, at the beginning of term, the same procedure was invariably repeated. As I responded to my name, the teacher would say :-

"Ugo. What an unusual name! Ugo Neil Phillips. No relation I suppose to John Dayton?

"Yes sir."
I would quietly reply.

"I'm his brother."

"Well if you're half as good as your brother you'll do well."
I always believed I would never be 'half as good', academically, as my brother. At Lewis' School, the masters always set that benchmark for me.

I was always compared with my brother. I knew I would never be able to compete with his academic success. I hated the brotherly comparison. The school's attitude drove my brother and me further apart.

Dayton was not a particularly sporty person, though he did enjoy a game of cricket. He was a reasonable spin bowler and a good fielder, but, as I used to say,

"He couldn't bat for toffee apples."

It was my first summer term at grammar school and Dayton's last. Dayton had been selected to play, for the first time, in the school's first eleven at cricket. For someone who had spent all his youth studying, Dayton's selection was indeed a great achievement. Our parents were rightly proud. Dayton was in the first eleven to play at Quakers Yard School. Dad drove Dayton to the ground by car. I travelled with them to give additional family support to Dayton. I would spend the Saturday morning as a spectator watching my school's cricket team.

As Dad drove our family car over the hillside to the neighbouring valley, that housed the Quakers Yard School, it started raining. Initially it was only a slight drizzle. As we approached the school, the rain became heavier. Dad was the first to arrive. He was soon followed by other parents bringing their sons to the match.

"The rain's been really heavy on the way up. We almost turned back."

reported one parent to my father.

"I suppose the match will be cancelled."

said another.

The rains eased however and play commenced at the allotted time of eleven o'clock. The early morning heavy rain, lower down the valley, had obviously deterred some of the school's players from attending. At the start of play, only nine Pengam Grammar schoolboys were present. Our games master had not arrived. Our school could not provide an umpire. My Dad was nominated as an umpire. Ted Judge was the school's Cricket Captain. {Sadly, he was killed, a few years later, on active service.} Judge approached me.

> "You're John Dayton's brother aren't you? In Form 2C I hear. We're two short, so you'll have to play. I can't imagine that our two missing players will turn up now. Young Phillips you're playing."

Judge lost the toss and Quakers Yard decided to bat. I fielded on the boundary in my short grey trousers. I made no contribution during their innings. The ball never came in my direction.

School cricket matches were played out with each side having a maximum of one and a half hours batting. Needless to say, I was to be the last man to bat. I was at number ten. My brother, Dayton, was at number nine. Our school was still one man short. I was upset that my brother was batting at number nine. I knew that of the two of us, I was the better batsman. Wickets tumbled frequently during our innings. Runs seemed very hard to come by. Eight wickets were down with twenty minutes left to play, when I was called upon to bat. It was now impossible for our team to win. My job would be to bat out the last twenty minutes and play for a draw. The problem, I foresaw, was that my brother was batting at the other end. The good thing was, with the fall of the last wicket, I would be on strike. I suppose the sight of an eleven year old in short trousers coming out to bat, with pads that reached almost up to his middle was somewhat incongruous. If my presence gave the opposition some hope of a quick win, I was unaware of it. Before taking guard from the umpire at the bowler's end, who happened to be my Dad, I decided to have a word with my elder brother.

> "I think it's best if I take all or most of the bowling. Just be prepared to take a quick single at the end of the over so that I can remain on strike."

My brother was furious. Even my father, who overheard my remarks, was most displeased. Here I was, an eleven-year-old youngster instructing his seventeen year-old brother to play a subsidiary role. I was happy to accept the responsibility and play the senior batting role; age did not enter into it. I knew I was the better batsman.

As usual, I took middle and leg as my guard. I'd watched the bowler from the pavilion. I knew he was especially quick. The batsmen, who had been dismissed, said that he bowled mainly out-swingers. As the bowler peered at me from the far end of his run, I had not appreciated how tall he was. He must have been well over six feet. The rain started to fall again, but there was no possibility of Quakers Yard leaving the field. Victory would be theirs at the fall of the next wicket. The name of the bowler was Pope. He started on his long run, bowling me my first ball. I concentrated hard. At the crucial moment of the bowler's delivery, a drop of rainwater fell from the peak of my school cap, obliterating the flight of the ball. Instinctively, I resorted to the philosophy I had been taught, batting on the Red Ground and in the street -

"If in doubt, play forward."

I stretched my left leg as far down the pitch as my little legs would allow. The ball clipped the outside edge of my bat before skittling along the ground between the slips. There was no third man on the boundary. With my first stroke, I had scored four runs. In reality I had never seen the ball from the moment it left the bowler's hand. Pope was visibly upset. He thundered in, running more quickly, for his next delivery and bowled a really short ball. The ball reared off the pitch, clearing my head by several feet. I asked my father, at the bowler's end, how many deliveries were left in the over. He informed me there was one ball left. I nodded to my brother, who reluctantly acknowledged my signal. The whole Quakers Yard team took up fielding positions closer to my bat, in order to prevent a single run being taken off the last ball of the over. I surveyed the field noting there was no leg slip. There was a forward short leg and a short square leg, but no fine leg. If I could move across to the off side for the next delivery, I just might be able to tickle the ball down the leg side and score my desired single. Pope bowled. I moved across to the off side. My bat just tickled the ball down the leg side. The ball raced along the ground towards the boundary. With the grass being wet with rain, the ball came to a stop, inches from the boundary line, with not a fielder in sight. My brother and I ran our intended single. As we crossed my brother shouted,

"There's an easy two there."

I shouted back,

"Don't be stupid. One is all we need."
The fielder took so long to retrieve the ball, my brother and I could have run three runs. Nevertheless one run was all I needed to keep the strike. I refused to run more than the one run. The next over was bowled by a slow off spin bowler, which was quite a refreshing change from the fast pace of Pope. In the wet conditions, the off spinner found great difficulty in controlling the spin. Despite frequently rubbing the ball in the sawdust pile, and wiping it from time to time with a duster, the ball continually slipped from his hand. His bowling was most erratic. Despite being surrounded by close fielders, I comfortably played out the over, frequently reminding myself to keep my left elbow high and my bat at an acute angle, in order to smother the ball. The last ball of the off spinner's over was short and wide of the off stump. I stepped back, hitting the ball off my back foot through the close fielders into the covers area. Dayton and I easily achieved our single run. The overs slowly went by. I managed to survive five overs by resolutely blocking those deliveries on the wicket and leaving alone those deliveries that were wide of the stumps. At the end of each over, I managed to steal a single run, so keeping my brother away from the bowling. From my arrival at the wicket, my big brother had not faced one ball. I was really enjoying myself. My brother fumed at the bowler's end. The endless hours of practice I had given to my batting on the Red Ground, and in the street at West Hill, were certainly now paying dividends. It was nevertheless a relief when my father called,

"Last over"

Only six balls left. I was determined to stay. Equally determined was Pope. He would bowl the fastest over of his young life. All his team-mates surrounded my bat, eager to take a catch. They wrongly believed a little eleven year old, playing in short trousers, would not frustrate Quakers Yard through their final over. All these years later, I cannot recall each individual ball of that last over, but survive the six balls I did. Although Quakers Yard had scored more runs, in the allotted batting time, than our school, the match was declared a draw. I had faced six overs, scored nine runs and was not out at the close. I was deliriously happy. Dayton's score was nought not out. He was furious. In the last six overs he had not faced a single ball. I had protected him from all the bowling. He was not pleased. Surprisingly my father did not congratulate me on my innings. He merely said,

"You and I will need to talk later."

Dad's words had an ominous ring. They were however completely overshadowed by the delight I felt. I had ensured the school had escaped with a draw. Ted Judge, the school cricket captain, was full of praise for my efforts, as were all the other members of our team. The youngster from Form Two had played well.

The following day, a Sunday, in the evening after chapel, my brother was, as usual, engrossed in his schoolwork. I was daydreaming about my big innings of the day before at Quakers Yard.

"It seems like a good time for us both to have a talk." Dad said.

"Let's go into the front room where it's quiet."

I sat on a chair. My father sat opposite me.

"Yesterday, you batted really well in difficult circumstances." my father began.

> "You batted really well. I was really proud of your batting. What I was not pleased about however was the arrogant way you dismissed your brother. You know his cricketing strength is in his bowling. Dayton would be the first to admit, batting is not one of his strong points. That, however, is no excuse for belittling his ability in front of his colleagues. You made it clear to everyone that you, his younger brother by some six years, was a better cricketer. You should never belittle anyone as you did yesterday, let alone your brother."

Immediately I knew I was not going to win this argument with my father, but I did try.

> "Firstly, I did not belittle Dayton in front of his colleagues. My comments were made in the middle of the cricket square. There was not a Pengam Grammar schoolboy within hearing distance. My sole concern was to ensure the school did not lose. I know, and I'm sure you know, that if Dayton had been

exposed to Pope's bowling, the school would have lost the cricket match. As it is, Dayton was a not out batsman. His colleagues will be proud of him for that. Anyway, if anyone is belittled in front of his colleagues at school, it's me. Every day of my school life I am compared, by the masters, with their blue-eyed academically brilliant 'John Dayton'. I know Dad, I will never achieve Dayton's academic brilliance. I do know, however, I'm good at cricket. It's about the only thing I'm better at than my brother. Why don't you ask the masters at school to stop belittling me in front of my colleagues?"

My feelings had been pent up for nearly a year. Dayton had this brilliant academic record throughout his school life. It was a record I would never be able to achieve. My strength is my cricket. For the first time, at the age of eleven, I was aware of the conflict that sport would bring to my education. At that early age, I was unaware it was a conflict that would plague me throughout my life. Where would my priorities lie? I wanted to be a cricketer. I was not concerned about university life. I knew Mam and Dad would be disappointed. My desire to be a cricketer would not fit into their overwhelming desire that both their sons should go to university.

"I had no idea you felt that you were being belittled at school by the masters in front of your colleagues."

my Dad continued.

"That's not fair either. If you feel aggrieved about that, maybe you can appreciate how Dayton feels about you dismissing his ability as a batsman. You have introduced your own benchmark for his batting. You always compare his batting ability with your own and that's not fair. You have a talent for batting. Dayton doesn't. Dayton has a talent for academic success and maybe, just maybe, your academic prowess is not as good as Dayton's."

My Dad paused. There was a long eerie silence.

"I think the lesson to learn from all of this is that both you and Dayton are your own person, each with your own individual strengths and weaknesses. As individuals, each part of you makes up the whole. Each one of you is important to yourselves. Every person is important to themselves. We should never belittle them."

With a smile my Dad added

"You did bat really well."

Each day, at Lewis' School Pengam, began with a service in the chapel. The school chapel was magnificent. Each form had its own allocated pews; junior pupils at the front, senior pupils to the back. The Prefect's Pew was to the side of the elevated stage. My brother sat in the Prefect's Pew. As a Form Two pupil, I sat in the front pews. All the masters sat on the elevated stage. The elegant, golden lectern was to their left. The electric organ behind them. The prefects read the lesson from the golden lectern. Every Tuesday and Thursday, the whole service was in Welsh. When the whole school was assembled, a messenger was sent to knock on the headmaster's door. All the pupils rose to their feet. The headmaster made his dramatic entry to the centre of the stage. The format of the service was always the same. The school sang a psalm. A prefect read the lesson. The headmaster made his announcements. The service closed with a hymn. On Mondays, the headmaster's announcements were mainly a report of the school team's sporting achievements over the weekend.

On completing the gospel reading, the prefect returned to the prefect's pew. The headmaster, Leslie Stanley Knight, rose from his chair.

"Good morning school. There is only one announcement. It concerns the result of the school's first cricket eleven. The team were playing at Quaker's Yard last Saturday. Regarding the game, I have a very special announcement to make. As you will all be aware, last Saturday was not a very nice day. Heavy rain, interspersed with drizzly showers, occurred during the early part of the morning. The rain was so heavy, two of the first team players decided the game would not be played. Those two boys know who they are. I shall not embarrass them by naming them. As a consequence of their absence, the school only had nine players present. The school however was fortunate, very fortunate, in that one of our Form Two boys turned up to watch his brother play. Ted Judge, our cricket captain, quite rightly invited the Form Two pupil to play. This junior school pupil was the last man to bat. He batted at number ten. When called upon to bat, some twenty minutes of play remained. I am informed the school had no chance of winning. All the school's efforts were concentrated in batting out time, for a draw. I am pleased to inform you an honourable draw was obtained. Our youngster, from Form Two, batted out six overs and saved the match. The youngster scored nine runs. He was not out. The match against Quakers Yard was drawn. I'm sure the whole school would wish to show their appreciation to that junior school member. I call Ugo Neil Phillips to join me on the stage I want him to receive the congratulations of the whole school."

As I rose to my feet, my whole body was shaking. I shuffled past my fellow form pupils in order to reach the end of the pew. I walked towards the stage. I was aware of the loud applause from the whole school. In order to reach the stairs leading to the stage, I walked past the prefect's pew. I did not have the courage to look at my brother. I would never know whether he was smiling with delight, applauding like the rest of the school, or staring fretfully ahead. I climbed the stairs and, as I approached the headmaster's chair, the whole school came to an eerie silence.

"Well done Ugo Neil"

the headmaster said, in a voice the whole school could hear, as he shook my hand.

"The whole school is very proud of you."

The school spontaneously broke into an explosive burst of applause. The noise rang in my ears. It continued until I returned to my seat. My Dad was correct.

"I was important after all–if only to myself."

When the end of year examination results came out, I was bottom of the class. This position would be a familiar one for me throughout my time at Lewis' School, Pengam. My school report was atrocious. My Dad commented

"The only thing you have consistently gone up in, over the three terms of your first year is your height and weight!"

I asked him to look at my games report. It said,

"Ugo Neil has an exceptional talent at cricket."

In comparison Dayton obtained high grades in Physics and Mathematics at his Higher School Certificate. He won a place at St. John's College, Cambridge to study Engineering. My parents were delighted not only for Dayton, but also for themselves. Mam and Dad had achieved the first part of their dream. Dayton was going to university. The second part of their dream, getting me to university, would prove more difficult. Dayton would leave home for Cambridge at the age of seventeen and a half. As for myself, I was completely satisfied with the Games Master's report

"Ugo Neil has an exceptional talent for cricket."

Next year my brother would be at Cambridge. I would be at Lewis' school on my own. I too would be a success at school, but only because of my cricket and rugby. The conflict between my work and sport had begun. It was a conflict that would last forever.

Joe Hodges was my mother's father. Grandpa Hodges, as I called him, was a fearsome man. It was well known that half the men in the town also feared him. For the men who worked at Ty-Trist colliery, Joe's word was law. No one at the Ty-Trist coalface argued with Joe, even when they knew he was wrong. He was the man to whom they gave the utmost respect. Respect, it is often said, cannot be demanded. Respect has to be earned. The respect shown to Joe Hodges was the exception. Joe demanded and received respect. Over the years, Joe had done little to earn the respect of the miners. The respect he enjoyed from the miners was bred out of fear. It had not always been so.

Joe left school at twelve and went to work at the coalface of Ty-Trist colliery. At the age of twelve, he joined the night shift. There was nothing unusual in that. Virtually all the lads of that era left school at twelve to work underground; there was little else for them to do. Joe, like many of the lads of his day, worked at Ty-Trist. As a young adult, he worked at the coal face, hewing coal out of the underground seams with a pick and a shovel. It was hard, dirty work.

Joe began each day walking to the pit. The pit was some two miles from his home. Joe left home in the morning at five thirty, before the sun had risen. Each day, he worked at the coalface until four o'clock in the afternoon. In wintertime, it was dark when he left home in the morning, dark where he worked during the six day working week, and dark when he arrived home in the evening. Joe and his fellow miners saw little of the sun in wintertime. With no pit head baths, he and the other miners walked back from the pit to their homes in their working clothes. Those clothes were thickly impregnated with coal dust, from their day's work underground. The bottoms of their trousers, I vividly remember, were tied around with string, to prevent the coal dust rising up their legs. Their faces and hands blackened and covered with coal dust. Home, was the only place to wash and soak in a bath. Emily, Joe's wife, like all the miners' wives, would have the tin bath full of warm water waiting, in front of the fire for his arrival. The boiling of the water, for the daily bath, was a chore in itself for Emily. After lunch each day she would boil several pots of water on the coal fire in order to fill the tin bath.

Joe had worked at the coalface for ten years when the accident happened. The pit pony was pulling the drams, full of coal, away from the coal seam. Joe stood watching the drams as they passed him. Suddenly the wire rope, connecting the drams, leapt up and crashed into his face. The impact of the steel rope tore through his lower jaw smashing his lower jawbone into several pieces. The profuse bleeding was stopped at the mine's first aid station. The severe wound was covered with a pack of white gauze. Joe was taken home in the manager's car. The mine's doctor called, almost as soon as Joe arrived home. Close inspection revealed a wound covered with coal dust. The right sided lower jawbone was smashed into several pieces. Whisky, in copious amounts, was administered to Joe, not only to ease the pain, but also to act as an anaesthetic. Having signed the pledge, it would be the only time alcohol would ever pass his lips. Joe was a fanatical supporter of the Temperance Movement. With Joe lying on the kitchen table, the alcohol-induced anaesthesia enabled the doctor to remove pieces of bone from the distorted face. His days at the coal face were at an end. On returning to work, Joe was promoted. He was appointed to the post of Check Weigher. It was in that position he was able to rule the miners with fear. Miners at the coal face, in those days, worked in teams. Each team filled their drams with the coal they had cut from the coalface. When full of coal, they wrote their team name on the side of the dram in chalk. When the dram arrived at the surface, it became the responsibility of the checkweigher. He inspected the contents of the dram and removed any slag. He weighed only the coal left in the dram.. The men, at the coal, face were paid only for the amount of coal they produced in each dram. The check-weigher was thus all-powerful at the pit. If he disliked any member of the coal cutting team, he would not only throw out the slag, but also remove much of the coal. As a result of the check-weigher's illegal action, the miners would be credited with cutting less coal and receive less pay. Joe was more honourable than most check weighers, but in return he expected compliance from the miners, not only at the pit, but also in every part of their life. The miners, at the coalface knew Joe controlled their wage packet. It was a fact Joe Hodges frequently reminded them of. During his years, as the check-weigher, Joe's power and authority became total. At Ty-Trist colliery, Joe's word was law. No one disagreed with him. As a result of the accident, Joe's face was severely deformed. His lower jaw was foreshortened on one side with a large depression in it. The covering scar tissue contained many blue marks; the proof, if any was needed, that it had been impossible to remove all the coal dust from the wound at the time of the injury. He was a fearsome looking man. His domineering personality fitted well with his looks. Joe was my grandfather. He lived five doors away from our home, at forty-seven West Hill.

With so much power at work, it was inevitable that his power and domineering personality were carried over into his family life. He had four children. Edith, my mother, was the eldest. Ivor, was his only son. Elsie and Marion were his other two daughters. All four children were petrified of their father. Marion, the youngest child, always maintained that the reason she took up a nursing career in London was to get away from him.

SCHOOLDAYS

Edith, Ivor and Elsie lived in Tredegar. Throughout their entire adult life, all his children were genuinely in fear of Joe Hodges. There is no doubt that, when they were children, Joe had physically abused them. Even slight misbehaviour was met with lashings with a leather strap. The memories of such beatings remained with all his children. It was Joe's way of ensuring his word was law. His four children never argued with him. Even in adult life, when they were married and had children of their own, they accepted every decision Joe made. They never questioned his decisions. Joe ruled the whole family. All his children feared him, until the day he died.

Dad had promised my brother and me tickets for the Wales versus England Soccer International at Cardiff. It was typical of my Dad that he would obtain three tickets and then decide later they were for my grandfather, my brother and myself. I didn't know if my father wanted to see the game. In any event he had a meeting to attend at the Park Hotel in Cardiff on the same day. My grandfather, Dayton and I had the three precious tickets for the enclosure at Ninian Park. I was to witness my first soccer international. The war had deprived everyone of international football for six years. International soccer players had fought for their country. They had been unable to display their football skills to the crowds who longed to see them. The end of the war brought the return of football to Britain. With the absence of television, the public came in their thousands to see football in the post war era.

On the day of the game I was fifteen, my brother was twenty-one and grandfather was old. I knew the Welsh team by heart. Sidlow in goal. Lambert and Barnes the two fullbacks. The half-back line was Powell I, Jones T and Burgess. The forwards Thomas, Powell A, Lowrie, Bryn Jones and Edwards. As I stood on the terracing, near the players' tunnel on the halfway line, those eleven Welshmen were my heroes. I had come to see them defeat England. As I studied the match programme, the names of the England players evoked no emotion in me. Later I would be ashamed of my feelings, but I can only record how I felt at that time. England had Frank Swift in goal. Scott and Hardwick playing at fullback. The half-backs were Taylor, Franklin and Wright. The illustrious forward line was Matthews,

Mortensen, Lawton, Mannion and Finney. Such is the confidence of youth, I believed Wales would win. My heart certainly ruled my head.

The record books show that England won the match three goals to nil. Finney, Mortensen and Lawton scored the goals. Wales were outclassed. During the game, I warmed to the skills of Stan Matthews, Wilf Mannion, Tom Finney, Frank Swift and Billy Wright. I appreciated their talent. I felt privileged to watch them play, even though Wales had lost. I would be an England soccer fan forever. As I witnessed that game, as a fifteen year old, standing in the enclosure with my grandfather and Dayton, I had no idea what the future held for me. I just wanted to be a professional cricketer. The thought that in the future, I would meet with most of these England players was just unbelievable. The thought that, in years to come, I would be a doctor and Wilf Mannion would be my patient was just unthinkable. George Hardwick would be the Middlesbrough's youth team coach and I, a Middlesbrough director. Billy Wright and I would be travelling companions on many overseas tours. I would meet Stan Mathews and Stan Mortensen at International Club luncheons. Tom Finney and I would make our acquaintance through The Football Association. Of the Welsh team I would often meet Bryn Jones with his nephew, and my friend, the sports writer, Ken Jones. Finally George Edwards and I would become good friends, as fellow directors of Cardiff and Middlesbrough respectively. The future had much in store, but I digress. On October 18th nineteen forty-seven, I was a starry eyed, fifteen year old, Welsh boy. I had witnessed the talents of a great England football team. I enjoyed the experience.

I do not know how many people attended that international, but my memory is that Ninian Park was full to capacity. Certainly, in the enclosure, where we stood, it was very crowded. At times I feared the crowd would crush me. At half-time grandfather discussed, with Dayton and me, the tactics for leaving the ground at the end of the match. He suggested we could leave ten minutes before the end of the game, thus avoiding the crush. Alternatively we could leave at the final whistle and fight our way through the crowds. His third alternative was to stand where we were at the end of the game, wait for ten minutes, until the crowd dispersed, and then leave. The three alternatives were discussed. We agreed that we wanted to see the whole game. The best option was to see the game through to the final whistle, then wait for ten minutes, allowing the crowd to disperse. We could then leisurely walk back to The Park Hotel to meet Dad. The decision was made. I could see the whole game. At the final whistle, the three of us would wait ten minutes in the enclosure, until the crowd dispersed. It was the sensible decision to make.

The referee blew the final whistle. As the England players left the field, I clapped and clapped and clapped. I glanced at my grandfather. Immediately, I realised he was not pleased with my enthusiasm for the England team. In Wales, my grandfather was what we call, Welsh-Welsh. He really hated the English. My grandfather was really upset that Wales had lost. I probably annoyed him, in that I was clapping the England players. In grandfather's eyes, England was our opponents ; the enemy my grandfather hated. I cared not. I had witnessed the talents of a great England side. I felt privileged to have seen them. It was absolutely correct for me to applaud them from the field. The players were still in the process of leaving the field when my grandfather decided to leave the ground.

"Come on", he said, "We're leaving."
My reply was spontaneous.

> "Oh no, I said "We made an agreement at half-time. We agreed we would wait for ten minutes until the crowd had dispersed. That is what we agreed and that is what I am going to do."

The anger immediately showed on my grandfather's face. No one argued with Joe Hodges. No one disputed his decisions.

"We're leaving now. How dare you question my decision."
he bellowed. Addressing my brother, he said,

> "Come on Dayton, we're leaving now. If Neil doesn't come, we will leave him."

Immediately, it seemed they were gone. I was left alone in the enclosure at Ninian Park. Dad had taught me to measure time accurately. His advice was always to say,

> "One banana, two banana, three banana"

Each banana, he had told me, would measure one second. Sixty bananas would fairly accurately determine a minute of time. As the crowd dispersed around me, I counted six hundred bananas. I knew six hundred bananas would equate to some ten minutes. The crowd left the stadium. I left after six hundred bananas.

Ninian Park lies some two miles from Cardiff's city centre. Outside, in the streets, I followed the crowd as they made their way back to the city centre. The cold autumn air swept across my face. Inside my body was warm with the joy of having seen the great football artists of England perform. I had actually been there. Seen them for myself. I would never forget my first international soccer match.. In my youth there was no television. Football matches were not brought into the living room by modern technology. My previous experience of professional football had been listening to the commentaries, by Raymond Glendenning, on a crackly radio at home. At last I had seen footballers in the flesh. I had not been disappointed.

As I entered Queen Street, the Saturday shoppers were making their way home. I turned left into Park Street. Immediately I saw Dayton and my grandfather standing outside the entrance to The Park Hotel. No words were exchanged on my arrival. I spent the few minutes, skipping on and off the kerbside to keep warm while we waited for Dad. Father was eager to know the match result and whether we had enjoyed the game. Grandfather and Dayton expressed their disappointment with the Welsh team. They both thought Wales had played very badly. Their perception of the game was one of Welsh failure, rather than the appreciation of the brilliance of the England players. Eventually my father asked me,

"Did you enjoy the game Ugo?"

"I loved it." I replied.

"They were absolutely magnificent. Hardwick, Mannion, Finney, Mathews and Swift were a joy to behold. They were absolutely fantastic. England could have scored six. They were so good. I shall always support England at soccer. They are a fantastic side."

My declaration of support for England was met with stony silence. We were soon back at the car. Grandfather sat in the front with father. My brother and I sat in the back. It was dark. The journey back up the valleys of South Wales was miserable. The rain, which had threatened all day, suddenly arrived. It poured down and Dad needed to concentrate on the driving. Everyone was quiet. I fell asleep, in the hope I would dream of those England players. What a day it had been! My first international. I had seen a magnificent England team.

Sunday was dry and sunny. It would not have mattered if it had been snowing or pouring with rain. The Sunday ritual never changed. With Dayton at home, he had been asked to play the church organ, for morning service, at chapel. I would pump the bellows. Mam would sit in the back pew with grandfather. They did not sit close together. Grandfather always sat at the end of the pew nearest the centre of the chapel. Mam always sat at the other end of the pew near the aisle. Dayton played the organ very well. I must have pumped the bellows well, as the organ did not run out of air! When the service ended Mam, Dayton and I climbed the west side of the valley to our home. How I hated that climb three times every Sunday.

It must have been a special Sunday, as all five grandchildren congregated at forty-seven West Hill for lunch. It was the usual Sunday performance. The children gathered around the harmonium with grandfather. Dayton played the hymns. Grandfather led us in the singing. There we sang until Gramma announced lunch was ready. The dining table was laid. We each had our identified place. We were never allowed to sit at any other place at the table except our own. Grandpa and Gramma sat at each end of the table. The grandchildren knew where their places were. I went to my place. As I sat down, my surprise was uncontrollable.

"You've forgotten to lay my place Gramma." I said.
There was a silent pause. Grandfather then spoke.
"There will be no lunch for you, until you apologise for your outrageous behaviour yesterday in Cardiff."
I was astonished.
"Well?" he enquired,
"I'm waiting for your apology."

Then addressing my cousins, he said,

> "Yesterday in Cardiff, Ugo Neil defied my instructions. Ugino wouldn't leave the ground when I told him to. His behaviour was unacceptable and disgraceful. Ugino has no respect for his elders."

Turning again to me, he said,

> "Well, I'm still waiting for you to say 'sorry'."

"I've nothing to apologise for." I said.

"If my lunch depends on an apology, I shall have no lunch."

I rose from my chair and departed. As I closed the dining room door, I heard grandfather deliver his usual prayer before lunch.

Mam wanted to know why I was home so soon. I explained what had happened at the end of the football match. I told her how I had been left alone in Ninian Park after the game. I explained what had happened at lunch. Grandpa had told me there was no lunch for me, unless I apologised. As I believed I had done no wrong, I could not apologise. I left Grandpa's house and came home.

"Well there's no lunch for you here either." Mam said.

"Just go back this minute and apologise to your grandfather."

Dad was astonished. Addressing my mother, he said,

> "Grandpa Hodges didn't say anything to me yesterday, on the way home. Everything seemed quite normal in the car."

Mam ignored my father's intervention.

"Go back this minute and apologise to your grandfather." my mother repeated..

> "No-one argues with you grandfather. Ugino, you must always have respect for your elders and do as they say. Off you go, apologise, and be done with it."

My reply to Mam was crystal clear.

> "I'm really sorry Mam. No one can make me apologise. I haven't done anything wrong. I refuse to apologise for something I haven't done. I know you are upset, because he's your father. I'm really sorry, but I'm not going to apologise. Not today, not tomorrow. Not ever."

Mam admonished me further. I refused to apologise. I was sent to bed. I remained in bed throughout Sunday. It was the first time in my life that I had ever been absent from Sunday school. I also missed the evening service at chapel.

Without question, the following nine weeks were the worst of my life. Joe Hodges decided to send Mam, Dad and me into exile. There was to be no contact between us. Although we only lived five doors apart, in the same street, the daily visits from Gramma Hodges, Joe banned. He ordered Gramma not to speak to any of us. Joe blamed my mother and father for not making me apologise.

"Do you have no control over that boy?" he had told my mother.

"You need to discipline Ugino with a heavy hand. A good leathering, with a belt, would make him apologise. That boy will be nothing but trouble."

Joe made these statements with his usual arrogance and authority. As far as I was concerned, Joe ignored me completely. If we were walking towards each other in the street, Joe would cross the road and walk on the other pavement to avoid me. I did not attend Gramma's for Sunday lunch. I continued to attend chapel three times on Sundays, but even there Joe, who was the chapel's senior trustee, chose to ignore me. Worst of all, on Sunday evenings, as I congregated in the chapel foyer with the other teenagers, Joe would approach us carrying his paper bag of sweets. They were always 'Mint Imperials'. Each Sunday evening, he would offer each and every teenager an imperial mint, but always ignored me and passed me by. It seemed quite incongruous to me that he could adopt such an attitude. Having distributed his sweets to the children, excluding me, he would then enter the chapel and pray. Doubtless he asked God for the forgiveness of his sins, as he forgave those who had trespassed against him. His outright hypocrisy scarred me for life. It taught me the big difference between Christianity and chapel. It made me realise that regularly attending chapel did not necessarily make one a Christian. One could adopt a Christian way of life without attending chapel. Throughout all those weeks I felt so sorry for my Mam. She often asked me to apologise, but

I really couldn't. My Dad never asked me.

It was Christmas day. My parents always ensured that I had nice presents. Despite all the turmoil with my grandfather, this year was no exception. My brother Dayton was at home for Christmas. Our family enjoyed Christmas lunch together. It was traditional for all our family to visit Gramma and Grandpa Hodges for Christmas tea and supper The family had received the usual invitation. I was included in the invitation provided I apologised to Grandpa Hodges. It was reconciliation time. I decided however I would not be going. Mam tried to persuade me, but I would never apologise and so I couldn't go. Dad was concerned, as I would be left in our house alone on Christmas day. Being alone in my own home was a much better option for me, rather than apologising to my grandfather. I did not want to be in Joe's presence. In any case, my parents, would only be five doors away. I would be fine on my own. In reality, I was never to be on my own. Bonzo would be at my side. A stream of cousins, aunts and uncles, all of whom had been sent by Joe to explain the position, visited me. All I had to do, they said, was to apologise to Joe. If I apologised to Joe, they each said, he would forgive me. My apology would enable Joe, and the whole family to enjoy their Christmas together. It was traditional that the whole family, wherever they were, would return to Gramma and Grandpa's for Christmas day. I was polite to all the messengers, but I refused to apologise. Messenger followed messenger. It was seven in the evening when my brother came to see me. In conversation with Joe, Dayton had made it clear I would never apologise. Not this Christmas, not next Christmas, not any Christmas, not ever. If Grandpa Hodges wanted his whole family present for Christmas supper, then my brother convinced Grandpa Hodges that he could persuade me to attend, but there would be no apology. In fact, my brother made an agreement with Joe that the matter of my first international match would never again be mentioned. When Dayton came to see me, he told me I could return. No apology was required. The matter would never again be discussed. My brother accompanied me to Gramma and Grandpa Hodges' house. No apology was requested from Grandpa Hodges and I gave none. Joe and Emily Hodges enjoyed their Christmas supper with their entire family. My Grandpa had forgiven me

[58]

because it was Christmas day. The previous nine weeks of stress, anguish and hostility were forgotten; conveniently forgotten, because it was Christmas day. The Lord's Prayer asked Christians to be forgiven for their trespasses, as they forgave those who trespassed against them. Before retiring to bed that evening, I checked with my Dad. I asked him if there was any mention, in the Lord's Prayer, of waiting until Christmas day. My Dad smiled. Dad's smile of approval pleased me.

"I wish every day could be Christmas day." I said.

My father's smile became even broader. Sadly, for me, every subsequent Christmas day would remind me of my grandfather. I would never forget his arrogance, his lack of forgiveness and the manner in which he had treated my mother. Christmas, for me, would never, ever be quite the same again.

"Gramma & Grandpa Hodges with their entire family"

My first introduction to Sports Medicine was as a patient. I was aged seventeen. I had spent six years at Lewis' School, Pengam. Situated in the Rhymney valley, Pengam was some fifteen miles from home. It was a boys only school. A school with an excellent academic record. More importantly, from my point of view, it was also renowned for the quality of its rugby teams. Its sister school for girls, was at Hengoed. Lewis' School Pengam and Hengoed School for Girls both admitted the top thirty pupils, at the eleven plus examination, from the neighbouring county of Monmouthshire. As a consequence both schools were considered, by many, to be elitist schools. It was as if the academic cream of eleven year olds from Monmouthshire were rewarded with a place at the schools of Hengoed and Pengam.

The Tredegar children, who qualified and decided to be pupils at Hengoed and Pengam, would need to travel each day, on the public service bus, down the Sirhowy valley from Tredegar to Blackwood. There they would transfer into separate school buses; the girls travelling onward to Hengoed and the boys travelling separately to Pengam. The service bus left Tredegar each morning at five minutes to eight and returned at five in the afternoon. In nineteen forty two, Glenys Williams and I were new pupils to Hengoed and Pengam respectively. We travelled together in those buses on every school day for six years. Glenys and I were now both prefects in the sixth form. We would sit our Higher School Certificate examinations in June. It was now early February. Our final school examinations were just three months away.

Snow had been falling heavily throughout the day. With the cold air of early evening, the snow lay thickly on the roads in the valley. The hour-long bus journey from Pengam to Tredegar was coming to its end. The conversation on the bus, amongst the schoolchildren, as we approached Tredegar, was of the snow. Snow usually fell heavily in the higher reaches of the Sirhowy Valley. If more snow fell overnight, the buses would be unable to run in the morning. Travelling to school would be impossible. As the service bus eased its way into The Circle, at Tredegar, it skidded slightly, confirming our belief that tomorrow, and maybe for some more days, our time would be spent away from school. The Pengam boys and the Hengoed girls would be snowbound in Tredegar.

As Glenys and I alighted from the bus, the cold night air brushed against our faces. The covering of snow on the pavements made our walking a slippery process. In such circumstances, Glenys and I would hold hands. Glenys ensuring that she didn't fall, and me because I loved her. We had commenced grammar school life together aged eleven. She started at Hengoed on the same day as I commenced at Pengam. For six years we had made the daily bus journey to and from school. We both knew every inch of the Sirhowy Valley. For five of those years, we had always sat together on the journey. We were the best of friends. We shared our experiences, our disappointments and our successes. On those bus journeys, we would put the world to right. We would solve all the world's problems, even though we were unable to solve our own.

Every school morning, I would meet Glenys on the corner of High Street at a quarter to eight. The bus left the Circle at five to eight. The journey south to Blackwood was only eight miles, yet it took a good thirty minutes. As we travelled down the valley, we passed coal mine after coal mine. Ty-Tryst, Bedwellty, Markham, Argoed and Oakdale collieries followed one after the other. It was in those pits that most men in the valley worked. Glenys' father and many of my relatives worked in those mines. At the end of the school day, as we made the return journey home, the miners would occasionally travel on the same bus. Every one of the miners had completed a hard day's work underground. In those days there were no pithead baths. The miners travelled in the clothes they had worn underground, covered only by a raincoat, their faces black with coal dust and with the whites of their eyes shining through their blackened faces. As their clothes were impregnated with coal dust, they were not allowed to sit on the bus. They all had to stand in the aisle. It was an embarrassment to all the schoolchildren. We were not allowed to give up our seats to the miners. They had carried out a hard day's physical work underground and yet they were required to stand on the bus. We, who had been sitting at school most of the day, sat uncomfortably while they stood. It always surprised me that the miners accepted the position.

With teenage emotions I loved Glenys. She was my first love. I loved her continuously throughout my grammar school days. Glenys, though the same age as myself, was much more mature. Love, for her, was many years away. She was content to just be my friend. Mother did not approve of Glenys. In mother's eyes, Glenys was "the brazen hussy", intent on capturing me as some great prize. Mother seemed to believe Glenys was intent on whisking me off to some distant horizon. Nothing was further from the truth, but mother would never be convinced. In fact, mother had very little contact with Glenys. Mam's view was coloured by the fact that, at home, I always talked about Glenys. I know my mother was fed up with hearing her name. If anyone was to be whisked away at that time, it would have been Glenys. In my dreams I was always eloping with her. Glenys however was too mature for such thoughts. She always ensured we were, and always would be, just good friends.

Glenys and I slithered our way up Castle Street. We skated around The Red Lion corner, and soon reached the corner of High Street, where she lived. The snow was falling more heavily, with a bitter northerly wind blowing. I wanted to linger at the corner of High Street with Glenys. Time spent with her was so precious. The falling snow and the freezing wind was no deterrent for me. Time I spent with Glenys was time that should never come to an end. The snow on her legs made them red and sore. She was keen to reach the warmth of her own home. In a flash, she was gone. Glenys disappeared along High Street, covered in a cloud of falling snow. As she walked to her home. I lingered at the corner watching her every movement until, at last, she disappeared into the warmth of her house.

The walk from High Street to West Hill is short yet quite steep. In the snow it seemed endless. On the upper reaches of the valley, the cold air had quickly frozen the snow as it lay on the ground. The steep hill of Glandovey was in front of me. The hill had a deep covering of frozen snow and was difficult for me to negotiate. Each step seemed so much longer than the last. The snow was falling heavily. It was very slippery under foot. The wind was now very strong. As the wind blew the snow into my face, it quickly froze on my skin. As I reached the top of the hill, I knew he would be waiting. Whatever the weather, he would always be there; always waiting. Sitting on the wall in a blizzard would not deter him. As I turned into West Hill, despite the cold wind and the heavy snowfall, there he was, sitting as always, on the side wall of the house, waiting for my homecoming. During school terms, I cannot recall an occasion when he was not there. Dutifully he waited for that shrill whistle that would see him leap from the wall and race the length of the street to greet me. Tonight was no exception. The shrill whistle had hardly left my lips, when he leapt from the wall. For a moment he was buried in the snowdrift that had formed at the base of the wall. He soon reappeared from beneath the snow bounding along the street with the glee of a friend about to meet his best friend. The snow was matted to his black curly hair. His body felt cold. The warmth of his greeting made the cold night air, and the snow, melt into oblivion. Bonzo and I were together again. All at once everything seemed right with the world. The wagging of his tail told me so. We were soon in the warmth of our house. The snow would fall for days.

Dayton's so called friends often referred to him, as a swot. There was a certain envy and jealousy in their remarks. They resented his success at school. He obtained three distinctions in Higher School Certificate. My parents were justly proud of him. A natural academic, with so much ability, he motivated himself. He enjoyed the challenge that any form of learning presented. He was a true scholar. He did not enjoy playing games. Mainly because of the six year age difference between us, Dayton and I had little in common. In order to assist Dayton with his studies, through his grammar school days, Mam and Dad built a study for him at the back of the house. With his departure to Cambridge, his study became my study. Unfortunately for my parents, my ambitions contrasted markedly with Dayton's. I didn't want to study. I wanted to play rugby and cricket. My ambition was to be a professional cricketer. I had no desire to further my academic studies at university.

At the end of each evening meal at home, after what I always considered was a tiring day at school, Mam and Dad allowed me ten minutes, to wash and clean up, before being sent to that study. With the passage of time, I came to hate that room. Hours, that could, and should, have been spent on academic work, I spent reading cricket books. I hid my cricket books amongst the mass of my brother's academic books. I spent hours reading and inwardly digesting those books on cricket. Each evening, when my parents assumed I was diligently doing school work in the study, I was reading my cricket books. I had the same dedicated enthusiasm for those cricket books that my brother had for his academic studies. As a consequence of my passion for cricket, my Christmas terminal examination results had been a disaster. In the two Chemistry papers, I had only obtained thirty-five and twenty three per cent. In Physics, I only achieved twenty-nine per cent. Biology was my best subject, but even there I only scored forty-seven and fifty-one per cent. The headmaster's comments on my school report was as follows.

> "In view of the obvious difficulty Ugo Neil is experiencing with Physics and Chemistry, perhaps it may be advisable for him to take three years, instead of two, before sitting his Higher School Certificate."

The outlook for my Higher School Examinations in June was indeed bleak. The examinations were now a mere three months away. I knew I had made no real progress. I was struggling with Physics and Chemistry. I had no motivation to improve. Nevertheless my examination prospects did not alarm me. I had already reconciled myself to the fact I would not pass the exams. I consoled myself with the knowledge that, to be a professional cricketer, it wasn't necessary to pass examinations in Physics and Chemistry. In the solitude of my study, as the snow continued to fall outside, I was more intent on reading and learning the correct way to play a cover drive at cricket.

> "Place your left foot to the pitch of the ball. Keep the left elbow high. Keep your head over the ball. Always show the full face of the bat to the ball."

Homework and the revision of Physics, Chemistry and Biology held no fascination for me. My mind was always filled with cricket and of course Glenys. My school report, after the Christmas examinations, contained

the following Headmaster's remarks,
"Ugo",
that dreadful name again,
"tends to be too optimistic about the standard of his work.
He should realise hard work is essential throughout Form Six".

By the end of two hours study, I felt confident in being able to play the cover drive. Higher School Certificate seemed a long way off. I was sure it was beyond my capabilities.

A peep through the curtain revealed the snow falling more heavily. As I hid the cricket books away for another night, I knew school would not be possible for a while. The Pengam boys, and the Hengoed girls, would have a few days holiday.

It snowed for days. At night it froze. West Hill was covered with three feet of snow. At the street corners, where the wind blew ferociously from the mountain top, the snow had drifted up to the bedroom windows. What a time I had! With my friends, we built igloos in the street. Bonzo became my husky. Snowball fights were enjoyed by all. Tobogganing, on Glandovey Hill, was an exhilarating experience. The buses didn't run out of Tredegar for a week. Eventually, a rapid thaw occurred and the snow was gone.

As usual I met Glenys on the corner of High Street on the Friday morning at a quarter to eight. How I loved that girl. She had spent the week, she said, working hard at her revision. The weather had been too cold for her to venture out. She had spent the time profitably, revising all her schoolwork. As she described, in detail, the extent of her revision, pangs of guilt came over me. I realised another week had been spent studying cricket, when I should have been revising for my exams.

The school's first fifteen team, for Saturday's rugby match, was always posted on the notice board at one o'clock on Friday. The following day, the school was playing its most important rugby game of the season. Pengam were to play Caerphilly grammar school away. It was a day to be etched in my memory forever. Saturday March the twenty-sixth, nineteen hundred and forty-nine would be imprinted in my brain in more ways than one.

The First Fifteens of both schools were unbeaten during the current rugby season. When the two schools met at Pengam, the previous November, the game ended in a draw, at nine points each. A result on Saturday, for either team, would probably mean that team being undefeated for a whole season. The game was certainly a very important one. At Lewis' School, rugby was a religion. Years later, it is difficult for me to appreciate how important winning rugby matches, and the Caerphilly match in particular, was to everyone at school. As a famous football manager was to comment later,

"Winning a football match is not a matter of life and death.

It is more important than that!".

The first fifteen pool of players gathered round the board as the school's rugby captain, pinned his selected team to the board. As the captain turned away, he gave me a wink. I knew instantly I was in the team. A close scrutiny of the team sheet told me I was on the left wing, with D. J. White at fullback. I preferred playing at fullback, but any position would do. It mattered not. I was in the team. I would play against Caerphilly.

Dad was always supportive of my sport. Keen and interested in all I tried to do at games he was always willing to help and advise me. Above all, he would always give me the most precious thing he had to give, which was his time. He hated spectating and, as a consequence, rarely came to see me play. He was my best supporter, but not as a spectator. The Caerphilly match was different. The game had gripped the imagination of the population of the Sirhowy and Rhymney valleys. My father was not going to be left out. He would be a spectator at the game. Moreover, he would take me to the match by car. It was indeed an important game.

Like many an important game, the match itself was not a classic. There was too much at stake for both sides. Sadly that day, even at schoolboy level, there was a built-in fear of defeat. It was such an important occasion. The crowd at Caerphilly was incredible for a schoolboy match. Several hundred spectators turned up for the game. They all must have been disappointed. It was a drab game. Half-time came with no score and, playing on the wing, I had hardly touched the ball.

The second half was some ten minutes old when Keith Thomas, the

"The School's First Fifteen"

Caerphilly right wing, had possession. Keith came running straight at me. I launched myself straight at him in a head-on tackle. While I was flying horizontally through the air, straight at him, Keith decided to cross kick. His right foot was half way to the ball when my head intervened. I am unable to recall the crack of Keith's boot against my head. Friends talked of the crack for days, but I cannot recall the sound of the moment. My world instantly went black. I lay still. My whole mind filled with complete darkness. I was unconscious for only moments, but it seemed an eternity. In minutes, I was running around in a daze, not knowing who or where I was. I played by instinct. I did not know where I was, or for whom I was playing. I was concussed. The world was passing me by.

Through the haze I saw them coming. Three of them, in their yellow and black hooped shirts, and there was only one of me. The inside centre had the ball, with the outside centre and the wing to his right. They were bound to score. I decided to stand still and hope. As the inside centre closed on me, for some inexplicable reason, he decided to pass the ball. Suddenly I had it. I had intercepted the pass. My instinct told me to run. I ran. Later, I was to learn it was the length of the field. It seemed like a hundred miles to me. I ran until I could run no more. I heard the pounding of my heart, or was it those feet that chased me, all the way to the line. I collapsed, when I could run no more. It was fortuitous, I collapsed over the line. I had scored a try. Pengam had won. The team had won. The school were victorious. Pengam went undefeated throughout that season. Caerphilly lost just the one game. Our team was delirious.

Others can recall those moments, but for myself they are lost forever. Team mates still talk of that match and my try, but for me, the memory is no longer with me. The joy of that try, would never be mine to recall. I only recall the details now as they have been told to me by my Dad and fellow team members. I went to bed early. My head was sore, but not unduly so. The moment my head touched the pillow, I was asleep. The darkness returned. I was at peace. I awoke suddenly. I felt sick. My head was pounding like a sledge hammer. The pain was intolerable. I felt awful. I was convinced I was dying. I left my bed and walked to the bathroom. I did not arrive in the bathroom. As I tried to cross the top of the stairs, I fell. I rolled down the stairs from the top to the bottom. I lay still. If I was not concussed before, I certainly was now.

The noise of my fall woke my parents. They found me lying at the bottom of the stairs. I lay still; unable to move. My father telephoned for an ambulance. I was taken to Tredegar's Cottage Hospital. I remained unconscious for a week. My sole memory of that week in hospital is in the X-ray department. I had been taken there for a skull x-ray. As I was placed on the X-ray table, the coldness of the table on my back momentarily awakened me. I looked up to see the great black machine descending upon my head. I let out a loud scream and returned to my slumbers. A whole week passed by, and I was not part of it.

Wolverhampton Wanderers were playing at home in The Football Association Cup. Raymond Glendenning was the radio commentator. His voice echoed throughout the ward. My week of slumber was over.

During that cup tie commentary, I gradually came to my senses. Slowly but surely, I returned to the land of the living. I recall the pleasure on my parents' faces at visiting time. My week of slumber had been a week of severe distress for them. Unable to make contact with me, they had sat at my bedside doing little except being there. Hoping and praying I would get better. The smiles on their faces that Saturday evening have stayed with me forever. I realised that evening how much they both cared for me; how much they loved me. I have never forgotten their love.

When you are getting better, life in a hospital ward is fun. I was getting better. All the patients and staff in the ward were conversant with the Pengam Grammar School rugby team. They knew the names of my school team mates and even some of their positions in the team. It appeared that my week's slumber had not been entirely peaceful. Frequently, in my delirium, I would shout out the names of my playing colleagues for all to hear. On one occasion apparently, I had determined the bed was a scrum and endeavoured to push it over. The Ward Sister had restrained me.

I knew Glenys would want to visit me. I also knew that my mother would never allow her to visit. Mam would use the excuse that only two visitors were allowed, but I knew that would not be the real reason. In any event, Glenys did not visit. I knew it was not her fault. Early one morning, the nurse brought me the letter. The brown envelope is creased now and faded with the years, but that morning it was bright and shiny. I eagerly opened the envelope to read the letter. I looked at the page. It was blurred. Each word and individual letter appeared confused. The words were jumbled. I could not read. I could not see clearly. I cried. The nurse returned, thinking the letter had upset me. As soon as I explained what had happened, she realised the cause of my unhappiness. The nurse closed the curtains around my bed. She read the letter to me in a soft kindly voice.

> "Dearest Neil. I miss you desperately. There is no one to meet me on the street corner in the mornings. The journeys on the bus are lonely without you. Please hurry up and get better. When will I see you? Get well soon. Yours, until elephants fly, Glenys."

I still read the letter. With the passage of many years, the message has not changed. Then, I kept the letter under my pillow. I tried, every day, to read it. I wanted to confirm every word the nurse had read to me. Each day, while in hospital, I failed. I was unable to read the words Glenys had written. I wondered if she had really written those words.

"Dearest Neil".

"Yours, until elephants fly."

"I miss you desperately".

I tried every day to read Glenys' letter, but on each occasion I failed. I could not read the words she had written. Every time I tried, the words were double and blurred. I had double vision. The double vision remained for many months. The spring and summer would be spent under the care of doctors, nurses and, most of all, my parents. I would never return to Lewis' School Pengam. My schooldays were over; they finished on the rugby pitch at Caerphilly school.

I had been due to travel to Sheffield University for an interview at their Medical School on April 7th. I was unable to travel. The interview was cancelled. On the day of the proposed interview, I was still in hospital recovering from my head injury. Father wrote to The Dean of the medical school explaining my head injury and its complications. As I would be now unable to sit my Higher School Certificate in June, Dad had written, informing the Dean there was little point in pursuing my application at this time. My future as a university student was at an end. No one seemed to know what was going to happen to me.

Twenty days after my admission to hospital, I was discharged home. My eyes remained a problem. The surgeon at the hospital and our general practitioner, Dr. Bryant, were both concerned about my slow recovery. They were particularly concerned about my double vision. Dr. Bryant advised me there was to be no returning to school, no reading, and no sitting Higher School Certificate. Instead, I was referred to Professor Lambert Rodgers, the consultant neurosurgeon at Cardiff. I saw the consultant on the 6th. May. I was subjected to a very thorough examination.

The early summer was spent under the supervision of the neurosurgeon.

SCHOOLDAYS

My world had fallen apart. No school. No Higher School Certificate. No Glenys. No games and no cricket. Worst of all Mr. Lambert Rodgers told me I was never to play rugby ever again. He told me,

"Playing rugby will be too dangerous for you."

My response was always the same. I repeatedly told him,

"But I want to be a rugby player."

He was adamant.

"You are never, ever to play rugby again."

I wanted the professor to realise I was a rugby player who was desperate to play again. I believed he decided the safest option was to stop me playing any more rugby. I wanted him to find a successful way for me to return to playing rugby. I became tired of the medical advice.

"It's a matter of time."

Lambert Rodgers continually told me.

"You must continue to rest".

My parents diligently followed the neurosurgeon's advice. I rested.

She came to see me one Sunday afternoon. While still not allowed to read, my eyesight was now improved. My vision clear enough to see Glenys in all her beauty. She had met my father, by chance, in town. Dad had invited Glenys to visit me at my home. I assumed Mam was not too pleased, but she made no comment. Glenys was as charming as ever. We both sat talking in the front room all afternoon. I wished she would have stayed forever. Glenys brought me up to date with the happenings at school. She explained how hard she had been working. How she had decided to take up nursing as a career. She had been accepted as a student nurse at The Royal Gwent Hospital in Newport, provided she passed her Higher School Certificate. Glenys would commence her nursing career in September. She would leave Tredegar, to live in the nurses' home at the hospital. With me remaining in Tredegar, Glenys would be departing from my life for ever. I was very sad. There was no confirmation from Glenys of me being her "Dearest Neil"; no suggestion that Glenys wanted to be mine "until elephants fly". When she knew I was seriously ill in hospital, the words in her letter, she informed me, were merely intended to cheer me up and make me feel better. I was now getting better. I was back in the real world. Glenys' written words did not mean what they said. My life would continue without Glenys. I would never be her 'dearest Neil'.

"Glenys"

My vision gradually improved. I spent the summer on the hills of Tredegar playing and walking with Bonzo. During my illness, he had special permission to sleep on my bed at night. I didn't believe our relationship could have become any closer, but it did. We spent hours on the hills, in the rush fields, playing near the ponds or just sitting on the hillside wondering what the future would hold. As we sat, I looked out on the town below. The town where I had been born. The town where Mam and Dad had lived all their lives. People, it seemed, were born in Tredegar, worked there all their lives and died there. Some had never ventured more than a few miles from their homes in their entire lives. Surely, I thought, life has more to offer. I wondered what the future held for me. I was determined I was not going to spend my entire life in the valley. I had to find some way to leave. Unbeknown to me, it was at this stage that my father decided I needed some special help with my university application to Sheffield. Father knew Doctor Rocyn Jones, the Medical Officer of Health for Monmouthshire and decided to pay him a visit at his home outside Newport. I do not know what was discussed at the meeting, but the outcome was that Doctor Jones wrote to the Sheffield Medical School supporting my application. His letter to the university explained the seriousness of my head injury and asked that the university reconsider my application due to my personal health circumstances..

It was early July. I was better. My vision was clear. Lambert Rodgers, my Consultant Neurosurgeon, did not wish to see me again for six months. I could play cricket, but not rugby. He continued to advise me that I was never to play rugby again. My rugby days were over. I had scored my last try. The road to a full recovery was nearly complete. My parents had been extremely patient with me. They had cared for me through a very difficult period of my life. I was most grateful to them. I would never ever doubt their love for me.

"You are invited to attend for an interview on the 31st July." the letter said. The letter was from the Dean of Sheffield University Medical School. My father had informed the Dean previously that I was unable to sit my Higher School Certificate so what was the purpose of an interview. Unaware of Doctor Rocyn Jones' intervention, I thought the interview must be for admission the following year. In any event, I was delighted and so were my parents. I travelled to Sheffield by train. My brother, who then worked in Middlesbrough, met me at the Sheffield Midland Station. My brother duly ensured that I arrived promptly at The Dean's Office for my 3.00p.m. interview. The interview was a dream. No academic questions or discussions. The Dean and his panel carried out a detailed questioning of my head injury. What was my impression of life in hospital? How good was I at cricket? Why had I applied to be admitted to Sheffield? My interview was all about sport. I was good at sport. The interview went well. That evening, my brother and I caught a train to the northeast. I was to spend two weeks holiday with him in Middlesbrough. My Dad phoned during the second week. A letter had arrived at home from Sheffield. The medical school had offered me a place commencing in October. The letter informed me I would spend the first year studying for 1st. M.B., the equivalent of Higher School Certificate. I cared not. I was to start a new life in Sheffield. My university life was to begin after all. Dad enquired if he should write and accept the offer on my behalf. It seemed a silly question.

"Of course" I said,

"Please write".

October would see me in Sheffield. I would be known at university simply as "Neil". I decided Ugo and Ugino would be gone forever. I would not use the name again. I recalled "Alice through the Looking-Glass".*

"What's the use of their having names,"
the Gnat said,

"if they won't answer to them?"

"No use to them,"
said Alice,

"but it's useful to the people that name them, I suppose."

My name of Ugino had been more than useful to my parents; it was a name they treasured. A name that gave thanks for two lives saved, they believed, by Doctor Zanazi. My first Christian name would always remind them of Ugo Zanazi. However, my parents' pleasure was not mine. It was my decision. I would not use the name of Ugo again. I would be known simply as Neil Phillips. By moving to Sheffield, my close relationship with Glenys was also at an end. I was very sad. Glenys and I would go our separate ways; live different lives. We would both spend our futures caring for others. Caring for each other, however, was no longer an option. I would enter university without ever sitting my Higher School Certificate. At university, I would have many girlfriends, exceptionally nice girlfriends, but there would never be another Glenys. In my early years at university, I wished, oh how I wished, that elephants would fly; the reality is they never do.

---

*   Lewis Carroll : *Alice Through the Looking Glass.*

3

Medical School

The university placed me in digs, with three other students. The lady whose house we lived in and who cared for us was Mrs. Dickenson. She lived in a small terraced house in Thompson Road. The house was about a mile from the University. I was to share one of the two bedrooms with another medical student, who was in the year above me. The accommodation was just about adequate. There was no study. In the evenings, if we had academic work, the four students would study around the dining room table together. Mrs. Dickenson was a very caring person. She looked after us well.

The day before I left home to travel to Sheffield, my grandfather made a special visit to my home. He wanted to wish me well. Our relationship, since the time of my first international, had improved beyond measure. He gave me a present, carefully wrapped in a cardboard box. Grandfather gave me strict instructions not to open the parcel until I was in my digs at Sheffield. I wondered, throughout the train journey, what gift he had bestowed upon me. On arrival at my digs, I eagerly opened grandfather's cardboard box. It contained one apple, one banana and one orange. Mam had always instilled in me the fact that it isn't so much the present that counts, it's the thought. I gave my grandfather a wry smile while I ate the fruit.

It happened in my second week. I spent an hour before lunch reading some Physics in the university library. During the lunch hour, I went for a walk in Weston Park, next to the university. I could visualise it all in front of me as I walked through the park. Every word I had read, from the Physic textbook, was there in front of my eyes. The words were clear. As clear as they were printed in the Physic textbook. Every word recalled before my eyes. I could recite the chapters of that textbook word for word with ease. This had never happened to me before. It was a new experience. In the afternoon, I skipped the lectures and returned to the library. What I read was permanently implanted in my mind. I could recall the words exactly. There were no mistakes. What I had read was instantly recalled. It began to dawn on me, I had developed a photographic memory. The weeks and years ahead would confirm that. Provided I had read an article or chapter in a book, I could recall the words at will. I can give no explanation for this. Neither could the neuro-surgeon at Cardiff, nor any of my medical colleagues. I certainly did not possess this talent at school. It was a new phenomenon for me. My personal belief is that it developed from the kick on the head at Caerphilly. Whatever the reason, my confidence at academic work flourished. My philosophy became, 'read it and you know it.' I determined that attendance at lectures was, in the main, a waste of time. For myself, time spent reading was much more profitable than attending lectures. Sitting in a lecture theatre listening to lectures did not allow me to retain or recall the facts. Concentrated reading, however, allowed me to reproduce the words with ease. From being a struggling student at school, I became an academic high flyer at university. From being a schoolboy floundering at the bottom of the class, at medical school my examinations became relatively easy. At university, I was always near the top and more often at the top in all examinations. My secret was to read everything studiously. I could then reproduce it with ease at the examinations. The Christmas and Easter term examinations saw me at the top of the year in Physics, Chemistry and Biology. As the summer term approached, I was confident I would succeed at my first M.B. exams. I was not to know then, but my six years at medical school were to be an academic success. My progress through medical school was assured. I once flippantly told my parents

"If you want to get ahead, get kicked on it."

There is no medical reason why the kick on the head should have affected me in this way. All I know is it did. I was most grateful it had. During

MEDICAL SCHOOL

the summer term, I could concentrate on the love of my life; my cricket. Although I was now at medical school, my overriding ambition was still to play county cricket. At home in Tredegar, I had spent many hours studying those cricket books. I had practised and played on the Red Ground, and in the street; I was a successful batsman in the grammar school's first team. Everyone, at home, knew I was a keen cricketer. I was confident in my cricketing ability. I considered myself to be good at cricket. During the Easter holidays at home, I practised my cricket continuously. I was eagerly looking forward to returning to the university for the summer term. I was confident I would play cricket in the first eleven. I returned to Sheffield, armed with my cricket books, my favourite cricket bat and my cricket pads. I was going to enjoy the summer term. I had no doubts. I would play for the university's first eleven at cricket. With my photographic memory, I knew I would pass my examinations. I could read all the books I needed in the cricket pavilion. The pavilion would be no different to the university library.

In comparison with other medical schools, Sheffield's medical school was quite small. In each year there were some sixty students. All medical schools, in the early fifties, were male orientated. Medicine was, at that time, considered a profession for men. In our year, for example, out of some sixty students, there were only eight girls. Of the boys, only two had come straight from school; John Wightman and myself. In nineteen forty-nine, when we were admitted to university, most incoming students had already spent two years doing national service. Many of the students had served for a longer period in the forces during the war. John Wightman and I were the babies of the year. Most of our fellow male students were much older. One of them was thirty-three years of age. He had five children. Such was the age distribution amongst our students.

The cricket trials were held during the first week of term at the university playing fields, based at Norton, on the outskirts of Sheffield. I attended with all my enthusiasm for the game I really loved. Before I reached the cricket nets however, I knew I was out of my depth. As I changed in the dressing rooms, I realised that my fellow university cricketers were not schoolboys, but grown men. I changed next to Noble Sarkar, a fifth year medical student from Trinidad. Noble was in his early thirties. He had opened the batting for Trinidad. Rumours circulated, at the university, that Noble, at an earlier age, was a candidate for the West Indies Test Team. He was an opening batsman of outstanding talent and experience. In comparison, I had opened the batting for West Hill; the street where I lived in Tredegar. Noble was a friendly person. He introduced me to Jack Whitely, the university cricket captain. Jack had opened the bowling for the armed forces. Jack introduced me to Stan Norton, who had opened the bowling for the Yorkshire county second eleven. Whilst all these cricketers were university students, they were fully grown, mature men with a wealth of cricket experience behind them. I was, in comparison, still a schoolboy. I knew I could not compete. My dream was shattered. I had no chance of playing in the university first eleven. The best I could hope for was a place in the university second eleven. I might even end up playing for the medical faculty's own cricket team.

On the second Friday of the summer term, I did venture to look at the cricket notice board. My name did not appear in any of the cricket teams. The university had three cricket teams. My name was not present. I was not even selected for the third eleven. I was bitterly disappointed. My first summer term would be spent in the library reading the books of Physics, Chemistry and Biology. Read and succeed would be my motto. Cricket would have to wait until I was back home in the summer holidays. My university cricket dream was in tatters. I was heartbroken.

My routine at university was well established. While my fellow students attended lectures every morning from nine to eleven, I spent the two hours reading in the library. The remainder of the morning, and most afternoons, the students spent in the laboratories carrying out various experiments. I never missed those practical classes. Mid-morning, I would meet up with my fellow students in the university refectory for coffee. Coffee mid–morning was a university tradition.

The university's summer term was halfway through. The year-end examinations were a mere few weeks away. I had played no university cricket. My playing of cricket had been limited to the medical school's cricket team. My work was going really well. I was confident of doing well in the first year examinations. I had never felt so confident about my academic work.

"Do you know anyone who can keep wicket?"
Roger Cox enquired over a cup of coffee. Roger, an ex-serviceman, was a second year medical student. He played for the university's first eleven at cricket and was an excellent bowler. He had played for the Derbyshire second eleven.

"John Lowe, the university's wicket-keeper has his final degree exams in two weeks and he's called it a day. John's developed examinationitis; he's decided to give up his cricket to concentrate on revising for his exams and believes his cricket is interfering with his work. The university hasn't another wicketkeeper. Do you know anyone who can keep wicket?"
"I can keep wicket."
I said, although I had never kept wicket in my life.
"I used to do it at school." I added.
"I'll let the cricket captain know." Roger replied.
"He may call you up for a practice session."

I was desperate to play university cricket. If that required me being a wicket keeper, so be it. In reality, playing cricket had always been what I had wanted to do. Becoming a doctor, was of secondary importance to me. The following day, I walked into town. I bought my first pair of wicket keeping gloves. I also bought a pair of yellow chamois leather, inner, gloves to protect my hands. I would practice being a wicketkeeper. Oh how I practised! I spent every moment, available to me, in the fives court. I repeatedly threw a tennis ball against the wall of the fives court. I practised catching the rebound, from every possible angle. I practised there for two hours before breakfast, an hour at lunchtime and two more hours in the evenings. I practised and practised. Jack Whitely, the university cricket captain, invited me to a practice session at the university playing fields ten days later. The following Friday my name appeared on the team sheet. I had been chosen to play in the university first eleven. Although I had never kept wicket before,

I knew I would not let them down. I continued to practice in the fives court whenever I could. My first game, for the university was a success. I felt I had been keeping wicket for years. It all came so naturally to me. I took one catch. More importantly, I didn't drop any catches and there were only three byes. The other members of the team were impressed. I played wicketkeeper for the first eleven for the rest of the season. I passed my 1st M.B. examination. My first year at university had been a great success. Mam and Dad were pleased.

At home, in the summer holidays, I kept wicket for any local team that would give me a game. I would play for anyone, as long as I was keeping wicket. I needed as much experience as possible. I enjoyed the summer. I had passed my exams. When I returned to university, I would embark on two years of Anatomy, Physiology and Biochemistry, before sitting my 2nd M.B. examinations. I would establish myself as the university's wicket keeper. My life was complete, apart from the fact that elephants still didn't fly!.

It is generally accepted, by all medical students, that the two years work leading to the 2nd M.B. examinations are the most difficult years of the medical course. It's a hard slog. The volume of work is unbelievable. The majority of the work is factual. It has to be learnt by heart. Gray's Anatomy was one of our textbooks. It was a book of over a thousand pages. It had to be learnt by heart. We were expected to reproduce it at will. The details had to be read, learnt and inwardly digested. Each and every medical student was required to reproduce the words satisfactorily in the examination. Anatomy at Sheffield was special. The Professor of Anatomy, Francis Davis, was the editor of Gray's Anatomy. Prof. Davis had a reputation, amongst all the students, as a brilliant lecturer. Despite the decision I had made, in my first year, to miss lectures, spending the time instead reading in the library, I determined never to miss a Prof. Davis' lecture. It was a decision I never regretted. I recall his first lecture.

"My lectures commence at 9a.m." he said.

"They do not commence at five to nine, or five past nine, they always commence at nine. I expect you all to be here by nine.

No-one is admitted to my lectures after nine."

His message was loud and clear. At his second lecture, the Prof. entered the lecture theatre precisely at nine o'clock. He closed the door. His lecture commenced, as he said it would, exactly at nine o'clock. At ten past nine, the lecture door opened. In walked Charles Eccles. Charles was a fellow student, notorious for his lateness. Charles walked up the steps to the back of the lecture theatre, sat down, undid his briefcase and opened his notebook. Almost imperceptibly, as he delivered his lecture, and without appearing to hesitate at any time, the Prof. said

"I wonder if the student who has just come in, would mind ensuring that the lecture door is properly closed."

Charles rose from his seat. He walked down the steps, satisfied himself the door was properly closed, climbed the steps, back to his seat. As Charles sat down, the Prof. just added

"No. I wanted the student to close the door,

from the other side!"

Charles Eccles left the lecture theatre. No student arrived late for anatomy lectures again. I read Gray's Anatomy, all one thousand pages, from cover to cover. More importantly, I could reproduce it page by page. During the two years, studying for my 2nd M.B. examination, most lunch hours I spent walking in Weston Park with Alan Simpson or Philip Quinn, two fellow student. As we walked, we would question each other on Anatomy.

"What's the course of the ulnar nerve in the upper arm?"

one of them would ask me.

"Now let me see,"

I would say,

"It's half way down the left hand page. This is how it goes."

I could then reproduce the words with unfailing accuracy. Provided I had read the page, I could reproduce it. My photographic memory would not let me down. Whilst other students struggled desperately in those two years, I found the work relatively easy. Reading became my watchword. Of course there were many other elements to those two years of study. Anatomy brought my first encounter with a dead body. In Anatomy dissection, we worked in pairs and, over time, gradually dissected the whole body. We would dissect the arm, followed in subsequent terms with the leg, abdomen, thorax and head and neck. I loved dissecting.. I enjoyed, yes really enjoyed, the fortnightly oral examinations conducted by the tutors. The work of Physiology and Biochemistry, whilst still factual, involved much practical work which I enjoyed. My end of term exams were a success. I was always at or near the top in all three subjects. It was a new experience for me, after all those years of struggle at grammar school. The summer term, of my second year at university, would be devoted to cricket.

The Yorkshire County Cricket Club first eleven played each of the Yorkshire universities in a pre-season warm-up game. I just could not believe it. I would be playing against not only Yorkshire cricketers, but also England players. In the Yorkshire side were Hutton, Lowson, Wilson, Close, Watson, Yardley, Wardle, Appleyard and Trueman; nine test match players. I could not believe I would be keeping wicket to them. They were my schoolboy cricket heroes. The press would be there, intent on taking early season photographs of the Yorkshire batsmen. As the university's wicketkeeper, I would be in many of the photographs. I would have my picture taken, keeping wicket to Len Hutton and Willie Watson. I sent a photograph to my Dad. I wrote on the back

"Neil keeping wicket to Willie Watson."

I knew he would be pleased. Norman Yardley, the Yorkshire and England captain, came in to bat at number six. At the end of the over, having only played two balls, he turned round to me and asked,

"Have you ever played county cricket?"

"No." I replied.

"Well, I think you should." he said.

"I've been watching you this morning and you've played really well. Where do you live?"

"South Wales." I replied.

"If you're interested, we'll have a chat after the match." Yardley said.

MEDICAL SCHOOL

Yorkshire won the game easily. Noble Sarkar was the only university batsman who could comfortably play the Test bowlers Trueman, Wardle and Appleyard. Noble made forty. The rest of us didn't reach double figures. After the game, Norman Yardley sought me out at the bar.

"If you would like me to," he said,

"I'll write to Glamorgan suggesting you visit them in the summer holidays. The experience would be good for you, even if nothing comes of it."

I was ecstatic. I gave Yardley my particulars. I looked forward to the cricket season with even more enthusiasm. I would practice more and more. My father forwarded the letter some weeks later. The envelope was embossed with the bright yellow daffodil; the emblem of the Glamorgan County Cricket Club. Phil Clift, the former Glamorgan opening batsman, signed the letter. Clift had taken over the coaching duties from George Lavis, the official coach, who was seriously ill. Clift would be pleased for me to attend the nets at Cardiff Arms Park when the university term was finished. I was asked to inform him when I would be available. He would write again confirming the arrangements. I replied to his letter the same day. I informed Clift I was available the day after term finished. My summer, I hoped, would be spent playing cricket for one of the county teams. In the second year of my university studies, I played in every cricket match the first eleven played. I passed my second year exams. I was awarded my university cricket blue. To add to all this success at university, I was now off to cricket trials with Glamorgan. My life was full of happiness.

I reported to Cardiff Arms Park on the first Monday after the summer term finished. It rained all day. Phil Clift, and the second eleven players were most welcoming. I particularly got on well with Peter Walker and Norman Hever. Peter, who had arrived from South Africa, was good enough to be in the county's first eleven, but first had to obtain a residential qualification. Hever, who had previously played for Middlesex and been the opening bowler for Glamorgan, was now coming to the end of his career. Hever was assisting Clift with the development of the junior players. Although it rained continuously on my first day, we practised in the indoor school. In

Photograph Of Me Keeping Wicket
"What I was really good at"

those days, the Cardiff Arms Park was split into two halves. Cardiff Rugby Club played on one side of the main stand, the county cricket club played on the other side. The indoor nets were in the main stand between the two. A matting wicket was laid over the wooden floor. The noise, as each ball landed on the matting wicket, was deafening. Behind the batsman's wicket was a brick wall, with barely space for the wicketkeeper to stand. There was certainly no room for the wicketkeeper to stand back. As the wicketkeeper, I stood up close to the stumps for all the bowlers. The quick bowlers were difficult to keep to in such a cramped space, but I did my best. Hever and Clift seemed impressed with my performance. At the end of the day, Phil Clift discussed with me my availability for some second eleven matches. In those days, the second eleven was called the Club and Ground side. I was told I could travel to Cardiff on a daily basis to practice and the club would pay my travelling expenses. I was delighted at this, as I did not wish to burden Mam and Dad with additional expenses. I spent many happy days at Cardiff playing in the nets, both indoor and outdoor. I was particularly grateful to Clift and Hever, who helped me develop into a better keeper. Most of all however I was grateful to Peter Walker. In future years Peter would not only play for the county on a regular basis, but also for England. He was noted for his expert fielding and close to the wicket catching. My time, spent with him, involved catching practice on the wooden, slip cradle. We spent many an hour practising catching together after all the other players had gone home. We practised and practised for hours. The practice was hard work, but I enjoyed every moment.

My first game for the Club and Ground side was at Maesteg, a town in the Rhondda valley. Dad and Dayton decided they would travel with me. They were keen to watch the game. Dad would drive us to the ground by car. I sat in the back seat of the car with my cricket bag, containing my clothing, pads, bat and wicket keeping gloves. Dad's car was a small Austin Seven. I was cramped in the back with all my gear. Dad knew the way to Maesteg, but not the way to the town's cricket ground. We arrived in Maesteg in good time. As we entered the town, Dad stopped the car at the road side. My brother enquired of a man on the pavement as to the directions to the cricket ground.

"I'm going there myself."
the man replied.
"You could give me a lift."
Leaning over my brother, Dad replied by saying that our car was full. Sadly we had no room for an extra passenger. The man reluctantly gave us the directions. We drove off to the ground. Needless to say, I was eager to play well. It was very important for me. I needed to prove to myself that I could play successfully at this higher level. Glamorgan batted first. I batted at number eight. I scored seven runs. A googly ball from their leg spinner deceived me. I never read the disguised spin on the ball. I was made to look quite foolish. Still I had plenty of opportunity to show my skills at wicket keeping. When we took to the field, I realised that one of the

umpires was the very man my Dad had refused to give a lift in our car earlier in the day. In the Maesteg innings, I took five catches behind the stumps. Unfortunately, the umpire declined to give any batsman out. I was fortunate that Hever was fielding at first slip. He also appealed for each of the five catches I took, with the same enthusiasm as myself. Each catch was given 'not out' by the umpire. Hever could sense my obvious disappointment. After each catch he said,

"Well done. That was a bloody good catch."

Admittedly each of the catches received only the slightest nick from the Maesteg batsmen, but each batsman was definitely out. The umpire thought otherwise. Clift was fielding at cover point throughout the innings. When the fourth catch had been turned down, Clift was so concerned with my constant appeals, he surmised I was appealing for appealing sake. Between overs, he walked over to Hever and enquired what was going on. I heard Hever say,

"All four catches were genuine. I feel sorry for the lad. It's his first game. He could have had four catches. It's a right shame."

Despite the umpire's intervention, the Club and Ground side beat Maesteg easily. I should have made five catches, but ended up with none. On the way home, I made my Dad promise he would always give a lift to strange men in the future. My Dad and my brother laughed; I felt like crying. On returning to Cardiff the following day, I recounted the story of the umpire, and the fact that my father had refused him a lift, to the other players. They also laughed. I surprised myself by joining in the laughter. Clift had a quiet word with me. He told me he was pleased with my performance and told me not to worry about the umpire. He went out of his way to reassure me. It was most kind of him. Having spoken with Phil Clift, I felt so much better.

My last game for the Club and Ground side was against Panteg. Joining the team were two schoolboys from Neath-Tony Lewis and Alan Rees. The day after the game Mam and Dad were taking me on holiday to Bournemouth for two weeks holiday. I travelled to Panteg on the team coach, sitting with Peter Walker. We had become good friends. On arriving at Panteg, Clift told me how disappointed he was that I was unable to play for the first eleven, in a benefit match, the following Sunday, at Colwyn Bay. I was stunned. I had no knowledge that I had been selected for the game. I said I would love to play. It transpired that Wooller, the first team captain, had telephoned my home with the news of my selection for the first team. He spoke with my Dad whose reaction apparently was immediate. The family was going on holiday. I was unavailable. My father informed Wooller I had worked hard throughout the year at university and I was in need of a holiday. Clift told me my father's decision was final. Wooller had now selected Hayden Davis, the first team wicketkeeper to play at Colwyn Bay. The matter, Clift informed me, was now closed. I was devastated. All my life, for as long as I could remember, I had wanted to play county cricket. I dreamed, as many boys do, of playing for their county. I was now at the threshold of realising my ambition. My dream was on the point of becoming a reality. I had worked and practised for years to achieve my goal. All those hours of practice and now, when my dream was becoming a reality, my father had thrown away the chance I had worked all those years for. Dad had not even discussed the situation with me. My dream was being destroyed for the sake of a stupid holiday in Bournemouth with Mam and Dad. I could not believe it! I was livid. I played well at Panteg. I took two catches, stumped one batsman and made a few runs. We won the match in the last over. Tony Lewis took a magnificent catch, at cover point, diving full length to his right. Tony caught the ball inches from the floor; it was a magnificent catch. On the team coach back to Cardiff, I sat with Peter Walker. Peter agreed with me. I could not turn down the opportunity to play for the first eleven, holiday or no holiday. I walked up the aisle of the coach to talk to Phil Clift.

"I really do want to play on Sunday."
I said.
"I'll speak to my Dad, if you'll speak to Wooller."
Clift felt there was little he could now do, but agreed to discuss the situa-

tion with Wooller. Clift advised me to telephone the club secretary's office the following day, after I'd spoken to my father. When I arrived home my father and I had a long and, at times, angry exchange of views. In the end, he relented. I could play at Colwyn Bay. The following day I telephoned the secretary's office at Cardiff.

"The team for Colwyn Bay has been chosen. You are not selected"
I was informed.
"Haydn Davis is keeping wicket."
I was not invited to play for the county again. The holiday in Bournemouth was a miserable affair; I wanted to be in Colwyn Bay.

I returned to Sheffield in the October. A new hall of residence had been opened. I applied for a room in Stephenson Hall. My application was accepted. With some reluctance I left Mrs. Dickinson and her digs in Thompson Road. She had looked after me well. I was sad at leaving her. I would live at Stephenson Hall for the next four years. It was a wise decision. In hall, I lived with and met, on a daily basis, students from other faculties in the university who were studying the arts and sciences. My next-door neighbours on the staircase were Alan Fox, studying English and History and Dave Preston studying Geography. I enjoyed mixing with those students. It took me away from the medical student environment, which at times was overpowering. It broadened my outlook. It brought diversity and variety to my student life. It was a good environment. I was very happy at Stephenson Hall. To my surprise, when I returned to university, rumours about me were commonplace. The news of my involvement with Glamorgan had been blown out of all proportion. The main rumour, which concerned me greatly, had emanated from some of the students from Wales. They were aware of my playing cricket with Glamorgan. According to the rumours, I was giving up my medical studies to play cricket full time for Glamorgan. In the second week of term, I received a note requesting I make an appointment with Professor O'Gorman, a surgeon who worked at the City General Hospital. I was surprised at his request. I had not met Frank O'Gorman. I saw Frank

O'Gorman two days after I received his note.

> "I understand you have the opportunity to play cricket for Glamorgan."

he said.

> "I was in a similar position, when I was a medical student at Glasgow. I played for the Reserves at Celtic Football Club. Celtic wanted me to give up my medical studies to become a full time professional footballer. I reluctantly decided not to sign for Celtic. Instead I decided to stick with my medical studies. My advice to you is don't sacrifice your career in medicine for a career in cricket. You've only been here at medical school for just two years, but already the staff are speaking very highly of you. A promising medical career lies ahead of you. Don't waste the opportunity you have here. The cricket offer may be appealing, but my advice is 'turn it down'."

O'Gorman concluded.

> "I wish it was true" I said.

I explained to O'Gorman the happenings at Glamorgan throughout the summer.

> "The information you have been given, Sir, is pure rumour."

I informed him.

> "I wish it was different. I have received no offer. I shall be staying at medical school. I have received no offer from Glamorgan."

I thanked O'Gorman for his concern. He had put himself out to advise me. I was grateful. Most consultants would not have bothered. Eighteen months previously, I could not even get a game of cricket in the university's third team. I had tried, oh how I had tried, to become a top class wicketkeeper. I had succeeded beyond my wildest dreams. Eighteen months ago I had not even worn a pair of wicket keeping gloves. Now I was a successful keeper. Yet the doubt would always remain with me. Could I have made a success at county level? I would never know. I had tried, when success seemed impossible. I would endeavour, in the years to come, to content myself with my relative success as a wicket keeper. Many happy years of playing cricket lay ahead. I resolved to combine playing cricket with a career in medicine.

At the end of my third year, I passed my second M.B. exams. I was awarded my second university blue for cricket. I now commenced my three years of clinical studies. In the future, there would be no long summer holidays. No time to laze in the cricket sunshine. Cricket would need to be fitted in around my medical work. My impossible dream of a career in cricket had nearly become a reality. The doubt however would always remain with me. I would never know if I would have been a success playing cricket for my county. I would never know if I would have been a success at the highest level. My career in medicine had been finalised. The conflict, between medicine and sport, ironically, was only just beginning.

I entered my final year at Sheffield University Medical School with confidence. I read, learnt and inwardly digested the set textbooks. My photographic memory allowed me to reproduce the text at will. I had been awarded four university blues for cricket. I was secretary of the university cricket teams. All the different sports, played at university, were represented on the Students' Athletic Council, by their captain and secretary. As cricket secretary, I was a member of that council. I had sat on the Athletics Council for two years. It was quite a surprise however, when, at the commencement of my final year, I was elected, unopposed, as President of the University's Athletic Council. In my Presidential role, I would lead the students' negotiating team, in discussions with the University Senate, to determine the finances allocated to each individual university sport. As President, I would also represent Sheffield University on the British Universities Athletic Union Council. It was a demanding role to take on with my final medical examinations imminent. The fact that I accepted the role, without a second thought, reflected the confidence I had in passing my final examinations. In addition to this new role as President, I continued to play cricket throughout the summer term. Medicine and cricket were my life. At university, I enjoyed both to the full.

MEDICAL SCHOOL

"The University's First Eleven"

As Sheffield medical students, we were extremely fortunate with our clinical studies. The number of medical students in each of our academic years, compared to other schools, was quite small. There were just sixty students in each year. Sheffield had a surfeit of hospitals ; the Royal, the Royal Infirmary, the City General, the Jessop Hospital for Women, the Children's, Fulwood, Nether Edge and Middlewood; the list seemed endless. As a result, there were plenty of hospital beds. As clinical students we were allocated to a consultant's team. Usually two students were allocated to each team. This small allocation enabled each student being individually assigned to some twelve or more patients. This extensive clinical experience was invaluable.

For my last two clinical allocations, in General Medicine and General Surgery, I was seconded to the two Professorial units at the Royal Infirmary. I spent three months studying General Medicine with Professor Wilson and my last three months, immediately prior my final examinations, with

Professor Jepson, the Professor of Surgery. For four weeks I, and the other students, would live in the student's residence at the Infirmary. This residential period enabled the students to be on call for all the emergency admissions. As students, we worked under the direction of the House Officers and Registrars. Sheffield Medical School gave us an exceptional experience as clinical students. The attachments entailed long hours of clinical work, at a time when, simultaneously, there was the revision to be done for the final examinations.

Professor Wilson was the Professor of Pharmacology. He was one of the most respected physicians in Sheffield. His house physician was Fred Lees, a good friend of mine. The ward sister was the very attractive Rosa Greaves. When patients were admitted to the ward, the house physician and the registrar examined them. After their examinations, the patients were allocated to one of the students. As students, it was our responsibility to write up the patient's medical history in our clinical notebooks. We were also required to carry out a full clinical examination, and ensure that all the relevant investigations were carried out. Each day, we attended ward rounds with either the registrars or house physician. We were subsequently examined and taught on each case. Professor Wilson carried out his regular ward round twice a week. On the Prof's ward round, the students listened to the Prof's discussions, with his house physician and registrars, on the clinical aspects of each case. During the ward round, the Professor would often ask which student had been given responsibility for the patient. Prof. Wilson would then question the student on the various aspects of the clinical case. It was an environment I enjoyed. As students we were fortunate to experience such high standards in our clinical teaching.

Fred Lees, the house physician, allocated Michael as one of my patients. Michael was aged eleven. In reality, he should not have been admitted to an adult ward. It was rumoured that Michael's parents were friends of several medical consultants. Professor Wilson had agreed to take over Michael's care, as a favour to his parents. The first time I approached Michael, even on a cursory observation from the bottom of his bed, I knew he was seriously ill. His dark, black hair, contrasted with the whiteness of his face. He was ghost like. As students, we had been instructed not to make clinical judgements on patient's complexions.

"There are patients who have a normal, pale complexion. Some people are naturally pale and interesting."
we had been told.

"Never diagnose anaemia on a patient's complexion. Always examine the conjunctiva of their eyes. If the conjunctiva is pale, it's fairly certain the patient will be anaemic. A simple blood test would then confirm the diagnosis of anaemia."

I had been taught this clinical entity in the early years of my clinical studies. As I approached Michael, and sat on the edge of his bed, I was impressed with the colour of his teddy bear. As I approached Michael's bed, he clutched his teddy more firmly.

"What's teddy's name?"
I enquired. Michael smiled and said,

"He's called Freddie. I call him Freddie after my favourite Yorkshire cricketer, Freddie Trueman. My teddy's golden in colour, very golden. My father says 'Freddie Trueman's worth his weight in gold to Yorkshire.' That's why my Teddy's called Freddie."

"Well Michael, I've played cricket against Freddie Trueman. The University team play Yorkshire every year. I've played against Freddie Trueman four times now. Your Dad's right. He is worth his weight in gold to Yorkshire. Last year, he bowled so fast against me, I couldn't get out of the way in time. The ball landed full toss on the handle of my bat and broke my finger"

I asked Michael if I could hold his Freddie for a while.

"Of course you can. If you've played against the real Freddie Trueman, you can certainly hold my Freddie."

Michael and I were instant friends. All because of Freddie Trueman!

Michael's conjunctivae were pale. They weren't just a little pale, they were very pale. As I wrote down Michael's medical history in my student's case book and carried out my clinical examination of his pale frail body, the seriousness of Michael's condition dawned on me. His thin, white arms and legs were covered with scars. The scars, proof of the repeated blood transfusions Michael had received. Michael had leukaemia.

When I was a medical student, in the mid nineteen fifties, there was no treatment for leukaemia. What treatment there was, consisted of repeated blood transfusions given at ever reducing, shorter intervals as time went on. As the disease progressed, to its inevitable fatal conclusion, even the newly transfused blood cells would be unable to keep the body alive. The disease, in those days, was fatal. Michael was eleven. He loved cricket. He had brought into hospital his photographic album and newspaper cuttings of his favourite Yorkshire players. Each time I visited Michael, he would produce his team photograph of the Yorkshire players.

"I've played against all these players."
I said.

I related to Michael my experiences of playing against the Yorkshire team in the pre-season matches. Through cricket, Michael and I became good friends. In ten minutes of cricketing stories we were the best of pals. I was his favourite 'doctor'.

My first clinical examination of Michael completed, I retreated to the ward's office in order to write up my notes. It was only when the student had completed his own notes that he was allowed to read the patient's full hospital notes. The official hospital notes had been written by the house physician and the registrars. Michael's hospital notes were contained in a bulging folder. He had been first diagnosed with leukaemia at the age of eight. The disease had been treated at the Children's Hospital. Despite their expert care, the disease progressed. The blood transfusions had been given at ever decreasing intervals. They were now occurring every two to three weeks. Over the past three years, every available vein in Michael's arms and legs had been used, in the transfusion process. No suitable veins were now visible in his limbs. When a transfusion was now given, it was necessary to cut through his skin, under local anaesthesia, and search for a vein in the tissues of his limbs. When found, the vein was opened. A canula inserted in the vein and the transfusion commenced. It was a procedure Michael did not enjoy.

Michael's blood test, carried out by Fred Lees, was reported as showing a haemoglobin level of thirty five per cent. Michael was severely anaemic. It was decided Michael should receive a further transfusion. Fred Lees would carry out the procedure. At this stage in my career, I had not observed the so– called 'cut down procedure'. I asked Fred Lees if I could watch him carry out the procedure. Lees readily agreed. Sister Greaves set up the trolley with the necessary instruments. The blood was delivered to the ward. The curtains were drawn around Michael's bed. Lees and Sister Greaves were ready to start the procedure.

"I want him to do it."
Michael said, pointing a finger straight at me.
"If he doesn't do it, I won't have it done."
Greaves and Lees exerted their combined charm on Michael, but all to no avail.
"If he doesn't do it. I won't have it. I'll never have it."
Michael was adamant. I felt it appropriate for me to intervene.
"I've never done one of these, Michael."
"Don't care. You do it, or no-one does it."
The procedure was abandoned. Lees, Greaves and I retired to the office.
"I suppose you could do it under my supervision."
suggested Lees.
"How do you feel about that? Michael really does need the transfusion."
"I can only try, but you'll need to brief me thoroughly. As long as you are there, we could always do it together."
Lees briefed me over and over again. I went to see Michael on my own.
"Michael, are you really sure you want me to do this transfusion?"
"Yes please. You, and no-one else."
"Sister and Doctor Lees will have to help me. The 'doctor' always needs some-one to help him doesn't he?"
"That's all right, as long as you do it."

I carried out the procedure on Michael's right forearm. On Lees' advice, I gave him additional local anaesthesia to ensure the procedure was painless. I found a vein, opened it, inserted the canula, and tied the canula firmly in place. The blood transfusion commenced. Michael was as good as gold.

"There you are, I knew you could do it!"
Michael told me.
The new blood slowly dripped into Michael's frail body over the next three hours.

"Which student is allocated to Michael?"
Prof. Wilson enquired on his ward round.
"I am Sir."
I replied.
"Good. Then tell us about Michael."
The Prof. moved all the students to a corner of the ward, where I reported on Michael's history, his clinical findings, his most recent blood report and the blood transfusion.

"Very well," stated the Prof.
"Ensure his blood levels are checked tomorrow. I need to know if the transfusion has raised his blood level sufficiently. See the haemoglobin report is here, for my next ward round."
After the ward round was concluded, Lees approached me and said,
"In view of Michael's preference for you carrying out the cut down, would you take the blood sample tomorrow." I readily agreed.

Michael had been subjected to more needles than any patient I had previously met.

"Do you really have to do this test again?"
Michael asked me.
"I'm afraid so. The Prof. wants the report for later in the week. He wants to see what improvement has taken place in your blood following the transfusion."
I replied.
"We could make it up. We could pretend we have done it,

couldn't we? It always goes up following a transfusion. We could tell him it's gone up from thirty-five to sixty-five per cent. The Professor will never know you haven't done the test. I won't let on. I just don't want any more needles. I always feel better after a transfusion anyway, but then I always do for a while. Please don't do another blood test."

Michael's eyes pleaded with me. There was no alternative for me.

"O.K., but I hope the Prof. believes me."

Michael smiled widely and was content.

"What was Michael's repeat haemoglobin value?"

the Prof. enquired of me on his next ward round, as we all congregated at the bottom of Michael's bed.

"Sixty-five per cent." I confidently replied.

"Sixty-five per cent!"

the Prof. exclaimed.

"Phillips, are you absolutely sure?"

"Yes Sir, sixty-five per cent."

Prof. Wilson moved closer towards Michael. He sat on the side of the bed and held Michael's hand.

"Michael, you see the doctor, standing at the bottom of the bed, the one who has just said your blood test result was sixty-five per cent."

"Yes, I see him."

The Prof. continued.

"Well Michael, tell me, has that doctor stuck a needle in your finger and taken some blood away? I need to know."

Michael pondered for a moment, while I stood petrified at the bottom of Michael's bed. After a silence that lasted, as far as I was concerned, for seemingly hours, Michael confidently replied.

"If he says he has, then he has."

The entire team of doctors, nurses and students, who were gathered around the bed collapsed in laughter. The Prof. was embarrassed. He gently tapped Michael's hand and murmured

"I see. I see."

Although still a student, I was always Michael's favourite 'doctor.' Michael was certainly my favourite patient. We were the best of friends. Usually, two days after his transfusion, Michael was discharged home, only to return to the ward for another transfusion two to three weeks later. On each occasion, when re-admitted, Michael insisted I was the only 'doctor' allowed to carry out the cut-down procedure.

"If he doesn't do it, no-one does it."
became Michael's stock phrase.

Christmas approached. Each year, The Royal Infirmary held a competition, in the weeks prior to Christmas, for the best-dressed ward in the hospital. Doctors, nurses and medical students worked hard at dressing their wards. The prize, for the best-dressed ward, was a coveted one. It enabled the nurses and medical students, working on the winning ward, to attend the Hospital Ball with free tickets. Michael asked me to make Christmas 'very special' for him.

"I want our ward to win the competition."
he demanded.

It was Michael's suggestion. We dressed the ward out as 'Under the Sea', and who would argue with Michael. I brought the cricket nets to the ward from the university playing fields. Together, in the evenings, the nurses and medical students built a boat out of strips of wood, covered with thick brown paper. The oars were borrowed from the University's Rowing Club. The nurses made a mermaid, complete with fish tail, and long flowing blonde hair. The mermaid reclined in the boat. All that was lacking was some seaweed! A fellow medical student, who lived in Cleethorpes, was contacted. He was instructed to send, by rail, a cardboard box full of seaweed. When the box was deposited at Cleethorpes railway station, the medical student was asked to declare the contents of the box.

"Seaweed"
replied the student.
Turning to one of his fellow porters, the porter exclaimed
"Harry, there's a fellow here sending seaweed to a hospital in

Sheffield for Christmas. I've heard of them sending holly, but never bloody seaweed before!"

When the seaweed arrived on the ward, Sister Greaves insisted it could not go into the ward, until thoroughly washed and sterilised with a solution of Potassium Permanganate. The dried sterilised seaweed completed our dressing of the ward. Michael was impressed. The ward was finally decked out with nets, displayed a boat named "The Rosa- Lee", after the ward's sister and house physician, and everywhere the ward was covered with sterilised seaweed. The ward won the competition. The nurses and medical students were ecstatic-the free tickets for the Hospital Ball were ours. Michael was delighted too. Michael was discharged to spend his Christmas with his family.

That year, I spent Christmas living in the hospital's Students' Residence. It was the first Christmas I had not spent at home with my parents in Tredegar. It just happened that my two weeks of residency covered the Christmas period. Christmas, in the hospital environment, was great fun. All the doctors, nurses and students ensured that the patients had an enjoyable time. On Boxing Day evening, the resident students held a party with the nurses in the Students' Residence. It was a great party and, not unusually, a fair amount of alcohol was consumed, but not, I can assure you, by me. The nurses and medical students were all quite merry. I don't know who was the originator of the idea, but, once it was suggested, everyone agreed it was a great idea. The Royal Infirmary lay some considerable distance from the main Infirmary Road. A tortuous path led from the main Infirmary Road to the hospital buildings. The Surgical wards were in a block on the left with the Medical wards in a block on the right. The tortuous path, leading to the hospital buildings, was interspersed with three or four gas lamps. Our plan was to remove the mermaid from her boat on the ward. The nurses would then dress her up in full nurse's uniform. We, the medical students, in the hours of darkness, would then hang the dressed up mermaid, now in nurse's uniform, from one of the gas lamps. At the appropriate hour the deed was performed. We left 'the nurse' swinging gently from the lamppost, attached to a rope, in the night breezes. Unfortunately for us all, the Night Sister, during her nightly round, crossed from the Surgical to the Medical block. All she needed was a sideways glance down the tortuous path. There she would see one of her beloved nurses swinging by a rope from the lamppost. Night Sister did just glance. In her horror, she panicked, ran, not to the nurse, to cut her down, but to the Casualty department to alert the Casualty staff of the poor nurse's predicament. Needless to say, when Night Sister and the Casualty staff found that the hanging nurse was no one other than our mermaid, they were not amused. The resident medical students, myself included, appeared, some days later, before the Dean of the Medical School. He was not impressed with our antics. Not one student admitted responsibility. Our tickets for the ball were withdrawn. We maintained that the nurses were not involved. All the nurses went to the Hospital Ball. The medical students stayed at home.

Immediately after Christmas, my attachment to the medical wards was completed. I left to take up my final surgical clinical attachment with Professor Jepson, the Professor of Surgery. Jepson had only recently been appointed to his post, having previously worked in Manchester. Jepson was young. It was rumoured he was only thirty-five, a very young age for a Professor of Surgery. He had an interest in Vascular Surgery. Although my next three months would be spent studying Surgery under Jepson's guidance, my involvement with Michael never ceased. Whenever Michael was readmitted for a transfusion, Michael demanded my presence. I was still the only 'doctor' he would allow to carry out his 'cut down'. It was a fortnightly duty I was pleased to carry out. I did it for Michael.

"When I grow up,"
he would say,
"I'm going to play for Yorkshire. Not like you, playing against them. I'm going to play for them."

Whenever he talked of playing for Yorkshire, his eyes shone brightly through his ever increasingly pale face. I knew Michael would never play for Yorkshire. I knew Michael would never grow up. He could not go on forever being topped up with blood transfusions. Life was so unfair. Life

MEDICAL SCHOOL

was cruel.

I was about to start yet another cut-down on Michael when he exploded into angry conversation. The tone in his voice was quite aggressive.

"Do you really have to do this again?"

he angrily enquired.

"Of course. You always want me to do it. If I don't give you the blood, you won't get better."

"I'm not going to get better, am I? I'm never going to get better. Not really better."

Michael's voice was firm, but desperate.

"Michael, I can't lie to you. I don't know if you are going to get really better."

emphasising the word 'really'.

"I only know that after a transfusion you do feel better."

I thought I had been positive in my reply. Michael looked straight at me. His eyes held contact with mine. Those eyes that shone through his pale face. Eyes I can recall to this day.

"Please don't give me any more blood. I've had enough. I just want to go home."

In desperation, I said,

"You do know Michael that, if you don't have the blood, you won't feel any better. I can't make you completely better, but I can make you feel better."

Michael, aged eleven, smiled at my helplessness.

"I know."

he said.

"I've just had enough. I want to go home."

Michael's parents were sent for. All the doctors, including the Prof., came to see Michael. The issues were fully discussed, but Michael remained adamant. When the time came for Michael to leave the ward, I asked if I could be notified. Sister Greaves agreed. I wanted to say my goodbyes to him.

"Promise you'll come and see me at home."

Michael begged of me.

"Of course I'll come."
I replied
"but you'll have to ask me. Your Mum and
Dad will let me know."
Michael went home with his parents. I just cried. Life is so unfair. I was given the message eight days later. A written note came from the Ward Sister.
"Michael wishes to see you. Take a taxi to the address below,
as soon as possible."
Michael's father let me into the house. I climbed the stairs and entered his bedroom. The bedroom wall was covered with photographs of his beloved Yorkshire cricketers. Michael's face, pale and drawn now, was as white as the sheets on which he lay. His mother sat on the edge of the bed.
"Thank you for coming. Michael did so want to see you. I'll
make you a cup of tea."
Michael's mother left to make the tea. His father stood at the end of the bed. As I sat on the side of the bed, Michael's eyes opened. He gave me his usual smile.
"Where's Freddie?" I asked.
He pointed under the bedclothes. I peeped under the bedclothes. Freddie was there, lying between Michael's left arm and his frail body. The two were intertwined; Freddie and Michael.
"Thanks for making me such a nice Christmas.
How was the dance?"
Michael uttered no more words, but gently closed his eyes. His pale right hand moved close to mine. As our hands made contact, he gripped my hand as firmly as his weak body would allow. We clutched hands together, his hand firmly placed in mine. I do not know how long we held hands together. I was afraid to move my hand. I knew Michael gained some security from holding mine. We held each other's hands until all Michael's strength departed. His hand went limp. I knew Michael had gone. I continued to hold his hands for some time. I didn't want to let go. I wanted to hold his hand forever. Eventually I gently laid his hand on the bed. I felt the tears

roll down my face. Michael was gone forever. I had lost a friend. Michael's parents had lost their son. His father and I gently covered his body with the white sheet of his bed. I went down stairs for my cup of tea.

Michael's death affected me greatly. I had made the error of making a patient of mine, a dear friend. I had become emotionally involved in his care. For Michael, my pain was irrelevant. As I returned to my university life, I contemplated again how unfair life was. My life, at that time, was full to overflowing. Michael's had been taken from him.

He was the first person I had watched die. I had never been present through the process of dying before. It had a profound effect upon me. As I had contributed to the care of Michael over the previous months, I felt his loss personally. Above all, he had taught me one great lesson, a lesson that would remain with me throughout my medical life. As Michael's favourite 'doctor', I thought I knew what treatment was best for Michael. Alas, it was not. Michael eventually decided the treatment that was best for him.

"Doctors",
I would often reflect,
"always believe they know what is best for their patients. Unfortunately, it is not always what the patient feels is best for themselves."

In a relatively short period, Michael had contributed much to my life. I was very sad. I would always remember Michael.

Of all the clinical subjects I studied at medical school, Surgery was my favourite. Under Jepson's guidance my interest in Surgery, became a passion. On his wards, I worked extremely hard with much enthusiasm. Jepson, I knew, was impressed with my attitude and my developing knowledge. Jepson's House Surgeon was taking two weeks holiday. The Prof. asked me if I would like to deputise for him. Students, in their final year, were occasionally asked to deputise for the Houseman when he took annual leave, but to be asked to deputise on the Professor of Surgery's Unit was quite an honour. Although still a student, I would be acting as a House Surgeon. Needless to say the Registrars would closely supervise me. My role was basically to be on ward duty, twenty-four hours a day. I admitted and clerked all patients who were coming in for planned operations. It was my responsibility to ensure the clinical notes were up to date and the necessary examinations and investigations were carried out prior to the operations. I loved the work. I thrived on the extra responsibility Prof. Jepson had bestowed upon me. One great advantage, during those two weeks, was I personally assisted the Registrars when they operated on emergency admissions. As a student, I had watched many operations, but I had never before actually scrubbed up and assisted at the operation itself. I enjoyed the operative work. At the end of my two weeks, the Prof. took me on one side..

"I've been very impressed with you during the three months you've been with my firm. When you pass your finals in a few weeks' time, I'd like you to apply for my House Surgeon's post. I'd really like to have you working on the unit."

Jepson told me.

"If I pass my finals Sir, I shall certainly apply. Thank you very much Sir."

"Phillips! not if you pass your finals, when you pass your finals. Good luck."

The Prof. seemed confident I would pass my finals. I must admit, I felt pretty confident too.

It was the University's Jubilee. The Duke of Edinburgh and Princess Elizabeth would be visiting the University to join in the celebrations. The Duke and the Princess had expressed a wish to take afternoon tea with a small group of students. Six students were chosen to take tea. As President of Athletics, I was one of the chosen six. We rehearsed afternoon tea over and over again. We received instructions on how to address the Royals; how to bow; where to stand in the room, and how to hold our plate, cup and saucer. We were even advised how to eat and certainly not to speak with our mouths full. When the day of the visit arrived, the main ceremony took place in Firth Hall. The six students were closeted in a small room on the ground floor. We were locked in the room for over three hours. When the Duke and Princess eventually entered, Princess Elizabeth stood in one

MEDICAL SCHOOL

corner. Each student was called upon to speak to the Princess in strict rotation. The Duke, on the other hand, joined the group of six students immediately. The Duke spoke to us while we waited to be called to our audience with the Princess. I recall the Duke setting his beady eyes towards a jam tart on the cake dish. In his eagerness to eat the tart, it crumpled in his hand as he lifted it from the plate. The Duke's fingers were immediately covered in strawberry jam. He eagerly licked each finger. The students were relieved. Our lessons, on how to eat in the presence of Royalty mattered little. The Duke was human after all!

During my final year the new University Playing Fields in Weston Park were opened. A cricket match was held to celebrate the opening. The University Staff would play the University's First Eleven. Edward Bramley, whose name would forever be associated with those playing fields, bowled the first ball. A celebration dinner dance would be held in the evening. As President of Athletics, I was invited to propose the main toast. My speech was well received. The Jubilee celebrations had been a great success. At the end of the dinner, Professor Stuart Harris, our Professor of Medicine, congratulated me on my speech.

> "I am delighted a student from the medical school has been elected President of Athletics. So many of our students give up their sport as they approach their final examinations. I'm so pleased you have continued with your recreational activities. Your speech this evening was excellent. You are a credit to the Medical School. I look forward to seeing you in the final exams. I'm sure you'll do very well. Good Luck."

Now there were two Professors, and the main two at that, who had indicated I would do well in my finals. There was little time left, before my final examinations commenced.

Many years previously, Sir Arthur Hall was Professor of Medicine at Sheffield. He donated a cup, known as The Arthur Hall Cup. It was awarded to the best all round student in the final year. The award, Sir Arthur Hall had insisted, was to be decided upon by the final year students themselves. Each student, he determined, would have one vote. Sir Arthur argued that having lived and worked together for six years, the students themselves were the best judges of who was the best all round student. My fellow students elected me as the best all-round student. It was a very proud moment for me. Everything in my life was a great joy and delight. I really enjoyed the success. However, now the final examinations beckoned.

"Speaking At The Dinner to Open
The Edward Bramley playing fields."

The final medical examinations at Sheffield, took place over three and a half weeks. In my time, no marks were allocated for the course work we had carried out during our final year. The hospital consultants had, of course, formed opinions of all our abilities. Their opinions were however merely their own personal impressions. There was no formal written assessment of the student's work in the final year. In our final examinations, it was essential to perform on the day or, more correctly, on every day throughout the three and a half weeks. All the students accepted the final examinations would be stressful, but then so would our future work as doctors. We were being trained to work under stressful conditions. Working under stress would be part of our future daily lives. The stress of the final examinations was accepted as a good test of our ability to perform well under such stress. To add to that stress at Sheffield, the students were only allowed two opportunities to sit the final examination. Two failures at finals would mean no university degree. Failing students would be directed to sit the Conjoint Board Examinations in London. The threat of a double failure, after six years of study, with the loss of a university degree, considerably added to the stress.

The first week of the examinations was taken up with three hour written papers; two papers each day. At the end of the first week, I knew I had done well in all the written papers. Every question asked, was on a subject I had read. With my photographic memory, it was relatively easy for me to regurgitate the answers onto the examination paper. After the three-hour paper on Obstetrics and Gynaecology, my fellow students and I gathered in the refectory to mull over the examination paper. The general view was that, of all the papers we had sat, this paper was, by far, the most difficult.

"I must have got close to one hundred per cent."
I recall telling Alan Simpson. All the questions came straight out of Prof. Russell's textbook.

"I've just written down what's in his book. I've written it down, word for word. If the Prof. doesn't give me a hundred per cent, he'll need to rewrite his book!"

At the end of the first week, I knew I had done extremely well in all the written papers, but particularly well in Obstetrics and Gynaecology.

The second and third weeks were taken up with a multitude of oral and clinical examinations. I felt vulnerable in the oral examinations. After all, the examiners could easily ask questions, the answers to which I had not read. In such circumstances my photographic memory was of no help. Fortunately, the majority of the questions, asked of me, were from the recognised textbooks. Consequently, my performances in the oral examinations were relatively satisfactory. I knew I had done exceptionally well, thanks to the Professor's own textbook, in the written paper of Obstetrics and Gynaecology. Apparently in my oral examination, I was to be subjected to detailed questioning to ascertain if I qualified for an award of honours in the subject. In the oral examination, I failed at the first question. Professor McClaren, the external examiner from Birmingham, asked me,

"In a young girl, approaching puberty, which comes first, the onset of menstrual periods or the enlargement of her breasts?"

I hadn't read that anywhere. I hadn't a clue! It was, I suppose, something one would read in a girly magazine. My mind was blank. I should have replied

"I don't know."

but decided to take a fifty-fifty guess. I guessed wrongly.

"It's obvious Phillips,"

the external examiner smiled, as he replied,

"you do not have any sisters."

The rest of my oral examination went relatively well, but I knew the award of honours in Obstetrics and Gynaecology had eluded me.

In the final clinical examination for General Medicine there were two clinical sessions. One session devoted to the so-called long case and the second session devoted to five or six short cases. The long case was the important one. It was a tradition that to be successful, in the final examination for General Medicine, each student had to pass in their long case examination. My long case examination was to be at The Royal Hospital on Professor Stuart Harris' ward. On the morning of the examination, the Houseman, Roger Cox, greeted me in the corridor. Roger and I had played cricket together for the university over five consecutive years. He was a great medium pace bowler. Roger had qualified the year before. He was now house physician on the Professorial unit. Roger and I were good friends.

"I'm in charge of allocating the cases."

Roger informed me, as I waited outside the ward.

"Your patient is quite straightforward. Nothing difficult.

MEDICAL SCHOOL

You'll be all right."
When my time came, Roger ushered me into the ward. He introduced me to the external examiner.

"Now Phillips,"
the examiner began,

"take a history from the patient, and only examine the relevant systems. I do not want you to carry out a full clinical examination. I just want you to examine, what you consider, the important relevant parts. I'll come back in a little while."

The history, the patient gave, was typical of many patients I had seen during my clinical years at Sheffield. Working in the steel mills, breathing daily the polluted atmosphere, many steel workers presented, later in life, with a history of chronic cough, shortness of breath, blue extremities and no energy. The medical condition was Cor Pulmonale. Working in the polluted atmosphere, the patient's lungs had become diseased and fibrosed. This lung disease placed an added burden on the heart itself. Strained, over many years, the heart could no longer cope working with such damaged lungs. The clinical result was heart failure, secondary to chronic lung disease. The condition was prevalent in Sheffield. I had seen many such cases as a student. I decided to examine the chest and heart, as these were the two relevant systems. I examined them carefully in detail.

Clinical examination, it had been drilled into us, over and over again, during our student days, consisted of four distinct elements. The four elements were Inspection, Palpation, Percussion and Auscultation. Initially, you look and observe. Secondly, you feel with you hands. Thirdly you percuss, by tapping one finger on another, to ascertain the different areas of resonance and dullness. Finally you listen with a stethoscope. I diligently carried out these four elements in my examination of the lungs and heart. The external examiner returned as I was completing my examination.

Having given the examiner the patient's relevant personal details, I informed the examiner of the man's occupation and his medical history. The examiner seemed satisfied.

"Tell me what you found on Inspection of the Chest."

The question was one I had anticipated. Inspection first, then to be followed by Palpation, Percussion and Auscultation. I was quite prepared. I listed all the factors I had found on inspection of the chest. I was confident with my replies. On completing my answer, the examiner said

"Unfortunately, Phillips, you've left out the most important item. Try again."

I carefully repeated every item I had observed on the inspection of the man's chest. My answers I knew were exactly the same as previously.

"You've still left out the most important item. I'll give you one more chance."

The examiner's voice became more irritated by his perceived stupidity of the student before him.

"Unfortunately,"

the examiner stated,

"if you don't get it right this time, I shall have no option but to fail you."

Failure, in my long case, would mean I had failed my final examinations. The sweat poured from my brow. I carefully went through inspection of the chest again. I reiterated each item, realising, as I did so, that I was merely repeating the same answers I had given on the two previous occasions. I added nothing new. I racked my brain, but could not come up with the missing item the examiner needed. As I concluded, I said

"I'm sorry Sir, but I haven't come up with the answer you require."

In that moment, I knew I had failed my final examinations.

"I'm amazed,"

the examiner explained,

"you failed to mention the position of the apex beat of the heart."

I fumed inside.

"Excuse me Sir, I always include the position of the apex beat of the heart in Palpation of the chest, not Inspection. In fact Sir, the definition of the position of the heart's apex beat is 'the furthermost downward and outward point on the chest wall where one gets a true lift of the finger.' You can't get a true lift of the finger on Inspection, it has to be done under Palpation. In order to describe the position of the apex beat it is essential to palpate with the fingers. By definition, the position of the apex beat cannot be determined on Inspection, it can only be determined by Palpation."

I saw the examiner's face. He was not amused.

"Thank you Phillips, that will be all."

I left the ward knowing I had failed. I was distraught. I believed I was unfairly treated. For the first time in weeks, I didn't sleep at night.

Examinations continued around me. I continued to attend my oral and clinical examinations, but the bottom had dropped out of my world.

"What went wrong in your long General Medicine case?" Professor Jepson asked as he crossed the entrance hall of the main university building. I re-lived those terrible moments again. I informed Jepson of the details of the exchanges between the external examiner and myself. When I finished telling Jepson, he said,

"That's disgraceful. I don't think I can allow that as a reason for your failure. In similar circumstances, I would have given, or rather not given, the same answer. Leave it with me. I'll see what I can do."

With those encouraging words, Jepson departed. What can Prof. Jepson do, I thought. He's not even in the General Medical department. He's the Professor of Surgery. He can't possibly change what has happened. I was convinced I would still fail.

My last examination in finals was the short cases in General Medicine. There seemed little point in attending. I had already been informed I had failed my long case. I did however attend. I would be pleased now when the exams were over. The thought however of spending the next six months revising and re-sitting General Medicine was one I did not enjoy. The clinical examination for the short cases saw me returning to Professor Stuart Harris' ward at The Royal Hospital. On my arrival, I realised all was not well.

"Your appointment has been put back to later this afternoon. You're now last of the day. Instead of two o'clock, you're now down for three- thirty. If I were you, I'd go for a walk. A walk would be better than hanging around here."

Roger Cox, the Houseman and my cricket colleague, told me. Roger was as stern as I had ever seen him. I went for a walk in town. It seemed three-thirty would never arrive. Roger showed me into the ward. He handed me over to Professor Stuart Harris.

"Now then Phillips, we have a lot of work to do. Normally, each student has five or six short cases. In the circumstances in which you now find yourself, it has been decided that you will be examined on all the cases we have brought in for these examinations. I shall personally examine you. We have some twenty cases to see."

With the Prof. at my side we moved from bed to bed.

"Please listen to this heart. Feel this lump. Examine this abdomen. Listen to this chest. Examine this man's liver area. What's your impression of this swollen gland? Examine this man, to determine if he has an enlarged spleen."

The Prof. moved me from case to case in quick succession. My short case examination seemed to last for hours. The Prof. questioned me fully on each and every case. When we eventually finished, I was totally exhausted.

"Very well done."

the Prof. told me at the completion.

"You basically got every case correct. I'm so pleased for you. Well done."

I finished my final examination totally confused. I knew I had failed my long case, which meant I had failed my finals, yet the Prof. had said

"Well done. I'm so pleased for you."

I consoled myself with the fact that the three and a half week ordeal of the final examinations was over. As I knew I had failed in General Medicine, I comforted myself with the knowledge that I would not be starting full time work in two weeks time. There would be plenty of opportunity to play cricket throughout the summer, before I re-sat finals in October.

The procedure for receiving examination results at Sheffield Medical School, was bizarre. At the appointed hour, all the students congregated in the sunken garden at the back of the Dean's office. When the students had all gathered, the Dean emerged through the French windows of his office. He stood on the terrace above the students. The Dean would then proceed to read the names out in alphabetical order, stating, after each name, whether they had passed or failed. It was a yearly experience we had suffered throughout our time at medical school. For those of us well down the list alphabetically, it was always a harrowing experience. Friends, higher up in the list who the Dean announced had failed, brought fear and dread into one's mind.

"If he's failed, what chance have I got of passing."

was the immediate thought passing through one's mind. One just had to wait as the Dean progressed through the alphabetical list of students. I attended all such examination announcements throughout my six years at Sheffield. On the occasion of our final examination announcement, I was convinced I had failed, so I decided not to attend. I walked around the city of Sheffield alone, before going to the cinema to see a film. I returned to the University's Student Union for a coffee at teatime. Immediately, I met Alan Simpson, who enquired,

"Where have you been hiding? Didn't want to celebrate with the rest of us did you? Fancy getting a distinction in Social Medicine and Public Health. You should be ashamed of yourself!"

"What about General Medicine?

I asked

"No distinction there, just a straightforward pass."

I could not believe him.

"You're joking aren't you?"

"Neil! after six years of hard slog, our final examinations are not a subject to joke about are they? You must have known you would pass. If you hadn't passed, what chance would the rest of us have had?"

I smiled, and smiled, until my whole face displayed my pleasure. I was a doctor at last. I needed to phone my Mam and Dad.

Parents are always delighted when their offspring graduate at university. They feel a sense of pride, not only in the achievement of their offspring, but also in the knowledge they too have greatly contributed to the success. That was the case with my Mam and Dad. They were not only proud of my achievement, but also pleased for themselves. They had always been supportive of me. They gave me considerable love and understanding over many years. In a strange way, they felt justified, if justification was necessary, for giving me that name of Ugino. They had named me after the doctor who had saved my mother's life. Years later, their beloved Ugino had now become a doctor himself. It was, they believed, fate. Mam and Dad could not contain their pleasure.

Probably, because of my upbringing in chapel, or because of those visits with my Dad to the Italian Temperance Cafes, or more probably because I just wanted to be a professional cricketer, whatever the reason, the thought of celebrating my graduation with a glass of alcohol in my hand never occurred to me. A famous athlete once told me, on informing his father he wanted to win a gold medal in the Olympics, his father's advice was,

> "If you want to win Olympic Gold my son, you can drink as much alcohol as you like, sleep with as many women as you like and smoke as many cigarettes as you like, but only after the age of thirty-five!"

My Dad had given me no such specific advice. Nevertheless he had guided me along the same path without me realising it. I was now a qualified doctor but, because I had always wanted to be a professional cricketer, I had accepted the same principles. Aged twenty-three, I had gone through medical school without drinking any alcohol, never smoking and was still a virgin! My lifestyle had merely evolved because I wanted to be as fit as possible to play cricket. How times have changed! The evening I qualified, I did not attend the celebration party with my fellow students. My night was not spent in the alcoholic marathon such parties entailed. Having phoned my parents, I went to the cinema alone again. I saw two films that day. I had no celebration drink. I had no need for one. I wanted to enjoy and remember forever every detail of that day. I wanted always to be able to recall the pleasure of the day I passed my final examination. In a few days I travelled home to Wales. I had just over two weeks holiday before returning to Sheffield to take up my first appointment as a doctor. I was to become House Surgeon to Professor Jepson, the Professor of Surgery at the Royal Infirmary.

On my first day as a qualified doctor, I visited the Faculty of Medicine offices. I wanted to be absolutely sure my name was printed on the list of successful students. My name was there. It was true. I really had passed. Needless to say, I was the only newly qualified doctor to appear at the Faculty Office so early in the morning. All my fellow students were fast asleep in bed, sleeping off the effects of their alcoholic marathon. They would wake up later, with a thick head, a feeling of nausea and some memory loss of the night before. I was glad I'd missed the party.

At the Faculty, I filled in my application form for the post of House Surgeon to Professor Jepson. When completed, I handed it in to the Dean's office. The next day, I travelled home to South Wales. I looked forward to my three weeks holiday. For the first time, I would arrive home as Doctor Phillips. To Mam, I was still her beloved Ugino. During my holiday, I would even play some cricket. I knew, when work began, there would certainly be no opportunity for cricket. It was my only regret at being a newly qualified doctor.

Four days into my holiday, I received a telephone call from Professor Jepson. He regretted to inform me I would not be appointed as his House Surgeon. One student in our year, Kent by name, was the only student to obtain a first class honours. Kent had applied to be House Surgeon to Mr. Blacow Yates at the Royal Hospital. When applying for that post, Kent had indicated that, on the completion of that post, he would be applying to be Professor Wilson's House Physician at the Royal Infirmary. Professor Wilson apparently had decided he was only willing to appoint Kent, in six months time, provided Kent had spent the first six months as Professor Jepson's House Surgeon. Jepson informed me Kent's preference was to be appointed to work for Mr. Yates. However, his over riding desire was to work for Professor Wilson. Kent, with Professor Wilson's compliance, had now decided to apply for Professor Jepson's post. Following discussions with the consultants panel, Jepson informed me, Kent would be appointed as his House Surgeon. I had only applied for Professor Jepson's post, and had submitted no other application. I was now without a post. Jepson advised me to apply for Mr. Yates' post. Jepson said he would speak to Mr. Yates on my behalf. I was devastated.

> "Oh, and by the way Philips, well done in your General Medicine short cases. I managed to secure an agreement from Professor Stuart Harris that he would personally examine you on the short cases. The external examiner reluctantly agreed, but stipulated you would need to be examined on all twenty cases. It was also agreed that you would only be allowed two mistakes. Stuart Harris told me you didn't make one mistake. Well done."

Jepson gave me the impression he was genuinely sorry about the situation that had developed with Kent. I was shattered. The following morning I returned to Sheffield in order to seek an appointment with Mr Blacow Yates, the senior surgeon at The Royal Hospital. During my clinical years, I frequently attended Blacow's outpatients. Most of my clinical surgery, I learnt from Blacow. I believed we had a very good relationship. Throughout my student days, I believe because of my photographic memory, Blacow always referred to me as "Professor Phillips." I hoped Blacow would now accept my application as his House Surgeon. I met Blacow at his home in Northumberland Road. We walked in the garden together. Jepson had already fully informed Blacow of Professor Wilson's attitude and the situation his decision had now placed me in. Furthermore, Jepson informed Blacow that he, Jepson, had invited me to apply for his post. Blacow was furious with Prof. Wilson's attitude. Apparently Wilson commented to Jepson about my sporting prowess, saying he didn't think students should be appointed to Professorial units because of their sporting prowess; appointments, Wilson was reported to me as saying,

"Appointments should be made on academic ability alone."
After my discussions, Blacow assured me he would be pleased to accept my application. I would be appointed House Surgeon on his unit
"Go home and enjoy the rest of your holiday."
Blacow advised.
I returned to the Dean's office; filled in an application form for Blacow's post and returned by train to South Wales. Four days later, I received a letter from The Royal Hospital informing me I had been appointed House Surgeon to Mr. Yates starting my duties on Monday, July 18th 1955.

Mam and Dad were ecstatic now I was a qualified doctor. Certainly in Mam's mind, it fully justified my name being Ugino.
"I suppose its fate."
she kept telling me.
"From the first day you were born, Zanazi had such
an influence on you. It was inevitable you would become a doctor."
I could not recall Zanazi influencing my life at all. He left Tredegar in 1940 when I was eight. His influence, as far as I was concerned, was non-existent. While I could not agree with Mam, I allowed Mam her reasons without question. I wondered to myself,
"Whatever happened to Zanazi?"
I would find him, if I could.

During my six years at Sheffield, I had many girl friends. In my early years at university, I had longed for "elephants to fly". I then longed for Glenys to re-enter my life, but it was not to be. In those early medical student years, I enjoyed the company of many girls, but did not become too romantically involved with any. I had been brought up at home to respect girls. Pre-marital sex was frowned upon. The thought never entered my mind. My upbringing in the Methodist chapel always ensured moral behaviour and in any case I didn't want any girl interfering with my cricket. On reflection, I now realise how naive I was in all matters relating to female relationships. I attended university before the contraceptive pill was introduced. Sexual intercourse, I naively believed, was the only means by which children were created. The sexual revolution of the sixties was yet to come. In my student days sex, as a recreational activity, was non existent. Relationships with girls, at most, developed into a kiss and a cuddle. Nothing more. An indication of anything more, or if a girl wished our relationship to be more serious, resulted in me 'running a mile'. My last year, as a medical student, however was quite different. During my final year, I had regularly dated Gill Skelton, a medical student in the year below me. In those twelve months, Gill and I were inseparable. Gill was the daughter of a general practitioner, practising at Chapeltown, just outside Sheffield. We were constant companions for some twelve months. The Skelton family had a cottage at Grindleford, in the Derbyshire dales. I spent many happy weekends there with Gill and her family. I loved Gill, and would have been very happy if my love for her had been reciprocated. Whilst I'm sure Gill always enjoyed my company, I always doubted her commitment to me. I hoped our relationship would continue forever. I wanted the relationship to develop.

Our Degree Congregation ceremony was held at the City Hall, Sheffield on the 2nd July 1955. Mam and Dad came to Sheffield with all the other proud parents for the ceremony. The ceremony was for the whole university, not just the medical students. We were placed, as a group, in the middle of the proceedings. Each student, called out by name, walked forward onto the platform to receive his or her degree certificate. When our time came, to proceed to the platform, Douglas Alan Kent was called first. Kent was the only medical student qualifying with first class honours. The remainder of our year would be called in alphabetical order. As Kent walked forward, from his seat towards the platform, his fellow students broke into spontaneous boo's of derision. Kent deserved his first class honours, but, as a person, he was very unpopular with his fellow students. The spontaneous booing was an indication of his unpopularity. I secretly felt strange. For a moment I believed the booing was because he had done me out of Professor Jepson's job. It wasn't true. The other students had no knowledge of Wilson's intervention with the appointments. I felt ashamed at my feelings. For that moment, I hated Kent. My chance of working for Jepson had gone forever. I consoled myself in that I was to become a member of Blacow's surgical team.

MEDICAL SCHOOL

The evening of my degree-day, Mam, Dad, Gill and I went to Hathersage to The Marquis of Granby Hotel. We all enjoyed a celebration meal. My parents were staying at the hotel. Dad allowed me to drive Gill back to Sheffield in his car. I took Gill back to Stephenson Hall. As I drove Gill back to Sheffield, I was lost in thoughts of her. Our relationship would now inevitably change. We would no longer meet on a daily basis. No longer enjoy morning coffee together in the university refectory. No longer enjoy lunch together in t he Students' Union followed by the strolls in Weston Park. I would be working at the Royal Hospital and Gill would be in her final year. On returning to my room at Stephenson Hall, I decided Gill and I needed to talk about the permanence or otherwise of our relationship. We talked for hours. The longer we talked, the more I realised Gill was uncertain about the permanence of our relationship. Gill, I then knew, was not in love with me. We never quarrelled, we just talked. We parted that night with a goodnight kiss, as we always had done. Gill had been a very good friend. I knew however our relationship was over. It would not progress, as I wished. I had obtained a degree, but lost my girl friend. Regretfully, I never saw Gill again.

Before collecting Mam and Dad from Hathersage, I called at the University Library. The Medical Directory was the reason for my visit. I searched the pages for "Zanazi, Ugo" and there his entry was. The address was Claremont Buildings, Shrewsbury. I jotted down the telephone number. Dad and I shared the driving on the way home. On arrival at Tredegar, I phoned Zanazi. I explained who I was. I informed him I had just qualified as a doctor. He was delighted.

"Ugino!"

that dreadful name,

"You must come and visit me. I would love to see you. You must pay me a visit."

I told him I would visit. Mam and Dad were delighted at the thought of a reunion between Ugo and Ugino. I was not so sure. I handed the telephone to my Dad. Dad spoke at length with Zanazi. I promised Mam and Dad I would visit Zanazi in Shrewsbury.

4

I'm A Proper Doctor..........

Two weeks ago I was a medical student. As a student, my only concern was to ensure I passed the final examinations. Now I was a qualified doctor. Suddenly, I realised, people's lives were in my hands. Part of their care would be my responsibility. The thought filled me with excitement, tinged with fear and apprehension. I was apprehensive of the unknown. I felt totally and utterly inadequate. I had worked hard for six years to be in this position. I now wanted to enjoy working in my chosen profession. I wanted to prove to myself I was a good doctor.

The newly appointed house-doctors, all from our year, arrived in dribs and drabs throughout Sunday afternoon. Eight, newly qualified doctors, had been appointed as resident housemen at Sheffield's Royal Hospital. Together, with the resident registrars in Medicine, Surgery and Dentistry, we would form the 'doctors mess' for the next six months. Like all my newly qualified colleagues, I was enthusiastic at the prospect of taking up my first job as a house surgeon. John Wightman and I were the two newly appointed house surgeons. John was house surgeon to consultant surgeon Jock Anderson. I had a similar position with the senior surgeon, Blacow Yates. In just a few hours, I would be the first port of call for half the hospital's emergency surgical admissions. I was concerned as to how, and if, I would cope. The eight new resident house officers were all colleagues of mine. We had worked together, as students, for six years. John Wightman, John Rumble, Cliff Farrow, Doug Aldridge, Kath Gibson, Dilys Tattersall, Josh Gethin and myself. We all felt the same. We were eager to start in our new jobs, but afraid and apprehensive. As students, we had no personal responsibility for the patients. Now the responsibility would be ours. We had all worked hard to be in this position, yet it was only now that we were realising how little we knew. Our professional lives were just beginning.

Resident Doctors At The Royal Hospital
"Author Front Left"

The bedrooms, for the resident doctors, were on the first floor of the hospital. The bedrooms faced directly on to West Street, one of Sheffield's busiest main streets. The position of my bedroom was, to say the least, unfortunate. My bedroom window was directly opposite the tram stop. As each tram rumbled to a halt, immediately beneath my window, the noise was unbelievable. The bedroom shook, from side to side and from front to back. With the onset of darkness, the situation worsened. The tram's connection, to the overhead wires, flashed a brilliant blue colour. The yellow colour of the sparks penetrated the flimsy curtain covering the window. As each tram came to rest beneath my window, it appeared my room was in the middle of an electrical storm. Each doctors' bedroom was minute. Long and narrow, each room was filled with two stand-alone wardrobes; a single bed; a small writing desk and one easy chair. I unpacked my clothes from my small suitcase. I was concerned. I would never be able to sleep in this bedroom. The noise of the trams with their flashing lights, I feared, would always keep me awake. Yet this small room was to be my home for the next six months. Blacow Yates' surgical firm consisted of four doctors. Blacow was the consultant surgeon. He was also the senior surgeon in Sheffield. The senior registrar was Ben Fowler. Steve Leitch, the junior registrar, was also the Resident Surgical Officer. Steve lived in a room on the same corridor as myself. I was the fourth doctor and new house surgeon. The firm had two fourteen bedded wards; the Arthur Hall Ward for female patients and the Fred Osborne Ward for male patients. Both wards had two side wards. In addition the wards were serviced, from a nursing point of view, by several nursing sisters, staff nurses and nursing orderlies. As a student, I had attended Mr. Yates' outpatients and ward rounds on innumerable occasions. I knew Blacow, Ben Fowler and Steve Leitch quite well. It was a comfort to me that the junior registrar, Steve Leitch, was also resident in the hospital. His room was just along the corridor from my own. He was immediately available to me for advice, as and when I needed it. Initially I feared I would need a lot of advice! Steve became a great support to me. We enjoyed each other's company and worked well together. There was a knock on my bedroom door. It was Mr. Yates welcoming me to the hospital. Sitting in my lounge chair, while I sat on the edge of the bed, Blacow ran through the weekly programme of his unit. He set out the many duties expected of me.

"Spend tomorrow morning, on both wards. Familiarise yourself with the patients. Introduce yourself to the ward sisters, staff-nurses and make good friends with them. You will need their help and advice throughout your stay with us. There's one golden rule. If any of the nursing staff, or anyone at all, request you to visit a patient on the ward, always visit. If you don't visit how can you know what's wrong? Never, ever refuse a request to visit a patient."

I'm a "proper doctor"

Blacow quickly departed. I was pleased he had taken the trouble to personally welcome me. His visit made me feel I already belonged to his team. It made me feel content. The apprehension I experienced on arrival slowly disappeared. Blacow's visit was most kind. I was reassured and very grateful to him.

I studied my timetable. It consisted of clerking, examining and having day-to-day responsibility for all the patients on both wards. I would attend outpatients, operating sessions and ward rounds throughout the week. I was to be the admitting doctor for all the firm's hospital admissions whether routine or emergency ones. I would assist the consultant and both registrars in the operating theatre. I was the first point of contact for the nursing staff. I was on call for the firm twenty-four hours a day. Throughout the hospital, a system of lights and buzzers operated. The lights were strategically placed throughout the hospital. There was no escaping those lights, day or night. As Blacow's house surgeon, the flashing yellow light was allocated to me. When the light buzzed flashing yellow, I was duty bound to contact the hospital switchboard immediately. In theory, I was allowed one half day every week. In addition, every other weekend, I would be off duty from Saturday mid-day until Monday morning. John Wightman, the other house surgeon at the hospital, covered me on my half day and alternative weekends. I reciprocated and covered John's work on his half-day and weekend off. This arrangement ensured that, on each other's half-day and weekend off, John or I would be on call for all the hospitals' surgical patients. At those times John and I were not only responsible for all the patients on four surgical wards, but also responsible for every emergency surgical admission to the hospital. When covering for each other, our workload doubled. Work was now the order of the day. Although it was July there would be no time for cricket. Blacow Yates had an unusual tradition with regard to his own operating sessions. He insisted his House Surgeon, the most junior person on the firm, was the person who always assisted him at the surgical operations.

"The House Surgeon," he would often say,
"is the one member of my firm who has the most to learn. I need to teach my house surgeon personally."

The operating theatre tradition was further extended. When the registrars operated, Blacow would often assist them. Whilst, as House Surgeon, I was always Blacow's assistant, Blacow was not always the registrar's assistant. I frequently assisted at operations carried out by the registrars. As Steve and I both resided in the hospital, I always assisted Steve at all the operations relating to emergency admissions to our unit. The work, as Blacow's houseman, was hectic and unrelenting. I enjoyed every minute. All three senior doctors on the team were excellent teachers. I learnt quickly from them. The nursing staff were particularly helpful to me. However it was with Blacow I developed a special relationship. Our close relationship commenced in the operating theatre and, surprisingly, in the confines of my bedroom. Work wise, his surgical teaching was excellent. My operative techniques developed well under his guidance. He instilled in me a confidence, when operating, that exceeded all my expectations. I developed a love for working in the operating theatre. In addition to teaching me surgery, Blacow furthered my sporting interests. In addition to being a consultant surgeon, Blacow was Chairman of Sheffield United Football Club. At quiet periods in the operating theatre, he would frequently discuss football matters with me and in particular events at his beloved Sheffield United. He developed the habit, which I loved, of visiting me, in my bedroom, on a Saturday evening, following a home match at Bramall Lane. Blacow would sit in the only decent chair in my room and relate to me every kick of the game. As the weeks passed, my surgical knowledge improved and so did my knowledge of Sheffield United. I developed a love and respect for Blacow. My disappointment, at not being appointed Professor Jepson's house surgeon, gradually disappeared.

As Blacow's house surgeon, each day began at six. I allowed myself an hour to bathe in the residents' bathroom, dress and eat a bowl of cereal from the mess. I routinely arrived on the wards at seven. An hour was spent on each of the two wards, discussing cases with the nurses, examining, and assessing the progress of the patients. I also ensured that the case notes, of each and every patient, were up to date. Every morning, at nine, I commenced work either in the operating theatre or in the outpatient department. I worked there until lunchtime. Immediately after lunch, I prepared myself for the ward rounds. These rounds occurred on a daily basis. Steve, the resident surgical officer, and I also did a daily round at four in the afternoon. Ben Fowler, the senior registrar, did his ward rounds on Mondays and Thursdays. Blacow's ward rounds were on a Tuesday and Friday. The medical students were encouraged to attend the ward rounds, the outpatients and the operating sessions. In addition, medical students were attached to Mr. Yates' unit for their three-month clinical attachments. For two weeks of their attachment, they were resident in the hospital's student residence. During this time, like me, the students were on call twenty-four hours a day. They attended all emergency admissions. It was part of my role to allocate patients to the students. I also supervised the student's clerking and examination of the patients. The buzzing and flashing yellow light frequently interrupted my daily routine. That light always took precedence over whatever else I was doing. The light usually indicated I was required on the wards by the nursing staff, or that a general practitioner wished to admit a surgical emergency.

Blacow also required his houseman to be available on the wards in the evenings at visiting time. It was important, he believed, that the relatives had the opportunity to discuss the progress of the patient with the house surgeon. Each evening between six thirty and seven thirty, I spent half an hour on each ward being available to the relatives if they wished to discuss any matters with me. The relatives enjoyed this facility and so did I. It was unfortunate that supper, in the doctors' mess, was always at seven, in the middle of my relative's session. Each evening, I always arrived for supper some forty minutes late. I seldom, if ever, met with my colleagues at supper. Every day was a busy day. In addition to the hectic normal routine, I was on call, day and night, for the emergency admissions to our unit. It was also my role to sort out initially any post-operative complications that arose with the patients. It was not unusual to be called out of bed two or three times during the night. Some surgical emergencies required immediate operations in the operating theatre. I recall, on one occasion, assisting in the operating theatre throughout the whole night, and still having to attend outpatients at nine the following morning. During the six months I worked at The Royal Hospital, whenever I hit my pillow, I was instantly asleep. The noise of the trams I did not hear. Their flashing blue lights never disturbed me. My working hours were ridiculous. It was an extremely busy job. The reality was I actually loved the work. It was a privilege to work as Blacow's house surgeon.

Blacow admitted a forty-five year old man to the Fred Osbourne side ward. He had suffered with Chron's Disease for several years. The man was admitted for resection and removal of the diseased colon. He was listed, on Blacow's operating session, as requiring a partial colectomy. All such patients were admitted routinely three or four days prior to their operation in order to be properly prepared for the operation. In those days, the routine pre-operative procedures included the large bowel being evacuated with daily enemas. In addition, the patient was placed on Thalazole, a non-absorbable sulphonamide drug, which supposedly sterilised the lining of the bowel prior to the operation.

The forty-five year old man looked a picture of health. He and his wife had just returned from a three-week holiday in Barbados. He looked perfectly healthy. His skin was bronzed all over with the Caribbean sunshine. Abdominal examination however, revealed the clinical signs of Chron's disease. The X-rays confirmed the extent of his bowel disease. On the third day, following his admission, I was called from my bed, in the early hours of the morning. The man had collapsed with severe abdominal pain. The night nursing staff were concerned. On my examination, he was severely shocked, in obvious severe abdominal pain and semi-conscious. I set up an intravenous drip and telephoned Steve. Steve arrived at the bedside in minutes. Having carried out his examination, Steve decided the patient's condition was so serious Blacow should be informed. Blacow was on the ward in fifteen minutes. The man died ten minutes later. No operation had been carried out. The patient had merely undergone the routine pre-operative preparation. The only treatments he had received were the enemas and the pre-operative, routine administration of Thalazole, which I had prescribed. His death was reported to the coroner. The cause of death was unknown. A coroner's post mortem examination was arranged. Blacow and I attended the post mortem. As the bowel was opened, we were both shocked to see the whole lining of the bowel covered with hundreds of small ulcers, each one of which had been bleeding. The pathologist expressed the opinion to Blacow this was the extremely rare condition of necrotising jeju-ileitis. His opinion was the Thalazole had interfered with the normal bowel bacterial flora in such an alarming way the bowel lining had broken down everywhere. The patient had died as a result of the administration of Thalazole. The Chron's disease had not killed the patient; it appeared the pre-operative administration of Thalazole had. Thalazole, of course, had been used, as a pre-operative drug, in hundreds of cases previously. In those days, it was the standard pre-operative treatment for all patients undergoing bowel surgery. In all his years of experience, Blacow had not seen such a case before. Blacow assured me he would speak to the man's wife. I was so sad. I felt responsible. I was the doctor who had prescribed the Thalazole tablets. It proved to me, at a very early stage of my career, that even the most innocuous drug could prove fatal. Thalazole was classified as an extremely safe drug, yet it had been responsible for the man's death. Thalazole, a simple non-absorbable drug, had killed him.

Although entitled to two weeks, I had taken no holiday during the six months of my house surgeon appointment. Blacow insisted however I take the last two weeks of my employment as holiday. I was reluctant to take any holiday. I enjoyed the work so much, but Blacow insisted. I went home to South Wales. I spent Christmas and New Year with Mam and Dad.

Before leaving Sheffield, I applied for the house officer's post, in Obstetrics and Gynaecology, at The City General Hospital. If successful, I would work with two consultants; Professor Scott Russell and the Irish consultant, Bill Clancy. I discussed my application with Blacow. He agreed to be my referee. Blacow also assured me he would speak with Professor Scott Russell. While at home with Mam and Dad, I received confirmation that I had been appointed to the post at The City General. I was pleased with my new appointment and so was Blacow.

As medical students, we did little practical Obstetrics. I, like all final year students, was required to be present and assist the midwives at twenty normal deliveries during our final year. Each delivery was written up and submitted to the Professor's department prior to the final examination. As I took up my new appointment, I was conscious of the fact I had never been in sole charge of a normal delivery. Abnormal deliveries I had only occasionally seen. The midwives supervised the normal deliveries. The qualified doctors were involved with the complicated abnormal deliveries. I approached my new job with more confidence than when I commenced working for Blacow. Everyone, during my six months on Blacow's unit, had been impressed with my work. More importantly, I had developed an inner confidence, particularly when working under pressure. I was delighted with the progress of my operative skills. I really enjoyed working in the operating theatre. I was now competent carrying out many minor surgical operations and dealing with surgical emergencies. I had come a long way in six months. I was looking forward to my new job.

The two maternity wards at The City General were built on top of one another. Clancy's ward was upstairs. Scott Russell's unit was on the ground floor. The number of doctors on the Professorial unit seemed excessive. In addition to Professor Scott Russell, Jack Dewhurst was The Reader, Hugh Blakey the senior registrar, Allan Dutton the resident registrar, Ann Lawrence the resident senior house officer in Gynaecology, and myself as the houseman; six doctors in total. Upstairs there was Bill Clancy, the consultant, Reg Lunt, the senior registrar, Ann Lawrence, and myself.

If I considered my job at The Royal Hospital busy, the job at The City General was doubly so. Babies, despite my protests, preferred being born during the night. Most nights, I worked throughout with the midwives in the labour wards. Sleep, throughout the six months of Obstetrics, was always in short supply. I worked with a minimum of sleep. The nights were busier than the days. If I worked throughout the night, with no sleep whatsoever, it was no excuse for missing any of the day work. The pace of Obstetrics was unrelenting.

I'M A "PROPER DOCTOR"

The work on the Professorial Unit was unlike any I had previously experienced. Blacow was a very practical consultant. He always emphasised the need to solve the patient's problems. The patient's outcome was the most important factor to Blacow. He was always asking,

"How well has the patient done under our care?"

If the patient had done well, Blacow was satisfied. The patient's outcome to him was paramount. Working on the Professorial unit, the patient's outcome while equally important, a more meticulous approach to patient care was in place. Each and every doctor, involved with a case, was required to detail, in the patient's notes, not only the patient's outcome, but also how that outcome had been achieved. The progress of each and every pregnancy, whether normal or abnormal, was documented in every relevant detail. The indications and reasons for any clinical intervention by the doctor had to be written down and subsequently justified. Every Friday afternoon, Scott Russell chaired the weekly case conference. All doctors, working on the unit, attended. At this conference, the case notes of all the patients, who had been discharged during the week, would be critically examined. The actions of each doctor, involved in the case, were questioned and discussed by the other doctors. Decisions I had taken in the middle of the night, when I was utterly exhausted, would be questioned and critically examined in those meetings. Every action taken needed to be justified to my peers. It was my first experience of regular, detailed peer review. Initially, these sessions were threatening and intimidating. Over time, I realised the enormous benefit I learnt from those meetings, not least the value of accurate detailed note taking at the time of a consultation or clinical event. As the weeks passed, I really looked forward to the Friday afternoon sessions. It was there I would justify my week's work to my senior colleagues. I enjoyed the challenge.

The city of Sheffield had two large hospitals caring for the diseases of women. The largest, and main teaching hospital, The Jessop Hospital, was in the city centre. The Jessop dealt with the extremely complicated diseases of women. It was the medical policy, determined by the consultants of the day, that no abortions were admitted to The Jessop. All abortions were admitted to The City General. Abortions at that time were illegal and most were carried out by so called back street abortionists. It was argued these cases had a high risk of infection. The city's abortion philosophy was introduced so that the introduction of sepsis into the Jessop Hospital was kept to an absolute minimum. The introduction of sepsis into The City General, was apparently of less importance.

My first weekend on emergency admissions came far too soon. I had been in post for just one week. Immediately, I was the first point of contact for all the hospital's Obstetric and Gynaecological admissions. If my knowledge of delivering babies was small, my practical experience of Gynaecology was non-existent. My first emergency occurred within thirty minutes of taking up my responsibility. A General Practitioner telephoned requesting an emergency admission for a 'Back-street abortion.' With all abortions at that time being illegal, pregnant women, desperate not to proceed with their pregnancy, frequently fell into the hands of unqualified lay women who attempted to carry out an abortion. Known as 'Back Street Abortionists' their procedures were carried out with minimal medical knowledge and in poor sanitary conditions. There were frequent dire consequences for the pregnant woman.

My first emergency admission was the result of such a back street abortion. The patient, who was in her late teens, was said to have been three months pregnant. An unknown woman, who had disappeared from the patient's home by the time the general practitioner arrived at the house, had attempted to carry out an abortion. The general practitioner informed me the patient was in considerable abdominal pain, bleeding from the vagina and in a state of shock. Those findings I confirmed on admission. I decided to treat the shock immediately. I set up an intravenous transfusion. Subsequent examination of the abdomen revealed extreme tenderness and some early signs of rigidity. It was important for me to carry out a vaginal examination. I explained the procedure to the patient. The ward sister chaperoned me, while I carried out the examination. I was conscious of the fact this was the very first internal vaginal examination I had ever carried out. I was inexperienced at vaginal examinations. As a medical student, I had carried out precisely none. My vaginal examination proved difficult, as the young lady found it impossible to relax after the recent traumatic experience she had experienced from the Back-Street Abortionist. However, I could feel what I determined was a baby's arm or leg hanging down into the vagina from the neck of the womb. I knew immediately that this was not the case, as the teenager was only three months pregnant. A baby's arms and legs had not developed to this extent in a three-month pregnancy. I could however only report what I felt on vaginal examination. I needed to contact the registrar, Allan Dutton.

"I know this sounds stupid"
I began,
"There's a teenage girl with a septic abortion whose been admitted. Three months pregnant and severely shocked. I've put up a drip. There's marked tenderness and some rigidity in the abdomen. I've done a vaginal examination and there appears to be a leg or an arm hanging down from the neck of the womb. I know that's stupid, as she's only three months pregnant, but that's what I can feel."
"I'll be on the ward in five minutes."
Dutton replied.
On returning to the patient, her state of shock had worsened. Her blood pressure had fallen and her abdominal pain was much more severe. On examining her abdomen, Dutton confirmed my findings. He decided it was necessary for him to carry out a vaginal examination to ascertain what, if anything, was hanging down from the neck of the womb. Alas, his examination was not possible. The woman was in vaginal spasm. Dutton was unable to gain access into the vagina. Dutton said,
"We need to take her immediately to the operating theatre."
In theatre, under a general anaesthetic, the patient was totally relaxed Inspection of the vagina was easy as the anaesthetic had removed all the muscular spasm. Dutton carried out the vaginal examination. I was scrubbed up as his assistant. I felt stupid. How could I have felt an arm or a leg hanging down in the vagina? In a three-month pregnancy it was

impossible. Surprisingly, Dutton commented,

> "I can feel exactly what you felt. It's not a leg or an arm. I don't know what it is. Sister can I have a large artery forceps."

Dutton placed the forceps into the vagina. After a moment he began pulling on the forceps. The forceps was extracted from the vagina. The arm or leg I had felt was, in fact, the long rubber adapter from a bicycle pump! Dutton carried out curettage of the womb. The lady was prescribed intravenous antibiotics through the drip I had set up to counter her shock. Over coffee, Dutton explained to me that Back-Street Abortionists, not infrequently, carried out their abortions using a soap and water solution delivered into the womb with a bicycle pump. With the pump filled with soapy water, the rubber adaptor was inserted into the neck of the womb. When in place, the soapy solution was pumped into the womb. The pressure of soapy water from the pump, would then cause an abortion. Dutton believed, in this case, the delivery of the soapy water had caused so much pain, the patient had collapsed. With the patient crying out in pain, the Back-Street Abortionist panicked. She unscrewed the bicycle pump from its adaptor, leaving the rubber adapter held, by the neck of the womb, inside the vagina. The abortionist fled, taking the bicycle pump with her. The patient was left crying with severe abdominal pain. The rubber adaptor, from the bicycle pump, left inside her vagina. Despite all our efforts, over the next twenty-four hours, the young girl died. Death resulted from a fulminating peritonitis caused by the sepsis of a Back-Street Abortionist.

In those days, there was no oral contraceptive. The contraceptive pill had not been developed. The methods of contraception, available to women then, were sexual abstinence, the rhythm method, a condom, a Dutch cap or spermicidal cream. None of these methods, apart from total sexual abstinence, was totally successful. Abortions, even if performed by doctors, was illegal. Young women, with an unwanted pregnancy, had little alternative but to seek, in desperation, the so-called help of Back-Street Abortionists. This patient had been born twenty years too soon! In twenty years time, the contraceptive pill would be available to prevent unwanted pregnancies. Therapeutic abortions by doctors would be legalised. There would then be no need for women, to seek the work of an unqualified abortionist.

Most of my work, at The City General, was in Obstetrics. I supervised, with the help of the experienced midwives, the birth of many babies. The birth of a healthy baby is a joyous time for parents and families. I enjoyed playing a small part in achieving such happy outcomes. Working on the unit, I frequently whistled or hummed the current hit song of the day.

"Every time I hear a newborn baby cry, then I believe."
I was really happy in my work. I enjoyed working in my chosen profession. Every normal birth was such a happy occasion. Of course there were also very sad times. The birth of deformed or abnormal babies was always a traumatic experience. Mothers, who lost their babies by miscarriage or some complication of pregnancy, needed sensitive and careful counselling. Complications were always a possibility in any pregnancy. As obstetricians, it was our role to achieve a successful outcome in all such circumstances. I revelled in the challenge. As each week passed I became more competent in Obstetrics. The teaching I received was exceptional. I became more and more interested in a career in Obstetrics and Gynaecology. I felt confident in my role. I enjoyed the work so much I became convinced I could specialise in the subject. Eventually, I thought, with plenty of hard work and further examinations, I could become a consultant in the speciality. Spring was coming to an end. Summer would soon arrive. I was so engrossed in my work that, for the first time in my life, I had given little thought to playing cricket in the forthcoming season. Playing cricket would now be the pleasure of my past. My pleasure now was working in Obstetrics.

It was late April when I received the telephone call. It was from the University's Director of Physical Education. We were old friends.

> "As you know Neil, the University play Yorkshire County Cricket Club at the beginning of each season. The game's next Wednesday. The University has no wicket keeper. We want you to play. The team needs your experience. Can you play?"

I couldn't refuse to play against the Yorkshire First Eleven. My heart was racing as I listened to the request.

"I'll take a day's leave. I'll be at the ground at ten-thirty. Thanks for the invite."

I was back playing cricket again. I experienced the thrill of anticipation. I was delighted to be playing cricket against Yorkshire once more. My cricketing ability would be tested against the best. On the day of the game, the University players seemed so young. They had all arrived at University straight from school. There were no ex-servicemen in the team. The match was one of Yorkshire men against boys. The University was heavily defeated. I scored ten runs and took one catch. I had a good day behind the stumps. I satisfied myself that my talent for wicket keeping was still present. At the end of the game, Vic Wilson, the Yorkshire captain, very kindly gave me a lift back to the hospital in his car. I'd enjoyed every moment of the day.

It was while working at The City General I fell in love. It was there I met Sister Meg Ramsay, one of the midwives working on the Professorial Unit. During my six-month appointment Meg and I worked closely together, both on the ward and in the labour theatre. We worked together during the day and through most nights. It was a relationship that developed through our work. Of course, it was an unwritten rule in the hospital that close relationships between staff were not allowed under any circumstances. It was essential our personal relationship was unknown to any of the staff in the hospital. Nowadays we often laugh together at our first date. We arranged to meet outside the Hippodrome cinema in the centre of Sheffield at five o'clock. Unfortunately both Meg and I were on duty throughout the previous night. We worked together throughout the night. Meg and I had no sleep. I struggled throughout the next morning on the wards. I was relieved it was my half-day. Naturally, I eagerly anticipated my first date with Meg. I waited patiently outside the Hippodrome for her arrival. Imagine my surprise, and disappointment, when Meg's best friend, another Sister at the hospital, arrived instead of Meg. Her best friend, Anthea, informed me Meg was too tired to come on the date! I went to the cinema with Anthea. It was a wonderful way for Meg and me to start our relationship! Unbeknown to any of our friends or colleagues at the hospital, apart from Anthea, our relationship flourished during the six months of my appointment. We were both very much in love. As my appointment progressed, I convinced myself my future career lay in specialising in Obstetrics and Gynaecology. I thoroughly enjoyed the work. I flourished in the academic atmosphere of the Professorial Unit. Specialising in Obstetrics was to be my future.

When I was accepted for medical school in 1949, it was necessary to apply for deferment from National Service. Although the war finished in 1945, every able-bodied man, on attaining the age of eighteen, was required to spend two years in the armed services. When I qualified as a doctor, my deferment was at an end. National Service was still mandatory. Eleven years after the end of the war, and now having completed one year working in hospitals, the country still required me to enter the armed services for the mandatory two years of National Service. With my mind now set on specialising in Obstetrics and Gynaecology, I decided to apply for a further three months' deferment. I was eligible for and wanted to sit the post-graduate Diploma in Obstetrics of The Royal College. If granted a further deferment, I would spend the three months studying at home. My application for further deferment was granted. I went home to study for three months. Mam and Dad were delighted to have me at home.

Many of my medical colleagues decided two years of National Service, at this time in their careers, was a waste of time. They used whatever means was available to them to avoid spending two years in the services. All the doctors attended for a medical examination in Sheffield prior to their National Service. One of my medical colleagues spent two days, prior to his medical, hitting his right knee with a rubber truncheon. The resulting swelling in his knee was sufficient to convince the examining doctor that my colleague suffered from recurring fluid on his knee! He failed his medical. The examining doctor concluded my colleague suffered from a recurring effusion of the knee and as such he was unfit for National Service.

My own medical examination was a farce. A Sheffield General Practitioner carried out the medical. He and I had played cricket together on numerous occasions. We were good friends. When I entered the examination room, he greeted me with riotous laughter.

"You must be one of the fittest people in Sheffield."

he said.

"I hope you don't mind if I don't examine you. It would be a waste of time. If you are agreeable, I'll pass you fully fit. It's been a busy morning and I could do with a break. We'll both have a cup of tea."

The tea duly arrived. We chatted. Our conversation centred on cricket. I was passed as perfectly fit for National Service. Grade A1. I was never examined.

I received a letter, some three weeks later, instructing me to attend at Chester Military Hospital for a second medical examination. An Army doctor, I was informed, would carryout my second medical examination. I travelled to Chester by train. I waited in the waiting room of the outpatient department. The Army doctor, eventually arrived. He was over an hour late for my appointment.

"All hell has broken loose here today. Please accept my apologies for being late. I'm now miles behind with my day's work. Now let's see. At Sheffield, three weeks ago, you had a medical. You were perfectly fit then. Any illnesses since then?"

"No."

I replied.

"Good. In that case I presume you don't mind if I agree with the Sheffield doctor and declare you fully fit."

I said nothing.

"Many thanks for your understanding and co-operation. I know you have a train to catch, so thanks very much. I'll see the papers are duly completed"

My second medical ended. I had not been examined again. It was disappointing. At this second medical, I didn't even have a cup of tea! I had travelled over two hundred miles by train for the medical and hadn't even taken my shirt off..

Before completing my appointment at The City General, Professor Scott Russell asked to see me.

"I've been really pleased with your work on this unit."

he began.

> "Your work has impressed everyone. I realise you will be taking the Diploma, before commencing your two years' National Service. That's a very sensible decision. If, on completion of your National Service you are still interested in pursuing a career in Obstetrics and Gynaecology, I want you to know you will always be welcome on my unit. If you are interested, write to me before you complete your National Service. I feel sure we will be able to find a job for you. Well done and good luck."

The suggestion of a future post on the Professorial Unit in two years time was something only dreams were made of. I was delighted. Meg was pleased too. I left Meg working in Sheffield. I went home to Mam and Dad for three months. I studied every day for my post-graduate Diploma in Obstetrics. I played no cricket that summer. Revision was the order of every day. I succeeded at the examination. In addition to my medical degree qualification of M.B.Ch.B., I could now write the additional letters of D.Obst.R.C.O.G. after my name.

I left home for Aldershot to commence my National Service. It would be a very different type of life. My Dad wrote me a letter. It was the first I received at Aldershot. The envelope was addressed:–

"Lieutenant, Dr. U. N. Phillips (A to Z-Perm any three)."

It was my Dad's way of showing how proud he was of me.

My National Service began in November 1956. The Suez crisis was at its height. After six weeks of square bashing at Aldershot, I was posted to Catterick Military Hospital. I was given, as indeed were all the other National Service Medical Officers, the rank of Lieutenant. With my Diploma in Obstetrics, I was to work in The Families Unit of the hospital. My posting, I was assured, would allow me to continue with my career in Obstetrics. I arrived at Catterick on New Year's Eve in a snowstorm. On New Year's Day, as instructed, I reported to the Commanding Officer at ten o'clock. The Commanding Officer had taken a day's leave. I was told to return the following day. I reported to Colonel Vine the following day.

"I'm sorry, but we have too many doctors working in the Family Unit. It's quite impossible for you to work there. They're one doctor short in the Psychiatric Department, so I'll allocate you to Psychiatry. You'll enjoy working there."

I protested

"I've had no training in Psychiatry. Know nothing about the subject."

"Phillips! You'll soon pick it up. I see you've played rugby previously and still play cricket regularly. That's really good. I shall put you in touch with the relevant people. You could have a great time here. Catterick is a haven for sportsmen. We always need officers who can play games. You could be a great asset to us. Off you go to the Psychiatric department. You are dismissed."

I was dismissed.

On arriving at the Psychiatric department, I introduced myself to the staff. It was a long way from the hospitals in Sheffield where I had been so happy.

Psychiatry, for me, was a nightmare. For the patients, it was probably worse. My knowledge of Psychiatry was minimal. I had received little training in the subject. In the outpatient department, several young National Service men, who obviously did not want to be doing their National Service, confronted me. I recall one such youngster who had not returned to his unit from leave. Having been missing for several days, he was listed as AWOL—absent without leave. He was arrested by the Military Police and brought under escort to his unit at Catterick. His story, which he slowly unfolded to me, was that he was unable to return to his unit, as the "little green men" had tied him up in his garden. The little green men, he assured me, had arrived from outer space. I had no idea whether this was a convenient story he had made up or whether he had some sort of psychiatric disorder. I sought the advice of the consultant army psychiatrist.

"How on earth"

I began

"do you decide if a patient is so psychiatrically disturbed as to warrant being diagnosed as insane and entitled to be discharged from the Army?"

"It's easy."

the consultant informed me.

"Keep talking to them Phillips, until that moment arrives when you begin to wonder whether you are insane or they are. When you get to that point, certify them, and discharge them!"

The consultant was in fits of laughter. I could not see the funny side. I longed to be back in Sheffield. This type of medicine was not for me. Psychiatry and I were incompatible. I was rescued from my turmoil in the Psychiatric department because of my interest in sport. Four days after arriving in the department, I was summoned to the Commanding Officer.

"Lieutenant Phillips I have a deal for you. If you agree to spend two weeks on a Rugby Refereeing Course, and qualify as a Rugby Referee, then on your return, I will ensure you cease working in the Psychiatric Unit and will move you to another unit."

The offer was too good to refuse. I spent two weeks qualifying as a Class Three Referee. When I returned to the hospital, as a fully qualified referee, I was transferred to the Surgical Unit under Colonel Mathieson. The Commanding Officer had kept his part of the deal and I had kept mine.

During my absence on the referee's course, Colonel Vine had contacted headquarters of the Royal Army Medical Corps at Aldershot. Although I had not played any rugby since the age of seventeen, Colonel Vine had now recommended me for a trial for the Corps' Rugby Fifteen.

"You are to report to Aldershot on Tuesday next. You will be housed for two nights–Tuesday and Wednesday–in the officers' mess at Aldershot. The trial is on Wednesday. You can travel back to Catterick on Thursday."

"But I was told by the neuro-surgeon, Professor Lambert Rodgers, following my head injury in 1949, never ever to play rugby again."

"That's poppycock Phillips. You can't possibly do any further damage. Not ten years after your previous injury. Have a good trial. I hope you make the team."

With that, I was dismissed.

Colonel Vine kept his promise. I was transferred to the Surgical Unit. The consultant was Colonel Mathieson. My arrival in the surgical unit would now be delayed for another week, while I returned to playing a game of rugby. I played at Aldershot, but not very well. It was nine years since my last school game at Caerphilly. I wasn't chosen to play rugby for the Royal Army Medical Corps. I returned to Catterick. The experience of playing rugby at Aldershot confirmed what I already knew. My days of playing rugby had finished on the school playing field at Caerphilly.

Colonel Mathieson, the consultant surgeon, was brilliant. Extremely well qualified, he was most concerned that the National Service Medical Officers did not waste their two years while doing their army service. Mathieson instituted weekly tutorial sessions in Surgery for all the doctors working in his unit. The tutorials were held in the afternoons. The few I attended were of a high quality. The National Service Medical Officers were very bright, intelligent doctors. The majority wished to further their studies along the road to specialisation and eventual consultant status. The quality of the National Service medical officers at Catterick was exceptional. Tony Mitchell would later become Professor of Medicine at Nottingham. Bill Duncan would become the Professor of Oncology at Edinburgh; Keith Norcross an orthopaedic consultant at Birmingham; Roy Summerly a consultant dermatologist at Stafford; Terry Buffin a consultant ear nose and throat specialist in Sheffield. Then there was me. My army training would endeavour to make me a consultant in sport.

My attendance at Mathieson's tutorials was most infrequent. As a qualified Class Three Rugby Referee, Colonel Vine ordered me, yes, ordered me, to referee rugby matches throughout the Catterick Garrison on three afternoons every week. It was for the good of the Royal Army Medical Corps, he informed me.

"What an asset you are to us."

he repeatedly told me.

"A qualified Rugby referee and a great cricketer."

My involvement in rugby became all consuming. Colonel Vine was responsible for that. He recommended me to Catterick Headquarters, as a well-qualified rugby officer. I was appointed to serve on the selection committee for Catterick Services' Rugby Team. As such, I was expected to attend as many unit matches as possible throughout the garrison. I reported on the performances of various players at selection meetings. As I was already refereeing three afternoons a week, the other two afternoons were taken up with watching rugby matches or attending selection meetings. In addition to these rugby commitments, I was expected to take my turn, with the other members of the selection committee, travelling with the team to their matches. On my commanding officer's orders, and with his pride and blessing, my week became totally dedicated to rugby. My work, in the Surgical Unit seemed totally irrelevant to my Commanding Officer. He wanted me to spend all my time involved in sport.

Because of my involvement in sport, Colonel Mathieson appointed me in charge of the monthly Sports Injury clinic. This clinic was carried out by Major Bass, the Northern Command's Specialist in Physical Medicine. Alan Bass was based at York. He visited Catterick Military Hospital once a month for the Sports Injury Clinic. The clinic consisted of difficult sporting injuries referred by the doctors working in the Surgical Unit. It was my role, in preparing for the clinic, to ensure all the patients' notes were available for Major Bass. I attended the clinic on every occasion. Major Bass and I worked very well together. We became good friends. We learnt from each other. I looked forward to the clinics as it ensured, for at least one day a month, I was involved in clinical work. Not even my Commanding Officer could interfere with my attendance at Major Bass's clinic. Alan Bass and I developed a great respect for each other's clinical judgements. We developed an excellent working relationship.

Before entering the Army, and on obtaining my post-graduate degree in Obstetrics, Meg and I became engaged. We were married at Sheffield on February 16th. 1957. Meg's Dad was unable to attend the wedding. He was terminally ill in Dundee with lung cancer. As we had no money there was no honeymoon. I rented a cottage in the beautiful village of Brompton on Swale, some six miles from the Catterick hospital. It was there we spent our honeymoon and set up our first home. My involvement with garrison rugby became all consuming. I regularly refereed unit rugby matches and became more and more involved with the Catterick Services Rugby Team. With the advent of summer, I played cricket every day. I rarely attended the hospital for any medical work. If not actually playing cricket, I was travelling the length and breadth of the country in order to play in a game. Specialising, practising and furthering my skills in any branch of Medicine was impossible. Improving my medical knowledge and skills became a fading dream. The whole summer was spent practising and improving my cricketing skills. I captained the hospital team, played for the village team, Catterick Services, the Royal Army Medical Corps and various army teams.

In the autumn, Colonel Vine transferred me from the Surgical Unit to the Families Unit. I was so pleased. I had excelled at cricket throughout the summer and my Commanding Officer was proud of my achievements. I was rewarded with an appointment in the Families Unit. I now was able to practise some clinical Obstetrics. From a career viewpoint it was a year too late. My first year in the Army was spent as a full time sportsman. Colonel Vine continued to ensure my involvement in sport took precedent over all my hospital duties. It is easy for me to blame Colonel Vine for ordering me to be totally involved in sport during my two years at Catterick, to the detriment of my clinical work, but that would be grossly unfair. He did always insist that my involvement with sport took precedence over my clinical work but, in reality, I needed little encouragement. I had always wanted to be a full time cricketer. The summers at Catterick more than satisfied my childhood ambitions. There, during the summer months, I was, for the first time in my life, a full time cricketer. If my medical work, at the hospital, interfered with my cricket, Colonel Vine soon rectified the problem. My Commanding Officer's enthusiasm for my participation in sport, eventually landed him in serious trouble. Colonel Vine made a serious error of judgement.

I'M A "PROPER DOCTOR"

The hospital cricket team, which I captained, reached the semi-final of the Army Hospitals' Cup. Our semi-final match was against a hospital in Belfast. The team would travel by coach and ferry. The trip would take four days. The hospital's consultant obstetrician, and my immediate boss, was on annual leave during those four days. As I was the only doctor remaining in the Families Unit with a post-graduate qualification in Obstetrics, I was in sole charge of the Families Unit. I informed Colonel Vine I was unable to play in the Belfast match. For once my medical duties would have to take precedence over my cricket.

> "You must play. It is inconceivable, having brought the team so far, that you are now unable to play in such an important game. There must be a way you can play. I cannot allow a situation to develop which could jeopardise the team winning and reaching the final. Phillips, you are aware, are you not, this hospital has never reached the final before. I am not going to miss the opportunity now we are so close. I will find a way. You must play. Give me a couple of days."

I was dismissed. Colonel Vine sent for me two days later.

"Phillips, you are to play in Belfast."

The Commanding Officer's instructions were clear.

> "I appreciate you cannot be absent from the hospital for four days. Four days absence would be unacceptable, when you are in sole charge of the Unit. However the Unit can manage without you for a day. No one is indispensable for one day. The team will leave by coach as arranged. On the morning of the game, I have arranged for you to fly to Belfast from R.A.F. Dishforth. You will leave Dishforth at 0800 hours. Arrive Belfast one hour later. A car has been arranged to transport you to the cricket ground. Play the game. Captain the side. Return to Dishforth on an evening flight. You're only absent during the day. It's simple. We'll easily cope for a day without you."

There was no point in my arguing with my Commanding Officer. In my two years at Catterick I had learnt, by bitter experience, there was no point in arguing with the Commanding Officer. One just accepted his orders, no matter how ridiculous they seemed. I would fly to Belfast on the morning of the game. The Families Unit would be left without a properly qualified person in charge

The day of the cricket match duly arrived. In the early morning Brompton-on-Swale was engulfed in thick fog. Meg was thirty-seven weeks pregnant with our first child. She was glad it was foggy. The flight would be cancelled. Meg would not worry. I would remain at Catterick in the Families Unit, where I belonged. The fog was very thick as I travelled by car to R.A.F. Dishforth. I was convinced the flight would be cancelled.

"It's a beautiful day up there."

The R.A.F. officer informed me, pointing to the sky.

> "We shall be flying in one of our training planes. You're the only passenger. It will probably be the only time you'll have a whole aircraft to yourself."

We left Dishforth at 0800 hours. I sat at a desk, usually occupied by trainee navigators. The noise of the aircraft was intense. I was the sole passenger. Thirty minutes into the flight a member of the crew came back to see me.

"We've received a message. We don't really understand."

The message reads:–

> "Rain for the past twenty-four hours. Still raining. Pitch unplayable. Passenger to return to Catterick."

> "Prior to departure we were informed you were a visiting Obstetrician to the Belfast hospital. It now appears we are transporting you to play cricket. Our Commanding Officer at Dishforth is not pleased. You are to report to him on landing."

The plane returned to R.A.F. Dishforth. I reported to the station's Commanding Officer.

It became apparent that Colonel Vine had requested a plane to take me, as a visiting Obstetrician, to the hospital in Belfast. No mention had been made of the cricket match. The Commanding Officer of Dishforth made it quite clear to me that if a flight had been requested to transport a

[144]

cricketer, the flight would have been refused. Fortunately he appreciated I was the innocent party. He informed me he would personally speak to Colonel Vine conveying his displeasure. The Catterick Hospital's cricket team played the following day without me and lost. The Belfast hospital team would play in the final. Colonel Vine was a very unhappy man. His actions confirmed my belief. He would go to any limits to ensure I played games in preference to working at my chosen profession.

It was during my two years of National Service that Margaret and I frequently visited Doctor Zanazi at his home in Shrewsbury. It was a convenient stopping place for Margaret and myself on our visits to South Wales from Catterick. Over many visits he reluctantly informed us of the happenings following his arrest in Tredegar immediately after Italy entered the war. Following imprisonment at the local Tredegar jail, he was transferred, with many other Italians from South Wales, to a barracks near Cardiff. As so many Italians were interred at that time, the British Government decided to transfer them, with many German prisoners of war, to Canada, aboard a liner, the Arandora Star. With fifteen hundred German and Italian prisoners of war on board, the ship set sail from Liverpool in early July of 1940, without any escort. The liner was torpedoed in the Atlantic, by a German U boat within forty-eight hours of leaving Liverpool. Thirteen hundred passengers, aboard the Arandora Star, were lost. Zanazi survived. He was picked up by a Canadian destroyer, but his hands were frozen to the ropes of a rubber ring which had ensured his survival. He then spent many months having plastic surgery to his hands before making a full recovery. He was subsequently imprisoned in an internment camp on the outskirts of Shrewsbury. At the end of the war he was offered a partnership in a General Practice in Shrewsbury, were he worked for the remainder of his professional life. He was anxious for me to join him there, at the completion of my National Service, but his very kind offer did not attract me.

Our first child, Shelagh Christine, was born in the Family Unit of Catterick Military Hospital on the third of September 1958. Meg and I were delighted. Shelagh was my Mam and Dad's first grandchild. They too were deliriously happy. Meg's mother was also delighted. There were only two months left of my National Service. Before entering the Army, Scott-Russell had asked me to contact him, prior to my discharge, if I was still keen on specialising in Obstetrics and Gynaecology. He assured me he would do all he could to help me return to his unit. I wrote to the Professor. He replied by offering me a Senior House Officer post in Pathology at The Jessop Hospital in Sheffield. I was to start in October. I would forego my terminal leave. The offer was too good to refuse. I was accepted back into a teaching hospital post with the Professor backing me. I was on the bottom rung of the ladder to specialise in Obstetrics. My professional future seemed bright.

I should have known better. It is sad for me to recall what had happened to me during my Army service. My two years of National Service, or should I say full-time sport, was at an end. For the two years of their National Service my fellow colleagues had regularly attended the tutorials and seminars conducted by Colonel Mathieson. They had worked really hard. They studied at every available opportunity. They had used their period of National Service to further their careers. While I was continuously involved with rugby and cricket, many of them sat and passed further post-graduate examinations. In contrast, my time had been spent on the playing fields. I had done little clinical work for two years and certainly no studying. I had improved, beyond my wildest dreams, as a cricketer. I held rugby referee qualifications. I became knowledgeable of rugby. Progress with my medical career however had been non-existent. Without realising it, my professional career had deteriorated. My desire to dedicate myself to specialising had disappeared. I had carried out no academic study for two years. Now it was time to return to the real academic and clinical world of medicine. It was time for intensive academic study. My involvement in sport would inevitably decrease. The conflict in my life between medicine and sport would just not go away. In his letter, Scott-Russell apologised for the fact he was unable to offer me a clinical post at The Jessop Hospital. He suggested however that one would be available for me at the completion of my six months in the Pathology Department. I started work at the Jessop in October.

I'M A "PROPER DOCTOR"

Margaret and Shelagh remained in the cottage at Brompton-on-Swale. I took up residence in the hospital. There was no accommodation for doctor's families. We were separated as a family for the first time. Meg and I were extremely unhappy at this separation..

The consultant in Pathology was Dr. Payne. He was recognised as one of the top pathologists in the country. He was also an excellent teacher. I liked Pathology and enjoyed the work. Work was intense. Returning to academic study and residence in the hospital and separation from Meg and Shelagh I found extremely difficult. I was on call twenty-four hours a day and every other weekend. I was entitled to one half day a week on Wednesdays. The volume of my work was such however that although I supposedly finished work at lunchtime, on my half day, it was nearer tea time when I set off in my car to make the journey from Sheffield to Brompton-on-Swale. I missed Meg and Shelagh tremendously. I would travel from Sheffield to Brompton-on-Swale every Wednesday afternoon to see them. After only a few hours with Meg and Shelagh, I left home, in the very early hours of Thursday morning, returning to the hospital by eight o'clock in time for breakfast. In addition to my work in the Pathology Department, I was expected to study every evening after my day's work. If I was to travel the road of specialisation, I needed to study and pass several more postgraduate examinations. When I studied for my Diploma, I did nothing other than study. I had no day job during that three months of study. I lived at home in Tredegar with my parents. For the past two years, I had done no academic study. I found the re-entry into academic work and the need to study long into the night, after a hard day's work, impossible. In addition, the separation from Meg and Shelagh was unacceptable to me. As the weeks passed, I became more unhappy. I realised specialisation may not be for me. Three months into my job, Scott-Russell sent for me.

> "Neil, I've been planning the next six years for you. In April, on completing your Pathology you will become my Senior House Officer here at The Jessop. Provided you pass your Primary Fellowship of The Royal College of Surgeons, you will then move to Oxford. I have arranged for you to work

then, as a registrar with the Professor there. After two years at Oxford you should by then have obtained your Membership of The Royal College of Obstetricians and Gynaecologists. A post of Senior Registrar is then possible for you at St. Mary's Hospital in Manchester. Of course I cannot promise all of this will happen. So much depends on the progress you make yourself."

Scott Russell was being most generous. He had laid out a future plan for my career. The plan would take in the next seven years of my life. My future in Obstetrics would be all consuming. It would need total commitment from me. The Prof. had presented me with a wonderful opportunity. The posts he had suggested, and which he had provisionally arranged for me, were some of the best in the land. He offered me a wonderful opportunity. I thanked Scott-Russell. I said I'd think very carefully about his suggestion. He told me how pleased everyone was to have me back. He emphasised what a high opinion everyone had of my work. I remained extremely quiet. I was unsure. I did not know if I wanted to travel along the road he had so kindly planned for me.

"It's a wonderful opportunity."
was Meg's initial reaction.
"You know the Prof. has always had a high opinion not only of your work, but also of you as a person."

Dad was delighted when I told him of the opportunity the Prof. had given me. The days that followed placed my mind in mental turmoil. I made enquiries at both Oxford and Manchester. There was no married accommodation at either hospital for the resident registrars in Obstetrics. The registrars lived in the hospital, their wives and families lived in private rented accommodation, at their own expense. The thought of living apart from my wife and family for the next seven years had no appeal for me. My over-riding concern however was whether my own personal commitment was sufficient to succeed along the hard road ahead. I could not commit myself to the necessary academic study that was required of me, particularly after doing nothing academically over the past two years. My short time in the Pathology department made me appreciate how much I had lost the zest and discipline for continuing with academic study, to the exclusion of all else. Sadly, I realised I had lost the desire and the discipline required of me. The Army, Colonel Vine and myself, though not necessarily in that order, had seen to that. Meg and I talked, on the telephone, long into many a night debating the issues.

> "I shall be happy whatever you decide."

Was Meg's standard reply. Over those agonising days, I came to realise I wanted more from my daily life than total devotion to academic study. I wanted a life, living with my family. I wanted an involvement with sport, particularly my cricket. In my heart of hearts, I knew I could not rekindle the total commitment to Obstetrics the Prof was now offering me.

My interview with Professor Scott-Russell was as friendly as always, but his disappointment showed, as I declined his kind and generous offer.

> "I have realised that the specialisation road to a consultant post is not for me. The dedication and sacrifice required of me and my family is too great. I have decided to enter general practice. By doing so, I will continue practicing medicine, and have a full family life. I might even be able to continue my involvement with sport. With your permission I will leave the hospital at the end of my appointment in Pathology. I'm sorry for the inconvenience and embarrassment I have obviously caused you"

Scott–Russell said how disappointed he was with my decision.

> "We shall miss you. I understand and respect your decision.
> I thank you for your honesty."

The Prof. wished me well.

I left The Jessop Hospital at the end of January. My ambition to specialise was at an end. I would seek a post in General Practice.

5

General Practice........

As January 1959 ended, I moved with Margaret and baby Shelagh to Redcar, a seaside town on the North Yorkshire coast. My dream of specialising in Obstetrics and Gynaecology was over. I had decided on a career in General Practice. Despite Scott-Russell's very generous career opportunity, I made a conscious decision to enter General Practice. Subsequent to my discharge from the Army, I had re-entered the hard, intense life of clinical work and academic study at The Jessop Hospital. That life was not for me. Senior medical colleagues, at the hospital, had spent years studying for their postgraduate degrees, to the exclusion of everything else in their lives. They were highly qualified medical personnel capable of being consultants in their own right. Alas, there were no consultant posts for them. They were caught in a blind alley, with nowhere to go. Most decided to be part of the 'brain drain' emigrating to Canada or the USA.

I decided I wanted a much fuller life, with my family, and my cricket. Specialisation could not be part of that. Cricket meant as much, if not more, to me, than the practice of medicine. The desire to commit myself to full time academic study had disappeared.

Entry into General Practice, in the late fifties, was no easy matter. There were far too many applicants for each vacancy. Appointments were difficult to obtain. After two unsuccessful applications, I was appointed an assistant, with a view to partnership, in a well-established four doctor practice at Redcar. The practice was based at The Green House, an extension of the home of the senior partner, Ian Mackinlay. The practice vacancy occurred as a result of the junior partner, John Garwood, joining the 'brain drain'. He emigrated to Canada. There were many applicants for the vacancy at Redcar and I considered myself fortunate to have been appointed. The practice appeared to be thriving. I eagerly looked forward to a settled family life in General Practice. As a bonus, I would continue playing cricket in Yorkshire.

The interview, or more correctly interviews, for my appointment, occurred on a cold, frosty Sunday in December. The three partners were keen, not only to interview myself, but also to meet my wife. Wives, in those days, were such an important element in the running of a general practice. Margaret and baby Shelagh accompanied me for the interviews. We first met with the senior partner and his wife, Ian and Sal Mackinlay. Their interview, took place at their home over morning coffee. Ian Mackinlay and I chatted in one of the consulting rooms in the adjoining surgery premises, Sal Mackinlay entertained Margaret and Shelagh in the lounge of their home. The interview with the senior partner and his wife was followed with a second interview, over lunch, at the home of Reg and Kathleen Cutts. Reg was the junior of the three partners. Shelagh behaved impeccably. Margaret and I enjoyed the company of Reg and Kathleen Cutts. After lunch, Reg directed us to the home of the second senior partner, Alistair Young and his wife Doreen. This third interview of the day, went particularly well. Alistair had previously worked in the same post as myself at The City General Hospital, Sheffield. We had much in common.

As we drove back to our rented cottage in Swaledale on that cold December day, Margaret and I hoped we would be offered the post. The practice seemed ideal. The appointment would give us a wonderful opportunity to have a settled family life together at the seaside. The three separate interviews had made the day a very long and tiring one. As we arrived back in Swaledale at dusk, Meg commented how much better it would have been if all three partners had interviewed me together, instead of having three separate interviews. Although striking me as somewhat odd, I read nothing further into the way the interviews had been conducted. Three days later, I received a telephone call from Ian Mackinlay. He offered me the post. I was delighted to accept. My acceptance did not further my curiosity into the interview process; a reflection, I suppose of my naivety in always accepting matters at their face value. Ian Mackinlay informed me Reg Cutts, the junior partner, would confirm the details of my appointment, in writing. The letter arrived two days later.

The letter informed me I was to become an Assistant in the Practice, commencing work on the 1st. February 1959. The terms of my appointment, with which I was extremely happy, at the time, are interesting to reflect upon all these years later. My appointment, as an assistant, was with a definite view to partnership after one year. My salary, during the year's assistantship, was £1,300 per annum. The practice would provide me with an unfurnished, semi-detached house, for which the partnership would charge me a rent of £200 per annum. The house would be rate free. Telephone expenses would be paid by the practice. The partnership suggested that my revised salary, of £1,100 per annum, be divided into two elements; £900 per annum as salary and the remaining £200 per annum as car expenses. As a result of this arrangement, Income Tax would not be deducted from the expense fraction. The letter concluded, 'all the Partners wish that you and your wife will be happy in your new work and the surroundings you have chosen.'

After only one week working in the Practice, I realised why my family and I had been subjected to three separate interviews. The three partners, Mackinlay, Young and Cutts hardly spoke to each other. They appeared never to socialise together. I had entered a Practice where great conflicts existed between the three of them. I was however grateful for the job. I would endeavour to make the best of it. At least all three partners individually made Margaret and myself feel welcome. I felt privileged that all three partners spoke freely with me. It was a privilege they did not extend to each other.

In the Spring, Ian Mackinlay kindly took me to Redcar Cricket Club. At the bar, he introduced me to the Club officials. Redcar played in The North Yorkshire and South Durham League, a semi-professional league. Each team, in the league, was allowed, if they so wished, to employ one professional. Redcar chose not to employ a professional. The standard of cricket throughout the league was high. I was keen to play. The partners in the Practice had agreed to my playing cricket on a Saturday, provided I was on call for the Practice every Sunday. I was so keen to play cricket I readily agreed with the arrangement. My cricket credentials were of a high order. As a wicketkeeper, I had five university cricket blues. I had played for the Glamorgan County Second Eleven, Catterick Services and the Royal Army Medical Corps. Entry into the Redcar cricket team, I considered a formality. How wrong I was! Geoff Grabham was the first eleven captain. He explained to me I would 'have to prove myself'. Grabham would initially play me in the third eleven! Such was the way of cricket in Yorkshire.

The summer of 1959 was the most miserable summer I could remember. I worked in an unhappy Practice, where the personal relationship between the three partners was non-existent. The summer was gloriously hot and sunny. The weather was ideal for cricket. Unfortunately, I played little cricket. Most Saturdays I spent on the beach with my family. What cricket I did play was usually in the Redcar third eleven, with an occasional game in the second eleven. As far as the cricket club was concerned, I was in the process of proving my ability. What made matters worse was the fact that the Redcar first team had a miserable season. They lost match after match. The team finished the season close to the bottom of the League. To be fair, the first team did have an excellent wicketkeeper in Colin Rose, a local schoolmaster. The club was happy for Colin to be their first eleven wicketkeeper.

Realising my unhappiness during the summer, Margaret was keen that my unhappiness did not continue into the winter months. In order to accommodate my love of sport, Margaret suggested I buy a season ticket for Middlesbrough Football Club.

> "Get yourself a season ticket for Middlesbrough F.C. Enjoy your Saturdays, through the winter, watching Middlesbrough Football Club. You never know, you might even prefer watching football to playing cricket".

For myself, I knew there was nothing better than playing cricket.

Nevertheless, I decided to follow Margaret's advice. I would purchase a season ticket and become a regular supporter of Middlesbrough Football Club. It was a boiling hot, mid July day, when I presented myself at the general office at Ayresome Park, the home of Middlesbrough Football Club. A friendly, jovial Geordie, who was most helpful, met me across the office counter.

> "The ground is completely open at the present time. The two stands are fully accessible. Very few seats have been taken for next season, so why not go walk around the stands and choose your own seat? I'll give you a plan of the seating. The seats taken, are marked in red. Take your choice of the remainder. I'd suggest the South Stand. You'll get a better view from there; fewer poles in the way. Go have a look. If you're back within half an hour, I'll still be here."

In twenty minutes I'd decided on a seat. Exactly on the halfway line my seat was in the South Stand. I returned to the general office. There, true to his word, was my jovial Geordie friend. I confirmed the booking and paid my cheque.

> "Full name and address please" the Geordie enquired.
>
> "Dr. Neil Phillips, 190, West Dyke Road, Redcar."

His head rose from the counter. His eyes glistened with anticipation.

> "I don't suppose you're a real doctor are you?"

The question was not unusual on Teesside. There were many doctors of chemistry employed at the I.C.I. works of Wilton and Billingham.

> "Yes, I'm a real doctor."

I replied.

> "I work in a General Practice in Redcar. The Green House.
> Near the clock in the town centre.".
>
> "Could you spare a moment? Please come into my office."

he replied.

He lifted the office counter. I followed the Geordie into an inner office.

> "My name is Bob Dennison. I'm the Secretary/Manager here. Have a seat."

GENERAL PRACTICE

I sat in the chair.

"I don't suppose you could get me some salt tablets could you? In my opinion our players need extra salt. They are well into pre-season training now. Working in this extreme heat, they are sweating profusely and feeling very tired. Two players had severe muscle cramps after yesterday's hard training schedule. Our club doctor doesn't believe the players should be given extra salt. He's more interested in his horses. I think he's wrong. What do you think?".

I was thoughtful before replying,

"Well obviously I wouldn't want to get into a conflict with your club doctor. After all, I only came here today to buy a season ticket! However, excessive physical work in severe heat can result in salt depletion, until the body acclimatises to the high temperature. In the short term some extra salt would be beneficial. Though I have to say taking salt tablets, even when they are dissolved in water is not very pleasant"

"How soon could you get some?

"I'm sure I could get a supply by tomorrow."

"Excellent".

The manager was obviously pleased.

"Shall I deliver them here tomorrow?"

I enquired.

"Why not come to the Hutton Road training ground tomorrow morning. We'll be there 'til noon. Come and watch us train. Meet the staff. See the players."

It was an offer I could not refuse.

I delivered the tablets to Bob Dennison the following morning. I met Harold Shepherdson and Mickey Fenton, the two trainers. I also met Jimmy Gordon, the coach in charge of the juniors. I watched the players train; Brian Clough, Alan Peacock, Eddie Holliday, Mick McNeil, Bill Harris, Willie Fernie, Peter Taylor, Derek Stonehouse, Ray Yeoman and many more. Bob Dennison made me very welcome. I enjoyed the experience. So began two very differing friendships. One with Bob Dennison, the other with Harold Shepherdson, the Middlesbrough and England Trainer.

Bob's friendship was restricted to Bob. I rarely met Mrs. Dennison and, when I did, it was always on the doorstep of their house in the Acklam district of Middlesbrough. It was always a case of "Hello" and "Goodbye". Harold, and his wife Peggy, quickly became good friends of Margaret and myself. My friendship with Bob Dennison was mainly confined to Wednesdays. My half-day in the Practice was fortunately every Wednesday; the day when most mid-week football matches were played. Most Wednesdays, I would meet Bob at Ayresome Park. We then travelled together to watch a football match. Bob obviously chose the match. He may have needed to see a particular game, in order to watch a specific player. More frequently, it was to observe a team Middlesbrough would soon be playing. I really enjoyed those trips. I learnt so much from the conversations we had together on those long car journeys. It also made the Middlesbrough home matches more interesting. I frequently saw teams at Ayresome Park I had seen a few weeks previously. Bob Dennison's assessment of those visiting teams, discussed on the car journey home, added greatly to my enjoyment of the home matches. In a season, Bob and I travelled all over the country, frequently returning in the early hours of Thursday morning. Sitting in the car with Bob, I listened to his views on football for hour after hour. I learnt much about the game from him. We discussed the players, the staff, team formations, tactics and the politics of football. Bob was a real gentleman. I enjoyed his company. Wherever we went, he was always keen to introduce me to other managers, coaches and professional footballers. Through him, I gained many acquaintances. My trips with Bob were a real joy.

Harold Shepherdson's friendship was more as a friend. We would dine out together with our wives. Invite each other to our homes. We involved our children in each other's company. Occasionally, Harold would invite me to travel with him to a football evening, when he was giving a talk on his experiences as the Middlesbrough and England trainer. Harold was a good speaker and I enjoyed his talks. As with Bob's friendship, through Harold's friendship, I gained much knowledge about the professional football game. Bob Dennison and Harold Shepherdson became good friends of mine. I felt privileged and grateful that they had so readily involved me in the world of football. Throughout the winter, my Saturday afternoons were spent in the South Stand at Ayresome Park as a season ticket holder. Occasionally, my eyes would drift away from the game to the dugout, where Harold sat, or to the front of the directors' box to watch Bob. They were both across the field from me in the North Stand. I was so pleased Margaret persuaded me to buy a season ticket.

Unfortunately, my happiness in sport was not matched with happiness in General Practice. I discovered, early in my assistantship, that the three partners barely spoke to each other. Ian Mackinlay and his wife Sal, Alistair and Doreen Young kept very much to themselves, having their own close circle of friends. Reg and Kathleen Cutts lived in a fantasy world, centred on world cruises, exotic cars, and much entertaining. There was no socialising between the three partners. It was interesting to see how they kept their social lives apart from each other. Ian Mackinlay was a director of the Redcar Race Company and President of Redcar Rugby Club. His social life, quite naturally, centred on racing and rugby. Reg Cutts was President of the local British Legion Club and a keen swimmer; his social life centred at those two establishments. Alistair Young, I knew only for a short while and thereby hangs a story.

Reg Cutts and his family had gone on an early summer cruise, leaving Ian Mackinlay, Alistair Young and myself, as the assistant, to run the practice. I was not on duty, but, at two o'clock one morning, I received an urgent call from Doreen Young. She informed me Alistair was poorly, with abdominal pain. She asked if I would be kind enough to visit Alistair.

"What about Ian Mackinlay?"
I enquired.
"He's the partner on call."
Doreen was curt with her reply.
"Alistair specifically asked for you."
I was at the Young's house within ten minutes. Alistair had acute appen-

dicitis. In normal circumstances such an illness would be quite straightforward, but not in Alistair's case. It was well known that Alistair had suffered with very bad asthma for most of his life. At the time of his acute appendicitis, he was being treated with ACTH, adreno- corticotrophic hormone. Surgical operations, on patients under treatment with ACTH, were fraught with complications. Alistair's simple appendicitis was therefore quite a serious surgical condition. I admitted Alistair to the local surgical unit. I personally spoke to the consultant detailing to him Alistair's complicated medical condition particularly Alistair's treatment with ACTH. Alistair was operated on the same day. With Reg Cutts on holiday, Ian Mackinlay and I were now left to run the four-man practice.. Reg Cutts was enjoying his cruise. The workload for Ian Mackinlay and myself was incredibly difficult. Three days after his operation, Alistair Young collapsed and died. Reg Cutts returned from his holiday on the day after Alistair's death. In order that Ian and Reg were able to attend the funeral, I remained on duty in the Practice. Two days after Alistair's funeral, Ian and Reg asked to meet with me. It was the first time in five months that any of the partners had officially met with me.

"Originally,"
Ian informed me,

> "you came here as an assistant, with a subsequent view to becoming a partner after twelve months. Obviously, with Alistair's death, we need a partner immediately. Reg and I have discussed the matter. We both would like to offer you a partnership immediately. Your terms, on becoming a partner, would be those we drew up initially."

There is no doubt I was flattered at being offered a partnership after such a short assistantship. Unfortunately, I did not realise the desperate situation Ian and Reg were now in. I did not realise I was in a very strong negotiating position. I should have tried to negotiate better financial terms than in my original agreement. I did not realise my negotiating strength and their weakness. I gladly accepted their offer of partnership, on the terms of my original agreement.

"We will of course need a new assistant, with a view to partnership. We presume you realise the need for such a person. Also, you need to know that at the private meeting Reg and I held we decided to bury our past differences. We both intend to start afresh for the good of the practice. With two new young doctors to be in the Practice shortly, we need a fresh start."

The three of us shook hands, as if the gesture was some symbolic event. Ian left to go to his beloved rugby club.

"It was a tragedy I went on holiday."

Reg began,

"There is no doubt in my mind that if I had been here, Alistair would still be alive. If I had been here, Alistair, when taken ill, would have telephoned me. I would have dealt with the case more successfully than you were able to do, as the assistant."

Needless to say, I was furious at Reg's statement. A row exploded between the two of us. I was so angry. I left in disgust.

Reg and Ian had yet another altercation a week later. On this occasion it was over a house call to a private patient. Each of them believed the patient belonged exclusively to them. It was immediately evident I was to become a partner in a Practice, where two of the doctors would inevitably distance themselves from each other. They would only speak to each other when it was absolutely necessary. I was glad I was taking the family home to South Wales for our summer holiday. I needed a break. It had been a hectic, traumatic first six months in General Practice.

Although I was only on holiday for two weeks, I was astonished on my return to find, in my absence, Ian and Reg had appointed a new assistant with a view to partnership. They did not consider it necessary or desirable to involve me in the selection process.

"After all,"

they said,

"you haven't signed the partnership agreement yet, so technically you are not a partner."

The new assistant was David Whitehouse, a Leeds graduate. David was older than me. Life in General Practice continued to be difficult.

At the time of David Whitehouse's arrival in the Practice, Margaret was pregnant with our second child. Ann was born on Boxing Day, one month before I completed my first year at Redcar. In years to come, I would reflect on why I did not leave such a Practice torn apart by petty squabbles. In essence, I did not leave for several reasons. Jobs in General Practices were difficult to obtain at that time. With two children, I had responsibilities to provide for the family, and then, as there always was, there was my involvement in football. That involvement increased week by week. It gave me great pleasure. The local cricket scene also beckoned. On balance, I decided to stay. It was such a shame that the bread and butter of my existence, General Practice, provided such an unhappy environment. I should have been able to fully enjoy both medicine and sport. Alas, in Redcar, it appeared enjoying medicine was extremely difficult.

Early in the football season, I returned home late on a Wednesday night, or more correctly early Thursday morning. Bob Dennison and I had been to Bury watching a game. Our house was in darkness. Margaret was in bed, but wide-awake, she had a message for me.

> "Ian Mackinlay, the senior partner, phoned about ten. Thought you ought to know Colin Rose, the Redcar wicketkeeper, sustained a very nasty eye injury last evening. Apparently he was playing in a charity cricket match at Loftus. Somehow, he was struck in the eye with the cricket ball. Ian thinks he's got a detached retina and thought you ought to know. How was the match at Bury?"

> "The match was great. Bury aren't a very good side. Middlesbrough should beat them easily in two weeks time. Bob was great company. I enjoyed it."

In no time, Margaret and I were fast asleep.

Colin Rose would play no more cricket. Next summer, I would play for Redcar at cricket. I would be the first team wicketkeeper, but that was a whole winter away. I would continue to enjoy a winter of football with Bob

Dennison, and Harold Shepherdson. Strangely, doubts began creeping into my mind. From early childhood, cricket had totally enveloped my life. It was the be all and end all of my existence. Even in winter time cricket was uppermost in my mind. Once, when asked what her younger son did in the winter time, my mother replied

"He oils his cricket bats".

Summer and winter, I lived for cricket. Now, for the first time ever, I could see a conflict developing between playing cricket and my involvement with football. I liked the idea of the conflict. Football, I thought, might even take over. A new life might begin. Cricket may not be that important to me. Margaret was right. I might, I just might, prefer watching football to playing cricket.

The last Sunday in February 1961 would certainly change my attitude to the two games. I received an evening telephone call from Harold Shepherdson. Unknown to me at that time, it was a telephone call that would change my whole life. The England Under Twenty-three soccer team was staying at Saltburn by the Sea, prior to playing Scotland at Ayresome Park, Middlesbrough on March 1st. One of the England players, who was doing his National Service, had arrived at the team's hotel with a septic wound on his leg. Harold contacted the Middlesbrough club doctor, requesting him to visit the player. Imagine Harold's astonishment, when the doctor informed Harold the England football players were not his responsibility. In any event, the twelve miles from Middlesbrough to Saltburn were too far for the doctor to visit. The Middlesbrough club doctor advised Harold to contact a more local doctor. Harold wondered if I would be prepared to visit. I was at the hotel in fifteen minutes. As I drove to the hotel in Saltburn, Blacow's words rang in my ear.

"If the nursing staff request your presence, always visit."

At the hotel, Harold took me to the player's room. I was introduced to Johnny, 'Budgie', Byrne of West Ham. When playing the previous week in an Army game, he had sustained a grass burn on the outside of his leg. The grass burn was now septic. It was oozing pus. Having satisfied myself 'Budgie' had no allergies, I took a swab from the pus and gave him a

Penicillin injection. I dressed the wound with a tulle gras dressing.

"I'll come and see you in the morning before breakfast."
I told 'Budgie'.
Before leaving the hotel, Harold introduced me to Walter Winterbottom, the England Manager. Walter enquired if 'Budgie' Byrne would be fit to play on Wednesday. I replied,

"I would hope so. I'll need to assess the situation on a daily basis. I will visit the player early tomorrow morning, before my morning surgery. I will then report on his progress. I am optimistic. I believe he will be fit to play on Wednesday. Much depends of course on how he responds to the treatment."

"Budgie" Byrne progressed well over the next two days. The Penicillin together with the twice-daily dressings with sofra-tulle cleared the local sepsis. I informed the player and Walter Winterbottom in my opinion the player was fit to play. 'Budgie' and Walter were delighted.

"I wonder if you and your wife, would like to be my guests at the match."
Walter Winterbottom enquired of me.

"Depends if we can get a baby sitter. Could I telephone you later today?"

"Fine. Telephone me before four o'clock."
I telephoned Walter at three. Margaret and I would be delighted to attend the match as his guests. Walter informed me to pick up the two tickets at the 'Directors' Entrance.'

"I would also be pleased if you and your wife would join me for a meal at The Alexandra Hotel after the match."
Walter added.
With our baby sitter's permission, we were able to accept the invitation.

England lost to Scotland, by one goal to nil. Denis Law scored a penalty for Scotland. "Budgie" Byrne played well. He showed no indication of his leg injury. After the game, Margaret and I dined with Walter Winterbottom and Len Shipman, the chairman of Leicester City and a member of The Football Association's Senior International Committee. Walter and I spent the whole time discussing various aspects of Sports' Medicine.

"Why does the England team not have a doctor travelling with them?"

I asked.

"Why not, indeed."

was Walter's reply.

Walter informed me of the medical courses The Football Association ran each year at Lilleshall, for prospective football trainers. The tutors on the course were two fully qualified physiotherapists, Bertie Mee, from the Arsenal, and Paddy Armour, the Wakefield Trinity physiotherapist, who worked at Pinderfields Hospital in Yorkshire. A Dr. Summerville, from London, who was the medical advisor to The Football Association, examined the students at the end of their course. Walter told me, Dr. Somerville found his honorary appointment to The Football Association difficult to fulfil owing to his hospital commitments. He apparently ran a Rehabilitation Unit in London.

"I wondered if you would like to attend one of the medical courses at Lilleshall? You could give me an assessment of the course. The course lasts two weeks. It would be a great help to me if you could carry out a detailed assessment of the course."

"It would mean taking two weeks holiday from my Practice. I would have to arrange the holiday with my partners. I would need to seek their agreement, but yes, I would help, if it's possible."

Walter agreed to send me the details.

"One condition." I said.

"If I attend, I would want to attend as plain Neil Phillips. I would not want anyone to know I was a doctor. Wouldn't be fair to them."

"I agree"

said Walter.

With great anticipation, I waited for the information to arrive. In three days, Walter and I had developed a good relationship. He was obviously impressed with my opinions, and I liked him as a man. He was someone I could trust. I did not realise then how much more he would help to further my career in football.

Although Middlesbrough Football Club languished in the Second Division, they had many good players. Players of international quality. There were three players knocking on the door of the England team–Brian Clough, Alan Peacock and Eddie Holliday. In defence, Middlesbrough had three left fullbacks–Mick McNeil, Gordon Jones and Cyril Knowles–fighting for places at international level. It was quite natural therefore that, at every available opportunity, the England manager would cast his eye over the performance of these players. Walter Winterbottom was a frequent visitor watching Middlesbrough play. In the boardroom at every game, when he met the Middlesbrough directors, Walter would enquire how that young Dr. Phillips from Redcar was doing. Initially the Middlesbrough directors had no knowledge of me, but on his frequent visits, Walter kept reminding them.

"If you have any sense,"
Walter would tell them
"I would suggest you involve Dr. Phillips in your Club in
some capacity. He would be a great asset to you."
Walter utilised every opportunity to further my involvement with the Middlesbrough directors and the football club. I was totally unaware of his support for me.

I attended the medical course at Lilleshall as plain Neil Phillips, no one knew I was a doctor. I was impressed with both Bertie Mee and Paddy Armour, the two chartered physiotherapists who led the medical course. The content of the course was adequate. The two tutors showed great enthusiasm towards the students. The course took three years to complete. An initial introductory year, was followed by an intermediate year. The third and final year led to the certificate of The Football Association in the Treatment of Injuries. I revelled in the experience of Lilleshall. I rubbed shoulders, for two weeks, with the true stalwarts of the game. Not only were there professional footballers attending the medical course, but also others attending the main football coaching course. These prospective coaches were endeavouring to obtain their Football Association coaching certificate. Their instructors were some of the top coaches in the game. It was at Lilleshall I met Ron Greenwood, Bill Shankly, Malcolm Allison, Walter Winterbottom, George Smith, Harry Potts, Billy Wright, Nat Lofthouse and Jimmy Adamson, to mention but a few. I mixed with them all socially in the evenings. I learnt from them by just listening to their conversations. They discussed all aspects of the game; training methods, systems of play and individual players. Most of all I enjoyed their banter.

I enjoyed my fortnight at Lilleshall. I wrote my report for Walter. I approved of the course, but expressed my concern that the students, when they completed the course, would only have a certificate from The Football Association in the Treatment of Injuries. In the world outside of football they would be classed as unqualified medical personnel. I felt it was necessary to find a way to encourage more fully qualified Chartered Physiotherapists to be employed in the professional game, as Bertie Mee was at the Arsenal. Having sent my report to Walter, I assumed that was the end of my involvement.

During the summer, I played regularly for Redcar Cricket Club as the first team's wicketkeeper. Colin Rose had retired. He decided not to risk another blow on his already damaged eye. Although I played regularly for the team, like all the other players, I did not enjoy my cricket. Geoff Grabham, who had been a great servant to the club and a good cricketer, was the club captain. Much older than the rest of the players, he belonged to a previous generation As the captain, he became very unpopular with his fellow players. His man management left much to be desired and there was no team spirit. Geoff ignored any advice the senior players gave. Towards the end of the season, when playing at home, matters came to a head. Geoff refused to inform the players the batting order. He told us, he would decide who batted next when a wicket fell! The scene in the dressing room was bizarre. Every player stood poised, waiting for an instruction from the captain. Amazingly, the next batsman could have been anyone. Redcar again finished near the bottom of the league, which was a shame, as I considered the team had many talented players. As the summer

DOCTOR TO THE WORLD CHAMPIONS

Group Photograph At Lilleshall
"I'm one of the Professionals- but only for two weeks"

ended, I was glad to return to my football routine. On a Saturday afternoon, I would be in my seat in the South Stand. My Wednesdays were spent travelling the country watching football matches with Bob Dennison. The family friendship with Harold and Peggy Shepherdson developed further. I really enjoyed my involvement in football with Bob and Harold. Nineteen sixty two was a World Cup year. England, with Walter Winterbottom as Manager and Harold Shepherdson as Trainer, would be departing to compete in Chile. During the cricket season and immediately prior to the World Cup commencing in Chile I received a postcard from Chile. I assumed it was from Harold. In fact it was from Walter Winterbottom. Walter had still found time to write to me even though he was extremely busy with the England Team's preparation. I was impressed.

At the end of the cricket season, Geoff Grabham indicated he would play no more cricket. Prior to the Annual Meeting of the Cricket Club, a small group of players approached me to ask if I would stand as their Captain. My response was immediate.

"I will only accept, if that is what all the players wish."

It was the wish of all the players. I was appointed Captain of Redcar Cricket Club.

By the summer of nineteen sixty-three, the Redcar cricket team had been transformed. In the two years I had been captain, the players had developed into a side challenging for the championship of the North Yorkshire and South Durham League. Gone were the days when the team languished near the bottom of the league. It was early August. The cricket team, my team, was lying in fourth position of the league. A few wins in August and the team would be in a good position to win the league. The team had been strengthened, at the beginning of the season, by two excellent all-rounders. Jack May, an opening batsman and medium-paced bowler, had moved to Redcar from Normanby Hall. The star acquisition, however, had been Tony Wade, a South African. Tony, the son of Herbert Wade, the former South African test captain, was an exceptional cricketer. A fast opening bowler, a good middle order batsman, and a brilliant fielder, made Tony an asset to any side. At Redcar, his arrival had made the team championship contenders.

If Redcar were to make their challenge for the championship, it was essential for the team to win away to Middlesbrough in early August. Although I captained Redcar, it was the Middlesbrough cricket team I admired most. Their team was almost invincible. They had been the most successful team in North Yorkshire for many years. They had many league titles to show for their efforts. It is now many years since I played against them, but those years have not dimmed the names of their team. Although I only ever played against them, their names are still embedded in my mind. When I captained Redcar, I spent many an hour checking on their individual strengths and weaknesses. The Middlesbrough cricket team was undoubtedly the best league side I ever played against. Harry Bell, an ex-

Middlesbrough footballer, and David Ellis, their captain, opened the batting. They were a formidable pair. They also were the regular opening batsmen for the Durham County side. Pat Briggs, a Cambridge rugby blue and Cheshire county cricketer, was at number three. Tony Allison, the Redcar grammar school's sports master batted at number four. Numbers five, six and seven were the Old brothers. Alan, who went on to be the England's outside half at rugby ; Chris, who played for Yorkshire and England at cricket and Malcolm, in my humble opinion, the best cricketer of the three brothers. Eddie Fuller, the club's professional and a former South African test bowler, was at eight. Brian Bainbridge, a superb off spin bowler, who played for the Yorkshire second eleven, was at nine. The wicket keeper, Bernard Gent, batted at ten. Michael Tate, the Durham County leg spin bowler batted at eleven. Middlesbrough was indeed a formidable team. If Redcar was to challenge for the title, a win at Middlesbrough was essential. Redcar needed to win to give ourselves the required impetus for a championship challenge.

Acklam Park, Middlesbrough, was being prepared as a Yorkshire County ground. In August, the ground was a picture. Middlesbrough were so professional in their approach to each game. They always prepared two wickets on their cricket square. This gave their captain a choice of two types of wicket on which to play any game. One wicket would be heavily watered during the week, and the other wicket left quite dry. A hard fast surface would favour Fuller, and the young Chris Old. The watered wicket would assist Bainbridge and Tate, the two spinners. On the day of our match, both pitches were prepared but, as Tate, the leg spinner, was playing, David Ellis elected to play on the watered wicket. As Redcar's captain, I was happy with their choice. I had every confidence in our own bowlers. Wade would open with Neil Brand, followed by Jack May. I also had two excellent spinners, Colin Bainbridge and Peter Davidson. I won the toss and decided to ask Middlesbrough to bat. My confidence in our bowlers was immeasurable. I felt Middlesbrough might regret choosing the wetter of the two wickets.

Over forty years have passed since that game was played. The details of the individual batting and bowling performances have long since faded from my memory. I recall however our bowlers did a fantastic job. We dismissed the Middlesbrough team for a relatively low score. Redcar's batsmen batted resolutely. Redcar won the match with several wickets to spare. Redcar had beaten Middlesbrough at Middlesbrough. It was unbelievable! The championship race was now wide open and Redcar would be involved in it. As their captain, I felt an inner sense of pride. The team had achieved much. It had been a privilege for me to lead them. The team were no longer 'also rans'. Redcar's team had become a well-balanced, competent side. We were a match for any of the other league teams. I was full of inner contentment at our victory.

David Ellis, the Middlesbrough captain, and I were good friends. As opposing captains, we accepted each other as fierce, but fair competitors. Win or lose, David and I would always be friends. He was an excellent cricketer, but more importantly he was a nice man. It was no surprise therefore when, after the game, David and I found ourselves in each other's company. Our players sat at innumerable tables in the club bar. David and I sat on two stools at the bar. He drank his beer. I supped my usual ginger beer and lime. We discussed cricket. We both loved cricket and enjoyed each other's company. Reg Hunt was one of the jewels at Middlesbrough Cricket Club. A respected league umpire, Reg had, for many years, coached the players at Middlesbrough. Many of the present Middlesbrough team owed their cricketing prowess to Reg. Like all good cricket coaches, he was a quiet, unassuming man, but one whose knowledge of the game was infinite. Reg joined David and myself at the bar.

"Neil, Mr. Thomas would like a word with you."
Reg said.
"Who's Mr. Thomas?"
I asked.
David Ellis smiled and said,
"I suppose some people would say Mr. Thomas is Middlesbrough Cricket Club. He's our Chairman. He's also Chairman of Middlesbrough Football Club. Come on, I'll take you over and introduce you."

David led me to a corner table, at the far end of the room. Sitting at the table was a fat Dickensian figure clutching a pint of, what appeared to be, a 'Black and Tan' in both hands. Bald and bespectacled, his several double chins and obvious excess weight, gave proof of a sedentary life style, associated with an over indulgence in his favourite 'Black and Tan' beverage.

"Eric, I wonder if I may introduce you to the Redcar captain, Dr, Phillips. Neil, this is Eric Thomas, our chairman ; Eric, this is Neil."

David, having completed the introductions, returned to the bar. Eric Thomas did not rise from his chair. He merely gestured to the three men seated with him.

"I wonder if Dr. Phillips and I may be left alone for a few minutes."

The three men departed. Mr. Thomas gesticulated to a chair.

"Sit yourself down,"

I sat.

Mr. Thomas' eyes scanned the room, ensuring no one was in earshot.

"How would you like to become a Director of Middlesbrough Football Club?"

These were the first words Eric Thomas spoke to me. There was no introduction, no small talk, he came straight to his point. While I thought of a suitable response,

Mr. Thomas continued,

"Over the past two years, I've watched you transform Redcar Cricket Club. That was a good win for you today, and I mean you. You have built up a really good side. Your personal leadership has been outstanding. I want you to do the same for Middlesbrough Football Club. What do you say? Would you consider becoming a Director of the Football Club? Think about it. If you can turn Redcar Cricket Club around, you can do the same for the Football Club."

I was astonished.

"Problem is, I don't play football." I replied.

It was now his turn to smile.

"I know you don't play football, but you could help us succeed."

"I'm flattered of course, but football directors need to be wealthy and I'm not. I've no money. I'm young, married with two children, just moved into a new house, have a mortgage. I'm just establishing myself."

Eric Thomas interrupted,

"We don't need your money-we need your brains."

I thanked him for his invitation and said

"I'll think about it. My initial reaction is to accept, but I need to think about it."

"I shall contact you later in the year. Please keep this conversation confidential. I will telephone you in a few months' time. I do hope you will be able to join us at the Football Club. I'll be in touch."

It was obvious our conversation was at an end. I returned to the company of David Ellis at the bar.

Redcar did not win the North Yorkshire and South Durham League. The team finished fourth. In many quarters, fourth position would have been hailed as a great success. Only a few years previously, the Club had finished next to bottom Considerable improvements had been made. The players now enjoyed their cricket. Success, however, brings its own problems. Relative success increases expectations. Players and Club officials now expected the team to win every game. Winning games became the normal expectation. Losing brought the inevitable inquisitions and criticisms. On taking up the captaincy, it had been my over-riding philosophy that all the players should, above all else, enjoy their cricket. My belief was if the players enjoyed what they were doing, then their performances would be so much better. I had personally set out to make the team a happy one. I wanted to lead a team that enjoyed its cricket. Happiness and enjoyment would, I believed, increase the level of performance of each player. Success would follow. It proved to be so.

The end of the cricket season saw my return on Saturdays to my seat in the South Stand at Ayresome Park. From there, I looked directly across to the Directors' Box in the North stand. Immediately prior to each game, I watched, as each Director took his seat in the front row. There were eight directors. Eric Thomas was the only director I had met. Unaware of Walter Winterbottom's continued support for my involvement in the Club, I often reflected on my conversation with Eric Thomas. Why had he contacted me and invited me to become a Director? I had no local connections with the Club. I was from South Wales, young and with no financial resources. I could not understand why he should ask me. If he was genuine, in wanting me on the Board, why had he not invited me to meet with the other Directors? As the football season progressed through to the winter months, I wondered if our conversation at the cricket club had really taken place. Eric Thomas may have changed his mind. After all, Redcar had finished fourth in the league. Perhaps he now believed I hadn't done such a good job, as the team's captain. It certainly seemed very odd to me that, following our conversation in the summer, no contact whatsoever had been made between us. I was extremely unhappy with Eric Thomas' treatment of me.

Middlesbrough Football Club started the season badly. Brian Clough, the top goal scorer for many seasons, had been transferred to Sunderland. Clough had averaged nearly forty goals a season for Middlesbrough and now the Club had let him depart. He was sorely missed. You couldn't afford to be without a man who regularly scored forty goals every season My Wednesdays continued to be spent travelling with Bob Dennison. Bob had taught me a considerable amount about the professional game. We enjoyed each other's company. Over several years, we had spent endless hours, talking about all aspects of the game. We discussed matches we had seen together, the various systems team's played and individual players. The political happenings, within Middlesbrough Football Club, Bob chose never to discuss with me. Bob was a very loyal person. The internal business of the Club, its directors, staff and players he never discussed with me. I respected him for holding that position, but I wondered why he had ever let Brian Clough leave. The Club's internal business remained excluded from our conversations. I, for my part, reciprocated by refraining from asking any questions relating to the Club's business. I did know however the poor performance of the team was causing Bob considerable concern. He and I both knew his job as Manager was under threat. With Bob's reticence to discuss Club business, it came as a big surprise, when, returning from a match in Lancashire, Bob threw out a question relating to the business of the Club. We were returning from a game late at night when, following one of those long pregnant pauses that occur on car journeys, Bob delivered his question.

"Do you know who the next Director of Middlesbrough Football Club will be?"
he asked.
"I haven't a clue,"
I said.
There was a long pause before Bob replied,
"You. You are to be the next director of the Football Club."
I was stunned. Apart from my wife, I had told no one of my conversation with Eric Thomas. I could not believe Eric Thomas, as the Chairman of the Club, had discussed our private, confidential conversation with his Manager. There was again another prolonged silence.
"Does that surprise you?"
Bob asked.
"It certainly does."
"Mark my words, Neil, you are to be the next Director of Middlesbrough Football Club."
Sadly, from my own personal point of view, Bob Dennison was sacked the very next week. Bob Dennison's dismissal meant I had lost a good friend. Raich Carter was very quickly appointed the next Manager of Middlesbrough Football Club. The appointment had not been mentioned to the new prospective Director. It appeared my brains were not required for such an important appointment.

Towards the end of October 1962, on the 29th. to be precise, my father was ecstatic. Not just genuinely pleased, but really ecstatic. Dad and Mam, in their married life, had produced two boys; my elder brother Dayton and myself. My brother was single. I had married aged twenty-five. Our first two children were daughters, Shelagh and Ann. Our third child, Michael, was a son born on the

29th October 1962. The birth of our son enabled the 'Phillips name' to be carried forward for a further generation. It was a fact that did not concern Meg and myself, but, for my father, it was of extreme importance. While he was delighted at the birth of our two daughters, my Dad was ecstatic at the birth of Michael. Margaret and I were genuinely pleased. Our family was complete. Michael's arrival however had a very special significance for my Dad. He was the eldest of the eight children. His five brothers had married, but none had produced a son. Howie, his youngest brother was killed at sea in 1941 when his ship, H.M.S. Sikh, was sunk off Tobruk. Howie's marriage to Myrtle was childless. Billy, the miner, considered by some to be the black sheep of the family, spent more time in the clubs and pubs than was good for him. His only child was his daughter, Barbara. Cliff was Chippenham's Borough Surveyor. His marriage to Mary was childless. Dodda, my father's other brother, married so late in life that having a child was out of the question. My brother Dayton and I, were the only 'Phillips' boys of our generation. The arrival of Michael ensured that the 'Phillips name' would be carried forward for another generation. Such an event had a great meaning and significance for my father. It was of no significance to either Margaret or me. My father was delighted at the births of Shelagh and Ann; he was ecstatic at the birth of Michael.

"The Phillips name is safe for another generation."
he commented. Michael was indeed special to my Dad.

Michael's first Christmas was my father's last. It was a wonderful time. The memories of that Christmas remain forever. Both my parents decided to travel from South Wales to Redcar. They would spend Christmas with their three grandchildren. The Christmas of nineteen sixty-two, was the only one we would all spend together. It was my Dad's last Christmas. He was not ill. In fact he was in good health enjoying his retirement. Mam and Dad, but Dad especially, enjoyed every moment of their festive holiday. Christmas is for families, but especially for children. Michael was just two months old. He was oblivious to the pleasures Christmas brought. Shelagh and Ann were old enough and yet young enough to believe in the wonder of Father Christmas. My mother and father saw to it that Father Christmas brought all our three children lovely presents. It was a Christmas to enjoy.

Over the Christmas period, I discussed, with my father, the conversation that had taken place between Eric Thomas and myself. Like Mags and myself, he did not understand the silence.

"Perhaps the New Year will be different"
he said.
The New Year was different. Unfortunately he would not be alive to witness it all.

It was a Thursday afternoon in mid February, some six months since I had played cricket at Middlesbrough. I had just commenced my evening surgery in the Practice when the phone rang in my consulting room.

"It's a Mr. Eric Thomas for you,"
the senior receptionist informed me. She put the call through.

"Good evening, Dr. Phillips speaking."
"Hello Neil, it's Eric Thomas. How are you?"
"I'm fine, just fine."
"Neil, you will recall the conversation we had at Acklam Park last August. I need to check that you're still interested in becoming a Director of the Football Club."

My mind raced. The August conversation, between Eric Thomas and myself, had after all taken place. My doubts were completely unfounded. I had not dreamed it all, but why the weeks of total silence? I wondered, but did not enquire.

"Yes, I remember our conversation well, and yes I am interested."
"Good, I'm very pleased. Where will you be this evening?"
"I shall be at home. I will be at home all evening. I come on duty at 10.30p.m. for the Practice. I'm on call for emergencies through the night, but I shall be at home all evening."
"May I please have your home number?"
I gave Eric my home telephone number.
"Thank you. Tonight will be the night, when you become a Director of Middlesbrough Football Club. We have a Board meeting this evening. I'll give you a ring at home later this evening."

With those words, Eric's conversation ended. Before replacing the telephone, I repeated my home telephone number, thus ensuring Eric had the correct figures. He repeated the number to me. There could be no mistake. Eric had my home number. I continued with my evening surgery, though my mind found it difficult to concentrate.

I finished my evening surgery at a quarter to seven. I arrived home shortly after seven. Immediately I was involved in the normal family activities. Michael was four months old. He was in the middle of a breast-feeding session. Shelagh and Ann had completed their bath and were in their pyjamas, waiting for me to arrive. When at home, I always read their bedtime story. The two girls were demanding their bedtime story. It was not appropriate to talk of telephone calls and Middlesbrough Football Club. Shelagh and Ann shared a bedroom sleeping in single beds. The sharing of a bedroom had a distinct advantage for me. Shelagh and Ann heard the same bedtime stories. The one reading satisfied both daughters. It was a time I really enjoyed. On weekdays, it was the only time we shared together. They were precious moments for my daughters and myself. Our story session always ended with excerpts from 'Now we are Six'. Our last story was always 'Have you been a good girl?' Shelagh and Ann agreed it was their favourite. While reading their stories, my mind wandered back to my earlier conversation with Eric Thomas. My ear was tuned for the ring of the home telephone, but the telephone did not ring. The girls were tired. They soon were fast asleep. I tucked them in their beds, gave them a goodnight kiss and left them to their slumbers. I think they were asleep before I closed their bedroom door. Downstairs Michael's breast-feed was over. Michael too was fast asleep. The three Phillips children were asleep. Peace reigned. Margaret and I worked well as a team. We were a happy family.

Over supper, I recounted to Margaret the telephone conversation I had earlier in the evening with Eric Thomas. The questions flew backwards and forwards between us.

"It is a wonderful opportunity for you."
she said, but there were so many unanswered questions we needed answers to.

"Why the total silence and lack of contact by Eric Thomas,

from August to February?

Why had Eric Thomas not invited us both to a match at Ayresome Park?

Why had I not been invited to meet the other directors?

How many shares would I need to buy and how much would they cost? Would we be able to afford them?

The questions just rolled off both our tongues.

"Eric Thomas did say, didn't he that they didn't need your-money, but needed your brains?"

"Yes, he did say that."

"I hope he's right–your brains will cost us nothing!."

Margaret said, and repeated the sentence again, doubtless to seek further reassurance.

After supper, we sat, like two little kids, by the telephone. We waited for the phone to ring. The telephone did not ring. We checked the telephone line. Was our line out of order? At ten- thirty, I came on call for the Practice, but no calls came. We waited by that phone until one o'clock in the morning. The phone did not ring. Eric Thomas did not telephone. Even worse, he did not ring to say why he hadn't. We both eventually went to bed in the early hours of the morning.

The following morning was another day. I was working as a General Practitioner in Redcar. Margaret would be devoted to bringing up our three children at home. Eric Thomas would not contact me. He was becoming renowned for his silence. I continued to watch Middlesbrough Football Club from my seat in the South Stand. Margaret and I were left wondering why he had not telephoned. We both wondered why Eric Thomas had said 'Tonight's the night', when it was not the night. Why had Eric Thomas not rung to apologise for not ringing? His silence was quite distressing. Silence or no silence, I still considered myself a potential new Director of Middlesbrough Football Club. Independent of each other, the Chairman and Bob Dennison had told me so. It was very odd however that, knowing it was possible I would be joining a Board, the directors of which were making major decisions, which would affect the Club for several years, and yet there had been no consultation with me. Bob Dennison, my friend and the Manager, had been sacked. Raich Carter had been appointed the new Manager. I inevitably thought

> "Why do these directors need my brains, when they have made such monumentous decisions without me?

It was a very strange way to run a business!

Under the new Manager, Raich Carter, the team improved. At the end of the season, they finished just four points short of a promotion place to the First Division. Eric Thomas' silence continued. My Dad had retired from teaching some eighteen months previously. He was enjoying his retirement. Dad suggested, during one of our telephone conversations, he and my mother would like to treat my family to a summer holiday. Mam and Dad would pay, he informed me.

> "On the holiday, your mother and I could baby sit for you both in the evenings. That way, you and Margaret would have a good holiday."

"Sounds like a good idea."

> "I'll have a word with your mother. I'll give it some thought and suggest the details when next we speak."

I missed my regular Wednesday trips with Bob Dennison. On occasions, I accompanied Harold Shepherdson, when he was speaking to a sports organisation. Harold had invited me to accompany him as he was visiting the York Referee's Association. After an enjoyable evening in Harold's company, I arrived home quite late at night. Margaret was waiting for me. As I came in through the back door she said, through her tears,

> "I have some terrible news. Your father has died. The Tredegar police, telephoned at about seven o'clock, saying Dad was dead. They said he had committed suicide. Dr. Bryant, your father's General Practitioner, rang later to say he had visited your home. He said your father had died as a result of an accident. Dr. Bryant was quite definite. Dad had not committed suicide. I'm so sorry."

Margaret cried. I cried with her.

> "Dr. Bryant insists you telephone him, whatever time you

come in. He wants to explain everything to you. I've written his number down. It's by the side of the phone."

"Good evening. Is that Dr. Bryant?" I enquired.

"It's Neil Phillips. I'm ringing about my Dad."

I sat in the chair and listened; there was little for me to say. With tears rolling down my face, it would have been difficult for me to speak. I was grateful for Dr. Bryant's full explanation of the accident.

Dr. Bryant gave me the full story.

"Your mother left home early this morning. She went on a chapel outing to Barry. Neighbours saw your father working in the garden during the morning. He was his usual self, speaking to the neighbours over the garden wall. Your mother had prepared a rice pudding for him to cook, as part of his lunch. At some time during the morning, I believe, he went into the house to check how the rice pudding was cooking. On opening the oven he discovered the gas had run out. His pudding was only half cooked. You know the gas supply to the house works with a shilling in the slot gas meter. The meter is situated under the stairs. Apparently your mother and father kept a tin of shillings in the dining room sideboard, to be used when the gas ran out. Your father opened the sideboard, found the tin, extracted some shillings and left the tin on top of the sideboard. He then went under the stairs and placed several shillings into the gas meter replenishing the supply. Your mother says he always placed three shillings in the meter when carrying out this task. Having filled the gas meter with shillings, your father returned to the kitchen to re-light the gas in the oven. He picked up the gas lighter on his way and placed it in his right hand. Unfortunately, as he entered the kitchen, he tripped on a loose carpet mat, falling head first towards the open door of the gas cooker. As he fell forwards, he hit his forehead on the corner of the open gas cooker door. His glasses were smashed in the fall. He had a laceration on his right forehead where he hit the oven door. The blow was sufficient to knock him unconscious and he lay in front of the open gas cooker. The three shillings' worth of gas killed him. He died with the gas lighter in his right hand. When your mother returned from her trip, she found your father dead in front of the gas oven. There was a strong smell of gas throughout the house. The police were called. Unfortunately, the gas lighter lay in your father's right hand and this lay under his body. The policeman did not move the body until I arrived. The policeman missed the gas lighter held in your father's hand. The policeman assumed the worst and that is how you received a message to say your father had committed suicide. I was called and on my way I knew your father would never commit suicide. I've known him most of my life. I moved your father's body and found the gas lighter in his right hand. I said to the police, 'You don't commit suicide with a gas lighter in your hand.' I then found the tin of shillings on top of the sideboard. Your mother confirmed that when she left home this morning, the tin was in the sideboard. The story, as I've told you, is the one I honestly believed happened. It's such a tragedy. I've given your mother a strong sedative for the night, so I suggest you call her first thing in the morning. When you eventually come home, please come and see me. If there's any further news, I'll give it to you then."

I thanked Dr. Bryant for his kindness and thoroughness. I confirmed I would visit him when I arrived home. It was close to midnight when I phoned Dr. Mackinlay, my senior partner, to inform him of my father's death.

"I shall travel home to Tredegar through the night. I need to be with my mother when she wakes in the morning. I shall return immediately after the funeral.

"Of course. Take care driving through the night. I feel so sorry for you."

GENERAL PRACTICE

If any funeral could be beautiful, my father's was most beautiful. Generations of pupils, whom he had taught over thirty-seven years at Georgetown School, turned out to pay their respects. Members of The Loyal Order of Moose, of which he was a founder member, came from all over the country. His family and friends turned out in great numbers. They were all grateful to my Dad in their own way and they would miss him. I was more grateful than them all. I would miss him the most.

I returned to Redcar and the Practice, after five traumatic days at home, knowing that the personal relationships between the partners were deteriorating month by month. Nevertheless, I was astonished, on my return to work, when I was told, that my five days absence at my father's funeral would have to count towards my annual leave. I pointed out that if one of the four partners had taken all of their annual leave in any year, prior to their father dying, they would not be allowed any time off to attend their own father's funeral. The stupid suggestion was withdrawn immediately! The incident merely highlighted the bad relationships that existed in the Practice. I was a partner in a very unhappy Practice.

"My Dad"

6

I Become A Football Club Director……

Eric Thomas, the Middlesbrough Chairman, telephoned me four weeks after my father's death. His telephone call came, like his previous telephone call, in the middle of a busy Thursday evening surgery.

"Neil, how are you?"

"I'm fine Mr. Thomas. Just fine."

I was astonished. There was no apology. Eric Thomas gave no reason why he had not telephoned me that evening in February, three months previously. He gave no explanation for the total silence that had taken place between us. There was no explanation and no apology.

"Neil, are you still interested in becoming a Director of Middlesbrough Football Club?"

"Yes of course. I haven't changed my mind."

"Then I'd like you to be at Ayresome Park at six-thirty this evening. Come to the main office. The Directors will be holding their Board meeting there. I would like you to join us. The Directors will co-opt you this evening. When you arrive, come straight into the main office. We will be expecting you. Are you able to be at the ground for six-thirty?"

"Yes. I'll be there."

"See you at six-thirty then."

With those words, the conversation was concluded. My instinct was to immediately telephone my Dad with the news. Alas he was no longer there. He had missed my appointment by four weeks. I telephoned Margaret. I explained why I wouldn't be home for supper. I apologised for not being able to read the girls' bedtime story. I continued with my surgery consultations.

After work, as I drove to Middlesbrough, the rain poured down. I arrived at Ayresome Park in the midst of a torrential downpour. I had no raincoat and no umbrella. I parked my car in Ayresome Street and ran to the main office. George Camsell, the former Middlesbrough centre-forward and now the club's Assistant Secretary, stood at the entrance. I spoke to him.

> "Good evening. I'm Dr. Phillips. I've come to see Mr. Thomas in the main office at six-thirty."

> "Well you can't go in there. There's a Board meeting in progress."

> "Yes, I know. Mr. Thomas is expecting me."

> "Well, my instructions are to ensure that no one goes into that office until the meeting is over. As far as I'm concerned, you can't go in. I'm not going to disturb them."

> "But they are expecting me."

I pleaded.

> "No. My instructions are that no one is to enter that room until the meeting is finished. It would be more than my job is worth to let you in. You'll just have to wait."

I waited in the narrow corridor. George Camsell stood firmly in front of me, barring the way to the main office. We stayed facing each other. No further words were spoken. Eventually the boardroom door opened. The portly figure of Eric Thomas, the Chairman, emerged into the narrow corridor.

> "Neil! Why on earth are you waiting out there in the rain? I told you to come straight into the boardroom when you arrived."

> "I'm afraid Mr. Camsell would not let me enter."

"You idiot George! You should have let Dr, Phillips come straight into the boardroom."

George did not reply.

I followed Mr. Thomas into the boardroom; my wet shoes squelching on the carpet as I did so. The Chairman gesticulated to an empty chair at the bottom of the table, while he walked to his seat at the head of the table. The room was full of smoke. I looked around that table at the sea of faces confronting me. There were nine men. Two officers and seven Directors. They sat around the table. The Manager, Raich Carter, and the Secretary, Harry Green, I had not met. The seven Directors present were the Chairman, his brother Harold, Bob Rand, George Winney, Geoff Wood, Jack Hatfield and the recently appointed George Kitching. I had only met two of them previously. I had met the Chairman of course, but only the once at the cricket ground. I knew Jack Hatfield, the local sports outfitter, as I had bought a few cricket bats from him. The other Directors I had not met. No introductions were made. I could not believe these men were inviting me to be one of their fellow Directors. I didn't even know them! Even worse, I suppose, they didn't know me! The situation, in which I found myself, was bizarre!

"Now then Bob, I believe you have something to say."

With this statement from the Chairman, one of the men sitting at the table, who looked quite elderly, burst into tears.

"Oh come on Bob, we don't want any of that emotional stuff. Just tell us what you have to say."

Bob Rand composed himself.

"Well, Mr. Chairman, the time has now come for me to resign my position as Director of this wonderful football club. Having been the Club's Scout, it was a great honour for me to join the Board all those years ago. I have enjoyed every minute of my time on the Board. It is very kind of you all, now I am leaving, to ensure, for the rest of my life, I shall have a complimentary ticket for the Directors' box at every home game."

I didn't know if Bob Rand wanted to say anything else. In the event, the Chairman cut him short.

"We now welcome to the meeting Dr. Neil Phillips. Neil has kindly agreed to become a Director of the Club. Would someone now propose that Dr, Phillips becomes a Director. Someone else will then second him."

I have no idea who proposed or seconded me. I do know, when the Chairman asked if all the Directors were in favour, they all raised their hands. My eyes were fixed on the boardroom table. It reminded me of the table in the saloon bar of a Western film. Glasses and empty beer bottles were scattered across the table. Interspersed between all the bottles, were several ashtrays full of cigarette stubs. It was obvious to me that a large quantity of beer had been consumed during the meeting. The room stank of cigarette smoke. It was an atmosphere I was totally unaccustomed to. It was an environment I had avoided throughout my life. One, I knew instinctively, I would not enjoy.

"Neil, perhaps you would like to say a few words to the Directors."

"Well, Chairman, I am most surprised you have invited me to join the Board. I hope, in the years to come, I will be able to justify the faith and trust you have placed in me. I hope we shall all enjoy working together."

With my statement completed, the Chairman closed the meeting.

"Gentlemen,"

the Chairman said

"The Reserve Team kicks off in five minutes, against Halifax Reserves. I shall send the pressmen down to the boardroom. The Secretary and Dr. Phillips can deal with the press and make the announcement of our new Director. Neil, when you've finished with the press, come and join us in the Directors' box."

With his final statement, the room emptied. I was left in the room with Harry Green, the Secretary. As Harry gathered together his papers, he said

"I'm really sorry. Your appointment is a complete surprise to me. I had no idea the Directors were appointing a new Director this evening. As we have never met before, and I know nothing about you, I think it would be to your advantage if, when the press arrive, you deal with them on your own."

Within minutes, three members of the press came into the boardroom. I was fortunate. I knew Bernard Gent, the Middlesbrough wicketkeeper, who worked for the local Gazette newspaper. Bernard led the questioning. He was most kind. The questions were completed in ten minutes. I left the boardroom, joining my fellow directors in the Directors' box. I saw Middlesbrough Reserves play Halifax Reserves. At half time I was astonished at the amount of alcohol consumed by some of the Directors.

I became a Director of Middlesbrough Football Club on Thursday May 9th. 1963. I was aged thirty-one. As I drove home after that match, which incidentally Middlesbrough won two goals to one, I found it difficult to believe what had happened. I had no shares in the Club. I did not know the majority of the Directors. I had no money. Somehow I had been appointed a Director of Middlesbrough Football Club, but I did not understand why. I knew I would need to buy at least five shares. Five, was the minimum number of shares, required to be held by a Director. I wondered if I would be able to afford them. Can you believe, I worried if I could afford five one-pound shares! My gross salary, at that time from General Practice, was £100 per month! I had no money in the bank. I did so want to telephone my Dad. He would have been so pleased for me, and so proud. My Mam would not be so interested. I didn't telephone her. I would use the excuse, and excuse it would be, that it was too late at night. It would save me from hearing the comment she always made.

"Time you gave up all this sport lark
and concentrated on your work!"

The following day, at the end of morning surgery, I informed two of my three partners of my appointment: Ian McKinlay and David Whitehouse. It was Reg Cutts' half day. Ian seemed unusually anxious to leave the surgery. I assumed he needed to get on with his work, visiting patients. Ian's intention, however, was immediately to visit the Coatham Hotel in Redcar. He wanted to inform the hotel's owner of my appointment. The owner was Charles Amer. He was a millionaire businessman, who had been trying to become a Director of Middlesbrough Football Club for many years. Ian, my senior partner, took great delight in informing Charles Amer that I, a Welshman with no local connections who had only lived in the area for four years, had been co-opted to the Board of Directors. Ian reported to me later in the day, with some relish, the displeasure with which Charles Amer greeted my appointment. The local newspaper reported my election. The article placed great emphasis on my youth. I was, the report said, one of the youngest directors in the Football League. The announcement listed my achievements at cricket and reported I had given medical lectures for The Football Association at Lilleshall. To my surprise, the article stated my appointment was as a replacement for Harry French, who had died some weeks previously. I believed, from the Board meeting, I was a replacement for Bob Rand, who had made his emotional resignation speech immediately prior to my election. Fortunately, the article made no reference to the fact that I did not know the majority of the directors, or that I had no shares in the company. I pondered the situation. If I was not Bob Rand's replacement, but a replacement for Harry French, there must still be a vacancy on the Board. It was most odd that not one of the directors had discussed the situation with me. The attitude of the directors was, to say the least, bizarre! It was a view I would confirm on many occasions in the future.

When I became a director, Board meetings were always held weekly on a Thursday evenings at seven. The day and time suited me. I had an evening surgery every Thursday, but it usually finished at six o'clock. This gave me time to travel the ten miles to Middlesbrough for the meeting. I was not involved with emergency duty on a Thursday evening. I came on duty every Thursday at ten thirty and remained on duty for emergencies throughout the night.

My first Board Meeting was held on 16th. May 1963. My initial fears were confirmed then. Throughout the meeting large quantities of alcohol were consumed by most of the directors; George Kitching, Jack Hatfield and George Winney being the exceptions. As the meeting progressed, innumerable empty bottles lay on the table. Cigarette smoke filled the boardroom. Some directors chain-smoked throughout the meeting. At that initial meeting, my main concern, was the club's financial position. The bank statement showed the overdraft at the bank was £56,000. In the previous three months, payments out had exceeded receipts in by £51,000! As one of the seven directors, I realised I was now liable for one-seventh of the overdraft, namely some £8,000. This, at a time, when I was concerned at purchasing five one pound shares in the company! Eric Thomas's words to me at the cricket club, the previous year, were of little consolation

> "We don't need your money, we need your brains."

he had said.

Within weeks, another stranger to me appeared at the Board meeting. No one had told me of his arrival. I had not met him previously. I did not know him. The Chairman announced

> "I'm sure we all welcome Ernest Varley to the Board. Ernest is our latest and newest Director. He replaces Bob Rand. We are now back to our full complement of Directors. Ernest, would you like to say a few words?"
>
> "I'm grateful for your kind invitation to join this Board. I look forward to working with you. I hope we can make our Club one of the more successful ones in the land."

As the meeting began its business, I reflected on the recent happenings. In the space of a few weeks, three new directors had been co-opted. George Kitching was the first. George was the nephew of the previous Chairman, Mr. Gibson. Stanley Gibson was the major shareholder of the company and George Kitching now represented his interest. On George's appointment, Stanley Gibson was elected Club President. I was the second person to be co-opted. Ernest Varley was the third. Such swift changes, in the composition of the Board, were unprecedented in the history of the Club. The appointments of the three co-opted directors' would have to be confirmed, by the shareholders, at the Annual General Meeting of the company. This meeting would take place in early August, a mere ten weeks away. There seemed to be no place for the Teesside millionaire, Charles Amer, who despite showing an interest had been overlooked. According to my senior partner, Charles had not been happy with my appointment. How would he now react to the appointment of Ernest Varley?

In the following days, several rumours circulated throughout Teesside.

I BECOME A FOOTBALL CLUB DIRECTOR

Many of the established directors reported that a consortium, headed by Charles Amer, had been formed to oppose the election of the three new directors. The press soon reported, that the members of this consortium included Charles Amer, Lesley French, son of the late Harry French, whose place on the Board I had taken, Albert King, a catering and property agent of Redcar and Walter Grosvenor, a physiotherapist and chiropodist. Confronted with this consortium, the established directors at the Club began to panic. The Thomas brothers, Eric and Harold, together with Geoff Wood, and Jack Hatfield, reported that shares, in the football club, were changing hands at grossly inflated prices. They reported, the one pound shares were changing hands for as much as fifty pounds, but they had no concrete evidence. The consortium was reported as asking many of the current shareholders to sign proxy forms, supporting the consortium at the forthcoming Annual General Meeting of the company. At that meeting, two of the established directors, the Chairman, Eric Thomas, and Geoff Wood, would be retiring, by rotation, from the Board. Both would need to seek re-election. As a consequence, five of the current eight directors would need to seek election and the support of the shareholders at the forthcoming meeting. Rumours associated with the consortium, and particularly those rumours circulating about the purchase of company shares, sent the senior members of the Board into turmoil. There was now an established state of panic amongst the club's directors. The consortium, known locally as "The Ginger Group", had created consternation amongst the senior members of the Board. To my astonishment, the senior directors were now wondering whether they held a majority of the shares to withstand the opposition from the consortium! It was an amazing situation! As a newcomer, I was appalled. How could the senior directors co-opt three new directors and then begin to realise whether they had sufficient authority, in the number of shares they held, to do so? Middlesbrough Football Club was a limited company and the company's situation, as it was in 1963, needs explaining.

In 1876, when Middlesbrough Football Club was formed, two thousand one pound shares formed the share capital of the company. For reasons best known to the directors at that time, only 1,485 shares were issued for purchase by the shareholders. Five hundred and fifteen shares were not issued when the company was formed and eighty-seven years later, in 1963, those five hundred and fifteen shares had still not been issued. When the shares were originally issued in1876, most people in the town, being mainly supporters, bought just a single share. These shareholders, when they died, left their single share to no one. In reality, the share had died with its owner. The individual share had never been transferred. As it was now eighty-seven years since those shares had been issued, surprisingly the present Board had no idea how many of these shares were still in circulation. The major shareholders, amongst the directors, were the Thomas brothers, George Kitching and Geoff Wood. Now, when threatened by the consortium, they were unsure as to whether collectively they had a controlling shareholding in the company. As the weeks progressed towards the Annual Meeting there was real concern amongst the senior directors. Their concern was whether the consortium held more shares, and hence more votes, than themselves. If this proved to be the case, the consortium would outvote the present directors at the Annual Meeting. As a result, the five directors, seeking election, would be voted off the Board. The five members of the consortium could then elect themselves. It was a situation too risky for the senior directors to accept.

The annual report of the company, to be presented at the Annual Meeting, would give plenty of ammunition to the consortium. Whilst Raich Carter, the newly appointed manager, had led the team into a respectable fourth position in the Second Division, missing promotion by only four points, the company had made a record financial loss in the year of £47,679. The directors, in their report, blamed this financial loss, on a twenty five per cent increase in player's wages and bad weather! The bad weather had resulted in an extension of the season to accommodate some previously cancelled fixtures. The directors' explanation seemed flimsy in the extreme. The consortium would interpret this record financial loss as one of gross mismanagement by the directors. The panic amongst the established directors worsened; the consortium remained quiet and kept their counsel. Their activities were based on rumour. No one at Board level had any facts.

I BECOME A FOOTBALL CLUB DIRECTOR

It was a ridiculous way to be running the business. The Board of Directors was in a mess. A mess of their own making. As a new director, I was not impressed with their business acumen.

As summer approached, it was time for my now annual visit to Lilleshall for The Football Association's Coaches and Trainers Course. The Football Association had now appointed me a lecturer on the Treatment of Injury Course. The students were mainly ex professional footballers. The three-year course was still organised and led by Bertie Mee, and Paddy Armour. I looked forward to my few days at Lilleshall. I would meet again with the professionals of the game. They were the real people of the game; the managers, coaches, trainers and players. In the previous two years, when I had visited Lilleshall, these men were the ones who had befriended me. However, in 1963, my reception by them was, to say the least, cool.

> "How on earth could you agree to becoming a director of a football club? Fancy joining that lot!"

was the view expressed by the majority of the professionals.

> "We can't understand you becoming a Director. You must be mad!"

I personally had not changed. In the eyes of the professionals however, I was a different person. I was now a director of a football club. To them, I was on the other side of the fence. I could no longer be 'one of them.' In the previous two years, I had joined in the fun and games with the other professionals at Lilleshall. Now these same professionals looked upon me as some form of outcast. I no longer really belonged with them! It was a reflection of the great divide existing between the professionals in the game and the amateur directors who controlled it. Personally, I was very sad at the reaction of the majority of the professionals, but fully understood their point of view. I had days before left the directors at Middlesbrough in a business mess of their own making. They had been amateurish in their approach, when co-opting three new directors. As a director myself, I would be now be classed as a member of an inadequate team. It was the penalty of becoming a director. The situation I experienced personally at Lilleshall illustrated the enormous chasm that existed in the game between the professionals and the amateur directors. I vowed to become as professional, as a director, as was humanly possible. I recalled a book, Len Shackleton, the famous England International footballer wrote. When writing a chapter about the game's directors, and their knowledge of the game, his book presented a blank page! I determined that, as a director, I would become as knowledgeable about the game as possible.

Alan Bass, the Major who I had worked with at Catterick, on leaving the Army, had been appointed a consultant at St. Mary's Hospital, Paddington in London. Alan had also been appointed the club doctor at Arsenal Football Club. When Alf Ramsey was appointed Manager of the England Team, he appointed Alan as the Team Doctor to the England international team. It was the first time a doctor had ever been appointed to the England team. Alan had also been invited by The Football Association to lecture at Lilleshall. I was looking forward to meeting him again. We had worked so well together at Catterick Military Hospital running the monthly Sports Injury Clinic. When I met Alan at Lilleshall he had some news for me. Following discussions with Alf Ramsey, they both now wished to offer me the Team Doctor post to the England Under 23 Team. We had worked well together, during our time at Catterick. We both had a high regard for each other professionally. Working with Alan would be a pleasure.

> "Unfortunately there is one condition Alf insists you must fulfil prior to you being appointed. Alf Ramsey wants you to resign your directorship at Middlesbrough."

I enquired of Alan why my resignation as a director was a pre-requisite to my appointment as the Team Doctor to the Under 23's.

> "Ramsey is of the view that if you continue as a Middlesbrough director there could be a conflict of interests in your role as a Team Doctor. There's always a possibility you could use your close contact with the England players to Middlesbrough's advantage. I suppose Alf Ramsey feels you could persuade a player to seek employment at Middlesbrough"

I asked Alan to convey my response to Ramsey.

> "Please tell Alf Ramsey, I have no intention of resigning my

post as a director at Middlesbrough. If my position, as a director, precludes me from being one of his International Team Doctors then so be it. If Ramsey believes I would use the position of Team Doctor to persuade players to transfer to Middlesbrough, then obviously I am the wrong person for the appointment."

Alan was obviously disappointed at my response. He did however assure me he would accurately convey my views to Ramsey. Throughout his stay at Lilleshall, Alan enthused about his England appointment. He seemed genuinely disappointed at my turning down the conditions of my appointment. I believed Alan would do a great job for England.

I knew we could work well together, but I was not prepared to give up my directorship in order to accept this new position. For me it was a matter of principle. I would have loved the job, but I would not accept it on the terms Ramsey had laid down.

I returned home refreshed, as always, in body and spirit. I really enjoyed my visits to Lilleshall. I was nevertheless saddened by the attitude towards me by some of the professionals, including Alf Ramsey. Lilleshall is such a beautiful place. Completely isolated in the Shropshire countryside, with its beautiful extensive grounds, the main house and facilities are some two miles from the main road. When at Lilleshall, I enjoyed total isolation and peace. In those days, the public were denied access to the centre when The Football Association courses were in progress. The whole estate was exclusively ours for the duration of our stay. There I always re-charged my batteries.

I enjoyed the friendship and fellowship of the managers, trainers and coaches involved in football. In the main, I felt they were my sort of people. I enjoyed their company and learnt much from them. I knew, as I returned home to Redcar, that the unhappy relationships in the Practice would continue. There would also be turmoil on Teesside over my appointment as a Director. Interesting days lay ahead!

During my absence at Lilleshall, Eric Thomas decided, with the approval of his fellow directors, to meet with the leader of 'The Ginger Group.' The directors were anxious to learn, at first hand, the true intentions of Charles Amer and his consortium. Charles Amer was invited to a meeting with the Chairman. The meeting was yet to take place. I was updated of the situation at a casual meeting with Harry Green, the Secretary, and the Chairman. At my informal meeting with them, I offered a partial solution to the problem. I informed Eric and Harry of the conversation that had taken place at Lilleshall, between Alan Bass and myself. I suggested I resign from the Board. My resignation would then enable me to be appointed Team Doctor to the England Under 23 Team, under the conditions Alf Ramsey had laid down. If I resigned immediately, the heat would be partially taken out of the situation with the consortium and the probable confrontation with 'The Ginger Group' avoided. Eric Thomas refused to accept my resignation. I was to remain a Director of Middlesbrough Football Club. Later Harry Green said,

> "I am amazed. You are appointed a Director at the age of thirty-one and four months later you offer to resign. I find it difficult to comprehend."

I was deeply concerned about the forthcoming meeting between the two parties. Charles Amer was an astute businessman. Ian Mackinlay, my senior partner, had informed me, on more than one occasion, that in business terms, Charles could 'eat people for breakfast'. Ian advised me he was a person I should avoid. I felt Charles Amer would outwit our Chairman at the forthcoming meeting. Charles was too strong a person in comparison to the Chairman. The outcome of their meeting was, from my perspective, disappointing. As I suspected, Eric lost any initiative the directors may have held over the consortium. Charles Amer and Eric agreed a strategy at their meeting, resolving the confrontational issue. In exchange for a quiet Annual General Meeting, requested by the Chairman, Eric agreed that Charles Amer, and one other member of the consortium, would be appointed as directors shortly after the Annual Meeting. As a result Charles gave an assurance the consortium would not oppose the election of the five directors seeking re-election. Within days of their meeting, the consortium decided to present their case to the public. The media headline

I BECOME A FOOTBALL CLUB DIRECTOR

read,

'Middlesbrough FC Get A Ginger Group'.

The report listed the five members of the consortium. The consortium confirmed the run on the company's shares, but denied their intention was to oust the present directors. Their intention, it was said, was to spur the present directors into action. The group wished to ensure Middlesbrough Football Club gained a place in the First Division. The media confirmed that Charles Amer had met with the Club's Chairman. Following the meeting the consortium was now satisfied the present directors were doing all they could to return the Club to the First Division. The consortium confirmed they would not be submitting any nominations for election to the Board. No mention was ever made of a deal having been agreed.

Frequently, after evening surgery, I loved to run on Redcar's beach. I usually ran from the Redcar pier to the pier at Saltburn-by-the Sea. Along the beach it was probably a distance of four miles. The firm sand was ideal for running. The sound of the sea, as the waves crashed on the beach, together with the sea breezes blowing across my face added to the enjoyment of the run. Whenever I ran on the beach I called it my thinking time. It was the time I was most relaxed. It gave me the opportunity to think through the issues of the day.

"Why can't we issue those five hundred and fifteen
un-issued shares?".

I thought.

There seemed no reason to me why those un-issued shares at the football club could not now be issued. The shares could be issued to the current eight directors. Sixty shares could be purchased by each one of the present eight directors. They could be issued immediately after the Annual Meeting, when the company's books reopened, to the exclusion of the two members of the consortium. As I ran along the beach, I knew there was no reason why those shares could not be issued immediately after the Annual Meeting and before the two consortium members joined the Board. The present directors could, immediately after the Annual Meeting, issue the four hundred and eighty un-issued shares to themselves. With the addition of nearly five hundred shares to the present directors' holdings, their security of tenure would be assured. These newly issued shares could not be used at this year's Annual Meeting, but they could be used in the future. If my fellow directors adopted this policy, the consortium would never ever again be in a position to threaten the Board on a share vote.. The issue of these new shares seemed essential to me for the survival of the present directors. It seemed a simple solution. My mind was in turmoil. I slipped on the wet sand and fell flat on my face!

I completed my run and returned home. I telephoned Eric Thomas and made an appointment to see him.

The following day, I put my proposal to the Chairman. Eric was a solicitor in Middlesbrough and, after careful consideration, he could see no legal reason why my suggestion could not be implemented. He was obviously delighted with my proposal. Eric Thomas had experienced a very difficult few months. I presented him with a solution to his problems. There were now bright lights for him at the end of a very dark tunnel. An emergency Board Meeting was arranged at which Eric presented my proposal. The directors unanimously agreed to the issue of four hundred and eighty shares. Each of the eight directors agreed to purchase sixty of the newly issued one pound shares. The new shares would be issued at a Board Meeting immediately following the Annual Meeting. Eric Thomas took me to one side and thanked me for my initiative. He was delighted. With two solicitors, Eric and Geoff Wood, and five experienced businessmen on the Board, I wondered why one of them had not come forward with the suggestion of issuing the shares. It was a very simple business solution. I was the youngest director, and the least experienced in the business world, yet the idea had come from myself. Eric smiled and said,

"I told you, we didn't need your money,
we needed your brains."

I was left to ponder how I would find the sixty pounds required to purchase the new shares.

The Seventy-first Annual General Meeting of Middlesbrough Football Club was a friendly affair. The fireworks, expected from the consortium, became a damp squib. The stormiest Annual Meeting in years had been forecast, but it never materialised. The meeting lasted just forty-five minutes. The Chairman explained to the shareholders why three new members had been co-opted during the year. He told the meeting that following the death of Harry French and the retirements of Stanley Gibson and Bob Rand, the Club was placed in a most unusual position. The Club's constitution required the Board to be composed of at least eight directors. He acknowledged the co-option of three new directors had been a contentious matter and explained to the shareholders why these three new directors had been chosen. In the case of George Kitching and Ernest Varley, they were appointed because they were experts in the entertainment business. The third appointment had been made because the appointee was a medical man. The directors thought, the Chairman continued, it necessary for a doctor to sit on the Board. Eric Thomas then spent an inordinate length of time explaining why I had been co-opted. He told the shareholders,

> "Whilst there is no Faculty of Sports Medicine in England, Dr. Phillips was one of only two medical men in Great Britain who were called upon by The Football Association to lecture on the treatment of football injuries. We are very fortunate to have him at Middlesbrough Football Club."

One of the shareholders asked the Chairman if the Board might extend the number of directors from eight to twelve. Eric Thomas's response was non-committal. The whole of that Annual Meeting was a sham! A sham, because the majority of the shareholders were unaware that a deal had already been agreed upon between the Chairman and 'The Ginger Group'. Charles Amer and one other member of the consortium would be given a directorship. The present directors would now, after the Annual Meeting was over, issue four hundred and eighty shares to themselves. The directors would inform no-one of this new share issue, until it appeared in the next year's annual report! The issue of these additional shares had been my original idea. I felt ashamed of the part I played in the deceit. I was beginning to dislike the politics of being a director. Probably Alf Ramsey, and the professionals at Lilleshall, had been correct.

"How did I ever become one of them!"

Immediately after the Annual Meeting, a Board Meeting was held with the express purpose of issuing the four hundred and eighty new shares. Each director purchased sixty shares. I visited my bank manager and negotiated a loan of sixty pounds to purchase my shares. I was fortunate in that my bank manager was a season ticket holder. It was nevertheless a fact; the Club did need my money after all! The day following the issue of the new shares, a second Board Meeting was called. The minutes of the previous meeting were approved and confirmed. The following week a third meeting was held. At that meeting, the co-option of two more directors, Charles Amer and Albert King, was agreed. It was an invite Charles and Albert were expecting and one they would immediately accept. The issue of four hundred and eighty additional shares exclusively to the present directors had placed them in a strong position regarding the control of the company. The Board, Eric Thomas's Board, now had the controlling interest of the Club's. In future years, the consortium, or anyone else would be unable to defeat the present directors on a share vote! The only criteria needed was for those directors, who had participated in the new share issue, remain loyal to, and supportive of, each other.

Shortly after the seventy-first Annual Meeting, a statement was issued from Middlesbrough Football Club. Charles Amer and Albert King had been appointed as directors of Middlesbrough Football Club. The Chairman's announcement said,

> "Considerable work is envisaged over the next three years at the Football Club. As a consequence, the number of directors has been increased from eight to ten. This will enable the Club to carry out its future developments and give representation to minority interest. Charles Amer has had a vast experience of the entertainment industry and Albert King is well versed in the catering requirements. Both gentlemen have a lifetime interest in local football and the Board feel their presence will enable us to carry out our future plans more easily."

The reality was that both the new directors had forced their way onto the

I BECOME A FOOTBALL CLUB DIRECTOR

Board. They would now sit as directors for a whole year, oblivious to the fact that four hundred and eighty new, additional shares had been issued to their fellow directors. The original eight directors would have control of the Club for the foreseeable future.

I felt quite sad for Eric Thomas. He tried to appoint his own team of directors. He had failed. He now had on his team two men who, a few weeks previously, had threatened his own and Geoff Wood's re-election. The consortium had also threatened the co-option of George Kitching, Ernest Varley and myself. It was a sad day. Needless to say Charles Amer and Albert King were delighted with their appointments. The ten-man Board now consisted of five directors who had no previous experience as directors of the Football Club. It was a ridiculous situation. Fifty per cent of the Board, myself included, were inexperienced in the business affairs of professional football! It was a most unusual scenario, but one of the directors' own making.

It came as a complete surprise to me, at one of the Board meetings, in the pre-season period, when the Chairman introduced a discussion on the Club doctor, Glyn Williams. The Chairman wanted to know if the directors wished to renew the club doctor's contract. No discussions had taken place on the subject with me previously.

I was unaware the issue was being raised at the meeting. In the general discussion that followed, it became apparent the Chairman and the senior directors were dissatisfied with the performance of their club doctor. I, and the five newly appointed directors had no first hand knowledge of the club doctor's work. In fact, I had not even met Dr. Williams. As a result, half of the directors were unable to contribute to the discussion.

Because of my silence, throughout the discussion, the Chairman was forced to question me directly on the issue. I was astonished when the Chairman asked me to comment on the professional competence of the doctor's work. I responded, to what I considered was an outrageous question.

"I have no knowledge of the doctor's work. I have only been
a director for a few months and those months have been in

the close season, when the club doctor rarely visits the Club.
I have never met Dr. Williams and no one has introduced me
to him. I therefore am unable to express a view."

To my even greater surprise, the Chairman persisted with questions directly addressed to me.

"If you are unable to give a view on whether the contract should be renewed, perhaps you could respond to this question. If we decide not to renew the contract, would you personally be prepared to take over as the Club's Medical Officer?"

There were of course, two separate issues before the directors. Firstly, the issue of whether the present doctor's contract should be renewed. Secondly, if the directors determined that his contract should not be renewed, then, and only then, a new doctor would have to be appointed to the role.

"First things first."

I said.

"Decide on the renewal or not of the contract. If it is
not to be renewed, we can then discuss a successor."

The directors determined not to renew Dr. Williams' contract. I abstained during the vote. The Chairman then asked if I would be prepared to take on the role. He asked if I would take up the role of the Club's Medical Officer 'as a director'. I stupidly believed, the Chairman's remark inferred that if I was appointed to the medical role, I would still continue as a director. The Chairman did not mean that at all! In those days, directors of football clubs were not allowed to earn money from the Club 'as a director'. The Chairman was wanting me to accept the role and provide my medical services for free! It was a misunderstanding that would cause friction between the two of us throughout the many years of my directorship. At the meeting, I was unaware of his meaning of my becoming the club's medical officer 'as a director'. Many supportive views, to the Chairman's proposal, were expressed by several of the directors. I was appointed to the additional role of Club Doctor. Dr. Williams left the following week. I informed the directors that, under no circumstances, would my partners in Redcar play any part in the Medical Officer's role. When I was not available, the Club

I BECOME A FOOTBALL CLUB DIRECTOR

would have to find a deputy. The Board accepted the arrangement.

As I drove home, after the meeting, I wondered if my appointment as the Club's Medical Officer was the real reason why I'd been invited to join the Board in the first place. The Chairman, at our first meeting informed me he didn't want my money, he just wanted my brains. He had now captured my medical knowledge to the advantage of the Club. However, I was content. I would endeavour to provide the professional footballers at Middlesbrough with the best possible medical care. I was delighted at the prospect.

My initial task was to make a full appraisal of the medical facilities within the club. The medical accommodation was non-existent. There was just one room. The so-called 'treatment room'. It had two beds and two infrared lamps. There was no consulting room where players could see the doctor in private. There was no gymnasium where remedial work could take place. The players' medical records were non-existent. The only medical records were the numerous consultants' letters following a player's hospital referral. No routine medical examinations had taken place. Simple, yet essential preventative work, for example the protection against tetanus infection, by the giving of routine immunisations, had not occurred. The staff, who carried out the players' treatments, were Harold Shepherdson, the England Trainer, and Mickey Fenton, a former celebrated Middlesbrough centre-forward. Harold had obtained The Football Association's Treatment of Injury Certificate, but Mickey Fenton had no qualifications in the treatment of injuries. I was extremely unhappy with the situation. Much work needed to be done. At least I knew I was commencing my role where little had been done previously.

After the political trauma during the weeks leading up to the Annual Meeting, all ten directors approached the 1963–64 season with high expectations. In January 1963 Raich Carter succeeded Bob Dennison as the new manager. The team's performance, under Raich's management, steadily improved throughout the season. Middlesbrough finished fourth in the Second Division with forty-nine points–three points behind Chelsea who were promoted to the First Division. Stoke City were the Second Division champions. Stoke had fifty-three points. The board of directors believed that, if Raich Carter had been the manager for the whole season promotion to the First Division would have been achieved. If Raich Carter could maintain the team's form into the coming season, then promotion to the First Division was guaranteed. It proved to be a false hope.

Raich Carter was an exceptional footballer. He was probably one of the best inside forwards ever to play for England. Unfortunately, like many players of his time, his international caps were limited as, at the pinnacle of his career, the Second World War intervened. International football matches were cancelled during the war. Raich was only capped thirteen times for England. He began his career as a Sunderland player. He freely admitted he was born with a natural talent for football. He was reputed to have possessed the best left foot of any footballer. In 1936, at the age of twenty-three, he inspired Sunderland to the First Division Championship. The following year, he captained Sunderland in the F.A. Cup Final against Preston. Sunderland won by three goals to one and, while Carter only scored once, he was the team's inspiration throughout the match. After the war, Raich was transferred to Derby County. There he formed a formidable inside trio with Stamps and Peter Doherty. In one of the best cup finals ever seen at Wembley, Raich was instrumental in ensuring Derby won the 1946 final by four goals to one. He did not score in that final, yet he personally dominated the game from start to finish. No one, who saw that game, doubted Raich Carter possessed an exceptional football talent. It appeared, Middlesbrough was fortunate to have him as their manager. Outstanding players, however, do not always make outstanding managers. Nevertheless, everyone at Middlesbrough Football Club was expecting a highly successful season, leading to promotion into the First Division. The directors were very optimistic.

The first player who consulted me medically at Middlesbrough Football Club was Alan Peacock. Alan was an England international player. He was a playing member of the 1962 England World Cup party in Chile. He was, without question, one of Middlesbrough's best players and essential he be fully fit for the ensuing season. Alan had suffered with a troublesome knee throughout the latter half of the previous season. Dr. Williams, my predecessor, referred Alan to Matt Leitch, the local consultant orthopaedic specialist. Mr. Leitch formed the opinion that Alan's knee would improve with rest during the close season. No definite diagnosis had been made on his knee and, apart from rest, no treatment had been recommended. When I referred to the consultant's report, Mr. Leitch had written,

> "There is no need for me to see Alan Peacock again.
> He will fully recover with rest during the close-season."

As pre-season approached however, Alan remained very unhappy about his knee. It was causing him pain and discomfort. The knee had not improved with rest during the close season. On examination of his knee, I was also concerned with his problem. Working on the principle I wanted nothing less than the very best medical advice for the Middlesbrough players, and knowing Mr. Leitch had written,

> "There is no need for me to see Alan Peacock again."

I decided to refer Alan Peacock to Alan Bass, the England team doctor and a specialist at St. Mary's in London. Following this consultation Alan was diagnosed with an inflammation of a bursar at the back of the knee and treated accordingly. Needless to say Alan's visit to London was reported in the sporting press. On reading the press report, Mr. Leitch was furious. The day following the press report, I received a telephone call from Matt Leitch's secretary asking me to make an appointment to see him. Mr. Leitch, I was informed, wished to discuss matters of mutual interest regarding the football club. I made an appointment for the following Wednesday. The appointment was most unpleasant. No sooner had I sat down in his office when Mr. Leitch said,

> "I think you're nothing more than a young clever-dick! In the few months you have been at Middlesbrough Football Club, you have initiated the sacking of Dr. Williams who is a very competent doctor. You have subsequently had the audacity to send one of my patients, Alan Peacock, to another specialist without first consulting with me."

I was astonished. Inside I was very angry, but outwardly I remained calm. I pointed out to Mr. Leitch that, while I was present during the discussion relating to the renewal of Dr. Williams's contract, I made no contribution to the discussion. Certainly I did not initiate the sacking. The sacking of Dr. Williams, I pointed out, was a decision of the directors. I abstained from voting on the issue. I further pointed out to Mr. Leitch that in his last letter to Dr. Williams, regarding Alan Peacock, he had written,

"There is no need for me to see Alan Peacock again."

I informed Mr. Leitch it was my intention to provide the Middlesbrough players with the best possible medical service at all times. If this resulted in players being sent to Timbuktu–so be it! It would be nice, I said, for the players and myself if Mr. Leitch continued, as part of the medical team, but if he did not wish to do so I would fully understand. In those circumstances I would obviously have to seek the services of another orthopaedic surgeon. After a lengthy discussion, in which I stated what I required of him and which he stated what he required of me, Mr. Leitch agreed to continue as part of the medical team. It was the beginning of a very happy professional relationship. The relationship lasted for many years. During those years, the respect we developed for each other's medical expertise was phenomenal. It proved to be a very happy working relationship.

I often wonder how directors of Football Clubs choose their Managers. From my experience, albeit short lived in the game and now many years ago, few directors have any experience of watching and assessing coaches in their work. I was fortunate in that I had observed the top British coaches working at Lilleshall. In addition, I had learnt much from listening to their views in the evenings at many a Shropshire pub. Even so, my knowledge was minimal. It was my opinion, my fellow directors at Middlesbrough certainly had no knowledge as to what constituted a good football coach or how they would assess one. Raich Carter's appointment at Middlesbrough was one that confused me greatly. Raich did not believe in coaching. He did not believe in team tactics. He did not believe in systems of play. Tactical formations he considered a waste of time. Raich only believed in the natural talent of players.

"Good players don't need coaching. They don't need tactics."
he often told me.

I BECOME A FOOTBALL CLUB DIRECTOR

In those days, driving a car was essential for every football manager. Raich hated driving. For car journeys, of any long-distance, Raich required a chauffeur. With the majority of midweek games played on a Wednesday, my half-day in the Practice, inevitably I became his driver. Whenever he wished to travel to watch a mid-week game, he would invite me to be his chauffeur. It was a role I enjoyed. Early in the season, Raich recommended the directors to purchase Don Ratcliffe, a forward from Stoke City. He had seen Ratcliffe play for Stoke the previous season, and had been very impressed with his performance. Having obtained the agreement of the Board, and with a fee agreed with Stoke City of £20,000, a meeting was arranged between Ratcliffe and Raich Carter at Manchester. As the meeting was arranged on a Wednesday, Raich asked if I would drive him to Manchester. I readily agreed. We met with Don Ratcliffe at the Station Hotel in Manchester. After a private discussion with Raich, the player agreed to sign for Middlesbrough. The press had been anxiously waiting for the outcome of the discussions between Raich and Ratcliffe. A photograph of Ratcliffe, signing his contract with Raich Carter was arranged. Raich suggested I join the photograph. The photograph appeared in the national newspapers the following day. My fellow directors were furious; angry at the publicity I personally had received. The Chairman confronted me on the issue.

I told the Chairman my only reason for being in Manchester was because the manager didn't like driving. I informed the Chairman, the manager frequently telephoned me on a Wednesday requesting I drive him to various locations in the country. On this particular occasion, it was to Manchester. I suggested to the Chairman if any other director was prepared to drive the manager, I would be perfectly happy to stay at home. As I expected, no volunteers from my fellow directors were forthcoming. The attitude of the Chairman and my fellow directors raised the issue, in my own mind, as to what directors actually did. I knew what I did. I now looked after the players medically. Most of my fellow directors appeared to me to do very little. I believed the attitude of the Chairman and my fellow directors was pathetic. Unfortunately the Chairman was not finished.

"Another issue concerning the directors is the number of visits you make to Sunderland Football Club. As a matter of principle, our directors do not visit Sunderland unless Middlesbrough is actually playing there. You seem to visit Sunderland at every opportunity. Are you aware, that in 1910, Sunderland reported Middlesbrough to The Football Association? As a result, of the subsequent inquiry, our then Chairman and Manager were permanently removed from office. Ever since then, relationships with Sunderland have not been very good. As Middlesbrough directors we tend to stay away."

I could not believe what I was hearing. I was furious and angry.

"Eric!, the reason why the then Chairman and Manager were removed from office, by The Football Association, was because they had offered the Sunderland Captain a bribe. They requested the Sunderland captain to throw the match and ensure Middlesbrough won the game! The Sunderland captain was quite correct to report both of them to his own Club and subsequently to The Football Association. Our then Chairman and Manager were in the wrong. The F.A's decision was quite correct. In any case all this was over fifty years ago! The Sunderland directors have been most welcoming towards me. I enjoy watching games at Roker Park and will continue to do so."

I informed the Chairman I had every intention, for my own personal benefit, of attending as many matches as possible. I needed to learn as much as possible about the professional game.

Eric Thomas was not pleased with my response. I even surprised myself with my replies. I didn't care whether he was pleased or not. I thought his attitude was confused and ridiculous. The attitude of the Chairman and some of my fellow directors confused me. They were, of course, some thirty or more years older than myself. They belonged to a different generation. I was never very happy in their company. I was much happier mixing with the professional staff and particularly with the players. They were more of my age. In fact they were my kind of people.

During the season, I continued to drive Raich Carter all over the British Isles. We enjoyed each other's company. Raich was a great raconteur. He loved talking about his playing days; the matches he played in; the goals he scored. Over and over he regretted the day he stopped playing.

"Life has never been the same since my playing days."
he frequently told me. Once he said,

"When I gave up playing, they should have shot me."
As much as I was impressed with Raich's reminisces, he was equally impressed with my driving. During one trip to Scotland, he wondered why I had not entered the Monte Carlo rally!

"You'd stand an excellent chance of winning.

Your driving is excellent."
On occasions, his requests for my driving were excessive. Raich was interested in signing Jimmy Townsend, a player at St. Johnstone in Scotland.

"I need to see him play. The scout's reports are excellent, but I need to personally see him play. His next game is at Perth on New Year's Day. Do you think you could drive me there? The fixture starts at 3p.m. We would need to leave Redcar at about 4a.m. on New Year's morning. It would mean you would be unable to celebrate New Year's Eve. Can you do it?

I was off duty on New Year's Day and the surgery was closed. No other director would offer to drive the manager to Perth and back in a day. On the team's performances to date, Raich certainly needed to strengthen the side. He was keen on Townsend, but had not seen him play. Knowing Raich would not drive himself, I agreed to drive.

We left at 4a.m. on New Year's morning. The plan was to stop in the Jedburgh area for coffee, but nowhere was open. It was, after all, New Year's Day! Plan B was to have lunch at The North British Hotel in Edinburgh. When we arrived, at lunchtime, the cleaner was the only person present. She was cleaning up from the night before. No lunch was available for us in Edinburgh on New Year's Day! We arrived at Perth in good time to see the game. Hungry, but in good time! Raich was very impressed with Townsend. At the end of the game, we both stayed on and relished the tea and sandwiches provided. We arrived back in Redcar at 4a.m. on January 2nd. I was exhausted. Apart from the game, I had driven continuously for some twenty-four hours. Apart from the sandwiches at St. Johnstone, we had not eaten. It was indeed like driving in a rally, except that Raich slept most of the time on the return journey. Middlesbrough agreed to sign Townsend at the next Board meeting. Raich informed the Board he had watched Townsend at Perth on New Year's Day. No director enquired as to who had driven Raich to Perth. I said nothing.

Despite the optimism at the beginning of the season, the team played disappointing and inconsistent football throughout the season. At no stage did they threaten a promotion place. The team finished in tenth position with forty-one points. It was a disappointment for everyone at the Club. The presence on the board of Charles Amer and Albert King had not ensured a place in the First Division.

Initially, as the club's medical officer, my fears, regarding the treatment room staff, were fully justified. Mickey Fenton, a loyal servant to the Club and a great centre–forward in his playing days, had no medical qualifications whatsoever. Harold Shepherdson's role at the club was now more as the Assistant Manager and first team Coach. It was a role in which Harold excelled, especially as Raich did not believe in coaching. Harold was the provider of whatever coaching the players received. I formed the opinion we needed a fully qualified, full time physiotherapist to be in charge of the treatment room. I knew the person I wanted. George Wright was the Superintendent Physiotherapist, at Middlesbrough General Hospital. We had played a little cricket together at Redcar, though George's cricketing ability was limited. I approached George with the offer of being the Club's Physiotherapist. The Club offered him an increase to his yearly salary of £500. The directors appointed George to the newly created post. The appointment of a Chartered Physiotherapist to a football club, at that time, was unusual, but I knew George would prove a great asset. The injured players would greatly benefit from his expertise. The medical

I BECOME A FOOTBALL CLUB DIRECTOR

staff at Middlesbrough General Hospital were not so happy. I had stolen their Superintendent Physiotherapist. The Club's gain was inevitably the hospital's loss. With the arrival of George Wright, Mickey Fenton decided to retire. He had served the Club well.

In addition to my commitments at the Football Club, I was of course still working as a full time General Practitioner in Redcar. During morning surgery, towards the end of April 1964, I received a telephone call from London.

The voice said,

"My name is Ramsey. Alf Ramsey. I am the England Team Manager. We haven't met, but I've heard good reports of you from many people. My purpose in telephoning is to ask if you would be prepared to travel with the England Under 23 Team on their summer tour to Hungary, Israel and Turkey. Joe Mercer, the Manager of Aston Villa, will be in charge. He will manage the team. I will be on tour with the Senior Team. The Under 23 Team leave on May 11th., and return on the 21st. It's a ten-day tour. Obviously I don't expect you to decide now, as I'm sure you will need to discuss this appointment with your wife and family and also your partners. Could you telephone me at The Football Association on Friday morning with your decision? About 11a.m. would suit me."

Alf Ramsey did not mention my resigning as a director of Middlesbrough Football Club. I did not raise the issue with him.

"Thank you for the invitation. I'm quite flattered."

I replied,

"I will contact you on Friday morning at 11a.m."

I replaced the phone and contemplated my position. In the past year I had been appointed a director at Middlesbrough Football Club. Following my appointment as a director, I became the Club's Medical Officer. Now I was offered a medical role with The Football Association in London. Alf Ramsey had asked me to be Team Physician to the Under 23 Team. It was like a dream. I pinched myself to ensure it was real! I hadn't made it as a professional cricketer, but now I was being offered a medical role with the cream of England's professional footballers. I was just thirty-two years of age. How I wished I could have phoned my Dad. Instead I rang the waiting room bell for my next patient. As I consulted with the patient, I was soon back in the real world. When I told Margaret of Ramsey's telephone call she was delighted.

"It's a job you must accept."
she said.

My three partners were also agreeable. No other partner wished to be on holiday in May. Provided I took the ten days as holiday, they were quite agreeable. I phoned Alf Ramsey on the Friday morning. He was delighted when I told him I was able to accept his invitation. He informed me he would contact Joe Mercer with the news. Joe Mercer would telephone me in the next few days. I informed Eric Thomas. He also seemed pleased. My career with England and Alf Ramsey was about to begin. It was April 1964.

In the past year, in addition to becoming a football club director, I had been appointed medical officer to both Middlesbrough Football Club and the England Under 23 Team. None of the three posts had been advertised. People just came and asked me. I had received no specialised training for any of these three posts. At that time the British medical profession had ignored Sports Medicine. There was no formal post graduate training in Sports Medicine. No course I could attend. No examination I could sit. No diploma I could obtain. Sports Medicine, Sports Science and Sports Psychology simply did not exist, at this time, in England. I was a cricketer who had qualified as a doctor. I was on my own. I knew however I wanted to provide both the Middlesbrough and England players with the best medical service that was possible. I was now on the international stage. It was an enormous challenge, but one I looked forward to.

Joe Mercer telephoned in the middle of a busy Monday morning surgery. The waiting room was full of patients, anxious to consult with me. It was not an ideal time to be talking about the details of the impending Under 23 football tour to Hungary, Israel and Turkey. Monday morning was always a very busy time in General Practice. On talking to Joe, I soon became aware he was not well. There was no sparkle in his voice. Joe Mercer was renowned for his humour. There was no humour in this conversation. He expressed no enthusiasm for the tour. His sentences were hesitant. During our telephone conversation, there were many long, silent pauses. Initially, I became irritated by the slowness of the conversation. I was conscious of the crowded waiting room with large numbers of patients wanting to see me. The more I listened to Joe Mercer's conversation, the more concerned I became for his well being. I was aware Joe had been under considerable pressure throughout the latter part of the season at Aston Villa, the Club he then managed. His team had been in danger of relegation. It had required all of Joe's managerial skills to save them from the drop. Skilfully, he steered them away from what, at one stage, seemed inevitable relegation to the Second Division. Aston Villa finished the season fourth from the bottom in the First Division. It became obvious to me the stress of the relegation battle had taken its toll. Joe Mercer seemed mentally exhausted. Nevertheless, Joe was kind enough to say he was looking forward to working with me. He assured me we would discuss matters in greater detail when we met in London. I was now running twenty minutes late with my appointments. There was standing room only in the waiting room. The receptionists and the patients were not pleased with me. Three days later, I received a call from Alf Ramsey.

"Mr. Mercer will not be going on the Under 23 tour. John
Harris, the Manager of Sheffield United, has replaced him."
The stress of being a Football Manager had taken its toll on Joe Mercer. He had been advised to take a long rest. I made a mental note. Always be aware of the mental stress Football Managers are subjected to. On my first tour, I would now work with John Harris. The England Under 23 touring team was in a unique situation. There were only three staff looking after the players. Of those three, the only Englishman was Les Cocker, the Leeds United trainer. John Harris was a Scot and the Team Doctor was Welsh!. Les would no doubt endeavour to keep the English flag flying!

In many ways, the change of Manager was fortunate for me. I had not met John Harris but his Chairman, at Sheffield United, was none other than Blacow Yates. Blacow was the consultant surgeon I had worked for in Sheffield. When Blacow knew John and I were to work together on tour, he was delighted. Aware that John and I had never met, Blacow spent some time briefing John on me as a person and my medical credentials. I knew whatever Blacow had said about me would be good. John therefore had learnt much about me before we had even met. His briefing from Blacow was, as I expected, thorough. John seemed to know more about me than I knew of myself!

The touring party was instructed to arrive at The Windsor Hotel, Lancaster Gate, London in time for dinner on Sunday evening the 10th. May 1964. I travelled to London by train. I wanted to arrive early. I arrived at the hotel shortly after mid-day. I was the first to arrive. My enthusiasm at being involved with an England team was obvious. The hotel bedrooms were not even ready for occupation. I decided to leave my luggage in the Porter's Lodge before taking a walk. I spent an hour or two walking in Hyde Park, just across the Bayswater Road from the hotel. My wife and our three children I had left at home. It was the first occasion I had left them. Aged thirty-two, I had only been abroad once before. My only overseas trip had been on a ferry across the channel to France. I had never flown in an aeroplane. With the knowledge of the Manchester United air crash, a few years previously, I convinced myself that when I had said goodbye to my family, it was probably for the last time. One of the planes, I determined, was bound to crash. In the next ten days, I would fly on seven different aircraft. Some of the planes would not even be British! One plane out of seven, I reckoned, was bound to crash. I spent the early afternoon walking around Hyde Park, taking in the May sunshine. For myself, this tour was a big adventure. As I walked in the park, I asked myself the same question over and over again,

> "How come, when there were over twenty thousand doctors in England, I had been chosen to be the Team Physician to the England Under 23 team?"

I realised I was in a very privileged, yet responsible position. I determined never to let Alf Ramsey or the England players down.

John Harris, Les Cocker and I met later in the afternoon. We had afternoon tea together. All the young England players arrived in time for the evening meal. When the meal was finished, John Harris arranged a team meeting for the players and staff. He requested I attend the team meeting. It was the first occasion any doctor had accompanied an England Under 23 Team on tour. Ramsey had informed John Harris that he wanted the doctor totally involved with every activity of the players. At the first team meeting, John introduced me to the players. John informed them if they had any medical concerns they could, if they so wished, approach me directly. The doctor would subsequently liase with the Manager. All the players reported fit and well. No injuries were reported. The touring party numbered twenty-four. In addition to the three members of staff there were sixteen players.

The goalkeepers were Peter Bonetti (Chelsea), and Jim Montgomery (Sunderland). The Backs were Len Badger (Sheffield United), Paul Reaney (Leeds United), and Keith Newton (Blackburn Rovers). The Half-backs were Mike Bailey (Charlton), John Talbut (Burnley), Graham Cross (Leicester), and Alan Deakin (Aston Villa). The forwards were David Wilson (Preston), Bobby Tambling (Chelsea), Geoff Hurst (West Ham), Martin Chivers (Southampton), Alan Ball (Blackpool), Alan Hinton (Nottingham Forest), and Terry Venables (Chelsea).

The Football Association officials accompanying the party were Ike Robinson, Lt.Col. Mitchell, Lt.Col C.F. Linnit and Squadron Leader Hadley. They were all members of the Under 23 committee at The Football Association. The committee was chaired by Ike Robinson. Stan Whitehorn, a member of the F.A. staff, completed the party. Everyone had been sent a printed itinerary of the tour. John Harris confirmed the detailed arrangements of the tour to the players. After the team meeting it was a case of an early retirement to bed. We were due to leave the hotel for Heathrow Airport the following day at 0830 hours. I phoned home to speak to Margaret and the children. Who knows, it could have been for the last time! What a pessimist I was.

We left Heathrow, aboard Flight BE 624 at 1020 bound for Cologne where, to my surprise, we arrived quite safely, at midday. A transfer to a different airline ensured we took off again from Cologne bound for Budapest. Flight SN787 arrived there, again safely, at three in the afternoon. There seemed nothing to this flying in aeroplanes.

Hungary, at the time, was of course behind the Iron Curtain. Apart from politicians, diplomats, sportsmen and some businessmen, few British people were able to visit the Eastern European countries. A few years previously, Hungary had been invaded by Russia. As we travelled in the coach from the airport to the Gellert Hotel, the scars of the Russian invasion were evident throughout the city. Numerous shell and bullet marks were easily identified on the walls of many buildings. As we approached the Gellert Hotel, situated on the side of the Danube, I noticed many of the bridges across the river were in various states of repair. Apparently the Hungarians, to prevent the advance of the Russian soldiers during the invasion, had blown up most of the bridges across the river. These bridges were now in the process of being rebuilt. Once settled in the hotel, a training session at Budapest's Nep Stadium was arranged for all the players.

As we checked into the hotel, one of the players, informed me,

"I don't feel too well."

"Give me your room number."

I said,

"I'll come and see you in five minutes."

At the completion of my examination, I could find no clinical abnormality. The player had no temperature and no abnormal clinical signs. I was unable to make a diagnosis. The player was convinced he was developing a cold. He thought it wise to remain in bed and miss the training session. I said I would discuss the matter with John Harris. I spoke with John.

"The player thinks he is developing a cold. I've examined him and can find absolutely nothing wrong with him. He says he wants to rest in bed and miss the training session."

"I've heard reports of this player from his Club. He doesn't like training!"

replied John Harris,
"I'll go and see him."
The Manager departed to visit the player in his room.

We all congregated in the reception area prior to boarding the bus taking us to the Nep Stadium. Every player travelled with the party. There was no need to enquire of the conversation between John Harris and the player. The player with the developing cold took a full part in the training session

"The Under 23's"

and suffered no ill effects. He played against Hungary two days later.

After a second training session on the Tuesday morning, we returned to the Gellert Hotel for lunch. The afternoon was spent on a conducted walking tour of Budapest, led by officials of the Hungarian Football Association. The spokesman and leader of the tour however, was a Russian Army Officer. He led us up a steep hillside just outside the hotel. At the summit of the hill, a statue of Russian soldiers had recently been erected. The army officer proudly showed us the statue. Russian soldiers supported the figure of a person holding aloft an olive leaf. The statue had been erected, we were told, to remind the Hungarian people it was the Russians who brought peace to Budapest. From the high vantage point, above the Danube, it was visible from most areas of Budapest. At night, the statue was floodlit. The Russian officers informed us it was to remind the Hungarians of the brave Russian soldiers who had given their lives setting free the Hungarian people from the tyranny of their own government. It was also explained to us that all the bridges across the Danube, which were clearly visible from the vantage point of the statue, were now in the process of being repaired by the voluntary labour of the Hungarian people. As he made this remark, I noticed one of the Hungarian Football Association officials smiling to himself. Later that evening, I enquired of the Hungarian official why he had smiled when the Russian officer said the bridges were being built by 'voluntary labour'.

"Ah well",

he said,

> "The Russians have a different interpretation of the word 'voluntary' to that of the Hungarians. Their meaning of the word is different to ours. In reality, when the war ceased, all the bridges needed to be rebuilt. At the end of each working day, all the able-bodied people of Budapest were ordered to report to the bridges. They worked on rebuilding the bridges until sunset. It was work for which no-one was paid. Because no-one was paid, the Russians believe the bridges were rebuilt by 'voluntary' labour!

After our escorted walking tour, Les Cocker and I explored the facilities within the Gellert Hotel. One of the hotel's outstanding facilities, we thought, was the outside swimming pool. The pool lay in a beautiful, terraced amphitheatre at the back of the hotel. We noticed ladies, dressed in nursing uniforms, placed at strategic places throughout the amphitheatre. The pool was extremely busy. We were told the pool was no longer an exclusive facility of the hotel, but was now a facility available to the general public, but only on the production of a doctor's certificate. Les and I visited the pool's waiting room area. There we saw people waiting patiently for their turn to be admitted to the pool. Many sat clutching their doctor's certificate. The thought of having a similar situation in England filled me with horror. General Practitioners in Britain were already required to provide too many certificates for their patients. The idea of having to provide a medical certificate for a swim in the public swimming baths did not bear contemplating!

In a very evenly fought game at the Nep Stadium, attended in the main by soldiers, we lost by two goals to one. After the game the England party were guests of the Hungarian Football Association at a banquet. The banquet finished well after midnight. Immediately the banquet finished, it was straight to bed for everyone. With no players injured, I had little work to do in Hungary. I did however learn of the workings of a country behind the Iron Curtain. We were due to leave the hotel at 0600hours the following morning en route for Israel. We would be flying all day, on three different airlines, via Vienna, and Istanbul. We were scheduled to arrive in Tel Aviv at 2105 hours on Thursday 14th. May. It would be a tedious and tiring day. The day was spent sitting in aircraft and waiting at the different airports. It was a relief when we tumbled into our beds, close on midnight, at the Ramat-Aviv Hotel in Tel Aviv. It had indeed been a tiring day! I had now flown on five different aircraft and there had been no crashes so far! I began to accept that flying was indeed a very safe way to travel.

Tel Aviv in May is hot. Even in the early morning it is hot. The temperature was high enough for our breakfast to be served in the hotel garden, under the shade of canopy tents. Even in the shade of the tents, it was still very hot. At mid morning, when we trained at the Hapoel Bloomfield Stadium, the heat was extreme. The temperature was close to one hundred degrees. Fortunately I had advised the players of the extreme heat and made them aware of the need to consume adequate quantities of fluid prior to the game. The increased fluid intake would compensate for the fluid lost with profuse sweating. A little more salt, taken with their food was also advised.

The match against Israel was played in the late afternoon. The temperature in the stadium, immediately prior to the game, measured one hundred and two degrees. The game was very physical. Some of the tackling, by the Israel players, was completely out of order. The England players coped well with the extreme heat and ran out easy winners by four goals to nil. The England players were delighted. Apart from several bruises, there were no serious injuries. After the game, we all attended another formal banquet provided by the Israeli Football Association. It was another late night. I found, as did the players, these post match banquets tedious, especially the long speeches by the various officials.

Most unusually, when on an England tour, the day following the international in Israel was a free day. John Harris decided all members of the party have the day off. The Israelis gave us several options as to how the day could be spent. Most of the players decided on a day at the beach. Les Cocker and I decided we would visit Jerusalem. The Israelis would provide Les and myself with a taxi for the journey. Unbeknown to us, the road journey involved travelling along 'The Road of Courage', so named in memory of all the Israelis who had been killed building this road to Jerusalem. The road, the taxi driver informed us, was extremely dangerous. Travellers were still, on occasions, subjected to sporadic sniper gunfire. On entering 'The Road of Courage', we noticed, at the side of the road, several burnt out lorries, trucks and tanks. These vehicles had all been destroyed, our driver informed us, by the Arabs firing from the high mountains on either side of the road. Throughout the "Road of Courage" the taxi travelled at an alarming speed. On occasions the speedometer recorded a speed above one hundred miles an hour. Les and I were relieved when we arrived in Jerusalem. The taxi came to a halt at the base of the Citadel. We were keen to climb the steps of The Citadel. The view from the top was well worth the climb. Although we were unable to visit the Golden Dome, due to the divided nature of the city, it was clearly visible as was The Mount of Olives. Apparently, word quickly spread that members of the England International Football Team were visiting The Citadel. An Israeli official approached us. We confirmed we

I BECOME A FOOTBALL CLUB DIRECTOR

were with the England Football Team. The official asked us to follow him. He led us up some stairs to a room securely locked. This room, he informed us, is believed by some to be the room where the last supper was held. He opened the door and led us in. The room bore no resemblance to the paintings I had seen of the last supper. The room was tiny. There was a small brick altar on one side of the room and a cylindrical stone pillar, otherwise the room was bare. We thanked the official for his kindness and left. We were both somewhat bewildered. We did not relish the thought of the taxi journey back to Tel Aviv. The taxi journey appeared more dangerous than flying! At least I would be able to tell the family I had been to Jerusalem and successfully travelled along the 'Road of Courage", twice in a day!

On every England tour, many of the country's Sports Writers accompany the official party. The Under 23 tours were no exception. The Football Correspondents always travelled on the same aircraft with us. However, they stayed at different hotels and travelled on different coaches to and from the airports. During this tour, I established good, trustworthy relationships with several of the nation's Sports Writers. Some of those relationships developed into genuine friendships. Some have lasted throughout my own life and theirs. On this tour, I developed lasting relationships with Ken Jones, Reg Drury, Frank McGhee, and Frank Taylor. It was no surprise therefore that, on Flight LY 331 from Tel Aviv to Istanbul, I found myself sitting next to Frank Taylor. It was just after 0730, when the pilot repeatedly revved the plane's engines at the end of the runway, immediately prior to take off. In a strange way, Frank's presence gave me a certain reassurance. Frank was a survivor of the Manchester United air crash at Munich. He suffered some horrendous injuries, the most significant of which affected one of his legs. As a result of those injuries, Frank wore a special shoe on his foot. Frank walked with a gait unique to Frank Taylor. As our plane hurtled down the runway on that warm May morning, I anticipated another safe take off. Half-way down the runway, the whole aircraft shook and shuddered. The pilot firmly applied the brakes. The plane slewed from side to side before coming to a standstill, close to the perimeter fence. After what appeared an inordinate length of time, the aircraft slowly taxied back to the start of the runway.

"That was like Munich all over again."
said Frank,
"No need to worry Doc."
he reassured me,
"We'll be O.K. next time."

The pilot revved the engines repeatedly, before setting off down the runway once more. This time we were O.K. and safely flew to Istanbul Airport where we arrived some two and a half hours later. Tuesday the 19th. May 1964 will however remain the day I, and many more, nearly came to grief on an aircraft. When Frank and I have met subsequently, over many years, we always recall our first attempt at taking off at Tel Aviv airport. The experience is deeply imprinted on our minds. At Istanbul, we stayed at the Hilton Hotel. From my bedroom, high up in the hotel, I had a wonderful view over the river Bosphorus. From my window, I witnessed the ferries travelling in minutes from Europe to Asia across that narrow stretch of river.

The football pitch at the Mithatpasa Stadium in Istanbul was a disgrace. John Harris was not happy. The pitch was grassless and very hard. The surface was deeply rutted in many places. John expressed his concern to the Turkish officials. There was undoubtedly a danger in playing on such a hard irregular surface. The Turks were unmoved by his complaints. The match was a disaster for England. Turkey won by three goals to nil. Inevitably there was an official banquet after the game. At the end of this banquet I began to understand what the managers, coaches and trainers had told me back at Lilleshall. They had criticised me for becoming a football club director. In Turkey, I began to understand why.

During the ten day tour the staff and players had seen little of the four Football Association officials. Of course, I had been formally introduced, at the beginning of the tour, to the Chairman, Ike Robinson, and the three directors Colonels Mitchell and Linnett and Squadron Leader Hadley. Since leaving London however our paths had hardly ever crossed. The officials rarely attended the training sessions; a role I believed was most impor-

I BECOME A FOOTBALL CLUB DIRECTOR

tant for them. They made their own arrangement for meals and spent their evenings away from the main party. Invariably they were being wined and dined by the officials of the host Football Associations. At the end of the Istanbul banquet however, I was drawn, at their request, into their circle. I can only assume it was my status as a director of Middlesbrough that drew me close to them. The Chairman, Ike Robinson, informed me, a serious error occurred during the Istanbul banquet, relating to the receiving of gifts from the host Association. Unbeknown to me, it was established by the four directors that at each banquet there would be five presents to be received by our directors from the host nations. The first present, the largest, would always be for The Football Association in London. The second present, and the next largest, at all three countries would be the personal gifts for the Chairman. At each of the banquets the third present would always be larger than the fourth and the fourth larger than the fifth. The three directors had agreed with the Chairman they would rotate in receiving the third, fourth and fifth presents during the tour. They had agreed apparently that Hadley would receive the third present in Hungary; Mitchell in Israel and Linnitt in Turkey. When the presentations were made at the Istanbul banquet it was Colonel Linnit's turn to receive the third present. Colonel Linnett had noticed however that Squadron Leader Hadley's present was larger than his. The view, expressed to me by the Chairman, Mitchell and Linnitt, was that Hadley had now received two of the larger presents while Linnitt had received two of the smaller ones. The Chairman and two directors had not mentioned this error to Hadley at the end of the banquet. Hadley had now retired to his bedroom. The Chairman then asked me to go to Hadley's bedroom and retrieve this third present from Hadley, and exchange it for the smaller present which then Linnitt handed to me. The Chairman explained it would be better if I visited Hadley in his bedroom because if one of The Football Association directors went to collect the present, an embarrassing situation might develop between the four officials. On the Chairman's instructions, I was designated to retrieve the present from Hadley's room. Standing at Hadley's door, I explained the situation to Hadley, who appeared as surprised as I was. He hadn't even noticed the size of the presents he informed me. Hadley happily exchanged the presents. Hadley gave me the large present. I exchanged it for the smaller one. Returning to the dining room, larger present in my hands, the F.A. Officials were greatly relieved. Linnit was pleased with his larger present. The Chairman was pleased with my efforts. My intervention avoided embarrassment between the four officials. Such was the main concern of the F.A. directors on tour! My job accomplished, I wondered if such tasks were included in my job description, but then I didn't have a job description!

There were no injuries after the Turkey game Every player reported a clean bill of health. Flight PA1 from Istanbul to Heathrow landed safely on Thursday 21st May at three in the afternoon. I travelled on the evening express train from Kings Cross to Darlington. Contrary to my fears, before leaving home, I arrived home safe and sound. My first England tour was completed.

I worked well with John Harris and Les Cocker throughout the tour. Although a doctor on tour with England was a new innovation, brought in by Alf Ramsey, I believed the players readily accepted me. I enjoyed being with them. It was in their company I felt at ease. During the tour I made lasting friendships, or perhaps better described as good acquaintances, with Mike Bailey, Terry Venables, Martin Chivers, Peter Bonnetti, Geoff Hurst and Alan Ball, which would last throughout my life. The Sports Writers had been most kind and co-operative. A doctor travelling with the England team was also a new experience for them. As a result of my first tour with England, I had developed life long relationships and friendships with some of the Sports Writers. Every player returned fit and well to their Clubs. Although, from a results point of view, the tour was not a great success, I was quite satisfied with the personal outcome of my first tour.

The summer of 1964, apart from my annual visit to Lilleshall for the Treatment of Injury Course, I spent with my family. I played little cricket. The cricket season was well under way when I returned from the England Under 23 tour. Redcar had another wicket keeper and a new Captain. I played only occasionally. There was much work to be done improving the medical care of the players at Middlesbrough. I wanted to provide them with the best possible medical care. With George Wright, appointed as our new Physiotherapist, I was confident it was a goal we would jointly achieve.

After a few weeks at home, I received a cheque from The Football Association for being the Honorary Team Physician on the Under 23 tour to Hungary, Israel and Turkey. In addition to my return rail fare from Redcar to London, the cheque was for £22. Although I had never been officially informed, apparently I was entitled to a daily allowance of two pounds a day, but only when abroad with the team. The players received a match fee of £20 and the reserves £10. The Football Association valued the players, who actually played, at £20 a game. For the medical care I provided for the entire party, over the eleven days of the tour, my services were valued at £22! In my discussions with Alf Ramsey no mention of remuneration had been raised and I sought none.

The Middlesbrough directors approached the 1964–65 season with some apprehension. The most senior directors persisted with their false optimism. They believed promotion for the team to Division One was a real possibility. The reality was quite different. The facts spoke for themselves. In the1962–63 season, Raich Carter's first season as Manager, the team had finished fourth. At the completion of the following season, Middlesbrough slipped to a mid table position. With Raich still believing that coaching and tactics were a waste of time, I could see no improvement occurring. All the Coaches and Managers I had met at Lilleshall passionately believed in coaching and tactics. Raich Carter was the odd man out.

It was during the 1964–65 season I first met Alf Ramsey. I received notification from The Football Association I had been appointed the Honorary Team Physician for the Under 23 game against Wales at Wrexham on the 4th. November; a game England won by three goals to two. During the team's three-day stay at Wrexham, Alf set aside two hours for a personal meeting with me; he wanted to discuss my role as he saw it. He assumed and expected I would provide a high quality of medical care for the players. He also wanted me involved in all the players' activities.

"Whatever the players do, and wherever they go, I want you to be there with them."

I was to attend all training sessions, and team meetings. My meals would always be taken with the players. I was to attend all the players' social functions. He trusted I would become, over time, just another member of the squad.

"Most of all, I suppose, I want you to become 'the players' friend.' I want them to be able to discuss matters with you they may not wish to discuss with me and the coaching staff. If you have any concerns, at any time, please do not hesitate to discuss them with me."

During our time at Wrexham, the differing contrasts in the approach of Alf Ramsey and Raich Carter, two players of the same era, was immediately obvious to me. At Alf's team meetings, the system of play he wished to adopt, was fully explained to the players. Every conceivable event that could possibly occur during a game he covered. He made each player aware of his individual responsibilities during the game. He discussed with them who would take free kicks, corner kicks and penalties. Players would know if they were to be part of the defensive wall or not. He decided which players would mark, in defence, the near and far posts. At our corner kicks, individual players would know who would attack the near post and who would position themselves at the far post. Additionally, he always spoke individually to the players during the training sessions. Those conversations always remained private between Alf and the player. He spoke at length of the way he expected the opposition to play. He addressed the individual strengths and weaknesses of each opposing player. He discussed the system he believed the opposition would play. Nothing was left to chance. His detail was unbelievable. Alf covered every aspect in his team meeting. During the training sessions, I was particularly impressed with his organisational and man management skills. I felt, as a doctor, privileged to listen to his expertise on professional football. His approach to the game was so different to that of our own manager at Middlesbrough. Raich Carter's philosophy to our players was always the same,

"There's the ball, now go out and play! Enjoy yourselves.
As the season progressed I enjoyed being associated with Alf Ramsey. He confirmed the views I had learnt from the many managers and coaches at Lilleshall. In contrast, at Middlesbrough, it turned out to be a disastrous season. They won only thirteen of their forty-two matches. The team finished sixth from bottom in Division Two; we had thirty-five points. Our points tally was only two points better than Swindon Town who were relegated. Oh how I wished the Middlesbrough players could have played to a system with the addition of proper coaching of their talents. Unfortunately Middlesbrough had a Manager who did not believe in such matters. It would have been completely unfair of me, if I made a sole comparison between Alf Ramsey and Raich Carter. I now worked for both managers, but my assessment was much broader than that. For three years, I had regularly attended courses at Lilleshall where, particularly in the evenings at the local pub, I had listened to innumerable managers and coaches discussing, with enthusiasm, the various playing systems and coaching techniques. I refused to believe they were all wrong and Raich Carter was right. As a consequence, Middlesbrough became a very unhappy place for me. I formed the opinion the Club's future prospects seemed quite bleak.

7

Triumph and Disaster............

As a Middlesbrough director, I approached the 1965–66 season, with fear and apprehension. As one of the five new directors, it was with much enthusiasm that I, and the other four, had initially set about the task of directing Middlesbrough back to the First Division. The five's initial enthusiasm, however, was frustrated by the team's performance and, more importantly, by the attitude of the senior directors. These directors believed promotion to Division One was always 'just around the corner.' They had been the members of the Board who had appointed Raich Carter as Manager, prior to the five newest directors–Kitching, myself, Varley, Amer and King–being appointed. They were desperate for Raich to succeed. Success for the team would vindicate them, in appointing Raich Carter as the Manager. Promotion to Division One, they believed, at the beginning of the 1965–66 season, was a distinct possibility. The facts however were stacked against such optimism. Past results stared them in the face; they were there for all to see. The senior directors however refused to believe the facts.

In the pre-season period, as an incentive to the players, the Chairman persuaded the Board to introduce, for the first time at Middlesbrough, a winning bonus system for the team. Eric Thomas believed the incentive of a financial reward would encourage the players to play better. I naively believed no player would be able to improve his game simply because he would earn an extra ten pounds. I always played sport to the best of my ability. Every game I played I wanted to be the best I could be. Money for me was not a factor. I failed to see how a player could play better if a ten pound bonus was dangled in front of him. Nevertheless, the Board agreed the Middlesbrough players would receive a £10 bonus for every point they obtained during the season. If the team won a game, in the days when there were two points for a win, a twenty pound bonus would be paid to each player. For a drawn game, the players would each received a ten pound bonus. In the three seasons of Raich Carter's management, the team had become progressively worse. In those three years in Division Two, the team had finished fourth, tenth, and seventeenth respectively. A schoolboy could have told the Board, on those performances, the team was becoming gradually and consistently worse. The senior directors refused to accept the reality of the situation. They seemed unable to accept the seriousness of the situation.

>"If the Manager does not believe in playing to a system, or improving the players by coaching, what can he do to improve the team's performance?"

I repeatedly asked.

For me, Ayresome Park became a depressing place! As the season progressed, it became apparent to me, as I visited the dressing room daily, the players had lost confidence in the Manager. I recall, immediately prior to one game, Raich Carter enquiring of Ian Gibson, the team captain, as he sat quietly in the dressing room,

>"What are you waiting for?"

>"The team talk, Boss."

Ian replied.

>"Don't be ridiculous. You never do what I tell you anyway. Just go out and play. Go and enjoy yourself!"

If Raich was still a player, that is exactly what he would have done. It was Raich's philosophy. The greatest pleasure in his life, he often told me, was playing in a game of football. His talent, as a player, was exceptional. Everything came so easily to him. He could never understand any player who wanted to make the game more difficult or complicated by playing to a system or undergoing individual coaching.

Middlesbrough's disastrous start to the season, forced the senior directors into some action. The senior directors reluctantly accepted that their Manager, the manager they had appointed, did not believe in coaching players. After much deliberation, the directors, who exerted considerable pressure on Raich Carter, decided to purchase Stan Anderson from Newcastle United and appoint him as the Player-Coach. Left to himself, I am sure Raich would not have agreed to this appointment. How could he? He didn't believe in coaching. In my opinion, Raich just went along with the directors' idea. Three months into the season, Stan Anderson was transferred from Newcastle to Middlesbrough. He was immediately appointed Club Captain and the Club's Coach. At Stan Anderson's request, Ian Gibson remained the Team Captain on the field of play.

On arriving at Middlesbrough, Stan became the only player to captain all three north-east sides—Middlesbrough, Sunderland and Newcastle. With Raich continuing as Manager, Stan's role was, in my opinion, impossible. In fact his appointment was ridiculous. How could Raich and the Board agree to appoint anyone as a Coach when everyone knew the Manager didn't believe in coaching! I questioned my fellow directors repeatedly regarding Stan's appointment as Coach. In appointing Stan Anderson as the Coach, the directors had given him an impossible task.

In contrast with the frustration I experienced at Middlesbrough, my involvement with the England Under Twenty-three team throughout the 1965–66 season flourished. I was involved with the team at eight internationals, all under the management of Alf Ramsey. The Under Twenty-three team was very successful. Only one game was lost, against West Germany, at Frieburg on the summer tour. The team played four home games against Scotland at Aberdeen; Czechoslovakia at Leeds; France at Norwich and Yugoslavia at Southampton.. On the summer tour they played West Germany at Frieberg, Czechoslovakia at Liberec, and Austria in Vienna. It was a busy season for the Under Twenty-three Team, as Alf Ramsey was determined to use these matches as part of his preparation for the 1966 World Cup. With Ramsey's encouragement, I became a full participant in preparing the England team for the 1966 World Cup tournament. At every international match, I spent three days with the team, enabling me to build an excellent working relationship with Alf, Les Cocker, the trainer from Leeds United and most importantly the players. With Alf insisting I was to be 'just another member of the squad', I became well know to the players. I joined in all their activities. My relationship with each individual player improved as the season progressed.

At the end of the season England would host the World Cup Competition. It was the first occasion the tournament would be held in England. During July 1966, the best football teams in the world would play in England for the Jules Rimet trophy. As hosts, England automatically qualified. It was a tournament Alf Ramsey had publicly stated England would win. Alf involved me totally in the build up for the competition. In particular he involved me totally in the pre tournament preparation which was to take place at Lilleshall. The chosen squad of players would spend two weeks at Lilleshall, carrying out extensive training. We worked on the most minute detail of the training programme.

"People may say we are not be the best team in the Competition,
but I want to ensure we are the fittest."
he told me.

He kept telling me I was very much a part of England's preparation. Although Alan Bass was the Senior Team Physician, Alf knew it was quite impossible for Alan to be present with the team throughout the whole competition. I was nominated by Alf to be the deputy. It was quite likely I would be put in charge medically of the players for their two week's training at Lilleshall. As a result of hosting the World Cup tournament, there would be no Under 23 tour at the end of the 1965–66 season. In fact, there was only one Under 23 international in 1966. That solitary match would be at Blackburn in April. The opponents would be Turkey. From my own personal point of view, with only one Under 23 game to look forward to, the forthcoming season appeared bleak. Middlesbrough's prospects were, in my opinion, poor. Similar to the majority of football supporters, I resigned myself to watching the World Cup games on television. Of course there would be World Cup games to watch in the North-east of England. Much to the annoyance of my fellow directors, The Football Association choose Sunderland and Newcastle as the venues. Middlesbrough were left out in the cold!

As I had predicted, Middlesbrough's season began badly and became worse. Matters were further complicated for Middlesbrough when, through no fault of their own, Newcastle United were forced to withdraw as a venue for the World Cup matches. Newcastle United was having difficulties with their City Corporation, regarding the lease of their ground. With the withdrawal of Newcastle as a World Cup venue, The Football Association appointed Middlesbrough as the replacement. Newcastle's loss was Middlesbrough's gain. Sunderland and Middlesbrough would now be the venues in the north-east for the World Cup games.

The Middlesbrough directors were delighted. Ayresome Park was to be a World Cup venue. Sadly Middlesbrough had been, of necessity, chosen some twelve months later than all the other venues. To improve Middlesbrough's ground, to the required standard for the World Cup, a tremendous amount of work needed to be done and there was so little time left before the competition commenced. Work began immediately at Middlesbrough following the announcement that matches were to be staged there. Inevitably, the ground, throughout the remainder of the playing season, became a building site. A subcommittee of three directors was formed to deal with the ground improvement scheme. It consisted of the Chairman, Eric Thomas, and two directors, Charles Amer and Ernest Varley. With generous financial assistance from The Football Association, these three directors worked tirelessly ensuring all the ground improvements were completed on time. The trio succeeded in the very difficult task they were given. I seized on some of the financial assistance given to the Club by The Football Association. I requested the building of a medical centre at the ground. With the pressure of the impending World Cup, my request was immediately granted. In the space of a few months, a new medical facility was built adjacent to the home dressing room. The medical centre consisted of an emergency medical room, a private consulting room and separate treatment area, together with a remedial gymnasium. In 1966, the building of such a medical centre at a football ground was considered quite revolutionary. To my surprise, the development warranted a request from The Football Association that I write an article on its development for The Football Association News. It was suggested to me the development could become one for other Clubs to follow.

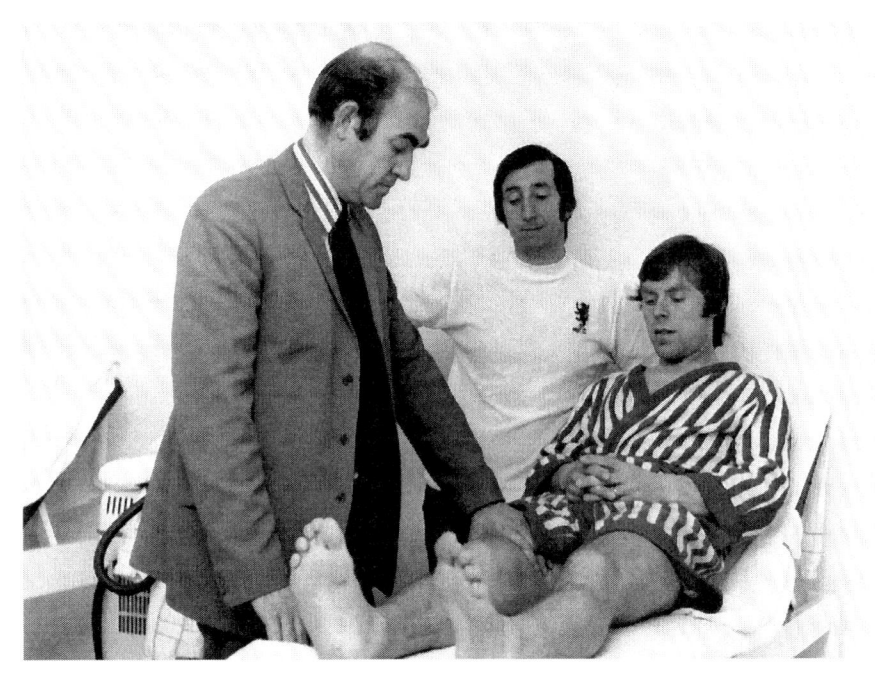

"Examining Frank Spraggon in the New Medical Centre"

With the hurly burly of the ground developments, there is no doubt, the Middlesbrough directors took their eye off their main responsibility, namely the performance of their own team. When January arrived, there was a real danger of relegation to the Third Division. Even the senior directors, the ones who had appointed Raich Carter manager, now realised the seriousness of the situation. The players had lost confidence in the Manager. Stan Anderson's role as player, Club Captain and Coach had proved impossible. Stan had been given some authority, but had no overall responsibility. The Manager had no belief in coaching. Stan tried to achieve an improvement in the team's performance with coaching, but the Manager did not believe in what he was doing. The team were demoralised and their performance was on an uncontrollable downward slide. A crisis meeting of the directors was called. The Board unanimously decided to immediately terminate Raich Carter's contract as Manager. It was a sad day for the Club.

The obvious immediate replacement as Manager, from within the Club, was Harold Shepherdson. The senior directors however were opposed to such an appointment. They were prejudiced against Harold. They used the excuse that his involvement as Trainer with the England team, in the build up for the World Cup, precluded him from being appointed. The view was expressed that Harold would be fully involved with the preparation of the England team for the World Cup, and would be unable to devote the necessary time to Middlesbrough's predicament. With three directors actively involved with the ground developments, the Board decided on an astonishing solution. They decided not to appoint any one person in charge of the team! The Club would be run without a Manager! The Board decided that all playing and team matters would be placed in the hands of a four-man committee! The committee, the directors decided, would consist of Harold Shepherdson, Stan Anderson, and two directors–Geoff Wood and myself. This committee would be responsible for all playing matters, including the selection of all the teams playing in the Club's matches. In managing people, it is my opinion, committees never work. This committee was no exception. The Board had given the four members of the committee the responsibility, but no individual on the committee had absolute authority. The result was disastrous. With Stan Anderson still playing, it was impossible for him to have responsibility for disciplinary matters involving the other players. The players were confused, as no one individual had authority over them. When this arrangement began, I told Harold and Stan they should select the team. I would always agree with their choice. Throughout the remainder of the season, Harold and Stan selected the team. They presented their selected team to Geoff Wood and myself. We always agreed with their selection. Unfortunately the issue of discipline was not so easily resolved. At the request of the other three, I became the person responsible for disciplinary matters. It was a role for which I was frequently criticised in the national press! The team, now under the direction of the committee, continued to play and perform badly. At the beginning of April, Middlesbrough's relegation to Division Three became more of a probability than a possibility. The whole disciplinary situation exploded in my face as the Club approached crucial relegation matches. I received a call from the Cleveland Police in the middle of the night. Such a call was not unusual for me as I was for a time a Police Surgeon locally. It was three o'clock on a Saturday morning and we were playing a vital game at home later in the day. I was informed that a Middlesbrough player was in custody on a drunk and disorderly charge. The player, who had been selected to play for the Club's first team, later in the day, had requested my presence. Having been assured by the policeman the player was not in any medical danger, I refused to attend. Later in the morning, I informed both Stan Anderson and Harold Shepherdson of what had happened. The player was replaced in the team for the home game later in the day. He did not play for Middlesbrough again.

It was somewhat of a relief, from the serious situation at Middlesbrough, when I received a letter from The Football Association inviting me to attend, as Honorary Team Physician, the Under 23 game at Blackburn against Turkey. I spent three days in the company of the England players and Alf Ramsey. It was such a refreshing change from the depressing atmosphere at Middlesbrough. During my eighteen months involvement at Under 23 level, Alf and I had developed an excellent personal working relationship. It was a joy to work with Alf. His football knowledge, enthusiasm, organisational skills, man management, and above all his integrity and honesty were qualities I admired. How I wished I could take some of them, even a small amount, back to Middlesbrough. Alas, it was not possible. It was at Blackburn Alf informed me he definitely wanted me involved with the full England team during the World Cup tournament. Apparently, Alan Bass, the senior doctor, was experiencing difficulty obtaining release from his consultant role at St. Mary's Hospital in

London. Alan had obtained leave for the pre-tournament European tour and the World Cup itself. He had informed Alf he was definitely unavailable for the two weeks of training arranged for Lilleshall from the 6th. to the 17th. June. Alf requested I provide the medical care for this two-week period. He wanted me to live with the players during those two weeks and be 'just another member of the squad'. I was excited by his invitation. I assured him I would discuss the matter with my wife and partners and, subject to their agreement, I would be available. As I retired to my hotel bedroom at Blackburn, my mind kept repeating,

"Me, Doctor to the full England International Football Team. I just can't believe it!"

It might only be for two weeks, but it was still unbelievable! How I wished I could have phoned my Dad. He would have been so pleased and proud. England beat Turkey by two goals to nil at Blackburn. On returning home, my partners were happy for me to spend two weeks at Lilleshall, provided I counted the two weeks as part of my five-week holiday entitlement. Margaret readily agreed to the family missing out on two weeks holiday with me. Her support for my involvement with England was exceptional. We agreed, while I spent the two weeks at Lilleshall, she would take the three children to Southport for a holiday. The family, minus Dad, would have two weeks at the seaside.

Middlesbrough continued playing badly. The committee idea just did not work. The last match of the season was an away game at Cardiff's Ninian Park. Cardiff, managed at the time by Jimmy Scoular, was also in danger of relegation. They were in exactly the same situation as Middlesbrough. Both Cardiff and Middlesbrough needed a win in this, the last match of the season to avoid the dreaded relegation into the Third Division. The committee decided to gamble with the team selection. Dickie Rooks, one of our centre-halves, was selected to play as a bustling centre-forward. It was a gamble that nearly worked. Dickie Rooks scored a hat trick. The team however lost the match five goals to three. Middlesbrough was relegated to Division Three for the first time in its one hundred-year history. Cardiff City, as a result of winning the game against Middlesbrough, remained in Division Two. Middlesbrough was relegated with thirty-three points. Due to the introduction of the Chairman's new bonus system, the Club paid each player bonuses of three hundred and thirty pounds. A bonus for being abject failures! Bonuses paid for achieving relegation! So much for the belief that players would play better if they were awarded ten pounds for each point they achieved during the season!

I, like most people in Middlesbrough, was absolutely devastated. The following week, circular head and shoulder photographs of all the Middlesbrough directors were individually portrayed on the front page of Middlesbrough's local newspaper. The heading, above the directors' photographs, was 'The Guilty Men'. We were portrayed as criminals. In the eyes of many, that is exactly what we were. As a Board of Directors we had turned out to be a disastrous failure. It was a very sad day for Middlesbrough Football Club.

The nineteen hundred and sixty-six World Cup draw did little to lift the despair of relegation at Middlesbrough. The four teams allocated to play their matches in the north-east were Chile, Italy, Russia and the totally unknown North Korean team. Three matches would be played at Middlesbrough. All three games would involve the North Koreans. They would play all their matches at Middlesbrough. Chile, Italy and Russia would each visit our ground only once, and that when they played their game against North Korea. With Koreans being completely unknown as a footballing nation, the proposed fixtures at Middlesbrough were hardly exciting. It did however give the Middlesbrough public the opportunity to adopt the North Koreans as their home team. This they did with great enthusiasm.

As the preparations continued for the tournament at Middlesbrough, I received a letter from The Football Association. The letter certainly lightened the personal gloom and despair I experienced with Middlesbrough's relegation to the Third Division. The letter, dated the 10th. May 1966 informed me of my selection to be a member of The England World Cup Squad.

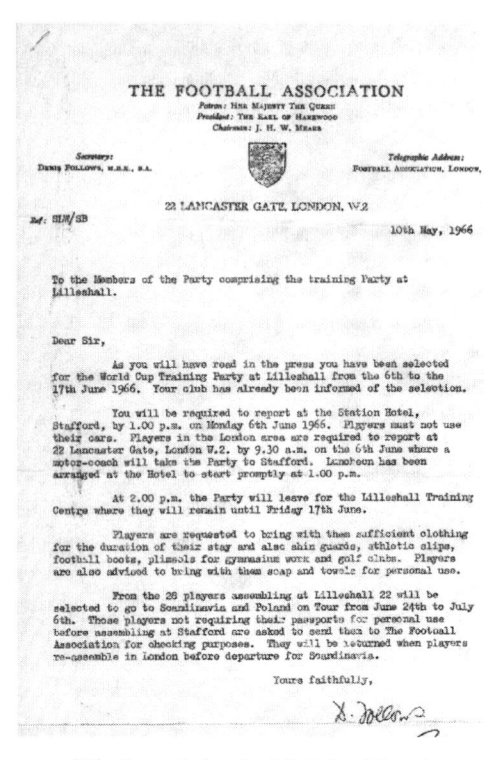

"The Letter Informing Me I Am Selected
For The 1966 World Cup Squad."

There it was in black and white. I really was going to be 'Doctor to the England International Football Team.' It would only be for two weeks, but what an honour and what a thrill! My feeling was similar to when I had received the first letter from Glamorgan County Cricket Club fourteen years previously. Then I had been selected to play for their second eleven. This time however my excitement and pleasure was ten fold. I would keep the letter forever.

The Football Association now gave Alan Bass, the England team's senior doctor, the arduous task of ensuring medical services were readily available at all the regional centres where World Cup games were to be played. All visiting teams needed to be assured they would be provided with adequate, and immediate medical, surgical and hospital facilities as required. Each visiting team required a written list of all the relevant medical specialists and hospitals prepared to provide such a service. Every region would have an appointed 'Regional Medical Advisor' who would liase with the visiting Team Doctors. Alan requested I be responsible for carrying out this organisational work for the four teams playing in the north-east. Working closely with Dr. Scott of Sunderland, it was a task quickly accomplished. We both provided the four Team Doctors with a list of the hospitals and consultants we regularly used during the season at Sunderland and Middlesbrough. All these consultants agreed to provide their services for free.

With the north-east organised, from a medical point of view, I travelled to Lilleshall by car accompanied by my family. I deposited my wife and three children at The Griffin Hotel on the sea front at Southport. They would have two weeks holiday at Southport, while I worked with the England team at Lilleshall. The England staff consisted of Alf Ramsey, Harold Shepherdson, Les Cocker, Wilf McGuiness of Manchester United, and myself. There were twenty-seven players in the party. They all reported fit, with the exception of Ray Wilson who had 'a stiff back'. The whole estate and facilities of Lilleshall were available for the exclusive use of the England party. As always, the grounds, playing pitches and gardens were absolutely beautiful. Lilleshall was the ideal place as a training camp. Two weeks hard work would take place here. Whilst Alf Ramsey and I had frequently discussed together the fourteen day training programme to be implemented, I received no instructions from Alan Bass, regarding the medical programme to be carried out with the players. Apparently, at the last get together of the senior England team in May, when England beat Yugoslavia at Wembley by two goals to nil, the only medical decision taken was that while at Lilleshall, there would be a daily weighing of the players and an inspection of their feet! Apart from that, no medical programme had been decided upon. An even bigger surprise for me occurred when, on arrival at Lilleshall, I discovered we had no medical supplies with us; not even a roll of Elastoplast! The only medical supplies available were those in my own personal medical bag. The bag I used as a General Practitioner in Redcar!.

I assumed, quite wrongly of course, that The Football Association would have a standard case, or rather cases, full of medical equipment for the team's use. Alas I was wrong. There was absolutely nothing! My first morning, with the full England team at Lilleshall, was spent at a chemist's shop, in nearby Newport. It was there I purchased the necessary medical supplies for the party's two-week stay. The chemist was delighted with my bulk purchases. Nothing had been provided by The Football Association for the players. Such was the medical care of the players at the time. Apart from two afternoons, set aside for press, radio and television interviews, all our training was carried out in private. Alf, Harold, Les and Wilf McGuiness and myself had drawn up with Alf, a detailed training programme for each day of the two weeks. I recall Alf telling the players at the first team meeting, what he had often told me in the previous twelve months.

> "We may not be the best team in the world, but I assure you when we finish our preparation and training here, we will be the fittest."

Alf's organisational skills at Lilleshall were exceptional. In addition to the organised programme of training and coaching, he divided the players into four teams. The teams competed against each other at games of lawn tennis, badminton, mini golf, table tennis and snooker during the two-week period. Prizes would be awarded to the members of the winning team. Competition in these activities was intense and extremely competitive. Sadly, out of the twenty-seven players at Lilleshall, five would be told at the end of the two weeks, they were not selected in the final twenty-two players for the competition proper. Those five players would return home. The selected twenty-two players would leave on a pre-tournament European tour to Finland, Norway, Denmark and Poland. In addition to the five unselected players, Wilf McGuiness and I would also be returning home.

With twenty-seven players competing for twenty-two places, it was unlikely any player would report an injury during our stay at Lilleshall. Every player wanted to be in the final selection of twenty-two players. An injury would seriously lessen their chances of selection. In the two-week stay at Lilleshall, no one reported any injuries. Ray Wilson's stiff back was the only condition requiring treatment. In addition to the usual remedial back exercises, I carried out with Ray, he and I spent some time swimming and exercising in the indoor heated pool at neighbouring R.A.F. Cosforth. With treatment, Ray quickly improved. I was grateful to the R.A.F. for allowing me to use their facility. Apart from the routine early morning weighing and medical inspections, most of my time at Lilleshall was spent with the staff and players in their training programme. Specifically, I was given a role by Alf to carefully observe the players during training and report to him any suspicion I had of any player having an injury. I had none to report.

The only adverse report I made, during the two weeks, concerned Alan Ball and Nobby Stiles. In the early evening on one occasion, I strolled down alone to the football pitches to practice my golf. While practicing, I noticed Nobby and Alan, both of whom I knew very well from the Under 23 team, breaking camp and walking to the Lilleshall Golf Club for an early evening beverage. It was a place Alf had ruled out of bounds to the players. When I reported the incident to Alf, he was annoyed. A quiet personal warning to Alan and Nobby by Alf was all that was required. They never ventured to the Golf Club again. I recall, with some personal amusement, and also some guilt, when Alan and Nobby told me of their personal reprimand from Alf. Neither player could explain how Alf had found out about their visit to the Golf Club and I chose not to tell them!

On our last day at Lilleshall, the final twenty-two players were selected by Alf for the tournament proper. Alf, personally and privately, informed the five players who were not selected. The five players to return home were 'Budgie' Byrne (West Ham), Bobby Tambling (Chelsea), Peter Thompson (Liverpool), Gordon Milne (Coventry) and Keith Newton (Blackburn Rovers). Alf took Wilf McGuiness and me aside, before we left, for our personal chat. He thanked us both for the contribution we had made and said,

> "I shall send for you both when we get to the final stages of the World Cup. At Lilleshall, you have both made significant contributions to the team's preparations. You, doctor,

have been involved in the preparation of the team for the past three years. I am most grateful to you both. I want you both to share in the team's success, so I'll see you at the final."

There were no ifs and buts. Alf had spoken. He had told us,

"I shall send for you both when we get to the final stages of the competition."

There was no doubt in Alf's mind. He emphasised 'when' we get to the final stages. Such was the firm conviction of the England Manager. Alf, Harold, Les and the twenty-two selected players left for their homes prior to joining up again in London for their European tour. I returned to Southport. I collected Margaret and three children from their two-week holiday at the seaside. The family had enjoyed their holiday. I also had experienced a great time. The contrast between working for England and Middlesbrough was unbelievable. I would return to Middlesbrough—now a Third Division side—to officiate at the World Cup matches in the north-east.

George Wright, Middlesbrough's physiotherapist, was given a new appointment for the World Cup tournament in the north-east. He was appointed Liaison Officer to the North Korean Football Team. He would live with the North Koreans at the Teesside Airport Hotel for the duration of their stay in the north-east. Thereby hangs an interesting tale!

The North Koreans arrived in England, accompanied by innumerable crates of their special brand of 'Ginseng'. I recall at every game, played at Middlesbrough, the home directors were always encouraged to sample this drink. The bottles had, what resembled, a diseased carrot suspended in the fluid. At their first hotel dinner, where introductions were the order of the day, George was asked if he was married and if so for how long. George replied,

"I've been very happily married for over twenty years."

"How many children do you have?"

enquired the North Koreans.

"None."

was George's reply.

"None!"

the North Koreans exclaimed,

"None! You must drink our Ginseng!"

George's delightful wife, Margaret, was a career girl. She had a very responsible post with a furniture firm in Redcar. George was plied with Ginseng at every opportunity by the North Koreans during their two week stay. Every time George sat down for a meal, he was encouraged to drink Ginseng. When the North Koreans eventually left the north-east, George was relieved his daily consumption of Ginseng was at an end. Exactly nine months later George Wright was blessed with the birth of Christopher, his son. So much for the power of North Korean Ginseng!

The gloom surrounding everyone at the Middlesbrough Football Club was certainly lifted by the performance of the North Koreans. No one knew very much about the North Koreans prior to the World Cup tournament. Following their first World Cup game at Ayresome Park, against the U.S.S.R., which they lost by three goals to nil, nothing much was really expected of them. The Russians, who dominated the game throughout, were easy winners. As the underdogs however, the people of Middlesbrough took the Koreans to their hearts. Although heavily defeated, the Koreans left the field to rapturous applause. Their second game was against Chile. The support the Koreans received from the Middlesbrough crowd was phenomenal. Losing one nil, with two minutes of the game against Chile remaining, Pak Seung Zin scored the goal ensuring the Koreans a creditable draw. The Middlesbrough crowd was delighted. The Koreans third game at Middlesbrough was against Italy. It seemed a mere formality the Italians would win. Class would tell. The enthusiasm of the Korean players, supported by the Middlesbrough crowd, could not possibly match the talent of the Italians. Although Italy lost one nil to Russia at Sunderland, it was inconceivable Italy would lose to North Korea. With Rivera, Mazzola, Facchetti and Bulgarelli in the Italian side, talent would obviously win the day. Italy rested Salvadore. For Italy, calamity struck after thirty minutes. Bulgarelli was stretchered off with severe damage to his knee ligaments. With no substitutes allowed, Italy would play the remainder of the game with ten men. The Koreans became inspired. The Italians became dejected and demoralised. Seven minutes after Bulgarelli had been stretchered off, Pak Doo Ik scored the only goal of the game. The Middlesbrough crowd roared the Koreans on. When the final whistle sounded, one would have thought Middlesbrough had won the league! The reality was Middlesbrough had been relegated to the Third Division. The Koreans would move to Goodison Park to play Portugal.

I did not see Pak Doo Ik score his goal. Stan Anderson, the Middlesbrough Coach and I were on hand in the Italian dressing room, ready to assist the Italian medical staff involved with Bulgarelli. When it became obvious Bulgarelli's injury was too severe for him to return to the field of play, all the Italian medical team burst into tears, fell to the floor and sobbed. I remarked to Stan Anderson,

"If the pressure ever gets to me like that Stan, insist I retire!"

During the regional games I saw all the other three qualifying matches at Sunderland. Italy beat Chile two nil; Russia beat Italy one nil; and finally Chile lost to Russia two one. Incredibly the two teams qualifying for the quarterfinals from the North-east would be Russia and the previously unknown North Koreans. While the Koreans would lose their quarter final 5–3 against Portugal, I watched Russia beat Hungary in the other quarterfinal at Sunderland. None of the games, apart from the enthusiasm given to the North Koreans at Middlesbrough, were of a very high standard. With England also qualifying for the quarter finals, it was reassuring to know I had seen nothing for the England team to fear from the five teams I had seen playing in the north-east.

England won their quarter final game against Argentina by a single goal, scored by Geoff Hurst. England would now play Portugal in the semi final. The phone rang at home,

> "Doctor, it's Alf Ramsey. I'd like you to join us for the final stages of the competition. We have a room available for you at the Hendon Hall Hotel. I've also invited Wilf McGuiness. When we later get to the final, I'd like your wife to travel to London and join in the celebrations with the players' and staff's wives. Let The Football Association know when you

are arriving. I shall look forward to seeing you."

I thought, what an amazing man! It was now seven weeks since I had left the England party at Lilleshall. Alf had told Wilf McGuiness and myself then, he would send for us "when we get to the final stages". Despite all the pressures he had been under during the tournament, he had remembered us. I was to be a member of the England party at the World Cup Finals. I was to rejoin the team.

I always enjoyed playing sport. At various times in my life, I competed, with moderate success, in athletics, tennis, fives, squash, golf, bowls, soccer, rugby and my beloved cricket. My Dad instilled in me the view that winning was not important. He always said,

"It's the taking part that's important."

I disagreed. I always enjoyed taking part, but it was the winning that gave me the greatest pleasure. When playing any sport winning was all-important to me. I fully participated in Middlesbrough's disastrous relegation season to the Third Division. Whilst not a player, my involvement in the Club's failure brought me no pleasure whatsoever. I had not enjoyed the taking part. On the other hand, I was now to be an integral part, albeit a small part, of England's success in the World Cup. England's success would give me the ultimate sporting pleasure. Success in sport for me was paramount.

I travelled alone to London by train. Accommodation, Alf had said, would be available for me at The Hendon Hall Hotel. Margaret would travel to London on the morning of the final. Throughout my rail journey to London, I reflected on my five-year journey in football. The journey initially started because I could not secure a place in the Redcar Cricket Team. That first hot summer in Redcar, I was miserable. There was no regular game of cricket for me. My wife encouraged me to buy a season ticket at Middlesbrough. There I met Bob Dennison and Harold Shepherdson, who befriended and encouraged me to become more involved in professional football. They involved me in every aspect of the game. Subsequently there was the emergency medical call, received in March 1961, to treat Budgie Byrne at Saltburn prior to the Under 23 game against Scotland at

Middlesbrough.

"If the sister or nurses request you to visit-always visit."

Blacow Yates taught me. I readily accepted the call. My successful treatment of 'Budgie' led Walter Winterbottom to invite me to attend the Football Association's Treatment of Injury Course at Lilleshall. That initial visit, together with the report I submitted to Walter, led to my yearly involvement at Lilleshall. There I enjoyed so many happy hours in the company of managers, trainers and coaches. I learnt so much about the professional game from them. Later Eric Thomas invited me to become a director at Middlesbrough Football Club, and subsequently the Club's Medical Officer. Eric had said,

"We don't need your money, we need your brains,"

To date, Middlesbrough had used very little of my brain. My appointment as Honorary Team Physician to the England Under 23 team quickly followed. My recent role had been preparing the England team at their two week World Cup training camp at Lilleshall. This gave me a close involvement with the England team. My five-year journey was beyond my wildest dreams. The England Manager had now invited me to be part of the England team for the final stages of the World Cup competition. I had been on an unbelievable journey! My only regret was my Dad did not share the journey with me.

When I arrived at The Hendon Hall Hotel, Alf was delighted to see me.

"I'm so pleased you could come."

he said.

"Since you've been looking after the Under 23s, you have been so much a part of England's success. I wanted you here to share in, what I believe will be our ultimate success."

Of course there was the small matter of a semi-final match against Portugal to overcome. The Portuguese were the best side, I had seen, in the tournament, albeit on a television screen. Their quarter final at Everton against the North Koreans had been one of the most bizarre games of the competition. In the first half, the North Koreans were ahead after just sixty seconds. Pak Seung Zin was the scorer. Within the first half hour, two more goals were scored for the Koreans by Li Dong Woon and Yang Sung Kook. Portugal were three goals down. Everyone was stunned. It was Eusebio, the genius of the Portuguese side, who responded. He refused to accept defeat He scored a superb goal which completely rattled the confidence of the North Koreans. Panic set in amongst the inexperienced Koreans. As half-time approached Torres, the Portuguese giant centre-forward, was felled in the penalty area. Eusebio took the penalty and scored. The half-time score was 3–2. Early in the second half, Eusebio received a pass from Simoes and scored his third goal of the match to level the scores. The Koreans became desperate. Within minutes, as he weaved his way passed several defenders into the Korean penalty area, Eusebio was felled by a frustrated Korean defender. Eusebio scored his second penalty of the game. Portugal won the game 4–3. Eusebio had scored all four goals. Portugal would now meet England, at Wembley, in the semi-final.

The semi-final game against Portugal was one of high quality. Played in an atmosphere of great sportsmanship, it was probably the best game of the whole competition. In the semi-final, both England and Portugal played football of the highest quality. Fouls were non-existent in the game. It was well into the second half before any England player committed a foul. The England defence was superb. Nobby Stiles, in particular, completely obliterated the danger of Eusebio. His fellow Manchester United player, Bobby Charlton, was in magnificent form. Some fifteen minutes before half time Pereira, the Portuguese goalkeeper, in attempting a save, slid the ball with his feet into the path of Bobby Charlton. Bobby scored England's first goal. It was the seventy-ninth minute of the game when England scored their second goal. Geoff Hurst broke clear on the right. He made a superb pass into the path of Bobby Charlton. Bobby's superb strike gave the goalkeeper no chance. England were two up. The last ten minutes of the game were tense. Jack Charlton gave away a penalty for handball, with just eight minutes remaining. Eusebio, who else, scored with the spot kick. England were worthy winners in what many observers believed was the best game of the tournament. It is interesting to note that Eusebio's penalty was the first goal England conceded in the tournament. Gordon Banks, and the back four of Wilson, Moore, Charlton and Cohen were superb. Nobby Stiles' extinction of Eusebio was magnificent. Wembley was ecstatic. The supporters sang, danced, waved flags and embraced one another. The players embraced and hugged each other. There was such a feeling of relief. All the hard work, carried out in the England camp over the previous three and a half years, had almost come to fruition. England was in the World Cup final, just as Alf Ramsey had told us at Lilleshall. For England, a World Cup Final, against Germany, now beckoned.

Ramsey's man-management always impressed me. He had the knack of making you feel, when he spoke with you, no one else in the world mattered. For those moments you, and you alone, were the most important person in his world. Although I had been away for a few weeks, he immediately integrated me into his England family. It was as if I had never been away. In every sense he made me feel I was an integral part of the squad.

With the passage of time, the mind plays tricks with reality. It is however a fact that in the World Cup Final of 1966, no substitutes were allowed. This presented Alan Bass and myself with a major problem. The only medical facilities for the players at Wembley stadium lay on a table in the home dressing room. The home dressing room was behind one of the goals, and at the furthest away point from the field of play. It was at the end of a long tunnel. Ideally a medical room should be available on the half-way line. Alan and I debated the problem at length. What would we do if an England player was injured in the final at the furthermost point away from the dressing room? Suppose the player required some stitches to a lacerated wound. To take the player the full length of the field, down the tunnel to the dressing room would take several minutes. The stitching procedure, and the return from the dressing room to the field of play, would result in the player being absent from the game for a considerable time. We both agreed the time taken for such a simple procedure would be too long. Alan and I decided, the doctor would take the stitching kit with him onto the bench. The doctor would then be able to stitch the player's wound on the touchline. Millions watching on television would witness the procedure, but that was the policy we agreed upon.

Played at the end of July, the day of the final was warm, but interspersed with frequent heavy showers. It was unbelievable, on such a momentous footballing day, I was strolling, immediately before the final, on Wembley's hallowed turf with the England players. It was a long, long way from the Red Ground in Tredegar covered as it was with red iron ore shale. The reception from the crowded stadium was awesome. Flags waved; player's names were chanted; songs were sung and there was a wonderful carnival atmosphere. The crowd was full of expectations. Throughout the final I sat alongside Wilf McGuiness. At football matches, whether with Middlesbrough or England, my emotions were always well under control. The World Cup Final however was different. I experienced more differing extremes of emotions, during that game, than at any other football match I had attended. Outwardly, I showed no emotion, but inwardly my mind and body were in turmoil. When Germany scored their first goal after thirteen minutes through Haller, I was depressed. It was the first occasion, in the whole tournament, the England team had been a goal down. I suddenly realised that all the work, I had been involved in with Alf, might, after all, be unproductive. My deep depression lasted just six minutes. Bobby Moore, having been fouled by Overath, immediately floated a beautiful thirty yard free kick directly onto Geoff Hurst's head. Geoff made no mistake and England levelled the score at 1–1. The score remained the same at half-time. My depression was followed by a long period of anxiety. It lasted throughout most of the second half. There was only ten minutes of the game remaining, when Alan Ball, who I had helped nurture through his Under 23 career, won a corner. Ballie took the corner which was headed free by a German defender straight to Geoff Hurst. Geoff's shot was deflected by a defender into the path of Martin Peters. Martin's shot hit the back of the net. England were leading Germany 2–1, with ten minutes remaining. My prolonged anxiety was replaced by joy and wondrous elation. Much has been written about the German equaliser, scored with only one minute of the game remaining. Jack Charlton certainly gave a free kick away as he climbed up over Held, though many thought the referee's decision harsh.

From the German free kick it appeared, that as the ball shot across the penalty area, it was handled by Schnellinger. Instinctively Bobby Moore raised his hand to the referee, indicating handball. The ball ran free and Weber toe poked it past Gordon Banks levelling the score at 2–2. The final whistle blew immediately. My mood returned to one of abject dismay and utter depression. It was twelve minutes of utter despair in extra time before my depression was again lifted. Nobby Stiles made a long raking pass out to Alan Ball. Alan, with his socks rolled down, raced towards the corner flag before crossing to Geoff Hurst. Geoff had his back to the goal, but managed to control the ball before swivelling and instantly hammering his shot against the crossbar and down onto or inside the goal line. At such a crucial time it was, to say the least, unfortunate the referee was unsure as to whether the ball had crossed the goal line. A lengthy discussion ensued between the referee and the linesman. During that discussion, I, like all the England supporters in the stadium, died a thousand deaths. It seemed an eternity before the referee and linesman decided it was a goal. England 3, West Germany 2. The players, on both sides were now physically exhausted. With tension running high, the minutes ticked away until, with the referee looking at his watch, Bobby Moore made a superb through pass for Hurst. Geoff dribbled the ball towards goal. He unleashed a fierce shot that left Tilkowski, the German goalkeeper, helpless. England 4 West Germany 2. The final whistle blew. England had won the World Cup. Ramsey had been in post just three and a half years. He had promised the country his team would win the World Cup and now he had delivered. As Bobby Moore collected the Jules Rimet Cup from the Queen, the Wembley crowd continually shouted 'Ramsey, Ramsey'. A tear rolled down my face. The hero of the Wembley crowd, had made sure I was a part, if only a small part, of England's success. Alan Bass and I were relieved no player required suturing with stitches on the touchline during the game!

The England dressing room was one of controlled happiness. There was no yelling or screaming, just the quiet chatter of celebration amongst the players and staff. We were all there. Not only the eleven players who had performed so magnificently, but the eleven reserves, who had contributed so much during the previous eight weeks. In addition, the five members of staff, Ramsey, Shepherdson, Cocker, Bass, McGuiness and myself, were also present. It is disappointing for me to report that The Football Association failed to appreciate the great contribution the eleven reserves had made to the team's success. A bonus of one thousand pounds, The Football Association decided, would be paid to each England player if the Jules Rimet trophy was won. This bonus payment however, would only be paid to the eleven players who actually played in the final game. The eleven reserve players would receive nothing. On learning of the F.A.'s decision, on their own initiative, the players themselves decided this bonus payment was grossly unfair. The eleven players, who actually played in the final, decided the bonus payment would be divided between all the players. Each player in the squad would receive five hundred pounds. The players realised each member of the squad had made a massive contribution to the team's success.

"We'll be getting a bonus."
I heard Alan Ball say to Nobby Stiles.
"Do you know, I'd forgotten about the bonus."
Nobby replied.
"I just wanted England to win."

England had won, and history had been made on that July day. The team's names would be embossed on everyone's memory forever. Banks, Cohen, Wilson, Stiles, Charlton J., Moore, Ball, Hurst, Charlton R., Hunt and Peters. The names of the other eleven players in the squad would sadly fade away with time. They had however made a significant contribution to England's success. I would never forget their names. Springett, Bonetti, Armfield, Byrne, Flowers, Hunter, Payne, Callaghan, Greaves, Eastham and Connelly. Those reserve players had lived in the shadow of a great England team. Each one of them and every member of Alf's staff was proud be so closely associated with England's success.

We left Hendon Hall Hotel in the early evening, en route to meet our wives at the Royal Garden Hotel in Kensington, where the official World Cup banquet were held. The north London public were aware of our route into town and lined the streets. As our coach passed the Hendon Fire Station, for the last time, the firemen, as they had done when we travelled to every game during the tournament, lined up outside the station. As usual, they waved to us with a chamber pot. The pot was their very own 'World Cup.' There was no open top coach ride for the England party. We travelled into London on our usual England coach driven by Sid, the usual driver. As we entered Camden Town his driving became impossible. Thousands of people lined the streets. In places, on both sides of the road, the people were seven or eight rows deep. The public were deliriously happy. They waved hundreds of flags. Many clashed dustbin lids together as we made our slow progress towards Kensington. The coach's progress was reduced to a snail's pace as, in places, the crowds had spilled onto the road. As Sid carefully brought the coach to a standstill at the Royal Garden Hotel, the chants of 'England, England' from the massive crowd were deafening.

The players and staff had naturally assumed that, on arriving at the hotel, they would all be reunited with their wives, but this was not so. The Football Association decided, in their wisdom, there was no room at the banquet for the wives. The wives were to eat in a separate dining room away from the official banquet! The players, having been separated from their wives for some eight weeks were, to say the least, extremely disappointed. At the banquet, I sat on Table 23 between Alan Bass and George Cohen. Also seated at our table were Bobby Moore, George Eastham, Ray Wilson, Bobby Charlton, Geoff Hurst, Alan Ball, Harold Shepherdson, and Terry Paine. We were all anxious for the banquet to end so that we could rejoin our wives. In any event, our meal was frequently interrupted. The crowds, outside the hotel, demanded the team make appearances on the hotel's balcony. At our first balcony performance, lead by Alf Ramsey, I was conscious of the advice the Medical Defence Union had given me, when I was originally appointed an England Team Physician.

"You should avoid having your photograph
taken with the team."
they had advised.
"It could be construed as advertising."

Advertising was not allowed for the medical profession at the time. Advertising by doctors could lead to disciplinary measures. As the players and staff lined up in single file along the hotel balcony, I positioned myself at the extreme end of the line and ensured there was a wide gap between Peter Bonetti, the last player, and myself. The Jules Rimet trophy was passed along the line from player to player. As each player held the trophy aloft, the packed crowds below cheered with increasing volume. Peter Bonetti handed me the trophy. I held it aloft. As last in the line, I imagined I received the loudest cheer. As I held the cup aloft, my eyes caught the stars shining brightly in the clear night sky of the July evening. The stars twinkled. I imagined one of them winked at me. I wondered if it was my Dad, somewhere up there. It was a great shame, he'd missed my big day.

The team made several balcony appearances during the evening. On one

The Balcony Scene
"Victorious England On Balcony–Author Extreme Left"

occasion, the wives joined us for our balcony appearance. Not to be outdone, Prime Minister Harold Wilson joined us. In order to gain entrance to the balcony everyone had to squeeze through a very small opening at the back of the balcony. Margaret, my wife, observing protocol, allowed the Prime Minister to precede her through the small opening onto the balcony. Unfortunately, Harold Wilson became stuck in the narrow opening. I witnessed my wife helping Harold Wilson onto the balcony by pushing, with both hands, on his buttocks! The memory has remained with her ever since.

Eventually the formalities of the banquet were over. Alf had given us all a list of numerous nightclubs and restaurants where we would be most welcome. Inevitably Les Cocker and I gravitated together. I say inevitably as Les and I were great friends, having worked consistently together with the Under 23 team during the previous three years. Les, his wife Norma, Margaret and I opted to visit the Bunny Club in Park Lane as their guests. Before leaving the banquet I had one duty to perform. I was conscious, during the meal, that sitting at a table in the room were four of my fellow directors from Middlesbrough. They had been invited to the banquet as directors of a Club hosting regional matches in the competition. It was important I crossed the room to meet with them. The four directors were Eric and Harold Thomas, George Kitching and Ernest Varley. As I approached their table I could not believe my ears.

"We hope you haven't come over here to ask Middlesbrough
to play football like this England team. We thought the way
England played was absolutely dreadful!
said the Club's Vice Chairman, Harold Thomas.
I made no comment. It needed no comment. England had won the World Cup. Middlesbrough had been relegated to the Third Division. I had contributed to both in no small measure. One a triumph, the other a complete and utter disaster.

At the Bunny Club, we required no food, haven eaten at the banquet. Much to the dismay of the Bunny Club's staff, who offered us free champagne, Les and I both decided we would drink orange squash. I recall saying to Les,

> "I want to remember every moment of this day. I do not want to wake up in the morning through a haze of alcoholic stupor. The memories of this day must remain clear in my mind forever."

Les agreed. We chatted through every kick of the final. We reminisced about our experiences, during the past three years, with the Under 23's. Les and I drank orange squash all night. Our wives enjoyed the champagne. The conversation between Les and me was so intense we both missed the arrival at the club of Ray Wilson and Bobby Charlton with their wives. Ray's presence was soon noticed by everyone however. As the cabaret came to a close, Ray mounted the stage giving an excellent rendering of Al Jolson songs. Ray brought the house down! It was a fitting climax to the day. The memories of the day remain forever.

8

Who wants to be a Millionaire............

The euphoria, of being involved with England's success in the World Cup, contrasted alarmingly with the depression I experienced with being involved with Middlesbrough's relegation. On returning home, from London, and throughout the summer, Middlesbrough Football Club was a depressing place. The depression affected all the directors, but I felt it more than most, because I had been so intimately involved with England's World Cup success. Try as I might, I found it difficult to treat those two impostors -Triumph and Disaster- as just the same. On Teesside, the euphoria of North Korea's success, and the success of staging the World Cup matches at Middlesbrough, was replaced by the harsh reality of the Club playing in the Third Division. I believed the directors were largely responsible, with the players, for the Club's demise. I was one of those directors.

My spirits were raised however when I received a thank you letter from Alf Ramsey. He expressed his thanks to me for my co-operation and assistance during the past weeks. It was a letter to treasure.

On returning from London, I was astonished to learn Stan Anderson had been appointed the Manager of Middlesbrough, while I was away from Teesside. I was not consulted on the appointment, merely told of the appointment by the Chairman, when I returned. The Chairman informed me,

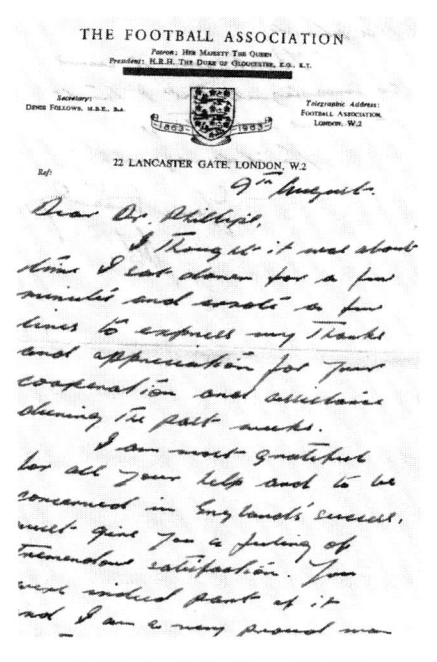

"Alf's Thank You Letter To Me"

"All seven Directors were in favour of the appointment, so your opinion was unnecessary."

The Chairman continued,

"I knew you would probably be against the appointment, as Stan Anderson does not have the Coaching Certificate of The Football Association. Your involvement with The Football Association gives you a jaundiced view. Like everyone at the Football Association, you would believe no-one should be appointed as a manager, unless he held The Football Association's Coaching Certificate."

So much, I thought, for the Chairman needing my brains! The appointment of a new Manager is the most crucial decision football directors make, yet, although a director, the issue of Stan's appointment had not even been discussed with me. The Chairman gave as his excuse that a decision had to be made quickly. It was unfortunate, he said, I was away on Football

Association duty. I wondered if he had ever heard of the telephone!

During the summer, I received a letter from a Jimmy Headrige, an ex player of East Clydebank in Scotland. Jimmy, whom I had never met, had been forced to retire, at quite a young age, with a severe knee injury. His letter enquired if there was a possibility of him being employed as a trainer at Middlesbrough Football Club. His own injury, he wrote, had given him a great interest in the treatment of injuries and he was now seeking employment, in that sphere, with a football club. With Harold Shepherdson becoming Assistant Manager to Stan Anderson, and Mickey Fenton having retired, George Wright was the only member of the Treatment Room Staff I had at my disposal. I replied to Jimmy's letter, informing him we might be interested. I asked him to attend for an interview. George Wright and I spent a day at the Club with Jimmy. Although he had no experience, both George and I were very impressed with him as a person. More importantly, George believed he could work well with Jimmy on a day-to-day basis. George was prepared to act as his tutor and train him in the ways of a qualified physiotherapist. Equally, Jimmy was enthusiastic to learn. I recommended to the Board that Jimmy Headrige be employed as the Reserve Team Trainer, succeeding Mickey Fenton. The Board agreed with my recommendation. It was the best appointment I made. At the football club. George Wright and Jimmy Headrige worked well together. Jimmy's enthusiasm for learning every detail of all aspects of Sports Medicine, was exceptional. In George Wright he had a first class, experienced, well-qualified physiotherapist to teach him. The two worked well together. The situation was ideal. It was the beginning of the three of us, George, Jimmy and myself, providing the Middlesbrough players with an exceptional medical service.

We developed a strategy for the care of all the players at the Club. Our recently introduced routine medical examinations would be further extended. In addition to a clinical examination, all the players would undergo heart and lung function tests. Blood tests would be carried out at regular intervals. The players' immunisations and vaccinations would routinely be kept up to date. We developed a new philosophy regarding the treatment of injuries. Great emphasis would be placed on the prevention of injuries. We decided to introduce pre-training warm up sessions to include stretching exercises; a novelty in those days. Injured players would have a personalised, active, full time programme of rehabilitation. No injured players would have any afternoons off. The rehabilitation from injury would be a full time occupation. We ensured injured players, undergoing rehabilitation, would work harder than when they were fully fit and in training. The incentive and hard work rate, we created, ensured the players were keen to leave their rehabilitation programme and resume normal training. Normal training would be easier than the rehabilitation programme. A system of medical records was introduced at the Club, so that every injury was properly recorded together with its treatment and outcome. We introduced new diets for the players and stretch exercises before, during and after training. Routine stretch exercises were unheard of at the time. Together the three

"Jimmy Headrige and I Introduce Stretch Exercises To The Juniors."

of us would ensure the success of these new innovations. With the pre-season training programme completed, the 1966–67 season opened with Middlesbrough in the Third Division playing away at Colchester.

With Stan Anderson as our new Manager, the early part of the season was a disaster. The away win at Colchester, in the first game of the season, was followed by only one win in the next nine games. After ten games, Middlesbrough were bottom of the Third Division. Prior to the season commencing, Stan Anderson had made three new signings. John O'Rourke, a centre forward from Luton, David Chadwick, a winger from Southampton and Willie Wigham, a goalkeeper from Falkirk. Several first team players from the previous season had left the Club. After ten games, with the team languishing at the bottom of Division Three, the Manager informed the Board he needed to further strengthen the team. He recommended the Club purchase John Hickton, a centre-half, from Sheffield Wednesday for twenty thousand pounds. In the previous season, Hickton played for Sheffield Wednesday in most rounds of the F.A. Cup, but had been dropped, in favour of Sam Ellis, for the Wembley final against Everton. Hickton considered he had been badly treated and, quite naturally, wanted to leave Sheffield Wednesday. When Stan Anderson brought his proposal to the Board, I was the only director to oppose his recommendation. At the time, Middlesbrough had three centre-halves at the Club; Dickie Rookes, Billy Gates and Alec Smith. I could see no logical reason for having a fourth. I believed the team needed someone who was a goal scorer. I was told Hickton was a very versatile player. He could play at full back, centre-half or even centre-forward. When I questioned the Manager however, he admitted it was as a centre-half he needed Hickton.. After a very lengthy discussion, the Board agreed to purchase Hickton from Sheffield Wednesday. Hickton made his Middlesbrough debut, in late September 1966 and scored on his debut. Stan Anderson quickly realised Hickton was an exceptional goal scorer. Tactically, for the remainder of the season, the Manager played Hickton as a centre-forward, sometimes with a number two on his shirt, supposedly to confuse the opposition! Billy Gates played twenty-five games for the Club during the rest of the season and in most games Billy was at centre-half.

Following Hickton's arrival, the team steadily improved. Promotion, back to Division Two however seemed impossible, owing to the disastrous start to the season. Towards the end of the season, with only six matches remaining, Middlesbrough was in its highest league position. They were seventh in the table. With only six matches remaining, the next game was an away fixture at Peterborough. It was a game Middlesbrough won. It was also the game that changed my relationships with my fellow directors forever. From the date of the Peterborough game, until I left the Club, my rapport with the directors would never be the same. The Peterborough match completely destroyed the relationship I had with my fellow directors.

In my dual role, as the Club's Medical Officer and Company Director, I often had divided loyalties. As the Medical Officer, I was a daily visitor to the dressing room. I always considered it a privilege to share in the players' environment. It was their company I enjoyed most of all. I especially loved, and entered into, their banter, humour, and everyday conversations. I gained much information from my visits to the dressing room. Often it was valuable information. The other directors rarely visited the dressing room, and so were unaware of such information. In the early days, following my appointment, I decided that my over-riding loyalty would always be to the players, the Manager and the dressing-room staff. That loyalty always took precedence over any loyalty I had to the Board and my fellow directors. In addition, I was always aware of the fact the players were my patients. They, quite rightly, expected I would treat them, at all times, with dignity and respect. During medical consultations, the players often discussed confidential and personal matters with me. Such matters always remained private and confidential. Over the many years I worked at Middlesbrough, I never disclosed the confidentiality of any player's medical consultation, without the agreement of the player. My over-riding loyalty to the players was paramount. Working in such a high profile role within the Club, it was essential the players had complete faith and trust in me. My medical integrity would at all times be beyond question. The confidentiality of the doctor patient relationship was supreme. The players expected it of me. I would never let them down.

During the years I worked in the dressing room, several people tried to compromise my medical integrity. I certainly was aware, on many occasions, of my divided loyalties. I had a loyalty to the Chairman; a loyalty to the Board of Directors; a loyalty to the Manager and the dressing room staff. Most important of all however was my loyalty to the players. The professional footballers were my patients. As such, they were always entitled to discuss matters with me in complete confidence. Of course, I needed to discuss the players' injuries with the Manager, Coaching and Treatment Room Staff and the players accepted that. There were however many matters players discussed with me that remained forever confidential and of which no one else would ever be aware. With all the pressures, and there were many, from the Chairman down to the players, I would never allow my medical integrity to be compromised. As a result, the players had the utmost confidence in me. I earned the respect of the Middlesbrough players over many years and I know they appreciated my professional confidentiality. My medical integrity was what I valued most. However it was placed under the severest threat, following the away win at Peterborough.

Billy Gates, a player at Middlesbrough, was the first schoolboy to sign a contract, as a professional footballer, for fifty pounds a week. In 1961, it was, for a professional footballer, an enormous weekly wage. At that time, to my knowledge, there was only one footballer in England, Johnny Haynes of Fulham, earning one hundred pounds a week. Billy Gates, a promising centre-half from Spennymoor Grammar School, was signed by Bob Dennison. Gates signed for Middlesbrough two years before I became a director. His personal contract, ensured that the Club would enable him to continue with his academic aspirations. Billy, in addition to wishing to be a professional footballer, also wanted to be an accountant. As a young professional footballer, he had it written into his contract he would be articled to a local firm of accountants. Gates was an unusual professional footballer! Articulate, academically very bright, forthright in his views and determined to succeed in both of his professions, Billy would play three hundred and twenty-three league and cup games for Middlesbrough's first team. He was the ideal person for the other players to choose as their Players' Union representative.

I came to know Gates extremely well. He originally lived at Hartburn, a district of Stockton-on Tees, with his wife Judith. During his time at Middlesbrough, Billy sustained several very serious injuries, which I supervised and treated. He fractured a bone in his spine; fractured an ankle; fractured a toe; had a cartilage operation on his knee, when there was no micro-surgery; developed a deep venous thrombosis in his leg and suffered numerous attacks of tonsillitis. Billy certainly had his share of serious injuries and illnesses. I nursed him through them all. He was always a difficult patient. He intelligently questioned every treatment I suggested. When in hospital, he frequently upset the medical and nursing staff with his forthright, inquisitive nature. As with all the Middlesbrough players, I enjoyed an excellent relationship with Bill. On one occasion, owing to the severity of an injury, a consultant erroneously informed him he would never play football again. I spent hours, at his home, convincing him otherwise. He responded with his usual determination. Within weeks of being given this shattering news, by the consultant, he was back in the first team playing again. When he later moved with his family to Marske-by-the-Sea, his family became National Health Service patients of mine; an indication, I suppose, that Bill Gates and his wife respected me as their medical advisor.

Nevertheless, it was a great surprise to me when Bill, while still a player at Middlesbrough, approached me to become his partner in a business venture. "Reeds", a sports shop in Redcar, was for sale. Bill wanted to buy the business. He wanted me to be his partner. We would be equal partners. Bill believed my position with the England International Team and The Football Association would be advantageous to the business. We met on several occasions, sometimes with our wives, to discuss all the business issues. Our intentions were well known to Charles Amer and George Winney, fellow directors, who supported the idea. In fact, it was Charles who originally suggested to Gates, he should discuss the purchase of the business with me. Following our discussions, I and my wife were tempted to join Bill in his new venture. We spent many an hour together evaluating the three previous years' accounts of the sport business.

When Middlesbrough was relegated to the Third Division, Billy Gates wanted to leave. Playing in the Third Division, Billy considered, was below the standards he had set for himself. Billy was a better player than the average Third Division player. He refused to sign a new contract. Rumours circulated he wanted a greatly improved financial contract to stay at Middlesbrough. He decided to seek a transfer. Stan Anderson, the Manager, informed Gates the directors would refuse any transfer request he made. As Manager, Stan Anderson would oppose any transfer of Gates. The relationship between Gates and Stan Anderson rapidly deteriorated. The ill feeling generated between both men rumbled on for many weeks during the season. Gates, as only Billy Gates would do in such a situation, bypassed the Manager. He sought the advice of two of the Club's directors, George Winney and Charles Amer. Gates was unsure how to proceed with his transfer negotiations. He wanted a new contract at Middlesbrough, with a substantial increase in his basic salary, or he wanted to be transferred. Surprisingly, when he discussed these issues independently with both directors, they both advised him to discuss the matter with me. Gates approached me for a meeting. I was reluctant to agree. I had no authority to discuss contractual issues with him or any other player and told him so. I certainly could not agree the terms of a new contract for him. Billy however thought a discussion of his situation with me would be helpful. As always, my time was limited. The only time I had available was an evening at my home, when I was on emergency call for the Practice. I saw Billy and his wife Judith at my home. We had a late afternoon tea together followed by a lengthy detailed discussion.

Middlesbrough was now playing Peterborough away, on a Saturday in the Third Division. Although the relationship between the Manager and Gates was strained, Gates was chosen in the squad for the Peterborough game. With one of my partners away on holiday, I was on weekend duty in the Practice. I did not travel to Peterborough. George Kitching was the director nominated to travel with the team. I heard the match result on 'Sports Report'. Middlesbrough had won 2–1 away from home. I was delighted.

After Monday morning surgery in my Practice, I made my way to Ayresome Park to examine the injured players. Gates was the only player I examined. As usual, I saw the player with George Wright, our physiotherapist. Apparently Bill had collided with a Peterborough player, early in the game and injured his thigh. He was forced to leave the field, with 'a dead leg' having played for only a few minutes. On clinical examination, he had a typical haematoma in the quadriceps muscle of his thigh. The muscle movements were limited and his thigh muscle was extremely sore. Treatment was agreed with Gates and the physiotherapist. As the team was playing at home to Leyton Orient on the Tuesday evening, it was obvious Bill Gates would not be available for selection. There were no other injured players for me to examine. Before returning to Redcar, I called in at the Manager's office to inform him of the situation with regard to Gates' injury. The Manager was in the office with the Chairman. I informed them both, Gates was unfit to play against Leyton Orient. The Chairman and Manager made no comment. I returned to Redcar to carry out my home visits.

The match against Leyton Orient was an exciting game, which Middlesbrough again won. After the game, in the directors' room, Ernest Varley, a fellow director, asked for my opinion on "The Billy Gates Affair". I informed Ernest I was unaware of any affair relating to Gates. Ernest was surprised. He then informed me that, in the dressing room at Peterborough the previous Saturday, a big row had occurred between the Manager and Billy Gates. Apparently, Stan Anderson had selected Gates to play at right full back. When Gates was informed of the Manager's decision, he refused to play. Gates apparently wanted to play at centre-half. If he wasn't playing at centre-half, Gates informed the Manager, he would not play. Gates was of course out of order. A heated argument ensued, immediately before the game in the dressing room area, between the Manager and Gates, with both parties yelling at each other. The Manager eventually informed Gates that, if he refused to play, it would be a disciplinary matter, which he would report to the Board. The stand off between the two men continued right up to the time the Manager was due to submit his selected team to the referee. Realising the impossible position he had placed himself in, Gates reluctantly agreed, at the very last minute, to play at right full back. Having reluctantly agreed to play at full back, Gates was then removed from the field of play, after just a few minutes, with what, the Middlesbrough people present, considered was a trivial injury. I told Ernest I was unaware of any argument at Peterborough between Gates and the Manager. I informed Ernest, I had examined Gates on Monday morning and no-one, but no-one, had informed me of the background to Gates' injury. The Manager, George Wright, the Physiotherapist, and Gates himself had not told me of the row. When I examined Gates on Monday morning, I diagnosed a badly bruised thigh; the so-called 'dead leg' and at present, as far as I was concerned, he was unfit to play. At this point in our discussion, the Chairman joined Ernest and myself. The Chairman was obviously in a bad mood. He informed both Ernest and myself,

> "There is absolutely nothing wrong with Gates. He feigned the injury at Peterborough because he did not want to play at right full back"

I immediately contradicted the Chairman,

> "Gates has a badly bruised thigh and presently is unfit to play."

The Chairman continued with his argument,

> "That is simply not true. This morning you told the Manager, in my presence, all the players were fit, including Gates."
>
> "That is a lie."

I said.

Addressing me specifically, he said,

> "I'm not surprised at your attitude and diagnosis of Gates and I will tell you why! When a director invites a player, and the player's wife, to his home for afternoon tea, the director's opinions is then bound to be coloured by such social connections. You know, only too well, there is nothing wrong with Gates. It's a cover up."

I was astonished at the Chairman's remarks and very upset. I am not ashamed to say I cried. The Chairman had compromised my medical integrity. He had questioned my honesty. My honesty and medical integrity was of the highest importance to me. How dare the Chairman question my medical opinion! My integrity in medicine was far more important to me than my relationship with the Chairman, my fellow directors, the Manager, the Physiotherapist or Gates himself. I was not prepared to have my medical integrity and my medical opinion, questioned by any of my fellow directors, let alone the Chairman. I was absolutely furious. I drove home. In my mind, I questioned whether I would ever return.

On arriving home, although it was late at night, I phoned Matt Leitch, the orthopaedic surgeon. I asked if he would kindly see Gates the following day. Matt readily agreed. I wrote the referral letter to Matt, requesting his opinion on Gates' thigh and the likely prognosis with regard to returning to match fitness. I gave Matt no information of the politics surrounding Gates' injury. I did not want Matt's view clouded, in any way, by extraneous information. It was the first time ever in my career I had referred a patient to a consultant seeking simple verification of my diagnosis. I slept little that night. I could not recall when I had felt so angry.

I saw Gates at the Club, the day after the Leyton Orient game. I informed him he had an appointment with the orthopaedic consultant at three o'clock that afternoon. Gates was not pleased. He did not wish to miss an afternoon at his accountancy training. He could see no reason why he should be referred to the consultant. Gates was happy for me to be in sole charge of his treatment. I, however, insisted. I received Matt's report the next morning. His report confirmed my diagnosis. Mr. Leitch also stated, in his letter, that in his opinion, Gates would not be able to play for the next two weeks. The weekly Board meeting was scheduled for the next day as usual.

I prepared a written statement for the Board meeting. The statement, which I read at the meeting, described, in detail, the happenings of the previous few days. In my defence, as if I needed any, I informed the directors the reason Gates and his wife came to my house was because two of my fellow directors recommended to Gates he speak with me on his contractual dispute. The two directors, Charles Amer and George Winney confirmed this at the meeting. I confirmed, I had informed both the Manager and the Chairman, on Monday morning, that Gates was unfit to play against Leyton Orient. The Manager agreed this was the case, despite the Chairman having told me it was not. I read Mr. Leitch's medical report on Gates to the Board. They were stunned to hear Gates would not play for a further two weeks. My lengthy statement confirmed I would not tolerate my medical opinion being questioned by the Chairman, or any of my fellow directors. My statement, which I still have, concluded,

> "For anyone to suggest my medical opinion of Gates, or any other player at this Club, is tainted or biased, because of any relationship I have with them socially, is ridiculous. For the Chairman of this Club to have done so, I find both deplorable and incomprehensible. For the Chairman to suggest I was involved in a cover-up is unbelievable. The events of Monday evening deeply hurt me. I have laid before you the facts as I know them. You will hear other views and from them you will have to judge the situation for yourselves. However, I must make it completely clear I will not allow such allegations, as were made against me by the Chairman, to go unanswered."

To my amazement, the end of my statement was met by stony silence. Not one of the directors said a word. Eventually the Chairman said,

> "I think it's wisest if we close the meeting at this point."

The Manager took me on one side and said,

> "Well done. You'll feel a lot better having got all that off your chest!"

I was not so sure. I felt vulnerable and isolated.

Later that day, the Chairman asked to see me. I met him at his home. He was full of apologies.

> "I made a big mistake."

he said,

> "It was all George Kitching's fault. He was the director on duty at Peterborough. He reported Gates' actions to me and his row with the Manager. It was George who informed me

of your private relationship with Gates. I acted with undue haste, and I regret my actions. I can only apologise."

"Apology accepted."

was my curt reply. There was little else I could say.

I nevertheless expressed my concerns to the Chairman. The whole episode was unsavoury. Instead of me covering up for Gates, as had been suggested, I had been set up by one of my fellow directors. No one had informed me of the true facts surrounding the background of Gates' injury at Peterborough. Those facts had been deliberately kept from me. I was not prepared to accept such behaviour. More importantly, I wanted the Chairman to know I would never tolerate, at any time, my medical integrity being brought into question. My relationship with the Chairman was never the same again. He and George Kitching had set a trap for me. Their behaviour was totally unacceptable. While I accepted the Chairman's apology, I would always be wary of their behaviour in future. I realised I was never going to be "a director's man". My place was in the dressing room with the players. They were my kind of people and Billy Gates was one of them. The professionals attending Lilleshall had been so correct, when they told me,

"How could you have become one of them?"

You must be mad!"

They were correct. The actions of some of my fellow directors convinced me that I would never be one of them. Amongst the directors at Middlesbrough, I felt very isolated.

Gates remained a Middlesbrough player, and gave valuable service to the Club for many years, after the so-called "Billy Gates Affair". As far as I am aware, Gates is still unaware, as I write this, of the problems his simple injury caused me. He is unaware the Chairman brought my medical integrity into question and the rift that occurred, at the time, between the Chairman and myself. I gave Gates no reason as to why I referred him to the specialist for what both he and I knew was a simple straightforward injury.

The away win at Peterborough was followed by a run of successes which elevated the team to fourth position in the League; their highest of the season. Only one game remained. It was a home game against Oxford.

Immediately prior to that last match of the season, Middlesbrough had fifty-three points. Queens Park Rangers were already promoted as champions with sixty-seven points. Watford was in second position with fifty-four points and Reading third with fifty-three points. Both Watford and Reading had completed their fixtures. The only outstanding match left to play in the League was our match, at home to Oxford. Ayresome Park was packed with a record 39,683 spectators for that final Oxford game. With a goal average inferior to Watford, Middlesbrough had to win the match; a draw would not be good enough. Middlesbrough won the game four goals to one. With a victory in the last match of the season, Middlesbrough returned to Division Two. Everyone at the Club was ecstatic. It seemed incredible Middlesbrough had gained promotion as, prior to the last match of the season, the team had never been higher than fourth in the league.

I shall never forget the scenes at the end of the Oxford match. The crowd surged forward across the pitch, towards the North Stand. They demanded to see the players. The players appeared over and over again in the Directors' Box waving to the crowd, who continued surging forwards in front of the stand. The pressure of the crowd against the enclosure wall eventually caused the wall to collapse. Supporters, at the front of the crowd, were hurled downwards into the enclosure. Bodies were stacked on top of each other. Several people were crushed. Many people suffered from various degrees of asphyxia. While the players, directors and staff celebrated our return to Division Two, I, together with the Physiotherapist, Trainer, Harold Shepherdson and St. Johns Ambulance men, were extremely busy in the medical rooms treating the injured spectators. Some spectators were so severely injured they required immediate hospital admission. It was ironic that with the whole Club celebrating the victory, the evening was disturbed by the sound of the ambulance sirens ferrying patients from the ground to the local hospital. Fortunately none of the injured died. Some of the injured remained in hospital for several days. A fatal disaster at Ayresome Park was narrowly avoided.

Middlesbrough was now back in Division Two. The purchase of Hickton had been vindicated. The reason, the Manager gave, for buying Hickton had been to play him at centre-half. John Hickton became an excellent centre forward for Middlesbrough. He contributed greatly to the team's promotion. My fellow directors believed I had made an error of judgment in opposing his transfer. Some of my fellow directors would never allow me to forget it. In return, I would never forget the 2–1 away win at Peterborough; the win that elevated the Club from seventh position to a promotion seeking possibility, with just five matches remaining. Football can be a funny old game!

I did not go into business with Billy Gates. He went ahead with the purchase of "Reeds" sports shop on his own. Billy, as I knew he would, made a great success of it. The year he stopped playing, he expanded his sports shop business by opening another sports shop in the Dundas Arcade at Middlesbrough. He became a very successful businessman. Gates' accountancy training made him eminently suited to the business world. Coupled with his in-built determination to succeed, he opened further sports businesses in Newcastle, Washington, Gateshead, Manchester, Liverpool, Birmingham and Nottingham. He became the sole owner of quite a sports empire. Many years later, Bill Gates sold his sports empire to Blacks, the outdoor sports chain. It was reported to me, the price was one of several millions of pounds. Billy now lives in the Cayman Islands and Florida. He is a millionaire. If I had gone into partnership with Billy, at the beginning of his business adventure, it is possible I could be writing this book in some exotic island living the life of a millionaire. Alas, it is not so. At least my medical integrity remains intact. No one can put a value on medical integrity. For me it was certainly worth more than a million!

Middlesbrough's promotion, back to the Second Division, in May 1967 was quickly followed for me with the Under 23 tour to Greece, Bulgaria and Turkey. Bill Nicholson, the Tottenham Manager, was in charge of the team. I met Bill Nicholson at the Cavendish Hotel in Lancaster Gate on the afternoon of Sunday May 28th. Les Cocker, the Leeds United trainer, was also present. Bill Nicholson discussed with us details of the tour prior to the arrival of the players. Bill already knew that four of the selected players would not be making the trip because of injuries. He discussed, with

Les, the various players who might be called up as replacements.

The players originally selected for the tour were Jim Montgomery and Peter Springett (goalkeepers); Hindley, Knowles and Reaney (full backs); Hurst, Mobley, Newton, Harvey and Greenhoff (half backs); Coates, Clarke, Husband, Marsh, Storey-Moore and Sammels(forwards). Reaney, Greenhoff, Marsh and Storey-Moore were the four players unable to travel owing to injury. They were replaced with Tommy Wright, Frank Sibley and John O'Rourke, the Middlesbrough centre forward.

It was nice to have a Middlesbrough player in the party. The members of the International Under 23 Committee, who travelled with the party, were Messrs. Robinson, Smith and Davis. I was very impressed with Bill Nicholson throughout the tour. Bill was not only a very astute coach, his experience was immense and above all he was a nice man. We became good friends. I valued his friendship for many years.

The first two internationals on the tour were drawn; a nil-nil draw against Greece and a one-one draw against Bulgaria. The match against Bulgaria was particularly physical and not without incident. Cyril Knowles was injured during the game, following a vicious Bulgarian tackle. Les Cocker, the England Trainer, went on the field to attend to the injury. Almost immediately he called on me to assist him. On the field, as I was examining Cyril's injury, a posse of Bulgarian first aid men came onto the field and began dragging Cyril from under my examination on to their stretcher. Les was enraged, and gesticulated to the Bulgarians to leave the player alone. As the spectators witnessed the altercations on the pitch, between the first aid men and Les Cocker, the crowd became enraged. Stones, cans and bottles were hurled on the pitch aimed at Les and myself. I was relieved when Cyril Knowles got to his feet and the game was able to continue. Missiles continued to be thrown at Les and myself, as we walked around the pitch back to the dug out. Fortunately all the missiles missed their intended target. Imagine my wife's surprise, back in England, when she saw the headline in one of the national newspapers the following day. It read,

"England Doctor Stoned in Bulgaria!"

and me almost teetotal!

At half time in the Bulgarian game, Bill Nicholson's experience shone through. In the first half, the game had been particularly physical and some of the tackles made on the England players were totally unacceptable. Imagine Bill's surprise when, at half time, the referee accompanied by some of the Bulgarian officials asked to see Bill Nicholson. They requested Bill to instruct the England players to be less physical in their tackles during the second half! Bill very diplomatically suggested, through the interpreter, they had come to the wrong dressing room!

In Ankara, Bill Nicholson gave John O'Rourke, of Middlesbrough, his first Under 23 cap against Turkey. As a Middlesbrough Director, I was immensely proud and delighted for John. I was even more delighted when he scored one of the three goals in the defeat of the Turks. We returned home on the eighth of June.

I had no sooner returned from the tour when it was time for my annual visit to Lilleshall for the Treatment of Injury Course. My visit, in the summer of 1967, was just for one day. I was to lecture on "The Pathology of Injury" and "How I Treat Muscle Injuries". I was also to expose myself to a question and answer session with the students. Despite my family commitments, and those with Middlesbrough and the England Under 23 team, I always looked forward to visiting the National Sports Centre at Lilleshall. This would be the fifth year I had attended, but my role had now changed. I was now a staff lecturer. Lilleshall remained such a beautiful place. The centre lies in acres of grounds in the Shropshire countryside. One lived there in total isolation, away from the madding crowd. For me, it was the place to rekindle my soul. All my memories of Lilleshall are happy and fond ones.

In 1967, Paddy Armour, the Principal Physiotherapist from Pinderfields Hospital in Wakefield, and Bertie Mee, the Arsenal Physiotherapist continued to run the medical course at Lilleshall. They had, over many years, established the course as one of high quality and one with which I was pleased to be associated. Throughout my short visit in nineteen sixty seven, Bertie Mee, who had become a great friend of mine, hinted over and over again that Alan Bass, the Arsenal doctor and Senior England

Team Physician, would, in all probability, be emigrating to Canada. Bertie worked closely with Alan, on a day-to-day basis, at Arsenal. Alan, Bertie told me, was disillusioned with the state of the National Health Service. Bertie was aware Alan was actively seeking an appointment in Canada.

> "You'd better prepare yourself for taking over responsibility of the senior team."

Bertie told me,

> "I'm sure Alan will not be around for the World Cup in Mexico. All the medical problems associated, with playing in Mexico are going to land on your shoulders. Just mark my words."

I was stunned. I had frequently discussed England's medical matters with Alan. I had telephoned him on innumerable occasions, but I had never been aware of his unrest with the National Health Service. He had never given me any indication as to the validity of Bertie's remarks. Alan had always seemed to me quite content with his life. More importantly, Sir Alf had not discussed with me the possibility of Alan leaving. Although I worked for Alf, Alan Bass was, in effect, my medical boss. Alf and Alan had given me no indication Alan was about to leave. I left Lilleshall confused. I remained convinced, in my own mind, there was no truth in Bertie's remarks. I believed, that if Alan had any intentions of leaving for Canada, he would have informed me of his intentions.. No such discussions had taken place between us. If all the medical problems of playing in the Mexico World Cup were to land on my shoulders, I was completely and utterly unaware of the possibility.

After my Lilleshall visit, it was back home and a summer spent working in the Practice. As a family, we did manage a week's holiday in Scarborough. Most of my holiday entitlement, during the year, had been taken up travelling with the Under 23 team. It was nice to spend some time with the family, if only for one week. Playing on the sands at Scarborough, with my wife and three children, the medical problems associated with playing football in Mexico seemed far, far away.

9

Promotion For Me............

The first Under 23 game in the 1967–68 season was against Wales at Swansea. Owing to my Practice commitments, I was unable to attend. England won the game by two goals to one. The first occasion I joined up with Sir Alf, during that season, was for the Under 23 game against Italy at Nottingham on December 20th. At Nottingham, I raised with Alf, the issue of Alan Bass's emigration to Canada. Alf was totally unaware of any such intentions. Alan Bass, he assured me, had not discussed any such matters with him. Alf had spent three days with him, two weeks previously, when England played the Soviet Union at Wembley. Like myself, Alf had not detected any unrest in Alan's life. As always, Alf believed, Alan was totally committed to the England cause. Having raised the issue with Alf, I was reassured. Surely, I thought, if Alan was even contemplating emigrating to Canada, he would have discussed the matter with Alf. The absence of any such discussions confirmed my belief that perhaps Bertie Mee had gained the wrong impression. Certainly Alf had no idea of any such proposal.

Immediately after the Italy game at Nottingham, I had a meal with Alf, prior to driving back home to Redcar. Bobby Robson, the then Manager of Ipswich, joined us for the meal. During the meal, Bobby and Alf discussed various players and their international potential. I was pleased to hear Bobby Robson speak so highly of Willie Maddren, our young centre back at Middlesbrough. Bobby had a very high opinion of Maddren's play. It was after two in the morning when I snuggled into bed, back at Redcar, beside Margaret. I would be in morning surgery at eight-thirty.

The Mexico World Cup was now just over two years away. The medical problems associated with playing there were enormous. To date, I was unaware of any medical discussions having taken place regarding the England team's preparation for Mexico. Alan Bass had not discussed any of the problems with me. I was strongly of the opinion that at least one of the two England Team Physicians should attend the 1968 Olympic Games in Mexico. I decided to telephone Alan Bass with my suggestion.

On speaking with Alan, he was not enthusiastic. I believed one of us needed to study, at close quarters, the whole environment of Mexico. There was a need, I told Alan, to assess, at first hand, the performance of the athletes competing in the Olympics. If one of us was present at the Games, we could learn so much from the competing athletes. We needed to know the problems they had personally experienced. By talking to the athletes we could learn the details of their preparations for the Games. It would be essential to know how much time they had spent acclimatising at altitude prior to the games; where they had carried out that altitude training and what form of training had taken place. It was important for me to ascertain and evaluate their training programmes during the acclimatising period. Someone, with a medical background, I argued, needed to listen to and evaluate the views of the athletes themselves. We needed to know, from the competing athletes, how the environment of Mexico City had affected their performances. If either Alan or I was present at the Games, we could visit the hospitals provided for the athletes and assess whether their facilities would be suitable for our players during the World Cup. We needed to assess the quality of care that was provided. I believed it was essential to personally meet with the Mexican doctors, in the various hospitals, to learn how their medical practice and treatments compared with our own. There was so much we needed to know. As one of the doctors responsible for the England team, albeit at Under 23 level, I considered a visit to the Olympic Games in Mexico essential. Visiting the Games would provide Alan or me with the opportunity to study all the problems at first hand. Prior to the Olympics, much had been written, in the medical journals, about the problems of gastro-enteritis in Mexico. Concerns were expressed regarding the Mexican food and the country's hygiene standards. By being present at the Games, I believed we could personally gain so much medical information. That knowledge would be of invaluable benefit to the England team. I stressed over and over again to Alan how essential it was for one of us to be present at the Games. Unfortunately, Alan disagreed.

> "I see no real point. There will be plenty of medical reports following the Games. We will be able to learn all we need to know from those reports. We will still have two years to prepare. In any event, Alf and Denis Follows, I understand, are going to the Games. Let's leave it to them"

The Football Association agreed with Alan. They decided Sir Alf and Secretary, Denis Follows, would attend the Mexican Olympics. The presence of one of the England Team Doctors, The Football Association decided in their wisdom, was unnecessary. Sir Alf would observe the football games. Denis Follows would make all the necessary administrative enquiries. The thought of Denis Follows, who had no medical qualifications, making a valued assessment of the hospital and medical facilities appalled me. I held the view that a great opportunity was being missed. The presence of a medical observer, with intimate knowledge of the medical requirements of the England team, was, I believed, absolutely necessary. The presence of Alan or myself would have gained much needed information for the England team. Unfortunately Alan, and The Football Association, decided otherwise. Instead of visiting the Olympic Games, in the summer of sixty-eight, I watched highlights of the Games on television. Anyway, the medical problems facing England in Mexico would be for Alan Bass to resolve. I would be staying at home.

In March 1968, I received an unexpected telephone call from Sir Alf.

> "I wonder if you could make yourself available for the European Championship game against Spain at Wembley on the 3rd. April? Alan Bass will be in charge medically, but I need you to be present also. We shall be discussing, and determining, our strategy for Mexico. I would like you to be involved in those discussions. It would be helpful if you could

attend for the three days. We shall meet up at the Hendon Hall Hotel on the Sunday and disperse after the game on Wednesday evening. I would be delighted if you can come."
Alf said.
"Provided I can take the three days as holiday from my Practice, I'll be there. I will confirm in the next few days."
I telephoned Alf later in the week to confirm my availability. Most unusually he seemed somewhat uncertain on the telephone.
"I'm glad you can come. I'm not sure at present, but it seems possible Alan Bass may not be available. If he's not available, will you act as Team Physician?"
"Of course."
"Thank you doctor."

The present situation seemed very strange to me. In the past, on the rare occasions when Alan was unavailable, he had always contacted me personally. Previously, it had always been Alan who asked me to deputise. I was suspicious. Maybe Bertie Mee was correct. Maybe Alan Bass had become disillusioned and was, after all, contemplating emigration.

At Alf's request, I spent three days with the England team during their preparation for the European Championship game against Spain at Wembley. In the three days prior to the game, the weather was atrocious. It was very cold. It snowed heavily throughout the day prior to the game Alan Bass was rarely seen during those three days. He continued working, during the day, as a consultant at St. Mary's Hospital in Harrow. Alan called at The Hendon Hall Hotel each evening on his way home from work. He wanted to ensure all was well with the team. Alan did not discuss with me any of the medical problems relating to Mexico. He was too busy! For the game against Spain, Alan was medically in charge. I sat, on my own, in the stand at Wembley. I was just one of the supporters cheering England to victory. England beat Spain by a solitary goal, scored by Bobby Charlton. It was Bobby's forty-fourth goal for England. It enabled him to equal the all-time record for an England goal-scorer. With only a one goal lead, in the two legged European Championship match, the second leg in Madrid, in four weeks time, would be very difficult.

I returned home extremely disappointed. The purpose of my spending three days in London, Alf had said, was to be involved, with Alan Bass and the staff, discussing the problems confronting the team in Mexico. No meaningful discussions had taken place. The medical problems, associated with the Mexico World Cup had still to be addressed. It appeared to me that, following the World Cup victory in 1966, two years, that should have been used preparing the England team for Mexico, had been wasted. The lack of medical preparation was of great concern to me. Alan Bass and I, the only two medical people involved, had not discussed any of the medical problems confronting the England team in Mexico. It was now April 1968; time was running out. At this time, neither Alan nor I had even been to Mexico. The ultimate responsibility however for preparing the England team medically for Mexico was Alan's. He was the Senior Team Physician. All the medical problems were his responsibility. I was just the deputy.

In April 1968, Bertie Mee's opinion, expressed to me at Lilleshall the previous year, proved to be correct. The telephone call confirmed it. It was from Sir Alf.

> "Good morning doctor. It's Alf Ramsey. I'm afraid Alan Bass is not available for the return fixture against Spain in Madrid. He's given me no reason, just said he is unavailable. Could you be available for the game in Madrid? We meet up in London on Sunday May 5th. and fly out the following day. We return on the 9th. May. I would appreciate it if you would let me know if you are available."

> "I will be available."

I said.

There was no way I would not be available. I could not miss the opportunity to be "Doctor to The World Champions." With the co-operation of my partners, I took four days holiday to be with the team, for the second leg of the European Championship game in Madrid. The two games against Spain, would result in my using up one whole week of my holiday entitlement from the Practice. That was the penalty of being an unpaid

Honorary Team Physician, with no contract or job description with The Football Association

Two days later, I received a telephone call from Alan Bass. He confirmed his unavailability for the second leg in Madrid. He was travelling to Canada, he said, and would not be returning until the 17th. May. To my surprise, he did not know if he would be available to travel with the England team during June, on the summer tour. Alan suggested, if he was unavailable, I should step up, from the Under 23 team, to care for the senior team. Alan suggested, in such circumstances, Dr. Boyne of Chelsea should take my place with the Under 23 team. Throughout the conversation, Alan was very vague as to his availability for any of England's matches and, when I pressed him for further information, he was quite guarded in his response. I wrote to Alf Ramsey reporting the details of my telephone conversation with Alan.

The game against Spain in Madrid, was the first occasion I was totally responsible, medically, for the England team. I travelled, with Harold Shepherdson, to London by train on the Sunday. On arrival at the hotel, I was immediately confronted with several medical problems. Colin Bell and Peter Bonetti reported to Alf they had received injuries the previous day. Colin had injured his ankle playing for Manchester City against Tottenham at White Hart Lane. Although he reported to the hotel, Colin was doubtful if he was fit enough to play. The ultimate professional, Colin had attended Tottenham Hotspur on the Sunday morning for treatment. The opinion of the Tottenham Physiotherapist was he was unfit to play. It was an opinion I shared. Colin returned to Manchester. Peter Bonetti's injury was, as reported in the Press. He had received a knock on his left thigh in Chelsea's home game. He had attended Chelsea for treatment, on two occasions during Sunday, and would attend there for further treatment on Monday morning. Peter's opinion, and that of the Chelsea Physiotherapist, was he would be fit to play. Peter would not report to the team's hotel on Sunday, but stay at home resting and visit Stamford Bridge for further treatment on Monday morning. His Club informed Alf, he would meet up with the England party at Heathrow Airport on the Monday morning prior to departure. More worrying for Alf, was the absence of Gordon Banks and Jack Charlton, both of whom, we were to learn later, were also injured during their league games the previous day. Alf contacted Jack and Gordon's Clubs. The Clubs confirmed both players were injured. Banks and Charlton, Alf was informed, were unfit to travel. Peter Bonetti, who had only played three times for England previously, would deputise for Gordon Banks, provided of course he was fit to play. To add to Alf's woes, Manchester City informed us Mike Summerbee was also unfit. Four players, selected for this very important game in the European Championship, had withdrawn with injuries sustained in league matches played on the previous day. Of the sixteen players, Alf had selected for the game in Spain all, except Keith Newton, had played the previous day. In contrast, Spain had cancelled their League programme for the current week, thus enabling the Spanish players to have ten days together preparing for the game against England. As replacements, Alf sent for Alec Stepney, Manchester United's goalkeeper, and Peter Thompson, the Liverpool winger. Like Peter Bonetti, they would meet up with the team on Monday at Heathrow Airport.

The main party did light training, during Monday morning, at Loftus Road, the home of Queen's Park Rangers, Joined by Peter Bonnetti, and Alec Stepney we all lunched, in a private room, at Heathrow Airport. Peter Bonetti reported the physiotherapist at Chelsea considered he was fit to play. I agreed with that decision. There was no reason why Peter would not be able to play. Peter and I informed Alf he was fit to play. Alf told Peter he would deputise for the absent Gordon Banks.

At the airport, Les Cocker drew Alf's and my attention to a report in a London newspaper relating to Dr. Alan Bass, the England Team Doctor. The paper reported Alan was flying to Canada on the same afternoon we were flying to Spain. Alan Bass, the paper reported, was being interviewed for a post at Kingston University in Ontario. Alan was indeed leaving for Canada. Neither Alf nor I knew if it was a temporary or a permanent absence. The medical problems associated with playing in Mexico could now, as Bertie Mee had told me one year earlier at Lilleshall, land on my shoulders. Peter Thompson, the newspaper said, would fly out to Madrid on Tuesday morning to join up with the England party. Flying, in a chartered Trident, we left Heathrow, arriving at Madrid in the late afternoon. The England party stayed at The Felix Hotel. Following supper, on the Monday evening, we all went for an evening stroll prior to retiring to bed at ten-thirty. I arranged to see the injured players before breakfast on the Tuesday morning.

My early morning clinic, on the Tuesday, involved three players. Norman Hunter had a sore ankle. Bobby Moore was troubled with a slight swelling in his left knee and Peter Bonnetti's thigh was fully recovered. None of the three injuries were serious. All three players were available for selection. Alf had given the players the morning off. As the players appeared for breakfast, I enquired if anybody had any medical problems. None were reported. I went for a walk before lunch, prior to the team meeting at 2.30p.m. On the completion of the team meeting, we all left by coach for the Real Madrid training ground. The facilities there were fantastic. The First Division Clubs in England would envy the facilities at Real Madrid's training ground. They were so much better than any facilities I had seen in England. Peter Thompson arrived in time to take part in the team's training session. Not unusually, on the evening prior to a game, Alf arranged a visit to the cinema. The players would have an early supper at six o'clock followed by the cinema visit to see the film "Half A Sixpence." I would be with the players at the cinema. The doctor was always with the players.

On returning from the training ground, the solitary Football Association director, who was present in Madrid, approached Alf Ramsey with a problem. The Spanish Football Association had invited the officials travelling with the England party to an evening meal at a Madrid restaurant. As the other officials were not due to arrive in Madrid, until the morning of the game, this solitary director would have to attend the dinner alone. Attending alone, he informed Alf, was not an option, as it was insulting to the Spanish authorities. The director made his request to Alf. As I was a director of Middlesbrough, The Football Association director considered I was an acceptable person to accompany him to the restaurant and be a guest of the Spanish Football Association. Surprisingly, Alf agreed with this suggestion. When Alf approached me on the matter, I was not happy.

> "My place is with the players. I'm not here to accompany The Football Association officials to a party."

I said.

Alf was unimpressed.

> "We are only going to the cinema. I have the restaurant's telephone number. If we need you, I can contact you there. Your presence at the restaurant would be a great help to the Football Association Council Member."

Reluctantly I agreed to be one of the two guests of the Spanish Football Association at the restaurant. It was a beautiful meal, which I did not enjoy. I kept thinking I should be with the players. At any moment during that meal, I expected the phone to ring. An England player would be injured; a player had collapsed at the cinema! The call never came. Such official functions drag on for ages. It was in the early hours of the morning when I returned to the Felix Hotel. There were no messages for me. I was soon fast asleep.

Geoff Hurst knocked on my door as I was shaving before breakfast.

> "I wonder if you can have a look at my toe? It's been getting worse, since we left England. When I returned from the cinema last evening, I looked for you, but you weren't here. My toe seems to be so much worse this morning."

Although I had not seen his toe previously, I understood why it had worsened overnight. The big toe was red and swollen with inflammation. On one side of the toe there was a small pocket of pus. I drained the pocket of pus and dressed the toe. I gave Geoff a course of antibiotics.

> "I don't think you can play with that toe."

I told Geoff.

> "I tend to agree. It's much worse this morning than last night."
> "I'll inform Alf."

I said.

My meeting with Alf was not a happy one. We had always agreed, from the first time we met five years earlier, my place was always to be with the players. Last night, when Geoff Hurst needed me, I let him down. I was not available for him. Instead, I was swanning around in a restaurant deputising for The Football Association Directors! When I told Alf of the condition of Geoff's toe, he was not pleased.

> "Why didn't Geoff report the matter to Harold Shepherdson or myself last night. We were both with him last night. Geoff didn't mention it to us. If he had, I would have telephoned you at the restaurant"

I was quite angry, but managed to keep my composure.

> "Geoff did go looking for me on his return from the cinema, but, when he needed me, I wasn't there. I was at a function for the F.A. officials. Please don't let it happen again. My place is always to be with the players. On this occasion I have let Geoff Hurst down and such behaviour, on my part, is totally unacceptable."

The press were informed Geoff Hurst was unfit to play. His place would be taken by Norman Hunter. When Alan Ball was informed who was deputising for Geoff Hurst, he made the classic comment,

> "For what they are about to receive, may the Lord make them truly thankful!"

I believed I would be crucified in the press. The press were informed of Geoff's injury and learned of my absence when Geoff returned from the cinema. Some of the reporters were already writing the story of 'the absent doctor' for their newspapers. I forecasted the press reporters would make a great story out of the facts. I had been absent, when one of the players needed me. I feared the press would report it was the doctor's first senior international in charge and, instead of being with the players, he was out 'enjoying' himself in a Spanish restaurant! Fortunately for me, England beat Spain at the Bernabeu Stadium, in front of 120,000 spectators, by two goals to one. Miracle of miracles, the winning goal was scored by Geoff Hurst's replacement, Norman Hunter. It really was a miracle, as

Norman scored with his right foot! Instead of writing about the absence of the England doctor for Geoff Hurst's injury, the papers were full of Alf's tactical replacement and Norman's winning goal. I was particularly pleased for Peter Bonetti. Relatively inexperienced, at international level, he had stepped into Gordon Bank's shoes at short notice. Peter shrugged off his injury and, apart from some initial nervousness, in the intimidating Bernabeu Stadium, performed really well. In his entire career, Geoff Hurst gained 49 caps for England. If it had not been for me, Geoff might have had fifty caps. Despite England's win, I was not happy with the role I had played.

Matt Busby and Louis Edwards, the Manager and Chairman of Manchester United, joined Alf, Harold and myself for a meal after the game. Everyone was delighted England had now qualified for the European Championship Finals in Rome. After my confrontation with Sir Alf, over my absence at a Spanish restaurant, I doubted if I would be with the team.

On the flight back home Alf came and sat next to me.

> "In view of Alan Bass's departure, I wonder if you could be available for the game against Sweden at Wembley in two weeks time. The game is on the 22nd May. We shall assemble on the Sunday evening and depart after the match."

My mind immediately returned to my Practice in Redcar. I did not think any of my partners were on holiday then, but I wasn't absolutely sure. Two weeks wasn't much notice for my partners but, if no one was away, it might be possible. If I was available, another three days would be used up, from my holiday entitlement at the Practice, for the game at Wembley.

> "If I can take a few days holiday, I'll be there. I'll let you know as soon as I've spoken with my partners."

I replied.

> "Doctor, I now also have a problem for the European Championship Finals in Italy. It does appear Alan Bass has left us. Is it possible for you to be with us for the finals in Rome from 30th May to 9th June?"

Alf enquired.

> "It will all depend on the arrangements, if any, my partners have made regarding their holidays.

I replied,

> I will speak with them on my return. I'll let you know if I am available, as soon as I can."

If I was to travel to London, for the Sweden game, and Rome, for the European Championships, I would use up another three weeks of my five weeks holiday from the Practice. I would need to speak with my wife and my partners!

On returning back in London from Spain, Alf, Harold, Les and I made our way to the Football Association headquarters at Lancaster Gate. We were busily returning the team's kit to an area in the basement, when Denis Follows, the Secretary, joined us. I then witnessed, at first hand and for the first time, the animosity that existed between Alf and Denis. Pointing to several blue boxes, embossed with golden Football Association Shields and stacked on the shelves, Alf enquired as to their contents. Denis informed us each box contained eight table and drink mats, depicting, in colour, the grounds where all the World Cup matches had been played in England. Alf asked if he could see them. Denis opened one of the boxes. Inside the box were eight beautifully coloured aerial photographs of all the World Cup grounds. All the aerial photographs had been hermetically sealed and the mats were of a very high quality. Pointing to Harold, Les and myself, Alf addressed Denis,

> "I'd like you to give a set of these mats to each of my staff."

> "I'm sorry,"

said Denis,

> "You and your staff can't have any. They have been produced for the F.A. Council Members and visiting overseas dignitaries. You and your staff do not qualify."

Alf exploded,

> "That's ridiculous. The players, and my staff, won the World Cup, not the F.A. Council Members. We've now qualified

for the finals of the European Championship. Are you really telling me we can't have a set of tablemats! I want each of my staff to have a set."

"I'm sorry but that is not possible."

said Follows, who then closed the box and returned it to the shelves. The box rejoined the innumerable other boxes on the shelves. Follows refused Alf, and his staff, to have a box. I found the situation unbelievable!

My second game, in sole charge medically of the senior team, the one against Sweden at Wembley, was almost as disastrous as my first. I assumed all the medical arrangements for the admission of injured players to hospital from a Wembley international, would be subject to a standard procedure. Alas no formal arrangement existed! With Alan Bass working as a consultant in Harrow, he called upon his fellow hospital consultants whenever a player needed hospital treatment. I knew of only one of Alan's fellow consultants, the orthopaedic consultant, Nigel Harris. Nigel and I had met once at Lilleshall on a medical course. The day before the Sweden game, I telephoned Nigel to enquire if he would be available, on the evening of the game, to assist with any hospital admission, should one be needed. Fortunately, Nigel was available and readily agreed.

It became a great concern of mine that, with so many games played at Wembley, under the jurisdiction of The Football Association, no standing formalised arrangements existed for hospital admissions. When I enquired what medical arrangements were in place for matches, other than internationals, such as the F.A. Cup Final, the League Cup Final, the Amateur Cup Final and the Varsity match, to name but a few, no one seemed to know! On the night of the Swedish game at Wembley, I enquired of the Wembley staff what medical procedures were in place for these matches. I was informed,

> "If anyone breaks a bone, or has a serious injury, we send for an ambulance and they are taken to Wembley Cottage Hospital."

So much for my dream of providing the best possible medical service for professional football players.

When I first visited the dressing rooms at Wembley years previously, I thought they were an absolute disgrace. No improvements had taken place. There was no medical room in the dressing room area. Instruments for suturing, and the various sterile dressing packs and bandages required, were placed on a small table in the home dressing room. There were no showers for the players, only a communal plunge bath. The toilets and the plunge bath were at a higher level than the changing room, but essentially in the same room. During each game, after half time, the Wembley staff filled the plunge bath with hot water. The steam rose from the surface of the plunge bath during the second half of each game circulating throughout the players' changing room. When it was time, at the end of the game, to change back into civilian clothes, the steam, from the plunge bath, had made all the clothes damp. At Middlesbrough, I had utilised some of the World Cup money, allocated to the Club, to build a new medical department in close proximity to the dressing room. I never understood why The Football Association had not used some of their money in a similar way. Spending money on facilities for the players in those days was regrettably never a priority at The Football Association.

I was pleased I had the foresight to make arrangements, prior to the Sweden game, for hospital admissions, should any be necessary. Inevitably, during the game, a severe injury did occur. The Swedish goalkeeper collided with Alan Mullery injuring his neck. I considered it part of my role to be on hand for any arrangements the Swedish doctor wished to make for his player. We both examined the player and agreed it was likely he had damaged one of the bones in his neck. I was on the point of phoning Nigel Harris, to arrange hospital admission for the goalkeeper, when the Swedish doctor informed me he had made his own arrangements for his players to be admitted to the Charing Cross Hospital near Hyde Park Corner. The Swedish player was duly admitted there. X-ray examination did reveal a small crack in one of the bones in his neck. After stabilisation, the player recovered sufficiently to return to Sweden. England beat Sweden by three goals to one. Roger Hunt, Martin Peters and Bobby Charlton scored for England.

During the three days in London, prior to the Sweden game, Alf, Harold Shepherdson and myself met with Gigi Peronace. I had met Gigi previously, when Italy played in the World Cup matches at Middlesbrough. Gigi was to act as our liaison officer during our stay in Italy for the European Finals. England would play their semi-final game in Florence. Gigi pointed out the heat in Florence would be quite severe in June. He suggested the team stay outside of Florence, at Montecatini, where it would be much cooler. We decided to take Gigi's advice. He would make all the necessary arrangements with the hotel in Montecatini and liase with Alf. Following the Sweden game, I was only at home for seven days, before departing for the European Finals in Italy.

The England team reassembled in London on the 28th. May 1968. Manchester United were playing Benfica, of Portugal, in the final of the European Cup the following day at Wembley. With Nobby Stiles and Bobby Charlton playing for Manchester, Alf thought it sensible for all the England party to attend the European Cup Final. Nobby and Bobby would join up with us immediately after the match. Alf invited my wife Margaret to London for the European Cup Final. It was a rare treat for Margaret. My wife and I sat together watching Manchester United win the European Cup by four goals to one, in extra time. The day after Manchester's magnificent victory, the England team flew to Hanover. Margaret returned to Redcar and our three children.

Following their extra time marathon against Benfica, Nobby Stiles and Bobby Charlton were excused from the first day of training in Germany. Both players requested a massage. Through the good offices of the German Football Association, I made an appointment with the massage clinic, recommended by the German officials. I accompanied Nobby and Bobby. I too would enjoy the luxury of a body massage. Travelling in the taxi, the three of us imagined beautiful female masseurs attending us. Unfortunately, we were bitterly disappointed. On entering the massage clinic, our masseurs turned out to be three very hefty German men! Massages completed, we returned to the British Army's military camp, where the England team were completing their training.

DOCTOR TO THE WORLD CHAMPIONS

England lost one nil to West Germany in Hanover. The solitary goal was scored some nine minutes from time. Beckenbauer scored it with a long range shot, which was deflected off Brian Labone past Gordon Banks. The defeat was England's first in Europe since 1963. It was also the first time Germany had beaten England. For the German team, a great psychological barrier had been broken. A fact that would haunt the England team for years to come. Our stay in Hanover was quickly followed with a flight to Rome on Sunday June 2nd. The England party travelled by coach from Rome to Florence, stopping at an auto-grill, at Pavesi, for an evening meal. We left Pavesi at 8p.m. arriving at Montecatini just before midnight. We stayed at the Hotel de la Pace, a truly magnificent hotel.

The first morning, in Montecatini, both Nobby and Bobby reported sick. Their bodies were covered in a skin rash. Nobby's rash was the worse. His torso was covered with innumerable pinpoint septic spots. Bobby's main complaint was of a small tender swelling in his groin, as one of his lymph glands tried to counteract the skin infection. Both players required immediate treatment. So much for the relaxation of a massage! The skin sepsis had obviously been caused by the German masseurs. Bobby played in the semi-final against Yugoslavia. Nobby did not.

The semi-final game against Yugoslavia in Florence was played in stifling heat. It was one of the most physically intimidating games of football I had ever seen. The marking was tight, on both sides, and the Yugoslav tackling was ferocious. At half time, Alan Ball reported he had a foot injury resulting from one of the many Yugoslav harsh tackles.

"Take your boot off and I'll have a look at it."
I said.

"Please don't do that Doc, I'll never get my boot back on for the second half."
was Alan's reply.

Alan played well throughout the second half. He gave no indication he was injured. He played his usual competitive game. His attitude spoke volumes for the courage of the man. The game itself was closing, in what appeared to be an inevitable draw, when, with only four minutes remaining, Holcer's cross from the left wing landed on the chest of Dzajic, at the corner of the six yard box. Dzajic controlled the ball and scored the only goal of the game. England had lost. The World Champions of 1966 would not be the European Champions of 1969. In the final four minutes of the game calamity struck. Alan Mullery was unfairly and ferociously tackled by Trivic, who stamped on Mullery's foot. Alan Mullery turned and kicked Trivic. The Spanish referee sent off Alan Mullery for retaliation. When one considered all the ferocious tackles that had taken place during the game, Alan's retaliation, by comparison, was trivial. In football, however, retaliation is unforgivable and Alan received his marching orders. Alan Mullery thus became the first England player to be sent off in a full international. It was also the first time England had suffered two successive defeats under Alf Ramsey's management.

After the game, I examined Alan Ball's foot. His instep was black in colour and, when released from the constraints of his boot, the tissues visibly swelled further before my eyes. I feared he had broken a bone in his foot, but this was not the case. Despite treatment however, Alan would take no part in the one remaining game of the tour.

The day following the defeat against Yugoslavia, Alf requested a meeting with me. He wanted me to confirm my acceptance of the position of Honorary Team Physician to the Senior England team. He explained the position would be an honorary one. No payment was ever likely, in his opinion, from The Football Association. Alf told me how impressed he was with my medical services to the England team at Lilleshall in 1966, and for the four years I had been responsible for the Under 23 team. He always found me easy to work with and was satisfied the players were happy with the services I provided for them. In fact, he said, apart from the excellent medical services you provide, you fit in with the squad extremely well. I wish, he continued, your appointment would be simple and straight forward, but unfortunately that is not going to be the case. Denis Follows objects to your appointment. He is endeavouring to convince the members of the Senior International Committee you should not be appointed. As you know, on my appointment as England Manager, I insisted both the Senior and the

Under 23 teams had Team Physicians. It was the first time, in the history of The Football Association such appointments had been made. Prior to 1963, the England teams travelled, home and away, without a doctor being present. You are aware of the medical problems that occurred in Chile during the World Cup of 1962. There, one of the England players suffered from Septicaemia. I did not want any England player to suffer a similar medical condition without a doctor being immediately on hand. On my appointment, as England Manager therefore, I insisted a doctor would always accompany every team. Unfortunately, after I appointed Dr. Bass, he was separately approached by the Secretary of The Football Association and encouraged to accept the additional post of 'Honorary Medical Advisor to The Football Association'. Dr. Bass unfortunately accepted this additional post, without discussing the matter with me. Alan Bass therefore had a dual role. He was an Honorary Team Physician for me and an Honorary Medical Advisor to The Football Association. Alf was unable to tell me what Alan did in his medical advisory role. Very firmly he said,

> "The Honorary Medical Advisory role has nothing to do with me. I'm only concerned with Team matters and the position of the Team Physicians. The Team Physicians are my own personal appointments and they will continue to be so."

Alf went on to say Denis Follows had a problem now of his own making. When I appointed Alan Bass, as my Team Physician, Denis Follows appointed him as the Medical Advisor. Alan had the status of a Consultant, working in London, readily accessible to Follows. The Secretary now believes, it is not appropriate to appoint a General Practitioner, from Middlesbrough, to the Medical Advisor's role. Denis Follows is therefore against your appointment as Team Physician to the Senior team. I could see Alf was furious.

> "I am not in the least concerned with who is appointed Medical Advisor to The Football Association. My only concern is who is appointed as a Team Physician. I want you in that role. I need to know if you will accept that position. If you accept, I can assure you I will win the battle with Follows."

Sadly, I was not able to give Alf an immediate answer. Whilst it was a position I would love to accept, there was my work in my Redcar Practice to consider. I needed to discuss the appointment with my partners, and not least my wife. Since Alan Bass's departure to Canada, just four weeks previously, I had, of necessity, taken three and a half weeks holiday from my Practice. That commitment, to the senior team, was required for the matches against Spain in Madrid, Sweden at Wembley and presently the three matches on this tour against Germany, Yugoslavia and Russia. Prior to my standing in for the Senior Team, I had attended two Under 23 matches in 1968, against Wales at Wrexham and against Scotland in Glasgow. In total, my five weeks annual holiday had been devoured by my England duties. As a consequence of the commitment I had given, on my return to England, my wife and three children would holiday on their own. In addition there was my role as a Director and Medical Officer at Middlesbrough Football Club to consider. A long list of important appointments, none of which I was going to be paid for! There was also my part time appointment, as a medical officer to I.C.I. Apart from being present with the England team, when they played, there would be an enormous amount of medical preparation necessary for the World Cup in Mexico. As Alf was aware, Alan Bass had carried out no medical preparations for the Mexico World Cup, now just two years away. It was impossible for me to commit myself immediately to Alf's request, even though I knew I would be delighted to accept the position he was now offering me. I told Alf I would very much like to accept his offer, but would need time to assess whether I could give the role the commitment required. Alf agreed I needed to discuss the appointment with several people back in England, but he stressed how much he wanted me to accept the role. I agreed to inform him of my decision as soon as possible, after my return home. I requested he send me details of all the dates when the senior international team were scheduled to play matches from now until after the completion of the 1970 World Cup. Alf agreed to do so.

England played Russia in Rome, for the dubious distinction of coming third or fourth in the European Championship. For this play-off in Rome, Nobby Stiles, who had now fully recovered from his skin sepsis, replaced

Mullery; Tommy Wright replaced Keith Newton at right fullback and Geoff Hurst replaced Alan Ball. The Russian game commenced at seven in the evening in Rome's Stadio Olympico, to be followed immediately with The European Championship Final between Italy and Yugoslavia. The whole England party would remain in the stadium to watch the final. England beat Russia 2–0. England played exceptionally well. Bobby Charlton and Geoff Hurst each scored a goal. The final, between Italy and Yugoslavia, commenced at 9p.m., and was a disappointing 1–1 draw. A replay between the two teams would take place two days later, when we were safely back in England.

With England playing against Russia at 7p.m. our pre-match meal had taken place at four o'clock in the afternoon. The meal consisted of tea and honeyed toast. When the whistle blew, at the end of the final Alf, Harold, Les and I, not to mention the players, were starving! The players drifted off to the centre of Rome, while Alf informed Gigi Peronace of the staff's need for food. In the early hours of the morning, Gigi bundled the four of us into a taxi. We ended up in a narrow deserted street in Rome at two in the morning. The street was in total darkness. Gigi rang the doorbell. There was no response. Gigi continued to hold his finger firmly on the bell. A light eventually appeared in an upstairs window. The window opened. A middle-aged lady, dressed in a nightdress, held a conversation in Italian with Gigi, as he stood on the pavement. The window closed. Suddenly the whole house became alive with electricity. Gigi entered the restaurant.

"We will be able to eat in half an hour."
Gigi said.

We were ravenous. We enjoyed a fantastic meal of Minestrone Soup, Escalope of Veal, with delicious potatoes and vegetables, followed by Italian Ice Cream. Our hunger was more than satisfied. Alf thanked Gigi and the lady owner for their kindness. It was four in the morning when we returned to our hotel. Our flight home to London departed in five hours. I hardly slept.

I slept on the flight home. It was my chance to dream. Mam always said I was a dreamer. Unlike extremely talented sportsmen, I was blessed with no more than average talent. Any success I achieved in my life, whether at cricket or in medicine, resulted from hard work. The hard work partially compensated for my limited talent. Dedication, commitment, hard work and self discipline was the road I personally had to travel in order for me to achieve any of my life's dreams. The limited talent, I possessed, would not, on its own, have been sufficient to achieve any of my goals. My life had been full of dreams, but they only became a reality with a minimum of talent and the absolute maximum of dedication, commitment and hard work.

In my youth, my goal was to be a professional cricketer. It was my boyhood dream. There was nothing unusual in having such a dream. Hundreds, nay thousands, of boys dream of becoming a professional sportsman of one sort or another. I chose cricket. I loved the game. Most of my school friends wanted to play rugby for Wales. None of their dreams came true. They had the vision, and most had more talent than me, but their desire and commitment was insufficient. They were diverted, from their dream, by evenings spent in the pubs with their mates and girl friends. All my friends were reluctant to carry out the hard work necessary to achieve the high level of physical fitness required of a professional sportsman. As I grew up, I was determined to be a professional cricketer; my desire and commitment was total. Being a professional cricketer was my dream. Nothing, and no one, deflected me from making it a reality. My desire and commitment was never questioned. Even as a teenager, I realised if I was to make my dream a reality, hard work would always be required of me along the way. I would need self-discipline to stick to the task. The lengthy process of following my desired goal would always, every day, require hard work and my total commitment. The process involved reading all I could about cricket. I practised each and every day, indoors and out, for as many hours as I was able. My dedication was total. Nothing else in my life mattered. Girls, alcohol, smoking and sadly my academic study at school would, at no time, deflect me from the process of becoming a professional cricketer. I wanted to achieve my dream more than anyone else. Now that my youth has long since passed, and my days of playing cricket are finished, I regret none of the endless hours I spent working to achieve the goal I had set myself in my youth.

At medical school, I developed another goal. I dreamed of being the best doctor there ever was. I wanted to be a Harley Street Specialist, in either Surgery or Obstetrics. It was another of my dreams. While at university therefore, I had two main goals. I still wanted to be a professional cricketer, but I also wanted to be a brilliant surgeon. The two dreams created conflict in my life. To achieve my medical dream, I dedicated myself to the academic process for over seven years. My medical dream however never replaced my desire to be a professional cricketer. My dedication, desire and passion for playing cricket, to the best of my ability, remained supreme. In comparison, my desire and commitment to achieve my medical dream was never as all consuming as my desire to become a professional cricketer. At a crucial time in my medical career, I gave up on my dream of becoming a top class medical specialist. I realised I was not prepared to dedicate myself one hundred per cent to the task of specialising in medicine. Cricket meant too much in my life. When faced with the ultimate choice, I chose to continue playing cricket. I would always choose cricket! From the experience however, I learned. if I was to reach the very top, in any sphere of my life, total desire, commitment, dedication and hard work were absolutely essential from me. I did not have that commitment for specialising in Medicine. That was the main reason I had entered General Practice.

On my appointment as the Medical Officer at Middlesbrough Football Club, and a few months later to the England Under 23 team, I had another dream. I wanted the players, under my care, to have the best medical services available. I had grown up, as a player in a variety of sports well aware, from the player's perspective, how poor the medical services for sportsmen really were. At the time of my appointment to these two posts, Sports Medicine was not a speciality in Britain. There was no academic course to follow. No examination to sit. No postgraduate degree to obtain. The medical profession, in Great Britain, ignored Sports Medicine. Most doctors involved in Sports Medicine, at that time, were, like myself, sportsmen who had qualified as doctors. Fortuitously, we had become involved in treating sportsmen. We were now practising Sports Medicine in our own particular individual way. My appointment to the England Under 23 team had however projected me into the front line of International Sports Medicine. Against some countries, I knew I was competing against full time, properly trained, and highly qualified Sports Medicine doctors.

Alf Ramsey was now offering me a new challenge. If I accepted his offer, my new dream would be to provide the England football team with the best Sports Medicine service in the world. No other international football team, would have better medical care. Achieving that aim would become yet another of my goals, yet realising this new dream, like in all my other dreams, would require my total dedication and commitment for the next two years Alf was asking me to achieve the impossible. The task was tremendous. In setting out to achieve this new dream, nothing and no one would be allowed to deflect me from the process. It would be essential for me to be totally committed to the process. Nothing else was acceptable. The sacrifice required of me and my family would be immense.

Pam Darch, the air hostess, gently rocked my shoulder. I awoke.

> "We're just making our descent to Heathrow Airport. You've slept for most of the flight. I hope you've had nice dreams. It would be helpful if you would fasten your seat belt."

Alf's offer to take up the appointment of Honorary Team Physician to the Senior Team might become a new challenge for me. I was unsure however whether I could give the role the dedication, commitment, self-discipline, desire and hard work, I knew I would demand of myself. There were so many issues to discuss. So many other people to consider. Margaret would need to be consulted first. She had once said of me,

> "He always has to have a challenge. He treats every challenge as if he's climbing a mountain. He always needs, in his life, a mountain to climb. Trouble is, when he's climbed the mountain, he doesn't stay long enough to admire the view. He's always off to climb another mountain, with yet another challenge."

Alf was now asking me to climb Everest! I didn't know if I was up to the task.

I returned to Teesside with Harold Shepherdson. The remainder of the summer would be spent at home. I'd used up all my holiday entitlement. Alf departed with Denis Follows to Mexico observing the Olympic Games. I should have gone with them. Instead, I would watch excerpts of the Olympics on television.

It was a sobering thought. The present World Champions were now third in Europe, behind Italy, who won the European Championship 2–0 in the replay, and Yugoslavia. England's task now was to focus on the World Cup in Mexico. The competition was just two years away. I was unsure if I could be part of the team.

There was never any doubt, in my mind, Margaret would want me to accept the post Alf Ramsey had offered me.

> "If at all possible, you must accept. How many doctors are ever offered such a post? I know it will mean extra work for you, but it's a once in a lifetime opportunity. You must accept."

she said.

Before he left for the Olympic Games in Mexico, Alf sent me the proposed fixtures of the England team for the remainder of 1968, the whole of 1969 and 1970. It was quite extensive. If I was to be present at all the games, it would require a massive time commitment from myself. In the two years up to and including 1970, I would need to be away from the Practice for ninety-five days, which was five days more than my total holiday commitment. If I accepted the role, there would be no possibility of the family having a holiday together for two years. It was a lot to ask of my wife and three children, aged ten, nine and six and my partners.

There were two matches still to be played in 1968. An away fixture in Romania and a home game at Wembley against Bulgaria. As a result of Alan Bass's sudden departure to Canada, and my involvement with the team in Madrid and Italy, my holiday entitlement from the Practice had already been used up for 1968. The commitment still required of me was another seven days later in the year. Working on the premise a home international at Wembley necessitated my presence for three days and an away international, with its associated travel, four days, the 'holiday' commitment required of me, the following year in 1969, was 39 days. As the total, of my yearly holiday entitlement from the Practice was thirty-five working days, I would be four days short. In 1970, including the World Cup in Mexico and the associated one month's acclimatisation, the team would require my presence for forty-nine days. Ninety-five days, in two years, away from the Practice was certainly some commitment.

In addition to my requested presence with the team, I was very concerned about the associated work and study I needed to do. There would be innumerable medical reports and research papers to read; specialists in England to be approached and visited for advice; hospital facilities in Mexico to be visited; training programmes to be worked out; players' and staff's medical examinations to be carried out at regular intervals; immunisation programmes to be agreed and organised; and regular blood tests to be arranged. The list seemed endless. In addition, I was well aware I would have to do all this work in an honorary capacity with no financial reward. Alf had stressed to me, on more than one occasion, The Football Association considered the role of Team Physician was a purely voluntary and honorary one.

Such a commitment from myself to Sir Alf and the team would have a major effect on my wife and three children, together with each of my partners in the Practice. On every occasion, when a partner was away, the workload on the remaining partners increased substantially. Lengthy discussions with my partners would be required to determine whether it would be possible for them to allow me such a privilege. Throughout the summer of 1968, the issues were discussed at several meetings with my partners. They were extremely cooperative and understanding, but it was a massive undertaking for them, as well as for myself. The discussions continued throughout the Olympic Games. For my partners, it necessitated them, and their families, ensuring whether they were all able to arrange their holidays around the fixtures of the England team. It was an extraordinary request I was asking of them. Whilst Sir Alf and Denis Follows attended the Games in Mexico, discussions continued with my wife and partners in Redcar.

At Lewis' School Pengam, the grammar school I attended, Geography was taught badly. That was not only my personal opinion, but a view shared by many of my school chums. In Geography, Alan Protheroe always had the distinction of coming bottom of the class. His school report once contained the written comment from the Geography master,

> "Alan amazes me that he can find his own way home from school!"

My Geography was only marginally better than Alan's. I did learn however, from my Geography, one knowledgeable item. La Paz, the capital of Bolivia, I learned, is the highest capital in the world. It lies, in a natural basin surrounded by the mountains of the Andes, at 12,400 feet. Visitors to La Paz, I read, will, at first, feel some discomfort from the rarefied air. The advice for people flying into La Paz, from sea level was simple.

> "On arrival, it is sensible to spend the first few hours resting in bed."

This initial period of rest, it was claimed, allowed the body to adjust to the altitude. The rarefied atmosphere, I was later told, though I can't remember the origin of the story, was the reason why the runway at La Paz airport was two miles longer than a comparable runway at sea level. The air, at the 12,400 feet of La Paz, is so thin, the aircraft landing have difficulty in stopping. On landing, all aircraft lower their wing flaps. The lowering of the flaps forms a resistance to the air, enabling them to act as a brake for the aeroplane, thus assisting the aircraft in coming to a stop. The air, at La Plaz, is so thin it presents little resistance to the aircraft's wing flaps and so, aircraft landing there, require a much longer runway in order to come to a satisfactory stop. I was aware the thin, less resistant, air at altitude allowed objects to travel more easily and faster through the air than at sea level. Golfers found this to be the case when they played at altitude on Swiss and Austrian courses. A five iron shot became a seven iron shot.

> "Take two clubs less."

was the golfer's cry.

> "When you hit a golf ball at altitude, it just keeps going and going."

A football, like a golf ball, would travel further through the rarefied atmosphere at altitude, as compared to sea level, and at a faster rate. Football skills, acquired over many years at sea level, in passing the ball, would need to be adjusted at altitude. A twenty-yard pass at sea level, could become one of thirty yards at altitude. Players would need time to adjust their skills to the thinner air. In addition, physical exercise at altitude would be severely affected.

Physical exercise, from a medical view point, may be divided into two distinct types.

Firstly, there are those physical activities requiring little or no oxygen during the activity. In this type of exercise, the body's exertion is so explosive and intense, but of such short duration, the breathing in of air, is not necessary. Consider the athlete who runs in the one hundred metres. Athletes complete the hundred metres in less than ten seconds. How many times can an athlete breathe in less than ten seconds? It is probable the one hundred-metre athlete only breathes once, or at most twice, during the whole race. A supply of oxygen appears not to be needed. The athlete completes the run without a supply of air. Such an athlete, apart from natural talent and good technique, requires muscular strength and power. The muscular effort is confined to a time span of just ten seconds. Such explosive, severe muscular effort is not dependent on the body receiving a supply of oxygen. Athletic races, of distances up to four hundred metres take place under similar physical circumstances. Medically, these physical activities are classified, as "Anaerobic Exercises"–physical exercise that takes place without the need for a regular supply of oxygen.

Secondly, in prolonged physical exercise however, particularly in those athletic events over four hundred metres, the body requires to receive a steady supply of oxygen whilst the event is taking place. The muscles of the human body are unable to sustain prolonged exercise without receiving a steady, regular, supply of oxygen from the atmosphere. Such prolonged exercise is medically described as "Aerobic Exercise"- exercise that can only take place with the body receiving a regular supply of oxygen during the event. In simple terms, the air at altitude contains less oxygen than at sea level. The higher the altitude, the less oxygen there is in the atmosphere. The atmospheric pressure is also reduced at altitude. For people born and living at sea level, severe, prolonged exercise at altitude is extremely difficult, even when they are given an adequate period of acclimatisation. At La Paz, the air is so thin and the oxygen content and pressure so low that, on arrival from a sea-level destination, even prolonged walking is difficult. Consequently travellers, arriving in the city, are advised to spend a few hours resting in bed.

The Mexico Olympic Games of 1968, were held in a city high in the sky. Mexico City lies in a basin surrounded by mountains. The mountains rise up to some 17,000 feet. Mexico City, lies in a flat basin, at an altitude of 7,434 feet. Mexico City is therefore some one and a half miles in the sky. The decision to hold the Olympics and the World Cup at Mexico City required competitors to compete one and a half miles up in the sky! The air, at such an altitude, is thinner and less dense and provides less resistance for objects travelling through it. Compared to the air density at sea level, the air density in Mexico City is reduced by some twenty per cent. The atmospheric pressure is also reduced. These factors lead to less oxygen being available to the human body than at sea level. Prior to the Mexico Olympics, it was feared athletes, from sea level countries, would be severely affected by the altitude and so it proved. Some reports, prior to the Games, suggested there was a possibility some athletes might even die! Those reports fortunately proved untrue.

Not all athletic performances were adversely affected by the altitude of Mexico City. Many athletic performances were greatly improved. It was a great advantage, to my improving knowledge of the effects of altitude on athletic performance, that all performances in the Olympic Games were scientifically measured. Athletes run a specific distance in an accurately measured time. Field events, whether the long, triple or high jumps are also accurately measured. Athletic performance is always accurately measured. In contrast, the game of football, in the 1960's, with the absence of computers and video analysis, was a game of impressions. Each spectator, at a football match, would inevitably have a slightly different impression of the game. Every individual watching, could have a different view of a team's or an individual footballer's performance. In athletics, the performance was accurately measured. The individual performances were recorded for everyone to see. The performances in football, in the years preceding the 1970 World Cup were not accurately measured.

Athletes involved in the explosive, anaerobic events, we have established, do not require a steady supply of oxygen to perform their event. These events were not adversely affected by the altitude of Mexico City. In fact, these athletic performances were enhanced. With the reduced air density at altitude, there is less resistance in the air for the athlete to run against. With the air at altitude so thin, any athlete running is subjected to less resistance. As he requires no oxygen in his explosive event, the performance would actually improve. Similar to the aeroplane landing at La Plaz, the athlete would travel through the air more quickly and may even have difficulty in stopping! In the long and triple jumps for example, when the athlete took off, there would be less air resistance for them to jump against. This decrease in air resistance, would allow the athlete to "fly through the air with the greatest of ease." The jumpers at the Mexico Olympics did not require a supply of oxygen to run down their runway. Like the sprinters, their performance would be greatly enhanced, simply due to the decrease in the air resistance. I believed, prior to the Mexico Olympics, all events requiring little or no oxygen supply during the event would be greatly improved. On the other hand, the endurance events, those requiring a steady supply of oxygen to the body during the event, would be adversely affected. In the Mexico Olympics, the times for every anaerobic event improved beyond my wildest expectations, and, I suspect, those of the competing athletes. The events requiring a steady supply of oxygen were much more adversely affected than I anticipated. The times, for these endurance events, were extremely poor.

The results of the Mexico Olympics warrant closer analysis. As I watched the Games on television I compared the results in Mexico with the results at previous Olympic Games. At this time of writing, I can also compare the Mexico results with the performances in subsequent Olympics. The comparisons are accurate, in that all the events had been timed or measured.

Hines, running in the 100 metres at Mexico, won in a new Olympic record time of 9.95 seconds. Despite three subsequent Olympics, all held at sea level, with all the improvements in training and coaching over the twelve year period, Hines' time was never equalled. Hines' time in Mexico remained the Olympic record twelve years later. Similarly, Smith's time of 19.8 seconds, in winning the 200 metres at the Mexican games, remained the Olympic record twelve years later. Evans' time of 43.8 seconds in the Mexico 400 metres was also still the Olympic record after the 1980 Olympics. For further confirmation of the effect of the thinner air, look what happened in the jumping events. Athletic supporters can readily recall Beaman's long jump at Mexico. Beaman leapt twenty-nine feet, two and a half inches. It seemed, when he took off, there was nothing in the air to stop him. The air was some twenty per cent less dense than at sea level. Less well remembered, though of equal significance, was the Russian Sancyev's performance in the triple jump. He took off at the end of his runway and leapt a staggering three quarters of an inch over fifty-seven feet. Despite all the improvements in the training and coaching of athletes that took place in the ensuing years, these Olympic records obtained in Mexico of Hines, Smith, Evans, Beaman and Sancyev were still the records twelve years later. These athletic performances confirmed to me that anaerobic events were greatly improved at altitude, directly due to the reduction in air density. The thin air in Mexico City worked to the advantage of these athletes; the air was simply easier to travel through.

If the less dense air at Mexico City improved the anaerobic athletic events, how did the aerobic events—those where the athletes needed a steady supply of oxygen throughout their event—perform? Their Olympic results confirmed athletes, competing in these events, were disadvantaged. Many athletes experienced severe distress. At the altitude of Mexico City the oxygen they needed, during their event, simply wasn't there. The reduction of the amount of oxygen in the atmosphere, together with the reduction in atmospheric pressure, worsened the athlete's performance.

Gammoudi won the Mexican five thousand metres. His time, of fourteen minutes and five seconds was the slowest time for any Olympic five thousand metres in the previous twelve years. Gammoudi's time was worse than in any of the previous Olympic Games of 1956, 1960, and 1964. The winner, of the ten thousand metres in Mexico, was Temu of Kenya. His time, of twenty-nine minutes and twenty-seven seconds, was the worst time ever recorded for the event in the previous twenty-four years of the Olympics. Wolde, of Ethiopia, was victorious in the Mexico Marathon. His time was a full eight minutes slower than the winner, in the Olympics, four years previously in Tokyo. From these times, it is obvious the endurance events were adversely affected by the altitude of Mexico City. The results, at the Mexico Olympics, was the scientific proof I needed. Athletic performance was severely influenced at altitude.

I called the 1968 Olympic Games, the "Unfair Games." Unfair, in the sense the Olympic records made in the explosive, anaerobic events were unfair on the previous and subsequent competing athletes. Future Olympic athletes, competing in the Games at a sea level city, would be unable to equal, let alone beat, such results. The times recorded, in the endurance events at Mexico, did not record the true ability of the competing athletes. If the Olympics of 1968 had been held at sea level, the times in the endurance events would have been so much better. The sea level athletes found, in Mexico City, their anaerobic performance improved in contrast to their aerobic performances which worsened considerably. In my opinion, the results of the Mexico Olympics should be completely removed from the Olympic records.

Football players require a steady supply of oxygen, during the game, to perform to their full potential. Football is a mixture of physical endurance, interspersed with sudden bursts of explosive physical effort. Football is thus a mixture of aerobic and anaerobic activity. Playing at altitude, ensures the usual supply of oxygen is not available for the players' endurance work. The endurance performance of football players inevitably suffers. They need a steady supply of oxygen throughout the game. The lack of oxygen at altitude would inevitably affect their performance. People watching football at altitude would give many different impressions of the effects of altitude, but it would only be an impression. In the absence of video and computer recordings of the day, football remained a game of impressions. The results in the 1968 Mexican Olympics gave me the scientific evidence I needed for the effects of altitude on athletic performance.

A long period of acclimatisation at altitude would be essential for the England team prior to the 1970 World Cup in Mexico. For how long, where and at what altitude that acclimatisation should occur, I knew not. The Mexico Olympics whetted my appetite. I wanted to gain more knowledge regarding the effects of altitude on athletic performance. I knew so little. The effects of altitude on athletic performance had not been a daily requirement for me working as a General Practitioner at the seaside town of Redcar! I was however aware of the existence of the Medlar database at Manchester University. There, records would be held of all the relevant articles which had appeared in the medical journals worldwide on the subject. Following a telephone conversation with a Mrs. Patterson, I wrote requesting a list of all the recent medical articles published on Acclimatisation to Altitude, and Athletic performance at Altitude. A return telephone call informed me there were over four hundred articles! I settled for a list of one hundred and fifty. Each and everyone of those medical articles I subsequently read. During the summer of 1968, I gradually became something of an expert on altitude and its effects on athletes!

When Alf Ramsey returned from Mexico, he immediately telephoned me to enquire if I was in a position to accept the post of Honorary Team Physician to the Senior England Team. Unfortunately, I was not. Discussions were still on going with my partners. No definitive decision had been made. I assured Alf my partners were being most cooperative but, to date, no final decision had been made. From a Practice viewpoint, it was a very large commitment to make. Some two weeks later, following further discussions with my partners, it was agreed I could commit myself to the England cause, albeit by taking my yearly holiday entitlement from the Practice. I was most grateful to my partners. On the 7th September 1968, I was able to write a letter to Alf, confirming my availability. My letter was as follows:-

PROMOTION FOR ME

Dear Alf,

Further to my letter of last week, I have now discussed the position with my partners and, not least, my wife, as regards to the medical commitment up to and including Mexico 1970. The outcome of these deliberations is that I should be available, as requested in your letter, with one possible exception.

You will appreciate that in 1968, I have taken all my holiday—in fact I am a little over as it is. I was unaware of any further football commitments this year until your letter of the 27th August.

My partners have however agreed to give me some extra holiday—how I need it!- so that I can go with the team to Romania from, I presume, November 4th-7th inclusive. Unfortunately however two of my partners are away in December during the period of the match on December 11th. If this match is at Wembley, I could still cover but not if it was overseas.

As regards 1969, the dates you have specified are alright, including the summer tour to Mexico, Uruguay, and Brazil.

The dates for the World Cup in 1970 have also been reserved commencing May 1st for the period of acclimatisation and the tournament proper.

It would appear therefore that December 11th. apart, I should be available until 1970. I am sorry to have kept you waiting so long for a reply, but I wanted to clarify the situation at this end before committing myself.

Perhaps we could benefit from an early discussion. I could travel to London on the next two Wednesdays—September 18th. or 25th, if this is convenient for you.

I hope you and Harold enjoy yourselves in the Channel Isles this week and trust you will not overdo the swimming and the sunbathing!

With Every Good Wish,

Neil Phillips

I met with Sir Alf in London on the 25th. September. He confirmed he wanted me to act as the Team Physician to the Senior Team. He informed me he was still having problems, with Denis Follows, with regard to the role of Medical Advisor to The Football Association. Alf said he was not interested in this role, as his remit was solely with the England Team and the care of the players. I had previously told Alf I was also only interested in being a Team Physician. I was not interested in becoming a Medical Advisor to The Football Association. He assured me, with his recommendation, I would be appointed as the Honorary Senior Team Physician. At our personal meeting, he gave me authority to prepare the England team, from a medical point of view, for the forth coming World Cup in Mexico.

"Start work immediately."
he said.

We had so much to discuss. Alf gave me his impressions of Mexico, together with the football matches he had attended. While in the country, he had visited Guadalajara, where, it was rumoured, our initial World Cup matches would be played. He had also visited Leon, and Puebla as these were two other World Cup venues.

While Guadalajara was at a lower altitude than Mexico City, a mere 5,400 feet above sea level, the heat there was considerable. At mid day, the temperature was over one hundred degrees. Playing there, Alf thought, the heat, rather than the altitude, would be the most significant factor to affect the players. Apart from developing an expertise on Altitude, I would now have to become an expert on the effects of Heat Stress and Heat Disorders. My involvement in my new role was increasing by the minute!

Following the international against Sweden at Wembley, I was extremely concerned at the lack of expert hospital personnel to call upon and the lack of availability for emergency hospital admission facilities. These I believed were absolutely necessary so that any serious injury would immediately have the best medical opinion available for the players. I reported to Alf that, while he was in Mexico for the Olympics, I had contacted the consultants at The National Orthopaedic Hospital in London. I had enquired of them if they would be willing to provide the England team with such a service. I had met with Mr. Wilson, an orthopaedic consultant based at the Stanmore branch of The National Orthopaedic Hospital and following our discussions, he, and his fellow consultant at Stanmore, Mr. Trickey, agreed to be on call for any orthopaedic emergencies occurring during any game at Wembley played under the jurisdiction of The Football Association. It seemed incredible to me that, if this arrangement was agreed, it would be the first occasion the provision of emergency medical facilities would be written down and available to all teams playing at Wembley. Mr Wilson had informed me of the extensive overseas medical network the National Orthopaedic Hospital possessed. Wilson suggested, should I ever need information regarding any overseas visits, he was happy to advise me on suitable orthopaedic specialists wherever and whenever the team played at home and abroad. Additionally, when overseas, I could tap into all the services provided by The National Orthopaedic Hospital simply by calling Mrs. Glen Hayes at the main hospital. I informed Alf I had invited Mr. Wilson to dine with the England party at Whites Hotel on the Sunday evening prior to our departure to Romania on the 4th. November. Any further arrangements, or clarification of the ones I had agreed, could be finalised then. The meeting would enable Sir Alf, his staff and the players to meet with Mr. Wilson. By involving Mr. Wilson and Mr. Trickey, in this way, I was satisfied the orthopaedic service available to the players would be second to none. The geographical proximity of Stanmore Hospital to Wembley, in the case of an orthopaedic emergency during a game, was an added bonus. It was astonishing to me that no standing arrangements were in place for the admission to hospital of serious injuries, particularly when one considered all the matches taking place at Wembley under the jurisdiction of The Football Association.

Whether or not I had been able to accept the position of England Team Doctor, I knew the players would need a series of vaccinations and immunisations prior to setting off for South America. I informed Alf I had contacted The London School of Tropical Medicine and they had readily agreed to give me all the advice and help needed. Their advice ensured all the players would be adequately protected against the known tropical diseases occurring in Mexico and South America. Dr. Roodyn, of the London School, had written to me giving me all the relevant up to date advice. He suggested many of the procedures could be carried out at the London School of Tropical Medicine, by himself, at a mutually convenient time. I reported to Alf I was due to meet with Dr. Roodyn shortly. Alf was delighted I had made all these arrangements whilst he was in Mexico. At our meeting Sir Alf gave me a copy of his report to The Football Association of his visit to Mexico during the Olympic Games.

As I had come to expect, with all that Alf did, his report was extremely thorough and covered every aspect to which professional footballers would need answers. Alas, and I did not expect any, there was no reference to any medical facilities and no appraisal of the standard of hospital care. Having stated the purpose of his visit was to assess conditions, inspect World Cup grounds, accommodation and training grounds, Alf reported he was delighted with the cooperation he had received from the British Embassy and the Mexican Football Association both of whom were most helpful. It would have been extremely difficult, he said, to have carried out the programme planned without their assistance. At Guadalajara, Leon and Puebla, local club officials went to some lengths to ensure that his visit was as beneficial as possible.

Alf had visited, throughout Mexico, all the grounds where it was possible England might play in the World Cup. He was particularly impressed with the Azteca Stadium in Mexico City which had a capacity for 100,000 spectators. Whilst the playing pitch was in good condition, Alf noted the stadium was bowl shaped and the seating rose from ground level to some considerable height. He believed this could possibly create a problem for the players, in that there was very little, if any, ventilation at the level of the playing pitch. At noon, the sun is directly overhead and the temperature, inside the stadium, at that time, was in the upper eighties. Alf had attended three games played there during the Games. All matches were played in the evenings and the floodlights appeared to be very satisfactory. He noted the time involved, in travelling from the centre of the city to the stadium was approximately forty minutes

Alf considered the Jalisco Stadium in Guadalajara to be excellent. Presently the seating capacity was for 50,000 spectators, but this would be increased by 20,000 for the World Cup. The playing pitch was in excellent condition and, in direct contrast with the Azteca Stadium, the buildings were not so high, thus giving more ventilation at ground level. However this could well be affected if 20,000 more spectators have to be catered for, as the only way this could be done was to build up on the existing foundations. Alf expressed his concerns that the floodlights on the main side of the ground were much lower than those opposite and could more certainly affect players' judgment. Guadalajara being 2500 feet lower than Mexico City was considerably warmer and the temperature frequently reached over 100 degrees during his visit.

The stadium in Leon is a small, newly built stadium close to the outskirts of the town, seating some thirty thousand spectators. The playing pitch was in excellent condition. The climate was comparable to that of Guadalajara. At Puebla, it was suggested to Alf, the stadium there would be completed by October 1968 and, from what Alf could see, it was being built on similar lines to that at Leon, accommodating thirty thousand spectators. The climate in Puebla varied little from that in Mexico City

Alf reported that he had visited many hotels in the four cities and it was apparent to him that if this type of accommodation was to be used, only a first class hotel would overcome the problems of sleep, food and drink. Most first class hotels have air conditioning, a necessary pre requisite in the heat, and he noted that sleep came much easier in Guadalajara than elsewhere because the Hilton Hotel there had a modern system of air conditioning, which was noiseless. A comparison, whilst staying at The Maria Isabel Hotel, also a first-class hotel in Mexico City, where the air conditioning proved to be very noisy. With regard to food and drink, Alf had been advised that stomach upsets will occur less frequently in first class hotels, where the food and drink should be of the best quality. In Guadalajara, except for the Hilton Hotel, there were few first class hotels on offer, but some new hotels will be built by 1970.

There were numerous training grounds in all the cities he visited, but in many cases they were of poor quality. However, in Mexico City, three training grounds were impressive. As it seemed almost certain England would be based in Guadalajara, Alf spent considerable time visiting various training grounds. Of these, the Atlas Sports Club had by far the best facilities. As a result an approach was made to the Secretary for the use of the ground. His reaction was most favourable and the grounds will be available for the England team in 1970. The Atlas Club has many facilities to offer in addition to a first class training ground and include tennis, table tennis, basketball, and a swimming pool. Areas visited in Leon and Pueblo were of a similar nature and the most likely training grounds, provided their condition is improved, are at the old Zaragosa Stadium at Puebla and the old Stadium at Leon. These grounds have been used regularly by all clubs in these towns prior to the completion of the new stadiums.

Alf was obviously concerned with the weather conditions he had experienced during his visit. Throughout, it consisted of bright sunshine, with temperatures varying from seventy to ninety degrees in Mexico City and seventy-five to over one hundred degrees in Guadalajara. During a visit to the latter, the temperature rose to more than one hundred degrees in the afternoon. It becomes dark about 7:30pm and the change from daylight to darkness takes place in little more than half an hour.

Alf's report concluded by listing the various altitudes of all the cities- Mexico City 7500 feet above sea level, Guadalajara 5000 feet, Leon 5500 feet and Puebla 6500 feet and whilst generally it was very hot in Mexico City and Puebla, the temperature in Guadalajara and Leon was much higher. Alf stated it is generally agreed physical exertion at high altitude will have an adverse effect on players' performances. Therefore acclimatisation is essential for all members of the team. A period of four weeks before the opening games would appear to be the minimum requirement. It was obvious from the five matches seen at the Azteca Stadium, one in the morning, one at noon, and three in the evening, that players responded much better at night when temperatures were lower than during the day. It would assist the players greatly if World Cup matches were played at night, but this seems unlikely as live television coverage of matches would be affected owing to there being a time difference of seven hours behind British summer time. Alf appeared to be more concerned now about the heat rather than the altitude

He was aware of the problems of occupying a group of players when abroad for any length of time, particularly if based in the same place. Training and matches apart, there are several cinemas with English speaking films, but little else of interest to professional footballers. With regard to the food, Alf recommended that local dishes should be avoided and only well-cooked food consumed. A diet, similar to that taken in England should be possible but salads, and unpeeled fruit and ice cream should not be eaten.

Hotels situated in a city centre, he commented, are not ideal for the purpose of preparing a team for matches mainly because of the tendency of the press, photographers, and broadcasting and television representatives to intrude upon all privacy. However, it seems that it will be necessary to stay in a first class hotel, which is modern and has silent air-conditioning. Equally important, as this type of hotel usually has many rooms, the players should be accommodated on one floor with rooms next to each other and arrangements made for private rooms to be available for eating and resting.

At our meeting, Alf expressed his disappointment, despite visiting many hotels during his visit, he had been unable to find suitable accommodation in Mexico City itself for the team. His obvious other concern was the heat in Guadalajara. Playing football in temperatures over a hundred degrees, with the sun directly overhead, was a daunting prospect. During the summer, I had read, learned and inwardly digested innumerable articles on altitude and its effect on athletic performance. I now considered myself knowledgeable on altitude. I now realised I would have to learn every detail of acclimatising to heat and all the associated problems of working in a very hot environment. It was a daunting task. I knew so little about the effects of working in extreme heat and how best to acclimatise to it

My knowledge of altitude, its physiological effects, acclimatisation and its associated problems had considerably improved during the summer months. Nevertheless, I was anxious to discuss the relevant issues with an expert who had personally been involved in all the planning of a previous expedition to altitude and the acclimatisation process. Such a person was Dr. Griffith Pugh, working at Hampstead in London. Griffith had been the physiologist advising Sir John Hilary and his team on the ascent of

Everest. He had taken part in that successful expedition. I needed to learn of Dr. Pugh's personal experiences. I sought his advice and informed Alf I had arranged to meet with Griffith Pugh at his office in Hampstead.

I finally informed Alf of the need to put in place the facilities for blood tests to be carried out on the England players and staff. These tests would need to take place on a regular basis during the eighteen months prior to our departure for the World Cup. With this in mind, I had contacted, Dr. Fielding, the consultant haematologist at St. Mary's Hospital in London. Following those discussions, I arranged to meet with Dr. Fielding to discuss the details of his involvement. We had subsequently arranged a programme of blood tests for the players and staff, which I gave to Alf for his approval. It was unlikely that many, if any, of the players had undergone blood tests previously. Dr. Fielding and I suggested the blood tests be carried out on all the players in London at the following times. In May 1969, prior to the South American tour. In December 1969 prior to the game against Portugal at Wembley. In January or February 1970, depending on the December results and any new players being called into the squad. In April 1970, during the home international tournament, thus completing the entire group of players and staff.. In addition, oral iron tablets would need to be given to those players with low blood levels from December 1969 onwards. In addition every member of the squad would commence taking oral iron tablets, two weeks prior to departure for the World Cup and continue to take the tablets daily during the four-week acclimatisation programme in Mexico.

Alf seemed pleased I had not been entirely idle while he was in Mexico! Sadly, I received no report from Secretary Denis Follows. The findings, of his visit to Mexico, were never given to me.

During his visit to Mexico, Alf had met Dr. Roger Bannister, the first man to run the mile in a time below four minutes. Roger had been at the Olympic Games as an observer. Alf was of the opinion I would be able to obtain much useful medical information from him. Apparently Roger Bannister had expressed his concern at the prevalence of gastro-enteritis in Mexico and the apparent lack of hygiene in food preparation. Bannister was aware the British Olympic team had used Streptotriad, as a preventative medicine, and was recommending the England team use Streptotriad also. Streptotriad is a combination of drugs—Streptomycin and three absorbable sulphonamides. It is administered orally as a pink tablet. The use of Streptotriad, as a preventative measure, was of great concern to me. Its use as a preventative drug seemed unwise to me. Streptotriad was such a powerful combination of drugs. If such a powerful drug was used as the first line in preventative treatment, what would I be able to use if a case of gastro-enteritis occurred subsequently? The most powerful treatment would have been used already. Previously, when football players under my care had been exposed to the dangers of gastro-enteritis, I had used a drug called Thalazole as the preventative treatment of choice. Thalazole was a non-absorbable sulphonamide that lined the gut, but was not absorbed into the body. It had worked well in the past. If gastro-enteritis subsequently developed, in a player taking Thalazole, I could then use Streptotriad as a curative treatment. It seemed quite wrong to me to use such a powerful drug as Streptotriad as a first choice prophylactic. I reasoned, if a player on Streptotriad developed gastro-enteritis, what drug treatment could I then use to cure the condition, if indeed drug therapy was indicated?

Alf informed me, at the meeting, of an additional problem. It was apparent Denis Follows was pressing for the appointment of the Chelsea Team Doctor to the position with the Under 23 team.

> "The selection of a doctor for the Under 23 team is my responsibility, not Denis Follows'. You do need a deputy however. I need you to advise me regarding a suitable person. There are two imminent Under 23 Internationals. One against Wales at Wrexham on October 2nd, and another at Birmingham, against Holland on November 13th. I wondered if you could cover both matches?"

As both matches were on a Wednesday, my half day in the Practice, it was agreed I would cover both matches, but only for the day of the game. As our meeting drew to a close, Alf impressed upon me whatever was necessary medically, in preparing the team for Mexico, we should discuss the matter first and, if we agreed, I should then proceed with the agreement. We had spent the day discussing the many medical problems confronting the players in Mexico. These problems were now my sole responsibility. I would seek the advice of many medical colleagues. The knowledge gained from them would be invaluable. The task facing me was incredible. At the end of the day however, on all medical matters, the final decisions were mine and mine alone. The buck, as they say, would stop with me. It was a huge responsibility.

On my train journey back north, my mind raced through the problems confronting me. My immediate concern was finding a suitable doctor to act as Team Physician to the Under 23 team. I contacted Ian Adams, the Leeds United doctor, for whom I had a very high regard. Ian wanted a salary. Sadly The Football Association was not interested in paying doctors. When a student, at Sheffield Medical School, I had a high regard for Professor Frank O'Gorman. Frank was one of the most highly qualified doctors in England, a director of Sheffield United, though not the Club Doctor. Nevertheless I decided to ask Frank if he would take up the role. Having discussed the appointment with his colleagues at Sheffield United, Frank accepted the position. I informed Alf of my recommendation. Frank O'Gorman, one of my student day professors, would become Team Physician to the Under 23 team, and my deputy. I was delighted. It seemed ironic that a former student was asking one of his Professors to act as his deputy!

As Alf had suggested, I contacted Roger Bannister with a view to discussing with him his views on the Mexico Olympics. His experiences, I said, would be very helpful to me in preparing the England team for the 1970 World Cup. He readily agreed to meet with me. We met at his consulting rooms in Harley Street. We had a full discussion on the problems athletes experienced when competing in Mexico City. We discussed the problems of altitude acclimatisation; the heat factor; the hygiene and food and the performances of the athletes. His views were most helpful. Most importantly, we had a very useful exchange of views on the use of the drug Streptotriad as the prophylactic treatment of choice. Bannister's view was the use of Streptotriad had been so successful for the British athletes in

Mexico, it was essential the England footballers were also given this drug daily throughout their stay in Mexico. Roger reported, out of two hundred and ninety four athletes in the British party, only six had acquired severe gastro-enteritis during their time in Mexico. Streptotriad, he stressed, had proved effective as a preventative measure. Reluctantly, I realised it was now a drug I would have to consider using in Mexico. I realised I would need to give Streptotriad a trial run with the footballers. I reported all the issues I had discussed with Bannister, including the use of Streptotriad, to Alf Ramsey. Alf and I agreed to give Streptotriad a trial with our players.

On returning home, I was somewhat consoled however by a Leading Article, published in The British Medical Journal,[†] which addressed the specific problem of 'Diarrhoea at the Olympics'. The article confirmed the view that Mexico had an unenviable reputation for producing in visitors some form of acute enteritis, the exact cause of which is not any recognised pathogen. Without going into the details of the various drug trials, carried out on North American students by the New York Physician, B. H. Kean,[‡] the results were very supportive of the view I held. Drugs used for the prevention of disease, it reported, should be completely innocuous when given to athletes and therefore drugs, which were not absorbed into the body, had a high preference. In terms of success rates, for a variety of drugs used in these trials, whilst no drug completely prevented the disease, the report concluded using Thalazole was the most beneficial in reducing the incidence of diarrhoea. According to the trial report, the incidence of diarrhoea amongst the students using Thalazole was reduced to 11.9% and severe cases of diarrhoea to 6.6%. The administration of a non-absorbable sulphonamide had apparently no undesirable effects on the athletes or their performances and their blood tests revealed no abnormal results.

Having read the detailed reports of the various clinical trials, I became more than ever convinced Thalazole would be the preventative drug of choice against gastro-enteritis in Mexico, but Streptotriad would have to be given, at some time, to the England players in a trial to ascertain whether it was acceptable to them.

[†] British Medical Journal. Leading Articles, 12th October 1968
[‡] Kean, B. H., Ann. Intern. Med 1963, 59, 605

10

The Medical Teams..........

The 1968 Olympic Games in Mexico were over. The British Olympic Association produced a medical report on their experiences. I eagerly awaited a copy of the report I had been promised. When the report arrived, I was extremely disappointed. It was a mere seven pages in length. Acclimatisation to the altitude was dealt with in ten and a half lines; the training of the athletes warranted just four lines; no reference was made at all of the heat factor, although a discussion on Sunburn was dealt with in fifteen lines. A statistical analysis of the various medical conditions, suffered by the athletes, covered two and a half pages. Only half a page was concerned with gastro-enteritis and tummy disorders. Another half page was devoted to the psychological factors which, the report stated, had played a large part in affecting some athletes.

The medical report, from The British Olympic Committee was, I considered, quite pathetic. The report did however confirm one serious issue I was aware of. Food Poisoning, the report said, was very common in visitors to Mexico! The illness was particularly debilitating. It was jokingly referred to as "Montezuma's Revenge". Food Poisoning, the report acknowledged, was a high risk factor in Mexico. Athletes, who contracted the disease, became seriously ill. They missed vital training days and their acclimatisation programme was severely affected. Ordinary visitors to Mexico were always given copious health advice. Tap water should not be consumed. Only bottled water was recommended. No ice should be placed in drinks. All fruit should be washed and peeled prior to eating. No ice-cream should

THE MEDICAL TEAMS

be consumed. The Olympic Report confirmed the information Roger Bannister had given me. The British athletes had been given two tablets of Streptotriad daily as the means of preventing the onset of gastro-enteritis.

Alf and I had decided we would introduce Streptotriad, as a prophylactic, at our next away international game in Romania. I would explain, to the England players, how successful the tablet had been with the Olympic athletes in Mexico. It was important, in that we had not used these tablets previously, to find out how effective they were and how our players reacted to them, if at all. England played Romania, in Bucharest, on the 6th November 1968. It was the first international of the season. Streptotriad would be used with the England footballers for the first time. I decided, for the visit to Bucharest, the players would be divided into two groups. One group would take the Thalazole tablets we had used previously and with which the players were accustomed. The other group would take Streptotriad. I explained to the players the reasons for introducing the new pink tablet of Streptotriad. Alf decided the players actually playing in the match would receive Streptotriad. The remainder of the players, the staff and the travelling officials would be given Thalazole. Everyone in the party commenced on the appropriate tablets immediately after the first team meeting in London. Everyone would remain on their tablets until our return. The players selected to play in the game were,

Banks, Wright, Newton, Mullery, Labone, Moore,

Ball, Hunt, Charlton. R., Hurst and Peters.

They all received Streptotriad.

Prior to our departure, on the Sunday evening at Whites Hotel, we entertained Mr. Wilson, the National Orthopaedic Hospital's consultant to dinner. At the dinner, Mr. Wilson confirmed to Alf, the staff and players, he and Mr. Trickey were prepared to provide orthopaedic services to the team. Should any hospital consultations, investigations or admissions be required by any member of the England party, prior to, during or after a Wembley international, provision would be available at Stanmore. Everyone was delighted with the arrangements. Knowing we were travelling to Bucharest the following day, Mr. Wilson gave me a letter of introduction to the Professor of Orthopaedics at the main hospital in Bucharest. Mr. Wilson informed me,

> "Many foreign orthopaedic specialists come to the National Orthopaedic Hospital for training and to attend international conferences. We have contacts worldwide and, should you so wish, we can always advise on suitable specialists to contact overseas, wherever you are."

Alf, the staff and players were delighted with the proposed arrangements and accepted his generous offer. Throughout my time with England, I used this facility whenever the team were travelling abroad. The service provided by Wilson and Trickey was excellent.

Bucharest in 1968 was a dismal place. As usual, when abroad, we trained at the national stadium on the Tuesday morning, the day before the international. The pitch and facilities were excellent. The training session went well. After training, I had arranged to meet with the Romanian Team Doctor. Fortunately, he spoke excellent English. He was very keen to show me their National Sports Medicine Centre. Equally, I was keen to visit their national facilities. With Alf's agreement, I arranged to visit the Sports Medicine Centre on the Wednesday afternoon, while the players rested. The Romanian doctor said he would send a taxi to the hotel for me at one-thirty. I looked forward to meeting the Romanian doctors and seeing, at first hand, the Romanian facilities.

The sixth of November 1968, was a cold, wet and miserable day in Bucharest. The taxi arrived on time. I was driven through the rain-drenched streets of Bucharest to the Sports Medicine Centre. The Romanian doctor was standing on the steps, under an umbrella, waiting for me. He and I first visited the hotel complex. On the day of my visit, the hotel was occupied by some two hundred gymnasts. They had been living in the hotel complex for two weeks. While resident at the hotel, they had undergone an intensive gymnastic training and coaching programme. In addition, during their stay, they had all undergone a thorough medical assessment programme. The Romanian doctor was unaware of the gymnasts' ages, but, to my eye, they ranged from five years old upwards. The senior international gymnasts were included in the party. Having visited the hotel complex, we then walked to the boardroom of the Sports Medicine Centre. The Romanian Team Doctor, had invited the Centre's doctors to meet with me in the boardroom. Ten doctors joined me. We had a full discussion on many aspects of Sports Medicine, including the medical problems relating to the World Cup in Mexico. I was surprised at the number of doctors working at the Centre. I enquired whether they were employed full time at the Centre. They laughed, as they assured me there were some twenty full time doctors working there. Furthermore, they informed me each one of them had been seconded to the Centre by their government, in recognition of the excellent work they had done previously in their particular field of medicine. I then realised I was in the company of the best doctors Romania possessed. All the doctors, I spoke with, considered it a great honour to be appointed to the Sports Medicine Centre. They were all dedicated to the support of all the national teams and their country's athletes. They were extremely frank and open in their discussions with me. They produced, for my inspection, medical files on the gymnasts who were presently at the Centre. From those files, it appeared to me, the Romanian gymnasts had visited the Centre at regular intervals throughout their lives. The gymnasts were not only subjected to a training programme commensurate with their development, but also underwent a series of medical examinations and investigations on each of their visits. The results of their individual training programme and medical tests were recorded and used as an assessment tool for their progress.

In the discussions I had with the medical personnel, it became apparent that while the Romanian national football team had their own Team Doctor, the expertise of all these full time, highly qualified Sports Medicine Specialists was also available to their national team. In the forthcoming Mexico World Cup, the Romanian team would be drawn in the same group as England. The Romanian footballers, I had now come to realise, would have a tremendous advantage over their England counterparts. The medical problems associated with competing in Mexico were enormous. Here, in Romania, they were being addressed by a team of full time medical consultants. The Romanian medical team was able to devote all of their time, twenty-four hours every day, to the problems of altitude, heat, gastro-enteritis and the other problems Mexico presented. In comparison, in England, the same responsibility was mine and mine alone. My full- time job was as a General Practitioner in Redcar. As far as The Football Association was concerned, I was a purely Honorary Team Physician, who had only been in the Senior post for a few months. Alan Bass, who preceded me in the post for the previous six years, was now permanently employed in Canada. As winners of the World Cup in 1966, Alan was aware England automatically qualified for the 1970 World Cup in Mexico, yet he had left no information regarding the preparation of the England team for Mexico. Likewise the Medical Committee at The Football Association produced no advanced planning. In fact no medical preparatory work had been done. The Football Association, or rather Alan Bass, had wasted two years. I was now virtually on my own. As far as medical preparation was concerned I was starting with a clean sheet of paper. I realised I was now on the medical platform of international football, competing with teams of full time doctors from Romania and other countries. The Romanian footballers inevitably would be better prepared medically for the World Cup in Mexico. On my own, I couldn't compete. I felt inadequate, isolated and vulnerable.

The Romanian Team Doctor drove me back to our hotel in Bucharest. I was depressed. I joined Alf Ramsey and Harold Shepherdson for a cup of tea. I related to them the findings of my afternoon visit.

> "It's just impossible for me to provide a level of medical support for the England team comparable to that which the Romanians will receive. Twenty full-time doctors are supporting their team. I'm a full time G.P. at Redcar. How can I provide a similar level of medical support? It's just impossible."

Ramsey leaned forward in his chair, his face moving closer to mine. I witnessed his steely eyes narrowing,

"I appreciate your problem Doctor."
he said.

THE MEDICAL TEAMS

"Nevertheless, I expect you to provide our team with the same level of support the Romanians have. In fact, I expect you to provide a much higher and better level of medical support. Our players must always have the best. I'm confident you will provide it. If I hadn't that confidence in you, if I had the slightest doubt, I would not have appointed you. Just ensure our players have the best medical support in the whole world."

Alf had set my objectives. I drank my tea in silence. I realised the enormity of my task. The next eighteen months would be eventful. There was so much work I needed to do.

Sixty-two thousand Romanians watched the international at the 23rd August National Stadium in Bucharest on a very wet November day. I sat in the director's box next to Alf throughout the match. The score was nil-nil at half time and nil-nil at full time. If the two teams had played for another ninety minutes, the score would, I believe, have remained nil-nil. It was a dreadful game. The Romanians certainly were the most dangerous side in the first twenty minutes, with Gordon Banks called upon to make many excellent saves. Tommy Wright was injured early in the game. He injured his ankle in a tackle and had to leave the field. The ankle was lacerated and badly bruised. I spent some time with him in the dressing room, during the game, repairing the wound with several stitches. Bob McNab, of Arsenal, made his England debut that evening when he replaced Wright. McNab, Brian Labone and Bobby Moore were superb in defence. The forwards, with the exception of Alan Ball, were very subdued. In the dressing room, after the game, the England players were silent. Every player knew it had been a poor team performance. Suddenly Alan Ball broke the dressing room silence,

"I know why we were so poor tonight."
explained Ballie,
"It was those bloody pink tablets the Doc gave us. That's what was different. We've never had them before. They're crap! Like the reserves, we should have been on the usual white ones."

Alan Ball had expressed his views and other players agreed. It appeared, as far as the players were concerned, Streptotriad was dead. Long live Thalazole! The England players had sought an excuse for their poor performance. They blamed Streptotriad. Of course, Streptotriad wasn't the reason for the team's poor performance, but the players convinced themselves it was. It seemed unlikely, as a result of the players' opinions, we would use Streptotriad again as a preventative for gastro-enteritis. Thalazole would be the drug of choice-the players had made the decision for me.

The dangers of gastro-enteritis in Mexico however had not disappeared. Roger Bannister's fears were confirmed when I received the F.I.F.A. report, on the amateur football played at the Mexico Olympics. Written and compiled by Dr. Dettmar Cramer, entitled 'Report of Final Competition in Mexico', it contained some interesting statements regarding the food and the prevalence of gastroenteritis in Mexico. Some Team Managers, the report stated, complained the food provided was unpalatable for their players. The report continued,

> 'Hygienic measures are of great importance. Intestinal complaints, with diarrhoea, occur very often. During a long stay of six to eight weeks, they are almost unavoidable.'

Dr. Cramer's report also gave certain recommendations for teams competing in the World Cup.

> "No drinking of tap water. Use distilled water for teeth brushing. Eat only peeled fruits. Do not take any ice cream. Take no salads cleaned in tap water. Do not drink fruit juice mixed with tap water. Do not take any ice cold drinks at all."

The last warning, the report concluded, is particularly important because the World Cup Tournament will be held from May 31st until June 21st., which is high summer time in Mexico and very hot. The report concluded,

> "Customary food should be taken with the teams, and if thought necessary, a cook or chef. Hotels, kitchens and servants should be carefully selected to fulfil the requirements."

It was a fact. The prevention of 'Montezuma's Revenge' in Mexico was going to be a very big problem for us.

THE MEDICAL TEAMS

Following my visit to Romania, Alf had made it perfectly clear to me the services I provided for the England team would have to be as good as, and preferably better than any other team competing in the competition. It seemed an impossible task. I realised I could not provide such a service alone. Ramsey had told me,

"Make sure our medical support is the best in the world; better than Romania's; better than any other competing nation."

It would become my new dream. I would endeavour to provide the England team with the best medical preparation and support in the world. No other international team, would have better medical care. I knew however to make this particular dream a reality, like all my previous dreams, my desire, dedication and commitment would need to be total. I decided to dedicate and commit myself to that process prior to the Mexico World Cup. My commitment needed to be total. The task was enormous. In setting out to provide this service for the players, nothing and no one would deflect me from the process. I was aware, for me personally to reach the very top, whether in playing sport or in my chosen profession, it was absolutely necessary for me to be totally committed. Nothing else was acceptable. I knew no other way. The sacrifice required would be immense. I decided the task was too big for me to achieve alone. With my full-time commitment as a General Practitioner, I realised, as the Romanians had done, I needed a medical team of exceptionally high quality medical men to assist me. I would approach and select the medical personnel for my team from the many specialist branches of medicine in England. Every significant medical area needed to be covered. Already, I had involved some medical people, but I now realised, following my Bucharest visit, I needed to form a much larger, comprehensive medical team. I already had the nucleus of a very good medical team. Wilson and Trickey, for orthopaedic services; Fielding, for all the haematological services; Griffith Pugh, for the altitude; Roodyn, for immunisations and tropical diseases; Bannister for advice and experiences of competing athletes. I would now add to my medical team as necessary. Frank O'Gorman was now my deputy, and together we developed a strategy for the composition of the medical team.

Although Frank and I met in Sheffield on several occasions, his appointment, was officially delayed because the relevant committee at The Football Association, required to ratify his appointment, was not scheduled to meet for a few months. As a result, I attended both Under 23 games against Wales at Wrexham and Holland at Birmingham. I was amazed, following my attendance at these matches, to become embroiled in controversy with The Football Association and in particular, Denis Follows. As I attended both Under 23 internationals with great difficulty, owing to my Practice commitments, Alf had agreed I was only to be present on the day of the game. Regarding the Wrexham and Birmingham games, having completed my Practice duties on the Wednesday morning, I travelled from Redcar to the venues driving my own car. I arrived at the venues in the early afternoon; had a pre match meal with the players; attended the match; dined with Alf after the game and left shortly after midnight, on both occasions, to return to Redcar, again driving my car. The following week I submitted my mileage to the Secretary at The Football Association, in order to claim my car mileage allowance. Imagine my surprise when my mileage claim was refused. I received a curt reply from the Secretary, informing me that, as a Team Physician, I was not allowed to claim any mileage allowance. Mileage allowances, he informed me, were strictly for Football Association Council Members and I did not qualify! I was only entitled to claim my rail fare. How the Secretary expected me to return to Redcar in the early hours of the morning from Wrexham and Birmingham, he failed to explain. I subsequently received a cheque for both rail fares, even though I hadn't travelled by train. I knew instantly where my place in the organisation, as perceived by the Secretary, actually was!

My relationship with the Secretary further deteriorated when I paid a visit, in January 1969, to The Football Association offices in Lancaster Gate. In the basement of the building, when checking what medical equipment, if any, was kept in stock, I came across many drugs lying loosely in a variety of containers within several boxes. Many of these drugs were classified, at the time, as Schedule Four Poisons and should have been kept under lock and key in a drugs cabinet, with a properly maintained drug register duly signed and the usage authorised by a qualified medical practitioner. I was horrified that such drugs were lying loosely in The Football Association's headquarters. I discussed the matter with the Chairman Dr. Andrew Stephens, a fellow General Practitioner, who was equally horrified at my find. He asked me to write a letter to Denis Follows. I wrote to the Secretary on the 21st. January 1969 as follows,

Dear Mr. Follows,

As you know I have been appointed Team Physician to the England football team, but there are two matters outside the province of the team which I feel it is my duty to bring to your attention.

As you are aware, The Football Association holds a stock of drugs which is kept in the basement at the Football Association offices. I do not know how long the present system of stocking drugs has applied, but I was most alarmed last week when I visited the offices to find that there were a large quantity of drugs present, which are classified as poisons and some are Schedule 4 poisons. The responsibility for these Schedule 4 drugs and poison drugs must, in my opinion, be that of a qualified practitioner and these drugs should be kept in a separate medical cupboard under lock and key and a proper poisons register kept up for those drugs so that no loopholes exist for the removal, usage, or loss of such drugs under any circumstances. I discussed this matter with the Chairman of The Football Association last week and he was of a similar opinion, so perhaps you would institute some form of procedure to put this matter right.

I would be pleased also if you would draw the attention of the Senior International Committee to the fact that the senior tour this year includes a visit to Mexico City. As you know, Mexico City is at 7500 ft altitude and there are considerable medical dangers for people, over the age of 60 who have had previous heart or lung disease, residing at this altitude. I feel it is right and proper that the members of the Senior International Committee should be informed of these dangers so that if they are in doubt as to their own physical fitness in making the trip, they may obtain medical clearance beforehand from their own Physicians.

If I can be of any further help in this matter to yourself or to any members of the committee, I would be pleased to advise you accordingly. I trust you will bring this matter to the attention of all members concerned

Yours sincerely

Neil Phillips

Although Alf had made it clear to me that my medical responsibility was solely to the players and his staff, inevitably, as the only medical practitioner with the party visiting South America, the day to day care of everyone, would be my responsibility. No-one at The Football Association had given me any details of such a responsibility.

The process of the medical preparation now became all consuming. The work involved completely took over my life. Nothing else mattered. My dedication and commitment, to preparing the England Team for the World Cup in Mexico, was total. My main occupation in life, throughout the two years of preparation, was of course as a General Practitioner in Redcar. My role as Team Physician with England continued to be in an honorary capacity. My remuneration from The Football Association, throughout my twelve years' service to the England team, was based on a daily allowance. When matches were played in England, my daily allowance was zero; no money at all! For matches abroad, my daily allowance was two pounds per day- so called 'out of pocket expenses'. The Football Association paid my travel (by rail of course) and hotel expenses, but I received no salary and no match fee. In fact the work, I was now involved in with the England team, was far more consuming than my work in General Practice. The fact that I was not paid for my England role began to annoy me.

My annoyance turned to anger when following the England v Scotland international at Wembley in 1969 I received a letter from the Secretary of The Football Association. The letter caused me much anxiety. When with the team for the England v Scotland game, I did not require my two complimentary tickets for the international, so I gave them to one of the players. Imagine my surprise when the letter from the Secretary informed me that sitting in my two complimentary seats was none other than the

THE MEDICAL TEAMS

ticket spiv, Mr. S. Flashman. It was obvious that I would not be prepared to inform anyone as to which England player was involved. I phoned Alf, informed him of the truth, without naming the player. He very kindly said he would deal with the matter. I heard no more.

In setting out, after my visit to Romania, to further prepare the England

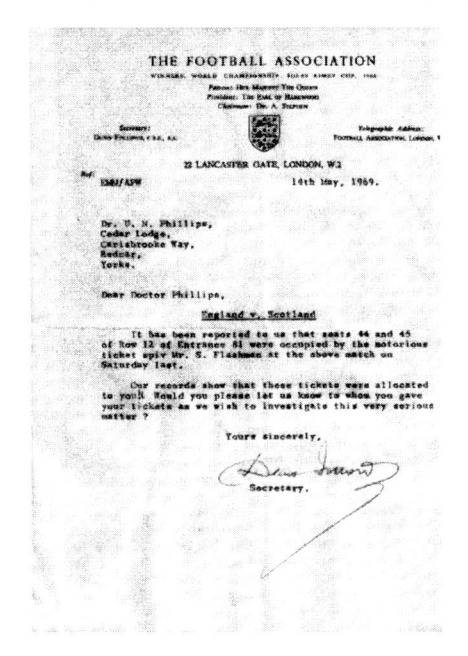

A Letter From The Football Association.

team for Mexico, my first port of call was back to the city where I trained as a medical student. My visit however was not to any of the learned professors of medicine, but to spend a day with Alan Brown, the Manager of Sheffield Wednesday. I had a high regard for Alan and sought his advice. He had previously taken Sheffield Wednesday on a three-week tour of Mexico, where they had played five matches and experienced all the problems of playing football at the altitude of Mexico City. Alan Brown, as he always was, had been meticulous in the preparation period prior to travelling to Mexico. In Sheffield, prior to leaving for their tour, he had subjected his players, and himself, to standard time trials over set distances with the objective of carrying out identical tests on a daily basis in Mexico. The comparisons he had well documented. It was apparent, from the figures he showed me, that over the first seventeen days in Mexico, the times for running distances above four hundred yards were quite adversely affected. The times for running these distances in Mexico were much slower than those in Sheffield. The players only began to approach their Sheffield times in Mexico, when it was time to come home! His players had then been at altitude for three weeks. His assessment of his team's performances was similar. The first game of their tour was played at Toluca. Toluca is at an altitude of 9,400 feet. It was one of the centres chosen for the World Cup. Alan reported all the players became distressed while playing at Toluca. It was of course what he expected. The game was played on the third day of the tour and too little time had elapsed to acclimatise. In all the initial games, Alan said, his team's performance was poor. The performances gradually improved with acclimatisation. He expressed the view it was not until the fifth game of the tour, played on the twenty-first day, the team put in their normal performance. Alan was of the opinion a period of at least twenty-eight days was essential for adequate acclimatisation. Some of the games, his team played, were in the afternoon and some in the evening. The afternoon games were played in high temperatures, whilst in the evenings the temperature was quite cool. He emphasised the fact that the goalkeepers found great difficulty dealing with shots. The ball travelled much faster through the rarefied atmosphere. Interestingly, he spent quite a time explaining to me his assessment of the players in the difficult playing conditions of Mexico.

"There is no doubt the conditions in Mexico are difficult. It sorts the men from the boys. Some players developed an 'acclimatisation neurosis' – mentally frightened of the altitude. These players were easily defeated by the conditions. Other players showed a fighting spirit. They were determined not to be beaten by the altitude. I learnt a lot about my players in Mexico. The ones with a strong personality shone through!"

Alan discussed the problems they had experienced with the food in Mexico;

the poor hospital facilities; the problems of smog pollution; the incessant traffic noise in Mexico City; and the boredom experienced by the players. The effect the extreme heat had on the players, when playing in the afternoons, was his greatest concern

> "If matches are played in the afternoon, the heat will be unbearable. It is a major problem."

After spending several hours at Hillsborough, Alan invited me to his home. There he had a large aviary. On entering the aviary, one of the birds immediately flew onto his shoulder. Alan flicked it away with his hand.

> "That's the cocky one"

he said.

> "Players are like birds. Some are cocky and you need to brush them away. Look at that bird in the corner. That's the timid one. Frightened to death. If I want to get him out of the corner I have to coerce him. I have players like that. That's what I mean about the personality and character of players. When confronted with the difficulties of playing at altitude, some players will need protecting. They are too cocky. They will take the altitude on, whether acclimatised to it or not. Other players you will need to coerce and encourage. The players are just like my birds."

It was a day well spent in Sheffield. Alan was a true professional. Even if he didn't wear the T-shirt, he'd been there, done that and his information was invaluable. Before leaving Alan gave me all the daily notes he'd made during the tour of Sheffield Wednesday to Mexico. I was most grateful to Alan Brown.

Many tropical diseases occurred in Mexico. I was totally inexperienced in Tropical Diseases. The reality was, in the whole of my professional career, I had seen a mere handful of such diseases. I needed to increase my knowledge of them. I decided to seek the advice of the Liverpool and London Schools of Tropical Medicine. At both schools there were medical experts, giving advice to travellers visiting exotic places worldwide. I needed them to be represented in my medical team. At Liverpool, I met with Professor

Magreith. In London, I had already made contact with Dr. Roodyn. Both agreed to act as advisors and joined my medical team. Throughout two year preparation period, they were both most helpful. In addition to his knowledge of tropical diseases, Professor Magreith had considerable experience in the study of the effect of heat on humans. He was particularly helpful to me in advising on, and overcoming, the problems presented by the extreme heat in Guadalajara. Dr. Roodyn was particularly helpful in the practical arrangements needed to actually carry out the necessary immunisation. He carried out these procedures himself, when the players were in London for international matches or training sessions.

My main advisor, for dealing with the problems of heat stress and heat disorders however was Professor Charles Leithead, the Professor of Medicine at Haile Sellassie University in Addis Ababa, Ethiopia. Living and working at 8,200 feet in Addis Ababa, he was very knowledgeable about the problems associated with living and performing athletically at altitude. His advice was invaluable. Together with Dr. Lind, Charles Leithead had written a book entitled "Heat Stress and Heat Disorders" * which, in the two years before the World Cup, I read several times from cover to cover. Their book became my main reference work for solving the problems presented by the extreme heat of Mexico. Helpful though Charles Leithead always was, he did live a long way away in Ethiopia and my contact with him was mainly by letter. I needed an altitude expert closer to home to consult with frequently.

On many occasions I sought the views of Dr. Griffith Pugh. Griffith had accompanied Sir Edmund Hillary on the ascent of Everest. He worked at a medical research establishment in Hampstead, and I visited him there on occasions when I was in London. An expert Altitude Physiologist, he was particularly helpful in determining, with me, the training programme we would carry out during our period of acclimatisation.

The National Orthopaedic Hospital at Stanmore, through the good offices of Messrs. Wilson and Trickey, were now providing emergency cover for all Football Association matches at Wembley. They always provided the England team with a high quality service. In addition to Mr. Wilson and

THE MEDICAL TEAMS

Mr. Trickey, I co-opted, into the medical team, the services of Stanmore hospital's Dental Surgeon, Mr. MacLachlan. He provided us with a superb dental service. He carried out routine dental examinations on the whole England party and made recommendations to the individual player's Club for the remedial work needed. When he initially carried out the routine dental examinations, several England players were found to have decayed teeth in need of urgent treatment. One player, he examined, had eleven decayed teeth! Many clubs, in those days, did not provide dental care or even dental supervision for their players. I spoke to the players regarding their dental hygiene. I did not want any dental emergencies occurring while we were acclimatising in Mexico. The players would prefer to be treated by their own dentist here in England rather than a strange dentist, they had never previously met, in South America. The findings of Mr. MacLachlan's dental inspections I sent to the player's Club. The requisite treatments were then carried out locally at Club level. Each player and member of staff, selected in the final party, was required to produce a satisfactory dental report stating all recommended treatments had been carried out prior to departure. All complied. Whenever the England team continued travelling abroad, Mr. Trickey and Mr. Wilson continued giving me letters of introduction to the orthopaedic staff at the hospital in the city where the team was playing. The system worked well and the service they both provided and their on call availability was exceptional. Dr. Fielding, the Consultant Haematologist, and I decided, in the eighteen months prior to the World Cup, routine blood tests would be carried out on the players and staff at frequent intervals. It was essential that prior to internationals at Wembley, these tests were arranged at St. Mary's Hospital for the players. I had been fortunate to enlist the enthusiastic support of Dr. Fielding who not only arranged the players' blood tests on a regular basis, but gave much valuable advice on the preparations needed for the players in the run up to the tournament. Additionally, he agreed to fly out to Mexico, towards the end of the acclimatisation period, in order to carry out further blood tests on the players. With these final blood results, taken in Mexico, he would be able to discuss with me how much extra red blood corpuscles each player had produced during the acclimatisation period. By agreeing to carry out the blood tests in Mexico himself, Dr. Fielding ensured those final tests would be repeated and read to the same standards as the previous blood tests in London.

My medical team was complete. Whether or not it would prove to be a better medical team than the Romanian's, as Alf had requested, would be for others to judge. Each and everyone of my medical team agreed to give their time, advice and expertise free of charge. They received no agreed remuneration from The Football Association for their services. To have such medical expertise available to myself, and through me to the England team, I considered a great coup. I was most grateful to each and every one of them. I submitted my team to Sir Alf. We met in London to discuss the medical team. He was very impressed.

To protect the players from the infectious diseases, prevalent in South America, both schools of Tropical Medicine drew up a plan of vaccinations and immunisations. Protection was needed against Smallpox, Typhoid and Paratyphoid Fever, Tetanus, Poliomyelitis, and Infective Hepatitis. Magreith, and Roodyn were aware that inevitably some players would react unfavourably to some of the procedures, particularly the Typhoid and Paratyphoid injection. Following that particular injection, a player could feel unwell for several days. Quite rightly the players' Clubs would not agree to these procedures being carried out during the playing season. Magreith, Roodyn and myself agreed that the immunisation and vaccination procedures should be carried out at the end of the playing season, when the England players returned from their tour to Mexico, Uruguay and Brazil. The immunisation procedures for Typhoid and Paratyphoid Fever would best take place at the player's own Club. There was however a major problem, from the playing point of view. The twenty-eight man squad, travelling to Mexico for the World Cup, would not be known at the end of the 1969 season. I discussed the problem with Alf Ramsey. He agreed to produce a list of some forty players for the immunisation programme, in the hope every possible player, being considered for selection, would be included. When I received the list of forty players, I personally wrote to all the Football Clubs involved requesting their support for implementing the immunisation programme. All the immunisations, with the exception of Yellow Fever and Infective Hepatitis, were carried out at Club level immediately after the 1969 summer tour. The immunisation against Yellow Fever, and the protection against Infective Hepatitis, would be carried out by Dr. Roodyn in London much nearer to our time of departure for Mexico. It is to the credit of all the Clubs and players that they cooperated fully with the immunisation programme. The programme was completed during the close season. In the event, not one player reported any adverse reactions to any of the procedures.

It was however a sad reflection on the care given to their players by some Clubs, in that several players were not even up to date with their Tetanus injections; an essential protection for a professional footballer. Some players admitted they had not had a booster injection since they were in school. At that time, even when players were transferred, few Clubs bothered to carry out a pre-signing medical examination. Routine medical examinations of footballers were rarely done at most Clubs. The treatment of some injuries was poor. The player's medical records were either non-existent or poorly documented. Routine dental examinations were few and far between. The medical care of football players, like all athletes at that time, was generally, in my opinion, poor.

When Dr. Fielding and I carried out the blood tests on the England players on May 5th.1969, it was the first time the England players, as a group, had undergone any blood tests. It was typical of the players that, on the day of the tests at St. Mary's Hospital, they decided to hold a sweepstake on the results! Every player contributed one pound in the sweep. The player with the highest blood level would scoop the pool. The player with the lowest level would have his pound returned! When the results were announced, Norman Hunter hit the jackpot and Brian Labone accepted the return of his entrance money. Typically, Jack Charlton objected to the result. He claimed all the Leeds United players had an unfair advantage. They had been taking iron tablets for several weeks. The medical care at Leeds, under the supervision of Dr. Ian Adams, was of a very high quality.

Jack's objection was overruled.

The results of the blood tests revealed wide variation in the players' blood levels causing great concern to Dr. Fielding and myself. Several players had values as much as twenty per cent below their colleagues. It was fortunate we had carried out these tests so soon in advance of the World Cup tournament. There were many months left during which the players, with low levels, could take the necessary daily iron and vitamin tablets to improve their blood levels. Further tests would be carried out over the ensuing months ensuring high blood levels were present in every player. Prior to embarking on any blood tests, I explained to the players how essential it was for their individual tests to be at the highest possible level. High blood levels, immediately prior to our departure for the World Cup, would be as important as a high level of physical fitness.

Alf Ramsey was most helpful to me in the eighteen months prior to the World Cup. We frequently had one on one discussions together, discussing the environmental and day-to-day problems confronting the players in Mexico. We both agreed it would be to everyone's advantage if the players were informed, throughout the months of preparation, of the measures we were taking to ensure everything that should be done was being done for their benefit. In the team meetings, at every get together of the players, I was given the opportunity of explaining the reasons for each and every medical action I was taking. The players were always asked for their views and no procedures were introduced by me without fully informing the players beforehand. Over time this information I gave to the players, built up their confidence in what we were trying to achieve.

In preparing England medically for the 1970 World Cup I strived, throughout the 1968– 69 season, to ensure everything that should be done was being done. Every spare moment of my life, was dedicated to England's medical preparation. It was essential I visited, on a regular basis, each member of my medical team. My Practice half days, when I should have spent time with my family, were spent travelling the country consulting with the individual doctors who had agreed to advise me. I certainly needed their advice. In addition, I wanted them to feel an integral part of my medical

THE MEDICAL TEAMS

team. It was important for them to realise they were actively involved in the team's preparations. Each one of them was an essential part of England's medical preparations. They all gave their time, and their undoubted expertise, freely. The Football Association employed none of my medical team, but then they didn't even employ me!

Throughout my time as Honorary England Team Physician, there existed at The Football Association, an officially constituted Medical Committee. Although I personally was involved with the England teams, in over one hundred international matches at home and abroad, I never met with any member of this committee. I was not invited to any of their meetings. With all the medical problems associated with the Mexico World Cup, they gave me no advice. In fact, I was unaware what the medical committee did, or what they were supposed to do. Several doctors were invited to join the committee, but I was never invited. I had no input into the appointment of doctors to the committee. My opinion was never sought. I was an Alf Ramsey appointment and was appointed by The Football Association as Honorary Team Physician, as were the players, on a match by match basis. In my twelve years of service, the medical committee of The Football Association, had no input whatsoever into the England players. It was astonishing to me, with all the medical problems associated with playing in Mexico, their contribution was absolutely nothing.

My greatest difficulty, when I acted as the England Team Doctor, was finding sufficient time to carry out the duties expected of me, or rather that I demanded of myself. Although I worked for Alf Ramsey, my main work was as a General Practitioner in Redcar. As a partner in the Practice, I was entitled, as were all my other partners, to five weeks holiday each year. Inevitably my holiday entitlement was used up accompanying the England team at all their international matches. Every year my holidays were arranged, with the cooperation of my partners, around England's fixtures. As a consequence, my wife and children suffered. Each year, the majority, if not all, of my holiday entitlement was taken up with my England duties. My wife invariably took our three children on holiday alone. Each of my three children, from time to time, even today, jokingly will say,

> "We never saw our Dad until we were teenagers! He was always away with England."

England's summer tour usually occupied two weeks. In addition, there were usually two internationals played away from home in Europe during the season. Each of these two fixtures took up another four days of my holidays. In addition there were the home internationals at Wembley; each one requiring my presence with the team for three days. Add all these days together and it's easy to understand how my five weeks holiday, from the Practice, was always taken up with my England duties. In old age, as I reflect on the commitment I gave to the England team, I even surprise myself. The Home International tournament, now defunct, best epitomizes the commitment I personally gave to the England team. I still recall, that one-week of football, with mixed feelings.

The Home International tournament involved matches against Wales, Northern Ireland and Scotland. The three international matches took place in the one week. Every other year, the matches were played at Cardiff, Wembley and Scotland. It was impossible for me to take yet another week's holiday to fulfill my commitment to the team. My holiday entitlement from the Practice was already committed to my other England duties. Alf, however, insisted I was with the team on match days. He did not want another doctor involved with the players. The first match was against Wales at Cardiff on a Saturday afternoon. The second game, against Northern Ireland, was played at Wembley on the following Wednesday evening. The third game took place three days later, on the Saturday, in Glasgow.

I worked a normal week in the Practice. On the Friday, the day before the game in Cardiff, I worked quite normally in the Practice. It was a typical day. Morning surgery was followed by several home visits. In the afternoon, I held another surgery. With a day's work completed, I left my home, at half past six. I then drove alone to Thornbury in Gloucestershire. The England team was staying at The Ship Inn. In those days, there was no M5 motorway; the journey was long and tedious. Having driven for six hours non-stop, I arrived at Thornbury after midnight. Alf was anxiously awaiting my arrival. As always he was pleased to see me. I went quickly to bed.

THE MEDICAL TEAMS

The trip mileage on my car registered three hundred and fourteen miles. On the Saturday morning, again driving my car, I followed the England motor coach, to Cardiff's Ninian Park. Some two hours after the game had finished, I commenced travelling again. I drove my car from Ninian Park to Redcar. On the three hundred and fifty mile return journey, Harold Shepherdson accompanied me. As usual, Harold slept for most of the journey. Having deposited Harold, at his home in Middlesbrough, I completed my journey to Redcar. I arrived there at two on the Sunday morning. I quickly fell asleep. First game completed.

On the Sunday morning at eight, I personally came on duty for the Practice. It was my turn to deal with the emergency calls throughout Sunday, until the surgery opened on Monday morning. Usually on a Sunday, the doctor on duty would make twenty to thirty house calls. Monday and Tuesday were normal working days in the Practice; morning surgery followed by house calls and an evening surgery. In addition, there were injured players to see at Middlesbrough Football Club.

On completing my Tuesday's work in the Practice, I set off travelling again. I caught the train from Redcar to Darlington. At Darlington, I boarded the inter-city express train to Kings Cross. Fortunately the train stopped at Hitchen, as the England players were now staying at a Welwyn Garden City hotel. The Football Association provided transport for me from Hitchin station to the hotel. I arrived at the hotel at midnight. On the Wednesday morning, I trained with the players and attended the team meeting. The international, against Northern Ireland was played on the Wednesday evening at Wembley. After the game I had a meal at Wembley Stadium. A taxi then took me to Kings Cross railway station. I caught the midnight sleeper-train to Darlington, arriving there at five in the morning. The early morning aptly named 'milk train' transported me from Darlington to Redcar. I walked, in the cold morning air, the four hundred yards from the station to my surgery. Second game completed.

As I commenced morning surgery, one of my patients commented,
"I thought I saw you on the television last night at Wembley,
but then it couldn't have been, as you are here now doing

morning surgery."

For me, Thursday was always a busy day in the Practice. Two, two hour surgeries and several house calls were followed by a night on emergency call. On the Friday, having been on emergency calls throughout Thursday night, I had the usual morning and afternoon surgeries and home visits. On completion of my Friday Practice duties, I again set off driving my car. I was now driving from Redcar to the west coast of Scotland. The team was staying at The Marine Hotel at Troon, having flown by air to Scotland. I drove alone in my car the three hundred miles to Troon. I fell into bed just after midnight. On the Saturday morning, at Troon, I walked beside the famous golf course. After lunch, driving my car, I followed the England motor coach to Hampden Park in Glasgow. Some two hours after the game, I drove my car, accompanied again by Harold Shepherdson, from Glasgow to Redcar. I arrived home at 0200 hours on the Sunday morning. Third match completed.

That was the week, for me, of the Home Internationals. I had taken no holiday from the Practice. I had been present at three England international matches at Cardiff, Wembley and Glasgow. My commitments, in the Practice, had been fulfilled. My wife and three children I had hardly seen. It was a ridiculous situation! How I envied those Romanian doctors at the Sports Centre in Bucharest with their full-time appointments. It appeared they had all the time they required. There were over twenty of them and only one of me. Yet somehow, Alf Ramsey, quite rightly, expected me to provide a better medical service for England! It was a tall order. It seemed an impossible task, but I now had my own medical team to help me.

In addition to all my medical work for the England team, there were of course several team functions I was invited to attend. Most notably, I joined with the players for the recording of "Back Home", a song written for the team prior to leaving for Mexico. Unfortunately, for the studio recording, Alf Ramsey and Harold Shepherdson were delayed and missed the recording. As the only member of staff present, I was in charge! We sang terribly. In addition to "Back Home", we recorded an album sounding equally bad. When the recordings were played back to us however, they sounded quite acceptable. It was amazing to us all how the electronic gear in the studio made our dreadful singing sound so good. The squad, me included, subsequently appeared on 'Top of The Pops' singing in front of 'Pans People'. "Back Home" became a number one best seller. Shelagh, Ann and Michael, my three children, were really proud of me. Their Dad was a Pop Star! "Back Home" sold so well, Pye gave us all a silver disc. Not many doctors have a silver disc for being a pop star!

In the summer of 1969, I accompanied the England team on their South American tour to Mexico, Uruguay, and Brazil. It was my first visit to Mexico. I still held the belief it would have been more helpful if I had been allowed to attend the 1968 Olympic Games as an observer. Prior to the World Cup, this tour was my only opportunity to visit Mexico and only four days would be spent in Mexico City. Additionally, three days would be spent in Guadalajara. I was looking forward to the experience. In addition to preparing the team for two internationals in Mexico, I was concerned that my assessment of the whole environment of Mexico City and Guadalajara would now have to take place in only seven, very busy days. As yet, no suitable accommodation had been found in Mexico City, by Alf or Denis Follows, for the team's four-week acclimatization period. I was extremely concerned no assessment of the hospital and medical facilities in Mexico had taken place. It seemed to me to be a ridiculous situation!

Flight BA 671 left Heathrow airport at 1015 on Wednesday 28th. May 1969 It was a fourteen-hour flight to Mexico. There were only fifteen. players on the flight, as the three West Ham players, Bobby Moore, Geoff Hurst and Martin Peters were already on tour with West Ham in America. Those three would be flying down from New York to meet up with us in Mexico. Gordon Banks of Stoke City, and Gordon West of Everton were the two goalkeepers. The four fullbacks were Terry Cooper of Leeds, Tommy Wright of Everton, Bob McNab of Arsenal, and Keith Newton of Blackburn. Colin Harvey of Everton, Alan Mullery of Tottenham, Jack Charlton and Norman Hunter of Leeds, Bobby Moore and Martin Peters of West Ham were the six half backs. The seven forwards were Jeff Astle of West Bromwich Albion, Alan Ball of Everton, Colin Bell and Francis Lee, both of Manchester City, Alan Clarke of Leicester City, Bobby Charlton of Manchester United, and Geoff Hurst of West Ham. There were three members of staff, Alf Ramsey, Harold Shepherdson and myself.

We arrived at Mexico City at 1700 hours, Mexican time. In reality it was well after midnight in England and, even with an hour stop in the Bahamas for refuelling, the journey had been very tiring. A motor coach transported us to the Del Prado Hotel, situated in downtown Mexico City. The three West Ham players were at the hotel waiting to greet us. During the long flight I had read again Alf's report on his visit to Mexico during the Olympic Games. Relevant aspects of his report were embossed on my mind. Most of the report, as I suspected it would be, related to an assessment of the local conditions, the World Cup stadiums, playing surfaces and associated training facilities, and, most importantly, trying to find suitable accommodation for the team for the long acclimatisation period. Many hotels had been deemed unsuitable, but no suitable accommodation had been found. Alf's staff had discussed the report many times. His report gave a detailed description of the Azteca Stadium, the main stadium in Mexico City. The 100,000 seated stadium, had an excellent playing surface, but the stadium was bowl shaped, with the seating accommodation rising almost vertically to a considerable height. Alf was concerned there would be very little, if any, ventilation on the playing pitch. I was looking forward to visiting the stadium. My first visit there was at noon. The sun was directly overhead. The stadium was very similar to a Spanish bullring. Standing in the centre circle felt as if I had been placed inside an enormous drum. The seating rose almost vertically from ground level. The stadium was claustrophobic. There was little air circulating at ground level. The temperature, registered on my thermometer, was eighty– four degrees. The Azteca stadium was an intimidating place!

During his stay during the Olympic Games, Alf had been unable to find suitable hotel accommodation for the team. Despite visiting several first class hotels, he had been unable to find a hotel suitable for the team's needs. The hotels, situated in the city centre, were not ideal for the purpose of preparing the team for the competition. City centre hotels would enable

THE MEDICAL TEAMS

the press, photographers, broadcasting and television representatives to intrude with ease on the players' privacy. Ideally, Alf wanted the players to stay in a secluded, secure, quiet, first class hotel, with silent efficient air conditioning. Finding such accommodation in Mexico City he had found impossible. My notes, made during our three day stay in Mexico City, reveal I visited, with Alf, Harold Shepherdson and members of the British Embassy staff, many first class hotels, including the Alameda, the Bamer, the Continental Hilton, the Maria Isabel and the El Presidente. All of them were unsuitable for the team, due to the very reasons stated in Alf's report. Apart from the problem of finding suitable accommodation, my main concern was to visit some hospitals to evaluate the medical facilities available and the standard of care provided.

On our second day in Mexico, Tommy Wright developed a dental abscess He had a badly decayed tooth. I gave him an intramuscular injection of antibiotics followed by oral antibiotics for five days. I made a note ensuring all the players would be subjected to follow-up dental examinations when we returned to England.

On the recommendation, of the British Embassy staff, I visited the American and British Cowdray Hospital, affectionately called the ABC. The Embassy staff expressed the view this hospital had excellent facilities, and the medical standards were of a high order. Accompanied by Mr. Vines, of the Embassy staff, I spent most of the Saturday, the day before the team played, at the hospital. Dr Deutsche, the Assistant Director at the hospital, very kindly spent the whole morning showing me all the hospital facilities.

The hospital had 57 beds, divided between General Surgery, Medicine and Orthopaedics. I visited the X-ray and Casualty departments; the wards dealing with Surgical, Orthopaedic, and Medical cases; as well as the Laboratory and Physiotherapy Departments. They were all satisfactory. Having visited the various departments with Dr. Deutsche, I was then introduced to the Director of the hospital, Dr. Herroz. He gave me details of the staff levels and the grades of staff working at the hospital. Both Drs. Herroz and Deutsche said they would be happy for the England team to use all the facilities at the hospital and confirmed the hospital's willingness to co-operate fully with the England team. The hospital was completely satisfactory from the facilities it had to offer, but there were considerable problems relating to the provision of in-patient care. My concerns related, in the main, to the nursing and domestic staff. In a full and frank discussions with Drs. Herroz and Deutch, I expressed my concerns. I was worried if a player required in-patient care. The level of nursing care provided was well below British standards. In the ABC Hospital, one nurse was provided for every eight patients. Many of the nursing and most of the domestic staff were Mexicans. The two doctors informed me that the incidence of carriers of gastro-enteritis or amoebic dysentery in these hospital staff ranged from twenty-five to fifty per cent. The food at the hospital was of course suspect, in that it was prepared Mexican fashion, by Mexicans. The two doctors said, the prevention of gastro-enteritis within the hospital was a difficult problem for them. They estimated twenty-five per cent of all admissions developed gastroenteritis during their hospital stay. Later, and admittedly anecdotally, some of the Embassy staff went further than the doctors, informing me they would not be happy about any of our players being an in patient for any length of time in any Mexican hospitals. I enquired of those staff what they would do personally if they had a serious illness or major injury.

"Catch a flight to Houston in Texas."
was their response.

"It's just over an hour away."

It became apparent to me I needed to develop a strategy for dealing with a major injury or illness requiring hospitalisation. While discussing medical issues with Dr. Deutche, I mentioned the problems we were having in finding suitable hotel accommodation for the team. I suggested to him we needed somewhere out of town, away from the smog and free of the hustle and bustle present every day in the city. We needed somewhere quiet, secluded and secure. He called over Mr. Vine.

"Wouldn't the Park de Prince Hotel be a suitable hotel for the
England team. It would appear to fit the requirements Dr.

THE MEDICAL TEAMS

Phillips is looking for."

Mr. Vine took the details of the hotel from Dr. Deutche. In the evening Mr. Vine, Alf and myself visited the Parc de Prince Hotel. It was an ideal home for the England party. Situated on the brow of a hill, with security gates facing the main road, no traffic noise was audible from within the grounds. The hotel had a central lawned area surrounded by individual bungalows. The bungalows were furnished to a high standard. Alf could not believe his luck. Alf informed the Hotel Manager, Mrs. Pugar,

> "I would like to book the whole hotel for the exclusive use of the England Football team for twenty-eight days in May 1970. Whatever deposit you require for the reservation The Football Association will provide."

She was delighted to accept the reservation.

The four days spent in Mexico City were full of administrative activity for the staff. Four days was too short a time for the players to acclimatize to the altitude. On each of the three days, prior to the international in Mexico City, the players trained. During the training sessions, all the players reported difficulty with their breathing. Their throats became dry and it was even difficult for them to swallow their own saliva. When players sprinted, they reported it took them longer to recover. The altitude also certainly affected their physical endurance. Both goalkeepers reported how different the speed of the ball was through the air.

> "It comes through the air quicker than at home. The ball is on you before you think it is."

was their comment. Alan Brown was however absolutely correct with his assessments. Some players will take the altitude on as a personal challenge, he had told me, when I spent that day with him in Sheffield. They will fight the altitude with utter determination. Others will succumb to the altitude and easily give up. The altitude of Mexico City, he had told me would sort the men from the boys. He was so right.

On the 1969 tour Alf's first choice, as deputy to Gordon Banks, was Gordon West of Everton. The two Gordons, Banks and West, were the only two goalkeepers selected for the South America tour. Alf preferred

Gordon West as Banks' deputy, in preference to the other goalkeepers, such as Peter Bonetti, Alec Stepney and the young Peter Shilton. Those three goalkeepers had all been left at home. The South American tour was designed, in part, to enable the players to experience the climatic condition of Mexico. The only two goalkeepers who would gain experience of the playing conditions at altitude on this tour were Gordon Banks and Gordon West.

Prior to visiting Mexico, Gordon West had only played in two internationals. He made his England debut against Bulgaria in December 1968. His only other international appearance had been against Wales, in the Home Internationals, at Wembley in 1969. He would make his third appearance in the Azteca Stadium against Mexico. Like all successful sportsmen, Gordon West had dedicated his life to becoming a great goalkeeper. He had committed himself to being the best in his profession. He was on the brink of achieving his ambition. He was England's second choice goalkeeper; second only to Gordon Banks–the world's greatest goalkeeper. In the Azteca Stadium, with a mid- day kick off on Sunday 1st. June 1969, Gordon West performed well. Unfortunately during the game, he was involved in a nasty collision, with one of the Mexican forwards. It appeared to be no more than any rough and tumble blow goalkeepers experience from time to time during a game. In the dressing room after the game, following my examination, I concluded that, apart from some bruising on his chest, there was no serious injury. Immediately after the international, the England party left Mexico City and flew to Guadalajara. We arrived at the Hilton Hotel in Guadalajara well after midnight. The following morning, with Gordon West still complaining of pain and stiffness over his chest, as a precaution, I arranged an X-ray for Gordon at The Santa Maria Hospital in Guadalajara. On the Tuesday evening, the England team was due to play a Mexican eleven in Guadalajara. It came as a great surprise to Alf Ramsey, the staff and myself when Gordon West declared he wanted to go home. He said he didn't like Mexico. He had no wish to return. Arrangements were made to fly Gordon West home to England. More seriously, Gordon West made it quite clear to Alf he did not wish to be considered for selection to the England team again. His international career was over. In his professional life, it appeared, he was content to be Everton's goalkeeper. He had no dream left to play for England. There is no doubt in my mind Alf Ramsey intended Gordon West to be England's second choice goalkeeper for the Mexico World Cup. However Gordon decided otherwise. He was honest enough to clearly state his position. He was content with his life at Everton. Playing at the highest level-that of an international player-was not for Gordon West. It was his choice. As a replacement, Alf sent for Peter Shilton. Peter had yet to make his international debut.

Our three-night stay in Guadalajara, was at the Hilton Hotel. The hotel is a first class hotel, with silent air conditioning. Its main disadvantage was it was in the centre of town, sited on a busy main road. At Guadalajara, I met with Dr. Williams, a local General Practitioner, who was also the British Consul in Guadalajara. He was of great assistance to me during my short stay. He gave me lots of relevant medical information.

"We have a major problem here in Guadalajara at the present time,

he told me.

"We can't always separate the drinking water from the sewage. If you have ice in your drinks, even in some of the hotels, it could be frozen sewage. I spend most of my working life here treating gastroenteritis."

he said.

Through his good offices, I visited two hospitals in Guadalajara. The El Carmen, where Dr. Williams worked, and the Hospital Santa Maria, where I had taken Gordon West for an X-ray examination. Both hospitals were reminiscent of a small cottage hospital in England. Facilities existed, at both hospitals for X-ray and in-patient care together with a small operating theatre. Neither hospital was as adequate as the ABC hospital in Mexico City. While at the El Carmen Hospital with Dr. Williams, I visited the children's ward.

"I want to show you how serious gastro-enteritis is in Guadalajara."

he said.

I had never before seen so many small babies and young children in one ward before. There were so many, the majority of them had no bed. They were lying on metal trays, tied in place by a single bandage, traversing over the babies, and tied in holes on each side of the metal tray. The majority of the children were so dehydrated they were on saline or dextrose-saline intravenous drips. Dr. Williams told me,

> "In the slum areas around here, humans defaecate in the dusty streets. Then the rains come. The sewage is washed into the soil. The water supply, in the slum areas is usually derived from a village pump. The pumped water is inevitably contaminated. What you see here, with these children, is the direct result of our poor hygiene in Guadalajara."

Both hospitals I visited, I would be happy to use, but only on an outpatient basis. They were more than adequate if I needed an X-ray examination or laboratory investigations. However, Dr. Williams confirmed the view, expressed to me in Mexico City, that very serious injuries and illnesses should be air lifted to America. Because of the Hilton Hotel's position, in the centre of town on a busy main road, Alf enquired of Dr. Williams if he could recommend any other hotel that might be suitable for the England team. He suggested we visit the Lake Chapala Hotel, some thirty minutes drive away from Guadalajara.

As it seemed likely England would be based in Guadalajara, for the preliminary rounds of the World Cup, Alf had spent some considerable time in the town during the Olympic Games. Alf had decided then the Atlas Sports Club in Guadalajara had by far the best training facilities in town. He had approached the Secretary of the Club and the England team had now been granted the exclusive use of their training facilities during the tournament. The Atlas Sports Club had many facilities to offer. In addition to the first class training grounds, there were ample facilities for tennis, table tennis, basketball, and a delightful swimming pool complex.

The Jalisco Stadium in Guadalajara, where the World Cup games would be played, is an excellent stadium with seating capacity for 50,000 specta-

THE MEDICAL TEAMS

tors. We were told this capacity would be increased by a further 20,000 for the World Cup, but no building work had commenced as yet. The playing surface was in excellent condition. In direct contrast to the Azteca Stadium, the surrounding buildings were not as high, thus giving more ventilation at ground level. The floodlights on one side of the ground were much lower than those on the opposite side and could possibly affect players when playing.

Until I personally experienced the sunlight in Guadalajara, I had no idea how very bright the sunshine really was. Even wearing Polaroid sunglasses I found the sun's glare extremely distressing. I walked around with my eyelids tightly screwed together. I concluded it would be necessary for all members of the squad to be issued with special sunglasses. Some optical firms, I knew were in the process of developing new sunglasses to overcome such severe brightness. I made a note to ensure theses new sunglasses would be available for every player during our stay in Guadalajara. The one factor causing me the greatest concern however was the intense heat. I went for a walk in the park at noon. The heat was unbearable. The temperature was in the upper nineties. The sun was directly overhead. There was no shade. Several inviting stalls were scattered throughout the park. They sold fruit and fruit drinks. The drinks looked especially tempting. The ice quickly melted in the intense heat. Imagine my surprise when the girl in charge replenished the ice, from a dirty sack lying in a rusty old bin, close to the stall. The lady in charge, had no facility for washing her hands. The concerns, which Dr. Williams had expressed to me with regard to public health and hygiene, were further confirmed to me when we went to the training ground. There, at the side of the training ground, a small stream was in full flow. Young girls, who may or may not have been married, used the stream to wash their clothes. The clothes were washed in a tub and the water supply delivered to the tub from the stream by a bright yellow tube. Just a few yards upstream from the girls however, was a horse. He was ideally placed to urinate or defaecate, or both, into the stream. The contaminated water easily flowed downstream straight into the weekly wash!

Everyone became aware, during our stay in Guadalajara, that if our games

DOCTOR TO THE WORLD CHAMPIONS

"Drinks In The Park–Ice In The Rusty Dustbin!"

in the World Cup were played at midday, as F.I.F.A. were suggesting, the heat factor would be very considerable. At the altitude of 5,400 feet, the heat would be a much greater problem for the players rather than the altitude. Particular attention would be needed to ensure the hydration of the players was adequate. Physical work, in extreme heat, leads to increase sweating. The increased sweating leads to water and salt being lost from the body. Replacement of the water loss and the provision of adequate salt, I considered, would be almost impossible. I formed the view, that players subjected to such severe heat during a game, might find it difficult to recover fully in two to three days as would be necessary in the World Cup. The use of electric fans in the dressing room prior to and during games would be essential.

Alf was keen to follow up Dr. Williams' suggestion and visit the hotel at

THE MEDICAL TEAMS

Lake Chapala. It confirmed the general view expressed by members of the party that the Hilton Hotel was not ideal, being in the centre of town and on a busy road. The whole squad travelled by motor coach to examine the hotel at Lake Chapala. It was a beautiful hotel, situated at the side of the lake. The hotel's large terrace extended down to the lakeside. Children swam in the lake. I have this lasting memory of Jack Charlton, fisherman extraordinaire, leaning over the rail and watching the fish swimming in the lake,

"Let's stay here."
said the fisherman.
"If I bring a rod, I'll have a great time."
With a cool breeze sweeping across the lake, the hot environment seemed so much cooler than the city centre of Guadalajara. Harold Shepherdson's view was much more scientific.

"I'm sure there's sewage floating in the lake.
Harold informed Alf. Sure enough the lake was contaminated with untreated sewage. Further enquiries revealed untreated sewage, from many of the villages, surrounding the lake, was deposited straight into the lake. The lake was seventy miles long and fifteen to twenty miles wide. No one should eat fish from the lake we were told. It's a sure way to contract Infective Hepatitis. With innumerable flies circulating the surface of the water containing untreated sewage, in close proximity to the hotel's kitchen, it was decided there would be too great a health risk if we stayed at the hotel. Jack Charlton would not be bringing his fishing gear!

Fortunately the England team was not subjected to playing in the searing heat in the Jalisco Stadium. The match, against a Mexico Xl, was played in the cool of the evening. England won by four goals to nil. The only sad event was the sending off of Alan Mullery, close to the end of the game. Immediately after the game, we flew from Guadalajara to Mexico City. There we caught a midnight plane, Flight CP522, which would convey us the entire length of South America through the night, arriving at Buenos Aires at 1400 hours. It was a long flight. With all the problems Mexico had thrown at me, my mind was in a whirl. I did not sleep on the sixteen-hour overnight flight to Argentina. After a two-hour stop in Argentina, we arrived in Uruguay's Montevideo at 2000 hours. We were all tired after the very long flight.

We were in Uruguay to play another international. However everyone's mind was on Mexico and the problems it had presented. The players, staff, officials and sports reporters talked of little else. The players were now convinced the altitude definitely did affect their physical performance. The players concerns were many. At the team meeting, the players' comments included,

"It takes longer to recover following a sprint."

"My throat and mouth became so dry, I couldn't even spit."

"The ball travels through the air much more quickly than at home."

"Twenty-yard passes end up thirty yards away."

"The food's a big problem."

"Where are we going to stay in Mexico City?"

"Has anyone seen this Parc de Prince place?"

"What about the heat in Guadalajara and the intensity of the sunlight?"

"How much time will we have to acclimatise?"

"If a player gets a really serious injury where is he going to be treated?"

The goalkeepers had obvious problems dealing with shots at goal. The ball was onto them too quickly. The players' questions seemed endless. Alf encouraged the players to discuss openly all their concerns.

Having travelled with England teams for many years, many of the Sports Journalists had become particular friends of mine. One such friend was the late Peter Lorenzo. Peter had contacts with several of the Uruguayan press. He enthusiastically returned from one meeting with his foreign colleagues and handed me a copy of an Argentinean Medical Report, which had been given to him. In their qualifying matches for the World Cup, Argentina played Peru at La Plaz. The altitude there was 15,000 feet, almost twice as high as Mexico City. The Argentinean Medical Team carried out over eight hundred examinations and investigations on twenty international

THE MEDICAL TEAMS

footballers during a fifteen-day stay at La Paz, prior to the qualifying game. Included in the report were clinical, blood, X-ray, urine and electrocardiogram tests, which could be compared with the results obtained, on the same players, at sea level. There was little in the report that surprised me. The Argentinean results, were similar to those Griffith Pugh and I had discussed at length back in London.

The Argentinean Medical Team however made certain recommendations to the Manager of the Argentinean team. I just could not believe their decision! For every medical test, carried out on the players in La Plaz, each player was given a score. If you like, a mark out of ten. In addition, to marking each of the tests out of ten, the medical team gave their assessments on each player in three specific areas. These specific areas were classified as psychological, physiological and the blood changes occurring at altitude. Each player was also given an additional mark out of ten in each of these three areas. The Argentinean medical team then made their amazing recommendation to the Manager. Their report concluded,

> "It is recommended only players with an average score of 6+, on the assessments, be sent to La Plaz in July and that these players are sent two weeks before the game. Those players, with an average score of less than six, would be sent direct to Lima for the game against Peru later in the month."

I laughed at their recommendation. I shuddered to think what Alf would have said to me if I had told him Bobby Charlton and Gordon Banks, or any other player for that matter, should not be selected to play because they had not scored over six on a parameter of medical tests! While I always looked on my role as one of supporting the Manager, Staff and Players, it appeared in Argentina the doctors had completely taken over the selection of the team!

While in Montevideo, Terry Cooper developed a very nasty tonsillitis, with enlarged glands in his neck. Although he responded to antibiotics, he was unable to play against Uruguay and Brazil. In taking a detailed history from Terry it became apparent he not infrequently suffered with tonsillitis. At the end of the tour, I wrote to Leeds United suggesting Terry be referred to a Ear, Nose and Throat specialist. Terry was referred. He had his tonsils removed during the close season.

While in Montevideo, I was caught out medically. One of the players went deaf. Examination revealed his ears were full of wax. I had suitable eardrops, but had not included an ear syringe in my medical equipment bag. When the player and I visited the local hospital, we had to wait over an hour to see a doctor. I assured the nurses that, given an ear syringe, I was perfectly capable of syringing a ear full of wax. Alas the nurses refused. Their doctor, and their doctor alone, would syringe the wax from the player's ear. When he eventually arrived, their doctor carried out the simple procedure. The lesson, for me, was to ensure in future I carried an ear syringe in my medical case. England won the international against Uruguay by two goals to one, with goals from Lee and Hurst. We would now move on to Rio de Janeiro playing the mighty Brazil.

We arrived in Brazil during the evening of Monday 9th. June We were staying at the Hotel Gloria. England would play Brazil in the Maracana Stadium, on Thursday 12th. June at 2100 hours. I was surprised to learn the official name for the stadium was the Mario Filho Stadium. Although we were in Rio only to play a football match, the beauty of the city is inescapable. The city extends, for some six miles in a narrow strip of land between the aquamarine sea, with its wonderful beaches, and the rich green mountains. Rising in the harbour entrance is one of the largest mountains, being the1,230 feet Sugar Loaf Mountain, with its exciting cable car ride. In addition to the beautiful Copacabana beach, where beach football seemed to be played all day, the most spectacular site, for me, was the Corcovado. Hanging over the city is a hunch-backed mountain, over two thousand feet high. On the summit is a one hundred and thirty feet high statue of Christ. The statue dominates the city through the day and, at night, the floodlights ensure its domination continues. The statue apparently weighs one thousand two hundred tons. I digress however. Our purpose in Rio was to play and beat Brazil in their own back yard. Some back yard it turned out to be!

The Maracana Stadium is awesome. It seats one hundred and fifty thousand spectators. For the game against England every seat had been sold. It

THE MEDICAL TEAMS

must be every footballer's dream to play in such a stadium. For me, merely to walk on the hallowed turf during a training session was a phenomenal experience. Although I didn't see the other facilities within the stadium, I was told a covered gymnasium, where other sports were played, was also housed in the complex. This gymnasium facility comfortably accommodates thirty thousand spectators. The Maracana was indeed an awesome place.

Because the game against England was completely sold out, the Brazilian authorities requested, for security reasons, the England team arrive at the stadium no later than two hours before kick off. We agreed to their request. The England motor coach entered the stadium, as requested, two hours before the commencement of the game. The motor coach was driven down a long tunnel and parked directly outside our dressing room door. We alighted the coach and entered the dressing room allocated to us. As Harold Shepherdson carried the last of the kit into the dressing room, he heard the dressing room door lock behind him. Almost immediately it appeared the central heating in the dressing room became over active. As the temperature rose, the players began sweating. The heat was unbearable. It was similar to being in a sauna. We hammered on the doors. There was no response. Alf shouted threats to a brick wall.

"If we are not released immediately England will not play."

In order to cool the players down I instructed them to take a cold shower. Many players did so. Eventually, after about ninety minutes of great discomfort, the dressing room door was opened and a Brazilian innocently enquired why we were making such a fuss. When I now witness the video of the game, the England players are seen, dressed in civilian clothes wandering about the pitch immediately before the game. The commentator remarks he has never seen the England players so relaxed so close to the commencement of an international game. Little did he know the players had been sent out onto the playing surface to cool down, both in body temperature and from the genuine anger they felt at being locked in their dressing room. The behaviour of the Brazilians and the stadium officials was totally unacceptable. The England team played exceptionally well that night. Colin Bell scored to put England in front. Gordon Banks saved a penalty. England led by the only goal of the game, until Tostao equalized with eleven minutes left to play. The players had looked tired for the previous ten minutes. The heat and humidity in the stadium, not to mention the central heating in the dressing room, was taking its toll. With only four minutes remaining, Jairzinho scored, ensuring Brazil won the game by two goals to one. The England players were devastated. They had been within eleven minutes of beating Brazil in their own back yard.

Most unusually on an England tour our last day was a free day. The players were told they had a free morning. Most went on the cable car to the summit of the Sugar Loaf mountain. After lunch we had a team meeting. I received a lot of stick from the players, in relation to the restrictions I had placed on them, regarding the food that was safe to eat. A very healthy discussion ensued. We all agreed for our six-week stay in Mexico the food problem would have to be solved. Bobby Charlton agreed to send me, when he was back in England, the food he ate on a daily basis. True to his word, for the first four weeks after our return, Bobby sent me details of every morsel of food he consumed at every meal.

In the evening of our last day in Rio, we were invited to attend a reception at the British Embassy to celebrate the Queen's Birthday. It was a superb evening and a good way to end the tour. I was more than a little annoyed however when one of the Embassy staff congratulated me on the way England had manipulated their defeat.

> "The result is the best possible one for relationships between Brazil and England. The fact that you were leading and then allowed them to win near the end of the game was absolutely magnificent."

I'm glad the result pleased someone! It certainly did not please anyone in the England party.

Our Flight BR662 left Rio for Gatwick at midnight. During the flight home, I sat with Alf Ramsey. We discussed the main medical issues confronting the players in Mexico. If we were given twenty-eight days to acclimatise to the altitude, I was certain that would be sufficient. The two major problems, as yet unsolved, were the food and the intense heat of Guadalajara.

THE MEDICAL TEAMS

The problem for me was now to find the best way to acclimatise to the heat and how to ensure the water and salt, lost in the copious sweating, could be adequately replaced. I promised Alf I would consult with my medical advisors and report back to him accordingly. It was five o'clock in the afternoon on Saturday 14th. June, when we arrived at Gatwick. I was glad to be back home. There were so many medical problems to be addressed by my medical team and so little time left in which to solve them.

    Ref. British Olympic Association, Medical Report, Olympic games, Mexico City 1968

        Heat Stress and Heat Disorders, Leithead and Lind, Cassell & Co. Ltd., 1964

11

If You Can't Stand The Heat ....

There is no doubt the tour of South America had been tiring. It would have been ideal for me to have a few days rest immediately following the tour. Unfortunately, as far as the Practice was concerned, I had been on annual leave. My days with the England team were always taken as holiday. My return home therefore was immediately followed, the very next day, by work in the Practice. I was also immediately involved in my role as Director and Medical Officer at Middlesbrough Football Club. There was also a need to spend time with my wife and three young children. On arriving home, my first England duty was to submit, to the England Manager, my medical report of the tour. I also needed to write to all the Football Clubs, whose players had been injured or ill on the tour. Discussions, on the unsolved problems of Mexico, with my medical team would have to wait. In compiling my medical report to Alf, I limited my remarks to the issues relevant to the following year's World Cup competition in Mexico. In consequence there was little in my report concerning the visits to Uruguay and Brazil.

In the late nineteen sixties, no one doubted the need to develop a strategy for the prevention of gastro-enteritis, endemic in Mexico. A very harsh food discipline had been introduced for the duration of the tour of South America. I decided no water, other than bottled water, would be consumed. Teeth would be cleaned in bottled water. We found the Mexican bottled water was so bland, it had little refreshing properties. No salads, unpeeled fruit or ice cream was eaten. No meals were consumed, except those prepared and provided for the entire England party. I had advised the players never to be tempted to buy or eat anything from a stall or shop while away from the hotel. We developed a strict habit of washing our hands before every meal and particularly after using the toilet. An antibacterial solution, Phisohex, was supplied to every player to be used for washing purposes. In addition, for the South American tour, I had divided the England party into two equal groups. Each group took a different drug as a preventative measure against gastroenteritis. One group took the non-absorbable Thalazole and the other group took Streptotriad. During the tour, four players reported with slight tummy upsets. Two of those players were in the Thalazole group and two in the Streptotriad group. In every case, the player felt well, had no abnormal clinical signs, received no further treatment and recovered quickly with reassurance. My report to Alf included the following observations,

"For visitors to Mexico, the most recent medical research, available to me, still recommends the use of Thalazole as the preferred first line of defence against gastroenteritis. I would of course prefer no one take any preventative drug daily during our long stay in Mexico, but I do believe it is essential some form of preventative drug therapy is necessary. It is therefore my recommendation that we use Thalazole as our first choice of daily preventative medicine. The more powerful Streptotriad I would then use as a second line of therapy, if a definite case of gastro-enteritis occurs. The majority of my medical team agrees with this decision. Although it was difficult to accept the disciplines I imposed, with regard to food and drink, it was pleasing to note the players accepted the disciplines. In Mexico City, food is a tremendous problem. In Guadalajara, the Hilton Hotel presented fewer problems than was present during our stay in Mexico City. At the team meeting in Rio, the players, quite rightly, expressed their concerns relating to a satisfactory adequate diet. We will need to give detailed care and attention in working out a satisfactory diet for the players during our long acclimatisation period. F.I.F.A., in their report on the Olympic Games, suggested some countries might give consideration to taking some of their own food supplies for the World Cup competition and even their own chef. This is something I shall explore. Bobby Charlton has offered to help in the production of his present diet and he has promised to send me his daily diet for a month. I shall keep you informed of progress in this area. We were informed the fish in Mexico is particularly suspect, because of the danger of Infective Hepatitis. It may be however, if the party were inoculated with gamma globulin prior to departure, this danger would be overcome. I am making the necessary enquiries. As the players have stated, tins of baked beans and spaghetti would be of great help!

My visit to Mexico confirmed my belief, from a medical point of view, we must be totally self-sufficient while at the World Cup. I propose therefore making a comprehensive list of the drugs and medicines required for the World Cup in 1970. I will submit these in good time for dispatch to Mexico. Such drugs and medicines, I understand, will be admitted under diplomatic privilege provided we inform the British Embassy in Mexico of their impending arrival. I have submitted to you already a list of the medical supplies I left, in Mexico City, in the care of the British Embassy. These medical supplies will be available to me in 1970.

I have arranged with the Rank Organisation, through their medical subsidiary Stanley Cox, for the provision of infra-red, short wave diathermy and ultrasonic machines. Following the visit to Mexico City, it will be necessary for such equipments to have voltage adjusters, as the voltage in Mexico City may fall on occasions as low as 80 and rise to a maximum of 150. I have written to Stanley Cox informing them of this problem, in order for the necessary adjustments to be made to the machines. I will discuss the dispatch and packaging of the equipment with Stanley Cox. While the ABC hospital in Mexico City, and the two hospitals in Guadalajara have adequate outpatient facilities, considerable problems could arise if a member of the party required in-patient care of any duration. Suggestions were repeatably made, to me, by the doctors and lay people I met, that, in the event of a serious injury or illness, the patient should be evacuated to The Methodist Hospital in Texas. I shall discuss this matter with my medical team and advise you later of our discussions. Before leaving Mexico, I put in place arrangements for suitable air transport should this evacuation strategy be decided upon.

There is no doubt the altitude, of 7500ft in Mexico City and 5400ft in Guadalajara affects, performance in the following ways:–

In the amount of physical work that can be performed.

The rate at which such physical work can be performed

The increased length of recovery rate after physical work is carried out.

The physical and psychological reactions of the players.

The speed and distance the ball travels through the air.

I can only hope that, following a period of twenty-eight days acclimatisation at altitude, sufficient improvement will occur to enable the players to physically perform at a level similar to that in England. A minimum of twenty-eight days altitude acclimatisation is recommended both by Griffith Pugh and myself. It is interesting to note, of the four players most affected by the altitude during the game in Mexico City, three were known to have low blood levels prior to departure, and the fourth player subsequently developed, the following day, a very nasty tonsillitis. It would be silly to correlate absolutely performance with blood levels, but nevertheless it is essential all the players have high blood levels before departing to Mexico in 1970. The players will also need to attain a high level of physical fitness immediately before leaving. Dr. Fielding and I are presently in the process of arranging suitable dates for further blood tests to be carried out over the next twelve months. I will commence remedial treatments immediately, if they are indicated, from the results of the blood tests. There is sufficient time for me to ensure everyone's blood level is satisfactory before we leave next May. Every individual's blood group will also be known, so that, in the unlikely event of a transfusion being necessary, the blood group of every player will be readily available.

During the game in Mexico City, and to a lesser extent in Guadalajara, some players complained of dryness of the throat and mouth and an inability to swallow. These symptoms became worse as the game progressed. Following discussions with the players, it was suggested by them a pocket could be made in the shorts into which a piece of lemon, or fruit sweets could be carried which might then be sucked from time to time relieving this dryness. It may be of course these symptoms disappear with adequate acclimatisation.

Personally, the big surprise of the tour for me was the intense heat at Guadalajara. If the games in Guadalajara are played at midday or four o'clock in the afternoon, as F.I.F.A. are suggesting, the heat factor will be considerable. In such circumstances particular attention will have to be paid to the hydration of players before and during every game. In the Olympic Games the long-distance runners found the heat a particular problem. The substantial increase in sweating will easily result in water and salt depletion, both of which might be extremely dangerous. With the difficulty of the water supply in Mexico and the bland, unpalatable taste of their bottled water, sufficient fluid replacement will be difficult. Even more difficult will be the replacement of the salt lost in sweating. It has proved in the past that to add more than five grams of salt daily to food makes it unpalatable. Some physiologists estimate, in un-acclimatised men, between fifteen and twenty-five grams of salt daily is required when working in extreme heat. As a normal European diet contains about ten grams of salt daily, there could be a daily deficit of salt, in the first week of working in the heat, of some five to fifteen grams. The provision of sufficient salt, to replace that lost, could be a major problem. In fact it might prove impossible. I am in discussion with Professor Leithead as to how we might solve this problem. As there may be only three days between games in the World Cup, players may find it difficult to fully recover between games. The use of electric fans in the dressing room prior to and during matches would be a considerable advantage. The brightness of the sun in Guadalajara is another problem. I am presently exploring whether appropriate sunglasses can be provided for the entire squad.

As you are aware, all members of the Senior and Under 23-teams, selected for the summer tours, have been vaccinated against Smallpox. I have written to all the relevant Club Medical Officers requesting that they carry out the immunisations, against Typhoid and Paratyphoid Fever, during the close season on the forty players you have nominated. Hopefully this will be done."

IF YOU CAN'T STAND THE HEAT

There then followed, in my report, a summary of the injuries sustained by six players during the tour, the treatment they had received and the progress made. I confirmed I had written to all the players' Clubs, informing them of the injuries sustained. For the three players, who had been taken ill on the tour, I also confirmed I had written reports to their Clubs. I had also written thank you letters to Dr. Deutch, at the ABC hospital in Mexico City and Dr. Williams in Guadalajara.

I had gone on the South American tour of 1969 convinced the altitude of Mexico would be the major problem facing the team in the World Cup competition. On my return, I was confident that, given the twenty-eight days to acclimatise I had requested, we would adjust to the altitude as well as any other European team and better than most. The team's visit to Guadalajara however had presented me with an even greater problem. The intense heat of Guadalajara, I considered to be a greater threat to a player's performance than the altitude, particularly if, as we were told, F.I.F.A. were insisting the World Cup matches would be played at mid-day or four o'clock in the afternoon. At those times, the temperature in Guadalajara would be in the nineties and on occasions in excess of one hundred degrees. Our one game at the Jalisco Stadium in Guadalajara, against a Mexican eleven, was played in the cool of the evening. At that time of day, the conditions were ideal for European footballers. England had played well in the cool of the evening. They had won the game, by four goals to nil. Having visited Guadalajara, my main concern now was definitely the heat factor. The intense heat would have a devastating effect on the players.

I could not believe the organising committee would insist on the games being played at mid-day, when the heat was at its most intense. The F.I.F.A. officials however appeared more concerned to receive vast amounts of money from Eurovision, than being concerned for the players' welfare. The organising committee was already in negotiations with the European television companies., who, quite rightly from their viewpoint, were insisting on televising the matches live in Europe at peak viewing time. It would be the first time, in the history of the competition, World Cup matches would be televised live throughout Europe. These matches would be screened at eight o'clock in the evening in Europe. With the eight-hour time difference, that required games to commence at midday in Mexico. At mid-day in Guadalajara, the sun would be directly overhead with no shade. The players would be exposed to considerable heat stress. On the tour, we had trained in the late morning at Guadalajara. The temperature was ninety-eight degrees.

"I sweated like a stuffed pig."
was the general comment of the players.

"I was exhausted after half an hour in that heat."
several of the players reported. F.I.F.A. seemed unconcerned at the players' reactions. Their only concern appeared to be negotiating the most lucrative financial contract possible, from the European television companies. There seemed no concern whatever for the welfare of the players. I didn't realise it then, but it was the beginning of television running the game of football. In my report to the England Manager, I wrote,

> "There is no doubt that if our games in Guadalajara are played at midday, the heat factor will be considerable. In such circumstances, particular attention will have to be given to the hydration of players before and during the games. The replacement of water and salt, lost in sweat, will be a particular problem. The players will find it difficult to recover fully, in a period of two or three days before the next game, as will be necessary in the World Cup competition."

The human body, exposed to working in extreme dry heat, responds by producing more sweat. As the increased sweat evaporates on the surface of the skin, it cools the body down. It is the evaporation of sweat on the skin, and its cooling effect, that maintains the body temperature. Working in temperatures approaching one hundred degrees, the increase in sweating is considerable. Playing in the extreme heat of Guadalajara, there was a real danger of water and salt depletion occurring in the players due to the excessive sweating. In my correspondence with Professor Leithead, he advised there was a real danger the increased sweating may lead to such depletion in the players, unless preventative measures were taken. He suggested it would necessary for the players to consume extra fluid and salt every day during exposure to this heat. Taking extra fluid in Mexico however was a big problem. We were advised not to drink the tap water. Dr. Williams had told me, in Guadalajara,

> "We can't separate the water from the sewage. If the players have ice in their drinks, they could be drinking frozen sewage!"

Although I had insisted, throughout the tour, the players drank only bottled water, it was tasteless and bland. The taking of additional salt on a daily basis had presented an even greater problem. Salt, in sufficient quantity, is almost impossible to take by mouth. It is best disguised in tomato juice, but even then it was quite nasty to take regularly in sufficient quantities. Inevitably, some of our players didn't even like tomato juice! Leithead's suggestion was to dissolve two grams of salt in a litre of citrus fluid to be taken twenty minutes before every game. The players were however resistant to drinking a litre of any fluid immediately before playing, let alone one containing two grams of salt. I personally tried it and certainly would not have looked forward to playing a game of football after drinking such a large quantity of the solution. Salt tablets, with a thick coating, the so-called enteric-coated tablets, had been used in the past in the belief they would reduce the feeling of nausea that occurred following drinking a salt solution. Previous research had shown these tablets did prevent the feeling of nausea, but unfortunately, when abdominal x-rays were taken some six hours after taking them, the tablets were still lying within the lumen of the intestine. The enteric coating was so strong the tablets remained intact and no salt had been absorbed into the body. The tablets were inadequate as a salt replacement.

The problem of replacing the water and salt lost in sweat, in playing in the heat of Guadalajara, presented me with a very difficult problem. I had expressed my concerns to Sir Alf while in Uruguay and Brazil. On our return from South America, Alf gave a television interview, during which he emphasised the problems the heat would cause, if our matches commenced at noon in Guadalajara, Alf said,

> "The heat in the Guadalajara stadium at mid-day is intense. The players will lose large amounts of water and salt in their

sweat. Replacing the water and particularly the salt, presents the team with a serious problem."

Sitting at his home in South London, watching Sir Alf on television, was the Professor of Medicine of Charing Cross Hospital, Hugh de Wardener

"I might be able to help the England players" he thought.

The following day, he contacted Sir Alf at The Football Association. Alf referred Professor de Wardener to me. I received a letter from de Wardener dated the 15th August 1969. In the letter de Wardener explained he had worked on Sodium (Salt) metabolism for many years. Like Sir Alf, he too was concerned. He wrote,

> "the gross dehydration and salt deficiency, caused by increased sweating in extreme heat, could cause muscle cramps and exhaustion in the players. I have an idea how this situation may be prevented which, I think, might be worth looking into. I wonder if we could meet some time for me to explain what I have in mind."

I phoned de Wardener's secretary the same day. I made an appointment to meet him in London the following Wednesday. We were to meet at his office in Charing Cross Hospital. The matter was urgent for me. It was September 1969. Tall and elegant, with a friendly disposition, deWardener explained he had a daily problem in the hospital with salt depletion. As Professor of Medicine, he had special responsibility for the Renal Unit and in particular for renal dialysis. He informed me, patients with kidney failure are unable to remove the waste products from their blood. Patients are placed on the dialysis machine, so that the machine removes the waste products from the body. Unfortunately, during the dialysis process, the machine not only removes the waste products from the blood, but also removes sodium (salt) as well. During dialysis therefore, some patients become salt deficient. In order to overcome this salt deficiency during dialysis, the patients are given a concurrent intravenous infusion of saline. From the patient's viewpoint, it is yet another needle inserted into them. For some time de Wardener and his staff had been working on a new tablet concept, to do away with the need for an intravenous infusion of saline.

"The idea is to make a new salt tablet, the structure of which is based on a honey comb. The walls of each cell in the honeycomb would be made of wax, but having different thicknesses. Each cell of the honeycomb would contain salt. The wax honeycomb would be covered with a, pleasant-to-take, sugar based layer. The tablet would be nice to take orally with no nausea or sickness occurring in the patient. As the wax walls in the tablet dissolved, the salt would be released and absorbed into the blood stream. With the wax walls of the honeycomb having a variety of thickness, the absorption of the salt occurs over a period of time."

"How soon after swallowing the tablet would the salt be absorbed into the body?"

"At this stage I don't know. The tablet is not fully developed yet. More research needs to be done, but I think we could complete all the work before the World Cup next June. My department has a very good relationship with Ciba, the pharmaceutical company, who are presently involved in developing the tablet. The tablet will be called 'Slow Sodium'."

I explained to deWardener I was already involved with Ciba. The England players were already taking the company's slow release iron tablet -Slow Fe–for improving their blood levels. I suggested as soon as the Slow Sodium tablets were ready I might be able to use the tablets, with the players at Middlesbrough, in order to establish whether they were acceptable to professional footballers. Later, I would be interested in carrying out an acceptability study with the England players. Ideally, I would like to introduce the tablet to the England players when England play Holland in Amsterdam in November.

de Wardener was enthusiastic. He agreed to contact Dr. Burley, the Senior Medical Officer at Ciba, informing him of our discussions and the urgency of the situation.

A copy of de Wardener's three-page letter to Ciba arrived at my home two days later. de Wardener described the discussions we had in London.

He outlined to Dr. Burley some of the issues to be addressed. de Wardener would personally endeavour to establish the rate of absorption of the sodium into the body, following the ingestion of Slow Sodium. He would use labelled (radio isotope) sodium in some of the studies. I had raised with deWardener the fact that exercise may affect the rate of absorption, and studies would be needed during exercise. de Wardener believed he could persuade some of the Charing Cross Medical School Football team to swallow the tablets and exercise for an hour and a half during the study. He believed the research could begin as soon as Ciba provided him with the isotope tablets. He also informed Ciba I was prepared to carry out an acceptability study with the Middlesbrough players. He requested 6,000 Slow Sodium tablets be sent to me at Middlesbrough. de Wardener suggested to Ciba each of the tablets should contain 600mgms of salt. The dosage would enable us to provide the players, and de Wardener's patients, with the required replacement of salt either lost in sweating or when on the dialysis machine. Three weeks later, six thousand Slow Sodium tablets arrived at Middlesbrough. The research was on its way!

My task, in the research, was simple. I discussed with the Middlesbrough Manager, Stan Anderson, and then the players their willingness, or otherwise, to participate in the acceptability study.

"You will only be swallowing a simple salt tablet, tasting of sugar."

I told them.

The Manager and players agreed to try out the tablets initially, prior to their training sessions. No reaction was reported by any of the players on taking the tablets. It was subsequently agreed, Middlesbrough players would each take four tablets with their pre-match meal, before a league match. The tablets were taken three hours before the commencement of the game. Again no adverse reactions were reported. Some players actually thought they felt less tired and fatigued during the game. No nausea was reported. The Slow Sodium tablets were certainly acceptable to the Middlesbrough players. I informed Ciba and de Wardener of the success of my acceptability study. They were delighted, as indeed was Alf Ramsey.

The irony of the situation amused me. Initially, when I was approached, by Alan Bass to become involved with England, he told me Alf had expressed doubts about me continuing as a Director at Middlesbrough. At that time, before I'd even met Alf, he felt I could utilise my position as Team Doctor to England for the benefit of Middlesbrough Football Club. Now, five years on, I was using my position at Middlesbrough Football Club for the benefit of England. Football certainly is a funny old game!

The research, which Ciba and de Wardener needed to carry out, was much more difficult and scientific than my acceptability study. At the Charing Cross Hospital they needed to ascertain the absorption rate of the salt from the stomach into the blood stream and whether the absorption rate was affected by exercise. Firstly they rendered the Slow Sodium tablets radioactive by neutron bombardment in a nuclear reactor. Without going into the technical details, following the swallowing of the tablet, the radioactivity levels were accurately measured, over the abdomen and in the blood stream. A fall in the count rate of radioactivity, over the abdomen, reflected the rate of absorption of Slow Sodium. Repeated blood tests, taken at intervals following the swallowing of the tablets, would reflect the level of radioactive Sodium in the blood stream. It was also important to know if the absorption rate was different, according to the number of tablets taken. The main problem de Wardener had was who would be willing to swallow radioactive salt tablets; be exposed to repeated blood tests; exercise for an hour or so and spend half a day undergoing all the tests. He and Dr. Jewkes, head of the isotope department at the hospital, approached the members of the Charing Cross Hospital Football Team. With the promise of a ticket, for the next international at Wembley and in the knowledge this research needed to be done for the benefit of the England team in Mexico, six of the team, together with Dr. Jewkes, volunteered for the study. The England team, and many of the dialysis patients at the hospital, would be for ever grateful to Dr. Jewkes and students Brooks, Burke, Kaye, Rooker, Sinnett, and Sillance for volunteering. Their efforts enabled the research to go ahead promptly.

The studies showed Slow Sodium tablets had a predictable pattern of absorption at rest and on exercise. If taken without food, most of the salt was absorbed over the first two or three hours, but the absorption was not complete for six hours. If taken with food, the absorption pattern was similar, but subject to an initial delay of up to two hours. The results of the trial were available to me in good time. I discussed the outcome of the research with Sir Alf Ramsey prior to the next international against Holland in Amsterdam on November 3rd 1969. With the results of the research, and the acceptability of the tablets with the Middlesbrough players, Alf suggested I talk to the England players prior to the Holland game. If the players agreed, I would introduce the tablets to the England players at the Holland game.

Having spoken with the England players, they were eager to try out the tablets. Each player received four tablets, with their pre-match meal, before the international against Holland in Amsterdam. As with the Middlesbrough players, the England players reported no adverse reactions. The England players found the Slow Sodium tablets perfectly acceptable. With an absorption delay, occurring when taken with food, the tablets could ideally be given with the pre-match meal. Absorption of salt into the blood stream would then commence two hours later and continue for up to six hours. Whatever salt was lost in the sweat, with correct dosage, would be replaced into the body as the players were actually playing. Salt lost from the body in sweating would be replaced at the very time the loss was occurring. Slow Sodium was a success.

Having introduced the England players to the Slow Sodium tablets in Holland, I administered the tablets to all the players prior at all subsequent international matches. No side effects were ever encountered. They were able to take increasing amounts without any problems. In Guadalajara, the players would be exposed to water and salt deficiency problems due to the increased amounts of sweat produced. It now appeared I could prevent salt deficiency occurring by the use of Slow Sodium. The water deficiency I decided would be prevented or overcome if we shipped fifteen thousand bottles of Malvern water to Mexico for our use. I would use Slow Sodium tablets and bottled Malvern water in Mexico, to overcome the problems of water and salt loss.

IF YOU CAN'T STAND THE HEAT

The management of the players in the heat of Guadalajara was along the lines described by Leithead and Lind in their book 'Heat Stress and Heat Disorders.' Hatch,[§] another researcher, suggested and recommended in 1963 that if one single measurement was used as an index of the physiological strain when working in the heat, then the change in nude weight, over a known exposure time, had much to commend it. I would use this simple measurement throughout our time in Mexico.

"Bobby Charlton Protects His Head By Training In A Trilby!"

The players would be weighed in the nude before and after every training session and game. After some training sessions and games, a weight loss of up to twelve pounds was recorded in some players. My aim throughout was to ensure this weight loss was regained by the administration of Slow Sodium and Malvern Water on a daily basis.

§ Hatch: 1963

Knowing the problems we had experienced on the tour in 1969 with the heat, Freddy Goodwin, the former Leeds player and Manager of Birmingham City, wrote to offer some help to Alf Ramsey. Freddy was managing a football team in Florida and was experienced in coping with players working in extreme heat. His suggestion was to use a glucose saline drink called 'Gatorade'; unheard of in England at the time. The company producing Gatorade in the United States quickly made supplies available to us. It was a pleasant lemon drink, which the players enjoyed. Unfortunately when de Wardener carried out a scientific analysis of the drink, its salt content was only equivalent to two Slow Sodium tablets if one drank a litre of Gatorade. The salt content was too low to act as a total salt replacement on its own. Nevertheless, because it was such a pleasant drink I decided to use it in Mexico. The requisite bottles of Gatorade were ordered. Unfortunately, when the Mexican authorities learned we were bringing Gatorade into their country, they said there was no licence for the use of Gatorade in Mexico. We would not be allowed to bring bottles of Gatorade into their country The company producing Gatorade however overcame the problem for me. They produced a supply of Gatorade, in powder form, and in sufficient quantities for the entire tour. All I was required to do was dissolve the powder in Malvern water and hey presto we had Gatorade! It was so much more pleasant for the players to drink than plain water.

    I ensured that in order to prevent the cumulative loss of water and salt during our stay in Mexico, the players would need to drink liberal quantities of Malvern water and Gatorade. The players were advised to drink until their thirst was quenched and then to drink a further one and a half litres during the day. In addition, when exposed to the extreme heat of Guadalajara, each player would be given a daily dose of eight Slow Sodium tablets; four to be taken each night and four prior to training or matches. In order to prevent the acute salt loss occurring during training or playing in Guadalajara, the players would be given a loading dose of Slow Sodium three hours prior to all training sessions and matches with the pre match meal. In addition the players would drink half a litre of Gatorade during the two hours before playing. A further half litre would be available to them at half time and they were encouraged to drink copious amounts of Gatorade or Malvern water at the end of the game.

In order to cope better with the heat, and following discussions Alf had with the players, it was decided to redesign the playing shirts and shorts. The clothing would be in light colours as these colours reflect the heat, while dark colours absorb radiant heat. When exposed to heat, light colours are more beneficial. Alf registered England's playing colours as white and light blue. The shirts were designed in cotton with an overall aertex design, so allowing more ventilation. The shorts also had aertex bands at the sides and contained a pocket, as requested by the players. Playing in the heat presented us with major problems but, in the twelve months prior to the competition most of them now appeared to be solved.

"*I Measure Wet and Dry Bulb Thermometer Temperatures, While The Players Train.*"

12

It Takes Time To Be Accepted......................

The first senior international of the 1969–70 season was an away fixture against Holland. Surprisingly, the Dutch team had failed to qualify for the World Cup in Mexico. In the qualifying rounds, Holland had been drawn in Group Eight, with Luxembourg, Bulgaria and Poland. Their two matches against Luxembourg, the weakest team in the group, had both been won. More difficult games followed for Holland, against Bulgaria and Poland. Bulgaria proved the tougher opposition. Holland were defeated two nil in Bulgaria and could only manage a draw, 1–1, at home. Against Poland, Holland won 1–0 at home, but then lost 2–1 in the away fixture. Holland finished third in their qualifying group with seven points. The two teams qualifying for Mexico, from Group Eight, would be Bulgaria and Poland. Holland would be staying at home. It was a great tragedy. The 1970 World Cup in Mexico would be deprived of seeing this extremely talented football team.

Sunday travel, by rail from the north-east to London, was always tedious. Harold Shepherdson and I travelled down to London together. Train journeys always provided me with plenty of thinking time. As the train journeyed from Darlington to York, I reflected on my position with the England team. Since my appointment, as the Senior Medical Officer, just twelve months previously, the work had become all consuming. The detailed medical preparations, required for the World Cup competition in Mexico, were taking up the whole of my spare time. I kept recalling my visit to the Romanian Sports Medicine Centre in Bucharest in November 1968. There, their medical team, of over twenty medical specialists, would be working full time preparing the Romanian footballers for the problems to be encountered in Mexico. In comparison, whilst I had invited several highly qualified medical consultants in England to advise me, I was conscious all my medical advisors, like myself, were unpaid part timers. I was nevertheless satisfied the medical team, I personally had appointed, was composed of an exceptional group of doctors. Each one of them was an experienced consultant, whose views I greatly valued. Moreover, they were all enthusiastic in their support for the team and for what I was trying to achieve. Each consultant had accepted my invitation, to advise me, without hesitation. The Football Association was paying none of them. The efforts and advice from my medical team were voluntary. Their main role, like mine, was working in the National Health Service. For many months, I had devoted every Wednesday, my day off from the Practice, and every spare moment at weekends to the England team. I had spent those days, travelling all over the country, visiting the various members of the team who had agreed to help me. Even with their expert and willing advice, it was still difficult for me to believe I was providing the world-class medical support Ramsey was demanding. I was always acutely aware of the quality of the full time medical support other countries, particularly those from the communist block and those in South America, were receiving. Our medical preparation for Mexico was going exceptionally well, but, as a part- timer with the England team, I believed it was impossible to devote the time required for the proper preparation of the team. There were never enough hours in the day for me. Ramsey's words, following my visit to the Romanian Sports Centre, kept ringing in my ears and haunting me.

> "I don't care how you do it. Just make sure our medical preparation is better than that of the Romanians. In fact, make sure they are better than any of the other competing teams."

It was easier said than done. Ramsey induced such loyalty in his players and staff, it was inconceivable for me to let him or the team down. I was also conscious of the lack of time I spent with my family. Our three children were growing up and I was always away from home. My England role had taken over my life. There was no doubt, my bread and butter work of General Practice was suffering. In addition, there was my part-time medical appointment at I.C.I., and the daily work at Ayresome Park, in my dual role as Medical Officer and Director. Individually, each of those roles was all consuming. When added together, it seemed they were impossible to manage. The England role, I genuinely believed should have been a full-time appointment. With all my other commitments, I knew I was unable to give the England role the commitment I knew it needed. My life appeared to be on a non-stop roundabout and I couldn't get off!

The train rumbled on. Shep was sound asleep. Shep slept anywhere. On Middlesbrough and England duty, I travelled the world with Harold Shepherdson. At home or abroad, he could fall asleep just anywhere. In a car, bus, train, aeroplane, or chair, Shep could nod off at a moment's notice. I envied his ability to take a quick nap, wherever he was. As the train travelled on through the Midlands, I continued to reflect on my role. Shep continued to sleep.

It was six years, since I had first met Alf Ramsey. During those years he and I had built up an excellent relationship. In most respects, I looked upon my job, not as working for The Football Association, but working for Alf.. He was a wonderful person to work for. His loyalty to the staff and players was supreme. He inspired me. He engendered in me a reciprocal loyalty. We respected each other and the differing roles we played. Our working relationship was first class. He left all medical matters to me; the football was his business. Where the two overlapped, full discussions always took place between us. The final responsibility, he said, was always his. Alf, I knew, would never let me down. I would always strive not to let him down. As Shep slumbered on, I recalled the conversation Alf and I had, in Wrexham and Aberdeen, when he first invited me to join the England team.

> "I want you to give good medical advice and treatments to the players. I want you to be someone they can trust. Someone they can converse with. Someone they have full confidence

in. I want you to be a full member of the squad. Most of all, I want you to be the player's friend."

At Under 23 level, this was relatively easy. The players there were young and keen to impress at international level. The step, from Club to international level, was a huge one for them to take. They all had varying degrees of anxiety as they progressed to full international level. All those players were anxious to do well; keen to be accepted by the management. It was important for them to impress the management team ; the doctor included. At senior level, it was quite different and my integration there had proved more difficult.

On my appointment to the Senior Medical Post, most of the senior England players were well-established stars. Most had been involved in the World Cup winning team. Although I had been involved with them in their training and preparation for the 1966 finals and in the preparation for the final itself, Alan Bass was then the Senior Medical Officer and the senior players, quite naturally, related more to him. I knew the players were disappointed when he left them and decided to emigrate to Canada. I now had to relate to a far more experienced group of professionals; players who had already established themselves as international players. They were the established stars of the game. Their respect I had to earn over time. At this stage, some eighteen months after my appointment, I believed my relationship, with all the players was coming together nicely. I had developed, with most of the senior players, an excellent relationship. There were exceptions of course. One such exception was Jack Charlton. Jack, I had always found, difficult to get to know; difficult to get close to. He was a model professional. Always did his training with enthusiasm. He played every practice game as if it was a real match. He contributed frequently in team discussions. Yet, when the work was over, he kept very much to himself. He would frequently isolate himself in some quiet corner of the hotel, seemingly engrossed in the most recent paperback. Jack and I had never been involved in a private conversation. We, of course, exchanged daily pleasantries like "Good Morning.", "Hey", and "See you", but no meaningful conversations. I had previously admired watching his coaching sessions at Lilleshall on the summer courses; admired his forthright clear comments, but, of all the players, Jack was the one I least knew. As Shep slumbered and the train hurtled ever onwards through the countryside, I decided I would set out to correct my relationship with Jack at the earliest opportunity. A look at the current itinerary made me realise it would not be on this trip. Brian Labone of Everton was in the party, as the centre-half and big Jack was not. Ah well, maybe some other time.

"Fancy a sandwich?"

I enquired of Harold, as he awoke from his slumbers.

"Don't mind if I do"

As we walked along the corridor of the train to the buffet car, I reflected on my lack of friendship with Jack Charlton. If the opportunity arose, I would make every effort to get close to him. It seemed strange that, over the past eighteen months, I had developed good relationships with the entire team except Big Jack. It was a situation I needed to correct.

The England squad met at Whites Hotel in Lancaster Gate on the Sunday evening. Alf was not a happy man. Several of the selected players had been injured on the Saturday. Their managers had been in contact with Alf. Many of the players, Alf had chosen, would not be making the trip. To date, five of the sixteen players selected had withdrawn. The playing squad was reduced to eleven players. Brian Labone was one of the five players injured. He had withdrawn from the squad. Alf informed Harold, Jack Charlton would be taking Brian Labone's place. Jack would be joining the squad late on the Sunday evening. That evening, at Whites Hotel, there were only eleven players present. The Football League, in those days, gave no concessions to the international team. Prior to every mid-week international fixture, The Football League insisted on a full programme of Club fixtures. While most European and South American Leagues would cancel their league programmes immediately prior to an international, no such privileges were given to the England team. Inevitably, Ramsey was always prevented from having adequate training and preparation time with his team. Three days before an international match, the players were required to play for their Clubs. Injuries were always a possibility. On this

IT TAKES TIME TO BE ACCEPTED

occasion, injuries had accounted for several players withdrawing. Ramsey's problem was not only the lack of training and preparation time, but actually assembling a full team. What a ludicrous situation! What a way to prepare the national team!

Harold and I saw little of Alf in the early evening. He was ensconced in his room, telephoning the various managers seeking replacements for the injured players. As it was a Sunday evening, many of the managers were unavailable. If the manager was available, invariably the player Alf wanted could not be contacted. After all, the players would not be aware of their late selection and were, in all probability enjoying a Sunday evening with their families. When Alf appeared for a late dinner, he informed us it had been impossible to contact all the replacement players he needed. Messages had been left with the appropriate Club officials. It would however be Monday morning before we knew whether the replacements were available. The final composition of the squad would probably not be known until lunchtime on Monday.

The Monday morning training session was held at the Bank of England's Sports Ground in Richmond. It was confined to the eleven fit players. Alf had used the Bank's sports ground at Richmond over many years. The facilities were excellent. The staff there were always friendly and helpful. The meals they provided were first class. Their roast beef and Yorkshire puddings were magnificent.

Our flight from Heathrow left on the Monday at three-thirty. As flight BE 463 climbed into the November sky, on its way to Amsterdam, there were only twelve players on board. None of the replacements, apart from Jack Charlton, travelled with us. They would all travel on a later flight. Those players would join us, at the Amsterdam Hilton, at lunchtime on the Tuesday. Our flight to Amsterdam was uneventful. Shep, as usual, slept most of the way. Our arrival in Amsterdam was in the midst of a torrential rain storm. It was a miserable welcome; wet and cold. On the Tuesday morning, Alf had arranged a training session at the Olympic Stadium, where the international game was to be played. The weather conditions were appalling. It didn't just rain, it poured down. Alf Ramsey was never one to give in to the elements. He had organised a training session and a training session would be held, rain or no rain.

"so let's get used to it."
he said.
The Dutch authorities, however, had other ideas. When we arrived at the Olympic Stadium the pitch was waterlogged. The training session was cancelled. We were not allowed to train on the Olympic Stadium. The Dutch authorities did, however, suggest we could train on a pitch outside the stadium, though that pitch was more saturated and certainly muddier.

"That's most kind of you, we'll train there."
said Alf.

A full training session took place. It was cold, wet and windy. The pitch was muddy. It was not an ideal morning for training. With the players running about on the pitch, the training ground soon became a sea of mud. After the usual warm-up and physical exercises, Alf organised the players into a six a side game. One of the players, with a bruised thigh, remained in the dressing room area receiving treatment from Harold Shepherdson. As a result, one of the two teams was a man short. Alf would referee. I was instructed to make the numbers up by going in goal. Jack Charlton was on the opposing team. Realising I was in goal, Jack moved to centre-forward. He and I would be in direct and close contact. As the six a side game progressed, I was subjected to Jack at his most wicked. There is no doubt, in my mind, Jack set out deliberately to provoke me. He wanted me to experience, at first hand, the physical contact of the professional game. At corners, he jostled, pushed and shoved me. At one of the corners, he actually stood on my foot. I was unable to move. On one occasion, Jack received the ball just outside our penalty area. I, the temporary goalkeeper, was the only defender in his sight. Jack and I confronted each other, eyeball to eyeball. As he approached, I advanced. Jack could easily have scored, by sliding the ball to either side of me. That was not Jack's style. He was out to prove a point. His mind was firmly set on me. When the easy option for him was to slide the ball either side of me, Jack took dead aim, from short range. He blasted the ball straight at me. I never saw the ball. I experienced a searing pain as the ball struck my abdomen. The ball rebounded into the mud. I instinctively dived at the Big Fella's feet. I somehow clutched the ball close to my body. I looked skyward. I was confronted by the biggest grin I had ever seen on Jack's face. The pain in my stomach was severe. No matter how severe the pain, I was determined to show Jack I was not hurt. He had set out to show me the physical hardness of the game. No quarter was asked of either of us and no quarter was given. On a sea of mud, with rain and sleet pouring down, we played for some twenty minutes. The icy wind continued to blow. Jack Charlton continued his attacks on me. Equally, at every opportunity, I took what he had to give. I was determined to give no indication of the pain he had inflicted on me. I had not experienced such physical contact since my grammar school days. Then, playing at full back for the first fifteen at rugby, I was the school's last line of defence. In such circumstances, physical contact was inevitable, but that had been twenty years ago. It was a great relief to me when Alf blew the final whistle. The training session was at an end. I trudged off the field, covered in mud. I was cold, wet, battered and bruised. My whole body ached and especially my stomach. As I trudged off the field, towards the warmth of the changing rooms and the prospect of a nice warm bath, a long arm stretched across my shoulders. Immediately I felt the warmth of the embrace.

"That were bloody great. I really enjoyed that. It were great fun. You never moaned once. You'll do for me."

It was Jack Charlton.

In Amsterdam that was a very special moment for Jack Charlton and myself. It was the moment when our very special friendship was sealed. A friendship that would last for years. We developed, over those years, a great respect for each other. We would never become what my father would call "buddies". We would never socialise privately; never go out for a drink together; never enjoy a private meal alone. Ours was a very special friendship. We understood and respected each other. I knew he was my friend. I knew that friendship would last forever. It was sealed in the mud of Amsterdam.

DOCTOR TO THE WORLD CHAMPIONS

"Jack Charlton's Shot Really Hurts My Stomach!"

On the Tuesday afternoon, the Team Doctor of the Holland team invited me to visit Holland's Sports Medicine Centre in Amsterdam. He arrived, to collect me by car, shortly after lunch. I was whisked away through the wet streets of Amsterdam. Alf held a short team talk with the players, after which they were free to shop in Amsterdam. The Sports Centre in Amsterdam, was everything I could wish for. There was an abundance of outdoor and indoor training facilities. They possessed a comprehensive Medical Centre, with all the investigatory facilities one would expect of an English district hospital. The medical equipment, required for the rehabilitation of injured players, was modern and extensive. The Centre had two large gymnasia. All the staff at the Centre warmly welcomed me. Having toured all their facilities, I was taken to one of the conference rooms. There I met with some of their full-time doctors and physiotherapists. As in

Romania, our conversations focused on the medical problems facing teams in the forthcoming Mexico World Cup. From my discussions with them, it transpired the Netherlands Olympic Committee, with finance from the Netherlands Sports Federation, had carried out a research project, prior to the 1968 Olympic Games. I was told a ten man medical team, mainly from the Universities of Amsterdam and Utrecht, had carried out the research on fourteen people. Ten of the people were Olympic athletes and four others acted as controls. The Olympic athletes selected for the research project came from the disciplines of athletics, swimming, canoeing, and cycling. Coaches from these disciplines had also been involved in the project. The project had been completed over a nine-week period. Four weeks of tests had taken place in the Netherlands, followed by a further four weeks of tests in Mexico. The transporting, from Holland to Mexico, of all the investigatory medical equipment, took a further week. The tests, originally carried out in Holland, were repeated at intervals during the four-week stay in Mexico. Comparisons of the two sets of tests had been made. The effect of altitude on athletic performance, in many parameters had been scientifically assessed. The research project, I was informed, had four main aims:–

- Firstly, to study the effects of the altitude at Mexico City on maximum athletic performance.
- Secondly, to detect any possible harmful effects and suggest measures that should be taken to avoid these.
- Thirdly, to investigate methods by which to bring and keep participants in optimal condition for competition in Mexico, with special reference to the time required for acclimatisation.
- Fourthly, to define the precautions to be taken, in order to prevent gastrointestinal disorders.

I tried to appear calm and unconcerned. They had what I had been looking for during the previous twelve months. Nowhere in England had I been able to find such detailed scientific investigations on athletes, prior to, and during the Olympic Games. I had received the official British Olympic medical report of the Games. It was a pathetic report; totally inadequate. It told me absolutely nothing. It had been unfortunate, in that Dr. Owen, the British Olympic Medical Officer, had been taken seriously ill following the Games. I had been unable to visit him, owing to his illness. Here, in Amsterdam, I had found what I needed. The Dutch research team had carried out all the investigations I required. They had left no stone unturned. Immediately, I suffered an attack of verbal diarrhoea. The questions flowed from my tongue.

"Had they investigated this and that?."

"Yes of course."

Every test, I enquired about, they had performed.

"Where was the report? Where were the research findings?" I tentatively asked.

"I knew you would ask that."

replied the Dutch Team Doctor,

"and we are pleased to give you a copy of our report. Remember, the research was carried out on our Olympic athletes, not our footballers. The work was commissioned before the 1968 Olympic Games commenced. Now our national football team has failed to qualify for the World Cup in Mexico, we are happy to share our research with you. We trust you will find the report of value".

I could not believe my luck. I was presented with their research book. It was entitled,

"Report on Physiological effects of Altitude".

The book contained over one hundred pages. It was the full report of the Dutch research team. The entire medical investigations, and their results, were there for me to study. The comparisons of athletic performance and medical tests at sea level and at altitude were there, in the fullest detail. The conclusions the Research Team had come to and the recommendations they had given to the Netherlands' Olympic Committee were all recorded. I was delighted. I would study the report at my leisure. It would save me a considerable amount of work. Before leaving the Centre, I thanked everyone for their generosity. It was an afternoon well spent.

IT TAKES TIME TO BE ACCEPTED

On the return journey to the Hilton Hotel, I repeatedly thanked the Dutch Team Doctor for his kindness. Obviously, on my return to the hotel, I was on a high. I could hardly contain myself. I was now the possessor of a very valuable, detailed, scientific, informative report. I had also been impressed with all the facilities at the Sports Centre.

Enjoying their afternoon tea, in the lounge of the Amsterdam Hilton were the five Football Association officials, sitting with Denis Follows, the Secretary. Each of the five officials was a director of an English Football Club. They were all friends of mine. In that we were all Football Club Directors, they regarded me as one of their own. They invited me to join them for afternoon tea. I enthused to them about my visit to the Sports Medicine Centre. I expressed my delight at being given the Dutch medical report. I was aware the Director of Coaching at The Football Association, Alan Wade, wished to build a similar Football Academy and Sports Medicine Centre in the Midlands. I had attended preliminary meetings with Alan. Alas he had told me The Football Association was not enthusiastic regarding his proposal. Having just visited the Dutch Sports Centre, I enthused to the officials about the wonderful facilities the Dutch possessed. I said,

> "What an advantage it would be if we had a similar Sports Medicine Centre in England."

It soon became obvious, from the response of the officials, Alan Wade's proposal would have little chance of success. Forty years on, there is still no such facility, although The Football Association is still discussing the proposal.

> "After all Neil",

Dr. Andrew Stephen, the Chairman of The Football Association, informed me,

> "I don't think we can learn much from the Dutch. They haven't even qualified for next year's World Cup. What you have seen this afternoon, is just window dressing. Read the report by all means. Learn what you can from it, but don't ask us to follow their ideas. Remember we are The Football Association."

his voice emphasised the word "the".

"We were the first Association in the world. Remember, we are the present world champions, not Holland."

Andrew Stephen, was a General Practitioner in Sheffield. He was a director of Sheffield Wednesday. A man I had known from my student days at Medical School. Andrew was a friend of mine. I sat there in disbelief. The Dutch, I believed, were years ahead of us. I made no comment. Inwardly, I felt angry and yet, at the same time, very sad. In years to come, the Dutch international team would excel in World Cups, when England would not even qualify. The Dutch were laying their foundations here in 1969, but their time was not now. Their time would come. Andrew's comments, I would frequently recall in the years ahead. Holland would grace the World Cup arena in future years, while England would flounder. The time of the Dutch might not be now; they were preparing for the future.

The Holland game in Amsterdam, was the first occasion the England team took tablets of Slow Sodium. I spent some time at the team meeting explaining the need to take Slow Sodium in the heat of Guadalajara. In the freezing cold of Amsterdam, salt replacement was unnecessary. The giving of Slow Sodium was merely to ensure the tablets were acceptable to the England players. I reported to the team, the Middlesbrough players had been taking the tablets with their pre-match meal for several weeks and no adverse reports had been made by the players. The England players each received four Slow Sodium tablets, three hours before playing. As with the Middlesbrough players, there were no adverse reactions. Slow Sodium was acceptable to the England players.

England beat Holland, one goal to nil, on bonfire night, at the Olympic Stadium in Amsterdam in front of 35,000 spectators. It poured with rain and was freezing cold. Colin Bell was the goal scorer. The England team was:–

> Bonnetti (Chelsea), Wright (Everton), Hughes (Liverpool),
> Mullery (Tottenham), Charlton J. (Leeds), Moore (West Ham),
> Lee (Manchester City) sub. Thompson (Liverpool),
> Bell (Manchester City), Charlton R. (Manchester United),
> Hurst and Peters (West Ham).

IT TAKES TIME TO BE ACCEPTED

I didn't know it then, but England would never subsequently beat Holland in Holland.

I travelled back to Middlesbrough avidly reading the Dutch report. I was fascinated with its content. The report was excellent. The investigations the Dutch carried out were very detailed. England had won another international. I had the report. Slow Sodium had been accepted by the players. As Shep slept on the way back to Teesside, I contemplated the visit to Holland. In addition, and more importantly, I had a new friend. It had not been a good trip but an excellent one. It had taken a long time with Jack Charlton, but I'd been accepted. Our friendship was one that would last and flourish in the years to come. As I arrived back home, my stomach still hurt. Jack Charlton had made his mark. His mark would remain with me forever. It had been a very good trip.

England's return international with Holland, on the 14th. January 1970, was at Wembley. As usual, the England staff and players assembled three days before the game. On the Sunday evening, everyone seemed in good spirits. Our medical preparations for Mexico were progressing exceptionally well; better than I ever envisaged. The Dutch medical report I had repeatedly studied and discussed with members of my medical team. The report had been very helpful in our medical preparations. I was looking forward to renewing my acquaintance with their Team Doctor. I would be able to report all medical matters were on schedule. All the procedures, planned with my medical team, were progressing well. I was satisfied the England players would be well prepared. Alf called a staff meeting. The purpose of the meeting was to ascertain the present position with every aspect of our preparation. Harold Shepherdson, Les Cocker and myself were the only persons attending the meeting with Alf. We were Alf's entire staff. Every aspect of the team's preparation was discussed. The progress made on each and every issue was reported to the group. All the outstanding issues, were resolved as the meeting progressed. At the meeting Alf put forward a new proposal. He suggested we play two pre World Cup tournament matches at a higher altitude than Mexico City. The first game would be against Columbia. The second against Ecuador. I was fully sup-

[385]

portive to the proposal. Bogotá, Columbia's capital, is at an altitude of 8,661 feet, some 1,200 feet higher than Mexico City. Quito, the capital of Ecuador, was even higher at 9,500 feet; 2,000 feet higher than Mexico City. Playing two internationals at a higher altitude would give the players further experience. The higher altitude of Columbia and Ecuador could only further benefit the players and improve our altitude acclimatisation. The meeting had progressed well and was coming, I thought, to a close when Alf dropped his bombshell.

"You need to be aware," he said,

> "a problem has arisen with some players. It involves the four London players–Bobby Moore, Geoff Hurst, Martin Peters and Peter Bonetti. These players have been involved, with private companies, in promotional work for the World Cup. Instead of receiving a fee for their services, the companies have agreed to fly their wives to Mexico for the tournament. Their wives will arrive a few days before the tournament commences. They will be based in Guadalajara. The wives will stay at a different hotel to the players for the duration of the tournament. As far as I know, no other players are involved."

Harold, Les and myself were stunned. The silence was unbelievable. Eventually, Les Cocker broke the silence. Hesitatingly Les said,

> "Well, if this is the case, I think the four players should be told, they will not be selected. The arrival of just four wives, after we have been away from home for over four weeks, will cause chaos. What will the other players think? It's disgraceful. It could ruin all our plans. It certainly will affect team morale. The presence of four wives will unsettle everyone. They should be told they can't do it. It is unacceptable."

Harold was of a similar mind to Les. Agreeing, with Les and Harold, I suggested it should be an all or nothing situation. Either all the wives came out to Mexico or none came. The arrival of just four wives in Mexico, would be a disruptive and disturbing influence, not only for the four players, but also for

IT TAKES TIME TO BE ACCEPTED

all the other players. The dedication, commitment and single mindedness of the team could be distracted. The World Cup tournament required a total commitment on everyone's part. With all the difficulties associated with playing in Mexico, it was absolutely essential that nothing and no-one should deflect us from the job in hand. I knew, from my own personal experiences, the job required total dedication and commitment from each and every individual in the party. Nothing and no one should be allowed to interfere with that commitment. The arrival of four players' wives was unacceptable.

Surprisingly Alf did not agree. Despite the views expressed by Harold, Les and myself, Alf was reluctant to take any action against the four players. He was not prepared to accept our views. He would not inform the four players of the views we had expressed. The four wives, Alf informed us, had already made their travel arrangements. The arrival of the four wives in Mexico was, in fact, a fait accompli. Harold, Les and myself were extremely unhappy with the situation presented by these four players.

The Holland game, at Wembley, ended in a nil-nil draw. It is interesting to note only one of the four players, Martin Peters, was selected to play in the international against Holland, although Geoff Hurst did come on as a substitute for Mick Jones.

In private conversations, Harold, Les and I continued to express our disapproval of the visit of the four wives. The three of us decided we would raise the issue again at the next staff meeting. Our concerns however were never raised. At the next staff meeting, before the issue of the four players' wives was raised, Alf informed us his wife would also be travelling to Mexico for the tournament. Lady Ramsey would arrive at a similar time to the four players' wives we were told. Apparently, Alf had been involved as Starter with the World Cup Motor Rally. As part of his agreement with the organisers, his wife would be travelling to Mexico for the tournament. With this new information, it was impossible for us to discuss our concerns regarding the visit of the four players' wives. How could Alf now complain about their arrangements, when he had made similar arrangements himself? The three of us could do nothing. The wives of five men, out of a total thirty-two men, would be flying out to Mexico. The five wives would arrive one week before the competition started. Although they would be staying at a different hotel to the team, their very presence, I was convinced, would cause major difficulties. It all seemed so unfair. The wives of all the other players and staff would remain back home in England. The decision to allow this to happen was, in my opinion, a major mistake.

During the whole of my professional career, the hardest, most concentrated work I personally experienced took place in the ten months immediately prior to the Mexico World Cup. Alf had arranged seven internationals during that period. The first game against Holland sealed my friendship with Jack Charlton. The opponents at Wembley, in December and January, were Portugal and Holland. There followed, in February, a visit to Brussels, where England played Belgium. The Home Internationals against Wales in Cardiff, Northern Ireland at Wembley and Scotland in Glasgow completed the programme. Of these seven internationals, England won four games and drew the other three. In the seven internationals, prior to leaving for Mexico, England was undefeated.

Throughout the year, with Alf's encouragement, I used the team meetings to educate the players on the problems facing them in Mexico. Following my discussions with the players, I wrote and produced a player's handbook. The relevant medical advice for the players was clearly set out in the handbook. Subjects addressed included the travel arrangements, the altitude of the various venues, the vaccination and immunisation programme, the need for a high level of physical fitness prior to departure, the acclimatisation programme, the need for satisfactory blood levels, the prevention of tummy upsets, the heat factor in Guadalajara, and the problem of dry lips, noses and throats. In addition, in the free time from my Practice duties, I travelled the country discussing the few unresolved problems with the members of my medical team. Their contribution was considerable. As a result of those discussions, I made a decision regarding hospitalisation in case of a medical or surgical emergency. I forwarded my recommendation to Alf. I recommended that any major injury or serious illness arising in any member of the England party would be evacuated to The Methodist Hospital in Houston, Texas. The flight time from Mexico to Houston is one and a half hours. The hospital in Houston is of a very high standard and world famous. I had made contact with the Methodist Hospital in Houston. They agreed all the facilities of the hospital would be available to me. My recommendation to the England Manager was that in the event of a serious injury or illness, requiring operative or in-patient care, this method of dealing with the problem should be adopted, as I considered it to be in the best interests of the players. The entire medical staff, I had spoken with in Mexico, agreed with this policy. It had always been my dream to provide the best medical care for the players and, by adopting this strategy, I would be able to achieve my aim. I reaffirmed to Alf my intention to use, on an outpatient basis only, the facilities of the ABC hospital in Mexico City. Similarly, when in Guadalajara, I would use the facilities at the El Carmen Hospital.

For a four-week period, Bobby Charlton religiously sent me details of all the food he consumed on a daily basis. To satisfy Bobby's needs completely, I formed the opinion it would have been necessary for his wife, Norma, to travel with the team and act as our chef! Nevertheless Bobby's dedication changed the approach to the provision of food in Mexico. For our possible eight-week stay in Mexico, Findus, the frozen food firm, were approached to enquire if they could provide all the food necessary. I attended several meetings with the representatives of Findus, until a final agreement was reached. Findus agreed to supply all the food for our eight week stay. The frozen food would be shipped to Mexico, where Findus had facilities to place the food in cold storage. Meetings continued to take place, in order to quantify the amounts of food required. In those days, Nutritionalists and Dieticians were not attached to the team. Surprisingly, the role was delegated to my wife Margaret! She had several meetings with Findus to finalise the quantities and types of food required. My wife held one such meeting at the Cleveland Golf Club in Redcar. Imagine her surprise when her first task, immediately prior to the meeting, involved keeping the press reporters from attending the meeting!

While my wife struggled with the diet of thirty active men for eight weeks, I met with Alf at meetings with Umbro, the sports kit provider.

They fully co-operated with our suggestions. The playing shirts and shorts would be made in an aertex format. The shirts would be made in white and light blue. I had meetings with representatives of C.Z. Scientific Instruments. This firm produced Zeiss sunglasses. Interestingly the firm were bringing into production at the time much improved sunglasses. These glasses were able to cut out the more damaging rays of the ultra-violet spectrum. Every member of the party received two pairs of Zeiss Umbral sunglasses. These glasses absorbed three quarters of the sun's damaging ultra-violet rays. They were a great success. I also coped with the flood of correspondence I received from well meaning managers, coaches, doctors and physiotherapists who wrote to me offering advice. Numerous pharmaceutical companies also wrote suggesting I use their products. With no secretary, dealing with my England work, I personally had to respond to each letter. In addition, I was determined to read every medical report, available to me, relating to the Mexican Olympics. My reading, which continued into the early hours of every morning, involved research papers on the acclimatisation to altitude and heat. The medical papers, on the problems of gastro-enteritis in Mexico, fascinated me. I read them all.

My workload, in the early months of 1970, had become unacceptable. One month before the World Cup, when the medical preparations were almost complete, I informed Alf, in a private conversation, of my intention to resign, from my post of Honorary Team Physician, when we returned from Mexico. With all my other commitments, back home in Redcar and at Middlesbrough Football Club, I would be unable to continue with my England role. The work over the previous eighteen months had killed me off. I was totally exhausted. My dedication and commitment to the England team had overtaken my life. Alf was not prepared to accept my resignation. With his usual smile, he said,

"There will be plenty of time for me to change your mind when we're in Mexico."

I genuinely believed he was wrong.

IT TAKES TIME TO BE ACCEPTED

"Alf & I enjoy a Cuppa"

13

Acclimatisation, 1970 Style......

The preparations were complete. The final day had arrived. All my medical preparations, and the expertise of my medical team, would now be put to the test. The World Cup party for 1970 assembled at London's Whites Hotel on Sunday May 3rd. Immediately, there was work for me to do. Several of the players required my attention. Alan Ball and Nobby Stiles had received minor lacerations while playing for their Clubs, which had been sutured at the time of the injury. It was now time for the sutures to be removed. Two players were suffering with bruising in their right thighs from knocks they had received. One was unwell with a severe headache and one player discussed with me his fear of flying and the need for me to give him some tablets to prevent airsickness. None of the injuries or illnesses presented any serious problems.

We left London Airport at 1300 hours the following day for our long flight to Mexico. There would be two stops en route. The first was at Bermuda, where we arrived at 2040 hours. The second was at Nassau, where our arrival was just before midnight. Departing from Nassau at 0105 we arrived in Mexico City at 0410, although, because of the time difference, the time in Mexico was 2110 hours. The flight had taken sixteen hours. When we arrived in Mexico, we were all extremely tired. A motor coach transported us to the Parc de Prince Hotel. We arrived there at 2300 hours Mexican time. The arrangements at the hotel seemed confused. I was allocated a bungalow in the grounds, as previously arranged. On entering the bungalow, I found Billy Wright already in residence. Billy was covering the

World Cup for ITV. In the confusion, the hotel management explained a mistake had been made. Billy was asked to pack up and leave! It was a great embarrassment to me! Billy Wright left.

Everyone in the England party, fell into bed as soon as possible after arrival. The flight from London had been tiring and tedious. Early in the morning however, long before I was due to wake, I heard the singing of religious hymns close at hand. I leapt out of bed to investigate. Could it be the England players were taking the mickey or playing a prank? Seated on rows of chairs, besides the swimming pool, was the Mexican Football Team. Dressed in their international football shirts, they were attending early morning mass. The Mexicans had worked on the principal that if the Parc de Prince Hotel was good enough for the World Champions, it was good enough for them! They were also now staying at The Parc de Prince. They had been resident for several days. So much for the agreement Alf had made with Mrs. Pugar during our visit twelve months previously. Then, she agreed with Alf, the England team would have the exclusive use of the hotel. Now we were expected to share the hotel with the Mexican team and their staff. Instead of each England player having a bungalow to themselves, they now had to share their bungalow with another player. It was a most unsatisfactory situation.

Further inspection of the hotel grounds revealed the builders on site. With the Mexican team subsequently booking their accommodation at the hotel, the hotel management decided the ground floor restaurant could not accommodate both teams. In their wisdom, they decided to build a second restaurant above the first one; in effect on a second floor. Needless to say, the building was unfinished. The second restaurant was uninhabitable. Building equipment and ladders surrounded the ground floor restaurant.

There were twenty-eight days remaining before our first match. Each member of the party had commenced taking Thalazole and Iron tablets two days prior to our departure. Everyone would continue taking them on a daily basis throughout our time in Mexico. On our first day, the England staff met with the British Embassy staff to discuss our requirements. As usual, the Embassy staff were exceptionally helpful. Lunch, at a second sitting in the restaurant, was followed by a visit to The Reforma Club, where

"The Mexican Team at Early Morning Mass"

most of our training would take place. Alf was keen for the players to see the excellent facilities there. Following his tour, we settled into one of the meeting rooms for a team meeting. It was my opportunity to hammer home, once again, the importance of personal hygiene. No food was to be consumed and no fluid taken unless obtained from our official sources. It was important minor tummy upsets were reported to me immediately and this point was stressed again to the players. It was also essential no-one missed their daily dosage of tablets. Frequent washing of the hands with Phisohex was also encouraged. All the players seemed happy with the regime.

The morning of day two, I spent completing, with Harold and Les, the unpacking of the various crates that had been shipped out from England. I was delighted to find the Physiotherapy equipment had travelled well. All the machines were in working order. Medically, we were now completely independent. After lunch, we all travelled by coach to the National Park, high in the mountains surrounding Mexico City. A cricket match was organised, as a light form of exercise for the players. As far as I was concerned, the presence of the whole party at an altitude of 12,000 feet for three hours was an added boost to our acclimatisation process. The effect of the altitude on the players was soon apparent. When Alan Mullery and Bob McNab were batting, they both decided on a run, but neither player was able to complete the twenty-two yards quickly enough. They were both run out and stood together, in the middle of the wicket, arguing as to which player should be dismissed. Alan Ball was needed to adjudicate! Following the cricket match, Alan Clark reported with a sore ankle. I instituted treatment immediately. In the evening, we all returned to the Reforma Club to watch a live television transmission of Brazil playing a team from Guadalajara. Brazil won by three goals to nil.

Mullery and McNab Run Out–Ballie adjudicates!

At our first team meeting, I emphasized to the players the need to report any slight tummy upset immediately. On day three, four players reported with a slight tummy upset. No player was particularly ill and no additional treatment was indicated. On day three, I carried out, on all the players and staff a full clinical examination, including electrocardiogram and skin fold measurements. The afternoon was spent at a beautiful ranch, where the owner and his family entertained us to a rodeo. Monte Fresco, one of the sports photographers, loaned me some of his telephoto lenses, enabling me to take some superb photographs of the rodeo. While at the rodeo, I received the news that all the food from Findus had arrived safely in Mexico and was now in cold storage. Unfortunately the Mexican immigration officials had inspected all the food. In their wisdom, they had decreed the Findus beef burgers, bacon and sausages were unfit for human consumption. They were all ceremonially burnt at the point of entry. I travelled, with a British Embassy official, to the responsible immigration department where I was asked to sign confirmation of the destruction of this part of our food. The immigration official informed me these meat products had been destroyed as England was a 'foot and mouth country'! As such, our meat products were unfit to enter Mexico. We now had no bacon, sausages or beef burgers for our eight week stay in Mexico. In the evening we watched the Mexican team play Borussia Dortmund on TV at the Reforma Club.

On the fourth day, the three slightly injured players, had recovered sufficiently to join in the first day of training activities. Alf had arranged that this training session would be an open day for the Press at the Reforma Club. Many sports writers, from various countries, attended. They were keen to interview Alf and the players regarding their first impressions of Mexico. Having had three days of relative inactivity however, the players were more keen to start some proper training and experience, at first hand, the effects of altitude. Under the watchful eye of the four staff members, the players did their usual warm up exercises, followed by ten minutes of interval running. This gentle warm up was followed by a practice match of thirty minutes. I was pleased there were no complaints from any of the players regarding their breathing. The three players previously injured came through the session well. With the Findus food, minus the meat products, having been delivered we tucked into a lunch of fish fingers, croquet potatoes and mixed vegetables, followed by English ice cream at the Reforma Club. Back at the Parc de Prince Hotel, I received a visit from Dr. Perez, one of the officiating World Cup committee doctors, who briefed me on the medical procedures introduced for the competition proper. In the early evening, we returned to the Reforma Club to play tennis, cricket and badminton. The players were in good spirits. With the help of Findus, we enjoyed an evening meal of soup, roast lamb, jacket potatoes, sprouts and sliced beans. The players were delighted.

Day Five brought our first major casualty. In continuing to unpack the various heavy boxes of equipment, Les Cocker, the Leeds United trainer, injured his back. Clinically, I formed the opinion he was suffering from a prolapsed disc in his spine. I arranged an X-ray at the ABC Hospital. I travelled with Les to the hospital. Although Les assured me he had no previous history of back trouble, the X-ray revealed a major defect in his lower spine. This defect in the spine had not been previously discovered. In his younger days, Les had been a Professional Footballer. The fact he had gone through his career without any back problems and that the defect had not been previously discovered frankly amazed me. Les would be confined to bed for several days. While the players enjoyed their day at the Reforma Club, playing football, cricket and tennis, I returned to the Parc de Prince to care for Les. He would be unable to take part in the training programme for several days. This would inevitably place an extra burden on Alf, Harold Shepherdson and myself. In the evening, I rejoined the players at The Reforma Club where we all enjoyed a Findus Fish and Chip supper.

A fun football match, was arranged on Day Six, at The Reforma Club. An 'England Select XI' would play the British Press. Before play commenced, I advised the Sportswriters to respect the altitude and take things easy during the game. It was important for them, a distinctly unfit group of individuals, to accept that the altitude would affect them. The Sports Writers, I advised, should not try to be silly by competing physically with the England players. My friend Ken Jones, an ex professional footballer himself, wanted to prove me wrong. He raced around the pitch like a frightened rabbit. Ken was intent on proving all the reports of altitude affecting physical performance were a myth. Come what may he was going to prove the altitude would not affect his own personal physical performance. Ken ran and ran continuously, during the game, until his breathing became impossible. Inevitably, he eventually collapsed in a heap on the pitch. Ken has the distinction of being the only person, during our entire time in Mexico, to whom it was necessary for me to administer an emergency supply of Oxygen. With the administration of a pure Oxygen supply, Ken was revived in minutes. Following the match, which the Select XI won easily, the players did an extra fifteen minutes training. After another delicious lunch, England played The Reforma Club in a Sunday afternoon cricket match, which they also won. It had been a good day for the players. Back at the hotel, Les had remained in bed all day. He was a little better. On returning to the hotel, four players and one member of staff reported some looseness of their bowels. On examination I found no abnormality with any of them and no treatment, other than reassurance, was indicated.

We had now been in Mexico City for a week. The training programme we had planned, back in England, had gone well. The training would now be increased in intensity. At The Reforma Club, Alf and Harold put the players through a hard training session, followed by fifteen minutes of seven a side football. None of the players appeared distressed and none reported any unusual symptoms. The acclimatisation process appeared to be going exceptionally well. Gatorade, mixed with Malvern water, was proving a very acceptable drink for the players during and after training. I always ensured a copious supply of Gatorade was available. The President of The Mexican Football Association and some of his staff joined us, after training, for lunch. They were anxious to officially welcome us to Mexico and to ensure all our needs were being met. It was a very pleasant lunch at The Reforma Club. In the afternoon, a motor coach took the party into Mexico City for an afternoon of shopping. Although Alan Clarke had participated fully in the training session, he still felt a little unsure regarding his ankle. Although his ankle appeared completely normal, I decided to reintroduce some physiotherapy treatment. Three more players reported with a slight tummy upset, but as with the previous players I found no abnormality and no treatment was initiated. Les remained in bed, but was much improved.

Alf arranged for the team to play an eighty-minute practice match at The Olympic Stadium at four o'clock on our eighth day. We spent the morning at The Reforma Club doing light training. After lunch, the players rested in their rooms. It was now important for the players to adopt, what was completely new to them, the habit of being well hydrated before playing in a game. The players were advised to consume the bottled Malvern water, issued to their rooms, on a daily basis. With their pre-match meal, they were now quite used to taking four Slow Sodium tablets, which had become standard practice. My advice to the players was it would be wise to consume at least half a litre of Gatorade at half time. The practice match was our first opportunity to introduce this new phenomenon. I was concerned as to how acceptable it would be to the players. The practice match was played in a recorded temperature of eighty degrees. The players performed well. All of them, on their own volition, consumed more than adequate amounts of Gatorade at half time and again at full time. Many players were anxious to consume more. Gatorade was proving to be a very popular drink with the players. In the evening, we all went to the Anglo American Institute to see the film "Guns of San Sebastian." Alf was pleased it was a Western film-he adored cowboy films.

Alf and his staff were well aware, from our planning discussions, at the altitude of Mexico City, the football travelled through the air much more quickly than at sea level. A shot at goal arrives more quickly than goalkeepers, used to playing at sea level, are accustomed to. It takes goalkeepers varying lengths of time in training to acclimatise to these atmospheric conditions. Some may never completely acclimatise to the problem. In the weeks of the acclimatisation programme, Gordon Banks adjusted best of all. The three other goalkeepers all struggled to acclimatise to the increased speed of the ball through the rarefied air. The problem is best understood by examining two photographs I took during a training session in Mexico City. The photograph of Gordon Banks shows him making a secure save.

His body is totally behind the ball. The ball is secure within his grasp. Gordon has made his customary good save. He has judged the increased speed of the ball accurately. In contrast, the photograph of Peter Bonetti shows he has misjudged the speed of the shot. As he endeavours to get his body behind the ball, the ball hits his chest much sooner than he anticipates. The ball has travelled through the rarefied air more quickly than at sea level. As can be seen clearly from the photograph, the ball bounces away from Peter's chest. Peter is left clutching nothing but the rarefied air.

Certainly the impression I personally gained, from observing the goalkeepers during the period of acclimatization, was Peter, Alec Stepney and Peter Shilton all found it difficult to adjust to the problems the rarefied air presented. With constant practice however, in Mexico, Columbia and Ecuador, there is no doubt all the goalkeepers improved, but Gordon Banks adjusted best of all.

"Gordon Banks–Safe As The Bank Of England"

ACCLIMATISATION 1970 STYLE

"Peter Bonetti Struggles With The Effects Of Altitude."

During the planning process in England, I raised with Alf the need, during our first week, for only gentle exercises and light training to be the order of every day. In the first week, the players would need time to acclimatize to the altitude, time change, and environmental conditions. With such a light training programme, during our first few days, it was inevitable the fitness levels of the players would decrease. This was a great concern to the staff and myself. On our ninth day therefore, we spent the training session several miles from Mexico City at a Sports Centre in Oaxtepec. This was where the equestrian events had taken place in the Olympic Games. The main advantage, in training at Oaxtepec, was its altitude was 5,400 feet, the altitude of Guadalajara and 2,000 feet below Mexico City. Here, I believed, the lower altitude would not be a problem for the players and a hard physical training session could be held. This decision was made well in advance of our visit. At Oaxtepec, forty minutes was spent on exercises, running and sprinting, followed by several five a side games of a very competitive nature. The players enjoyed the day's extremely hard workout. They were oblivious however to the real reason for our journey to Oaxtepec. I considered the visit was essential to maintain the players' high level of physical fitness. The temperature at Oaxtepec was eighty-one degrees. The players came through the day extremely well.

The day following our visit to Oaxtepec, one player reported with a sore calf and another with slight soreness over the medial side of his knee. Treatment was commenced for them both. Knowing all the players would have experienced a hard day's training at Oaxtepec, the following day was planned as a quiet, relaxing day. In the morning, during a light training session, to which the Press had been invited, the players were divided into equal teams to compete in a mini-Olympics athletic competition. It proved very competitive. The players seemed to be enjoying their training programme. The Government minister, Lord Chalfont accompanied by Lady Chalfont, visited us during the morning session. He conveyed to us the very best wishes of the British Government. The afternoon was spent at La Hacienda Country Club, where we played golf and tennis. At night we relaxed watching the film 'High Society'.

Keeping the players occupied and happy during the long period of acclimatisation was always going to be difficult. In those days, everyone had simple pleasures. There were no mobile phones, laptops, and play-stations to amuse the players. They enjoyed playing football, training, playing other physical games, cards, reading, watching TV and seeing films. The British Embassy staff believed the players would enjoy a visit to the Aztec Pyramids. The visit was a disaster. A long hot bus journey eventually deposited us at the Pyramids, which as one player advised me,

"I suppose they are quite nice but, in reality, they are only a large block of rock!"

There were innumerable steps to climb to reach the top of the pyramids, but, in the searing heat, very few players attempted the climb. On returning to Mexico City, the players were much happier training in the afternoon heat, at The Reforma Club. The training session, conducted by Alf and Harold, was as intense and hard as that at Oaxtepec. All the players enjoyed the session and felt comfortable, even though the temperature was again in the mid eighties. At night, we all played Bingo. During the day, I met with the Findus representatives.

"Ask no questions, tell no lies.",
they said,
"We now have a supply of sausages for you. Also we have a supply of bottled soft drinks, baked beans, spaghetti, fish and ice cream. These supplies will last you throughout your stay in Mexico. We have also arranged a further supply of Malvern water and Gatorade."

I was most grateful.

Day Twelve saw our first, full ninety-minute football game. The game took place at the Olympic Stadium. Every player participated at some time during the game. The practice match was played in a temperature of eighty-two degrees. The players coped well, both with the altitude and the heat. They were now well into the routine, established months previously in England, of taking four Slow Sodium tablets with their pre-match meal. The drinking of copious quantities of Gatorade at half and full time was also well accepted by the players. I did not have to remind the players to drink plenty of fluids. It had all become quite natural to them. They all enjoyed drinking Gatorade. No adverse effects were ever reported with Slow Sodium. Sadly, following the practice match, whilst signing autographs for some children, Jack Charlton reported he had lost his football boots. The boots were never found. Alf arranged an afternoon visit for Harold and myself to a jeweller's factory. The factory imported ladies Omega watches and placed them in Mexican white gold bracelets. The owner of the factory wished to present me with one of the watches. Unfortunately, I had no idea how long the bracelet needed to be to fit around my wife's wrist.

"Phone her in England from my office."
he advised.

In my excitement, at obtaining a really valuable present for my wife, I phoned. I woke her at three in the morning to ask if she would measure her wrist! At that time in the morning back in England, it took her some time to find a measuring tape!

"Six and a half inches."

She eventually replied. When I informed the factory owner, he said,

"That's impossible. Six and a half inches is larger than the wrist of most men."

"That's my wife."

I replied.

Reluctantly, he made a six and a half inches white gold bracelet; the longest, he informed me, the factory had ever made. Into the bracelet he fitted the smallest Omega watch I had ever seen. It fitted my wife perfectly when I returned to England.

The late afternoon was spent at the races. The players were in their element at the horse racing. We all enjoyed the relaxing afternoon at the Hippodrome America. One of the difficulties being the Team Doctor surfaced after the races. As the only English doctor immediately available to the touring party, it was expected I would be available to diagnose and treat any of the Sportswriters accompanying the team. I was asked if I would be kind enough to see Gerry Loftus. When I saw Gerry, he was obviously suffering from a deep venous thrombosis of his leg. I arranged for him to have some anticoagulant therapy. I advised him his World Cup adventure was at an end. He should return back home to England immediately. In the evening we all watched a recording, on television, of a recent Brazil versus Bulgaria football game.

Day Thirteen in Mexico was lucky for some and unlucky for others. The day was lucky for Les Cocker. He was now well enough to return to training with the team. The unlucky one was Bobby Moore. The day was our last in Mexico City, before departing on the tour of Columbia and Ecuador. Following a morning of training and playing seven a side football, it was decided we would all have a relaxing afternoon back at The Parc de Prince Hotel. There I had a meeting with the Findus representative to ensure further food and drink supplies would be available for us on our return to Mexico. The various food provisions were quickly agreed. Delivery was promised both in Mexico City and Guadalajara on our return. In the afternoon, Billy Wright of ITV interviewed me. The interview went well. It was mainly concerned about how successful our acclimatisation programme had been. I was pleased to report that, to date, it had gone better than I could ever have imagined. The evening was spent at a farewell Dinner Dance hosted by members of the Reforma Club. There were to be fifteen tables with just two members of the England party allocated to each table. The players eagerly anticipated the freedom of an evening's dancing. The smell of aftershave filled the air. When the players were informed there was to be a dance, their wicked streak appeared. They decided two players, Mullery and Ball, would assess the female talent in the room. These two players would choose who, in their opinion, were the prettiest, dowdiest, thinnest, youngest and oldest ladies present. The players drew lots as to who would be nominated to dance with the chosen lady. As luck would have it, Bobby Moore drew 'the dowdiest' lady and promptly informed the remaining players he would opt out and refuse to dance. The players however were determined he would fulfil his obligations. Bobby, as the Team Captain, would dance the first dance with the selected partner. During the dinner Ball and Mullery instructed all the players to remain seated when the band introduced the first dance until Mooro had completed a full circuit of the dance floor with the chosen partner. The band began playing. Bobby Moore remained seated. Not one player rose from his seat. The members of The Reforma Club were confused. No England player would dance. Alan Mullery came to the rescue. He approached the chosen lady thus,

"Excuse me, but I am the Team Captain's lackey. Our Captain, Bobby Moore, has asked me if you would do him the honour of dancing the first dance with him."

Overwhelmed, the lady agreed. She was led by Alan to Bobby Moore's table. Confronted with the immediate presence of the lady, Bobby had no option but to dance. He danced a full circuit of the dance floor to rapturous applause from the other players. It was the beginning of a superb evening. It was a wonderful opportunity for the whole squad to say a big thank you to the Reforma Club for the exclusive use of their facilities. We had thoroughly enjoyed our two weeks of training there. The acclimatisation programme had gone well. One surprised lady would always recall the evening she was chosen to dance with the England Captain!

Our flight from Mexico to Columbia, on an Argentinian flight, departed Mexico at 0720 hours. We left The Parc de Prince Hotel at the unearthly hour of 0545. Most of us were still asleep. We breakfasted on the plane. Our flight was due to arrive at Bogotá at 1210. Unfortunately there was an accident on the runway at Bogotá and our aircraft was diverted to Panama. We stayed at Panama Airport for some two hours. While in the airport building I witnessed Alf giving a dressing down, in public, to a group of players. He had found them in the airport lounge with ice in their soft drinks. Ice in drinks had been banned from our first day in Mexico. The players had made a genuine mistake. Alf would have none of their excuses.

"You all know, ice in drinks is banned. Put those drinks back on the bar."

he told them.

Other passengers, in the airport lounge, wondered what all the fuss was about. In twelve years working with Alf, it was the only occasion I can recall him discipline any player in public. The offending drinks were returned to the bar.

With our diversion to Panama, we eventually arrived at Bogotá Airport at 1600 hours. We were booked in The Tequendama Hotel. There we were met by Andrew Stephens, Chairman of The Football Association, and Denis Follows, the Secretary, who had travelled to Bogota independently. Having ordered dinner of Tomato Soup, Fillet Steak, French Fries, Peas and Carrots followed by Crème Caramel, I wandered into the foyer. I noticed the two Bobbys—Charlton and Moore—window-shopping inside a small jewellery shop, within the precincts of the hotel. I joined them in the shop. As there was nothing in the shop to interest us, the three of us left the shop. The three of us sat on a settee in the hotel lounge, immediately outside the jeweller's shop. Within minutes, a very angry and distressed shop assistant confronted us.

"Which one of you has taken the emerald and diamond bracelet?"

she enquired of us.

"It was you, wasn't it?"

she said, pointing a finger at Bobby Moore.

"You have stolen the beautiful bracelet. I must notify the police."

We were astonished. I told Bobby Charlton and Bobby Moore to speak to no one, until I collected Alf from the basement, where I knew he was unpacking the kit with Harold Shepherdson.

"Alf, you'd better go straight upstairs to the lounge. There's a lady there accusing Bobby Moore of stealing an emerald and diamond bracelet from the jeweller's shop in the lobby."

Alf left immediately. After supper, I attended a meeting with Alf and the two Bobbys. Alf insisted the three of us report exactly what, if anything, happened in the jeweller's shop. We all claimed total innocence. Before retiring to bed, another player reported a slight tummy upset. Again I could find no clinical abnormality and reassured the player. It had been quite an eventful day!

The morning of our first day in Columbia was spent training at an Army Camp. Although Bogotá was 1,200 feet higher than Mexico City, none of the players experienced any breathing difficulties during quite a hard, forty-five minutes training session. The only person to complain of some breathing difficulties during training was the Manager himself! The players felt fine. The training session was followed by a reception at The Columbian Football Association. The players and I found such receptions totally boring. After lunch, Alf had another meeting with myself, Bobby Moore and Bobby Charlton. We each repeated our view of the happenings within the jeweller's shop. Alf was satisfied we three were totally innocent of any wrongdoing. It was at this second meeting Bobby Charlton reported he had lost his wallet containing cash and credit cards. It never rained but it poured in Bogota! At tea, Alf informed all the players of Bobby Charlton's lost wallet. He asked every player to check if Bobby's wallet was in their possession. In the evening we watched a dreadful Burt Lancaster film in the hotel ballroom.

Our sixteenth day of acclimatisation was our second day in Bogotá. At breakfast, Bobby Charlton's wallet was returned. It had been found on the bus, used yesterday to transport us to the training ground. The wallet and its contents were intact. No money or credit cards were missing. The day saw my first real case of Gastro-enteritis since leaving home. My patient however was not a player, but the Chairman of The Football Association. He had been up all night with diarrhoea, had a high temperature and some vomiting. He would remain in bed all day. For the players, it was a match day filled with their normal routine. A light training session in the morning, with an afternoon spent resting in their rooms. I wandered out into the streets of Bogotá, but not for long. I was followed everywhere by disabled children and adults persistently begging of me to give them "Peso, Peso, Peso". I noticed one of the young children had an amputated right arm. Closer inspection revealed the stump of the amputation had no muscle covering. It was flat and covered by a paper thickness of scar tissue. The stump did not have the usual rounded appearance. Later in the day, I was informed some parents deliberately mutilated their children in order that their children could legitimately beg in the streets. The thought of a parent amputating an arm, for the purpose of begging, appalled me.

Alf was keen for every England player to play in a competitive game at altitude. As a result, he had arranged two separate games following each other on the same evening. The first game England won 1-0, with a goal scored by Jeff Astle. The second game England won 4-0, with goals scored by Peters (2), Bobby Charlton and Ball. Both games were against Columbian national teams. The players reported their breathing, during the games, was quite comfortable. As both matches were played in the relative cool of the evening, there was no problem with the heat factor. Our acclimatisation programme to the altitude appeared to be working well.

ACCLIMATISATION 1970 STYLE

The following morning, before breakfast, Bobby Moore was whisked away to the British Embassy. There he was to make an official statement regarding the disappearance of the bracelet. It had become apparent Bobby Moore, and he alone, was being accused of stealing the bracelet. Surprisingly, the jeweller had now produced a witness, who reportedly witnessed Bobby Moore stealing the bracelet. I say surprisingly, as the three of us, who were in the shop, saw no one apart from the girl assistant. Even more surprising was the fact that neither Bobby Charlton nor I were asked to make any statements, when everyone accepted the fact we were the only two witnesses.

Our flight from Bogotá to Quito, in Ecuador, left at 1245. We were all aboard, including our Captain. We arrived safely at Quito just over an hour later. We were staying at the Intercontinental Hotel. Playing in Quito, where the altitude was 9,500 feet, would be the ultimate test of our acclimatisation to altitude. In our eagerness to rush to our rooms, twelve of us piled into the lift. The notice in the lift clearly stated that the maximum number of people should be eight. The lift stopped between floors. The twelve of us were stuck in the lift for over twenty minutes. It was not a pleasant experience at 9,500 feet! In view of the increased altitude of Quito, we decided on a quiet relaxing afternoon and early evening around the swimming pool.

The players were told they could have a lie in during the following morning. Most took advantage of the suggestion. I wandered around the immediate vicinity of the hotel taking photographs. After lunch, the players trained at the stadium where the two games against Ecuador would be played. The training session was quite intensive and included a thirty-minute game. The whole session lasted an hour. A few players reported their breathing was more difficult than in Bogotá, but none were unduly distressed. In the evening we watched a Clint Eastwood film, before retiring to bed.

Saturday May 20th. turned out to be a disastrous and distressing day for the England party, but particularly for Alf Ramsey and David Sadler. Travelling with the England team throughout our time in South

America were several sportswriters employed by English newspapers. Within the group, there were a few Sportswriters who only wrote for the Sunday newspapers. These writers wrote only one article a week. With an eight hour time difference between Ecuador and England, it was essential these reporters filed their weekly report to their London offices early on the Saturday morning, Ecuador time. Filing their reports this early on the Saturday was the only way publication of their one and only weekly article could be ensured. Alf had informed the players he would announce his selection of the twenty-two players, selected for the tournament proper, to them at noon on Sunday, March 21st. It would be the final composition of the party for the World Cup Competition. Six players, who had been our colleagues throughout our time together would be dropped from the party. Those players would be disappointed and devastated. The six would take no part in the tournament proper. I had witnessed a similar procedure at Lilleshall in 1966. It was not a pleasant experience for anyone.

Representatives of the Sunday Sportswriters approached Alf enquiring if he would give them the names of the final twenty-two players selected, and therefore by implication the six who had not been selected, early so they could meet their publication deadline with the 'hot news' of Alf's final selection. If Alf agreed, it meant these reporters would be given the news before the players. The Sportswriters assured Alf they would all place an embargo on the final selection until after he had informed the players. Alf decided he would think about it and meet with the Press members concerned immediately after our Saturday morning training session. Alf's three staff, Harold Shepherdson, Les Cocker and myself already knew Alf's selection. It had been necessary for Alf to inform The Football Association officials and the British Embassy staff in Bogotá, in order they could convey the names of the final twenty-two players selected to the World Cup Organizing Committee and meet their deadline. The three of us had been sworn to secrecy. After training, during which the goalkeepers again found the flight of the ball difficult to judge, due to the high altitude, Alf met with the Sunday Sportswriters. I was not present at the meeting but Alf agreed to give them his final selection, provided all the reporters ensured there was an embargo placed, both on themselves and their offices, on the information until 1600 hours, when Alf would have informed the players. The press reporters readily agreed. Imagine Alf's surprise and dismay when his lunch was interrupted by a very angry David Sadler. David asked if he could see Alf in private. David had received a telephone call from his wife in England. She hoped he was not too disappointed at not being selected in the final twenty-two players for the tournament. David of course was unaware of the information his wife had given him! Mrs. Sadler had apparently been telephoned by one of the Manchester newspaper offices enquiring of her reaction to David's omission from the final party of twenty-two players selected for the tournament proper. Furious though Alf was, at the obvious leak of the information, he had no alternative but to apologise profusely to David. Alf called two meetings immediately. One meeting was with the Sunday Sportswriters, the other was a Team Meeting with the players. At the meeting with the Sportswriters, it became apparent Mike Langley, one of the reporters, had failed to emphasise to his office in Manchester the fact that the contents of his article were subject to a time embargo. Alf was furious with Mike Langley, as indeed were all the other Sportswriters. Alf had tried to cooperate with the Press and he had been badly let down. At the Team Meeting, Alf informed the players exactly what had happened with the Press and the embarrassing position in which he and David Sadler had been placed in. In front of the whole squad, Alf again apologised to David. He also apologised to all the players. He then had the unenviable task of informing the five players who he had not selected in the final selection of twenty-two. The five players were Ralph Coates, Brian Kidd, Bob McNab, Peter Shilton and Peter Thompson. I had great sympathy with them all. I was particularly sorry for Peter Thompson. Peter had been subjected to the same fate at Lilleshall in 1966. After supper we saw yet another film.

At a staff meeting, later that night, Les Cocker raised the issue of our future travel arrangements. From Quito we were due to travel back to

Bogotá. At Bogotá there was to be a delay of some six hours, before we caught a second plane from Bogotá to Mexico City. At Bogota, Alf had even arranged for the whole party to return to The Tequendama Hotel to watch yet another film, to while away the hours of our wait. In view of the Bobby Moore saga, Les suggested our travel arrangements be cancelled and we find a different flight, direct from Quito to Mexico City. Alf disagreed.

"Bobby didn't steal the bracelet."
he said.

"If we opt out of returning to Bogotá, people there will assume we have something to hide. They will assume Bobby is guilty."

Alf gained support, when Bobby was brought into the meeting. Bobby maintained his innocence and wished we all return to Bogotá. Our travel arrangements, flying from Quito back to Bogotá, remained in place. It had been a distressing day.

Two matches took place on the Sunday in Quito. An England B game, against an Ecuador XI, was followed by a full international of England against Ecuador. The matches were played around mid-day, when the temperature was in the mid seventies. At 9,500 feet it was the ultimate test, as to how successful our altitude acclimatisation programme had been. England won the first match by four goals to one. Jeff Astle scored a hat trick and there was one own goal. In the full international, England beat Ecuador, two goals to nil, with goals from Francis Lee and Brian Kidd. Alf was pleased with the team's performance. The players were happy with the way they had coped with the conditions. We all attended a reception in the evening at a tennis club. The reception was given in our honour by The Football Association of Ecuador. Unfortunately the hosts forgot to turn up! The England party ate alone. The meal of Melon, Fillet Steak and Pancakes was most acceptable.

On the Monday morning we left Quito at 1020 and arrived in Bogotá at 1120. A motor coach transported us back to The Tequendama Hotel, where we lunched on Vegetable Soup, Roast Lamb, Vegetables and Crème Caramel. We all assembled in the large meeting room and settled down to watch yet another film. On this occasion it was Shenandoah, starring

James Stewart. During the film, a commotion developed at the back of the hall. The noise lasted for just a few minutes and no one paid particular attention to the disturbance. When the film finished, we were aware that Bobby Moore and Alf were missing. Instructions had been left, by Alf, that we were to proceed to the airport as normal. Our flight was due to leave at 1750. We were all seated on the plane, when Alf returned. The departure of the plane had been held up for him. I was informed Bobby Moore had been arrested by the Columbian Police. Bobby was being charged with stealing an emerald and diamond bracelet, valued at two thousand pesos. Dr. Andrew Stephens, Denis Follows and the British Embassy staff in Bogotá would care for Bobby. There were only eight days left before our first game in the World Cup. We had now lost our Captain. Alf had no idea if, or when, Bobby would return. The word of Bobby's arrest quickly spread around the plane. The Press, on board the plane, now had the greatest news story of the tournament and probably of their lives. As they were all in mid air, and mobile phones had not been invented, there was no way they could contact their offices with the story. Transmission of the story would have to wait until we had landed at Mexico airport. Back at The Parc de Prince Hotel, Alf held a Team Meeting to inform the players and staff of the details of Bobby's arrest and detainment. Alf reassured us he would keep us informed of any news. The mood amongst the party was sombre and depressing.

The following morning, I had arranged for Dr. Fielding, our Consultant Haematologist, to take blood samples from each member of the party. Dr. Fielding had flown out to Mexico especially for this purpose. It was important he personally read the results, as he had done in England, thus giving uniform, consistent reporting standards of the tests. The effect of the altitude, during our acclimatisation, would be for the body to produce more red blood cells. The production of more red blood cells inevitably made the blood thicker, placing an added strain on the heart. The extra red blood cells were necessary however to ensure that the reduced amount of oxygen, in the rarified atmosphere, could be absorbed into the blood stream. Our daily intake of iron and vitamins tablets should have ensured everyone had the wherewithal to manufacture more red blood cells. The bloods tests were taken on Tuesday morning. Fielding took all the samples to the laboratory for analysis. Five pressmen, Reg Drury, Desmond Hackett, Ken Jones, Peter Lorenzo and Frank McGhee, had kindly agreed to act as controls. They too had been tested back in London and they were also tested with the players and staff now in Mexico. The only difference between the players and the pressmen was that the latter had done no training. Dr Fielding and I studied the results in the afternoon. Every player had produced more red blood cells during their time at altitude. From a haematological viewpoint they had responded well to the acclimatisation programme. Every player was now in a satisfactory position, regarding their blood tests, although there were three players who had not responded quite as well as the remainder. Dr. Fielding and I informed Alf of our findings.

The atmosphere at The Parc de Prince was bizarre. Our Captain had been arrested. Some reports said he was in jail. Others that he was confined, as a prisoner at the British Embassy building in Bogotá. During the blood testing procedure, Alf received a telephone call from the Chairman of The Football Association, who had remained behind in Bogota with Bobby Moore. He confirmed Bobby was confined to the British Embassy in Bogota. In reality, he was a prisoner within the confines of the Embassy. Alf was also informed that Lord Harewood, the President of The Football Association, and a relative of the Queen, had now involved the Prime Minister, Harold Wilson, in the Bobby Moore affair. Dr. Andrew Stephens had no news as to whether Bobby would be allowed to rejoin us. The two governments, British and Columbian were now involved in the case. Following lunch, we all left for a training session at The Reforma Club, but everyone's mind was focused on Bobby Moore back in Bogota. During the afternoon, Alf spoke with Bobby Moore and Denis Follows. The information was encouraging. Both Bobby and Denis informed Alf the matter was due to be resolved in the courts the following day. Alf kept the players updated of the situation. Following dinner we all watched, on TV, the friendly international between Romania and

Portugal.

There were six days remaining before we played our first game in the tournament. Twenty-three days had been spent at an altitude of 7,400 feet or above. It was time now to leave Mexico City for Guadalajara. The timing of our move to Guadalajara was critical. It was a medical decision. Research, carried out by Lind, and confirmed by several members of my medical team, indicated that acclimatisation to extreme heat could be achieved in five days if certain conditions were strictly adhered to. Those conditions required the players to work in the heat, at maximum intensity, for a period of one hundred minutes on each of the five days. Further sessions in the heat would gain no advantage and splitting the session into two fifty-minute sessions was also of no advantage. The players would be exposed to hard training sessions, of exactly one hundred minute duration, on each of the remaining five days. There would be ample supplies of Malvern water and Gatorade, prepared and cooled in my bathroom to the appropriate temperature. My bath was filled daily with ice until the Gatorade I had prepared was at the correct temperature. Slow Sodium continued to be prescribed for the players. Our luggage, and all the kit, was collected from The Parc de Prince hotel by a luggage van at 0900 hours. Following breakfast, our morning was spent training at the Olympic Stadium. At noon we were entertained to a reception at the British Embassy. It was our opportunity to say a big thank you to Sir Peter Hope, Mr. Vine and all the staff at the Embassy. They had all been so helpful during our stay in Mexico City. The Embassy staff had no news of Bobby Moore, other than he would not be returning to Mexico today. On returning to The Parc de Prince hotel, I was met by the Mexican representatives of Findus. At Guadalajara, they informed me, a fresh supply of frozen food and drinks awaited us. There were one hundred dozen bottles of Malvern water; eighty-six dozen ten ounce cans of bitter lemon; a similar quantity of twelve ounce cans of Orangeade; and fifty-six dozen ten ounce cans of lemonade. In addition there were supplies of English sausages, baked beans, frozen chips, steak and kidney pies. In Guadalajara I was to contact a Mr. Wieshofer of Oxidenta who would arrange the delivery of drinks and food on a daily basis to the Hilton Hotel.

Still without our Captain, we departed from The Parc de Prince at 1500 hours catching the1830 flight to Guadalajara. We arrived at the Hilton Hotel just before 2100 hours. All the accommodation for the England team was on one floor at the Hilton. Three players shared the same room. Security was tight. Mexican soldiers, armed with guns, sat outside the lifts on our floor. Rumours circulated that some left wing guerillas were intent on kidnapping a footballer during the tournament. Whenever we went to our rooms, it was necessary to gain passage from the soldiers. Harold, Les and I began unpacking the kit before retiring to bed.

Our first morning in Guadalajara I spent helping Alf, Harold and Les complete the unpacking. The four staff not only unpacked their personal possessions, but there was all the kit, films, games and footballs to be stored. Alf called a Team Meeting for mid-day. Again he stressed the need to be extra careful regarding the food, drinks and personal hygiene. The heat acclimatisation programme I again explained fully to the players. I placed great emphasis on the need to drink copious amounts of Malvern water and Gatorade. Following the players meeting, the staff had a meeting with the officials of The Atlas Sports Club. It was there we had arranged to carry out our daily training programme throughout our stay. A light lunch was followed by a period of rest for the players. We set off for our first training session, in the heat of Guadalajara, at 1530 hours. Malvern water and Gatorade, in abundant supplies and cooled to the requisite temperature, travelled with us in thermos flasks. Joe Mercer and Don Revie, who were working for the BBC, attended our training session. The temperature at The Atlas Training Ground was eighty-eight degrees. The medical team recommended, for rapid acclimatisation to the heat, one daily training session at a high work rate of one hundred minutes duration. Alf carried out our medical recommendation to the letter. Ten minutes was spent on running and a similar time on physical exercises, sprints and ball work, though the ball work ran over time

[416]

ACCLIMATISATION 1970 STYLE

by some five minutes. The session then stopped for five minutes, while fluid was replaced in abundance. The second half of the training session consisted of seven a side football, with each team playing the other three times, ensuring the players spent one hundred minutes in hard training. Fluid was replaced in abundance midway through the seven a side games and at the end of the session. In the evening, we received the good news that Bobby Moore would rejoin us in Guadalajara the following day. Findus were voted 'Top of the Pops' by the players, as they tucked into an evening meal of grilled English sausages, baked beans, and chips followed by apple pie and ice cream. In the evening, I spoke with Joe Mercer and Don Revie. They commented how surprised they were there had been that no concession had been made to the intense heat during the training session. I explained to them the reason for our one hundred minute training programme at a high work rate. It had been a good first day in Guadalajara.

With only four days remaining before our first game against Romania, Bobby Moore arrived at the Hilton Hotel, to rapturous applause from all the players and staff. We had all assembled inside the main entrance of the hotel to greet him. It was so good to have the Captain back with us. After Bobby had settled in, I carried out a complete medical examination on him, ensuring his five days absence in Bogota had not resulted in any medical concerns. My only concern, was he had lost some five pounds in weight. Up to his detention in Bogota, his daily weight, throughout the acclimatisation process had been very steady around 82 kilograms. His weight, on returning from his harrowing experience in Bogota, was now 79.5 kilograms; his lowest weight since we had left England.

I decided before and after every training session and match in Guadalajara, every player would be weighed in the nude. The weight loss recorded, during the training or match, would be an indication to me of the fluid loss sustained, as a result of the increased sweating in the extreme heat. Our second day in Guadalajara, involved another one hundred minute training session in a temperature of eighty-eight degrees. Every player lost over two pounds in weight during the session. Bobby Moore, whose weight loss was of concern to me before the training session, lost the most weight. Bobby lost a staggering five pounds. He was closely followed by Peter Osgood, who lost four and three quarter pounds. I informed each player of his weight loss during training. The players knew this weight loss was a good indication of how much they had sweated during training. Every player knew it was essential to replace their weight loss by drinking plenty of fluid and taking the prescribed Slow Sodium tablets on a daily basis. The players had been made aware of how the human body acclimatises, in the main, to the extreme heat by producing more sweat with each successive exposure to the heat. If our heat acclimatization process was to prove successful, the weight loss, occurring on each successive day, would increase in line with the production of more and more sweat.

Bobby Moore's weight loss was now a great concern of mine. He had lost five pounds during his stay in Bogota and an additional five pounds during his first training session in Guadalajara; ten pounds weight loss in total. Further discussions with Bobby revealed that during his stay at the Embassy in Columbia, he had trained every day in the Embassy garden. While Bogota was not as hot as Guadalajara, Bobby admitted he had sweated profusely during his training session and may not have consumed adequate fluids subsequently. Examination of his urine, by the Fantus test, revealed an absence of Chloride. While the accuracy of this test does not compare with that of laboratory blood sodium levels and urine by flame photography, it nevertheless is a rough guide as to the diagnosis of salt depletion having occurred. I therefore decided to markedly increase the supply of fluids and Slow Sodium tablets to Bobby. He readily co-operated. Within twenty-four hours his weight increased by four pounds and within forty-eight hours, he was back to his normal weight of 82 kilograms.

With just three days left, before we played our first game against Romania, the heat acclimatization process of carrying out one daily session of hard training for one hundred minutes continued. The weight losses recorded by the players, before and after training, increased. The players also reported they were aware of an increase in the amount they

ACCLIMATISATION 1970 STYLE

"My Bathroom—Filled Daily With Gatorade"

sweated. Every day, I continued to place great emphasis on the need for the players to drink plenty of fluids and ensured they all received adequate supplies of Slow Sodium tablets. My bedroom, early in the mornings, became a hive of activity. Each day, a large quantity of ice was delivered into my bath. Dr. Williams was still convinced its purity was very suspect. The ice was not to drink but to cool down bottles of Malvern water into which I had dissolved crystals of Gatorade. Daily, I made up some thirty one litre bottles of Gatorade. With my bath full of ice, the bottles were stood in the ice until the temperature of the Gatorade fell to a temperature of 12 to 15 degrees Centigrade. When this temperature was achieved, I transferred the Gatorade to innumerable thermos flasks. The flasks then accompanied me to the training sessions. It became a daily ritual for me during our stay in Guadalajara. At half and full time in the training sessions, the cool Gatorade was greatly appreciated by the players.

It was the last day of May. We had been away from our homes in England for twenty-eight days. It was the first day of the World Cup tournament in Mexico. Russia played Mexico, in the opening game. The match was played in the Azteca Stadium in Mexico City at midday. We all went to the television studios in Guadalajara to view the game. The first day of the tournament was the first time, during our stay in South America, a player developed genuine acute gastro-enteritis. The player was quite poorly. He developed frequent diarrhoea during the day, and had a raised temperature. He vomited on two occasions. I confined him to bed. He was placed on fluids only. His daily Thalazole tablets were replaced by Streptotriad. I ensured he had more than adequate supplies of cooled Malvern water and Gatorade. The other players trained at The Atlas Club, again for one hundred minutes, in the extreme heat of Guadalajara. The temperature at the training ground was ninety-one degrees. It was very hot and the sunlight extremely bright. In the evening everyone, with the exception of the ill player, tucked into Steak and kidney pie, chips and carrots, followed by an ice cream desert. The food provision from Findus was excellent.

On the first day of June, everyone had the morning off. The first player to suffer with Gastro-enteritis was much better. He had slept well. His diarrhoea had ceased. There was no further vomiting. He would remain on Streptotriad for a further four days. As most of the players decided on a lie in bed, Harold Shepherdson and I ventured into the town of Guadalajara to shop. After a light lunch Alf held a Team Meeting. He informed the squad which players he had selected for the first game against Romania. The team would play a 4–4–2 system. In the late afternoon, the whole squad had a thirty-minute training session, followed by various five-a- side games. Everyone was in good spirits. The ill player even did some light training with no ill effects. At night, on the eve of our first game, Alf made one of his rare mistakes. He had arranged for us all to see a film, at the local cinema, he personally highly recommended. The film was entitled "Paris is Burning." Unfortunately for Alf, the film was in French, with Spanish subtitles! We returned to the hotel after watching the film for just ten minutes!

"Alf's Final Briefing To The Players."

14

The Competition Proper.........

The five wives arrived in Guadalajara before the first game, against Romania, was played. The wives were accommodated at The Camino Real Hotel. No one had seen them. My personal wish was we would have no contact with them, until the tournament was over. The team's acclimatisation, both to the altitude and the heat, was all important to me and it had gone exceptionally well. The players and staff had been totally committed and dedicated to that task throughout the twenty-eight days of our stay. Our preparation had been the most important issue to everyone. All of us, in the party, had adopted a most professional attitude to achieving our aim. The players' confidence was high. The preparation period was now over. The players had come to terms with the difficulties of playing at altitude. Their bodies had made excellent blood responses. Dr. Fielding was delighted with the results of the blood tests. The five-day acclimatisation programme, to the heat of Guadalajara, had been completed with excellent results. I was initially worried as to whether the heat acclimatisation process, as recommended by Lind and Leithead, would be successful. I had not embarked on such a programme previously. I need not have worried. I religiously followed their research advice on heat acclimatisation, without knowing for certain if it would be successful. Their research advice had proved perfect. The risk, I had taken, was non existent. The players were coping extremely well with the intense heat. Water and salt replacement was highly successful. In the twenty-eight day period of acclimatisation there had only been one genuine case of gastro-enteritis. That player's ill-

THE COMPETITION PROPER

ness had occurred on day twenty-seven, two days before our first game. With treatment he made a swift recovery. Overall, the acclimatisation programme, prepared over two years by my medical team, had gone far better than I ever imagined.

Now a new factor appeared, over which I had no control. The four players' wives and Lady Ramsey, were now at The Camino Real Hotel. Many players, coaches and managers from England, were also staying at the hotel. The arrival of the wives immediately affected our players. During our four weeks acclimatization period, we had developed an unbelievable togetherness. With the arrival of the wives, our togetherness sadly, rapidly diminished. The day after the arrival of the wives, on returning to the Hilton Hotel from our routine training session, the four players immediately disappeared to the privacy of their rooms. They were, quite naturally, anxious to telephone their wives at The Camino Real Hotel and speak at length with them. It was their first concern. For the four players, it was a perfectly natural thing to do. Immediately however, Hurst, Peters, Bonnetti and even captain Bobby Moore, became separated from the main party. The remaining eighteen players and three staff had no such luxury of speaking with their wives.

Within hours of the wives' arrival, the issue was raised as to whether they should meet with all the players.

"Why don't we have a welcoming party for the five wives."
someone suggested to me.

"Don't ask me."
I said,

"Ever since I was a kid, I have always considered girls, alcohol,
smoking and parties a distraction from the job in hand."

Holding a party, was not part of our detailed preparations. In the two years of our preparation, holding a party for five wives had never been mentioned; never been in the planning. However with the five wives now living just a few hundred yards away, and their husbands not having seen them for over four weeks, for me to oppose an innocuous party, I knew, would be unacceptable. Nevertheless, I was extremely unhappy we were even contemplating having such an event. It would be a distraction from our main purpose. Our purpose, and my dream, had always been to retain the World Cup, in the hostile environment of Mexico. A party was not part of the preparation.

At breakfast, on the day of our first game against Romania, Martin Peters approached me.

"Kathy, my wife, is not too well. She has a tummy upset. I wondered if you would be kind enough to visit her. She's in bed at The Camino Real Hotel."

Over the two years I had been the Senior Team Doctor, I had developed a good relationship with both Martin and Kathy. I visited Kathy, who was suffering from acute gastro-enteritis. I advised her to stay in bed. I gave her the appropriate advice and treatment. I promised to visit her later in the day.

My main task, on returning to the Hilton Hotel, was to prepare sufficient Gatorade, at the correct temperature, for the players to drink before, during and after the game against Romania. When prepared, the drinks were transferred to innumerable thermos flasks. The flasks travelled with me to the game. As usual, four Slow Sodium tablets were given to the players with their pre-match meal. The Romanian game commenced at 1600 hours. The temperature in the stadium was eighty-one degrees, much cooler than if we had played at mid-day. No goals were scored in the first half. I was keen to assess the physical performance of the players in the heat. Everyone of them performed well. The Romanians were a very physical side. In the second half, the ferociousness of their tackles, particularly those of Mocanu, were unacceptable. He seemed more intent on sending an England player to hospital than allowing them to continue playing football. Mocanu committed a dreadful foul on Keith Newton. He tackled Keith at knee height, inflicting an injury resulting in Keith having to leave the field, unable to return. Tommy Wright replaced Keith Newton at right fullback. Keith had a severely bruised knee. The Romanians continued with their ferocious tackles and both Francis Lee and Terry Cooper were the victims of unacceptable tackles. Midway through the second half, following a cross

THE COMPETITION PROPER

from the right wing by Alan Ball, Geoff Hurst scored the only goal of the game. Geoff later told me the ball actually went through the goalkeeper's legs. England won their first game one goal to nil.

I weighed the players, in the nude, before and after the game and recorded each individual's weight loss. At the end of the game, Brian Labone and Bobby Charlton were the two players chosen for the dope tests. While all the players and staff returned to the Hilton Hotel, I took Keith Newton and Terry Cooper to hospital for precautionary X-ray examinations. Both X-rays were perfectly normal.

Before leaving the stadium, I met and chatted with the Romanian doctor, who had been so kind to me in Bucharest two years previously.

"How are your players coping with the extreme heat?"
he enquired.
"Very well."
I replied.
"We have found it very difficult."
he said,
> "A few Romanian players are suffering with quite severe water and salt deficiency. Their weight loss has been of great concern to me. Some of them have been unable to totally regain their weight loss. The replacement of adequate amounts of salt has proved to be very difficult; in fact impossible."

I inwardly smiled and privately thought of the wonderful work Professor de Wardener and his staff had done for us at The Charing Cross Hospital. I pondered. Maybe, after all, I had provided a better medical service than the Romanians, as Alf had insisted on that November day in 1968.

Although the X-rays, of Keith's knee and Terry's foot, showed no bony injury both Keith's knee and Terry's foot were extremely sore. A supper of Vegetable Soup, Grilled Sausages, Chips and Beans, followed by Apple Pie with Ice Cream, and Cheese and Biscuits proved very acceptable to the players. The Findus supply of food was working well. After supper, I revisited Kathy Peters. She was much improved. Martin was pleased and greatly relieved. His worry and concern disappeared.

DOCTOR TO THE WORLD CHAMPIONS

Bizarre stories, real or imaginary, were wickedly spread about on a daily basis by the eighteen players, whose wives were still at home in England. All these stories related to the wives of the four players residing now in Mexico. Stories of late night parties, nude bathing and fanciful behaviour with the other residents of The Camino Real Hotel were rapidly invented by many of the England players. If, for example, one of the four players, on phoning their wives, found the telephone line to be engaged, the other players would always have a spontaneous, wicked explanation ready.

"I heard there was a party at their hotel last night. Didn't finish until three in the morning. They were all playing games in the pool. The wives seem to be having a fine time. They'll be sleeping it off now. Too tired to answer your call"

There was no truth to these stories, but the effect of these stories on the four players varied enormously. These pressures, all caused by the arrival of the wives, were in addition to those of participating in the World Cup tournament in the hostile environment of Mexico. These pressures were completely outside our preparatory programme. As far as I personally was concerned, the presence of the wives was a disaster.

For the players, who played against Romania, Wednesday was a day of rest. The players in that group, who wished to, did only some light training; others just rested. For the players who had not played, there was the usual training session at The Atlas Sports Club. We trained there at mid-day. The temperature was in the mid eighties. During the day, several World Cup games took place. Belgium beat El Salvador three goals to nil. At Toluca, Italy beat Sweden, one goal to nil. West Germany struggled to beat Morocco, by two goals to one. We all decided to watch the game between Czechoslovakia and Brazil in the television studio at Guadalajara. Brazil easily won, by four goals to one. At the Team Meeting after supper, Alf talked to the players about the Brazilian and Czech teams. During the day, Peter Jones, working for Radio Wales, interviewed me. People in the principality were still intrigued to know how a Welshman was the doctor caring for the England players! Later, I visited Martin Peter's wife, Kathy, at the Camino Real. She had made a full recovery.

THE COMPETITION PROPER

Our eighth day in Guadalajara was most significant for me as two players became ill. We had carried out a normal training session at mid-day, in a temperature of eighty degrees. Everyone trained well. After lunch, we all watched a filmed replay of our game against Romania. Alf gave the players his usual thorough appraisal of the England team's performance. In the early evening, one player complained of a sore throat. Examination revealed an attack of Acute Tonsillitis. I treated him with a course of antibiotics. The second casualty had developed acute gastro-enteritis. We now had suffered two cases of gastro-enteritis since our arrival in Guadalajara. I was most concerned. I emphasised again, to all the players at the Team meeting, the need for everyone to maintain food discipline and personal hygiene. After supper, we settled into the hotel lounge to watch the film 'Grand Prix.'

On Friday June 5th, two days before our game against Brazil, the coaching staff decided on a light training session at mid-day. The normal routine was observed. Players were weighed in the nude, before and after training. Slow Sodium was now administered routinely. Gatorade, in plentiful supplies, was available. The temperature was eighty-eight degrees. The players were disappointed the training session was so light. They wanted to do more work! Spirits and morale, amongst the players was high. Keith Newton and Terry Cooper had responded well to treatment. Keith's knee and Terry's foot were now symptom free. They both completed the one-hour training session without any ill effects. The two players with Tonsillitis and Gastro-enteritis had improved sufficiently to attend the training session; they both insisted on doing some very little training. The players were given the afternoon off to shop. I advised the two players with recovering illnesses to rest in bed. I went shopping with Les and Harold. I bought nothing. In the evening, we watched the film of the Czechoslovakia versus Brazil game. Before retiring to bed, Alf gave me the news I had been dreading since the wives had arrived in Guadalajara. The manager of the Hilton Hotel had expressed the desire to have a party for the entire squad. Alf had agreed, with the manager. The party would be on the Sunday evening after the Brazil game. Alf had also agreed the five wives would be invited to the party. Alf knew I was unhappy with the arrangements. I believed the party would be a major distraction from the task we had to achieve.

The day before the Brazil game, Alf decided our training session would be at mid-day, the time of the Brazil game. The normal routine of salt and fluid replacement was maintained. The training session lasted just thirty minutes. In the late afternoon, Les Cocker took the players to the television studio to view the game between Romania and Czechoslovakia. Alf, Harold and I went to the stadium to view the game live. Romania won the game by two goals to one. We all returned to the hotel for an early supper.

The noise commenced as we finished supper. It was eight o'clock. It transpired hundreds of cars had encircled the roads around the Hilton Hotel. Many of the cars had people sitting on the car bonnets. They banged on drums and tin lids. The car horns hooted. Trumpets were blown. The crowd chanted 'Brazil, Brazil', to accompany this noise. The noise was deafening. The Mexicans and Brazilian supporters burnt flags in the street. Police were present inside and outside the hotel in considerable numbers. Despite our pleas however, the police refused to take any action. Two hours of incessant noise followed, before we realised this behaviour would continue throughout the night. No-one was willing to stop the incessant din, except Alfie Isaac, a West Ham supporter. The three West Ham players restrained him. Alfie was so annoyed, he wanted to fight everyone in the street! At ten o'clock, we decided a strategy was needed to ensure the England players would have a good night's sleep. Most of the noise was at the front of the hotel. We decided that all the players, sleeping at the front of the hotel and playing against Brazil, would change their rooms for the night. They would swap rooms with those players who were not chosen to play against Brazil and whose rooms were at the back of the hotel away from the main street. It was the only way the selected players would possibly get a reasonable night's sleep. The change of rooms was quickly accomplished. Players, and the substitutes, were moved into the rear bedrooms; players not selected to play or be substitutes, slept in the hotel's bedrooms at the front of the hotel. Six players selected-Gordon Banks, Colin Bell, Bobby Charlton, Emlyn Hughes, Brian Labone and Tommy Wright-decided to stay in their bedrooms, even though they were at the front of the hotel. While the players endeavoured to sleep, the noise continued unabated, until three in the morning. It was disgraceful behaviour. The decision of the Mexican police, not to intervene, merely aggravated the situation. During all this confusion, Les Cocker, acting in what he thought was in the best interests of the players, committed a major mistake. Les gave all the reserve players, sleeping in the front bedrooms, a sleeping capsule of Tuinal. Fortunately, the six players selected to play, who remained at the front of the hotel, did not receive a capsule. Tuinal is a barbiturate. The drug was one of those listed, in the competition, as a banned substance. None of these reserve players could now act as substitutes or be brought into the team at the last moment. They all ran the risk of failing the dope test. Les apparently had his own private supply of Tuinal. When Les reported his actions, Alf, to say the least, was not pleased. Fortunately, all the players selected to play, and those on the substitute's bench reported, at breakfast, they were fit and well. No replacements, from the players who had been given Tuinal, were required. One player did not appear at breakfast. He had developed acute gastro-enteritis. It was the third case of gastro-enteritis. I was very concerned at this development. The player remained in bed all day.

The game against Brazil was always going to be our most difficult in Guadalajara. We left for the stadium at ten thirty. On arrival at the stadium, the temperature was seventy degrees. In the hour, before the game, the temperature rapidly rose through the eighties. Ten minutes before the game commenced, I recorded the temperature at ninety-six degrees. Our heat acclimatisation programme would be severely tested. England played exceptionally well against Brazil, but lost to the only goal of the game, scored by Jairzinho. As an indication of the extreme heat stress, suffered by the players during the game, I measured their weight loss during the game. The weight loss gave me a good indication of how much water and salt the players had lost in sweating during the game. The weight loss, sustained by the players was considerable. Geoff Hurst lost 11.8 pounds or 6.5% of his pre-match weight; Bobby Moore lost 11 pounds or 6.25% of his pre match weight and even Jeff Astle, who only came on as a substitute, lost 9.9

pounds or 5.3% of his pre-match weight. The heat stress had been considerable. The players had coped with the extreme conditions exceptionally well. In the evening, at the Hilton Hotel, the party I had been dreading took place. The hotel manager acted as host. The party was short in duration. It was finished within an hour. Alf invited some of his personal friends to the Camino Real Hotel to have a drink with his wife. I was also invited. As usual, I drank orange juice. I was back at the Hilton by eleven and soon fast asleep.

The morning after the manager's party, I became very annoyed. It was our thirty-fifth day in Mexico. Throughout our stay, only one player had missed a day's training. He had been confined to bed for a day, when he had a genuine gastro-enteritis. Today was different. Two players remained in bed all morning. They both had self inflicted severe hangovers from the previous night's party. Neither player appeared for lunch. My Dad had been so right. Alcohol was a diversion and a distraction. It should be avoided, particularly in the middle of a World Cup campaign. Alf also discovered, after the manager's party, several players had used 'Room Service' for extra sandwiches. Room Service, at the hotel, had been banned; the risks were too great. Mexicans prepared the food supplied by Room Service. The food was not cooked. The sandwiches were garnished with salad and unpeeled fruit, which everyone knew was to be avoided. At the Team Meeting, Alf informed the players once more,

"Room Service is banned."

We trained at the Atlas Club at four o'clock. One of the players with a hangover remained in bed. His hangover prevented him training. The players, who had played against Brazil, enjoyed the luxury of lying in the baths at the Atlas clubhouse. They all enjoyed a relaxing hot soak. The remaining players, who had not played against Brazil, had an eighty-minute training session. In view of the severe weight loss incurred by the players during the Brazil match, their fluid intake was considerably increased and I gave all those players an additional four Slow Sodium tablets. After supper everyone settled for an early night. The streets outside the Hilton Hotel were quiet.

THE COMPETITION PROPER

Alf and I left the Hilton early in the morning. We were taken on a visit to a large privately owned ranch in the countryside. It had been suggested the ranch would be a suitable place to take the players for an afternoon's relaxation. The ranch however was not suitable. Undeterred, George Stirrup, the man whose idea it was, then drove us to a Golf and Country Club with magnificent facilities. In addition to the golf course, there was a driving range, large practice areas and several tennis courts. Alf decided it was an ideal venue for a visit by the players. We were back at the Hilton in good time to sit down with the players and watch the film of the Brazil versus England game. All the players trained at three-thirty at the Atlas Club. The temperature was eighty degrees. The training session lasted eighty minutes. At night we saw yet another film. The film, on this occasion, was another of Alf's favourite westerns-'Butch Cassidy and the Sundance Kid'.

On the third morning after the Brazil game, all but two of the players had regained their average weight. The two players, whose weight had not completely returned were given extra fluids throughout the day. The morning was spent at the Golf and Country Club Alf and I had visited the previous day. The players thoroughly enjoyed the facilities of the Country Club. Some played a few holes of golf; others practised on the driving range; some played cards under the protection of a large sun umbrella, while others played tennis with a football!

A late lunch was taken back at the Hilton hotel. Harold took the players to the television studio to watch the game between Brazil and Romania. Alf, Les and I went to the Jalisco Stadium to witness the game live. During the first thirty minutes of the game, the Brazilian played the most wonderful football I had ever witnessed. They attacked relentlessly. Their one-touch football was a joy to behold. The Romanians chased Brazilian shadows and offered only token interference to the Brazilian interchange of passing. As the game progressed, the Romanians became more and more of a threat, but in the end Brazil won comfortably by three goals to two. Brazil's win ensured they would achieve first place in the group. They would remain in Guadalajara for their quarterfinal game. England could now only qualify in second place, and that was dependent on achieving at least a draw against

Czechoslovakia. The England players now knew exactly what was required of them. They must not lose against the Czechs. In the evening, I weighed the two players whose weight loss concerned me. Both were back to their normal weight.

It was now thirty-eight days since we had left Heathrow Airport. It was the fifteenth day of the competition. England and Czechoslovakia would play their crucial game at four in the afternoon at the Jalisco Stadium. Alf Ramsey's team selection was very brave. He decided to rest Alan Ball, Geoff Hurst, Brian Labone and Francis Lee. Alf made five changes from the team that had played so well against Brazil. Keith Newton, who had fully recovered from his bruised knee, replaced Tommy Wright. In addition to Keith Newton, Jeff Astle, Colin Bell, Jack Charlton and Alan Clarke were chosen to play. The Team Meeting was held at eleven thirty. It was the fifty-second time I had acted as Team Physician to an England team. At Alf's insistence, I always attended the team meetings. Although I always listened intently to every one of Alf's team talks, I never spoke on football matters. My contributions at team meetings had always been, quite correctly, solely on medical matters. The team meeting was coming to a close, when Alf asked,

"Are there any further questions?"

There were none. During the ensuing silence, I slowly raised my hand.

"Yes doctor, you have a question?"

Alf asked.

Apprehensively, I said,

"In view of the fact Geoff Hurst is not playing, who is going to take the Penalties?

"An important point. Thank you doctor. Now who takes them at Club level?"

Alf's question was met with total silence.

"I assume no one takes them at Club level. Do we have a volunteer then?"

After a prolonged silence, Alan Clarke volunteered.

"I'll take the Penalties."

THE COMPETITION PROPER

he said.

"Alan, thank you for that. The team meeting is closed."

I had sat, throughout the team meeting, next to Les Cocker. As we rose from our chairs, Les said,

"Clarkie taking Penalties is ridiculous! At Leeds, he never takes them. At Leeds, he'd be our fifth or sixth choice!

England beat Czechoslovakia one goal to nil in the Jalisco Stadium on Thursday June 11th.1970, in a temperature of eighty-eight degrees. Bobby Charlton was substituted by Alan Ball and Jeff Astle by Peter Osgood. Alan Clarke scored England's goal from the penalty spot. It was my one and only intervention at a team meeting on a football matter in my entire twelve years of being a Team Physician. I was overjoyed. Alan had scored. England, having now qualified, would play West Germany in a quarterfinal match at Leon. Leon is at an altitude of 6,182 feet, half way, in altitude terms, between Guadalajara and Mexico City.

"Breakfast With Coleman, Revie and Mercer—From Mexico"

Back at the Hilton Hotel, everyone was in high spirits. During supper, the players enquired of Alf if they could have a quiet drink in one of their rooms, before retiring to bed. Their request was granted. The quiet drink would take place in the room shared between Bobby Charlton, Keith Newton and Gordon Banks. I went to bed immediately after supper. My mind was now focused on Leon. Alf had visited Leon during the Olympics and I had read his report. I had not visited Leon. No accommodation had been booked for us in Leon. Although we were due to move there in two days, we had no idea which hotel we would be staying in.

At breakfast, on Friday June 12th, Alf was not particularly happy. Our travel agent had been refused permission to fly the England party from Guadalajara to Leon. He was informed, by the World Cup organizing committee and the Mexicans, the runway at Leon Airport was too short to accommodate a plane large enough to accommodate the England party. Enquiries, the travel agent made, proved this information to be false. The West German party had flown directly into Leon from Germany at the start of the competition. The runway was long enough for them, but not apparently for England. We were instructed we would have to travel by motor coach to Leon, a distance approaching two hundred miles. We were told there was no alternative. Most of the journey would be through the dusty Mexican desert. The motor coach would inevitably travel through the heat of the day. At a time like this, the team needed the authority and influence of our senior administrator. Denis Follows, the Secretary of The Football Association, should have been on hand to assist Alf in his protestations. Denis could have used his undoubted influential position to persuade the responsible officials to allow us to fly. Unfortunately, Denis was nowhere to be seen. In fact we had seen little of the Secretary throughout our stay in Mexico. Denis' main role, accompanied by his wife, appeared to be responsible for and entertaining the President of The Football Association, Lord Harewood, who was also accompanied by his wife. The team's problems, Denis, no doubt, considered were Alf's responsibilities.

Breakfast had just finished when I received a call to visit Keith Newton. Immediately after breakfast, Keith had vomited. He had experienced one

THE COMPETITION PROPER

episode of diarrhoea during the night, had slight abdominal pain and was feeling quite poorly. He had acute gastroenteritis. Keith would rest all day in bed. Bobby Charlton and Alec Stepney also reported they had each suffered with two episodes of diarrhoea during the night. I wondered what had happened at the 'quiet drink' the night before. Three players now suspected of gastroenteritis. It was my nightmare scenario. Having instituted treatment for the three players, and advised them to rest, the remainder trained at the Atlas Sports Club at eleven o'clock. The afternoon, for all the other players, was spent watching films of the games West Germany had played against Peru and Bulgaria. West Germany had beaten Bulgaria by five goals to two and Peru by three goals to one. After the films, Alf called a staff meeting.

At the staff meeting, Alf informed us the World Cup and Mexican officials were adamant. We could only travel to Leon by motor coach. Flying from Guadalajara to Leon, we were told, was not possible. The motor coach would leave Guadalajara at 0830, allowing the journey to be completed in the cooler morning period. The England staff were aware, hotels in Leon had presented problems to the teams based there. Helmet Schoen, the Manager of the West German team, having visited the hotels in Leon prior to the tournament, decided his players would be accommodated sixteen miles outside of Leon at Comanjilla. Wisely, Schoen had also decided to bring a German chef with the team. The same chef they had employed four years previously in England. Peru, on the other hand, originally booked a hotel in Leon for the duration of the tournament. The Peruvians left their Leon hotel after only a few days, amid rumours that the gorgeous girls of Leon had infiltrated the hotel and were over friendly to their players. Peru moved their team to accommodation some thirty miles from Leon! The Bulgarians, whose manager incidentally was a Medical Physician, Dr. Stefan Bozkhov, stayed at a motel in Leon. Reports, mainly from the Press, indicated this motel was of a poor standard. The Bulgarians, I was told, suffered many cases of 'tummy upsets' during their stay. The powers that be, had now decided England would be accommodated at the Motel Estancia, the very hotel where the Bulgarians had stayed! The Bulgarians had failed to qualify for the quarterfinals; had vacated the Motel and returned home. The Motel was now allocated as suitable accommodation for England. The England staff were all unhappy with these arrangements. The arrangements had been imposed upon us without any prior consultation. When I learned we were to stay at the Motel Estancia, I consulted a travel handbook of South America lying on a table in the Hilton Hotel. Only two hotels were listed for Leon and the Motel Estancia was not one of them! The two hotels listed were the Hotel Leon and the Hotel Mexico. Both those hotels, we were informed, were fully booked and could not accommodate the England team. Despite our repeated protestations there appeared no alternative available. We would travel to Leon by coach and be accommodated at the Motel Estancia. The rest of the afternoon and early evening the four England staff spent packing.

After supper, the three players, Keith Newton, Bobby Charlton and Alex Stepney, two of whom shared Room 1208, were much improved.. The attack in all three was quite mild. They improved during the day. The fact that two players, from the same room were involved made me suspicious.

Late in the evening, Alf called a second Staff Meeting. He was really concerned about the Motel Estancia in Leon. Information, he had received during the day, from a variety of sources, questioned the wisdom of staying there. Alf suggested an advanced party be sent to the Motel Estancia, before the arrival of the players. The role of the advance party would be to sort out the accommodation. He also wanted the kitchens inspected and the chefs advised as to the meals required and the way they were to be prepared. Alf nominated Harold Shepherdson and myself to be the advance party. We would travel from Guadalajara to Leon by taxi, leaving at four in the morning. I protested. I had left the players only once before with disastrous results. My absence then resulted in Geoff Hurst being unable to play against Spain in Madrid. I suggested Les go with Harold. Les and Harold however were not happy carrying out a kitchen inspection. It was hardly a job they did at Leeds and Middlesbrough! With three players presently suffering with a tummy upset, I argued I should stay. My argument was countered by the fact I would be leaving at four in the morning, when

THE COMPETITION PROPER

the players would be asleep. The players were due to arrive in Leon at one o'clock. If the three players were all asleep at four in the morning, and their condition had not worsened in the night, it was decided I would travel with Harold. None of the players disturbed me during the night. Harold and I left the Hilton for Leon on the Saturday, at four in the morning.

Gordon Banks has stated that on waking in the Hilton, on the Saturday morning, he realised he was feeling unwell and consulted with me. That of course was impossible because I wasn't there! He also has revealed that during the motor coach journey to Leon his condition deteriorated further and he again consulted me on the coach. Again that was not possible, as I was probably in a taxi somewhere on the road to Leon, if not already at the Hotel Estancia in Leon.. The truth is that on that Saturday, I and no other doctor was available for Gordon. He would not see a doctor, until 1300 hours, when he arrived at Leon and then immediately consulted with me. A whole morning was wasted in treating Gordon and it was a major mistake.

The accommodation, at the Motel Estancia, was basic and sparse. Harold allotted rooms to the players. The accommodation was in bungalows, scattered around the grounds. The Motel's chef was particularly helpful. He spoke reasonable English. He understood our culinary wishes. The kitchen itself was not so satisfactory. It was easy to pick out areas in need of cleaning. The hotel manager was helpful, in that he quickly organised a group of cleaners, who thoroughly cleaned the kitchen under my supervision. The motor coach, conveying Alf, Les and the players, arrived at 1300 hours. It had been a hot, tedious journey for everyone, but particularly for Gordon Banks, who had been unwell throughout the bus journey. Although he had suffered no further diarrhoea, his stomach still felt queasy. Gordon immediately went to bed on arrival. His temperature was normal but, after examining him, I decided he should remain in bed for the rest of the day. After a light lunch of poached egg on toast, all the players, with the exception of Banks, trained at the Guanajuanta Stadium. At the stadium, before the training session commenced, Alf was informed the England players would only be allowed on the pitch for exactly thirty minutes. To confirm the instruction, as soon as the first England player set foot on the turf a large clock appeared at one end of the ground counting the time down in seconds from the thirty minutes.

On returning to the Motel Estancia, I visited Gordon Banks again. He had slept throughout the afternoon. He had suffered no further diarrhoea, was symptom free and feeling a little better. Clinically he had improved. I advised him to continue resting in bed. In the evening, after a very acceptable evening meal, Alf held a Team Meeting. Gordon Banks remained in bed.

Day eighteen of the tournament was the quarterfinal game against West Germany. I visited Gordon Banks before breakfast. He had slept well and was symptom free. I advised him to stay in bed during the morning. At breakfast, I was again diverted from my role as Team Physician. At the Staff Meeting, it was decided Les Cocker and I would take the kit to the Guanajuanta Stadium immediately after breakfast. Our role was to set out the kit in the England dressing room. I realised, I was now the 'Kit Man', as well as the Team Physician! With Les and myself at the Stadium, Alf and Harold remained at the Motel with the players. I was surprised, when I returned to the Motel, to find that Alf and Harold had subjected Gordon Banks to a fitness test. Alf and Harold informed me Gordon had passed the fitness test, with no ill effects. I was not given any detailed knowledge of the fitness test. I was simply told it had been successful.

"As far as we are concerned, Gordon is fit to play."

I visited Gordon in his room. He confirmed that, after the fitness test, he had agreed with Alf and Harold, he was fit to play, although he admitted the fitness test was merely a matter of collecting footballs that Harold had rolled across the lawn to him.

The Team Meeting was held in one of the bungalows. The room was quite small and the entire squad was packed into it. It was very hot and stuffy, even though all the windows were open. During the meeting, Gordon Banks became dizzy and fainted. He certainly was not fit to play. I took Gordon back to his room, decided he was not fit to play and advised him to remain in bed. When I returned to the Team Meeting, it was on the point of finishing. As the players departed, Alf, Harold and Les were engrossed in private conversation. It was then decided Peter Bonetti would play in goal, in place of Gordon Banks. It would be Peter's first game in any World Cup tournament and only his seventh international cap. Although Peter was relatively inexperienced at international level compared to Gordon Banks, who at this stage in his career had over sixty caps, no one doubted Peter's undoubted talent as a goalkeeper. Nevertheless, as the two teams lined up in Leon, I had great sympathy for Bonetti. He had been a member of the England squad for many years and had been a member of the 1966 World Cup squad, yet he had only made six previous international appearances. Alf had given Peter little experience on the big stage.

In the early part of the game, Bonetti made some good saves. Alan Mullery scored a great goal, to give England a one-goal lead at half time. In the dressing room at half time, I enquired of all the players if they were physically fine. Every player responded positively. England increased their lead in the fifth minute of the second half. Martin Peters scored at the far post, from a Keith Newton cross. The game had progressed to the sixty-eighth minute, before disaster struck. Beckenbauer scored for Germany, with what I had come to describe as a typical 'altitude goal'. I had always emphasised to the players, how the ball travelled faster through the rarefied atmosphere at altitude than at sea level. Beckenbauer, having swerved past Alan Mullery, shot for goal from an acute angle on the edge of the penalty area. It was the type of shot Peter Bonetti had easily saved a hundred times back in England. This was not England however but Leon, at an altitude of over six thousand feet. Peter dived to make his save, as he had done in England on innumerable occasions. Unfortunately the ball travelled faster in the rarefied air than Peter anticipated. When Peter dived to make his save, the ball was already past him and Beckenbauer scored. With the score at two goals to one, Germany was back in the game. Alf then made his first substitution. Colin Bell came on for Bobby Charlton. Almost immediately Bonetti made a good save from Muller. With only ten minutes remaining and England still leading by two goals to one, Alf made his second substitution. Norman Hunter came on for Martin Peters.

Within seconds, Germany equalised. Brian Labone made a bad clearance straight to Schnellinger. With Labone's slip, Bonetti was stranded in no-man's land for Schnellinger's cross. Seeler at the far post desperately leapt high to head the ball. I do believe the ball hit the back of Seeler's head. The ball looped over Bonetti and into the goal. Germany had drawn level and extra time would be played. In the second period of extra time, with eleven minutes remaining, Germany scored the goal that sealed England's exit from the World Cup. Grabowski, who had come on as a substitute for Germany, crossed from the right wing. At the far post Lohr, for Germany, and Keith Newton, for England, rose to meet the ball. The ball struck Keith Newton's head and came back across the goalmouth. Muller leapt in the air and volleyed the ball into the net. Bonetti, was a helpless onlooker, riveted to the ground, as the ball sped into the net. Although England attacked relentlessly, for the last eleven minutes, the players were unable to reduce the three goals to two deficit. England was out of the World Cup. West Germany had won in extra time, after England had earlier led by two clear goals.

England's dressing room was the saddest place in the whole world. West Germany would play Italy in the semi-final at the Azteca Stadium in Mexico City. England would be travelling home.

My first task on returning to the Motel was to visit Gordon Banks. Alec Stepney was also in the room. Gordon, sitting up in bed, was still watching our game on television. The broadcast was scheduled on television with a two-hour delay. England was still winning. Alec had told Gordon of our defeat. Gordon thought Alec was pulling his leg. I had the task of confirming to Gordon we had lost the game. Gordon could not believe it. Gordon felt much better and was keen to get up. There was now no earthly reason why he shouldn't.

When I rejoined the players in the Motel's garden, I was astonished. The four players, whose wives had flown out to Mexico, had packed up and left. They had been given permission to travel to Acapulco to holiday with their wives. The togetherness of the squad had suddenly disappeared. My mind recalled the evening, four years previously, after England won the World

THE COMPETITION PROPER

Cup in 1966. We all attended the celebration banquet at The Royal Garden Hotel together. We celebrated the victory together. We enjoyed the victory together. Our wives in 1966 enjoyed their banquet in a private room. We all joined our wives only when the official banquet was finished. Now, as we gathered on the lawn of the Motel, to communally share together the pain of defeat, Captain Bobby Moore, Geoff Hurst, Martin Peters and Peter Bonetti were travelling to the luxury of a holiday in Acapulco with their wives. It was so unfair. Over time, the players remaining at Leon, changed into swimming costumes and sunbathed on the lawn. It was a pleasure that had been denied to them for eight weeks. Even Alf took his shirt off. Slowly bottles of beer appeared on the lawn to ease the pain of defeat. I sat with the staff and players for some two hours, before retiring to the solitude of my room. The players needed to be free of my presence. I needed to be alone. I had lain on my bed for hours it seemed, mulling over the events of the past weeks, when the telephone rang. I assumed it was my wife, telephoning from England.

"Dr. Phillips speaking."

I said.

"Good evening, it's the Prime Minister, Harold Wilson. I've been unable to contact Sir Alf Ramsey. I wondered if you would give him the following message."

I quickly grabbed a pen and wrote the message on a blank luggage label. The following morning I gave the message to Alf.

The morning after our defeat, we travelled from Leon to Mexico City, by motor coach. Gordon Banks had fully recovered. If we were to play West Germany today he would have been fit to play. Twenty-four hours made all the difference. Before boarding the coach, I talked with Francis Lee. He looked out wistfully over Leon and made a very astute comment.

"You know Doc, a part, of each and everyone of us, has died at Leon. That part will never be replaced."

How true those words have become. On the motor coach, I sat alone at the front next to the exit door. As we travelled through the Mexican desert, Alan Ball stood at my side.

"Can you open the door Doc?" he enquired.

"They've given me this medal for losing the World Cup and I don't want it. I'm going to throw it away." Alan said,

"I know a lad in England who would love that medal." I replied.

"Yeah. Give it to Michael. I don't want it."

Alan Ball gave me his World Cup 1970 medal. From our first Under 23 international together, Alan had always given me his badges for my son Michael. Thirty-five years on, Alan's medal is still my son's prized possession. Many stories have been written over the years, concerning that medal. People believed, for it was written in the papers, it was lying somewhere in the Mexican desert. I can assure the reader however, it is still secure with Michael.

The bus journey to Mexico City was tedious. In Mexico City, we were deposited at the Motel Maria Barbara. It was the Motel, where the El Salvador team had stayed during the competition. Norman Hunter took advantage of the Motel's swimming pool. In diving into the pool, Norman lacerated his leg. The wound required three stitches. No one was interested in the injury, save Norman and myself. The Press had temporarily deserted us.

The following day, Tuesday June 16th, we departed Mexico City at midday. On its way to London, our plane would stop at Nassau for refuelling. It was noticeable the Secretary, Denis Follows, and not a single Football Association Council Member travelled home with us. We were told there were insufficient first class seats available, on our plane, to accommodate them. Travelling back home in economy class was perfectly acceptable for Alf, his staff and the players, but not apparently for The Football Association's Secretary and the Council Members. Their attitude was a disgrace. If ever they needed to be with the team, in their defeat, it was now, but they remained in Mexico. Later, I was told they travelled by first class air travel to Paris and thence to London.

15

With Hindsight Everything Is Easy ∙∙∙∙∙∙∙

The flight home from Mexico took fourteen hours. There was plenty of time to reflect. Alf sat next to me throughout the flight. During our time away, Alf had raised with me, on several occasions, the issue of my resignation. He made it quite plain he did not want me to leave. On one occasion, in the company of Harold Shepherdson, he said,

"You can't resign. If you weren't connected with the England team, you'd be a nobody!"

I had replied,

"Maybe that's what I now want to be!"

Throughout the fourteen hour homeward flight, the issue of my resignation, was never raised. Alf wanted to discuss the medical aspects of the World Cup competition. He enquired whether I had been entirely satisfied with the medical decisions I, and my team, had made during our preparations. As always, it was a frank, reasoned and open discussion. Inevitably there were some medical issues that overlapped into football matters. Where these two issues overlapped, he was always willing to discuss them with me.

My first concern, in my discussion with Alf, was obviously the illness of Gordon Banks. Alf could not deny, it was my responsibility to ensure every player was kept physically fit in Mexico. It was essential, I believed, that Alf had a full squad of players to choose from for every game. With Gordon's illness, resulting in his inability to play, I believed I had failed in my responsibility. Yet even with this case of gastro-enteritis, there were so many other factors for me to consider with hindsight. Medically, it could be argued, I should have used, as Roger Bannister had recommended, Streptotriad as the prophylactic drug against gastro-enteritis, instead of Thalazole. In my conversation with Alf, and even to this day, I still believe the non-absorbable Thalazole was the better drug of choice. All the research evidence available to me from America recommended Thalazole. It would of course had been better if no daily drug was indicated, but Thalazole seemed the best drug of choice at the time. Even using the non-absorbable Thalazole, I was always conscious of that man who died back in Sheffield while under my care. He developed necrotising jeju-ileitis after taking Thalazole for just a few days. To use such a powerful drug as Streptotriad, on a daily basis for eight weeks, I still considered unwise.

Should I have insisted, as the West Germans had done, to bring our own chef? A chef would certainly have been much more beneficial to the team than Sid, the bus driver, and the motor coach that would not perform at altitude.

Also, I should have discussed with the players, in the months before leaving England and obtained their agreement, that no after match parties or relaxing drinks would be held while we were in Mexico. During the competition, two parties were held. Following the Brazil game, the Manager at the Hilton had held a party. The wives were invited. The following morning, two players had hangovers and one of those players missed a valuable training session as a result. The second party, was the so-called 'relaxing drink' in Room 1208, after the game against Czechoslovakia. I was always aware the food disciplines, I imposed on the players, would be difficult for them to adhere to over an eight-week period. In the main however, the players had accepted them. 'In the main' however was, for me, unacceptable. The food discipline needed to be total. The possibility of contaminated food being given to the players, via 'Room Service', I had never contemplated. That was a major error on my part. Contaminated food was the only explanation I had to offer for the three players, in Room 1208, developing gastro-enteritis, the day following the 'relaxing drink' party. A sandwich, pieces of salad or unpeeled fruit, prepared by a Mexican, was, in my opinion, the most likely source of the infection. It was Alf himself who had re-emphasised to the players, the day following 'the relaxing drink', that Room Service was not allowed and then he banned it. I should have been aware of the possibility of this loophole being a possible source of infection. However, I had no definite proof Room Service was indeed the source of the infection. The evidence pointed to Room 1208, but I couldn't be absolutely certain. The conspiracy theory, with the involvement of the C.I.A., in 'getting at' Gordon Banks, I dismissed. Many subsequent reports, relating to Banks' illness, have suggested his illness was caused by this conspiracy. These theories are all based however on the assumption Gordon was the one and only England player to suffer with gastro-enteritis during our stay in Mexico. This assumption is of course untrue. Several players suffered with the disease during our stay. My personal view, as to the cause, centred around 'the relaxing drink' party that took place in Room 1208 of the Hilton Hotel, the evening after we had beaten Czechoslovakia. How else would the three players living in that room, develop gastro-enteritis within hours of each other. Only one other player, in the entire squad, succumbed to the infection at that time. In the Players' Handbook, under 'Tummy Upsets', I had written,

> "Diarrhoea is prevalent in Mexico. No meals are to be eaten, except those prepared and provided for the party. Never be tempted to buy or eat anything from a stall or shop while out from the hotel."

I should have added 'and do not use Room Service'.

I informed Alf, I considered it was a mistake to send me, as part of the advance party to Leon at four in the morning, to inspect the kitchens at the Motel Estancia., My departure resulted in my being absent when Gordon Banks awoke on the Saturday morning. He wanted to report on his illness to me early on that morning, but I wasn't there. If I had been present, I may have commenced treating him immediately. I was also absent on the coach journey to Leon, when Gordon's condition worsened. As it was, the first occasion I saw Gordon on that day was five hours later, when the team arrived by bus at Leon. Five hours treatment, which I considered critical, was lost. It now seemed tragically ironic that, in the Players' Handbook, I had written,

> "Any player, suffering from any unusual looseness of the bowels, must report to the Doctor at once. An infection, treated in the very early stages can often be cured simply and quickly, but to try to carry on, until the infection has become severe is simply to risk non participation in a game."

By sending me off to Leon at four in the morning, Banks was unable to report to the Doctor immediately. Sending me to inspect the kitchens at Leon was a mistake. My responsibility was always to be available to the players. I should have remained with them. My absence delayed the treatment of Gordon Banks for a critical five hours. Those five hours could have been vital in treating him and ensuring he was fit to play, but now I would never know. Alf thought I was being too critical of myself.

My absence from the Hilton Hotel, on the morning of Banks' illness, was another issue I raised. It would forever concern me. I would never know, not even with hindsight, whether, if I had been given the opportunity to treat Gordon five hours earlier, as I had done with his room mates Keith Newton and Bobby Charlton, he might have recovered in time to play. Keith and Bobby recovered sufficiently, with my treatment, in time to play against West Germany. Gordon did not. Ironically, Gordon Banks would have been fit to play the day after the West Germany game. The day after, however, was of no use at all. My discussion with Alf on Gordon's illness, even with hindsight, seemed full of ifs and buts. I repeated to Alf, that at the end of the day, it was my responsibility to ensure that every one of the players was fit, and available for selection, for every game. In that Gordon Banks was unfit to play against West Germany at Leon, the responsibility lay at my door. Alf argued that I couldn't accept total responsibility, as there were many other factors to consider.

The first issue Alf raised with me, on the flight home, was a football issue. It concerned his selection of Gordon Banks. Alf said that, when

WITH HINDSIGHT EVERYTHING IS EASY

he selected the England team, the first name he always wrote down was 'Gordon Banks'. Gordon was without question, he said, the world's best goalkeeper. As the world's best, it was natural he would be the first player Alf selected. It was obvious Alf wanted to talk at length on the subject and I allowed him to do so. I did not have access to the statistics on the plane, but the selection of Gordon Banks, under Alf's management, occupied our conversation for a considerable time. Subsequent study of the statistics proved very interesting to me.

Gordon made his England debut at Wembley, against Scotland, in April 1963. England lost the game 2–1. It was Alf's second game as England's Manager. Commencing with and including the game of his debut, seventy-eight internationals had been played by England, prior to the commencement of the 1970 World Cup. Gordon Banks was selected for fifty-nine of those games. In fact, Gordon had played in 75% of all England's internationals to that date. The only other goalkeepers to be selected for England, during this period, were Ron Springett who played four times, Tony Waiters who played on five occasions, Peter Bonetti who played six times, Gordon West on three occasions, and Alec Stepney who played once. Between the two World Cups of 1966 and 1970, thirty-five internationals were played. In these four years, excluding Banks, the only goalkeepers to win international caps were Bonetti, West and Stepney. In total these three goalkeepers only appeared on nine occasions between them. During the same period, Gordon Banks appeared on twenty-six occasions. Gordon was not only England's best goalkeeper, he was the best in the world.

"Banks"

Alf told me, he always considered

"was England's greatest strength."

On reflection, and with the advantage of hindsight, he said, England's greatest strength turned out, in Mexico, to be its weakness.

> "Over the years, I should have given the other goalkeepers more experience at senior level. More experience would have given them greater confidence. Greater confidence would have helped them."

The year before the 1970 World Cup, Alf's first choice, as deputy to Gordon Banks, was Gordon West of Everton. The two Gordons, Banks and West, were the goalkeepers selected for the 1969 tour of South America. West was then preferred to Peter Bonetti, Alec Stepney and the young Peter Shilton. Those three goalkeepers were left at home. Prior to that tour, Gordon West had only played in two internationals. He was an inexperienced international goalkeeper. Gordon West made his debut, as a full international, against Bulgaria in December1968. His second international appearance was against Wales, in the Home Internationals, at Wembley. His third, and last appearance, was in the Azteca Stadium against Mexico on the South American tour of 1969. The game was a 0–0 draw. It appeared then, that Gordon West was achieving his personal dream. Like all successful sportsmen, he had dedicated and committed himself to being the best in his profession. He was on the brink of achieving his ambition. He was England's deputy goalkeeper, second only to Gordon Banks—the world's greatest goalkeeper. In the Azteca Stadium, playing for England against Mexico, Gordon West performed well. Two days later, in Guadalajara, his international career was over. He decided to quit the tour after only one game. He informed Alf he wanted to return home. He did not wish to be considered for selection in any future internationals. His dream of being an outstanding England international ended.

When we left England, for the World Cup in Mexico, there were four goalkeepers in the party. Gordon Banks, had played on fifty-nine occasions, Peter Bonetti had played on five, Alex Stepney had played once and Peter Shilton was yet to make his debut. The world's best goalkeeper was an experienced international, the other three were not. After completing the four weeks acclimatization programme, Shilton was not selected in the final party. He returned home before the competition started. Between them, the two selected deputy goalkeepers, Bonetti and Stepney, had only played for England six times between themselves. Their international experience was severely limited. Their lack of experience at international level was unfair to them.

"Experience leads to confidence."

WITH HINDSIGHT EVERYTHING IS EASY

Alf repeated,

> "I should have given Peter and Alec, more opportunity at senior level but, when you have the world's best goalkeeper available for selection, it's very difficult not to select him."

I had every sympathy with Alf's dilemma.

Alf and I then had a lengthy discussion on the attitude of players at international level and how it might affect them. This discussion, in the main, resulted from some of the players stating Peter Bonetti's mind was not focussed enough on the job in hand at Leon. In our time, Sports Science and Sports Psychologists were only in their infancy and generally frowned upon. Playing, at the highest level, in any sport, affects players in many different ways. At its worst, the build up of pressure, before an important game, can affect some players alarmingly. I have witnessed players becoming so distressed, prior to a game, that on arrival in the dressing room, they have headed straight for the toilet. They sit on the toilet, seemingly forever, their insides being squeezed from their bodies in excruciating turmoil. The pressure of the big match causes them unbelievable nervous tension. Other players would merely feel minor degrees of tension and discomfort in the pit of their stomachs. These symptoms are minimal and usually relieved by a few deep breaths. In contrast, no amount of pressure seemed to affect some players. Bobby Moore, the England Captain, was the best example of this. Before, during and after all the matches in which he played, and I was associated with, he always appeared calm and serene. The pressures never appeared to affect Bobby. In fact, the greater the pressure, the more composed and serene he became. Whatever the pressures, Bobby always had them under his complete control. He had a marvellous temperament. Complete control under pressure was one of Bobby Moore's great assets. The fortunate ones, like Bobby Moore, give the appearance of absolute tranquillity. They have the ideal temperament. For them, the pressure and nervous tension, experienced by others, is always under their complete control. They are always able to keep the pressure under control. Bobby's attitude to any game was superb.

I mentioned to Alf one of the most talented young footballers I ever knew. He was a junior player at Middlesbrough. He joined Middlesbrough as a schoolboy. I had watched his development closely over several years. Managers, coaches and fellow players raved about his talent. In training and reserve matches his skills were unbelievable. He was quick, read the game well and was extremely fit. Everyone was convinced he was a future star. Alas, he never made stardom. When selected to play in the Middlesbrough first team, his game just fell apart. The roar of thirty thousand spectators tore at his personality. The pressure was too great for him. He was unable to control the pressure. His temperament collapsed. He became a shadow of his former self. I discussed the problem with the player on many occasions. I recall him telling me,

> "You see Doc, it's running out into that tunnel. When I hear the crowd roar, I get pains in the pit of my stomach. My legs turn to jelly. I feel really ill. I just cannot concentrate. I cannot perform"

That Middlesbrough junior did not become the star we all believed he would be. He possessed a great talent for football, but his temperament was unable to cope with the pressure.

The airhostess served lunch. Over lunch, I explained to Alf my own personal experience of playing in sport. My own experience was all I could draw upon. I digressed for a purpose. To achieve any of my dreams in life, it was always necessary for me to be totally committed. From an early age, my Dad had instilled into me, the fact that girls, drinking alcohol, smoking cigarettes and my attending parties, were all diversions and distractions that would prevent me achieving my dreams. Consequently, I always avoided them. There was no purpose to those distractions. Participating in any of those distractions, my Dad repeatedly told me, would always bring into question my dedication and commitment to realising my dreams. As a boy in South Wales, most of my school friends dreamed of playing rugby for Wales. None of them played for Wales. Undoubtedly, one or two had the talent, but they lacked the desire, determination and commitment. They were diverted, from achieving their dream, by evenings spent in the company of their girl friends. They smoked cigarettes, consumed large quantities of alcohol and were reluctant to train sufficiently to achieve the high level of physical fitness required of professional sportsmen. My school friends were not prepared to work hard or make the necessary sacrifices to achieve their dream. The sacrifices demanded of them were too great; the distractions too inviting. As a boy, my dream was to be a professional cricketer. At a very early age, I determined my desire and commitment would be total. I really, really, wanted to be a cricketer. That was my dream. Nothing, and no one, was allowed to deflect me from achieving it. My commitment and desire would never be questioned. I realised however my dream would never become a reality without years of hard work. The talent I possessed for cricket, limited as it was, even when accompanied by my total desire and commitment, was insufficient. In addition, I needed high levels of self-discipline to stick to the task. I strongly believed, that if my dream was to become a reality, there would always need to be a daily commitment to hard work. The process involved reading all I could about cricket. I practised each and every day, indoors and out, winter and summer, for as many hours as I was able. My dedication was total. Nothing else in my life mattered. Girls, alcohol, smoking and, sadly, my academic study at school, would, at no time, deflect me from the process of achieving my cricketing dream. Every day I trained hard to obtain a high level of physical fitness. I wanted to achieve my dream more than anything else. In my youth, cricket was all that mattered. Now that my youth has passed, and my days of playing cricket are finished, I regret none of the endless hours I spent working to achieve the dream of my youth. I believed, if I was to reach the very top in that sphere of my life, a total desire, commitment, dedication and hard work was absolutely essential. These were my beliefs throughout my school and the early part of my university life. They have remained with me throughout my life.

The closest I came to achieving my cricket dream was playing for the Glamorgan County Cricket Club's second eleven. I recalled, to Alf, the first time I played for them, as if it was yesterday. The match was at Maesteg. Alf had never heard of Maesteg. It was my big day. All the years of dedication, self-discipline, practice, sacrifice and endeavour, I had committed to, were now about to bear fruit. My dream was close to becoming a reality. I believed all the years of hard work would enable me to compete with anyone. On that day at Maesteg however, another factor entered my cricket preparation. I needed to be mentally prepared to perform at my very best, on that particular day. The excitement of playing for the County Second Eleven, and the pressure I inwardly felt was considerable. It was essential the excitement and pressure, I experienced, were completely under my control. As I sat in the dressing room, I reflected that this situation was what all my hard work and dedication had been for. The excitement, nervousness and pressure, I then experienced, needed to be under my complete control. The pressures must not ruin my performance. My Dad had taught me, over the years, about always being in control under pressure.

"To be in control, you'll need to give up control."
he repeatedly told me.
For years, I didn't really fully understand what he meant.
"Focus only on the job in hand."
he would say.
"Never get excited. Think only of the task lying before you.
Concentrate only on that. Allow nothing to distract you."
In the Maesteg dressing room, I sat next to Phil Clift, the Glamorgan opening batsman, whom I had admired throughout my youth. Phil was now the Coach and our Captain for the day. On the other side of the dressing room was Norman Hever. Norman had played for the Middlesex and Glamorgan first teams. He had played in an England trial, as a fast bowler. Sitting next to Norman was the young Peter Walker, the South African, who would later play cricket for England. In the midst was yours truly. I was excited, but my excitement was contained. I was ready to perform. Having gone through the process of hard work, over many years, it was now absolutely essential for me to put in a good performance on this particular day. Performance on the day was everything. I needed to be at my best on this particular day. Performing well tomorrow or next week would be no use to me. This particular cricket match could be my only chance to achieve my dream. I was looking forward to the challenge with confidence. Despite

the pressures and my inevitable nervousness, I was in complete control. I felt serene and ready for the task. Performing well, on that day in Maesteg, was all-important.

I played well at Maesteg. I was 'up for it'. Professional sportsmen often refer to their periods of peak performance as being 'in the zone'. Certainly that was my situation at Maesteg. I was relaxed; focused; 'in the groove'; concentrated, or any other term athletes use when they perform well. I had lost myself in the task of wicket keeping. I played well enough to be congratulated, after the game, by Phil Clift and Norman Hever. I would certainly be picked to play again. My dream was still on track. My mental approach and attitude on the day had enabled all those years of training, commitment, dedication and single mindedness to come to fruition. It was at Maesteg, I convinced myself I had the mental toughness to perform well at cricket when under pressure. People will argue the pressures of playing cricket at Maesteg were not great, but the game was a make or break game for me. Similarly, when I worked as a House Surgeon and Senior House Officer in the Operating Theatre, the pressure at times was unbelievable. People's lives were in my hands. One slip or mistake by myself could have resulted in devastating consequences for the patient. In all my operating sessions in the theatre, I always felt confident and focused. The pressures, from any situation that developed there, were always under my complete control. My senior surgical colleagues frequently told me I had a wonderful temperament; one that thrived when working under pressure. I was always aware a proper mental attitude was essential to perform well in any occupation. It was particularly important when one performed under pressure.

Over coffee I informed Alf I found it almost impossible to diagnose whether the attitude of a particular player was satisfactory before play commenced. I posed the question to Alf,

> "How does one diagnose, prior to a game, that a player is not one hundred per cent in the zone: up for it; or in the correct frame of mind to play.

It was a problem I found impossible to solve. I was not a qualified Sports Psychologist, in fact that profession hardly existed in England at the time.

I was confident at diagnosing players' physical fitness, but to diagnose their mental approach to a game I found impossible. Athletes realised themselves an exceptional performance only occurred when they were completely at ease, physically and mentally. Playing in such circumstances enables the athlete to become relaxed, and focused. Concentration is then at its highest level. Unfortunately, unlike a physical injury, I informed Alf, I was unaware of any scientific way, I possessed, to determine whether the athlete was or was not mentally at his best before competing. There are occasions when it is an easy matter to diagnose the fact that a player is not in the right frame of mind to perform. For example, in the extreme circumstance, as may occur with the sudden death of a close relative, an athlete, manager or doctor can say, with confidence, the athlete is not mentally attuned to compete. Nevertheless it remains, to a very large extent, an assessment by the athlete himself. Immediately before competing, any athlete may be perfectly satisfied he is fully prepared for the task before him. He believes his physical and mental states are in perfect shape for the forthcoming event. Often, he then finds it is not. His performance is poor. I fully realised a good mental attitude was as important as full physical fitness in order to produce a top athletic performance, but the problem I had was how, on an individual basis, do I assess the athlete's mental state accurately and scientifically beforehand? Sadly I knew of no way I could delve into a player's mind and satisfy myself his mental attitude was perfect. I could give an opinion when it wasn't perfect, but not if it was.

I then raised, with Alf, the problems created by the arrival in Mexico of the four players' wives. In my opinion, it certainly affected the unity within the squad and affected players to varying degrees. At the staff meeting, before the Holland game in January 1970, each one of the four staff should have prevented the four players bringing their wives to Mexico. At that meeting, it was left to Les Cocker to express his total opposition to their presence. On reflection, Harold and I gave Les only token support. On reflection I personally felt I too should have been much firmer in my attitude. Although, at the meeting, I expressed the view the appearance of the four wives in Mexico would be a distraction from our main task, I bitterly regretted not being more forceful in stating my opposition to the proposal. In my opinion we should not have allowed it to happen. Their arrival in Mexico had a disruptive effect on the squad of players. The four wives should not have been allowed to travel to Mexico. The decision should have been made that no wives would travel, or alternatively, everyone's wife would travel. The staff should not have allowed the situation to develop.

My discussion with Alf occupied most of the flight. We arrived safely at London. As usual Alf shook everyone's hand before they left for their homes. It was his personal way of thanking everyone for their individual contributions. Harold and I caught a flight to Teesside Airport. I had left Mexico forever. I arrived back home in Redcar on Wednesday June 17th. I had been away from home for forty-four days. I was back at work in the Practice the very next day.

Middlesbrough Football Club, in June 1970, was a bleak place. Everyone was on holiday. Inevitably, when I say everyone, I mean of course the Manager, Coaches, Trainer and the players. They were my kind of people. I was always content in their company. I wanted to discuss the World Cup with them, but they were enjoying themselves in sunny climes. My relationship with my fellow directors was, in comparison, poor. In meeting some of them, I gained the impression some of them were even pleased England had lost the World Cup in Mexico. I had been at home for some two weeks, when I received a telephone call from George Winney, a fellow director. George suggested we meet at the Billingham Arms for lunch. George was one of the few directors, for whom I had a high regard, so I readily accepted his invitation. George simply wanted my report on the World Cup. Over lunch, I explained everything that had taken place. George was intrigued. I ended my report to George by informing him I now intended to resign as the England Team Doctor. George was astonished. Two hours after lunch had finished, George was still trying to convince me I should stay. He appreciated how much time I had spent over the previous two years on the medical preparations for the Mexican World Cup and accepted the work involved had taken over my life.

"You must realise this situation will never recur."

he said,

> "No other World Cup will present the problems you have had to deal with. The next World Cup will be in Europe. No future England doctor will have to overcome the immense problems of altitude, heat, acclimatisation, food, boredom, and hospitals. In comparison your role in the future will be relatively simple. You will always provide excellent medical care for the players. Don't throw everything you have achieved away. It would be a disaster, not only for you, but also for Alf Ramsey and the England players."

Maybe George was correct, but I remained unsure. I was enjoying spending time with Margaret and our three children. Throughout the summer months, Margaret and I discussed the implications of me continuing in the England role. We reached no definite conclusion. As Stan Anderson and the Middlesbrough players returned for pre-season training, I again became involved in the dressing room atmosphere. The company of the players was what I enjoyed most of all. More and more, the thought of giving up, even a part of that pleasure, with the England team, seemed improbable. At various times in the pre season period, I discussed my dilemma with my good friend, Harold Shepherdson. He was of the same opinion as George Winney. Harold thought I should stay with England. As I reported the outcome of the World Cup to the individual members of my medical team, I also discussed with them my future role with the England team. Without exception they all advised me to stay. I suppose my mind was finally made up when I received a letter from Sir Alf. In that letter he wrote,

> "It was a pleasure working with you and no one could have done better or more than you did. It was not only a pleasure, but an honour to be associated with you."

I replied, informing him I would continue in my post, provided he was happy with my decision. I received a prompt reply.

> "Needless to say, I am very pleased indeed that you have decided to continue as the England Team Doctor, at least for the next four years, and feel sure that we will continue to

enjoy our association as we have done in the past."

The first match, at international level, in the 1970–1971 season was at Norwich on the 23rd. September. The Football League played the Irish League. The Irish League were defeated by five goals to nil. Jeff Astle scored two goals, while Peters, Brown and Hector scored one goal each. Following lunch, on the day of the game, the players retired to their rooms for several hours of rest. Alf suggested he and I leave Harold Shepherdson in charge, while we went for a walk. We were staying at Great Yarmouth. There, Alf and I walked the promenade for a couple of hours. He went over the events of Mexico again. You will recall, he said, in the immediate aftermath of the defeat against West Germany, in Leon, people criticised me saying,

> "I should have played Stepney. If I had played Stepney, there would have been no guarantee the result would have been any different. Alec Stepney had only played one international. Like Peter Bonetti, only more so, he was inexperienced at international level."

The goalkeepers, and particularly Alf's esteem for Gordon Banks, occupied most of our conversation. It was interesting to note, that for the game at Norwich, Peter Shilton had been chosen as the goalkeeper.

I was also subjected to a boosting of confidence by Alf. He knew I was bitterly disappointed when Gordon Banks was unfit to play against West Germany. You mustn't, in any way, blame yourself. No one could have done more for the players than yourself. Gordon's attack of gastro-enteritis, while most unfortunate, was not your fault. The medical service you and your self appointed team provided was magnificent. With a smile on his face, he said,

> "I'm sure it was better than the Romanians."

It was a long drive back home from Norwich to Redcar after the game. I had Shep for company, but in no time he was fast asleep. It was three in the morning, when I tumbled into bed. I was back on the roundabout I had said previously I couldn't get off. I fell asleep, consoled by Alf's words,.

> "I'm sure it was better than the Romanians"

16

The Lull Before The Storm.........

With no England Internationals scheduled in the early part of the 1970–71 season, it was an opportunity for me to further improve the medical services for the Middlesbrough players.

With the co-operation of Dr. Jenkin Evans, the senior medical officer at I.C.I. Wilton, more detailed medical tests were introduced for all the players. Previously, the players' blood tests had been carried out at Middlesbrough General Hospital, but these tests were now transferred to I.C.I. Wilton. The medical facilities at I.C.I. Wilton were made available to every player at the Club. It was there I commenced functional respiratory investigations and routine electrocardiogram examinations on the entire staff. Routine clinical examinations, I continued to carry out personally at the Club's medical centre. The reader may be surprised to learn that in 1970, routine medical examinations of football players were not carried out at many Clubs. Players were transferred, in those days, for quite large sums of money, without a medical examination ever taking place. Sports Medicine, as a speciality of medicine, still did not exist in England. Even medical record keeping by football clubs, of their players' injuries, was virtually non-existent. I did try to persuade The Football League, by writing to Alan Hardaker the Secretary, to introduce routine medical examinations prior to the transfer of a player, but my suggestion was turned down. The Professional Football Association were also surprisingly against any such proposal.

Following the World Cup in Mexico, I was invited to become a director of The Institute of Sports Medicine in London. I found it a peculiar organisation. Apart from holding regular meetings of the directors, it appeared to have no actual function. The Institute's Secretary was Peter Sebastian. He and I had little in common. One of my fellow directors at the Institute was Frank d'Abrue, a consultant surgeon from the Westminster Hospital. Frank was a medical adviser to The Jockey Club. We both had similar ideas on the broader aspects of Sports Medicine. We realised there was a need for the medical profession in England to embrace Sports Medicine, as a recognised speciality. We jointly suggested that a Diploma in Sports Medicine be introduced, recognised by the profession's various Royal Colleges, so that a medically accepted standard for the speciality be recognised in England. I took our idea to Lilleshall, where I had arranged a conference of Football League Medical Officers. They too were enthusiastic and would welcome recognition of the speciality by their peers. Many, at the Lilleshall conference, were keen to sit an examination for a Diploma in Sports Medicine. With my enthusiasm and Frank d'Abrue's professional contacts at The Royal Colleges of Surgery and Medicine, our suggestion quickly gained the support of the hierarchy in our profession. After three years of negotiation by Frank, the Royal Colleges agreed to introduce a one-year full time course for qualified doctors in Sports Medicine. An examination, for the Diploma in Sports Medicine, would be held at the end of the course. It was my one and only successful achievement during my time at the Institute of Sports Medicine, and most of the successful negotiating, with the Royal Colleges, was due entirely to Frank d'Abrue.

It was five months since England had been defeated, at Leon, by West Germany, when we all gathered in London at The Hendon Hall Hotel in London. It was three days before a home game against East Germany. There were many notable absentees amongst the players. Bobby Charlton, who had always been a permanent fixture in the England team had retired from international duty. Allan Clarke replaced him. Since returning from Mexico, Brian Labone, England's centre-half had lost his place in the Everton team. David Sadler, of Manchester United replaced Brian in the England squad. Peter Shilton, at the age of twenty, made his debut in goal.

There was no Gordon Banks, the world's greatest goalkeeper. The England team, Alf selected for the game, was, Shilton, Hughes, Cooper, Mullery, Sadler, Moore, Lee, Ball, Hurst, Clarke and Peters. In front of 93,000 spectators, England were enthusiastically cheered to a three goals to one win. Clarke, Mullery and Lee scored the goals. England's next fixture, in February 1971, would be the first game in the qualifying round of the European Championship.

England had been drawn, in the preliminary qualifying group for the European Championship, with Greece, Malta and Switzerland. Each team would be played on an home and away basis. No group is ever easy to win, but everyone expected England to win this group easily. It was early February when England beat Malta in Valetta by one goal to nil. Martin Peters scored the goal. The pitch had no grass on the playing surface. It was made of clay and, in places, was covered with sand. On the morning of the game, the groundsman had a full sized steam-roller going up and down the pitch endeavouring to make the surface flat! The international against Malta, again emphasised the difficulties under which Alf and the England players worked. A full League programme of fixtures took place on the Saturday, four days prior to the international. Of the players Alf originally chose, Ball, Clarke, Cooper, Labone and Lee all sustained injuries playing for their Clubs on the previous Saturday. As a consequence four players, Martin Chivers, Colin Harvey, Roy MacFarland, and Joe Royle, made their international debut. England struggled to win against Malta by the one goal to nil margin.

Back at Middlesbrough, expectations were high at the beginning of the season, as the team strove to gain promotion to the First Division. The team had finished fourth in each of the two previous seasons. As usual however, the team flattered to deceive. At the end of March, the team was close to the promotion target, but then failed to win a single game in the season's last eight fixtures. Middlesbrough finished seventh in the League. The positions of the team, in the Second Division, over the three previous seasons, had been fourth, fourth, and now seventh. It appeared the team was going backwards. Stan Anderson, in his fifth season as Manager was

THE LULL BEFORE THE STORM

bitterly disappointed. There was unrest amongst the directors. Most of their unrest was directed at the Chairman, Eric Thomas. In an effort to strengthen his coaching staff, Stan Anderson brought in, as the first team coach, Ian MacFarlane. Ian had previously been Manager of Carlisle United. The team would try again for promotion in the 1971–1972 season.

In April, England easily defeated Greece at Wembley by three goals to nil, and followed this up with a five goals to nil win, in the home fixture, against Malta. Qualification for the European Championship was going well. The season ended with the Home International Championship games. Allan Clarke scored the only goal in the away defeat of Northern Ireland. This was followed by a disappointing result against Wales, at Wembley, when no goals were scored by either side. England however recovered their form against Scotland, at Hampden Park and ran out easy winners by three goals to one. Martin Chivers scored two goals and Martin Peters one. There was no summer tour for England. I had the luxury of spending a normal two-week holiday in Cornwall with Margaret and the three children. It was great!

During the international season, England had involved me in all seven internationals. Alf's selection of goalkeepers during this time was interesting. Gordon Banks had been selected for five games and Peter Shilton for two. My medical role however was now substantially diminished. There were no problems to encounter relating to altitude or heat. The three qualifying matches for the European Championship had all occurred in the early part of the year, so the heat factor was totally absent. The food, in European countries, was not a problem. The standard of hygiene, wherever we played, was good. Boredom was not a problem, as the team was only together for three days, prior to each game. My role was mainly concerned with treating injuries and there were few of those during the year. It was essential I got to know the new players and they got to know me.

When I was first invited to join Alf's staff, he expressed concern with my dual role as a Middlesbrough director and the England Team Doctor. He would have preferred me to just be solely a medical officer at Middlesbrough and not a director. Alan Bass was Arsenal's medical officer, but not one of Arsenal's directors. Alf believed, with my position as a Middlesbrough director, there would be a conflict of interests. His view quickly disappeared however when Alan Bass approached George Cohen, the England right back, who was a Fulham player. Alan conveyed to George the fact that Arsenal would be very interested in signing him and Alan could act as a go-between. It was a request George declined. When Alf learnt of Alan Bass's intervention he was not pleased. As I pointed out at the time, it was not the fact that I was a director that should concern Alf, but whether my integrity would always be secure. It was a situation I jealously guarded. I was completely surprised therefore when Stan Anderson reported to the Middlesbrough directors he had purchased Nobby Stiles on a free transfer from Manchester United. I had no previous knowledge of the move, but was delighted Nobby was joining us. Middlesbrough supporters will argue that Nobby made little contribution to the team during his time at Middlesbrough, but that is not true. For the 1971–72 season, in addition to Nobby, Stan Anderson brought to the Club Stuart Boam, a tall centre-half from Mansfield, and John Craggs, an Under 23 international right back from Newcastle. With the Northern Ireland international, Jim Platt, taking over the goalkeeper role from Willie Whigham, the team had a totally different look to the previous season. In addition, four local junior players, David Armstrong, Joe Laidlaw, Willie Maddren, and David Mills would establish themselves as regulars in the team during the season. The away form of the team, during Stan Anderson's sixth season as Manager, was however abysmal. Only ten points were gained in matches played away from home during the entire season! The team finished in a disappointing ninth position. Middlesbrough had last played in the First Division in the 1953–54 season, almost twenty years previously. There seemed little prospect of an early return. As Nobby Stiles was coming to the end of his career, too much was expected of him as a player. His influence in the dressing room was however immense. The knowledge he imparted, particularly to John Craggs, Willie Maddren and Stuart Boam stood those players in good stead for many future seasons. The Middlesbrough public failed to appreciate Nobby's influence on the other players. He was judged purely on his on field performances.

The frustration of the directors, at Board level, resulted in a change of Chairman and Vice-Chairman. The two Thomas brothers, Eric and Harold, had held the positions of Chairman and Vice-Chairman respectively for some ten years. They had enjoyed no success at the Club. Their aim had always been to return the Club to the First Division, and they had failed to achieve their goal. In a relatively bloodless coup, Harold resigned, as a director, and Eric resigned as Chairman, but remained on the Board. George Winney was appointed Chairman and George Kitching, the Vice-Chairman. Every director was aware George Winney and Stan Anderson had a good, long standing relationship and it was hoped this relationship would be of benefit to the Club.

Three England internationals took place during the last three months of 1971. All three matches were qualifying games for the European Championship. The first game was played against Switzerland in Basle on 13th. October. England won the international by three goals to two. Having beaten Switzerland away, a victory against them at Wembley was expected. However, the difficulties of proper preparation for the England team surfaced once again. A replay, in the fourth round of the League Cup Competition was arranged between Tottenham and Stoke City for the Monday evening, two days before the home international against Switzerland. When he learnt of this, Alf was furious.

"I do not think it is appropriate,"
he said
"for any player to play four matches in eight days especially when the last one is an important international match."

As usual, his outburst fell on deaf ears. The fourth round replay went ahead. The three England players selected in the squad, for the game against Switzerland and involved in the fourth round replay, were Martin Peters and Martin Chivers of Tottenham and Gordon Banks of Stoke City. These three players played on the Monday evening and joined the England squad on the Tuesday; the day before the international. Having spoken with the three players, Alf decided to leave all three out of the team. Peter

Shilton replaced Gordon Banks in goal, Emlyn Hughes replaced Martin Peters, and Mike Summerbee replaced Martin Chivers. It was obvious to everyone, the England team, of that time, received little co-operation from the Football League. Conflict existed between The Football Association and The Football League. The relevant Secretaries, Alan Hardaker of The Football League and Denis Follows of The Football Association, were known not to get on with each other. As a result, Sir Alf and the England team suffered. The international was a poor game. England drew one goal each with Switzerland. Mike Summerbee scored England's goal and Odermatt equalised for Switzerland. England now shared first place in the qualifying table with Switzerland, who had completed all their qualifying games. England had yet to play Greece in Athens. England had a superior goal difference to Switzerland. Ramsey knew England could afford to lose to Greece in Athens by three goals and still qualify. In the event, when England played Greece in Athens in December 1971, England was the comfortable winner by two goals to nil. Martin Chivers and Geoff Hurst scored for England. England qualified for the quarter-finals of the competition as Group leaders.

It had been agreed, by U.E.F.A., that if England reached the last four of the European Championships, the latter stages of the competition would be played in England. The administrators, both at The Football League and The Football Association were keen for this to happen. When the draw was made in January 1972 however, England's quarter-final opponents were the old enemy, West Germany. The quarter-final was to be played on a home and away basis in April and May. The first game would be at Wembley; the away game would be played at Berlin in May. For those players, who had played for England in the defeat at Leon, it was a wonderful opportunity to seek revenge for that World Cup defeat. At least in these forthcoming two matches against West Germany, there would be no problems with the searing heat of Mexico or the Mexican food. Alf was delighted with the draw. Both he and Helmut Schoen, the German Manager, considered their individual teams to be one of the top teams in the World. They both eagerly awaited the contest at Wembley. The football administrators in

THE LULL BEFORE THE STORM

England were so enthusiastic to stage the final games of the European Championship in England that they cancelled all the relevant league fixtures, on the Saturday, prior to the international against West Germany. Alf was given the unusual privilege of having the England players together for a whole week before the game. However, Alf was more than a little concerned at the absence of his selected centre-half, Roy McFarland. Roy was withdrawn by his Manager, Brian Clough, who reported Roy was injured. There was no suitable centre-half replacement. Alf decided to play Bobby Moore as England's centre-half. McFarland's absence made the defence vulnerable. The England team contained only five players, Alan Ball, Geoff Hurst, Francis Lee, Bobby Moore, and Martin Peters, who had started the game against West Germany at Leon. Norman Hunter and Colin Bell were selected to play and these two had come on as substitutes in Leon. The four players selected, who did not play at Leon were Gordon Banks, Paul Madeley, Emlyn Hughes, and Martin Chivers. On the night, for unusually the game was played on a Saturday evening, England was totally outplayed. Hoeness scored Germany's first goal with a twenty yard shot, which was deflected off Norman Hunter wide of Gordon Banks. Francis Lee scrambled an equaliser, but then Germany sealed the game with a late penalty by Netzer and a goal from Muller. England had lost the home leg, by three goals to one. The task facing England, in the return fixture, seemed impossible. During the game Geoff Hurst was substituted with Rodney Marsh. Alf was furious, when the absent, injured, Roy McFarland played for Derby County two days later.

There is no doubt, in my mind, Alf approached the return fixture, played on May 13th. 1972 in a dull overcast Berlin, in defensive mode. He was determined England would not be beaten again by West Germany. The formation of 4–3–3, played at Wembley, was replaced by his more traditional 4–4–2 formation. Two strong defensive wing halves, Norman Hunter and Peter Storey played, and Roy McFarland played at centre-half with Bobby Moore alongside. Peter Storey was given the role of snuffing out the German playmaker Netzer, a role he admirably performed. With McFarland playing, the England defence was superb. If the defence had played as soundly in the home fixture, it is doubtful if Germany would have scored three goals. Defensive football however was unlikely to make England winners by the two goals they needed for a replay, or the three goal win, they needed for an outright win over the two legs. In the event, the match ended in a nil-nil draw. England was out of the European Championships. The final stages of the competition would not be held in England. In the after match discussions, with The Football Association Council Members, it appeared to me, they were more disappointed that England would not be hosting the final stages of the competition than they were at England's exit from the competition.

On the charter flight home, I sat next to Martin Peters. Martin mentioned to me a young player at Tottenham who was desperate for a transfer. Martin spoke very highly of this player, who originated from Edinburgh and wanted to live nearer to Scotland. Strong in the tackle, Martin thought he could be a great asset to Middlesbrough and suggested I mention the player to Stan Anderson, the Middlesbrough Manager. The player's name was Graeme Souness. Martin thought he could be available for about £25,000. When I returned to Middlesbrough, I discussed Souness with Stan Anderson. He was genuinely interested in purchasing the player. Stan would watch Souness play in the Tottenham reserves. Souness was transferred to Middlesbrough in December 1972 for £30,000. His purchase was probably the best transfer Middlesbrough ever made. At long last, after ten years, I had, if inadvertently, used my position of England Team Doctor for the benefit of Middlesbrough Football Club. Souness proved to be a great player for Middlesbrough and was, with other players, responsible for bringing eventual success to the Club. Stan Anderson had also brought to Middlesbrough Alan Foggon, an ex Newcastle United forward, then playing for Cardiff.

During the trip to Germany, some of the players approached Alf regarding the proposed summer tour to, amongst other countries, Turkey and Yugoslavia. Many players expressed the feeling they had played too much football during the season and were physically exhausted. Alf agreed with their request. Three days after the drawn game in Berlin, it was announced

THE LULL BEFORE THE STORM

by The Football Association, the summer tour had been cancelled. I could spend another summer holiday with Margaret and our three children.

The defeat, in the quarter-final of the European championship against West Germany, hurt everyone in the England camp. None more so than Alf Ramsey himself. There was little time to reflect, however, on the defeat, as the Home International games commenced seven days after the goalless draw in Berlin. The first game, in the Home Internationals, was against Wales in Cardiff. England comfortably won the game by three goals to nil. Emlyn Hughes, Colin Bell and Rodney Marsh scored the goals. Three days later, at Wembley, the England team performed poorly against Northern Ireland and lost by one goal to nil. The goalscorer, for Northern Ireland, was Terry Neill, then playing for Hull City. The crunch match was the away game against Scotland. Both England and Scotland could win the coveted Home International Tournament. Hampden Park was packed with 119,325 spectators. It is difficult to convey, to the non-footballing person, the hostility an England Scotland game generates, particularly when the game is in Scotland. In the nineteen seventies, many Scottish footballers played their football in England throughout the season; many Scottish internationals shared the same dressing room, week in and week out, with their England counterparts. Yet, in the weeks before an England Scotland game, tensions always mounted between players in the dressing rooms throughout England. In nineteen seventy-two, I worked, on a daily basis, with Jimmy Headrige, the first team trainer at Middlesbrough. We were great friends and had a very high regard for each other. Jimmy was a dyed in the wool Scot. He asked me to obtain two tickets for him for the international at Hampden. I was delighted to oblige. For weeks before, every day at Middlesbrough, Jimmy had riled me about the 'battle of Hampden'. I had arranged to give Jimmy the tickets at Hampden, on the day of the game. About an hour before the game was due to commence, I ventured outside onto the steps of Hampden Park, to be confronted by an enormous crowd of spectators cordoned off by the police. From my elevated position on the steps, I easily picked out Jimmy from the crowd. I beckoned Jimmy to come forward, to receive his tickets. Jimmy did not move. He beckoned for me to join him in the crowd. I beckoned him to come forward. Jimmy refused to move. As I was conscious of my responsibilities in the dressing room, I descended the steps, met Jimmy and gave him the two tickets.

"I didn't come forward,"

he said,

> "because I didn't want any of my Scottish friends to see me associating with anyone from England, on such a day as this!"

and Jimmy was my best friend! England won a tense game, by the only goal of the game, scored by Alan Ball. Both Scotland and England finished the tournament with four points each, but as England had a better goal difference, four-one, against three-one, England won the Home International Championship. It was scant comfort for missing out on the European Championship.

With England's failure to qualify for the finals of the European Championship and Middlesbrough finishing a disappointing ninth in the Second Division, the 1971–72 season was very disappointing for me, as disappointing as England's exit from the World Cup in Mexico in nineteen seventy.

England's task was now to qualify for the nineteen-seventy-four World Cup, to be held in Germany. It was the first occasion England had been asked to qualify since nineteen-sixty-two, when the competition was held in Chile. As hosts in nineteen sixty-six and the World Champions in nineteen- seventy, England had been excused qualification for both of those World Cups. When the draw was made, England was placed in a group with Poland and Wales. As England's summer tour, in nineteen-seventy-two, had been cancelled, there was only one scheduled international, before the qualifying games commenced. England would play Yugoslavia at Wembley in a friendly international in October. With the summer tour cancelled, I enjoyed the summer with Margaret and our three children.

Adopting his policy of playing other goalkeepers, besides Gordon Banks, Alf selected Peter Shilton to play in goal against Yugoslavia. The England side had a fresh look. Mills and Lampard were the full backs, Jeff Blockley

THE LULL BEFORE THE STORM

of Coventry was at centre-half. Joe Royle and Mick Channon played up front with Rodney Marsh. The game was an entertaining spectacle, but again England did not win. The match ended in a one all draw. Joe Royle scored England's goal.

A great tragedy befell England later in the month. Gordon Banks, undoubtedly the world's best goalkeeper, was involved in a car crash. His right eye was severely damaged. His sight was impaired. Gordon would not play football at international level ever again. He had represented England on seventy-three occasions. Not only was he the world's best goalkeeper, England would never have a goalkeeper to equal him in my lifetime. If Gordon's accident was a severe blow to England, worse was to follow. In the week before the important qualifying game against Wales at Cardiff, Peter Shilton was injured. Alf already knew Peter Bonetti was unfit. Ray Clemence, of Liverpool, made his debut in goal for England in the important game at Cardiff. Kevin Keegan, also of Liverpool, made his international debut. England's team was Clemence, Storey, Hughes, Hunter, McFarland, Moore, Ball, Keegan, Bell Chivers, and Marsh. Before the game, Dr. Andrew Stephens, the Chairman of The Football Association, presented Sir Alf with a silver salver to mark his one hundredth game as the England Manager. England won the game by a single goal scored by Colin Bell. Both Clemence and Keegan played well on their debuts, in what was otherwise an unimpressive win. A win is a win however and England was off to a good start in their qualifying group

An incident occurred at Cardiff, which hurt me greatly. Alf and I, as usual, had seats in the director's box. As we entered the box, the players were already out on the field. Everyone was seated in the director's box and our two seats were clearly visible as the only two empty seats remaining. Alf immediately noticed Brian Clough was sitting next to our two empty seats accompanied by Don Revie. Brian and Don were working as the pundits for television. As we walked up the gangway to our seats Alf said to me,

"You go in first Doctor, I do not wish to sit next to Brian Clough."
I did as my Manager asked. I shook hands with both Brian, whom I had known as a player at Middlesbrough, and Don, who had become a good

friend of mine over the years I had been involved in football. Suddenly Clough thumped me hard in the ribs with his left elbow.

"Why don't you go and sit down on the bench where you f****** belong. I want to sit next to Sir Alf."
said Brian Clough.
When I picked myself off the floor, my reply was curt.

"Brian, I've been in this game long enough to know I always do what my Manager requests."

I sat through the game with Clough on my right and Sir Alf on my left. Brian Clough and Don Revie left well before the end of the game to travel back to the television studios in London.

It is a cliché, held in football, that, in European and World Cup qualifying games, it is absolutely essential to win all your home games. Having beaten Wales in Cardiff, the return fixture at Wembley in January 1973, was assumed to be a comfortable home win for England. The game turned out to be completely different to everyone's assumptions. Alf selected the same side that played against Wales at Cardiff. Disaster struck England in the first half, when John Toshack beat his fellow Liverpool goalkeeper, Ray Clemence, to give Wales a one-goal lead. England drew level just before half-time, when Norman Hunter, of Leeds, beat the Leeds United goalkeeper, Gary Sprake, with a fierce shot from just outside the penalty area. It appeared there was no love lost with players from the same Club when playing against each other in internationals! At international matches, every professional is solely concerned with playing well for his own team! The match ended in a draw. England had made the fatal mistake of not winning all their home games in a qualifying competition. Needless to say, the England Manager was crucified in the press and media following the draw at Wembley. Our next international was at Hampden Park against Scotland, a game played to celebrate the centenary of The Scottish Football Association. The game would also see Bobby Moore make his one hundredth appearance as an England international. When we arrived in Scotland in February nineteen seventy-three, it was in the middle of a typical Scotland winter freeze. The pitch was frozen and, in my opinion,

THE LULL BEFORE THE STORM

dangerous for the players to play on. The centenary match went ahead. The night was so cold only 46,000 spectators turned up ; over 70,000 less than had watched the same fixture eight months previously. On the treacherous surface, England were rampant. England's goals were scored by Clarke, who scored two, Chivers and Channon with an own goal from Peter Lorimer. England won Scotland's celebration match by five goals to nil. After the game we were invited to attend a banquet, together with the Scotland team, as guests of The Scottish Football Association. We all duly attended. The meal we ate alone. The officials of the Scottish Football Association and the Scotland team did not appear. A taxi driver brought gifts for everyone in the England party. We each received a set of drinks mats and a brown tie embossed with the golden letters 'S.F.A.'. The irony of the letters was not lost on the England players. No further internationals were arranged for England prior to another Home International Championship Competition in May. The first game of the Home International was against Northern Ireland at Everton's ground in Liverpool. The game against Northern Ireland should have been played at Belfast, but the situation in Northern Ireland, at the time, was deemed too dangerous for England to appear.

The game against Northern Ireland at Goodison Park again brought me into conflict with Brian Clough, although I was unaware of it during the game. As I was tidying up, in the dressing room after the game, Jack Charlton appeared. He had been working for a different television company to Brian Clough. Jack asked if I could give him a lift, in my car, back to Leeds. I duly obliged. We arrived back at Jack's house in Leeds, just in time to watch B.B.C's 'Match of The Day' on television. Both Jack and I were appalled when, during the game, close up pictures of Sir Alf and me, sitting together in the stand, were shown on the programme. Our photographs were accompanied by Clough's commentary.

"Why is it," he asked,

"does Alf Ramsey have Dr. Phillips sitting next to him during a game. The doctor knows nothing about football, Alf should have a fellow professional with him to discuss football matters during the game. Look at the doctor now, he's looking at his watch. Anyone can get a watch from H. Samuels. Is the doctor's role to tell the time?"

Worse was to follow. The three television pundits that evening, on the B.B.C., were Brian Clough, Don Revie and Jock Stein. When the game had finished Brian continued his argument in a lengthy discussion with Jock and Don, as to why the doctor should sit next to Sir Alf at international matches! Jack Charlton was furious, as indeed I was. Jack said,

"I thought 'Match of The Day' was a football programme, not a discussion on doctors. It's disgraceful."

Sitting at my home, watching the same television programme, were my three children. They were so incensed, they wrote a letter to David Coleman, the match commentator, at the B.B.C. They posted the letter, without me seeing it. Part of the letter, they later told me said,

"We think, Sir Alf is very fortunate to sit with our Dad. We wish we could sit with our Dad at international matches too!"

The repercussions of that televised programmes caused ripples in the medical world. I had always been advised, by The Medical Defence Union, to avoid publicity in my role with the England team. Advertising, at the time of my involvement with England, by the medical profession, in any shape, manner or form, was frowned upon by the medical profession. As a consequence of Cloughie's comments, I had to write to Sam Leitch, the Head of Sport at the B.B.C., for a transcript of the conversations and discussions in the programme relating to me. Sam duly obliged. The transcript, I forwarded to The Medical Defence Union, with a written statement, from me, confirming the discussions and close up photographs had taken place without any prior knowledge on my part. It seemed irrelevant that England beat Northern Ireland by two goals to one. Martin Chivers scored both goals. Home International matches followed against Wales and Scotland. Both games, played at Wembley, saw England beat Wales by three goals to nil and Scotland by a solitary goal from Martin Peters. It was, of course, ironic that we had beaten Wales three-nil in the Home Internationals, but had only drawn the World Cup qualifying match with them four months

THE LULL BEFORE THE STORM

earlier. In that game, John Toshack's goal would prove decisive in preventing England's quest for qualification in the World Cup of 1974.

The Home Internationals were followed, almost immediately, by the summer tour to Czechoslovakia, Poland, Russia and Italy. I was continuing to use up my holiday entitlement from my Practice to accompany England. The game against Poland was a qualifying game for The World Cup. In Prague, the warm up game against the Czechs was a draw; one goal each. England was fortunate to achieve the draw. Allan Clarke equalising in the final minute of the game. The Polish manager, Kazimierz Gorski, who watched the game, was quoted as saying after the game,

"If England plays like that in our country, then they will lose."

The game against Poland, at Katowice, was played on the 6th. June 1973. Poland had lost their first qualifying game in Wales, by two goals to nil. For reasons best known to himself, Sir Alf informed me, following our arrival in Katowice, he was again going to raise the issue of me receiving a salary or match fee from The Football Association. Alf said,

"When I think of all the work you have done for the England team, it is disgraceful you do not receive a salary or match fee. I'm intent on putting matters right."

He did so on our first evening in Poland. Sir Alf and Dr. Andrew Stephen, the Chairman of The Football Association, were engrossed in conversation when I entered the hotel's lounge. Andrew beckoned to me to join them.

"Sir Alf has been telling me, it is his view you should be paid a proper salary or match fee for your services. How long have you been involved with the England teams?

Andrew Stephens enquired of me.

"Almost the same time as Alf's been Manager.

I replied.

"I have to say Neil, that over those years you have done an excellent job, but if The Football Association paid you thirty thousand pounds a year, you could not do a better job than you are doing now for nothing. So why should we pay you?"

There was no answer to Andrew's remarks. I was utterly flabbergasted!

The game against Poland was a disaster for Bobby Moore, for many years England's most reliable defender. After only seven minutes, a Polish free kick eluded Bobby in the England penalty area. The ball fell to the unmarked Banas of Poland who promptly scored. England was a goal down after seven minutes. At half time the players remained quietly confident. They had only been on the field for a minute, in the second half, when Lubanski dispossessed Bobby Moore, who seemed to hesitate on the ball. Although Lubanski took the ball away from Bobby, just inside the England half, he now had a clear run at goal. He struck a hard low shot, which gave Peter Shilton, in goal, no chance of saving. Poland led by two goals to nil. Worse followed for England, when Alan Ball was sent off, by the referee, with ten minutes of the game remaining. England lost the game by two goals to nil. It was a very disappointing result. After the game, I have never seen an England player so dejected as Bobby Moore. He felt personally responsible for England's defeat.

"I made two mistakes. Two mistakes that cost us the match." he said to me.

"I feel sick."

The following morning we flew to the capital of Russia; a country still, at that time, behind the 'Iron Curtain'. On arrival at Moscow Airport we were all warned by the British Embassy staff to be particularly careful, especially if any Russians, male or female, approached us in our hotel. In the hotel, the players were allocated rooms on several different floors. Initially this did not appear to be a problem, but it soon became a very big problem for me. As any one exited from the lift, on any floor, two Russians, sitting at a table, confronted them. On leaving the lift, everyone had to report to the table with the two Russians. They had a written list of all the people accommodated on their floor, together with the room numbers. If your name was not on their list, the two Russians escorted you back into the lift. As I needed to visit players in their rooms, on floors different to my own, I was frequently escorted back into the lift by the two Russians and refused access to the players. It took the management of the hotel two days to give me a pass to gain access to all floors!

THE LULL BEFORE THE STORM

Panic descended on the England staff in the early hours of our first night in Moscow. Alan Ball and Bobby Moore shared a room in the hotel. Alan awoke, in the early hours of the morning, to find he was the sole occupant of the room. Bobby Moore was missing. Alan and the England staff searched the hotel for Bobby. All to no avail. We then went out into the streets of Moscow. A park was near by. Imagine our surprise and disbelief, when we found Bobby sleeping on a bench in the park! At least he was safe. Bobby was so upset, with his performance in the Poland game, he couldn't sleep. He decided to go for a walk. Hence his appearance, sleeping like a tramp, in a Moscow park, in the early hours of the morning!

Prior to the international against Russia, the British Embassy in Moscow was keen for the England players to develop good relations with the Russian public. They had arranged for the entire England party to pay their respects to Lenin, at his tomb in Red Square. We all assembled mid morning, in the searing heat of a June day in Moscow, dressed in our official England suits. The British Embassy staff greeted us on our arrival. The queue of Russians, waiting to pay their respects to Lenin, was enormous. It stretched around Red Square and spilt over into an outside park. The Embassy staff endeavoured to negotiate for the England party to be led to the front of the queue. The negotiations took over half an hour, while the players, standing in small groups, sweated in their grey suits. The players became agitated as the prolonged negotiations continued. Having hung around for some forty minutes, we were eventually told the negotiations had failed. The senior Russian officer refused to allow the England party to take precedent over the queuing Russian public. The players had stood around for forty minutes in extreme heat for nothing. The Russian officer now instructed the England party to return to the hotel. We were prevented from paying our respects to Lenin! Immediately, the players departed back to the hotel. A soldier, of the Russian army, was intent on ensuring we all left Red Square immediately. He approached Les Cocker and myself. Les, irritated by the long fruitless wait, lost his rag! Addressing the Russian soldier face to face, Les bellowed,

"My uncle Charlie is buried in Leeds' cemetery. I wouldn't

[475]

even queue up to see him and he was a better man than Lenin!"

We both made a quick exit back to the hotel. England beat Russia by two goals to one. Khurtsilava scored an own goal for England and Martin Chivers scored the other.

Our next game was in Turin, against Italy. It was Bobby Moore's one hundred and seventh appearance for England. By playing against Italy, Bobby broke the record, for England International appearances, held previously by his good friend and playing partner of many years Bobby Charlton. To mark Bobby Moore's achievement, the entire England squad clubbed together to purchase and present him with a magnificent Cape de Monte ornament. The Football Association did not mark the occasion in Turin. Football can be a cruel game at times. After his disastrous game in Poland, Italy scored their first goal in Turin with a shot that went through Bobby's legs. Italy won the game by two goals to nil. The combination of the Home Internationals, followed immediately by the summer tour resulted in the squad being away from home for almost four weeks. After the defeat in Poland, it seemed like four years! June had not been a happy month for the England team.

On the same day in September, when England played Austria at Wembley in a friendly international, Poland beat Wales, at Katowice, in their World Cup qualifying game, by thee goals to nil. Poland now headed the qualifying group by one point from England and Wales, who were joint second. England knew they now had to beat Poland at Wembley in October to qualify for the nineteen seventy-four World Cup. England versus Poland was a vital match. Against Austria, England ran riot. Bobby Moore, England's long time captain was not selected for the game. The centre-backs were Roy McFarland and Norman Hunter. Martin Peters captained the England team. England scored seven goals. Austria remained goalless. The game was a confidence boost for the all-important next game against Poland.

In the two weeks prior to the crucial game against Poland, another row broke out between The Football League and The Football Association.

THE LULL BEFORE THE STORM

Alan Hardaker, Secretary of The Football League, announced the League would not cancel its fixtures three days before the vital game against Poland, as Alf had requested. The players, selected for the international against Poland, would have to play, for their Clubs, three days beforehand. The intensity of the dispute was highlighted when Hardaker made public the League's feelings. They were most unhelpful to the England cause. His outburst was,

> "This England game against Poland does not amount to a war. It is a game of football. If England lose, football in this country will not die. It will be awful for a few weeks and then everyone will forget it."

Thirty years on, no one seems to have forgotten England's game against Poland! I had the distinction, if distinction it was, of sitting in the Royal Box between my great friend Sir Alf, on my right, and Alan Hardaker on my left. Despite Brian Clough's remarks on television, Alf still wanted me sitting next to him.

Bobby Moore was not selected to play against Poland. I didn't know it then, but Bobby would only play one more game for England. His last game would be the home game against Italy later in the year. For the game against Poland he was on the bench. Much has been written about the game against Poland, played at Wembley on October 17th. 1973. For most of the game, the England players pounded the Polish goal, yet were unable to score. Tomaszewski, the Polish goalkeeper, described by Brian Clough before the game as 'a clown', had an unbelievable game. Throughout, he made one fantastic save after another. At half time, neither England nor Poland had scored. Ten minutes into the second half, Lato, of Poland, dispossessed, of all players, Norman Hunter. Lato sped towards goal, before passing to Domarski whose shot at goal went under Peter Shilton's body and into the net. Fifteen minutes later, following continuous pressure on Poland's goal, which Tomaszewski coped with brilliantly, England drew level with a penalty. Martin Peters, the England captain for the game, had been fouled. Allan Clarke scored from the penalty spot. The remainder of the game was virtually England against Tomaszewski, the Polish goalkeeper. He continued to make one magnificent save after another. Despite all their efforts, the England players could not score. The game ended in a draw. England had failed to qualify for the 1974 World Cup. Poland headed the group. They would go forward to play at Munich in the best football competition in the world. England would be staying at home. The England dressing room, after the game, was a depressing place to be. England players cried, as they realised the opportunity for them to play in a World Cup competition had disappeared. Some realised they would never now experience playing in a World Cup. At times such as this, it is important for the directors to show their support for the team. None was forthcoming. Not a single Football Association Council Member, nor any member of the Senior International Committee came to the England dressing room following the defeat. The players were left to grieve alone. The action of the senior Football Association members was despicable and totally unacceptable. Those football professionals at Lilleshall, all those years previously, had been so right when they questioned me.

'How could I have become one of them?'

Meanwhile, during the year, many dramatic events had occurred at Middlesbrough Football Club. I was intimately involved in them all.

17

Jack Charlton—A Matter of Trust.

In January 1973, Stan Anderson was in his seventh season as Manager of Middlesbrough Football Club. In the 1966–67 season, his first, with a win in the last game of the season, he had raised the team from the depths of the Third Division, to gain promotion to the Second Division. Six years later, Middlesbrough was still in the Second Division. At the beginning of the New Year, the team was languishing in the bottom half of that Division. The third round of the F.A. Cup would provide some relief from the rigours and disappointments of the League. In the F.A. Cup, the Club was drawn away from home. Middlesbrough would play Plymouth, of the Third Division. Middlesbrough lost the cup-tie, by the only goal of the game. They were eliminated from the competition at the first hurdle.

Stan Anderson was a bad loser. Whenever his team was defeated, he became quiet and sad. After the Plymouth game, he was at a very low ebb. It was not only the defeat, but also, and more importantly in his mind, the way his team had played. The performance against Plymouth had been poor. Middlesbrough was out of the F.A. Cup for another year. To be defeated in the third round of the F.A. Cup was not an unusual occurrence at Middlesbrough, but, on this occasion, they had been beaten by a team from a lower Division. In Stan's opinion however, the team had been playing badly for several weeks. He knew his team was experiencing the worst run of performances since he became the Manager. Whenever his team lost, Stan would retreat into himself. In the hours following a defeat, Stan became very quiet, and thoughtful. Everyone at the Club had learnt not to involve Stan in conversation immediately after a defeat. Losing hurt Stan tremendously. He frequently took forty-eight hours to recover. The Plymouth defeat was particularly humiliating. Stan was deeply affected by the inept performance and manner of Middlesbrough's defeat at Plymouth. The defeat hurt Stan more than his Chairman or any of his players realised.

The Middlesbrough team had flown to Plymouth on a charter flight from Teesside Airport. On the return flight, Stan Anderson sat at the front of the plane, in an adjoining seat to the Chairman, George Winney. Stan was singularly quiet. The Chairman was accustomed to Stan's post match solitude. The Manager's silence was not unusual. However, the Plymouth defeat had affected Stan more than even George Winney realised. The Chairman realised the time spent on the return flight to Teesside was not an appropriate time to discuss important issues with Stan. George decided the Manager was best left alone with his private thoughts. During the flight home, Stan closed his eyes. He would pretend to be asleep. In reality, his brain would race through every kick of the Plymouth game. He would reflect on every player's performance. Sleep for Stan was impossible, yet his eyes remained closed. George Winney assumed the Manager would sleep throughout the return flight.

As the plane commenced its descent to Teesside Airport, Stan Anderson's eyes opened. He turned to the Chairman and quietly said,

> "I've thought things over, very carefully, these past weeks. In fact, I've thought of nothing else. The team has been playing badly for the past two months. I've brought this team as far as I can. The players need a fresh impetus. It's now time for me to depart. The Club needs a new Manager. I've made up my mind. I wish to resign."

The Chairman was not surprised at Stan's comments. George Winney held the view however, that Stan's decision was a knee jerk reaction to the Plymouth defeat.

> "Resignation decisions need careful consideration over several days, if not weeks."

was the Chairman's initial response.

"You need time to reflect. Matters are not as bad as you think. You can easily pull things around."

"I've done all the reflecting I need"

Stan replied.

"I've thought the situation over and over for several weeks. It's time for me to go. I'd like you to inform the Board. I definitely wish to resign."

George Winney insisted,

"Stan, reflect on the matter for two weeks."

With great reluctance Stan agreed, but, with his usual sardonic smile, added

"I will not change my mind."

The Chairman and Manager agreed to meet in ten day's time to discuss the matter. The delay would give Stan additional time to reflect. Meanwhile, the Chairman and Manager agreed, the matter would remain confidential between the two of them. No one else would be informed of the discussion.

Stan Anderson was never a man to change his mind. I personally do not believe that Stan's decision was a knee jerk reaction to the Plymouth result. Stan was too sensible a person to make such a major decision on the result of one game. He would have carefully considered the team's performances over several weeks. Stan knew he had brought the team as far as he could. He honestly believed the team needed a new impetus. He knew he personally could not provide that impetus. Stan was an honest man and a realist. He had decided that a change of Manager was necessary. He had convinced himself of that fact and no one would change his mind.

George Winney, the Chairman of Middlesbrough Football Club, was a true gentleman. In all his personal dealings with me over many years, George was always honest and totally sincere. He was an extremely knowledgeable man, both of his timber business and of football. Of all my fellow directors at Middlesbrough, George was the one I admired most. Before he became Chairman, George was a great supporter of Stan Anderson.

They had known each other for many years. They were both good golfers. When Stan was a player at Sunderland and Newcastle, George and Stan had frequently played golf against and with each other. Because of this relationship, George mistakenly believed he could persuade Stan to change his mind and withdraw his resignation. George was convinced Stan Anderson was a good Manager. He wanted him to stay. He honestly believed, after ten days of reflection, Stan would change his mind. The Chairman was to be disappointed. Stan and George met the following week over lunch at the Billingham Arms. Stan had not, and would not, change his mind. All the Chairman's efforts, at persuading Stan to remain, failed miserably. Stan Anderson's resignation stood.

When the directors assembled for the weekly Board meeting, Stan Anderson was absent. I, like all the other Directors present, assumed Stan had been delayed at the training ground. It was a complete surprise to us all, when George Winney informed the Board of Stan's resignation. From their reactions, it was obvious that none of my fellow directors were previously aware of the Manager's decision. The Chairman's announcement surprised us all. As I was involved in the dressing room on a daily basis, some of my fellow directors quizzed me, as to how much I knew of the Manager's decision. They were keen to know if Stan had discussed the situation with me. I was able to confirm to them that I had not been privy to any such discussions with the Manager. Like all my fellow directors, the Chairman's announcement was a complete surprise to me. George Winney informed the Board of all the discussions he had held with Stan Anderson. The Chairman explained how he had tried to persuade Stan to change his mind, but had failed miserably. The Manager's mind was made up. Stan Anderson had resigned.

"The Club is now without a Manager and we need to put someone in temporary charge,"
George Winney informed the Board
"and it needs to be soon."

His comment was met with stony silence. The silence was a mixture of shock, at Stan's resignation, and fear at their own inadequacy in not knowing who might be his immediate successor. When Raich Carter was sacked as Manager, in 1966, the Board formed a Committee of four to replace the Manager. This Committee consisted of two directors, Geoff Wood and myself; the Player-Coach, Stan Anderson, and the Assistant Manager, Harold Shepherdson. Like the majority of committees, I have been a member of, making decisions proved impossible. The committee was a disaster. The team, under the committee's jurisdiction, was relegated to the Third Division. As far as I was concerned, another committee, to run affairs, in the short term, was not an acceptable way forward. The obvious choice, for a temporary Manager was Harold Shepherdson. Unfortunately, Shep had many enemies amongst the Directors. There were certain Directors who disliked his association with the England Team and particularly The Football Association. They envied, and were jealous of, the success Shep had enjoyed with England. They intensely disliked his involvement with The Football Association. Those directors had openly stated to Shep and myself, on several occasions, how they deplored the way the England team played under Ramsey. I knew they would not be supportive of Shep taking charge. The silence around the table was unbearable. George Winney, as Chairman, allowed the silence to continue. Eventually, I broke the silence.

"It has to be Shep."

I said, and waited for the reaction. To my surprise none came. I continued,

"I know some of you have grave doubts about Shep's managerial capabilities, but he's the only man for the job. A Committee didn't work last time and it won't work now. In order to manage the players, there needs to be just one person, in charge. That person needs to have the responsibility and the authority to act. You can give a committee the responsibility, but as far as the players are concerned the committee would have no day-to-day authority. Authority and responsibility needs to be given to just one person. That person should totally manage the team. I suggest we put Shep in charge and inform him immediately. I know many of you are prejudiced against Harold, but he is the Assistant Manager. He has years of experience at Club and International level and importantly has the good of this Club at heart. My suggestion is to put Harold to the test. I propose we ask Harold to take charge until a new Manager is appointed."

It seemed so obvious to me.

Some of my fellow directors, looked at me in stark disbelief! At least I had broken the silence. Eric Thomas, the previous Chairman, was opposed. Ernie Varley and George Kitching were lukewarm. Charles Amer, Albert King, Geoff Wood and the Chairman, George Winney, were in favour. Initially, the Board was split. After an hour's futile discussion, those who initially opposed Shep could not think of an immediate, acceptable alternative. Reluctantly those directors agreed with my suggestion. Shep got the job.

George Winney asked me to bring Shep from his office into the Board meeting. Harold came. The Chairman informed him of Stan Anderson's resignation. Harold was shocked. Shep, even though he was the Assistant Manager, had no idea of Stan's intentions. George Winney invited Harold to accept the post of Acting Manager. He duly accepted. Shep was to be in charge of all team matters. I was delighted. The Chairman impressed on Shep the enormity of his task. The team was in the bottom half of the Second Division. The possibility of another relegation was not to be contemplated. A press statement was issued immediately after the Board meeting.

"Stan Anderson has resigned as Manager of Middlesbrough Football Club. Harold Shepherdson has been placed in temporary charge, until a successor is appointed. Harold Shepherdson has the responsibility and the authority for all team matters. The Board wish to place on record their thanks to Stan Anderson for all the hard work he has done over the past six years as Manager, and wish him well in the future."

Three days later, on the Sunday evening, the Chairman rang me at home.

George Winney thought it would be a good idea if we had lunch together. He suggested we meet for lunch at the Billingham Arms on Wednesday. I agreed. It would mean another of my half days would be ruined. How my wife suffered!

Bill Forest, an ex Middlesbrough player, and his wife ran The Billingham Arms. He and his wife were delightful hosts and completely trustworthy. When they lived at Redcar, they were patients of mine. I knew them well. No one would ever know that George and I had lunched together. Lunch at the Billingham Arms was always a delight. George had arranged a private room for just the two of us. We had hardly sat down when George came straight to the point.

> "I've brought you here to discuss the appointment of a new Manager at the Club. Following the discussions that took place at the last Board meeting, it is obvious the directors would not be in favour of appointing Harold Shepherdson on a permanent basis. Every director, who initially opposed Harold's temporary appointment, have subsequently telephoned me, since the meeting. They have expressed their concern, even over his temporary appointment. We only just got them to agree to Harold being appointed on a temporary basis. We would have no chance of making Harold's appointment a permanent one. As you said, at the meeting, it is pure prejudice, but it's a fact of life. Those directors would never agree and I'm not prepared to take them on. In any event, I doubt if Harold would want the Manager's job on a permanent basis. The appointment of the Manager is the most important decision the Directors ever have to make. I am reluctant to have an open discussion at a Board meeting on the matter. After all, when one looks at our fellow directors, what knowledge do they possess to assess the credentials of a football Manager? In this field, they are merely amateurs. In the past, when the Club needed to appoint a new Manager, the Board have relied heavily on advice received from several

Sports Writers. I do not want to go down that road on this occasion. I personally cannot afford to make a mistake with this appointment. I want the next Manager to be the right Manager for Middlesbrough Football Club. The appointment has to be correct."

George had delivered his speech. It had been well prepared. I had not said one word. There was more to come from George.

"You're different from the rest of the Directors. You've now been involved with the England team for the past ten years. You've attended the summer courses at Lilleshall mixing with Managers, Coaches and Trainers for weeks at a time. England players, current Managers and Coaches know you and, more importantly, you know them. I need your advice. I respect your knowledge. You have a standing in the game, which the rest of our Directors do not have. Suppose I gave you a free hand. Who would you recommend as our new Manager? Suppose I said 'You choose the Manager. Who would you choose?' I need to know if we can determine this appointment between the two of us. Let's try and present one name to the Board. For starters, give me the three Managers you would recommend and then we will narrow it down to just one. Let's see if you and I can conclude the matter between the two of us. Let's try and present just the one name to the Board."

Mrs. Forrest intervened

"Are you ready to order?"

"Not quite dear"

said George

"Give us a few minutes."

We studied the menu and ordered lunch.

With a smile on my face, I began my response.

"I presume Cloughie is not acceptable"

I said, knowing that George had been a Director during the whole of Brian's time as a player at Middlesbrough..

"Definitely not."

replied George.

"Too much history at the Club. Several of the directors have ruled him out already. The Board would definitely not approve. Brian would be too much of a risk for them."

George was quite firm.

"It's not important."

I said

"Cloughie is not my first choice. My first choice would be Jack Charlton of Leeds. Jack's due to finish his playing career there at the end of this season. I know he will be looking for a position, in the game, as a Manager or Coach. Jack is an excellent coach. I've watched him at Lilleshall on many occasions. He's brilliant. Very forthright. He's contributed well and intelligently in the team talks at England level. He makes the game so simple. Jack knows what he wants and will move heaven and earth to get it. He doesn't suffer fools gladly. He could easily fall out with some of our Directors, particularly if they start expressing their views on football. Jack will be a difficult person to manage. He has a fiery temper. However, if you want to go places; go for Jack. In my view Middlesbrough need someone to tell them what to do. Jack will do just that."

"Whose your other recommendation?",

the Chairman enquired.

"Terry Venables"

I replied.

"He was a player on my first England Under 23 tour; the tour when John Harris was Manager. Terry is also an excellent Coach; very knowledgeable about the game. He's a complete extrovert. Has clear views. Is well respected by his fellow players. Very humorous, but very capable and, I repeat, an excellent Coach. Problem is, he's a Londoner. It will be difficult to prise Terry away from the bright lights of London"

The steak was, as always, excellent; the fruit–salad superb. Mrs. Forrest's coffee was delicious. The Billingham Arms had lived up to its reputation.

"I can't see Venables leaving London and fitting into the north–east."

said George over coffee.

"I'll take your first recommendation. Let's go for Charlton."

I could not believe George's response. I knew, if Jack would agree to come, we could do no better. All the frustrations, I had experienced over ten years as a director at Middlesbrough, could be at an end. Alan Brown, the Manager of Sheffield Wednesday had been so right when he told me in 1969,

"The most important role for a Football Club Director is to appoint the right Manager and then let him manage."

If Jack would come, I knew we would have the right Manager. I also knew that, as Chairman, George Winney would allow Jack to manage. The combination was ideal. I was delighted.

"I'll ring Harry Reynolds, the Leeds Chairman, when I get back to my office this afternoon. I'll ask his permission to approach Charlton."

George said.

"That would be your first mistake."

I immediately replied.

"Although Mr. Reynolds is Chairman at Leeds, Revie runs the place. If you approach Mr. Reynolds, Revie is likely to get upset. If we want Charlton you have to ring Revie first. I'm sure, at Leeds, that's the right approach. If Revie agrees, he'll speak to Mr. Reynolds and then set up a meeting with you and Jack."

It was obvious George was not happy bypassing the Leeds Chairman and going direct to Revie, but I persuaded George to approach Revie first.

"I'll ring Revie this afternoon."

JACK CHARLTON— A MATTER OF TRUST

Jack Charlton was to be our man..

George rang Don Revie in mid afternoon. Yes, Revie knew of Jack Charlton's wish to become involved in football management. He would speak to the player and inform him of Middlesbrough's interest. Don would speak to Jack Charlton over the weekend. Following his discussions, Revie would inform George Winney as to whether or not Charlton was interested in coming to Middlesbrough. Don Revie would be in touch. That evening George Winney telephoned to inform me of his conversation with Revie. I was delighted.

February 16th. 1973 was our sixteenth wedding anniversary. Margaret and I had planned the day for weeks; the baby sitter had been booked well in advance. Morning surgery would be followed by my daily visit to Ayresome Park to assess the injured players. The afternoon would be spent at Wilton I.C.I. Medical Centre carrying out my usual clinic. The clinic finished at four o'clock. I would be home for tea with Margaret and the three children. In the evening, Gladys, our daily help, would baby sit. I had booked a table for dinner at The Bridge Inn at Wetherby where we would celebrate our wedding anniversary. The day was well planned—or so I thought!

In the midst of a busy morning surgery, Miss James, our senior receptionist, telephoned through to my room. She informed me a Mr. Revie was on the phone and wished to speak to me. The brusque Yorkshire voice greeted me as a good friend would.

> "Is that Doc Phillips?. I've spoken with Big Jack about your interest in him becoming Manager at Middlesbrough. He's with me now. Trouble is Sheffield United are also interested. Big Jack and I have decided he should speak first with you and you alone. I've spoken to your Chairman, Mr. Winney, and he says its O.K. for you and Jack to get together on your own; just the two of you. If you want the big fella you'll have to see him today; tomorrow may be too late. I'll put Jack on."

"Morning Doc",
the big fella began.

> "I'd like to meet with you to discuss the job at Middlesbrough.

Only discuss you understand. There are lots of questions I need to ask. Don has given me his long list of questions to ask. We'll meet at The Fox at Wetherby at twelve o'clock. We can discuss it over lunch. I've loads of questions for you. Hope you can answer them. Do you know where The Fox is? It's two miles north of Wetherby on the A1. Left hand side coming down for you. Right hand side for me. See you at twelve."

He was gone. Come to think of it, he didn't ask me if I could make it. Not for the first time, my day would have to be reorganised because of football. It was however an opportunity I could not refuse under any circumstance. It was an appointment I could not miss.

The waiting room was full of patients and I was already running late. I could tell no one of my movements. No one, that is, except Mags. I could not ask one of my partners to deputise for me at the I.C.I. clinic. I could tell no one where I was going. In any case, it was too short notice for any of my partners to reorganise their schedule. Certainly no one at the Football Club should know where I was going. If anyone learnt of my meeting with Jack, it would be the main story on all the sports' pages of the national press. Tea with Mags and the children would not take place, or, at best, I would be late. Our wedding anniversary dinner at The Bridge Inn at Wetherby seemed secure. Now I would be travelling to Wetherby twice in a day! I thought about telephoning the Chairman, George Winney, but quickly decided against it. This was a mission I would carry out myself. I would inform no one. Miss James came into the consulting room.

"You're now running twenty minutes late and the patients are getting restive."

I got the message and pressed the bell for my next patient. It was always difficult, at times like these, to focus entirely on the patient. The words of Blacow Yates, the first consultant I worked for and the then Chairman of Sheffield United, echoed in my ears,

"Remember, patients are always important to themselves."

I tried hard to concentrate on the patients, but in all honesty my mind kept wandering back to Big Jack. Could I land such a big fish for Middlesbrough?

Surgery finished fifteen minutes late. After a quick cup of coffee with two of my partners I left for home. In that I was to attend the afternoon I.C.I. clinic, I was excused all house calls for the day. What a blessing! I returned home, to inform Mags of the change of plans. I would go to the Football Club and see the injured players as normal. I would ring I.C.I., from Ayresome Park, and cancel my clinic, giving no explanation. I would travel to The Fox at Wetherby direct from Ayresome Park. The rearranged plan seemed perfectly satisfactory.

As I travelled along the A19 from Middlesbrough to Thirsk, my mind thought of nothing else but Jack Charlton. I knew it was the right decision, but what about his questions? Revie was well known for compiling a list of them when his players went for a Manager's interview. As I drove, I wondered what those questions would be. More importantly, did I have the authority to answer and agree them? I had the responsibility for sure, but no authority of the Board. I was not the Club Chairman, or Vice Chairman, but merely a Director. Only the Chairman knew of our intentions, and even he knew nothing of today's meeting. I felt somewhat vulnerable, but I needed Jack Charlton for Middlesbrough. As I passed R.A.F. Dishforth, I thought how my life had changed. It was at this airfield in 1958, where I sat, as the sole passenger, on that training flight to Ireland to play cricket under the guise of a visiting Obstetrician. My life had certainly moved on. My main problem however had not changed over the years. It was the never-ending conflict I had between being a Doctor, on the one hand, and my constant involvement in and commitment to sport, on the other. How I wished I could combine the two into one full time appointment. As I drove, other cars flashed by. I drove automatically. My mind was in turmoil, constantly flitting from one thought to another. George Winney, at the Billingham Arms luncheon, had said he wanted my view and mine alone on the future Middlesbrough Manager. He said I was the only Director who knew about such matters. We had agreed to go for Jack Charlton. On my recommendation he had telephoned Revie. As I journeyed to meet Jack, I had no intention of letting George Winney down. My mind drifted back to Holland in 1969. Jack and I were opponents in a five a side match. I was in goal. The rain was pouring down. The pitch was a mud bath. I could still feel the pain in my stomach when he deliberately shot at me from just a few yards. Perhaps it was because of that friendship I was meeting with him today. I certainly hoped so.

I knew the exact location of The Fox Inn at Wetherby. I turned into the car park automatically, with the assurance of a daily visitor. The Fox was not there. Instead I was confronted by an Austrian Tyrolean building that was now a restaurant. My car came to rest in the car park, facing the dual carriageway of the A1. I was distraught. Was there another Fox? Where would Jack be going? What if we didn't meet! Would Jack be waiting somewhere else? Was there another Fox Inn at Wetherby? If we didn't meet, maybe Jack would end up at Sheffield United. How would I explain that to George Winney. My mind was in turmoil. Imagine, on my return, having to inform the Chairman,

> "Oh, by the way George, my meeting with Jack never took place. I got lost in Wetherby!"

I sat in the car in a state of panic. Two hundred yards down the A1 was a garage. I decided to walk down the dual carriageway to enquire where The Fox had gone.

> "Knocked down last year."

the garage attendant told me.

> "Stupid fella from the Dales built this bloody Austrian place. Not a patch on the old Fox. Wouldn't go in there for my lunchtime pint—not in a month of Sundays. That's where The Fox was though. There's no other Fox in Wetherby."

I walked back to the car.

I saw him coming up the A1, travelling north in his dirty grey Ford shooting brake. The right indicator was flashing to cross the dual carriageway. He joined me in the car park.

> "Hullo Doc. Where's The Fox gone?"

he said.

"Knocked down last year."
I replied.
"Let's go in and have some lunch. Don't forget you're paying.
We have to get this Director–Manager relationship right from the start don't we?"

Jack's remarks were accompanied, by a wicked smile. The same smile I had first seen beaming down on me as I lay in the mud in Holland in 1969.

We sat in the restaurant for three hours. The fellow at the garage was correct. No one came in for a lunchtime pint. Jack Charlton and I were the only persons in the restaurant. Revie had given Jack a list of questions to put to me. Jack was to seek answers and assurances on each and every question.

Would Jack have complete control of all playing matters?

What is the financial state of the Club?

How much money is available for new players?

What are the Directors like?

Would Jack and the Chairman be able to build a good working relationship?

Would Jack be encouraged to extend his managerial role over time to become the Manager of the whole Club?

There were questions I needed to ask of Jack, but I made little progress.

"What sort of contract do you want?"

I asked.

"I don't want a contract. I won't sign one. You and I will have an understanding. If I decide to come, I want to come for four years. I want an assurance from you that I will not be sacked in those four years whatever happens. I don't think a Football Manager's job is full time. I shan't work more than three or four days a week. Need to relax–shooting and fishing."

"Salary?"

I enquired.

"Not really interested in money. Ten thousand will do."

"Ten thousand is not enough."

I replied,
> "Not only do you deserve more, but if you're on ten what are the Assistant Manager, Coach and Training Staff going to earn?"

"Ten thousand is all I want and ten thousand it is to be."

"OK, and an additional ten thousand, if we gain promotion."

Ten and ten was agreed.

We chatted through every aspect of the job and every facet of the Club. The three hours seemed to fly by. Eventually Jack asked
> "One last question Doc. Why do you personally want me to come?"

I felt this was Jack's thousand-dollar question. There was a long silence before I replied.
> "Jack, I've been a Director at Middlesbrough now for ten years. During that time, people at the Club -Directors and staff–have always been telling the Manager what he should do. What Middlesbrough Football Club needs is a Manager who will tell them what to do. You can do that better than anyone I know. You know what you want. I know you will tell everyone at the Club what is required of them. Middlesbrough needs you."

The big fella smiled.
> "I'll come. Some conditions though. I'm due to finish at Leeds in three months; at the end of May. It's my benefit year and the last match of the season is my testimonial game against Celtic. The match is arranged for the Monday after the F.A. Cup Final. I don't want anyone to know that I'm coming to Middlesbrough until after the Celtic game. I'll arrive at Middlesbrough two days after the Celtic game. Until then, if anyone asks me, I'll say I know nothing about it and I want you and Middlesbrough to do the same. I shall look forward to coming."

We shook hands. I was delighted. I had got the Manager I wanted and Middlesbrough needed.

Throughout the lunch I had made copious notes in my diary. Everything we had agreed was written down. I looked at my notes and went through each item with Jack. I wanted to ensure it was correct. It was. This was our agreement. As we walked to our cars I said,

"When I get back, I'll report to the Board and put all this in writing for you."

"What for?"

"Well, none of the Directors at Middlesbrough know you and I want to ensure that everything we've talked about is agreed by the other Directors."

"Don't bother. We have our agreement. If they don't trust you, I don't want to come. I've agreed everything with you. I'll be there two days after the Celtic game; until then not a word."

My friend had agreed to come. I was ecstatic.

As I drove back to Redcar, I purred with inward satisfaction. My mission had been achieved. I knew, on reflection, I had been foolish to agree to one of Jack's suggestions.

"I will come for four years,"

he had said,

"but during that time I want you to promise I will not be sacked whatever happens."

I had given him that promise. On reflection, how could I ensure, with seven other directors involved, that would occur? As I drove home, I determined that, if there was any proposed sacking of Jack Charlton in those four years, I would also resign as a Director. Jack and I would be inextricably linked, at the Club, for the next four years.

I realised, of course, the main obstacle to Jack's appointment was yet to be confronted and overcome. George Winney, and I, had acted without any discussion with the six other directors. The Board would now need to approve the appointment. They would also need to agree every detail I had negotiated with Jack. Informing the Board, and obtaining their approval, would be George Winney's responsibility. For the present, I was extremely happy with the outcome of my meeting.

The children's tea was long finished when I arrived home. I related the outcome of my meeting briefly to Mags. I spent half an hour on the phone relating the outcome of my discussions to George Winney. He was delighted with every detail. George would inform the Board at its next meeting.

Gladys arrived. Mags and I said goodnight to our three children. We were off to celebrate our wedding anniversary. Back at Wetherby, this time at The Bridge Inn, Mags and I would drink a toast to the new Middlesbrough Manager. We enjoyed a lovely evening celebrating our anniversary together.

Middlesbrough Football Club do not realise, even to this day, the great debt they owe to their former Chairman, George Winney. It was George who made the unprecedented decision, following the resignation of Stan Anderson, that no discussion on the appointment of a new Manager would take place with his fellow Directors. It was George, who had the vision to use my experience, at international and coaching level, as to who should be Middlesbrough's next Manager. The other Directors were unaware that George and I had lunched at the Billingham Arms to privately discuss the issue. They were unaware that George and I, just the two of us, had decided that Jack Charlton was to be our man. George had subsequently given me the sole responsibility to negotiate with Charlton. Now it was George's responsibility, to present the appointment of Charlton to the other Directors as a fait accompli.

I considered George Winney a man of immense courage. He reported every detail of my discussions with Charlton to the next Board meeting, or to be more accurate, to a meeting held before the official Board meeting. The Club Secretary, Harry Green, and the Acting Manager, Harold Shepherdson, were not allowed to be present.

It would have been ideal if the Directors had been unanimous in agreeing to Jack Charlton's appointment, but that was not the case. Charles Amer, at that stage a Director, had definite reservations. His view, forcibly expressed at the time, was that Charlton had no experience as a Manager, and his appointment would be too much of a risk. Charles believed Middlesbrough needed an experienced, strong, proven Manager. Despite the reservations of Charles Amer, George Winney, the then Chairman, persuaded the Board to agree the appointment of Jack Charlton as their Manager. The terms of Jack's employment were to be exactly those he and I had agreed at Wetherby.

In Jack Charlton's autobiography, for reasons best known to himself, Jack describes, in some detail, the interview procedure he went through, or rather the interview procedure he put the Middlesbrough directors through, prior to his being appointed. None of Jack's report on the interview procedure is true. Jack did not come to Middlesbrough for an interview, let alone meet with the directors and turn the tables on them. He did not meet any of the directors or submit a list of questions to them at interview. He was never interviewed by anyone apart from myself. In fact, apart from myself, when Jack arrived in Middlesbrough in June 1973, on the day he took up his appointment, he had not met any of the then directors of Middlesbrough Football Club apart from myself. I would suggest to the reader that few, if any, manager has been appointed to a football club without meeting the directors at some stage, prior to their appointment. The circumstances surrounding Jack Charlton's appointment at Middlesbrough are, thanks to George Winney, unique, but then Charlton is a rather unique person himself. George Winney and I had succeeded in getting our man. It would however be four months before Charlton arrived at Middlesbrough. I had given Jack a promise that no news of his appointment would emanate from Middlesbrough until after his testimonial match in June. Those sixteen weeks were to be an eternity.

The Board's decision to appoint Charlton as Manager was made at the end of February. Harold Shepherdson was in charge of the team. Stan Anderson was at his home in Billingham. I continued to visit him and his family. When he was the Club's Manager, I had accepted medical responsibility for Stan's family. I treated them as private patients, but never charged them a fee. Despite his resignation, Stan and I remained, and still are, good friends. On one of my visits to their family home, he informed me he had received a telephone call from Bill Shankly, the Liverpool Manager, enquiring about one of our players. Apparently Shankly wanted to buy David Mills. Following his discussions with Stan, Shankly had intimated that he would be prepared to offer £150,000 for the player. Shankly asked Stan to sound out George Winney, our Club Chairman. Stan immediately informed George of his conversation with Shankly. George Winney telephoned me later.

> "You are aware that Liverpool are interested in Mills. It will be discussed at the Board meeting on Thursday. I do not want you to mention the fee of £150,000 to anyone. You'll realise why at the meeting."

At the Board meeting, George informed the directors of Liverpool's interest in Mills. He gave each director a blank piece of paper and asked each director to write on the paper their transfer valuation of Mills. George collected in the papers. George and I returned blank papers. The highest price any director placed on Mills' transfer was £120,000. One director was prepared to transfer Mills for £25,000! I expressed the view, at the Board Meeting, that any discussion on the transfer of Mills was irrelevant. Having agreed to appoint Charlton as Manager, it was essential he be consulted about the selling of any players. The Board agreed. The Chairman asked me to telephone Jack for his view on selling Mills..

"Mills? Who's Mills? Don't know him."

I gave Jack a detailed description of Mills.

> "I'll talk to the Leeds players about Mills in the morning. I'll ring you back tomorrow evening."

Jack rang the following evening.

> "Don't sell Mills. The Leeds players say he's a good player. Come to think of it, if Shank's is offering £150,000, he must be a great player."

Liverpool's request for the transfer of Mills was refused. Four years later Mills was transferred to West Bromwich Albion for a reported fee of £500,000. It just emphasised one director's football knowledge. He was prepared to transfer Mills for £25,000! It was one more fact confirming the view professionals in the game had of the directors.

The impending retirement of Jack Charlton, as a player from Leeds

United, produced much media interest and speculation. Almost daily, in one newspaper or another, it was reported that Jack was to become the Manager of one football club or another. The Middlesbrough directors became twitchy. They had nothing in writing to confirm Charlton's appointment at Middlesbrogh. The directors only had my word that he would arrive at Middlesbrough at the beginning of June. Jack and I had shaken hands on the deal. It was a matter of trust between the two of us. The directors were not involved in the trust. They felt vulnerable. They had no binding contract with Charlton. They just had my word.

"We should insist on him signing a contract."
The directors repeatedly stated at Board meetings.
"He wouldn't sign a contract, even if one was offered to him."
I always replied.
"What if he should go to another Club?"
my fellow directors at, and outside of, Board meetings, frequently asked me.
"If he decides to go elsewhere, we will look stupid."
was their cry.
"You just have to trust Charlton and myself."
was my consistent reply. It was a situation some of my fellow directors found hard to accept.

"If Charlton changes his mind, we, the directors, will have egg on our face. What would the supporters think of the Board? Months, when we should have been seeking a new Manager, would have been wasted. We are in a ridiculous situation."

The directors felt they needed to have some written agreement with Charlton. Meeting after meeting I resisted their arguments, but my fellow directors kept raising the issue at every opportunity. My trust in Jack was supreme. He had given me his word. We had shaken hands on it. I knew he would be coming. Reluctantly, very reluctantly, my fellow directors decided to go along with my belief.

Playing against Wolves in the semi-final of the F.A. Cup, Jack Charlton

DOCTOR TO THE WORLD CHAMPIONS

suffered a severe hamstring injury. He wouldn't play for Leeds United again. He would miss playing in the F.A. Cup Final against Sunderland. With Jack not playing for Leeds, George Winney wondered if Jack would like to meet him for lunch one Saturday prior to a Middlesbrough home game. George also suggested Jack might then attend the home game and watch the team play at Ayresome Park. When I telephoned Jack, he readily agreed.

"It would be good to have a look at the team."

A date was arranged. Under the temporary management of Harold Shepherdson, the team was playing well. Shep was doing a great job. The team was now in the top half of the table.

George Winney, Jack and I lunched at The Cleveland Tontine, immediately prior to a Saturday home game. George, who was meeting Jack for the first time, was most impressed. From my point of view I was delighted George and Jack got on extremely well together. Listening to the two of them discussing issues during lunch, I knew they would have an excellent Chairman to Manager relationship. After lunch, Jack left his car at The Tontine. I drove him into Middlesbrough for the game. We deliberately arrived in the Directors' Box as the teams were kicking off. When the press realised Jack was in the directors' box, photographers appeared at the front of the stand. Jack and I both left before the end of the game. I drove Jack back to his car at the Tontine.

"They're not a bad side, Doc. Could become quite a good side. I'm really looking forward to coming. I'll be there after the Celtic match. Who was that fella who kept touching me on my shoulder during the game?"

"Charles Amer."

"Whose he?"

"One of the directors. A millionaire."

I replied.

It had been a good day. George Winney and Jack, as Chairman and Manager, would be a formidable combination.

The fact that Jack had visited Ayresome Park, and seen the team play,

[500]

seemed to quieten the sceptical directors. They all started to believe that Jack was, after all, actually coming to Middlesbrough. On the Monday, the local paper printed a photograph of Jack Charlton sitting beside myself in the director's box. Privately the Sport's Editor told me,

> "The photograph looks like the next Manager is sitting with the future Chairman of the Club."

I simply laughed at the suggestion. I denied of course that Charlton was to become our Manager. Denial, was part of the deal I had made with Jack.

It was several weeks since I had met with Jack Charlton at Wetherby. The team was performing really well under Harold Shepherdson's astute management. The weekly Board meetings appeared quite straightforward, but I had learnt, over my time at Middlesbrough, that matters were never ever straightforward. I had no indication however of the shock announcement that was to be delivered to the Board by the Chairman, George Winney. George announced that he would be resigning as Chairman. His timber business had been severely hit by the recession. He needed to devote more time to his work. He would continue as a Director of the Club up to the annual meeting, but would then resign from the Board. Surprisingly, no Director tried to persuade George to change his mind. It was decided in the circumstances to close the meeting. Instantly, I knew, considerable in fighting would start amongst the remaining directors as to whom should become the new Chairman. I was very concerned.

Following the lunch at The Tontine, I knew Charlton and Winney would have formed an ideal partnership. As I looked around the table at my fellow directors, I couldn't see Jack forming a good relationship with any one of them. George's decision was, as far as I was concerned, a catastrophe. George Winney, the man who had ensured that Jack was appointed the Manager, would soon depart. Middlesbrough F.C., already without a Manager, now needed a new Chairman. The situation was serious. Until the situation was clearer, I decided not to inform Charlton of Winney's resignation. The Directors agreed to meet in a week, when the issue of a new Chairman would be fully discussed.

The shortened Board meeting allowed me to visit the dressing room earlier than expected. I was glad to seek the sanctuary and company of the players. It was there, in the dressing room, I was most happy. I really enjoyed being with the players and the staff. The dressing and treatment rooms were where I felt at home. The directors' room was a place I always tried to avoid. The inane conversations, I heard there, I found difficult to accept. Their authoritative pontificating on all aspects of football, when they had so little knowledge, I found difficult to tolerate. Knowing my fellow directors would now be holding their group conversations upstairs, I lingered in the Treatment Room with Jimmy Headrige, our excellent trainer, much longer than was necessary. I was reluctant to rejoin my fellow directors.

Only two directors remained, when I eventually did return to the directors' room. The two directors were the solicitors, Geoff Wood and Eric Thomas. Charles Amer always left immediately after any Board meeting. George Kitching usually left at the same time, as he and Charles invariably lunched together at the Marton Hotel and Country Club, one of Charles' three hotels on Teesside. If there were important issues to discuss, following a Board meeting, Ernie Varley occasionally would join them. Today, there was certainly an important issue to discuss. Whether Ernie had also left for Charles' hotel I knew not. In any event Ernie had also left. George Winney, having delivered his bombshell, had returned to his business. Jack Hatfield had returned to his sports shop. Geoff Wood, Eric Thomas and myself were the only directors still at the Club.

As I poured my usual non alcoholic drink from the bar, Geoff Wood made his statement,

> "There's only one person to take over the chair. Neil has to take it over. Don't you agree Eric?"
> "I agree. Neil, will you do it?"

Eric said.

> "Only if that is what the majority of the directors want. If I became Chairman, I would have to give up my position as the England Team Doctor. Nevertheless, if the majority of the directors want me to be Chairman, I would do it."

"Leave it to us"
Geoff Wood replied.
"We'll speak to George Winney."
As I drove back to Redcar, the prospect of Jack, as Manager, and myself, as Chairman, was one I anticipated with relish. The two of us would be a strong partnership. I awaited developments with interest.

George Winney phoned me at home the same evening.. He was aware, he said, of the conversation between myself, Geoff and Eric. He also was fully supportive to my being appointed as chairman. As George was still the Chairman, and would continue as a director for several weeks, the three most senior directors on the Board were in favour of my becoming Chairman. George and I agreed to meet the following day for lunch. At the lunch, George informed me that another director, namely Jack Hatfield, had also given his support to my appointment. With myself there were now five of the eight directors in favour of my becoming Chairman. The three directors who had not declared their position, nor indeed had been approached, were Charles Amer, George Kitching and Ernest Varley. Over lunch, George Winney agreed to approach each of these three directors individually to seek their support for my appointment. I approached no one.

At the beginning of the next Board meeting, the Secretary read out a letter from the Club's Bank Manager. The Club was overdrawn to the extent of £70,000. The bank was demanding equal financial guarantees from every director. Charles Amer was the only director prepared to give such a guarantee. If necessary, he said, he would be prepared to guarantee the full amount of the £70,000 overdraft. It seemed strange, but not one of my fellow directors, supported the suggestion I made at that meeting. I suggested we invite the Bank Manager to the next Board meeting to discuss the financial state of the Club. Not one director was in favour of having such a meeting. Even more strange was the fact that no discussion took place on the appointment of a successor to George Winney. The meeting was short. I left immediately for the sanctuary of the dressing room and the company of the players and staff.

I met Charles Amer, by chance, at The Hotel York, one of his hotels, later in the week.

"We need to discuss the situation at the Club."
he said.

To my astonishment, he asked me to give my support to George Kitching becoming the new Chairman. When I refused, Charles was not pleased. His tone became quite aggressive.

"George Kitching can guarantee the overdraft. You can't!"
he said.

I knew immediately that George Winney had approached Charles Amer to support my nomination. I also knew, at that moment, that Charles had refused to give his support. I nevertheless agreed with the statement Charles had made.

"Of course I can't guarantee the overdraft. However, the fact that I personally can't guarantee the overdraft, is no reason to appoint George Kitching as Chairman. In my view, George is not the person for the job."

It was, at that moment, that I realised I could never become Chairman of Middlesbrough Football Club. When Eric Thomas first approached me, at the cricket club, to become a director of the Club, he had said,

"We don't need your money, we need your brains."

Now it was clear. They did need my money. The reality was I didn't have any! My superannuable income in 1973, as a National Health Service General Practitioner, was £6,256. My conversation with Charles made it abundantly clear that, after ten years as a director, it was not "my brains" Middlesbrough Football Club required. Now they really did require my money. Charles was very annoyed with me. He obviously expected me to give my full support to George Kitching becoming Chairman. I argued that George Kitching would never be able to work with Jack Charlton and, I knew, that Charlton would certainly not be able to work with Kitching. During my discussion with Charles, I also was conscious of the fact that, including myself, five of the eight directors had given their support for me to be the Chairman. Why should I now support someone else? My attitude certainly annoyed Charles Amer. After a very difficult conversation, we agreed to differ.

Surprisingly at this time, the Managing Director of the local Middlesbrough newspaper telephoned me. He invited me to a lunch with himself and the paper's editor. They were both aware of George Winney's impending resignation as Chairman. At the luncheon, they both informed me that, of all the directors, they would only support my nomination as Chairman. They informed me of the number of Middlesbrough Football Club shares they had at their disposal. If necessary, they informed me, they would use those shares to support my nomination at a general meeting of the Club. It was gratifying to know I had their support, but I informed them it was extremely unlikely I would be appointed.

With four directors, out of seven, clearly supporting my nomination as Chairman, the decision made at the next Board meeting astonished me. Following the ongoing discussions on the Club's financial position, and the demand from the bank for financial guarantees, the directors appointed Charles Amer as Chairman. Immediately following his appointment, Charles informed the Board, as if it was his idea, that he would only become Chairman, if I agreed to be the Vice- Chairman. I was unaware at the time that the four directors, who had previously given me their full support, had met and agreed a deal with, the other three directors. No one told me such a meeting had taken place. I had been excluded from attending the meeting. At this informal gathering, the directors had agreed Charles Amer would personally guarantee the Club's overdraft at the bank. In return, he would become Chairman. As part of their agreement, the four directors, who had initially supported fully my nomination as chairman, negotiated with the other three, that I would become the Vice- Chairman. I was totally unaware that any such agreement had been made. Needless to say I turned down the directors' invitation. I politely refused to become Vice-Chairman. Rather than continue the discussion at the Board meeting, Charles Amer suggested he would have private discussions with me, in order to resolve the situation. I was bitterly disappointed. The four directors had let me down. Immediately after the meeting, Jack Hatfield apologised to me for what had happened. He was the only director to discuss the holding of this informal meeting with me.

I now had a very big problem. My instincts told me that the personalities of Charles Amer and Jack Charlton were incompatible. As Chairman and Manager, it would be impossible, in my opinion, for Charles Amer and Jack Charlton to have a good working relationship. Conflict would be inevitable. In addition, Jack was unaware that Charles was the only director at Middlesbrough who was not fully supportive and had certain reservations about his appointment. Charles Amer quite reasonably, believed the Club needed an experienced Manager, not someone who had just finished his playing career and who had no managerial experience. Although only two months had passed, it now seemed years since I had met with Jack at Wetherby. The situation at the Club had now dramatically changed. Believing, as I did, that the relationship between the Chairman and the Manager was crucial to any success, I now had a moral duty to inform Jack of my deep concerns. I would discuss the situation with Jack. When I did telephone him, my advice would have to be,

"Don't come!"

I was distraught.

In the ensuing ten days, my wife and I were invited, on several occasions, to spend time with Charles Amer. On each occasion Charles tried to persuade me to become his Vice-Chairman. He wined and dined Margaret and me at The York Hotel in Redcar, and the Marton Hotel and Country Club in Middlesbrough. Despite his efforts, Charles was unable to persuade me to accept the position. I dithered about phoning Jack. I wanted him to come so badly. I didn't want to advise him,

"Don't come!"

Margaret was most supportive of my decision not to become Vice-Chairman. In his efforts to persuade me, Charles arranged a private dinner for Margaret and me at another of his hotels on Teesside. On this occasion we were wined and dined at The Tall Trees at Yarm. It was at this dinner that Charles suggested a completely different role for me as Vice-Chairman.

"If you agree to become my Vice Chairman, I will ensure that you have sole and complete control of all football matters at the Club. I will run the business side of the Club and you will be the director responsible for running the football side of things. The Manager, the dressing room staff, and the players will be your sole responsibility. On behalf of the Board, you will be responsible for all football matters. In fact, I shall even ensure that no other director is allowed in the dressing room. You will have complete control. You would be, in essence, the Club's 'Director of Football.' If you and the Manager require money for transfers, you will come to me, as I will have overall responsibility for financial matters. You personally will have complete control of all football matters. The Manager will always initially relate to yourself."

"You won't get that through the Board. The other directors will never agree to it."

I said.

"If the other directors agree to it, will you agree to become Vice Chairman?"

he asked.

It was an offer I could not refuse. I already had a special relationship with Jack Charlton. The opportunity, for me to work so closely with him, I couldn't turn down. In this role, I would be the buffer between Charlton and the Board. I would be able to protect the Manager from confrontation with the Chairman. Jack would say, of course, he needed no protection; he was quite capable of fighting his own corner with anyone. Having been a director at Middlesbrough for ten years however, I was well aware of the destructive influence some of our directors had exerted in the past upon the Manager. With this new proposal, I could prevent any of that occurring. Charlton and I would work closely together. We would be inextricably linked. If Jack and the directors parted company, for whatever reason, I would also part company with the directors. Charlton and I would sink or swim together.

"If the Board agree to this new arrangement, I will accept."

I said.

Margaret was not pleased with my decision.

"You may live to regret that decision."

she said on the way home.

At the next Board meeting, Charles' suggestion was unanimously accepted by the directors, without any discussion or pertinent questions. The proposal went through on the nod, as it were. George Winney resigned both as Chairman and as a director. I was very sorry to see George leave. Charles was appointed Chairman. I became Vice Chairman and the so-called 'Director of Football.' I telephoned Jack to inform him of the changes. He seemed pleased that he would be working so closely with me. A brief statement was issued from Ayresome Park to the effect that George Winney had resigned from the Board and that Charles Amer would succeed him as Chairman. Dr. Phillips, the statement said, would be the Vice Chairman and have responsibility, at Board level, for football matters.

Two days before the F.A. Cup Final between Leeds and Sunderland, I travelled to London for The Football Writers Dinner. I had attended the dinner, at which The Footballer of The Year award is made, for the previous ten years. The Sportswriter, Ken Jones, had always extended me an invitation to attend as his guest. It was an annual invitation that would remain throughout my life. Ken and I had become great friends. As a previous winner of the award, Jack Charlton sat on the top table next to Jock Stein. I sat on Ken Jones' table with his other guests. Over the years, Ken's guests have included Terry Venables, John Hollins, Charlie George, George Cohen, Cliff Jones, Des Anderson, and Maurice Setters, to name but a few professional footballers. Additionally I met with many of Ken's business associates. Ken's invitation is one I always cherish and rarely refuse. It was always so refreshing to listen to, and be involved in, the football conversations of those professionals. I learnt so much from them. It certainly was a refreshing change from the conversations I heard in the directors' room at Ayresome Park. At the end of the evening, I mingled with some of the England players. They all congratulated me on becoming Vice-Chairman at Middlesbrough.

"Take good care of our Jack at Middlesbrough."
Bobby Charlton whispered in my ear.

I made no response. Even to Bobby, I kept the promise I had made to Jack at Wetherby. I wouldn't admit to anyone, that Jack was coming to Middlesbrough; not even to his brother. Bobby obviously thought my silence strange. Even though Jack's arrival at Middlesbrough was now just days away, I was determined to stick to the promise I had given him. The matter, as far as I was concerned was confidential between Jack and myself until after his Testimonial Match. Surprisingly, I did not speak with Jack during the evening.

18

Phenomenal Success & Utter Despair........

Four months previously, at Wetherby, Jack Charlton had told me he would arrive at Middlesbrough Football Club, at eleven o'clock in the morning, two days after his benefit match against Celtic. I had no need to check on his arrival. I knew he would be there. It was a matter of trust. Jack's career at Leeds was finished. A new challenge now awaited him at Middlesbrough.

Contrary to what Jack wrote subsequently in his autobiography, when he arrived at Ayresome Park, the home of Middlesbrough. F.C., to take up his appointment as Manager, Jack had not met any of the Middlesbrough directors apart from myself. George Winney, the previous Chairman had lunched with Jack on one occasion, but George was no longer at the Club. When he arrived to take up his appointment at the Club, Jack had not even met the Chairman, Charles Amer. Jack, accompanied by his wife Pat, arrived at 11a.m., the exact time I had informed Charles Amer, he would arrive. My initial role was to introduce Jack to Charles Amer. Jack, Pat and I retired to the Chairman's office for coffee prior to Jack attending a press conference.

Charles suggested that he, Jack and I meet on Friday evening for a meal at The Tall Trees at Yarm, one of the Chairman's hotels. Jack and I readily agreed. Charles Amer explained to Jack, not only had I been appointed Vice-Chairman, but I had also been given the role of the director with sole charge of the football side of the Club. Because of the relationship that existed between Jack Charlton and myself, the Chairman wanted us to work closely together.

"I want you two to run the football side of the Club."
I recall Charles telling us.

"I, as the Chairman, together with the other directors, will run the business side of the Club. You two will run all football matters. Neil will be, in reality, The Director of Football"

Charles Amer quickly established the principle that should we require any money for the transfer of new players, we were to seek such funds via the Chairman. Jack seemed pleased with the arrangement. I knew he and I could work extremely well together. I think Jack knew that too.

On the way to the Press conference Jack said quietly to me

"You realise the Chairman has put you in a precarious position. If things go wrong with the football, which is all the public are interested in, the Chairman will be able to say 'Dr. Phillips is the director responsible for the football side of things', and you'll be the director who will carry the can."

"I'm fully aware of that, but I have every confidence you will deliver the goods. Remember what I said at Wetherby, ' You are needed here, in order to tell us what to do.' So go to it and tell us!"

As far as I was concerned, I had kept completely to the agreement I had made with Charlton at our Wetherby meeting. Rumours had frequently surfaced that Jack was on his way to Middlesbrough but, when asked, I had always denied the rumours. Denial was the agreement Jack had suggested and the one which I had agreed with. I was not prepared to risk Jack's arrival at Middlesbrough by divulging the truth to anyone. I did not even divulge the truth to my trusted friend Harold Shepherdson. When Jack Charlton did arrive however, the two local football reporters were not pleased. They both considered I had misled them over several months. The two reporters, Ray Robertson, of The Northern Echo, and Cliff Mitchell of The Middlesbrough Evening Gazette, were particular friends of mine. Over ten years, I had developed an excellent relationship with them both.

There was a mutual trust between us. In their eyes, and in truth, I had betrayed that trust. I had denied, on many occasions, to them both any knowledge of Charlton coming to Middlesbrough. My loyalty was always to the agreement I had made with Charlton at Wetherby. Both Ray Robertson and Cliff Mitchell, who was also a patient of mine, felt I had misled them. I had let them down. I was sorry to lose the confidence of two friends, but delighted Jack had safely arrived at the Club. The temporary loss of Ray and Cliff's close friendship was a price I had to pay. The rebuilding of their confidence in me would take time.

At the end of the Press Conference, involving the Chairman and Jack Charlton, the local radio station requested an interview with myself. In answer to one of the interviewer's questions I said,

"If Jack Charlton cannot get this football club promotion,
then I believe no one can."

The Chairman thought my remark was stupid.

"That comment will haunt you forever."

he said.

At the time, the comment I made was what I genuinely believed. I consoled myself with the knowledge that the Chairman did not know Jack as I knew him. I had every confidence in our new manager.

On reflection, the timing of Jack's arrival at Middlesbrough was all wrong. In fact it was a disaster. The players had dispersed for the summer. Most were out of the country on holiday. Jack was unable to get all the players together. The Club's dressing room staff, at the time, was the Assistant Manager, Harold Shepherdson, whom Jack knew well. The two coaches were Ian MacFarlane and Jimmy Greenhalgh. The sole member of the Treatment Room Staff, and First Team Trainer, was Jimmy Headrige. Jack met with the staff. He informed them that he wanted them all to stay. They would all be given the chance to prove themselves. Jack was prepared to give each one of them a trial probationary period. If they proved satisfactory to him, they would continue to be members of his staff. They were all relieved to learn the new manager was not bringing in his own staff. Jack was giving them the opportunity to prove themselves to him. The staff were delighted.

PHENOMENAL SUCCESS AND UTTER DESPAIR

If the timing of Jack's arrival seemed wrong, the absence of the players did not allow him to become inactive. On the contrary, he spent the time diligently working on all aspects of the Club. At Leeds, Jack, and his wife Pat, had run a Club Shop selling club souvenirs and merchandise. Jack was surprised that Middlesbrough had no Club Shop. He and Pat promptly opened one. The Club possessed a house on the corner immediately opposite one of the entrances to the ground and this became the site for their new shop. With Pat's expertise, it immediately became a great success. The shop was greatly supported and quickly appreciated by the fans.

The Tall Trees at Yarm is a delightful hotel. Charles, Jack and I enjoyed a nice meal in a private room. The Chairman explained to Jack and myself our separate roles at the Club. Charles Amer and the other directors would run the business side of the Club. In addition, I would have responsibility, at Board level, for the football side. Jack would relate directly to me on a day-to-day basis. If we needed any money for players, or for any other reason, we were to ask the Chairman. Once during the evening I became irritated and annoyed. Speaking directly to Jack, the Chairman said,

> "Dr. Phillips is a very good doctor and has a wide knowledge of football, but he is not a good businessman. I understand, when he negotiated your terms of service, you both agreed that, in the event of the team gaining promotion to the First Division, you, Jack, will be paid a bonus of £10,000. I want you to have that bonus tax free. I will bet you now, £10,000 to a crate of champagne that you won't get promotion. As it's a bet, your £10,000 will be tax-free. I assume you have no objection."

That incident apart, the meal and conversation had gone well. Jack and I were almost on the point of leaving when the Chairman made a cardinal mistake.

> "Oh, by the way Jack,"

he said,

> "you need to know that Jimmy Greenhalgh, one of our coaches is not up to the job. You need to get rid of him."

Jack instantly became very angry. He leaned across the table and exploded into the Chairman's face.

"Don't you ever do that! Not ever! The dressing room staff are my staff. They are mine and mine alone. I have met with all the staff. I have assured them all, including Jimmy Greenhalgh, that they will be staying. Provided they satisfy me, they will stay. If they do not come up to my requirements, they will leave. In any event, I shall be the sole person to make that judgement. Jimmy Greenhalgh is staying"

The Chairman was furious at Jack's response. As Jack and I returned to our cars, we lingered in the car park.

"He's a clever devil that Chairman. He's absolved himself of any responsibility for the football at the Club. Put it all on our shoulders Doc. We'll fix it though! Whatever he suggests in the next three months, we'll say is a load of rubbish. Whatever it is! We can't have him interfering. See you on Monday. I'm off back to Leeds"

It had been an interesting first meeting. I was convinced I had made the right decision in becoming Vice-Chairman. I would always be the buffer between the Chairman and the Manager. I would ensure that there would be no interference from the directors with Jack. The Manager and I were in this together. I relished the thought.

Jack quickly formed the opinion Ayresome Park needed a face-lift. He made arrangements for the rusty, old, main gates to be replaced with new modern ones. He approached me, enquiring as to who was in charge of the Paint Division at I.C.I. Although I worked, at I.C.I., as a part-time medical officer, I knew no one in the Paint Division, but I knew a man who did. Dr. Jenkin Evans was the Medical Director at Wilton and my immediate boss, when I worked there. When I enquired, Jenkin readily made arrangements for us both to lunch at Wilton Castle with two of the relevant I.C.I. directors. Jack was in top form throughout the luncheon. He had both directors eating out of his hand. They quickly agreed to supply all the paint Jack needed for the ground. Even better, the supply of paint would be free! It

PHENOMENAL SUCCESS AND UTTER DESPAIR

was a major coup. Jack was delighted. He said,

"Free paint for the whole ground. Bloody marvellous! That was a luncheon well worthwhile having. However I hated the cold jellied consommé! They don't serve that in the mining villages of Ashington and Tredegar!"

When Jack reported his coup to the Board, the Chairman was furious. He said,

"I have a friend at I.C.I. who can do a better deal for us."

"How can you get be a better deal?" Jack asked.

"We're getting it all for nothing! We can have as much paint as we require. I've organised it with two of their directors"

It so happened that Charles' friend at I.C.I. Wilton, was none other than Dr. Jenkin Evans, the very man I had contacted. There was no point in Charles making any further contact. Jack and I had completed the deal. On such matters however, the Chairman wanted to be involved. He wanted to receive the credit for such successes. Charles was not prepared to allow Jack Charlton to receive the glory for what he considered was a business matter. Subsequently, the Chairman told me,

"Charlton's role is to coach the team. I don't want him involved in business transactions. Try and keep him to the football side of things."

I chose to ignore the Chairman's point of view. I knew Jack wanted to be totally involved in every aspect of the Club. He wanted to manage the whole Club.

In a very short time, the entire stadium was repainted. Blocks of seating were painted in red or white. The whole environment of the stadium was improved. It became a brighter, friendlier place.

Jack busied himself with the mass production of the Team's Fixture List. He arranged the production of large cardboard Fixture Lists in their thousands and then organised their distribution throughout the whole of Teesside. Every public building, public house, club, factory, garage, sports organisation, school and retail shop would have one of the new fixture lists.

Jack wanted everyone to know when his team was playing at Ayresome Park. He visited the bus companies to persuade them to improve their bus services on match days. Jack wanted the buses running at times more convenient for the fans. He also wanted the number of buses travelling on match days increased.

> "Why is Charlton involving himself in these business matters? He should stick to managing the team."

the Chairman and other directors repeatedly enquired of me.

> "At present, as it's the closed season, he has no team to manage. The players are on holiday. In any event, everything he does is for the Club's benefit. I fully support what he is doing."

I frequently replied.

The Chairman however was not happy. He did not want Jack involved in what he considered were "business", and not "football", matters. Worse followed!

Jack was not impressed with the Middlesbrough team shirts. Many years previously at Leeds, on his appointment as Manager, Revie had changed the Leeds' playing shirts, from blue and gold, to pure white. White shirts Jack, like Revie, believed made it easier to pick out your own players on the pitch. Middlesbrough's traditional playing strip was a red shirt with a narrow white cuff and a small white collar.

> "Not enough white on these shirts."

Jack told me.

So Jack changed the strip. Under Jack Charlton, Middlesbrough would continue to play in a predominately red shirt, but Jack now introduced a broad white band around the chest, a larger white collar than previously and a white V shaped inset below the neck.. The new shirts would continue to have white cuffs. Unfortunately, Jack and I did not inform the Chairman of the intended change. We both considered it a football matter. All their lives, the Chairman and the directors had supported the team playing in predominately red shirts. The entire Board, apart from myself, were traditionalists. They wanted the old, traditional shirt to remain. Following

PHENOMENAL SUCCESS AND UTTER DESPAIR

Jack's decision, I argued with Chairman and Directors that the new shirts would be an advantage to the players and could improve the performance of the team. In any event, I believed it was a 'football' matter. The decision had been made. I formed the opinion, with which Jack agreed, that the directors did not like anyone making decisions, apart from themselves!

When they had sat together at The Football Writers' Dinner, a few weeks previously, Jock Stein gave Jack some advice. Jock's advice to Jack was,

> "Get to know your players as quickly as possible. The best way, is to take them on a pre-season tour. Live with them for a week. If you do that, it's amazing what you will learn about them."

Jack heeded the advice. A series of pre-season matches in Scotland were quickly arranged. The players and staff would live together for a week. Middlesbrough would play Morton, Hamilton Academicals and Partick Thistle. The Manager, Players and Staff would live together for ten days. On their return from Scotland, other pre-season matches would be played against Newcastle United at home, and two away games at York and Grimsby.

In those initial weeks Jack formed a bad impression of Graeme Souness.

> "Graeme's too interested in the night life and too keen on the girls."

he told me. Surprisingly, in the six pre-season matches, Jack only selected Graeme Souness on one occasion. Souness's only appearance was playing at left fullback in the away fixture against York City. We lost the game, 2–1.

Even more disturbing, particularly to Harold Shepherdson the Assistant Manager, was the fact that for five of the pre-season matches, played under Jack's management, young Brian Taylor partnered Boam in the team's central defence. Taylor and Boam appeared to be Jack's first preference as the two centre backs. For the sixth pre-season match, Billy Gates partnered Boam. In all six pre-season matches, Jack played Willie Maddren in midfield. Harold Shepherdson, who had managed the team so successfully in the last four months of the season, implored me,

> "Have a word with Jack. Tell him Willie can't play in midfield. Playing him there is just stupid. Willie is not mobile enough. Maddren is a superb central defender. He should play alongside Boam."

Under Harold's management, he had selected Maddren and Boam as the two central defenders. They had played very well together. I respected Harold's opinion enormously and I knew he was correct. I also knew however that, over the ten years I had been at the Club, there had been too much interference, by others, on the Manager's thinking. I was determined Jack would never be subjected to such interference. I chose not to speak with Jack on the matter. Team selection was a matter for him and him alone. Of the six games played in the pre-season period, Middlesbrough won all three games in Scotland and the away game at Grimsby. Two games were lost; the one at home to Newcastle and the other game away at York.

The team's and Jack's first fixture, in League Division Two, was an away game at Portsmouth. Jack selected Boam and young Brian Taylor as the two central defenders. Maddren played in midfield. There was no place for Souness. The team won at Portsmouth, by the only goal of the game. Alan Foggon was the scorer. The team was off to a good start!

Souness was not happy at being left out of the side for the majority of the pre-season fixture and even more aggrieved when he was not selected for the first three league matches. He had not even been selected as the substitute. Souness sought a meeting with his Manager. Graeme was quite outspoken at the meeting about Jack's accusations.

> "Of course I like the girls and I enjoy a good night out, but, more than anything, I want to be a success in football. Women and booze will never interfere with my ambition to succeed. In football, I prepare for games as well as anyone and I will never let you down."

During their meeting Jack became impressed with Souness' attitude. For the next game, against Carlisle at home, Souness was on the substitute's bench. Maddren was still playing in midfield, with Boam and young

[518]

PHENOMENAL SUCCESS AND UTTER DESPAIR

Taylor remaining as the centre-backs. In my opinion, and that of Harold Shepherdson, but not of Jack Charlton himself, the Carlisle match was the turning point for the team's subsequent performances.

To succeed in any sport, you always needed a little luck. Jack, I knew, was an excellent coach, but I didn't know if he was a lucky one. Before resigning as Middlesbrough's Manager, Stan Anderson had sold Joe Laidlaw to Carlisle. Joe was playing for Carlisle in our fourth match of the season against his old Club. Ten minutes into the game, Joe's elbow accidentally hit Brian Taylor's eye with such force that he was unable to see properly. Brian was forced to retire. He was replaced by Graeme Souness. Souness went into mid-field. Maddren reverted to centre back, partnering Boam. During the previous season this was the team formation used so successfully by Harold Shepherdson. Middlesbrough beat Carlisle by the only goal of the game. John Craggs, our right full back, scored the goal direct from a free kick.

Following the Carlisle game, Willie Maddren played thirty-eight consecutive League matches at centre-back. Graeme Souness played thirty-four League games in mid-field. Poor Brian Taylor would not be selected to play in any League game again. Maddren, Souness, and Jack owed a lot to Joe Laidlaw and his accidental elbow in Taylor's eye! Jack had experienced his little bit of luck. I now knew that not only was Jack a good manager, he was a lucky one as well.

Within a week of the Carlisle victory, Jack made the greatest scoop of the season. Although he would frequently refer during the season to Boam and Maddren as "the two men who mind the shop for me." He knew that the success of his team depended on the quality of the mid-field players. In this area Jack felt he was at least one player short. He discussed the situation with his friend Jock Stein, the Celtic Manager. To Jack's surprise Jock Stein told him,

"I'll give you Bobby Murdoch on a free transfer! He'll need a signing on fee and if you can sort that out, he's your player."

Jack knew Bobby Murdoch was an outstanding right-sided mid-field player. Bobby was probably one of the best passers of a ball the game had ever seen. An experienced Scotland international, he was a member of Celtic's European Cup winning team. Jack could not understand Jock Stein's generosity and quickly set up a meeting in Glasgow with Bobby Murdoch. I received a telephone call from Jack,

"I want to sign Bobby Murdoch. He wants a signing-on fee. Can we sign him?"

"You know, as well as me, signing on fees are illegal."

I instantly responded.

"Well the Chairman told us if we ever wanted any money we should ask him. So let's test him out. Phone the Chairman and tell him the situation. Let's see what he says."

I phoned the Chairman. He needed background information as to who Bobby Murdoch was.

"If he is the player Charlton and you want, then bring him down. I can see him any morning at one of my hotels."

"What about the signing on fee?"

I enquired.

"Don't worry about that. We'll find a way."

The Chairman replied.

Bobby Murdoch, later that week, met with the Chairman on his own, for just half an hour.

"I'm happy with the outcome."

Murdoch informed Jack.

"I'll sign a three year contract."

Murdoch was a Middlesbrough player. He made his debut in the team's away game at Blackpool. Several Celtic supporters, who were on their way to the First Division game between Leeds and Manchester United, changed their plans and came instead to Blackpool to see Murdoch make his debut for Middlesbrough.. Such was the drawing power of Murdoch with the Celtic fans! Middlesbrough drew with Blackpool. No goals were scored during the game. Interestingly Harry Potts, the Blackpool Manager gave the "Man of the Match Award" jointly to Boam and Maddren.

"They perform extremely well together at centre-back."

he said.

PHENOMENAL SUCCESS AND UTTER DESPAIR

I was intrigued of course to find out how the Chairman had satisfied Bobby Murdoch's demand for a signing on fee. When the Chairman explained the arrangement to me, I was flabbergasted. He had agreed to sell Murdoch a house, on the estate he was developing at Normanby. Murdoch would have the house valued, by his own valuer, and the Chairman would allow Murdoch to buy the house at a discounted price. At the end of his three-year contract, with a rising house-price market, Bobby would be able to sell the house for more than the original valuation. The profit from the sale of his house would be tax-free. Murdoch's signing on fee demands were met by the Chairman's extreme generosity. The Chairman's action made me further realise I could never become Chairman of a Football Club. I just did not have the financial wherewithal!

Maddren played alongside Boam in central defence for the rest of the season. Graeme Souness played in central midfield, with David Armstrong on his left and Bobby Murdoch on his right. With these players in their best positions, the team went from strength to strength. At the completion of the tenth League game against Hull, we were top of Division Two by three clear points. Later in the season, Maddren was selected, as a central defender, for the England Under 23 team, and Souness played for the Scotland Under 23 team in midfield.

Jack introduced his own new system of playing. It proved most successful. Jack was aware, at that time, the game had changed. Defenders were concentrating on implementing the offside trap at every available opportunity, Defenders, on both sides, pushed up field regularly. As a result, the midfield, in every game, became totally congested with players. Instead of trying to carry the ball through them, Jack devised a system of delivering the ball beyond the defence, as they pushed up field. He employed a midfield runner to get in behind the defence as they came out. To make his system work, Jack needed a player of real pace. Such a player was Alan Foggon. He had tremendous pace and was the ideal person to get in behind opposing defences. Jack maintains it was Foggon's pace that made the team so successful. Under Jack's management the team was extremely successful on the field. With the team sitting on the top of Division Two, Middlesbrough was more successful than they had ever been in the previous twenty-two years, and it was all due to Jack Charlton.

Unfortunately, off the field, Jack's relationship with the Chairman and the other directors became fraught. With the team running away with success in Division Two, it was natural for the television companies to visit our home games. If Jack's involvement in the so-called business matters of the Club had upset the Chairman and some directors previously, they were now in for a further shock. During the latter part of our promotion season the television cameras visited our ground. Football supporters all over the country were anxious to see Middlesbrough play and the television companies duly obliged. When we did appear on 'Match of the Day', the pictures were abysmal. We had no proper facilities at Ayresome Park for the television companies. The cameras, of necessity, were sited at ground level. As a result the television pictures were totally unacceptable. Jack was now a football pundit with the television companies and was aware, more than most, of the need for the presentation of televised matches to be photographically professional. As there was no television gantry at Middlesbrough, Jack decided it was essential we had one built. He approached a Teesside businessman, Mac Murray, whose day job included building oilrigs for the North Sea. Jack, like he did with the paint from I.C.I., persuaded Mac Murray to build a television gantry on the roof of the South Stand for free. Needless to say Jack completed the deal without consulting anyone at the Club. He considered it was a necessity if the Club was moving towards the First Division. The fact that it would be built for free made the deal absolutely ideal.

When informed, the Chairman and some of the directors were furious.

"How dare the Manager make these arrangements without consulting with the directors."

The Chairman angrily said to me.

"He has no right to behave like this. He has no authority to make such decisions."

"But it's what we need and it's for free! It will greatly improve the appearance of our team on television."

PHENOMENAL SUCCESS AND UTTER DESPAIR

I replied.

The Chairman and the directors were not pleased. A fierce argument developed at the Board meeting when Charlton presented his agreed plan to the directors. The directors were totally opposed to Jack's idea. Jack could bear their anger no longer.

> "I've never heard so much rubbish spoken at these Board meetings. I can't waste my time listening to the nonsensical views you put forward. In future, I will not attend any Board meetings. If you have anything you wish to tell me, inform the Doc. He will relay the message to me."

With those remarks Charlton left the Board meeting. He did not attend another Board meeting for three years.

Charlton's departure from the Board meeting, accompanied by his outburst, stunned the directors into silence. I broke the silence.

> "I just do not understand your attitude. As directors we should be grateful to the Manager for negotiating such a deal. No building will proceed until the Board have sat down with Mac Murray and reached an agreement with him as to the actual siting of the gantry. May I suggest that, if any director objects to the proposal, they personally come forward with an alternative builder who will do the work for free and be able to complete the work before the start of next season."

The Chairman was absolutely furious not only with Charlton, but also with my support for his actions. Mac Murray built a superb gantry. The television pictures were outstanding. Unfortunately, as the television gantry went up, the relationship between the Directors and the Manager went down alarmingly.

My role as a buffer, between the Manager and the Board, increased considerably. Unfortunately the building of the television gantry was yet another item for the directors to file away in the 'Jack Charlton Interference Folder'. It was patently obvious they totally objected to Jack's involvement in anything other than the coaching of football. I considered my fellow directors' attitude pathetic. I could not understand why they could not just enjoy the success Charlton had brought to the Club. It always appeared to me they wanted the credit for the Club's success for themselves. They were reluctant to acknowledge that all the success we had achieved was due to Jack Charlton. The team, during Jack's first season, was unbelievably successful. Their success placed me in a very strong position with my fellow directors.

When I reflect on Jack Charlton's first managerial season at Middlesbrough, I still find it difficult to comprehend the success he achieved. Promotion to the First Division was achieved on March 23rd., some six weeks before the end of the season. David Armstrong's solitary goal at Oxford ensured Middlesbrough were back in the First Division. Jack Charlton and his team had fulfilled the statement I had made before the season started.

"If Jack Charlton cannot get Middlesbrough promoted, no one can."

So much for what the Chairman considered was a stupid comment! The team had only played thirty-six of their forty-two league games. Middlesbrough were crowned as League Champions the following week at Luton. Including the 'lucky' home win against Carlisle, when Brian Taylor was injured, the team achieved the longest unbeaten run in the Club's history. Twenty-four consecutive games were played without a single defeat. Middlesbrough won the League with sixty-five points, when a win was just two points. The points total was a record for the Second Division. Only eight goals were conceded at home in the entire season. The team recorded twenty-seven wins in the season; another club record. Jack was named 'Manager of the Month' for September and March, a fitting tribute to the success his team had achieved. After the Luton game, at which Middlesbrough were crowned Second Division Champions, Jack asked me to enquire about his bonus for achieving promotion. The Chairman presented Jack with his bonus at the Club's Celebration Dinner held at the Chairman's Marton Hotel and Country Club. Representatives of the Leagues' Clubs were present at the dinner.

The morning after the Club's celebration dinner, after completing a morning surgery, I made my way, as usual, to Ayresome Park. With the added responsibility of being the director in charge of football, such journeys had become a daily and frequently a twice daily occurrence. Surprisingly, as I drove the eleven miles to the ground, I was not in a particularly celebratory mood. In fact I felt quite depressed. Throughout the season, I had worked my socks off at Middlesbrough Football Club. I had been at the Club virtually every day ensuring Jack Charlton was not subjected to any interference from my fellow directors. Instead of being happy at the success I had achieved, I was quite resentful. My resentment was mainly concerned with the fact that I had carried out all my responsibilities for no financial reward whatsoever. I received no remuneration as the Club's Medical Officer. The Club received my medical expertise free of charge. As the so-called football director, no remuneration was possible in those days. I wondered why I had been doing all this work for nothing. All the staff were now, quite rightly, receiving financial bonuses for our success. I considered myself to be a member of staff, yet I was to receive no financial reward for my efforts. In that I was totally responsible for bringing Jack to Middlesbrough, and with all the success that had followed, I felt the Club owed me something.

"You don't look particularly happy."

The Chairman said, as I entered his office. We were alone.

"I'm not happy."

I said.

"I should be, but I'm not. I've worked really hard at the Club for the past year, and yet I have received no financial reward. It appears I can provide the Club with all my medical expertise and be responsible for all football matters, yet receive no payment whatsoever. Everyone seems financially better off with promotion, except myself."

The Chairman reached for his inside pocket. He threw his chequebook on the table.

"There you are. Write your own cheque. Write it for any amount you want. Three thousand, Four, Five or even Ten if you want. As a result of our promotion, I shall make a fortune next year. With the team playing in the First Division, my three hotels on Teesside are really going to prosper. You have contributed to our success more than anyone, so write your own cheque."

The chairman's chequebook lay on the table.

"I couldn't do that. I'd have to talk with Margaret first."

"Well talk to her. I'll still be here tomorrow. Let me know the amount then."

Charles Amer placed his chequebook back in his pocket.

Margaret and I talked long into the night. Eventually Margaret came up with a plan. We would ask the chairman for £2,500. If I received the cheque, we would then both seek an appointment with our bank manager. We would request the bank manager to enter the cheque into our account and, at the same time, record that this was a personal ex gratia payment to me from the Club Chairman for all the work I had done contributing to the team's success. The following morning I received the cheque. Margaret and I visited the Bank Manager. He recorded depositing the cheque according to our wishes. The Chairman had been most generous to me.

Despite the euphoria at Middlesbrough, before the season finished I was to receive catastrophic news. The news changed forever my love of the game. Despite Middlesbrough's fantastic success, I was on the brink of being plunged into utter despair. Football, for me, would change forever. For me the beautiful game was about to lose its gloss.

I had been on weekend, emergency call for the Practice. It had been tiring and frustrating. Week-ends on duty in the Practice were shared amongst the partners. The senior partner and I shared our weekend on call. He was on duty from the Saturday mid-day until eight on the Sunday morning. I was responsible for all emergency calls from eight on a Sunday morning until eight on Monday morning. Although I had the larger share of our weekend on duty, it suited me. I was always free to attend Saturday football matches. It also suited the senior partner because he had the smaller share of the on call duty. It had been a very busy Sunday with over thirty so called emergencies. I say so-called emergencies, for, in reality, none of the calls were for a patient with a serious illness. In the early seventies this was not an unusual occurrence for General Practitioners on weekend call. The majority of the emergency house calls had been to see children who were crying. Frequently throughout the week-end my mind wandered back to the days of my paediatric training in Sheffield with Professor Illingworth. One of the questions, set for us, in the final paediatric examination had been,

> "What are the commonest causes of crying in a three month old baby?."

The answers Illingworth would initially want from his students were not illnesses, but the simple everyday happenings in a baby's life.

> "The baby has a wet nappy and needs changing. The baby is hungry and needs feeding. The baby needs picking up and loving."

These were the simple things babies needed and parents should check first. Only when the normal things in life had been stated would Illingworth wish the students to consider illnesses. Placing illnesses before normality would, Illingworth had repeatedly told us, result in failure. Illingworth was an expert on the normal child. Certainly it appeared, after this very busy week-end, that many parents reacted to their child crying by saying,

> "We'd better send for the Doctor."

Over the weekend I'd seen many babies who just needed some tender loving care; the changing of wet nappies or proper feeding. Past experiences made all my partners realise the week-ends on call could be quite tiring and exhausting. As a result, the Practice had instituted an arrangement whereby following a week-end on duty, the on call doctor would have a half day on the Monday. As I drove to Monday morning surgery, I was quite looking forward to the half-day. Morning surgery passed off uneventfully and, with only a few house calls to make, a reasonably quiet day was in prospect.

The Monday sport injury clinic at Ayresome Park would be interesting. I usually saw all the injured players on a Sunday morning but, with being on call in the Practice, I had not seen them. Jimmy Headrige, the first team trainer, had phoned me at home however and given me a list of the walking wounded. I was quite looking forward to seeing them. I had seen the entire first team players after the home game on Saturday, but now there would be the reserves and juniors to examine. I loved looking after those footballers. In the main they all wanted to be fit. They hated being injured or ill. They, at least, wouldn't send for me unless they were really ill. As I examined each player, in the Club's medical department, I was conscious of Harold Shepherdson, the Assistant Manager, being present throughout. Harold was in his hovering mood. I knew he had something important to tell me. I also knew, from previous experience, Harold would not mention his important news in front of anyone else. The number of players needing to be examined was considerable and, when I had seen them all, Harold had disappeared.

It had become a ritual at the Club, when I had completed my examination of the players, I would report to the Manager. Jack was in good form and pleased to know that the first team pool of players was fit and all available for selection. Monday morning had also become a ritual for the Chairman, Charles Amer, and two directors, George Kitching and Ernie Varley. These three would spend their morning deep in conversation in the Chairman's office. It was usual for me to join them just before they went off for lunch. Today, however, was a half-day for me and I was intent on playing a few holes of golf in the afternoon. The sooner I got home the better. I merely exchanged pleasantries with the three directors and was on my way out of Ayresome Park, and on my way home, when I found Harold. He was now hovering around my car in the car park.

"Can we have a chat?" he enquired.

"Of course" I replied.

"But not here" said Harold. "Let's take a walk out onto the pitch."

We threaded our way through the home dressing room, walked down the player's tunnel and out into the centre circle.

"No-one will overhear us out here" Harold said.

PHENOMENAL SUCCESS AND UTTER DESPAIR

Whatever it was Harold was about to tell me was serious and his ultra caution, in not being overheard, confirmed the secrecy of what he was about to tell me. Even so, I was ill prepared for what was his message.

"I suppose you know what is happening at eleven o'clock on Wednesday"

Harold enquired.

I thought for a moment and replied

"I haven't a clue".

"Funny that, Alf seemed sure you would know".

"Know what?" I enquired.

Harold looked at me with sadness in his face.

"Alf is to be sacked on Wednesday morning. Alf telephoned me first thing this morning and told me."

Whilst I didn't want to believe Harold, I knew it was true. Harold's face told me it was true.

"I can't think why Alf would suggest I knew"

I mumbled.

"I had no idea. I'll give him a ring this afternoon."

"No. Alf doesn't want you to ring him. Made that quite clear. He doesn't want any contact made at the present time. He'll ring us if needs be."

Harold replied.

"What about the tour?"

I enquired, followed quickly by

"Well I don't think I'll want to go now. Who's going to manage the tour to East Germany, Bulgaria and Yugoslavia?"

"Don't know. Don't know."

said Harold.

We walked back across the pitch, through the dressing room and into the car park in silence..

"It goes without saying no-one's to know about this. The announcement is to be made on Wednesday. Strictly confidential till then."

Harold's words drifted into oblivion. Stupid Football Association, I thought. There'll never be another Alf. How can they do this to him? The Manager, who won the World Cup for them, they now decide to sack. How stupid can these directors become. They have a great Manager and they sack him. My half-day was in ruins. My round of golf was irrelevant. I knew Alf's life would be in ruins.

The announcement was made on the Wednesday. I drove onto the sand dunes at Redcar to hear the announcement on the radio. It was an eerie feeling waiting for some urgent, breaking news I had been aware of for two days. The radio announcement was made.

> "The Football Association has relieved Sir Alf Ramsey of his duties."

There were the usual platitudes from the Secretary of The Football Association. about what a great job Alf had done in 1966, but this was eight years on and it was time for change. The platitudes were meaningless. They had sacked Sir Alf. It was the end of an era. An era I had been privileged to be part of. The King was dead. Alf's contract was terminated by The Football Association with effect at the end of April. No decision had been made as to who would mange the team for the Home Internationals and the tour to East Germany, Bulgaria and Yugoslavia. The phone was ringing when I entered my home.

> "It's Les Cocker."

My wife informed me as she handed me the phone

> "Have you heard the news? Bloody disgrace. What about the tour? Shan't go myself now. They can stuff it. If Alf's sacked, so am I. Bloody disgrace."

I could do no other than agree with everything Les said.

> "I haven't heard anything officially."

I told Les.

> "Suppose they'll get round to us eventually. Like you however I shan't be going on the tour. If Alf's sacked, so am I. I'll let you know if I hear anything. Harold knows. I'm seeing Harold tomorrow at the Board meeting. I'll phone you

tomorrow night. Thanks for ringing. See you soon."
Les rang off.

It was not a day to be at home waiting for the phone to ring. I knew the phone would never stop ringing. I went for a walk on the beach with Margaret. My thoughts were private. I felt very sad.

"Joe Mercer to lead the England Tour"
was the headline on the newspaper boarding a few days later. Well at least he's been contacted I thought. Almost a week went by. Harold, Les and I had heard nothing from The Football Association. On meeting Harold however, he had a message from Alf for the three of us. Harold and Alf had talked about the tour on the phone. Harold had explained to Alf the three of us did not wish to be part of the tour. Alf however had a different view. He wanted the three of us to go. He had expressed that view forcibly to Harold. Alf believed, if the three of us opted out of the tour, there would be no continuity for the players. The players would suffer as a result.

"The three of you must go."
Alf was adamant.
The message was clear. Make your own minds up after the tour is over, but don't leave the players in the lurch now. Even in the hurt of being sacked, Alf's thoughts were, where they always were, with the players. I rang Les at night.

"It's all very well Doc"
said Les
"We haven't even been asked yet to go on the tour. Let's wait and see if we are asked."

The usual invite arrived at the usual time. There was no other contact. No information or remarks about Sir Alf's sacking. Just the usual letter informing me of my selection for the tour. Enclosed with the letter was the Itinerary Card setting out the daily routine of the tour, the flight times to the various countries and the members of the party. The participants on the tour were,

[531]

DOCTOR TO THE WORLD CHAMPIONS

The Officials, all of The Football Association, Sir Andrew Stephen, R. Wragg, E.M. Gliksten, F.A. Would and E.A. Croker

Team Manager: J. Mercer (Coventry City).
Honorary Team Physician: Dr. U.N. Phillips.
Trainers: H. Shepherdson M.B.E (Middlesbrough) and L. Cocker (Leeds United). Administrative Officer: A. Odell (F.A. Staff).
Players: C. Bell, S. Bowles, T. Brooking, M. Channon, R. Clemence, M. Dobson, E. Hughes, N. Hunter, K. Keegan, M. MacDonald, D. McKenzie, P. Madeley, R. McFarland, M. Pejic, M. Peters, P. Shilton, C. Todd, D. Watson, K. Weller and F. Worthington.

The tour was to East Germany, Bulgaria and Yugoslavia. All members of the party were to report to The Great Western Royal Hotel by 1900 hrs. on Sunday 26th May 1974. The party would return on Thursday 6th June.

I travelled to London with Harold Shepherdson. As usual, we caught the express train from Darlington. Harold had received no information other than the usual letter of invitation from the Football Association and the itinery. We were both surprised Joe Mercer had not contacted us. The reason for his lack of contact became apparent as soon as we arrived at The Great Western Hotel. Dick Wragg, the Chairman of the Senior International Committee, was waiting for us as we registered in the hotel. Joe Mercer was not very well. He had gone to his room feeling quite poorly. Dick Wragg informed me he would like me to go to Joe's room and examine him. Joe was not well. He had a high temperature and was sweating profusely. He had been vaccinated against Smallpox some days earlier and his upper arm was very swollen and the vaccination site, together with the surrounding area, severely infected and inflamed. I advised Joe to stay in bed. I gave him the appropriate treatment and said I would visit him after the evening meal. I assured Joe, Harold and Les, the two trainers, would ensure all the players had arrived by the allotted hour. Dick Wragg was extremely concerned to know of Joe's state of health. Dick wondered whether Joe would be fit to travel and act as Manager on the tour. Having sacked Alf,

PHENOMENAL SUCCESS AND UTTER DESPAIR

Dick Wragg stressed to me how important it was for Joe Mercer to be fully fit to take up the managerial duties. Dick Wragg's concern was a measure of the anxiety The Football Association officials had regarding the success of the tour. Their sacking of Alf would only be justified, in the short term, if this tour was a success.

Inevitably when the England players gathered for a match or tour, there were players who were unavailable because of injury or illness. The Sunday evening revealed that several players would not be making the trip. Various Club Managers had phoned in to say their players were injured and would not be making the trip. The players were Stan Bowles, Norman Hunter, and Paul Madeley. Before supper, Harold, Les and I visited Joe Mercer in his room to inform him of the situation and seek his advice as to which additional players were to be contacted, as replacements. Harold and Les were given the names of the players Joe wished to invite as replacements and after a considerable amount of phoning, Tommy Booth and David Mills of Middlesbrough were invited to join the party. These two players would arrive in time to catch the mid-day flight from Heathrow to Leipzig in East Germany on the Monday. Harold and Les greeted the other players on arrival and informed them of Joe's illness. Inevitably the conversation of the players at supper revolved around Alf's sacking. The players expected Harold, Les and I would be able to give them some more information on the sacking. They were astonished we had no more information than they already had. There was unease amongst us all.

Harold, Les and I, Alf's staff, had made no arrangement to sit together throughout the tour. At Heathrow Airport however, it became apparent we would be doing just that. The press reporters were still hounding the F.A. Officials for yet another slant on Alf's sacking. We three did our best to avoid any such discussions with any of the officials, press or players. We had no inclination to become involved in discussions with the F.A. Officials. The thought, of listening to their reasons for Alf's sacking, was abhorrent to us. The press reporters were divided into two groups. There were those reporters who had always been loyal to Alf and those who, by their writing and media pressure, had contributed to his downfall. We three were in no mood to communicate with either. The event had been too recent and the three of us felt as if we were going through a bereavement process. In the departure lounge, the three of us sat in a quiet corner together. Ted Croker, who was relatively new into the post of the F.A. Secretary, joined the three of us.

"During this tour"

he began

> "I'd like to have a fairly lengthy meeting with the three of you. After all, you three have been involved with the England Team for many years. I suppose for hundreds of internationals. Your knowledge is extensive and invaluable. I want to tap into that knowledge. Learn from you. I want you to tell me what you consider are the good things and inform me of the bad things. The things that have been done wrong in the past, so that I can prevent them happening in the future. I want to learn from all three of you. I hope you will all agree to co-operate with me to the full."

Harold spoke for us all.

> "Of course Ted. We'll be pleased to. You arrange the time of the meeting and we'll be there."

As Ted Croker sped out of earshot, Les was already jumping in with his ideas.

> "Wants us to tell him what's wrong does he? Well what about those table mats? Remember when we got back from Spain? Alf wanted Dennis Follows to give us a set of World Cup Table Mats and Follows refused. Remember? Follows said they weren't for the staff. Only for Directors and Visiting Officials. In my book, every member of staff and every player should have had a set. After all it was the players who won the World Cup aided by the Manager and the Staff. I'll tell him what's wrong. First rule–value your staff and your players. The F.A. should realise the players and staff are more important than the officials."

[534]

PHENOMENAL SUCCESS AND UTTER DESPAIR

The England party left Heathrow Airport on British Airways Charter Flight BCH 594 shortly after noon for the two-hour flight to Leipzig. In recent years the England party had always travelled by specially, chartered British Airways flights. Invariably British Airways gave us the same cabin crew. Over the years they had become our friends and always looked after us well. Pam Darch, the senior stewardess on board, had now been promoted to a Purser. She had also become a great family friend, having spent weekends with my family.

Joe Mercer was not well during the flight. His temperature remained high. He sweated profusely, but fortunately slept through most of the flight. On arrival at the Interhotel Astoria in Leipzig, Joe took my advice and went straight to bed. Harold and Les took the Monday evening training session. Although Joe Mercer was feeling better on the Tuesday morning, I persuaded him to stay in bed and miss the morning training session. Harold and Les would again be responsible. Joe would meet with the players at the afternoon team meeting when the team would be announced. Reluctantly Joe agreed to remain in bed at the hotel. The team meeting revealed the differing style of the two Managers. Alf was a master of detail. The opposing team would have been watched and he would go through their way of playing. He would also go through the opposing players individually, pointing out their strengths and weaknesses. Joe was not particularly interested in what the opposition was going to do. Having announced the team he had chosen Joe was mainly concerned with how England would play. His instructions however were in very general terms and there was little attention to the detail we had experienced with Alf over the previous twelve years. I recall at one stage during the meeting Les asking Joe which players were to form the defensive wall in the event of an opposing free kick just outside the penalty box. In Alf's team talks, each member of the defensive wall was nominated and each player would clearly be informed of his defensive responsibilities. Joe's response to Les's question was quite dismissive.

"These are professional players Les. Internationals to boot.
They'll sort themselves out. I have every confidence in them."

The players left the team talk not knowing who was to be in the defensive wall. Les and Harold sorted it out with the players later that evening. The team talk highlighted the problem Harold and Les now had. They had worked with Alf for some twelve years. They both were used to doing things according to the gospel of Alf. It was ingrained in the two of them. Now it was all change. Harold and Les had been given no time to adapt. With Joe not feeling very well they had no opportunity to sit down and discuss with him the details of how he wanted matters to be run. It was inevitable that comparisons would be made between Alf and Joe. Inevitable, but sad.

The match against East Germany was a dull, but hard fought, game and the England players fought a rearguard action to earn a commendable 0–0 draw. Immediately after the game, the players had hardly sat down in the dressing room when the entire party of F.A. officials visited them. Led by Sir Andrew Stephen the officials were delirious. The England Team had not lost. England, without Alf, had not lost! The officials had already convinced themselves, they could survive without Sir Alf. While none of them actually said so, their obvious delight at the 0–0 draw expressed their inward thoughts. I recalled the Poland game at Wembley; the game which decided England had missed out on being represented in the 1974 World Cup. No F.A. Officials visited the dressing room after the Poland defeat. Harold Shepherdson was to be presented that evening, in the dressing room, with a Silver Salver, to commemorate his one hundred appearances as England Trainer. Not one official turned up in the dressing room. The presentation did not take place. My mind recalled Rudyard Kipling's "If" that said

"If you can meet with Triumph and Disaster and treat those

two impostors just the same."

The F.A. Officials were obviously not students of Kipling. I felt sick at the hypocrisy of it all. They were obviously delighted with the draw. They believed the draw in East Germany justified the sacking of Alf. The King was certainly dead.

The meeting with Ted Croker, Harold, Les and me took place on Friday the 31$^{st.}$ May in Bulgaria. We congregated in Ted Croker's room, or rather his suite, in Sofia's Grand Hotel. The size of his room became the first item under discussion. Here was the Secretary staying in a suite with a large lounge, separate bedroom and en suite facilities. In comparison the room allocated to each Trainer was a single bedroom with en suite facilities. Into their rooms of course they had to accommodate the kit for the entire tour, together with the medical and physiotherapy equipment needed to treat the injured players.

> "Why can't the Trainers be allocated a suite similar to this? It would be so much easier. The kit would be easily accommodated and a proper treatment area could be set up within the lounge.

Ted accepted the point. In future he agreed that it was in the players' interest to have adequate treatment and storage facilities while on tour. Much of our discussion centred on travel arrangements.

> "Why,"

we asked,

> "do the F.A. Officials travel first class on the scheduled flights, and the players travel economy class?. After all, it's the players who, on arrival, have to play in the matches. Their travel should be as comfortable and relaxed as possible."

In relation to Alf's sacking, we discussed the lack of information given to us. We had to accept, from Ted, the need for secrecy until the official announcement had been made. However we felt that a personal letter to each of us, setting out the new arrangements, should have been sent prior to our departure. The meeting lasted for over an hour. We were on the point of departure, when Ted asked if there was anything else bothering us. That was the cue for Les to bring up the story of the World Cup tablemats. Les reiterated the story, that many months after the World Cup Alf, Harold, Les and I were in the storage rooms of the F.A. headquarters with Dennis Follows, the then Secretary. Alf pointed to several shelves of blue presentation cases, which were carefully stacked in the storeroom.

> "What are in those boxes" Alf enquired.

> "Those are the World Cup table mats." Follows replied.

Alf asked if he could see them. Follows then showed Alf the beautiful aerial photographs of all the World Cup grounds in England embossed on thermal resistant table and drinks mats. The set contained eight mats.

"I'd like you to give one set to each of the staff."

Alf had said.

"Oh, I'm sorry, they are only for the F.A. Council Members and visiting officials. I'm afraid your staff, and none of the players, can have them."

Follows replied.

"We won the World Cup,"

retorted Alf

"not the officials. Are you seriously telling me the staff who helped the players win the World Cup, cannot have a set of commemorating tablemats?

"Yes"

replied Follows.

"You and the staff cannot have a set."

It was obvious Les was quite resentful of this incident.

"Do you know",

said Ted Croker

"I do believe those mats, in their presentation boxes, are now covered in mildew in the garage at the F.A. On returning to London, if I can find three undamaged sets, I will send one to each of you. That's a promise."

With that promise the meeting ended.

"Some hope of getting a set"

said Les, as the three of us walked away down the corridor.

"I bet we never see a set."

It was also in Bulgaria that I requested a meeting with Dick Wragg, the Chairman of the Senior International Committee. I informed Dick that I wished to resign from my post of Honorary Team Physician to the Senior International Team and Medical Advisor to the Football Association. Dick and I had been great friends for many years. When Chairman of Sheffield United, he was also President of The Northern Intermediate League, a position he held for many years. When he resigned from that position, he very kindly proposed me as his successor. I was duly appointed to succeed him. We both had a high regard for each other. At our meeting in Bulgaria, Dick was anxious for me to remain as Honorary Team Physician, but my mind was made up. As I told Dick,

> "The reality is, for the past twelve years, I have not worked for The Football Association. I have always worked for Alf Ramsey. Now that Alf has been sacked, it is time for me to depart also."

Dick Wragg immediately assumed that my reason for resigning was a knee jerk reaction to Alf's sacking. While this was true to a certain extent, I pointed out to Dick that I had written to Alf four years earlier, in 1970, prior to travelling to the Mexico World Cup, indicating my desire to resign after that World Cup. I was of the opinion then, and it had not changed over the following four years, that the role of Medical Advisor to The Football Association and Team Physician needed to become a full time properly remunerated post. It was not possible, in my view, for anyone to perform the role properly on a part-time honorary basis. I pointed out to Dick I was a full time General Practitioner at Redcar; Medical Officer and Director of Football at Middlesbrough Football Club and a part time Medical Officer with I.C.I. Whilst I had enjoyed every minute of my time with England, it was time for me to move aside and let someone new take over. As I expected, Dick was not be prepared to accept my resignation. He said I should think it over. He asked me to reconsider my position over the next two weeks. I promised I would do so. We agreed that I would write to Dick in fourteen days time with my decision. As I was leaving the meeting, Dick put forward a suggestion for me to consider

> "If you do resign, why not stand for The Council of The Football Association. The representative for the north east is currently Wilf Dodds. He has been a good servant to the amateur game and the F.A., but he's well into his eighties now. It's time for Wilf to resign. With your youth, yet with your twelve years' experience at international level, you would be a

great asset to The Football Association. Think about it!"
Having seen how inadequate the F.A. Council members had been during my twelve years at international level, his suggestion interested me. While Dick was hoping that I would reconsider my position with the England team, I knew I would not be changing my mind over my resignation. My time with the England team was at an end. Dick Wragg and I agreed that our discussion would remain confidential, until I wrote to him. We would mention our meeting to no one. I knew however that the game in Yugoslavia would be my last. I would retire from the England job at the ripe old age of forty-two. It was not a rash decision. No knee jerk reaction to the sacking of Alf. It was a considered decision over many months. It was time for me to move on.

If the draw against East Germany had caused delight amongst the F.A. officials, it was nothing to the ecstasy that resulted from the 1–0 victory over Bulgaria. It was as if the team had won the World Cup all over again. In the officials' view, the sacking of Alf was now fully justified. England could win abroad without Sir Alf. The third match against Yugoslavia could see their decision totally vindicated.

The euphoria after the win in Bulgaria was such, that in response to a request from the captain, Emlyn Hughes, Joe agreed to the players having a night out in Sofia "to enjoy a few beers." Such relaxation would not have occurred with Alf Ramsey in the middle of a tour. The following morning, several bleary eyed players congregated in reception prior to our departure to Belgrade. It was a surprise to Harold, Les and me, that Joe Mercer had given the players permission to travel in casual clothing instead of the usual F.A. suits. We looked a right rabble. The discipline, which had been the hallmark of the England team in the previous twelve years, had just disappeared.

We left Sofia airport for Belgrade aboard a Bulgarian Airways flight at three fifteen on Sunday June 2nd. Encouraged by the euphoria of the F.A. Officials to the win in Bulgaria, the England party was in happy mood. It was if we were all on a summer holiday rather than an England tour. That old impostor "Triumph" had raised its ugly head again. Oh that people

PHENOMENAL SUCCESS AND UTTER DESPAIR

would learn to treat Triumph and Disaster in a similar way. During the whole of Alf's reign as manager, the consumption of alcohol was always kept under strict control. Certainly, on air flights, no alcohol was allowed for the players and they had become accustomed to drinking soft drinks during the flights. The one-hour flight to Belgrade however was different. At Sofia airport, the Captain, Emlyn Hughes, had asked Joe Mercer if it was in order for the players to have a drink while waiting at the airport and on the plane. Joe gave Emlyn the assurance he sought. In the Sofia Airport Departure Lounge a minority of players had far too much to drink and were quite inebriated when boarding the plane. During the flight, for this minority group of players, the consumption of alcohol got out of control. Harold, Les and I, sitting at the back of the plane, were powerless to do anything about the situation. After all, the Manager had given the players permission to enjoy a drink. In agreeing to Emlyn Hughes' request, Joe intended the players would have no more than a couple of drinks, but inevitably some players took advantage of the situation. There is no doubt a small minority of players had consumed far too much alcohol and were now not responsible for their actions. Three of the players, who were sitting together on one side of the plane, decided to play fancy free with a Bulgarian airhostess. The players complained the safety belt of the player nearest the window was jammed and he was unable to unlock it. As the air hostess leaned over the two outside players, to check the safety belt, the middle player fondled her breasts and the gangway player pinched her bottom. The players were so inebriated, they were in hysterics at their actions. The Bulgarian airhostess was not amused.

We arrived at Belgrade airport at four thirty in the afternoon. I was the last person to leave the plane. I was accompanied by Kevin Keegan who, I hasten to add was entirely sober and had not been involved in the drinking or in the episode with the safety belt. When Kevin and I came out of the plane into the bright sunshine, we could not believe our eyes. Yugoslavian soldiers surrounded our plane. They stood, rifles at the ready. As we disembarked from the plane, the rifles were pointing directly at Kevin and me,.

"What's all this about, Doc."

[541]

DOCTOR TO THE WORLD CHAMPIONS

said Kevin.

My response was stupid. I said

> "This is a communist country Kevin. Things are often like this in communist countries."

Little did we know that the players' prank with the airhostess had been immediately reported, by her, to the Bulgarian pilot on the plane. Immediately, he had informed the Belgrade airport authorities that the England players were drunk on board the plane and three players had attempted to rape one of the Bulgarian airhostesses! Hence the display of Yugoslavian soldiers, guns at the ready, on the tarmac at the airport.

When Kevin and I arrived in the baggage collection area, the players and officials were milling around waiting for the luggage to be brought off the plane. Outside, in the airport's public area, the British Embassy official party was waiting to greet the team and the officials. The arrival area was congested not only with the England party, but also with innumerable Yugoslav soldiers who were intermingled with our party. At that time, in Belgrade airport, the luggage was delivered to the arrival area on a single tracked belt. Eventually the belt began to move, an indication that our luggage was on its way. The movement of the belt was also the indication for Alec Lindsay, the Liverpool fullback, to jump up onto the moving belt and start running down it the wrong way. Lindsay's action was the moment the soldiers had been waiting for. In a flash, the soldiers dived at Lindsay. Alec obviously saw the soldiers coming towards him. He side stepped the soldiers, but as they missed Lindsay they grabbed Keegan. In a flash, Kevin was thrown over a wooden counter and frog marched into a back room. The room was one of see-through glass. I could see soldiers surrounding Kevin. He was thrown into a chair and made to bend forwards, his head between his knees. Through the glass petition we then witnessed the soldiers hitting and kicking Kevin repeatedly. I could see Kevin's face was covered in blood. His nose was bleeding profusely. I immediately contacted Joe Mercer and Ted Croker. A serious diplomatic situation developed. It was a matter to be resolved by the officials. Almost immediately, the British Embassy staff became involved with the Yugoslav authorities. Kevin would many years later say,

PHENOMENAL SUCCESS AND UTTER DESPAIR

"Even if I had been a convicted drug-smuggler, instead of the captain of the England football team, I would have had cause for complaint."

Of course he was not England captain on this tour, the late Emlyn Hughes was, but no human being should have been treated in the way the Yugoslav soldiers treated Kevin. Eventually, as a result of the intervention by the British Embassy staff, a bloody faced Keegan was released from the control of the soldiers and allowed to rejoin the England party in the baggage area. The Yugoslav officials made it plain however that, although Keegan had been released back to the England party, he was to be subsequently charged by the Yugoslav Justice Department. Immediately following the assault on Keegan, the players met. They were angry at the way Kevin had been treated and were determined to return home without playing. They were informed however, by the Yugoslavian officials, that while everyone else

"Keegan Exits From My Treatment At The Airport – I still keep A Watchful Eye On Him."

could leave Yugoslavia, Kevin would have to remain. Joe Mercer suggested to the players it would be much better if we all stayed, played the game and gave the Yugoslavs a match to remember. The players agreed.

Ramsey's no alcohol policy with the England players, had stood the test of time for twelve years. The policy was now in ruins. Kevin Keegan, a totally innocent party in all of this, had been the one to suffer. Ramsey's strict discipline policy had been destroyed. In future years, there would be similar instances of misbehaviour by England players. In my opinion, such behaviour began in Belgrade in nineteen seventy-four.

Once settled in our Belgrade hotel, the British Embassy officials paid the England party a visit. They confirmed what we had learnt at the airport. Keegan was to be charged by the Yugoslav Justice Department. Ted Croker called a meeting of the staff, which Joe Mercer, Harold Shepherdson, Les Cocker and I attended. At any time during our stay, the British Embassy staff warned the F.A. officials, Keegan could be arrested. Debate took place as to whether the England team should stay or withdraw from the fixture and return home. It was decided that whatever the outcome, if Kevin was arrested we would all stay behind with him. Eventually it was decided The Football Association would make a public statement. The statement would make it clear that Kevin Keegan was a vital part of the England team. It was essential he play for England in the forthcoming match with Yugoslavia. By issuing this statement the officials believed that Kevin was unlikely to be arrested before the match. If he was arrested, England would not fulfil the fixture and we would all stay in Yugoslavia with Kevin. Everyone, including the British Embassy staff, was of the view that the most vulnerable time for Kevin was in the post match period. Fortunately, after the international, there would only be some eleven hours before we departed Belgrade for London on our British Airways charter flight. Those eleven hours, immediately after the match, were considered the most dangerous time for the arrest of Keegan. The officials decided to draw up a plan to protect Kevin during the post match period. Croker and Joe Mercer and the F.A. officials would consult with the British Embassy staff to decide the details of the plan. Harold, Les and I would be informed later.

PHENOMENAL SUCCESS AND UTTER DESPAIR

The build up to the Yugoslav match was surrounded with rumour and counter rumour over Yugoslavia's attitude to Kevin. The plan, Ted Croker and Joe informed Harold, Les and me, was as follows. As Kevin had been injured at the airport, it was perfectly reasonably for us to appear concerned about his injuries on the Monday, Tuesday and Wednesday. To show the concern of his injuries, the Team Doctor, namely me, would always accompany Keegan when he appeared in public. I was, in effect, to be Keegan's minder for a few days! Immediately after the match, the team would return by bus to the hotel. It was estimated we would return to the hotel just before midnight. Every member of the party would be confined to the hotel; no one would be allowed to leave the building. British Embassy staff would be present at the hotel during the night. The following morning we would depart from the hotel at 08.30 en route for the airport. At the airport, Kevin would continue to be accompanied by myself. If no arrest had taken place, when our flight was called, no one would leave the airport lounge, until Kevin and I had successfully passed through passport control and entered the final checking area. Everyone else was to stay back until Keegan and I were aboard the plane. The whole England party would hold back ensuring Kevin and I went through without hindrance. Everyone, in the England party, needed to know right up to the last moment, Kevin had not been arrested. The plan had been agreed with all the officials and British Embassy staff.

The three days prior to the game passed off without any further diplomatic incident. Wherever Kevin went in public, I was at his side. I was supposedly concerned about his injuries. Kevin was so resilient, and so determined to play, no injuries would prevent him playing. When Joe announced the team, to play against Yugoslavia, Kevin was in the side. The atmosphere in the Belgrade stadium, with 90,000 people packed inside, was intense. The England team needed no motivation; the Yugoslav soldiers at the airport had provided them with all the motivation they needed. It was an exciting game. As usual the Yugoslav players were quite physical but the England players responded magnificently. In the two goal, drawn game, Channon and Keegan scored for England. Kevin proved his point to the Yugoslavians on the field of play.

The following morning Kevin was still with us. Together he and I boarded the bus to the airport. British Embassy officials accompanied us to the airport. At the airport, the final part of the plan was put into operation. Unimpeded, Kevin and I went through passport control together. When the flight was finally called we both handed in our boarding passes together. We boarded the plane. The rest of the party waited patiently until Kevin and I were safely aboard. On boarding the plane Kevin sat with the England players. I sat at the back of the plane with Harold and Les.

Sitting on Flight BCH 596 the whole party was relieved we were still all together. Most importantly Keegan was safely on board. The cabin crew were our usual British Airways staff. The senior airhostess on the flight was Pam Darch. Over the years I had flown with the England team, Pam had become a family friend. When on tour, she frequently brought me messages from my wife and family. Pam was the messenger when my daughters passed their eleven plus examinations. She had spent weekends at our home and her friendship remains to this day.

"Welcome aboard BCH Flight 596."

Her reassuring voice announced, over the loudspeaker system,

> "We shall be travelling at thirty-five thousand feet, and our estimated time of arrival at Heathrow Airport is at ten past one. During the flight we shall be serving a hot meal. One other thing,"

she said,

> "Our airhostesses have now been carrying the England team for the past ten years. We are all disappointed that to date no one has attempted to rape us!"

The message was received and well understood.

In future years, the Yugoslavian experience would have severe repercussions for Kevin Keegan. Later, Kevin would play for Hamburg, managed by the Yugoslavian Branko Zebec. In the Hamburg team were also Yugoslav players. After his traumatic experience in Belgrade, Kevin had said he would not return to the country. Inevitably, while at Hamburg his team were drawn against Hajduk Split of Yugoslavia in the European Cup. Although it was in doubt as to whether Kevin would play, it speaks volumes for the character of the man that he returned to Yugoslavia to play for Hamburg in the match.

During Flight BCH 596, back home to England, I became more convinced, than ever, it would be my last flight as the England Team Doctor

19

My International Resignation

On returning to Middlesbrough, I was due to travel with the newly promoted team to Norway. Middlesbrough would be playing matches at Stavanger and Bergen, as a First Division Club. It was a trip I was looking forward to. I would celebrate Middlesbrough's promotion with the players and staff during a relaxing week in Norway. In those euphoric days, following Middlesbrough's promotion, Jack Charlton gave innumerable interviews to the media. In one of those interviews, the interviewer congratulated Jack on being such a successful Manager. Immediately Jack corrected the interviewer.

"I'm not the Manager here, not yet anyway. I'm the Coach."

It was an innocuous, off the cuff remark, but I knew exactly what he meant. During his first year at Middlesbrough, he had tried to establish himself as the 'Manager of the whole Club' but, whenever he did so, the directors objected. When he involved himself in the so- called business matters of the Club, and there were many during the year, the Chairman and some of the directors objected. During Jack's first year, the Chairman told me on several occasions,

> "Charlton's job is with the team. Tell Charlton not to involve himself in the Club's business. That role is for myself and the other directors. His role is coaching the team. You and he deal with the football: I and the other directors will deal with all business matters"

I never relayed any of these messages to Jack. In my view Jack was doing a fantastic job. My personal view was that his involvement in the so-called business affairs of the Club was essential. I did not agree with the view expressed by the Chairman and my fellow directors. Jack's innocuous, off the cuff remark, during his media interview, did however have serious consequences. The situation confronted me on the first day of the Norwegian tour.

It was a surprise to the staff, players and myself, when Jack had withdrawn from the Norwegian tour at the last moment. He said he was staying behind in order to attend a meeting of First Division Managers. We left for Norway without him. On the tour, our first destination was the beautiful city of Stavanger. It was there that Ian MacFarlane, the first team's Coach, asked for a private meeting with me. Ian had been appointed Middlesbrough's Coach, when Stan Anderson was Manager. He was very experienced as he had previously been Manager of Carlisle United. A Scot, passionate about the game, Ian was a great motivator of players. When Jack arrived at Middlesbrough, he was happy for Ian to continue as the Coach. The two had worked well together throughout the season. Ian had made a significant contribution to our success. I was shocked therefore, when he told me,

> "I've decided to leave. Following our promotion, Jack has given me no credit whatsoever for all the work I've done as the Club's Coach. Jack even talked to the media and said of himself, 'I'm not the Manager at Middlesbrough I'm the Coach.' Well that was the greatest insult of my life. I had been the Coach all season. Jack's remark really hurt me. When we return from Norway I'm leaving. I'm going to Manchester City to join Tony Book. I've been appointed the First Team Coach at Manchester City. I wanted you to be the first to know. I've really enjoyed working with you."

I knew Ian would not change his mind. I thanked him for all he had done at the Club and wished him well in the future. Ian and I agreed we would tell no one of his decision until he had informed Jack personally.

Prior to leaving for Norway, I had discussed again with Margaret my resignation from the England job. We both agreed it was time for me to leave.

I was interested however in Dick Wragg's suggestion that I should stand as a candidate for the F.A. Council, as their representative in the north-east. I contacted Keith Collins, the Chairman of Sunderland, to seek his view and possible his support. Keith was very supportive. He said Sunderland would be willing to propose me. With Sunderland as my proposer, my own Chairman said,

> "Middlesbrough will be happy to second Sunderland's proposal."

With Sunderland and Middlesbrough supporting my nomination, I decided to stand for election. My election campaign needed to start immediately. I cannot recall how many votes in total would be cast in the election, but in addition to the five professional clubs in the region—Newcastle, Sunderland, Middlesbrough, Darlington and Hartlepool- there were innumerable amateur clubs, all of whom had an equal vote with the professional Clubs. I requested and received, from The Football Association, a full list of Clubs in the north-east, amateur and professional, who were eligible to vote. The number of amateur clubs was considerable. I decided that all my spare time, on the Norwegian tour, would be spent writing a personal, hand written letter to each and every club entitled to vote. It was a huge task. In my letter, I set out what I thought were my relevant credentials. These included being, a director at Middlesbrough for twelve years; Honorary Team Physician to the England teams for twelve years; Middlesbrough's medical officer; President of The Northern Intermediate League; and a Staff Lecturer to The Football Association. I felt my credentials were entirely appropriate for the post I was now seeking. Imagine my surprise when the result was declared. I only managed to achieve three votes; the votes of Sunderland, Middlesbrough and Darlington. Wilf Dodds was re-elected in a landslide victory. Not one amateur club voted for me. The lack of support from the amateur clubs did not surprise me. Wilf Dodds had been involved with all the amateur clubs in the north-east all his life. What did surprise me however was the fact that Newcastle United did not support my application. I took the matter up with their Chairman, Lord Westwood, when we next met. I was astonished at his response. Bill

MY INTERNATIONAL RESIGNATION

Westwood said,

> "The person who is responsible for your non election is Stan Seymour, one of my own directors. Stan and Wilf Dodds ran a campaign against your election. You know Stan Seymour is also a member of the F.A. Council. Like Wilf Dodds, Stan is now in his eighties and the two of them enjoy travelling to London together for the meetings. They're both from the same era, you see. They both like to chat over the old times together during the journey. They both intend to retire from the Council in two years. When they do retire, they will both be in their late eighties! On their retirement, they want you to know, they will support your nomination. At that time Newcastle United will also support your nomination."

Seeking election to the F.A. Council was the first time in my life I had set out to be elected to any organization. In future, I determined, I would always wait to receive an invitation to join any organisation. Whilst in Norway, I wrote my letter of resignation to Dick Wragg. England would need a new Team Physician.

It was in Norway we received the news that Jack Charlton had received 'The Manager of the Year Award'. He was first Second Division Manager ever to be given the award. I, like all the players and staff, was delighted for him. Although George Winney had now left the Board of Directors I knew he would also be thrilled. It was George's vision that had led to Jack being appointed at Middlesbrough in the first place. In my opinion, without George Winney's vision, the team would not have been promoted.

During the close season, Ian MacFarlane left for Manchester City. Jack appointed John Coddington as his successor. During the close season, I fully expected Jack to embark on a spending spree. The team, I believed, would need to be strengthened, if we were to survive in the First Division. Jack however had other ideas. He decided that he would stick with the players who had achieved the Club's promotion. The only new player to join us was Terry Cooper, the Leeds United and England full back. Terry joined on a free transfer. Don Revie was appointed England's Manager, to succeed

Sir Alf Ramsey, and my old friend Les Cocker was appointed the Assistant Manager. I assumed, quite wrongly as it turned out, that Ian Adams, the Medical Officer at Leeds United would succeed me as the England Team Doctor. It was a surprise therefore when I received a telephone call from Don Revie.

"I wonder if you would do me a favour."

Don enquired.

"I need your advice regarding the appointment of your successor. Could you travel down to London to discuss the matter with me."

We arranged a mutually convenient date to meet at the The Football Association's offices in Lancaster Gate. Over many years, Don had been most kind to me on my visits to Leeds United. He was also most helpful when I wanted Jack Charlton as Manager at Middlesbrough. We met a week later in Don's office.

Don informed me he had already approached two doctors. Ian Adams from his own Club of Leeds United and my deputy Frank O'Gorman from Sheffield United. He had offered the job to both doctors. Both had turned down the post. In the circumstances I recommended Peter Burrows of Luton Town, with whom I had worked and for whom I had a high regard. I discussed with Don his capabilities. Don agreed to approach Peter Burrows. I said I would also speak with Peter.

Dr. Burrows was appointed a few weeks later. As I was on the point of leaving Don's office, he asked me,

"By the way, how much did you get paid as the Team Doctor?"

"Nothing."

I replied.

"Oh, come off it. You've resigned now. You can tell me."

"Nothing."

I repeated.

Don pressed a bell push on his desk. The Secretary, Ted Croker, came into the room.

"Doc Phillips is trying to tell me that, over twelve years, he didn't get paid a salary or match fee, as the England doctor. He says he worked purely in an Honorary capacity. Is that right.?"

"Absolutely right."

said Croker.

"That's an absolute disgrace. I know how much time and hard work Doc Phillips has given to this job. I can't believe it!"

exclaimed Don.

Croker then expressed his amazement at the fact I had only received three votes in the election of the representative from the north-east to The Football Association Council. That's an absolute disgrace too. You could have been such a great asset to us here. Don Revie agreed. When Croker had left, Don told me,

"I'll see what I can do for you financially."

I then suggested to Don the England Team Doctor should always be paid a salary or match fee. He agreed. I had at least ensured The Football Association would regularly pay my successors. Alas it was too late for me.

Two weeks later, I received a telephone call from Dr. Andrew Stephens, the Chairman of the Football Association. He informed me that The Football Association wished to make me a presentation, in recognition of the twelve years service I had given them. The Duke of Kent, President of The Football Association, would make the presentation prior to Don Revie's first international at Wembley. Andrew informed me I could either have a silver salver, or a cheque for £500. I opted for the cheque. Andrew said I would receive an invitation in due course and my wife was to accompany me. Harold Shepherdson also received a similar invitation, but no mention was made to Harold, as to the presentation he would receive.

Harold, his wife Peggy, Margaret and I travelled to London together. Harold and I were presented to the Duke of Kent, prior to the international, in the Royal Box. I received an envelope. Harold received a small presentation box. Within minutes of leaving the Royal Box, Harold exploded.

"I can't believe it! They've given me a watch. I must have ten of these at home. What did you get?"

"A cheque for £500."

I said.

"I'm going to give the watch back to Croker and ask him if I can have the money instead."

Harold did just that. Croker was taken aback.

"If that is what you want, I shall send you a cheque for the purchase price, together with the invoice."

the F.A. Secretary informed Harold.

In due course Harold received a cheque for £39.50 and the purchase receipt for the watch from a shop in Cheltenham. Revie had seen to it that I received a cheque for £500. Together with the ex gratia payment of £500 I received following the Mexico World Cup, my total financial reward from the Football Association for twelve years service was £1,000. I was cheap at the price! Sir Alf Ramsey once told me, when I was discussing with him, what I considered was his own meagre salary,

"I do this job, for the love of the game."

I guess we both did it for the same reason. I certainly always believed I worked for Alf Ramsey and the England players, not The Football Association.

With only Terry Cooper added to our staff, I was extremely apprehensive as to how we would perform in the First Division. My concerns proved to be totally unwarranted. The team performed exceptionally well. At the end of our first season in the Division, the team was in seventh place. If it had not been for a stupid mistake in the last minute of our last home game, against Derby County, we would have qualified for Europe. Middlesbrough was leading one–nil with only minutes left to play. A win would have resulted in us qualifying for Europe. With the clock ticking to full time we were awarded a corner kick. Jack's instructions to the players, in such circumstances, I had heard over and over again in his coaching sessions, was

"Play it short."

He repeatedly told the players,

"Keep the ball near the corner flag."

MY INTERNATIONAL RESIGNATION

For some inexplicable reason, Bobby Murdoch crossed the ball into the Derby penalty area. The corner was headed clear to the Derby forwards. Collecting the ball Kevin Hector dribbled the ball half the length of the field and scored an equalizing goal with virtually the last kick of the match. It was ironic that Bobby Murdoch, who had contributed so much to the success of the team over two seasons, should make such an elementary mistake. Jack was furious. Middlesbrough had thrown away a wonderful opportunity to enter Europe in their first season back in the First Division. Finishing in seventh place, we amassed forty-eight points. We won eighteen games, drew twelve and lost twelve. We scored fifty-four goals and conceded forty. It was a very creditable performance.

During the season, I received a telephone call from George Winney. It was an invitation to lunch at The Billingham Arms. When I arrived Jack Hatfield, another of the directors, was also present. George explained to Jack Hatfield and myself that he wanted both of us to have his Middlesbrough Football Club shares.

"I want my shares to be transferred to you both in equally divided amounts between the two of you."

Jack Hatfield and I were surprised. George Winney's niece was married to Keith Varley, another member of our Board. Keith's father, Ernest, was also a Board member. It was generally assumed, by all the directors, that George Winney's shares would go either to Ernest or Keith. George however was adamant.

"I want all my shares equally divided between the two of you.

I don't want any other members of the Board involved."

George informed Jack Hatfield and myself that he would be responsible for submitting the necessary Share Transfer Forms to the Club Secretary.

At the end of our first, successful season in the First Division, Jack Charlton had arranged a close season tour to Australia. I had never been to Australia and was keen to accompany the team. A few days before we were due to depart, I received a strange telephone call from Jack.

"I can't tell you over the phone, but I don't want you to go to Australia. I want you to stay behind."

I was devastated. I had arranged two weeks holiday from my Practice and was keen to visit down under.

"I'll give you all the details at the ground tomorrow."

I was intrigued to hear the reasons for Jack's decision.

"I've heard a whisper." he began,

> "As soon as you and I are out of the country, I've heard the Chairman's building firm is going to knock down the offices, including the Club shop, near the main entrance. A new office complex and shop will be built in its place. I don't want that to happen. I want you to stay back and, if it does happen, I want you to phone me immediately."

"I can't see how that can happen." I replied.

> "I haven't missed a Board meeting. No such proposal has been discussed, let alone agreed, by the directors. I'm not aware that any planning permission has been sought. Your idea is unrealistic."

> "Nevertheless, I'd like you to stay back and monitor the situation."

I agreed to do so. The team left for Australia without me. My two-week holiday from the Practice, I cancelled.

Two days after their departure, the workmen arrived at the ground to commence demolishing the old offices. When I approached the Chairman, he informed me he wanted to smarten up the entrance to the ground and was intent on building a new office complex before the commencement of the 1975–76 season. I informed the Chairman that Jack would not be pleased. Over the two years since he became Manager Jack and his wife, Pat, had worked incessantly building up the Club shop from scratch. It was now a very successful business.

> "Jack needn't worry. I'm building a new Club shop. It will be bigger, better and more spacious than the present one. I'm sure he'll be pleased with the outcome."

[556]

MY INTERNATIONAL RESIGNATION

There was no need for me to phone Jack in Australia. I met Pat, his wife, at the ground the same day. She had already informed Jack of the situation. The new complex was built. Whilst I did not agree with the way the matter had been dealt with, the new complex was a vast improvement on the old one. The new Club shop was much better.

With Jack thousands of miles away in Australia, I cannot report accurately exactly what happened when he received the telephone call from his wife. The information, I received, was given to me some two weeks later, from the players and the directors, on their return. Apparently Jack received the telephone call while the rest of the party were eating a meal in the hotel restaurant. Armed with the information, Jack stormed into the restaurant, approached the directors and, in front of everyone present, verbally abused the directors over what was happening back at the ground. The players informed me that they were embarrassed to hear the dressing down Jack had given to the directors in front of them and in a public place. The directors, accosted by Jack, were horrified. It was yet another incident they would store, for future reference, in the Jack Charlton Interference Folder.

There is no doubt, despite the rift that had developed over the two years between Jack Charlton and the Chairman, I was delighted with the progress the team had made. Playing wise, Middlesbrough were playing better than they had ever done in the previous ten years of my time as a director. The fact that I had been responsible for bringing Charlton to the Club gave me great satisfaction.

If the rift between Charlton and the senior directors at the Club was considerable, the rift that was to occur in my General Practice was ten times worse. Unbeknown to me, the two junior partners in the practice, David Whitehouse and Cameron Davidson, had met and agreed to split away from the four-man practice. The most junior partner, Cameron visited me at my home and informed me of their intentions. Cameron invited me to join with himself and David to form a three-man practice. Such a decision would of course have left the senior partner, Reg Cutts, working on his own. He would have become in effect a single-handed practitioner. With all that had been going on in my life, I was totally unaware of the degree of ill feeling that had developed between the partners. Work wise, I would have much preferred to work with David and Cameron, but I was not prepared to subject the senior partner, at his age, to working single-handed. I declined Cameron's invitation. The two junior partners then began the difficult process of splitting the medical partnership. Dissolving a medical partnership is possibly more traumatic than a marital divorce and our dissolution was indeed traumatic for everyone involved. David and Cameron formed their own partnership. Reg Cutts and I formed our own. It was a sad occurrence.

In his third year as Manager, another of Jack Charlton's brilliant ideas came to a successful conclusion. The idea, or rather the way Jack presented it, caused more anger and consternation to the Chairman and senior directors. Jack had developed an idea of building Corporate Boxes at the ground. When I say developed, I mean just that. Jack, surprisingly, attended a Board meeting. He presented his completed plan to the Chairman and the directors. It was another of Jack's classic fait accomplis. Each corporate box, sold to business concerns, would accommodate up to eight people who would attend the matches in absolute comfort. It was a great idea and quite innovative at that time. Arguments developed between the directors, in private and at Board meetings, over his proposal. There were the usual initial comments as to Jack's interference in business matters. When convinced the idea was a good one, arguments raged as to where these corporate boxes should be built. Some directors preferred the South Stand, others the North. In my opinion, some directors opted for their preferred choice, purely and simply because it was not the one Jack Charlton had suggested. Those directors, knowing in which stand Jack wanted the boxes built, decided their preference was to be in the opposite stand. When the matter was eventually resolved, in Jack's favour, a second argument materialized as to the height of the boxes. Again Jack's view eventually won the day, but only after much heated argument. With Jack not attending Board meetings, much of the criticism directed at him inevitably fell on my shoulders. I rarely relayed to Jack the various views of the directors, but on this occasion I did. Even he and I then began to experience misunderstandings on the issues. As each

MY INTERNATIONAL RESIGNATION

month passed, I imagined the directors' 'Jack Charlton Interference Folder' was growing to enormous proportions! As we approached Jack's third season as Manager, expectations, at Middlesbrough, were high Having achieved a very respectable seventh position in the First Division the previous season, those expectations seemed fully justified. In the previous season, the team had only lost out on a place in Europe by one point and that by Bobby Murdoch's schoolboy error in the last minute of the last match of the season. The high expectations seemed fully justified. Jack determined that Bobby Murdoch could not go on playing for many more games. He decided to replace him with Phil Boersma from Liverpool. Boersma was not a success at Middlesbrough. He somehow lacked the passion Jack demanded. Jack's third season, in comparison to his first two, proved to be a great disappointment. Jack had set his goal on finishing in one of the first six positions in the First Division. He desperately wanted to be in Europe. We ended up as a mid table side and never looked like being in contention for the desired place in Europe. The team did achieve some success but, as far as Jack was concerned, the success achieved was unsatisfactory. We won the Anglo–Scottish Cup, beating Fulham in the final. We also had a very successful run in the League Cup, reaching the semi-final. In the two leg semi-final against Manchester City Middlesbrough won the home leg one goal to nil, but were then thrashed in the return fixture at Maine Road by four goals to nil. Following the second leg at Manchester, I stayed overnight at the home of Ian MacFarlane. I was guest speaker the following night at a sportsmen's' dinner organised by the Altringham Football Club. Needless to say, Ian was delighted Manchester City had beaten Middlesbrough. He seemed to think it proved how much better a coach he was than Jack! His departure to Manchester City, Ian believed, was Middlesbrough's loss. My after dinner speech at Altringham seemed to be well received.

It was during 1976 that I finally decided that my time at Middlesbrough Football Club was at an end. Jack had entered into yet another confrontation with some of the directors. Jack supported the action of one of the directors who replaced the flat advertising boards around the ground with angular frames. From every vantage point in the ground, the new angular frame gave the advertisements improved prominence. It was what advertisers wanted. The Chairman did not agree. Jack was convinced the Chairman's objection was due to the fact that he had not thought of the idea first! Yet another row ensued between the Manager and the Chairman. As usual, I was piggy in the middle.

In July 1976 however, I was completely taken aback at a Board meeting when a proposal was made to sack Jack Charlton. The list of complaints put forward by the directors was endless. In their view, Jack's interference in so many "business matters", had humiliated the directors. There was the I.C.I. paint; the television gantry; the change of playing kit; his outburst in Australia, humiliating the directors in public, when he opposed the building of the new offices; the ill feeling he caused with his interference in the building of the new corporate boxes; and more recently his interference with the advertising boards The directors were adamant. Jack Charlton should be sacked! At this point, I did what I always intended to do if Jack was threatened with the sack. I resigned. I had given Jack an assurance, when we met at Wetherby, that I would ensure he would not be sacked in his first four years at Middlesbrough. I intended to keep to my promise. It had always been my intention that, if he was threatened with the sack, I would resign. Having informed the directors of my resignation, I left the meeting. On the way out of the ground, I stopped at Mrs. Thompson's desk; dictated my resignation letter; signed it and left the ground. I was convinced it would be for the last time.

The Rolls Royce drew up at my home at nine o'clock the same evening. The Chairman arrived to inform me that he would not accept my resignation.

I told Charles,

> "I can no longer accept the behaviour and attitude of my fellow directors. In my opinion, every day of their lives, they should be on their knees thanking Charlton for what he has achieved at the Club. Without Charlton there would be no success at the Club. The directors should support him at every opportunity and let him manage."

MY INTERNATIONAL RESIGNATION

To my surprise, Charles agreed. He too said he was fed up with the attitude of certain directors and that visiting Ayresome Park was no longer a pleasure. He was obviously desperate for me to withdraw my resignation. The arrangement he had made, whereby I was in charge of all football matters had been a great success. He again gave me an assurance that no other director would interfere in any football matters. The Chairman apologised for the fact that certain directors had interfered with my role in suggesting the Manager should be sacked. The sacking of the Manager, he had told the other directors, would only occur if I made that recommendation to the Board. The issue of sacking Jack Charlton was therefore no longer an issue. The fact that Charles Amer had taken the trouble to visit me at home certainly impressed me. I gave Charles an assurance that I would reconsider my resignation and inform him of my decision within forty-eight hours. Two days later I informed the Chairman that I would withdraw my resignation. Charles Amer subsequently wrote me a letter. The contents of his letter are interesting.

13th July 1976

My Dear Neil,
Referring to the unfortunate situation which developed at our Directors' Meeting last Friday, 9th July, I have to agree with you that the pleasure of visiting Middlesbrough Football Club is gradually becoming worse. The pettiness and in my opinion deliberate friction which is being caused by certain Directors has, I think, got to be stopped or alternatively other measures will have to be taken.

It is perhaps unfortunate that Jack Charlton, who I am sure has the best interest of Middlesbrough Football Club at heart, has this tendency to develop ideas and finalise them before the Directors get to know. This of course will and does cause a great deal of ill feeling and you can well understand one or two of the Directors feeling very annoyed about it.

I know that the situation in your particular field, which you have been able to contain so admirably, should not in my opinion be interfered with at all and anything to the contrary that has been arranged in recent weeks will be stopped.

The embarrassment caused by lack of communication between certain members of the Board and the Manager led to this awful situation in which we find ourselves over the boxes on the south side of the ground, and I have come to the conclusion they did not want to be proved wrong and resented very much to find that they are.

Finally I more than understood your feelings last Friday lunchtime and am only too pleased that I was able to persuade you to change your mind. Having said all this I think it would be advantageous if the sensible members of the Board had a very extensive meeting with a view to putting the whole matter right.

Charles. Chairman

I greatly appreciated Charles' letter, but my decision to leave Middlesbrough Football Club remained. With the medical practice, I had originally joined, now split into two, I would begin looking for other medical appointment at home or abroad. The attitude of the Middlesbrough directors towards Charlton had convinced me there was little future for either of us at the Club. I did not inform anyone of my intention to leave, least of all anyone at the Club. Obtaining a suitable medical post, at the age of forty-four was not, I believed, going to be easy. How wrong I was. In the ten months from July 1976 to May 1977, I was appointed to seven different medical positions. All, except two, I turned down.

The first post I applied for, would remain my preferred option. It was a fabulous job and, when offered the post, I duly accepted. I was to work as a Regional Medical Officer for the Anglo-American Company in South Africa. Based at Newcastle in the southeast of the country it was a wonderful opportunity with outstanding fringe benefits. I was to be in charge of a group of doctors and have management responsibility for the regional hospital and medical services. As a family, we were eagerly looking forward to a new life in Southern Africa. Unfortunately, one week before our departure, war broke out between South Africa and Mozambique. Newcastle, the town where we were to live, was less than a hundred miles from the

Mozambique border. Being so close to a war zone, with so much guerrilla activity, I decided was too risky and I withdrew. Two separate Department of Health appointments followed at the new towns of Peterborough and Warrington. The Department Officials who appointed me, and there were some thirty who interviewed me, were looking for an experienced medical practitioner to set up, from scratch, medical practices in these new towns. At interview however in response to my questioning, the details of the appointments had not been thought through sufficiently well. It became obvious to everyone, at both interviews, that it was unclear how the responsibilities of the post would develop over time. In response to my questions, at both interviews, the members of the interviewing panel began arguing amongst themselves. No one seemed sure as to how these posts would develop. Although offered both posts I declined each one.

I then applied for two separate General Practice vacancies at Bournemouth, and Hastings on the south coast of England. Each post was for a single-handed practice, advertised by the then administrative organisations called Family Practitioner Committees. The interview at Bournemouth was particularly interesting. The practice had been previously run by a husband and wife partnership and was a very thriving and successful practice. Immediately after my interview at Bournemouth I returned by train to Redcar. The senior administrator at Bournemouth asked me to telephone him from Kings Cross station to enquire of him if I had been appointed. I duly telephoned.

"I'm sorry you were not appointed."
he said.

> "Although you were, by far, the best candidate. The interviewing panel decided to continue the Practice tradition and appoint a husband and wife to the vacant post. However the interviewing panel were so impressed with your application they would like to offer you a post on the outskirts of Bournemouth. Based at Ferndown, it would be to set up a completely new practice. Ferndown is to become a new town on the outskirts of Bournemouth and we would like you to be the senior partner of this completely new practice."

I was astonished. The committee had not appointed me to the post for which I had applied, but were now offering me a post that, as far as I knew, had not even been advertised! I declined the invitation.

More difficulties occurred when I was interviewed for the post at Hastings. Having visited the practice at Hastings, I was interviewed again by a Family Practitioner Committee, on this occasion, at Lewes. Again I was offered the post. When I declined the appointment, for what I considered were perfectly good reasons, the committee refused to reimburse my travelling expenses!

All these interviews required me taking, at the very least, a day's holiday from the Redcar Practice. My final application was to replace two doctors who were retiring at Malvern in Worcestershire. I was later informed that there were over three hundred applicants for the post. When advertised the information contained a statement that this area of the country was one of "outstanding natural beauty" and that is certainly the case. My interview took place in late December 1976 at Worcester. I was informed of my appointment immediately after the Christmas holiday. I was delighted.

Of course my endeavours to move to a completely new post, in a different part of the country, were completely unknown at the football club and my Practice in Redcar. As matters developed it was fortuitous that I had informed no one. Having received written confirmation of my appointment from Worcester a week later I received a second letter informing me that my appointment had been placed on hold. Apparently one of the three hundred or more candidates, who had applied for the post, had formally objected to my appointment. The letter stated that a formal investigation would now be set up, as demanded by Ministry of Health regulations and each of the applicants would have to be contacted to enquire if they also had any objections to my appointment. Under no circumstances, the letter advised me, was I to enter into any financial commitment at Malvern, until the matter was resolved. My life was in limbo. My work both in the Practice and at Middlesbrough Football Club would continue as normal. It was unlikely, I was informed from Worcester, that the Malvern issue would be resolved for several weeks. It was February 1977 and the new doctor appointed at

Malvern was due to take up his duties when the two incumbent partners retired at the end of April. I informed my partners and the Chairman of the Football Club that there was the possibility I would be leaving to take up an appointment at Malvern. As it was only a possibility, they did not seem to take the matter seriously. I asked them both to keep the matter confidential until I had some definite news. Surprisingly both parties did so.

In the weeks during which I was seeking a new appointment in medicine, the football team in Jack's fourth year were going nowhere. Rumours were circulating that Jack would be leaving the Club at the end of the season. The players were confused and, for the first time in his four years as Manager, the team was not performing very well. There was no danger of relegation, but Middlesbrough seemed to be settled in a mid table position. The directors were restless. They too were aware of the rumours circulating regarding Jack's future and sought clarification of the issue. I approached Jack, although I knew beforehand what his answer would be.

> "I'm definitely leaving at the end of the season. Four years in one of these jobs is enough for anyone."

Knowing that I too was likely to be leaving, I did not try to persuade him to stay.

> "Before I inform the Board of your decision, I want to be absolutely sure you will not change your mind. I am aware, Mike McCullagh has become one of your best friends and when informed by me, I'm sure he will say, 'I'll have a word and I'm sure I will be able to persuade Jack to stay.'

> "There's no chance of that. I'm definitely not staying. Come the end of the season I will be gone."

As Jack was still not attending Board meetings, we agreed that he would inform the players and I would inform the Board on the following Thursday. This we did.

Predictably, when I informed the Board, Mike McCullagh said,

> "I'll have a word with Charlton,. I know I can persuade him to stay."

With the players now knowing what was happening to the Manager, who had brought them so much success, they became more settled. The team performances gradually improved towards the season's end.

It was mid April when I received a telephone call from Worcester.

"You are cleared to start work at Malvern on May 1st. Obviously you will be unable to make all the necessary arrangements in the time remaining, so all the Malvern doctors have agreed to look after your patients until you eventually arrive."

"That's ridiculous. If that was to occur, when I do eventually arrive in Malvern, I'll have no patients left. They will transfer to the other doctors. Come what may, I will start my duties on May 1st. I'll definitely be there."

My last football match at Middlesbrough, and that of Jack Charlton, was the last match of the season; a home game, on a Friday evening, against West Ham. As usual Margaret and I attended the Chairman's pre match meal at The Marton Hotel and Country Club for our own and the visiting directors. Charles Amer was waiting for Margaret and me at the top of the stairs.

"Could I have a word in my office with both of you.?
he enquired.

"I can't really believe you are leaving tomorrow for Malvern, so I've a proposal to make to you. I want you to stay. Give up your medical practice in Redcar. I'll appoint you Chief Executive at the Football Club."

When I refused, he increased my proposed salary in stages until the salary was more than twice what I would earn in Malvern, but still I refused. Charles thought I was mad, but my mind was made up.

Immediately after the West Ham game, I attended a dinner at another of the Chairman's hotels–The Royal York, at Redcar. It was in aid of John Hickton's benefit. John was a great and distinguished servant to Middlesbrough and nothing would keep me from his dinner. Throughout the night, without them knowing, I said my personal goodbyes to each and every player. I would miss them. Oh how I would miss them! Sadly, after living there for eighteen years, there were very few other people I would miss.

The following morning I travelled to Malvern. I had left behind Middlesbrough Football Club and the medical practice in Redcar, where I had worked for all of those eighteen years. Regrettably, I had also left behind "The Jack Charlton Interference File."

20

Epilogue

I had been working in Malvern for eight weeks. I was thoroughly enjoying working, on my own, in my new Practice. As I drove around the beautiful rural countryside of Worcestershire, Radio Five interrupted its programme.

"Don Revie has relinquished his post as the England Manager."

The announcer reported.

Don had been England Manager for only three years. His record, at international level, was pretty abysmal. I knew a man who would be a great success as a Manager at international level. That man was Jack Charlton. I had worked closely with Alf Ramsey for twelve years and had detailed knowledge of what was required of an England Manager. I'd also worked on a day-to-day basis, for four years, with Jack Charlton. I knew he would be a great success as an England Manager.

I decided to write to my friend, Dick Wragg, the Chairman of the Senior International Committee at The Football Association. I would extol the virtues of Jack Charlton. I posted the letter two days later. I received no acknowledgement to my hand written letter. In fact, Dick never acknowledged or replied to my letter. I was unaware, at the time, that Jack had written to The Football Association applying for the England Manager's post. Jack Charlton wanted to succeed Revie. Like myself, Jack received no response or acknowledgement to the letter he wrote. Not even a thank you, but no thank you. The Football Association appointed Ron Greenwood.

EPILOGUE

Some two years later, I met Dick Wragg at an international at Wembley. It was the first time we had met since I had written my letter. He was full of apologies.

"I just couldn't reply to your letter." he told me.

"We did carry out an investigation regarding Charlton's application. I showed your letter to the Senior International Committee. The committee decided to seek the views of people back at Middlesbrough. I shuddered. The 'Jack Charlton Interference File' would have resurfaced and been commented upon. Inevitably there remained, amongst some people at Middlesbrough, their perceived interference by Jack in the business matters of the Club. The list could include the I.C.I. paint Jack had negotiated for nothing; the corporate boxes; the television gantry; the advertising boards; changing the playing strip and, worst of all, Jack's performance in the restaurant in Australia. No names were mentioned. Dick just informed me the message he received was a simple No."

Jack, I know, remains deeply hurt that The Football Association did not reply to his application. He blames The Football Association. The fault lay however, so Dick Wragg informed me, with Middlesbrough.

Jack subsequently became the Manager of Ireland. He was the most successful manager Ireland has ever had. His great delight was when Ireland beat England in Stuttgart in 1988 and then drawing with them at Wembley in 1991. I believe Jack would have been a great England Manager, but it was not to be.

The late Willie Maddren was a great centre-back during my time at Middlesbrough. He signed for the Club as a schoolboy and made great progress throughout his career. He was a cornerstone in Jack Charlton's promotion winning side. His talent and consistent performances were rewarded with selection to the England Under 23 team. Inevitably, Willie attracted a lot of attention from the Managers of other Clubs who appreciated his talent. Middlesbrough, an unfashionable Club at the time, found it difficult to retain such an outstanding player. I recalled an England Under 23 international at Nottingham, played in December 1967. England had beaten Italy 1–0. After the game, the then Ipswich Manager, Bobby Robson, joined Sir Alf and the England staff for a meal. During the meal Bobby Robson, enthused about Maddren. He thought Maddren was one of the best centre backs playing in England. Praise indeed! Willie certainly was a great player and Middlesbrough's promotion to the First Division in 1974 owed much to the consistent quality of Maddren's play.

Unfortunately, in the early seventies whilst playing for the England Under 23 team, Willie Maddren sustained a severe knee injury, which was to plague him for the rest of his professional career. Within two years of the injury to his knee, the X-ray was showing early evidence of arthritic change. The knee would need very careful supervision for the rest of his career.

During Jack Charlton's second season, it was something of a surprise when he informed me, as the director in charge of football at the Club, that Willie was reluctant to sign a new contract and wanted a transfer. There was a suspicion, within our Club at the time, that Willie had been illegally approached by other Clubs, who were prepared to offer him better financial terms than those on the table at Middlesbrough. Jack was very concerned at the thought of losing Willie Maddren.

"Well there's no point in him seeking a transfer. He wouldn't pass the medical."

I said.

"If you did agree to his transfer, I don't believe any Club would invest in Willie when they see the X-ray of his knee. The transfer would be called off."

"Is Willie aware of that?"

Charlton enquired of me.

"Well he's aware that his knee is suspect, following the injury he sustained playing for the Under 23 team, but no, he's not specifically aware that he would fail a medical, because of his knee."

EPILOGUE

> "Then I think, as the Club's medical man, you should speak with him. Tell him, in your opinion, he would fail the medical. Encourage him to sign the best four-year contract he can extract from me here at Middlesbrough. Tell him the truth. Tell him it is unlikely he would be transferred anywhere on account of his knee."

The following day I saw Willie. I explained I was aware of the discussions he was having with the Manager about a new contract, and the possibility of a transfer to another Club. Now, as far as I was concerned, I needed to inform him as to the state of his knee. I emphasised that I was speaking purely as his medical adviser.

> "In my opinion you wouldn't pass the medical. Your knee is showing early arthritic changes. No club would pay out the transfer fee required when you have X-ray changes, such as you have in your knee. With good medical care, you will probably be able to continue playing for, at most, another four years. You will then, in any event, almost be at the end of your career. My present opinion is that you would not pass the medical and this is confirmed by Mr. Leitch, our local orthopaedic consultant."

Naturally Willie was devastated.

> "What do you advise me to do.?"

he asked.

> "With my other hat on Willie, namely as Director of Football, I would advise you to obtain the best four-year contract you can from Jack Charlton and sign the new contract with Middlesbrough as soon as possible."

Within two weeks, Willie Maddren had signed a new four-year contract at Middlesbrough. Privately, on signing his new contract, Willie thanked me for the advice I had given him. He was pleased with his new contract. I was also pleased. I had been perfectly honest in my dealings with Willie. I had told him the truth. The outcome for Willie was financial security for the last four years of his career. Jack Charlton was also pleased at the outcome.

He had enlisted the services of one of the best central defenders in England for the next four years. Everyone was happy.

Twelve months after arriving in Malvern, I received a telephone call from Annette Iveson. Annette was the daughter of our family butcher in Redcar. I was now well established as a General Practitioner in Malvern.

"I wonder if you could help me?"

she enquired.

"I play hockey for Stockton Ladies and we have qualified to play in the European Finals in Brussels. Unfortunately, we are the only competing team without a doctor. I wondered if you could oblige."

Annette gave me the relevant dates. I said I would make some enquiries. I would need to find a locum to work my Practice in my absence, but in Malvern that may not be too much of a problem. Two days later, I telephoned Annette and agreed to be Medical Officer to the Stockton Ladies Hockey Team at the European Championships. Annette arranged a venue for the coach to pick me up outside of London. I was at the pick up point in good time. Imagine my surprise when the coach duly arrived. It was a "Maddren Coach". Sitting in the front seat was Willie Maddren. Willie was travelling as a relief driver. His family owned a fleet of coaches. He and I were delighted to see each other. We would spend three happy days reminiscing about the days we had spent together at Middlesbrough.

"I owe you a big apology."

Willie informed me one evening.

"You recall how you persuaded me to sign a new four year contract at Middlesbrough. You told me I had a dodgy knee. Well I didn't believe you. I was convinced at the time you were in cahoots with the Manager. I knew Jack Charlton wanted me to sign a new contract and I thought your story about my knee was most convenient at the time. Too convenient. I simply didn't believe you. At that time, I didn't think my knee was too bad. I sought the advice of Billy Gates, our players' union representative. He made a secret appointment for me

EPILOGUE

to see an orthopaedic specialist in London.
Needless to say, that consultant confirmed your opinion. I would not pass the medical. With two opinions now telling me that I had a dodgy knee, I had to accept it. That was why I signed the four-year contract. I apologise for doubting your medical opinion and your honesty."

I pondered my reply.

"Willie, imagine the position I would have been placed in if I hadn't told you the truth. Supposing I had concocted the story. Supposing I had been in league with the Manager. What would you have thought of me, if the London specialist had said 'There's nothing wrong with your knee.'? Throughout all my time at Middlesbrough I always considered the interest of the player first. The players were my patients. I would never compromise my medical relationship with them. That's why I had such a good relationship with them. I believe they trusted me. In my fourteen years at the club my medical integrity always remained intact."

The words "medical integrity" resounded in my mind. I recalled "The Billy Gates Affair at Peterborough" and how the directors had tried to compromise my medical integrity and Billy Gates' honesty. I had defended both. Later, without me knowing, Billy and Willie were prepared to compromise my medical integrity over the opinion I had given over Willie's knee.

The Stockton Ladies did not qualify for the final stages of the European Hockey Championships. I had no medical work to do. Willie and I enjoyed our three days together. Annette was pleased I had made the trip. The Stockton Ladies were happy with my presence.

Frank Spraggon was a competent left full back in Middlesbrough's promotion winning team. Frank married Linda, Harold Shepherdson's daughter. My wife and I have kept in close contact with them ever since I left Middlesbrough. In 2002 Frank and Linda went on a Caribbean cruise and called in at the Cayman Island. They visited Billy Gates.

"You don't happen to have the Doc's address."

Bill Gates and his wife Judith enquired of them. Linda and Frank duly obliged. Thus it was that in 2003, I received a letter from Billy Gates and his wife, Judith. We had not had any contact for twenty-six years. In replying, I asked if he would be kind enough to check out the details I had written in this book referring to the Peterborough match played in the Third Division. As Willie Maddren had sadly died, I asked him also to confirm the details Willie Maddren had given me when making the apology he had made in Brussels on the Stockton Ladies Hockey tour. I sent Billy a copy of the relevant chapters.

"I never knew I caused you so much trouble. I had no idea why you insisted I see the specialist, following the Peterborough match. As I said at the time, I was quite happy for you to deal with the injury. Yes, I did take Willie to London and your report is accurate."

After twenty-six years, Margaret and I have renewed our friendship with Bill and Judith Gates. They recently visited us in Malvern. The four of us enjoyed a very pleasant weekend together. Bill had no knowledge of the directors' attack on my medical integrity, following the Peterborough match, and I had no knowledge of Willie's visit to London until the ladies' hockey tour to Brussels. The delight is Bill, Judith, Margaret and I are still friends.

———•◆•———

The phone rang at three in the morning. I was soundly asleep. Immediately however, I recognised Madeline's voice. Madeline had moved from North London two years previously. Her London accent was easily distinguishable from the usual Worcestershire accents telephoning me. Madeline was not ill. She had a couple visiting her for the weekend from London. After going to bed, the man had been taken seriously ill with acute abdominal pain. Although the man was not a patient of mine, Madeline wondered if I would be kind enough to visit him. As Madeline lived only a mile from my home, I said I would be there in ten minutes.

Madeline greeted me at the front door. I followed her upstairs to the guest's bedroom. As I entered the bedroom, I could not believe my eyes! The patient writhing around in bed, with excruciating abdominal pain was none other than George Cohen, the England international who had played at right fullback in the 1966 World Cup team. George, who had no knowledge of my moving to Malvern, was as astonished to see me as I was to see him. In many ways George was greatly relieved at my presence as he anticipated he would be visited by a strange doctor who would not be aware of his medical history.

"I'm glad it's you."

George said.

"You know all about my abdominal problems. I suffer with this abdominal colic from time to time, but it's really bad tonight. The worst attack I've had in years."

Not only was George aware of the diagnosis, but he was also very knowledgeable about the most appropriate treatment he had received from his doctors back at home. He advised me as to the most successful treatment he had received in the past and requested I treat him along similar lines.

I examined his abdomen and confirmed the diagnosis both George and I suspected. I gave him the appropriate injection and informed him, his wife Daphne and Madeline he would now sleep. I would visit him again at about eight o'clock on my way to morning surgery. If George did not sleep, or the pain worsened, they would telephone me again. I departed for my home and as usual was asleep within minutes.

When I visited George, on my way to morning surgery, he was sitting up in bed, was pain free, and smiling at our encounter in the middle of the night. His tummy had settled and he had made a good recovery. As George and Daphne were anxious to return home to Kent, I gave them medical clearance to do so.

George and I occasionally still meet up in London with our mutual friend Ken Jones. George and Daphne have visited Margaret and me in Worcestershire and stayed the weekend with us together with Ken Jones and his wife Kathleen. George and I often enquire of each other what the chances were of our meeting up in our medical encounter some fourteen years after we had both been involved in the World Cup Final. It seemed ironic that at the 1966 celebration banquet at The Royal Garden Hotel, George and I had sat next to each other. When we next met, it was at three in the morning in a house in rural Worcestershire. Football is indeed a funny old game.

My son Michael is a keen golfer. Now a successful accountant, for many years he toyed with the idea of becoming a professional golfer. Following his A level examinations, at Millfield School, he wanted a year off to play golf. I persuaded him to go to university first, gain his degree and then have a year off. This was the course we jointly decided upon. Michael went to Southampton University and graduated in Economics and Accountancy. During his time at University, Michael was appointed Captain of the University Golf Team. The Worcestershire Golf Club in Malvern is rightly proud of him holding that office, as, at the same time, three other juniors from The Worcestershire were appointed University Golf Captains– Adrian Coleman at Manchester, Philip Guest at Birmingham and Philip Shurmer at Keele. Four juniors, from the same Golf Club, being University Golf Captains at the same time. Unfortunately half way through his year, as University Golf Captain, Michael sustained a very nasty spiral fracture of his Tibia when playing football at the university and his whole leg was placed in a long leg plaster for several months.

In order to help Michael with his rehabilitation, I wrote to my old friend, from the north east, Lawrie McMenemy, the then Manager of Southampton Football Club. I enquired if Michael could attend the Club's physiotherapy department and if they would help with his rehabilitation. Lawrie readily agreed. While attending the Club, Michael was introduced to Kevin Keegan.

"Oh I remember your Dad very well."
Keegan said.
"He was a very good friend of mine when I toured Yugoslavia

EPILOGUE

with the England team. I ran into a bit of trouble there and your Dad was very good to me. If I can do anything to help you, let me know."

Kevin was not only a great help to my son but his help was unbelievable. As Michael lost his plaster and began walking again, Kevin regularly fixed him up with match tickets for Southampton's home matches. During Michael's rehabilitation, they even played golf together at Stoneham Golf Club. My wife and I will be for ever grateful for Kevin's kindness to our son, at a very difficult time in his life.

I met up with Kevin at The Ryder Cup, when it was played at Walton Heath, so I was able to thank him personally.

"Don't mention it"

he said,

"You were a good friend to me in Yugoslavia."

When I had first met with Alf Ramsey, before I was officially appointed an Honorary Team Physician, he had told me,

"Most of all, I suppose, I want you to be the players' friend."

In Kevin's case I had achieved one of the goals Alf had set for me.

———•◆•———

Until the late nineteen sixties, the England international team, when playing abroad, travelled on schedule flights. The Football Association Council Members travelled first class and the players and management team travelled in economy class; an incongruous situation! Following the victory in the World Cup, in nineteen sixty six, Alf Ramsey persuaded the powers that be to charter a British Airways Trident, for our exclusive use, at all our European matches. The football correspondents, television personnel and a few selected supporters travelled in the same plane. We were fortunate in that British Airways invariably gave us the same crew and cabin staff for all our flights. On the summer tours, which usually involved at least three matches, the Trident would fly us to our first destination, returning empty to London. The Trident would then fly out, the day following our first match, and transport us to our second venue again returning empty to London. It was a system that worked extremely well and over time we inevitably developed relationships with the aircraft crew.

To describe Pam Darch, one of the British Airway stewardesses who always accompanied us on our charter flights, as beautiful, would seem, to many, to do her an injustice. Pam was stunningly attractive. Invariably on such European flights Harold Shepherdson and I would sit at the back of the plane. Occasionally Pam, in one of her few quiet moments, would come and sit next to us. Over time Pam and I became good friends.

In the summer of nineteen sixty eight, England's summer tour involved playing in the European Finals in Italy. Initially we were to play in Florence. Alf arranged a warm up game in Hanover against West Germany. Margaret and my three children remained at home. Shelagh our eldest daughter was expecting her eleven plus results the day of the game in Hanover, and I, as usual, was not at home to support her. On the flight from London to Hanover Pam came and sat next to me and I explained to her how guilty I felt at not being at home on such an important day for my daughter and how it would be several days before I knew if Shelagh had passes her examination.

"Give me your home telephone number."

Pam said.

"I'll ring your wife, before we fly back out to Hanover, and

give you the result on the flight from Hanover to Italy."

True to her word, Pam gave me my daughter's successful eleven-plus results during that flight. I was so pleased for Shelagh and indebted to Pam for her kindness. So began a close friendship between my family and Pam. She came and spent a weekend with us at Redcar. She also joined my wife and children when they were holidaying in Benidorm and I was away on yet another England tour. Pam became a close family friend. When Pam married Tony, our entire family was invited to their wedding in London. When the Ryder Cup was played at Walton Heath, Michael and I stayed at their home for three days. Ann our middle child, following her graduation at Sheffield joined the Civil Service and was posted to Slough. Rather than living in digs, Pam and Tony invited Ann to live with them. Ann lived with

EPILOGUE

Pam and Tony in Chiswick for two years. Pam and Tony often refer to Ann as their adopted daughter. Pam and Tony have visited us here in Malvern and been guests at my eldest daughter's wedding. They are true friends. A friendship that began on a flight with England and one that has lasted forty years. Not only was Pam stunningly attractive, when an airhostess, but she is, and more importantly, a very nice person and a true friend. Her friendship is one my family cherish to this day.

One of my best friends is Ken Jones, the Football and Boxing Correspondent. Ken was on the first Under 23 tour I went on in 1964. We have been close friends ever since. One year after I resigned my position as Honorary Team Physician at The Football Association, I received a telephone call from Ken. Not being much interested in Boxing, I was surprised when Ken asked if I would be prepared to help John H Stracey, in his quest to become World Welterweight Champion. Stracey, who I must confess I had never heard of at the time, was due to fight in Mexico City against Jose Napoles for the world title in December 1975. John Stracey's trainer was Terry Lawless and Ken had spoken at length with Terry of the problems associated with athletic performance at the altitude of Mexico City and all the associated problems. Ken had informed Terry how successful our training programme had been for the World Cup in Mexico and wondered if I would advise them on a suitable acclimatisation programme. I readily agreed.

Terry Lawless and I spent many hours on the telephone working out a daily training programme for their month's acclimatisation in Mexico prior to the fight. We discussed the programme in the most detailed manner in the weeks before they left for their acclimatisation programme. Although floored in the first round by Napoles, John H. Stracey recovered sufficiently to inflict serious damage to Napoles. In the sixth round, the referee stopped the fight as Jose Napoles eye had completely closed. Stracey was declared World Champion, winning with a technical knock out in the sixth round. When Terry and John returned to London from Mexico, they were both interviewed by Frank Bough on the Saturday afternoon television programme. Terry was kind enough to say that without the training advice given to them by myself, he doubted if they would have won the fight.

Terry invited me down to London when Stracey defended his title against Carlos Palomino. I had never been to a professional boxing match before and, although Terry was most kind in giving me two ringside seats, I did not enjoy it. J.H. Stracey lost his world title to Palomino on June 22nd. 1976. At least the acclimatisation programme I had designed, with the help of my medical team, was once again proven to be correct. It enabled John H Stracey to become a world champion.

———•◆•———

Thirty years after leaving Middlesbrough, I received a telephone call. The northern accentuated voice said,

"This is a voice from the dead."

It was Gordon Jones, the former Middlesbrough left back, who was Club Captain when I became a director in 1963.

"Alan Peacock and I, on behalf of The Old Players' Association, would like to invite you and your wife to be our guests at Middlesbrough's home game against West Ham on November 11th. Would you like to come?"

"We'd be delighted."

I replied.

Margaret and I visited the Riverside Stadium as Gordon arranged. We dined with Gordon, his wife May, and former player Frank Spraggon, with his wife Linda, in the Legends Room. After lunch Gordon interviewed me in front of over one hundred guests. As we watched a very poor game I remarked to Gordon I was no legend.

"To the players of my era you were."

he replied.

"You introduced new diets for the players; provided us together with George Wright and Jimmy Headrige, a superb

EPILOGUE

medical service; commenced routine medical examinations and blood tests; built us a new medical centre; and above all genuinely cared for us."

It was a kind remark and one I greatly appreciated. I had always wanted to provide the best medical care I could for professional footballers. The former Club Captain led me to believe I was,

"A former legend, who provided the players with a superb medical service."

If that was my epitaph, I would be more than happy.

My friendship with Alf continued until his death. Margaret and I stayed at their home and Alf and Victoria visited Margaret and me here in Malvern. In the latter days of his life I journeyed across to Ipswich to visit my friend and I was greatly saddened when he eventually died. In my professional career I had worked for many consultants, professors, millionaire businessmen and high profile managers, but none compared with Alf. He was a class act; head and shoulders above them all. I felt honoured and privileged when Victoria asked me to organise, together with the vicar, his memorial service, in Ipswich.

I endeavoured to carry out every detail of the service as requested by Victoria. The church was full. The service was attended by the majority of the players, who played in the 1966 World cup Final. George Cohen and Bobby Charlton gave the eulogies and I was asked by Victoria to read one of the lessons. The players and I, together with our wives, attended a private reception following the service, held by Victoria. Lady Ramsey, Margaret and I remain in contact to this day. Once, when in Mexico, I informed Alf of my intention to resign from my England position, he said to me.

"Think of it, if it wasn't for your association and involvement with the England team you'd be a nobody!"

I shall always be grateful and proud of my association with Sir Alf Ramsey. He made me somebody.

ISBN 142511261-7